Electronic Evidence:
Disclosure, Discovery and Admissibility

Electronic Evidence: Disclosure, Discovery and Admissibility

First edition

Stephen Mason
General Editor
Philip N Argy
Ruth Cannon
Stephen Coughlan
Robert J Currie
Brian W Esler
Lorna Goodwin
Julien Hofman
Manisha T Karia
Tejas D Karia
David Leung
Iain G Mitchell
Laura O'Gorman
Damian Schofield
Daniel Seng
Bryan Tan

LexisNexis®
Butterworths

Members of the LexisNexis Group worldwide

United Kingdom	LexisNexis Butterworths, a Division of Reed Elsevier (UK) Ltd, Halsbury House, 35 Chancery Lane, London, WC2A 1EL, and RSH, 1–3 Baxter's Place, Leith Walk Edinburgh EH1 3AF
United Kingdom	LexisNexis Butterworths, a Division of Reed Elsevier (UK) Ltd, RSH, 1–3 Baxter's Place, Leith Walk, EDINBURGH EH1 3AF and Halsbury House, 35 Chancery Lane, LONDON WC2A 1EL
Argentina	LexisNexis Argentina, Buenos Aires
Australia	LexisNexis Butterworths, Chatswood, New South Wales
Austria	LexisNexis Verlag ARD Orac GmbH & Co KG, Vienna
Benelux	LexisNexis Benelux, Amsterdam
Canada	LexisNexis Canada, Markham, Ontario
Chile	LexisNexis Chile Ltda, Santiago
China	LexisNexis China, Beijing and Shanghai
France	LexisNexis SA, Paris
Germany	LexisNexis Deutschland GmbH, Munster
Hong Kong	LexisNexis Hong Kong, Hong Kong
India	LexisNexis India, New Delhi
Italy	Giuffrè Editore, Milan
Japan	LexisNexis Japan, Tokyo
Malaysia	Malayan Law Journal Sdn Bhd, Kuala Lumpur
Mexico	LexisNexis Mexico, Mexico
New Zealand	LexisNexis NZ Ltd, Wellington
Poland	Wydawnictwo Prawnicze LexisNexis Sp, Warsaw
Singapore	LexisNexis Singapore, Singapore
South Africa	LexisNexis Butterworths, Durban
USA	LexisNexis, Dayton, Ohio

A CIP Catalogue record for this book is available from the British Library.

ISBN : 9781405718370

Typeset by Letterpart Ltd, Reigate, Surrey

Printed and bound in Great Britain by William Clowes Ltd, Beccles, Suffolk

Visit LexisNexis Butterworths at www.lexisnexis.co.uk

Foreword

In the last 15 years the penetration of computers and other electronics into commercial and domestic life has had a great impact on the practicalities of litigation. Documents are stored on computers, and leave tell-tale traces, so computers have to be searched for documents and, sometimes, their hard disks have to be investigated to find those traces. Mobile phones leave their own traces, both in terms of records of the calls (again, stored on computers) and in terms of being able to indicate their own physical whereabouts. Many more examples can be given.

These facets come into play at all stages of litigation. Computers have to be interrogated on, or as a result of, search and seizure orders; the volume of emails on the parties' computers creates an intolerable burden on disclosure, or a potential goldmine for the other side, depending on your point of view in the case in question; and the fruits of all these electronic wonders will provide important evidence for proving or rebutting cases at trial. Lawyers have had to learn new tricks. They have had to re-think what a 'document' is; they have to work out how to go about disclosure of electronic documents; and trial lawyers have had to learn how to read emails in trial bundles when their content is buried on a page full of disclaimers and other flummery, when their precise times are sometimes very important (and on occasions inaccurately stated) and when they appear in reverse chronological order. (In my view a small prize should be offered by the legal community to the person who writes a piece of software which enables a chain of emails to be presented in proper chronological order on the page, and a larger one to the person who procures that the irrelevant gubbins is removed so as to leave only important content).

This means that lawyers, and the investigators who assist them, have got to get to grips with the technology and its effect on their activities. The technical side cannot be ignored by anyone who expects to be able to conduct litigation in and out of court. All lawyers can be expected to be aware of some of the areas in which electronics have made a difference. In some cases a knowledge of how things work, even at a basic level, will make all the difference when it comes to winning or losing an application or a case, and not everyone has that. This book will help with all that. It is not just a textbook of legal principles. It contains technical introductions which assist an understanding of the underlying technology. It also contains some extensive recitations of the facts of certain cases which, while in some ways perhaps a little over-long in a normal legal textbook, nevertheless sometimes assist an understanding of the technology by placing it in context. Other chapters provide assistance on the legal principles and practicalities involved. In addition there are chapters about aspects of the law in various other jurisdictions—mainly, but not exclusively, common law jurisdictions. These are useful for at least two reasons. First, the law is having to undergo a fairly rapid adjustment to the sort of issues that arise in relation to all this, and it is happening in a number of jurisdictions. Lessons can be learnt from the experience of others. Second, electrons know no jurisdictional boundaries, and commercial cases may well involve cross-border communications. In that context it may be necessary to have a view as to the relevant law in another jurisdiction. I doubt if the authors and editors would claim that the foreign law chapters contain everything that it will be necessary to know, but they certainly provide a good base from which intelligent questions can be asked.

Those authors and editors are to be commended for pulling together the strands that they have pulled together in order to achieve this book. It will undoubtedly be very useful to the many lawyers who are likely to be having to get to grips with this technology and its effect on their practices.

The Hon Mr Justice Mann
March 2007

The abacus

'Your honour, I seek to exhibit the abacus.'

The judge looked over his spectacles 'Which form of abacus is it?'

The barrister looked perplexed and turned to his solicitor and whispered 'Which form of abacus? How do I know? Are there different types of abacus?'

'Oh yes' whispered the solicitor, 'it's a Chinese abacus.'

'Oh, right. Thanks.' 'It's a Chinese abacus, your honour.'

'Thank you, Mr Puffington. And what is the purpose of exhibiting the abacus?'

'Well, your honour, it's the item upon which the calculations were made to perpetrate the alleged fraud.'

'Indeed, but that does not mean the abacus ought to be exhibited. Have you a submission on this matter Miss Jawleyford?'

Miss Jawleyford stood as Mr Puffington sat down. 'Well, your honour, the defence does not seek to argue about an inanimate object.'

'Quite.'

'But what we must look to, in my submission, is the reason for admitting the abacus as an exhibit, your honour.'

'Indeed.'

'We have already had the opportunity of viewing the abacus, and take no point on the object itself. It is admitted that the defendant used the device. As a material object, it can be admitted into evidence. But the question is, what purpose is served in admitting the device. It is my submission that the presence of the abacus serves no purpose, because the device is merely a device. There is no record of what, if any, calculations might have been made on the device.'

Miss Jawleyford sat down. Mr Puffington stood. 'Your honour, in our submission, it's important to exhibit the abacus, because it will serve to make the members of the jury ask themselves why the defendant, a finance director earning over a million pounds salary a year, deliberately used such a device. It is our case that he used the abacus to avoid the creation of records that would implicate him in the alleged fraud. To that end, it's an important exhibit that ought to be admitted into evidence.'

Preface

Lawyers and judges now deal with digital evidence regularly, even if it is mainly in the form of email correspondence, the authenticity of which may not be in question. The short list of random examples cited below illustrates how many, and how varied, the sources of digital information are, and the purposes to which the evidence is put. Email has become ubiquitous and is now cited regularly in evidence across a range of civil and criminal cases, including allegations of defamation[1]; messages left on mobile telephone voicemail facilities have been tapped and subsequently misused in at least one case in England and Wales[2]; fugitives have been tracked down when using a Skype telephone[3]; a pastor has used text messages to incite his lover to murder his wife[4]; a professor has used the internet to search for the means to kill his ex-wife[5]; Khalid Shaikh Mohammed, accused of being the mastermind of the attacks in the USA on 11 September 2001, was arrested because he, together with his accomplices, used the same the SIM card in whatever mobile telephone they used, thus enabling the security services across a number of continents to track the use of the card[6]; evidence from the global positioning

[1] *Western Provident Association Ltd v Norwich Union Healthcare Ltd and Norwich Union Life Insurance Co Ltd* (1997) *Financial Times*, 18 July, (1997) *The Times*, 18 July; *Exoteric Gas Solutions Ltd and Andrew Duffield v BG plc* [1999] LTL 24 September 1999, (1999) *The Independent*, 24 June; *Takenaka (UK) Ltd and Corfe v Frankl* [2001] EWCA Civ 348, [2001] EBLR 40. Comments placed on web sites have also been the subject defamatory proceedings: *Jim Murray v Spencer, Steve and Pankhurst*, see 'Friends Reunited user pays damages' (2002) *BBC News*, 21 May, available online at http://news.bbc.co.uk/2/hi/uk_news/england/1999231.stm and an OFCOM Adjudication on a related matter: http://www.ofcom.org.uk/tv/obb/prog_cb/pcb_15/f_p/adj_jm.pdf; and for comments placed in chat rooms: *Michael Keith-Smith v Tracy Williams*, see Adam Sherwin 'Chat room insults lead to internet libel victory' (2006) *The Times*, March 22, available online at http://www.timesonline.co.uk/article/0,,2-2097470,00.html; Owen Gibson 'Warning to chatroom users after libel award for man labelled a Nazi' (2006) *Guardian Unlimited*, March 23, available online at http://www.guardian.co.uk/law/story/0,,1737445,00.html.

[2] *Relf v Rifkind; Hibbert v Rifkind* [2002] EWHC 2199 (Ch).

[3] Eric Bangeman 'Fugitive exec nabbed after Skype call' (2006) *Ars Technica* 24 August, online at http://arstechnica.com/news.ars/post/20060824-7582.html.

[4] 'Murderous texts send pastor to jail' (2004) *Reuters*, 3 August, archived by WorldWide Religious News online at http://www.wwrn.org/article.php?idd=7133&sec=71&con=48.

[5] Stacey Archambault and Jaime Pedigo 'Murray found guilty of murder' (2005) *KUJH-TV News* March 17, online at https://tv.ku.edu/news/2005/03/17/murray-found-guilty-of-murder; Jesse Manning 'Murray convicted of murder Jurors return guilty verdict following 3 days of deliberations' (2005) *Kansas State Collegian*, March 18, online at http://collegian.ksu.edu/collegian/article.php?a=5466.

[6] Don Van Natta Jr and Desmond Butler 'How Tiny Swiss Cellphone Chips Helped Track Global Terror Web' (2004) *The New York Times*, March 4, online at http://

device placed on a vehicle was admitted into the trial of the murder of Scott Peterson's wife and their unborn son[7]; Blake Ranking confessed on a blog to causing a car to leave the road, and subsequently entered a plea of guilty to manslaughter[8]; email correspondence helped the police find the person alleged to have killed Bobbie Joe Stinnet and remove the baby she was carrying from her womb—Lisa Montgomery had communicated with the victim by an exchange of instant messages and emails, which enabled the police to locate her through the IP address[9]; evidence of a video taken on a mobile telephone of a woman performing a 'lap dance' whilst naked saved three men from being tried for rape, and subsequently caused the alleged victim, Cinzia Sannino, to enter a plea of guilty to two charges of perverting the course of justice[10]; the trial of a Kurdish youth was dismissed when he played a recording of the comments made by the arresting officer, PC David Yates of the Territorial Support Group of the Metropolitan Police, the recording was made on his mobile telephone at the time he was arrested (PC Yates used abusive language to allege the youth was a robber and a rapist, was subsequently charged with a racially aggravated attack on a Kurdish man and found not guilty at a trial held at Southwark Crown Court in January 2007)[11]; digital evidence from a wide variety of sources demonstrated how Dhiren Barot planned to initiate a number of terrorist attacks in London and the United States—the evidence was so overwhelming, that he entered pleas of guilty to the charges[12]; allegations of industrial espionage by the use of 'spyware' will be considered by the High Court in London when the trial takes place in the dispute between Ashton Investments and Ansol against Rusel Management Company and others[13]; and in the divorce action of *White v White*[14], the husband failed in his application to have email correspondence suppressed on the basis that his wife unlawfully intercepted the email and intruded upon his privacy by looking through his files on the computer: Issenman JSC held that merely looking through files stored on a computer used by all members of a family

www.nytimes.com/2004/03/04/international/europe/04PHON.html?ex=1393736400&en=71c64fa22f23d30a&ei=5007&partner=USERLAND.

[7] 'Peterson Trial: Judge Allows In GPS Technology Evidence' (2004) *Foxreno.com* February 27, online at http://www.foxreno.com/news/2853360/detail.html; Diana Walsh, Stacy Finz and Kevin Fagan 'Jury recommends death for Scott Peterson 11 hours of sentencing deliberations cap six-month trial' (2004) *San Francisco Chronicle*, December 13, online at http://sfgate.com/cgi-bin/article.cgi?f=/c/a/2004/12/13/PETERSON13.DTL.

[8] 'Teen pleads guilty after blog confession' *MSNBC.com* online at http://www.msnbc.msn.com/id/10561564/.

[9] 'Web Led Cops To Stinnett Suspect' (2004) *CBS News* December 21, online at http://www.cbsnews.com/stories/2004/12/21/national/main662366.shtml.

[10] Simon De Bruxelles ' "Evil" teenager who cried rape is jailed' (2006) *The Times*, September 19, p 16.

[11] 'Officer suspended in racism probe' (2005) *BBC News*, 19 May, online at http://news.bbc.co.uk/1/hi/uk/4561131.stm; 'Policeman denies "racist attack" ' (2006) *BBC News*, 5 April online at http://news.bbc.co.uk/1/hi/england/london/4879946.stm; 'PC Suspended After Racist Rant' (2005) *Muslim Directory*, 8 June online at http://www.muslimdirectory.co.uk/viewarticle.php?id=40; 'Officer not guilty of race attack' (2007) *BBC News*, 31 January, online at http://news.bbc.co.uk/1/hi/england/london/6317751.stm.

[12] Sean O'Neill and Adam Fresco ' "Dirty" bomber's plot to hit stations and hotels' (2006) *The Times*, November 7, pp 1 and 6.

[13] *Ashton Investments Ltd v Rusal Management Co* [2006] EWHC 2545 (Comm).

[14] 344 N.J. Super 211, 781 A.2d 85 (N.J.Super.Ch. 2001).

did not constitute an act of interception and that the wife had an equal right and authority to view files on the computer in the same way as the other authorised users.

As the examples set out above illustrate, lawyers handle digital evidence every day, even though the vast majority of them are not aware that they do so. It is partly for this reason that this book has been written. The main aim of the text is to offer judges, lawyers, legal scholars and students an insight into the complexities of electronic evidence in its widest sense. For this reason, the content of the book sets out in brief the sources of digital evidence; identifies the characteristics of digital evidence; considers the issues involved with the investigation and reporting of digital evidence; discusses the evidential foundations for adducing digital evidence into legal proceedings; sets out and explains the use of animations and simulations using computers; and individual chapters put the admissibility of electronic evidence in each jurisdiction into context, placing electronic evidence into the framework that is familiar to participants in the justice system. For lawyers, it is hoped that this text will provide useful guidance that is sufficient to enable them to begin to understand what questions to ask of digital forensic specialists and to advise on electronic evidence confidently, competently and with assurance. It is also thought that the text may be of interest to law enforcement agencies, digital forensic specialists and the IT industry in general.

To further illustrate the nature of the topic, weeks before the publication of this text, Mr Justice King granted Norwich Pharmacal relief to the Campaign Against Arms Trade ('CAAT') against BAE Systems plc ('BAE')[15]. Ann Feltham sent an email on the 29 December 2006 to the members of the CAAT steering committee internal email list (caatcommiteee@lists.riseup.net), a private list not open to the members of the public and comprising only the 12 members of the steering committee and seven members of CAAT's staff. The email contained privileged legal advice that CAAT received from its solicitors. A copy of the email was sent to BAE. Solicitors for BAE returned a copy of the email printed on paper to CAAT's solicitors, by a letter dated 9 January 2007, received the following day. This was the first time that CAAT came to know of the leak.

The email returned to CAAT was incomplete, as described by Mr Justice King, at 31:

> It was a redacted version of that which had come into the possession of the Respondent and/or its own solicitors. All the routing information, the header address and so forth, which would give details of the email accounts through which the email had been received and sent before arriving at the Respondent and its solicitors, had been removed. Such removal must have been done either by the Respondent or by its solicitors acting on its instructions.

The source of the leak could only be the result of two possibilities, and CAAT did attempt, unsuccessfully, to trace the source, as described by Mr Justice King:

> 45. As Ann Feltham says, there are really only two broad possibilities: either the source is one of the authorised recipients of the email, i.e. a member of the Applicant's steering committee or staff, or the email was intercepted or retrieved by other means by a person or persons unknown, be it by improper access to the Applicant's or a recipient's computer system, interception at riseup.net or at some

15   *Campaign Against Arms Trade v BAE Systems plc* [2007] EWHC 330 (QB).

point whilst the email was sent over the internet. In her first witness statement she explains how she made enquiries of each of the authorised recipients who each denied forwarding the email on. Her second witness statement was made in response to that part of the Respondent's skeleton argument in which it is said that the Applicant has not done enough and that before seeking the present order the Applicant should have (skeleton para.27.) "examined the electronic data available to it on its own computer systems and those of 'riseup.net' and further should have asked any authorised recipients to provide it with access to their personal electronic data for purpose of determining whether their denials of involvement in the copying are accurate".

46. In this later statement Ms Feltham says she did check the 'sent folders' on the personal computers of the staff based in the Applicant's office, but explains that there was a major practical and logistical problem as regards access to the computers used by members of the steering committee. Unlike the staff they are not employees of the Applicant but volunteers who do not work in the office or use computer systems belonging to the Applicant. Some are members of other organisations who access emails from accounts and equipment owned by their employers. Some are based outside London. This all means that to have investigated further on the lines suggested by the Respondent, the Applicant would have needed access to computers to which the Applicant has no right of access and in any event the Applicant would have needed the "costly services of a computer expert to go on a fishing expedition for emails which might or might not have been sent which moreover would have been very time consuming".

The claim by BAE that CAAT ought to physically examine every computer to trace the route of the email is somewhat unrealistic, as explained above, and also fails to grasp the fundamental issue: that digital data knows no geographical, physical bounds. Returning the email without the source data is similar to returning a letter received through the post in an envelope, yet refusing to deliver up the envelope. That the routing and other technical data is 'similar' to the data included on an envelope is an understatement, because the routing and other metadata available in relation to an email is far more extensive than the metadata contained on an envelope. In this instance, Mr Justice King concluded that the order sought ought to be granted, although not in the terms requested.

This application, and the decision by Mr Justice King, illustrates the importance of the metadata associated with a digital object. Documents in digital format include metadata as a matter of course and it seems unrealistic for the recipient to refuse to deliver up the full document, including the associated metadata, in such circumstances.

The mix of common law jurisdictions included in this book serves to demonstrate that the same or similar problems occur in every jurisdiction. In planning the book, an outline of the topics was agreed (although this was subsequently amended as work progressed), subject to the different nuances peculiar to each jurisdiction that inevitably meant each author took a slightly different approach. The resulting text does not have a uniformity about it that might please the legal aesthete. In addition, the chapter on England & Wales is of much greater length than the other chapters, at the request of the publisher, although it is the editor's wish and intention to encourage the contributors of country chapters to expand on their treatment in future editions. It is for this reason that the reader is invited to offer comments regarding the usefulness or otherwise of the text so that, when future editions are planned, consideration can be given to suggestions from readers.

To summarise, evidence in a digital format fits into a number of categories:

(a) records of activities that contain content written by one or more people. Examples include email messages, word processing files and instant messages. From an evidential point of view, it may be necessary to demonstrate that the content of the document it is a reliable record of the human statement that can be trusted;

(b) records generated by a computer that have not had any input from a human. Examples of such records are data logs, connections made by telephones, and ATM transactions. The main evidentiary issue with such records may be to demonstrate that the computer program that generated the record was functioning properly at the material time;

(c) records comprising a mix of human input and calculations generated and stored by a computer. An example is that of a financial spreadsheet that contains human statements (input to the spreadsheet program) and computer processing (mathematical calculations performed by the spreadsheet program). From an evidential point of view, the issues are whether the person or the computer created the content of the record, and how much of the content was created by the computer and how much by the human. It is possible that the input could be hearsay and that the authenticity of the computer processing might be in issue.

It is possible to challenge the authenticity of digital evidence in a number of ways, although many reported cases appear to indicate that a lawyer will merely assert that the authenticity or reliability of the evidence is not to be trusted, and the court will then have to determine a suitable response to the allegation raised. Digital evidence can be challenged in a number of ways:

(a) it may be claimed that the records were altered, manipulated, or damaged between the time they were created and the time they appear in court as evidence;

(b) the reliability of the computer program that generated the record may be questioned; and

(c) the identity of the author may be in dispute: the person responsible for writing a letter in the form of a word processing file may dispute they wrote the text or, alternatively, it might be agreed that an act was carried out and recorded but at issue could be whether the person alleged to have used their PIN, password or clicked the 'I accept' icon was the person that actually carried out the action.

Finally, the vast range of information that is now available to lawyers can be helpful but, because of the sheer volume, difficult to manage. In England and Wales the system of justice is dependent on the assistance given by advocates to the court and advocates are required to bring relevant authorities to the attention of the court. The members of the Court of Appeal in the case of *Copeland v Smith*[16] had occasion to address this issue when it became apparent that a relevant authority had not been brought to the attention of the court, which meant it was assumed the judge could rule on a matter in the

---

[16]   [2000] 1 WLR 1371.

absence of any authority. Research carried out by both instructing solicitors and counsel failed to uncover a relevant authority. This was commented upon by Buxton LJ at 1372–1373:

> 'I cannot draw back from expressing my very great concern that the judge was permitted by those professional advocates to approach the matter as if it were free from authority when there was a recently reported case in this court directly on the point, which was reported not in some obscure quarter but in the official law reports. It is, of course, not only extremely discourteous to the judge not to inform him properly about the law, but it has also been extremely wasteful of time and money in this case ... I have, I fear, to say that the advocates who appeared below did not discharge their duty properly to the court in that they apparently failed to be aware of the existence of that authority.'

In his judgment, Brooke LJ made a number of observations respecting the introduction of the new Civil Procedure Rules then, at 1375–1376, addressed the point made by Buxton LJ:

> 'In these circumstances it is quite essential for advocates who hold themselves out as competent to practice in a particular field to bring and keep themselves up to date with recent authority in their field. By "recent authority" I am not necessarily referring to authority which is only to be found in specialist reports, but authority which has been reported in the general law reports. If a solicitors' firm or barristers' chambers only take one set of the general reports, for instance the Weekly Law Reports as opposed to the All England Law Reports, or the All England Law Reports as opposed to the Weekly Law Reports, they should at any rate have systems in place which enable them to keep themselves up to date with cases which have been considered worthy of reporting in the other series. If this is not done, judges may be getting the answer wrong through the default of the advocates appearing before them.'

Not only is it not in the interests of the system of justice that a relevant authority is missed but it cannot be in the interests of the client to miss a relevant authority (or authorities) when making submissions on their behalf before a court. There is a serious point to the comments made by the members of the Court of Appeal in the context of electronic evidence. The comments made by Brooke LJ inferred that the advocate that holds themselves out to practice in a particular field ought to be aware of recent authorities in that field. However, evidence in electronic format covers all areas of law and this means that every lawyer should make themselves aware of the nature and complexities of electronic evidence, because it is no longer a specialist area of legal practice, if ever it really was.

This text aims to help everybody involved in the justice system, either by reinforcing the strengths of their knowledge or, where they have no knowledge, to recognise the need to begin to understand the nature of the world they now inhabit before an action for negligence hits their in-box. If this book achieves either of these aims it will have justified the time spent in preparation.

Stephen Mason
Langford, Bedfordshire
February 2007
stephenmason@stephenmason.eu

Acknowledgements

I thank all of those that have kindly helped me to obtain and locate sources of information for the text of this book, including the members of staff at the libraries of Inner Temple, Gray's Inn, Middle Temple, the Institute of Advanced Legal Studies, the Maughan Library and Information Services Centre of King's College, London and LexisNexis Butterworths Tolley. Thanks also to those who have kindly responded to my requests for information: Bruce M Allman of Thompson Hine LLP; Jane Bailey, Assistant Professor, University of Ottawa, Faculty of Law; Michael Ives, Marten Walsh Cherer Ltd; Gregory P Joseph of Gregory P Joseph Law Offices LLC; John H Messing, Law-on-Line, Inc., Edward J Nison, Los Angeles County District Attorney Office; Rouhshi Low, Sessional Lecturer, Faculty of Law, Queensland University of Technology; Susan K Stahlfeld of Miller Nash LLP and Sir Richard Tucker. I also thank Kara Irwin, Director of Pro Bono at BPP Law School, for advertising for research help in the United Kingdom. Safia Iman, Kevin D Latham, Fiona Place and Rizwan Rahman took up the challenge of researching the topic of digital evidence and electronic disclosure. Each found a nugget of additional information that has added to the content of this text. My thanks also to Allen Lucas, a law student at the Appalachian School of Law, Virginia, in the United States of America, who took time off to conduct some very helpful research of areas relating to authenticity and cash machine fraud.

In particular, I thank the Institute of Advanced Legal Studies for renewing my Associate Research Fellowship for the academic year 2005–6, which permitted me unlimited use of the IALS Library and Information Services.

This text has had the benefit of constructive criticism from a number of people who have taken the time and trouble to read and comment upon various chapters (further acknowledgments are also included in country-specific chapters). They are: Ross Anderson, Professor of Security Engineering at the Computer Laboratory Research Group at Cambridge University; Brian Collins, Professor and Head of Department of Information Systems, Royal Military College of Science; Bruce Houlder QC; Janet Lambert of Barlow Lyde & Gilbert; Dr John A Mitchell, LHS Business Control; Nick Pope, IT Security consultant; Peter Susman, QC and Dave Walker, senior security consultant, Sun Microsystems UK Limited.

Acknowledgments

Further thanks are also due to Preston W Shimer, FAI, Foundation Administrator, ARMA International Educational Foundation; Richard J Cox, Professor, Archival Studies, Doctoral Studies School of Information Sciences, University of Pittsburgh, and Adrian Brown, Head of Digital Preservation at The National Archives, for their comments on various versions of an earlier version of the chapter on Evidential Foundations, which was prepared for the ARMA International Educational Foundation and presented at the ARMA International 51st Annual Conference & Expo, held in San Antonio, Texas in October 2006.

Naturally, I remain responsible for the text as it stands, with all of its imperfections.

I also take this opportunity to express my appreciation and thanks to the authors who have contributed chapters to this book. They have all taken time out from very busy schedules to prepare the text in accordance with a suggested outline that has, inevitably, altered over time.

Finally, I remain eternally grateful to my wife for her constant patience.

Author biographies

Philip N Argy

Philip N Argy is a senior partner in the Intellectual Property & Technology Group at Mallesons Stephen Jaques. He specialises in science and technology law, intellectual property, competition law and trade practices. He is also a renowned mediator in technology disputes and has been on the WIPO panel of domain name arbitrators since its inception. His website is at: http://www.mallesons.com/our_people/5486445W.htm.   E-mail Philip.Argy@mallesons.com.

Ruth Cannon

Ruth Cannon LLB (Dub) BCL (Oxon) BL is a practising barrister and member of the Department of Legal Studies, the Dublin Institute of Technology, Aungier Street. She is the co-author, with Niall Neligan, of *Evidence* (Thompson Round Hall, 2002), a textbook on Irish evidence law.

Steve Coughlan

Steve Coughlan is a professor at Dalhousie Law School, Halifax Nova Scotia. He is co-editor of the Criminal Reports, the National Judicial Institute's Criminal Law e-Letter, and the Canadian IT Law Association e-newsletter on law and technology. He is the co-author of several books, including *Learning Canadian Criminal Law* (10th edn, Scarborough: Thomson Carswell, 2006) with Don Stuart and Ronald J Delisle, and the *Annual Review of Criminal Law* with Gerry Ferguson. He has received a number of teaching awards, including the 2006 Association of Atlantic Universities' Distinguished Teacher Award.

Robert J Currie

Robert J Currie is assistant professor at Dalhousie Law School in Halifax, Nova Scotia. His teaching subjects include evidence, civil procedure, advocacy and international criminal law. He is a co-author of the latest edition of the leading Canadian international law textbook, *International Law: Chiefly as Interpreted and Applied in Canada* (Emond Montgomery, 2006), and is the author of *International and Transnational Criminal Law* (Irwin, forthcoming 2007). He has published articles in various subject areas, including evidence, law & technology, and professional liability.

Brian W Esler

Brian W Esler is a partner in the Intellectual Property Group at Miller Nash LLP in Seattle, Washington. His practice concentrates on disputes involving intellectual property and high-technology law, appellate advocacy and general commercial litigation. He received his LLM with honours in intellectual property law from the University of London (London School of Economics) in 2002, his J.D. cum laude from the Georgetown University Law Center in 1992, and his BA from the University of Pennsylvania. He may be contacted at brian.esler@millernash.com.

Lorna Goodwin

Lorna Goodwin is a researcher at the University of Nottingham. With a degree in engineering, her postgraduate work focuses on virtual reality reconstructions of road traffic accidents, with particular reference to the use of data visualisation techniques and the admissibility of computer-generated evidence. Lorna has recently worked on a two-year research project funded by the FBI into the analysis of craniofacial measurements from anthropometric data for security applications, and is currently working for the priority group on Crime, Security and Defence, University of Nottingham, http://www.cs.nott.ac.uk/~lmg.

Julien Hofman

Julien Hofman is an associate professor at the Department of Commercial Law, University of Cape Town, South Africa, and is responsible for the LLM programme in ICT Law. Over 60 South African and foreign students have graduated from this programme since it started in 2001. His interests are in the law governing electronic transactions, the effect of ICT on intellectual property law and access to knowledge. He wrote *Cyberlaw: a Guide to South Africans Doing Business Online* (1999) and a new book on this topic will be published in 2007.

Manisha T Karia

Manisha T Karia is a practicing advocate in the Supreme Court of India at New Delhi. She specialises in intellectual property law and information technology law. She completed her LLB from ILS Law College, Pune, India in 2000 and worked with a number of leading law firms in Mumbai, India until 2004. She is presently reading for her Masters of Business Laws from the National Law School of Bangalore, India. Manisha may be contacted at manikaria@yahoo.co.uk.

Tejas D Karia

Tejas D Karia is a senior associate with Amarchand & Mangaldas & Suresh A Shroff & Co, Advocates & Solicitors, New Delhi, India. He has completed his LLB from ILS Law College, Pune, India in 2000, and read his LLM from Gujarat University, India in 2002 and the London School of Economics, London, in 2003. He is a qualified advocate in India and solicitor in England and Wales, (non-practicing). He specialises in international commercial arbitration and information technology law. Tejas may be contacted at tejas_karia@yahoo.com.

David Leung

David Leung is the deputy section head of the Appeals Section, Prosecutions Division, Department of Justice, HKSAR. He was appointed an honorary lecturer of the Department of Professional Legal Education, Faculty of Law, University of Hong Kong in 2000. Mr Leung became chairman of the Information Security and Forensics Society ISFS (www.isfs.org.hk) in January 2003. He is currently the vice-chairman. He is also the secretary and one of the founding members of the Asia Pacific Chapter of the High-Technology Crime Investigation Association (HTCIA http://www.htcia.org.hk).

Stephen Mason

Stephen Mason is a door tenant at St Pauls Chambers, Leeds; Director of the Digital Evidence Research Programme at the British Institute of International and Comparative Law, and an Associate Senior Research Fellow at the Institute of Advanced Legal Studies. He is the author of *Electronic Signatures in Law* (Tottel, 2nd edn, 2007), *E-Mail, Networks and the Internet: A Concise Guide to Compliance with the Law* (xpl publishing, 6th edn, 2006) and the general editor of the *Digital Evidence Journal*.

Iain G Mitchell QC

Iain G Mitchell QC is chairman of the Faculty of Advocates Information Technology Group, the Scottish Lawyers' European Group and vice-chairman of the Scottish Society for Computers and Law. He was formerly joint editor of the E Law Review and writes and lectures extensively on e-commerce and Internet regulation. His other interests include history, politics, archaeology, walking, travel and writing. He is lay reader in the Church of Scotland, a trustee of numerous arts charities and is working on a screenplay. He may be contacted at igmitchell@easynet.co.uk.

Laura O'Gorman

Laura O'Gorman is a partner at Buddle Findlay, Wellington, New Zealand. Laura is a commercial litigator with specialist expertise in competition law, contractual matters, and international disputes. Laura has appeared numerous times in the High Court and the Court of Appeal in New Zealand. She has also worked in Singapore and the Channel Islands. Laura may be contacted at laura.ogorman@buddlefindlay.com.

Dr Damian Schofield

Dr Damian Schofield is currently an associate professor of Computer Games and Digital Media at the School of Creative Media, RMIT University, Melbourne, Victoria, Australia and a director of Aims Solutions Limited, Nottingham, United Kingdom. Dr Schofield's main research area involves the use of digital evidence in courts, particularly virtual reconstructions. For many years he has investigated the prejudicial effect of digital evidence, validation and verification procedures, admissibility of digital evidence and the mathematical uncertainty concerned with digital evidence.

Author Biographies

Daniel Seng

Daniel Seng, BCL (Oxon), is an associate professor with the Faculty of Law, National University of Singapore. He is an Attorney-General's Chambers Law Reform Consultant and has advised on information technology legislation, including the Electronic Transactions Act and the Evidence Act. He was director of research at the Singapore Academy of Law. When in practice, he was profiled for his work in information technology and intellectual property law. He teaches and publishes in these areas and has lectured for the WIPO and the World Bank.

Bryan Tan

Bryan Tan is an advocate and solicitor and managing director of Keystone Law Corporation, a leading Singapore law firm in the fields of IT and intellectual property and is also named by the Legal500 Asia/Pacific as one of the leading individuals in IT and telecoms law in Singapore. Bryan sits on the editorial board of the Digital Evidence Journal. He is also an author of Halsbury's Laws of Malaysia—E-Commerce, and can be reached at bryantan@keystonelawcorp.com

Contents

Table of Statutes

Paragraph references printed in **bold** type indicate where the Statute is set out in part or in full.

Table of Statutory Instruments

Table of Statutory Instruments

Table of European Legislation

Table of International Legislation

Table of Other Enactments

Table of Cases

xlv

Table of Cases

C

E

F

Table of Cases

I

J

K

Q

R

Table of Cases

Table of Cases

Table of Cases

D

Decisions of the European Court of Justice are listed below numerically. These
  decisions are also included in the preceding alphabetical list.

Glossary

A glossary almost seems to be superfluous since the advent of on-line encyclopaedias, such as Wikipedia (http://www.wikipedia.org/), Encyclopedia (http://www.encyclopedia.com/) and the Internet Public Library (http://www.ipl.org/div/subject/browse/ref32.00.00/). Where a word or term is not included in this glossary, it is recommended that the reader consider trying one of the online encyclopaedias, such as Wikipedia, which seems to be very useful for the discussion of technical terms.

Application software
Software that enables the user to use the computer.

Arithmetic logic unit ('ALU')
A calculator that performs logical and arithmetic operations in the processor of a computer.

American Standard Code for Information Interchange ('ASCII')
Letters, numbers and symbols are represented by either a binary or octal conversion table. The following examples demonstrate how this works.

Symbol	Octal	Binary
A	101	1 0 0 0 0 0 1
B	102	1 0 0 0 0 1 0
C	103	1 0 0 0 0 1 1
1	061	0 1 1 0 0 0 1
2	062	0 1 1 0 0 1 0
3	063	0 1 1 0 0 1 1
&	046	0 1 0 0 1 1 0
#	043	0 1 0 0 0 1 1

ASCII was developed by the American National Standards Institute to achieve compatibility between various types of data processing equipment. The ASCII tables assign certain combinations of ones and zeros to represent letters and numbers. Some tables that are in use may have symbols in different places in the table. The user will become aware of this if, for instance, they type " on some keyboards and the symbol @ is displayed.

Automated teller machine ('ATM')
An automated teller machine or automatic teller machine or automated banking machine or cash machine is a device by which a person can obtain access to their account remotely to undertake a number of transactions, including the withdrawal of cash, deposit of money or cheques, transfer of money between accounts, obtaining the balance of an account or to pay for

goods and services. The machines are located in banks and other public places and are linked to central servers. They purport to provide a secure method of undertaking a financial transaction.

Basic input and output system ('BIOS')

The basic input and output system is one component of memory. In most computers, the different programmes communicate with the central processing unit by way of the BIOS.

Control unit ('CU')

The control unit is a component of the processor of a computer that controls the processing of instructions by moving data between the different parts of the processor.

Extended Binary Coded Decimal Interchange Code ('EBCDIC')

EBCDIC is a code for representing characters as numbers. It is widely used on large IBM computers. Most other computers use ASCII codes.

Data log

Operating systems and computer programs have data logs (or 'logs') that record events. A data log consists of entries that include information of events that have occurred within a system or network. A data log can be generated by a variety of sources, including security software (anti-virus software, firewalls, and intrusion detection and prevention systems), operating systems, individual work stations, networking equipment and applications. The number, volume and variety of data logs have increased.

General Packet Radio Service ('GPRS')

This is a standard for wireless communications that can run at up to 115 kilobits per second. This is greater than the speed that can be achieved by Global System for Mobile Communications ('GSM'). A number of band-widths can be used over GPRS and this particular standard is good at sending and receiving small surges of data, as well as large volumes of data.

Global System for Mobile Communication ('GSM')

GSM is a digital cellular system that allows mobile telephones to connect to each other. It was introduced in 1991 and is now widely available across Europe and Asia.

Instant Messaging ('IM')

Instant messaging is the name of a software application, called a client, that sits on a computer. The software allows the user to maintain a list of people that they may wish to communicate with by way of the Internet. Messages can be sent to anybody on the list, providing the recipient is connected to the Internet at the time the message is sent. When the message is sent, a small window is opened on the screen. Messages are exchanged by each party through the screen. A user is also able to take advantage of a number of features offered by most of the instant messaging programs, such as:

(a) Instant messages: people can communicate with others over the Internet;

(b) Chat: a user can create a chat room for any number of others to take part in an online chat;

(c) Web links: a user can share links to web sites with others;

(d) Images: users can share files by sending them directly to people on the message list;

(e) Sounds: sounds can be played to people on the message list; and

(f)   Files: users can share files by sending them direct to each other.

It should be noted that instant messaging is an inherently insecure method of communicating or sending files over the Internet. This is because messages are passed between computers and the method of connection is by way of the servers maintained by the provider of the particular software program.

Interface unit or processor buses

This is a component of a processor in a computer. It is a collection of conductive wires that connect components together, permitting values to be moved from one element to another.

Local Area Network ('LAN')

A local area network links computers together within a defined geographical area, such as a home, office, or small group of buildings. Current LANs are most likely to be based on switched Ethernet or Wi-Fi technology running at 10, 100 or 1,000 Mbit/s (1,000 Mbit/s is also known as 1 Gbit/s).

In essence, a local area network tends to link computers together within a defined geographical area. There are different types of local area network. One of the most common for personal computers is the ethernet. An Apple Macintosh network will be based on the AppleTalk systems, which is built into Macintosh computers. A local area network can have a number of characteristics. The arrangement of the computers on the network can differ. For instance, computers can be connected in the form of a ring or in a straight line. Protocols will determine how data will be sent over the network. A network may use a computer-to-computer protocol, or each computer may act as a client to a central server. The physical connections may be by way of coaxial cable, fibre optic cable or via wireless technology. The aim is for each computer connected to the network (individual computers are called 'nodes') to obtain access to data and devices anywhere on the LAN. This enables many users to use a single printer, thus saving costs. A user can also communicate to any other user on the network, by sending emails or initiating and taking part in chat sessions. A LAN is capable of transferring data at very fast rates, providing the distance between computers is not too great.

Malicious software

Whether a person creates a malicious software (often abbreviated to 'Malware') for the sheer thrill of creating a destructive virus, to deliberately cause damage and inconvenience to computer users, or to boast about their ability, malicious software can be irritating at best and destructive at worst. Factors that helped cause the development and spread of malicious software include the increased us of personal computers, the use of bulletin boards over the Internet in its early stages, and the invention of the floppy disk—which is compatible across all types of computer.

It is possible to classify malicious software in a number of ways: how the software is executed, how it is distributed, what the software does. The groups overlap but the distinguishing feature of malicious software is that is causes unauthorized actions to occur in a computer or information system.

(a)   Backdoor: a backdoor is an item of software that permits an unauthorised third party to obtain access to a computer or system by bypassing the authentication procedure.

(b)   Spyware: this is a program that explores the files in a computer. The information that is gathered, such as which websites a user visited, credit card details or keystrokes, is then sent on to the address specified in the sypware program.

(c) Trojan horses: a Trojan horse is a program that purports to do one thing (eg, asserts itself to be a game) but can collect, exploit or falsify data. A program can also destroy data and erase the hard disk. A Trojan horse does not replicate itself automatically.

(d) Virus: a small piece of software that attaches itself to a program that reproduces itself when the program runs. A virus can destroy, change or alter data. They can also be designed to slow down or hinder other operations of the system.

(e) Email viruses: a virus transported by way of email. This form of virus usually replicates itself automatically. The Melissa virus demonstrated, in March 1999, how effectively a virus could be communicated. The virus was created as a word document and then posted on an Internet newsgroup. When a person downloaded the document and opened it, the virus would be activated. The virus was programmed to send the original document, incorporating the virus, to the first 50 email addresses in the address book of the computer. The mechanism also included an element of social engineering, as did the I LOVE YOU virus, because the virus sent out a message that included a friendly note to the recipient, using their name. As the recipient opened the document, so the virus would continue to spread.

The I LOVE YOU virus appeared in May 2000. This virus contained a code as an attachment to the email. When a recipient double-clicked on the attachment the code was then able to execute itself. The code did two things: it sent a copy of itself to every email address in the computer's address book and then began to corrupt all of the files on the computer. Arguably, this was a Trojan horse distributed by way of email.

(f) Worms: a worm is a computer program that can replicate itself from computer to computer. Worms are normally distributed by way of a computer network. A copy of the worm will scan the network for another computer with security holes. When it finds the type of security hole it is looking for, it will replicate itself through the security hole and on to the new network.

Metadata

The metadata refers to the data about data. It is a digest of the structure and subject matter of a resource. For instance, the metadata in relation to a piece of paper may be explicit from perusing the paper itself, such as the title of the document, the date, who wrote it, who received it and where the document is located; or implicit, which includes such characteristics as the typeface used, such as bold or italic; perhaps the document is located in a coloured file in order to denote a particular type of document; labels may also act as pointers to allow the person using the document to deal with it in a particular manner, such as a file marked 'confidential', for instance.

With electronic documents such data can include, and be taken automatically from, the originating application software or be supplied by the person that originally created the record.

For more information on metadata, see the Dublin Core Metadata Initiative at http://dublincore.org/; Understanding Metadata (National Information Standards Organization) the current version is available at http://www.niso.org/standards/resources/UnderstandingMetadata.pdf; the Wikipedia entry at http://en.wikipedia.org/wiki/Metadata; the Digital Curation Manual instalment on Metadata by Michael Day, Research Officer, UKOLN, University of Bath: http://www.dcc.ac.uk/resource/curation-manual/chapters/metadata/.

Multipurpose Internet Mail Extensions ('MIME')

Multipurpose Internet Mail Extensions is a specification for formatting messages that are not in the ASCII character set. This enables messages to be sent over the Internet. MIME is supported by a number of email protocols, enabling the protocol to send and receive graphic, audio, and video files over the Internet. In addition, web browsers also support various MIME types. These allow the browser to display files that are not in HTML format.

Operating system

The operating system comprises the various system software programs that manage the computer.

Personal Identification Number ('PIN')

A personal identification number is a secret shared between a user and a system that is used to provide some evidence that the user has the authority to obtain access to the system. It is a form of electronic signature. A PIN usually comprises a four-digit number in the range 0000–9999. There are 10,000 possible numbers.

Processor buses

See interface unit.

Random access memory ('RAM')

This is a chip that can be both written to and read from.

Read-only memory ('ROM')

A storage chip that is capable of storing programs once. It can only be read from.

Source code

Source code refers to the text written by humans that defines the functioning of a software program and which is either compiled or interpreted by other software programs into a form which can be executed on an appropriate computer or (in the case of hardware design languages) uploaded to a programmable gate array or used to create masks for microchip production. Source code for a program which has a useful purpose is almost always intended to be understandable by other software engineers who are skilled in the language in which it was originally written, so that the code can be maintained and new features can be added to it.

The term 'source code' is also the subject of a useful commentary by Jacob J at 286 in the case of *Ibcos Computers Ltd v Barclays Mercantile Highland Finance Ltd* [1994] FSR 275:

The program the human writes is called the 'source code'. After it is written it is processed by a program called a compiler into binary code. That is what the computer uses. All the words and algebraic symbols become binary numbers. Now when a human writes he often needs to make notes to remind himself of what he has done and to indicate where the important bits are. This is true of life generally and for programmers. So it is possible to insert messages in a source code. A reader who has access to it can then understand, or understand more readily, what it going on. Such notes, which form no part of the program so far as the computer is concerned, are called "comments." They are a kind of side-note for humans. In the DIBOL and DBL programs with which I am concerned, a line or part of a line of program which is preceded by a semi-colon is taken by the complier as a comment. That line is not translated by the compiler into machine code. The program would work without the comment. It follows that although computers are unforgiving as to spelling in their programs, they do not care about misspelt comments in the source code. If a line of operational code (a "command line") is modified by putting a semi-colon in front of it, it ceases to be operational. The computer treats the code as a mere comment. Computer programmers sometimes do this with a line which pre-exists when they no longer want that line, but are not sure they may not need it in the future. Or, if the programmer thinks he may want to add a feature to his program in the future he may put in a comment allowing for this. He is unlikely in the latter instance to put in detailed code only to comment it out. A general note will do.

Source code, being what humans can understand, is very important to anyone who wants to copy a program with modifications, for instance to upgrade it. It is the source code which shows the human how it all works, and he or she will also get the benefit of all the comments laid down by the original programmer. Software houses not surprisingly normally keep their source code to themselves and confidential.

Transport Control Protocol/Internet Protocol ('TCP/IP')

When a computer connects to the Internet, it uses a set of protocols called TCP/IP. This can be a considered as a common language that enables various types of network to communicate with each other.

Unicode Transformation Format-8 ('UTF-8')

Unicode Transformation Format-8 encodes Unicode characters and is the standard code used over the Internet. UTF-8 is also the default encoding for XML.

Unsolicited bulk e-mail ('spam')

Unsolicited commercial email is colloquially known as 'spam'.

Wide Area Network ('WAN')

A wide area network is a network of computers that cover a wide geographical area, linking a considerable number of computers. The difference between a local area network ('LAN') and a wide area network is size: one example of wide area network is the Internet. A wide area network is used to connect local area networks together. This enables users and computers in one location to communicate with users and computers in other geographical locations.

Chapter 1

THE SOURCES OF DIGITAL EVIDENCE

STEPHEN MASON

1.01 Different technologies are capable of creating evidence in a digital format. The aim of this chapter is to introduce the reader to a range of technologies, their underlying principles and the general characteristics that set evidence in digital format apart from evidence in analogue or physical form. It must be emphasised that the content of this chapter does not deal with any of these matters in depth. Neither is it meant to be a comprehensive review of the technologies that create digital evidence. The intention is to provide the reader with a broad introduction to some of the technical issues involved and to illustrate the types of issue that a forensic examiner should be concerned about when investigating digital evidence.

THE COMPUTER

1.02 Most of us tend to use the term 'computer' as a generic term that encompasses almost any form of processing unit. However, not all devices can necessarily be termed a 'computer': it all depends on how a computer is defined. To illustrate the point on a superficial level, a computer is defined by the Oxford English Dictionary as[1]:

> A calculating-machine; esp. an automatic electronic device for performing mathematical or logical operations; freq. with defining word prefixed, as *analogue, digital, electronic computer.*

In comparison, the Department of Computer Science at the University of Texas offer a shorter explanation: 'computer—a programmable electronic machine for processing information'[2], whilst one online computer dictionary tenders a longer meaning that includes various components:

(1)   a functional unit that can perform substantial computations, including numerous arithmetic operations, or logic operations, without human intervention during a run;

(2)   a functional programmable unit that consists of one or more associated processing units and peripheral equipment, that is controlled by internally stored programs, and that can perform substantial computations, including numerous arithmetic operations, or logic operations, without human intervention[3].

One further definition, offered by the website Virtual Nebraska, also provides a definition that distinguishes between the various components of a computer[4]:

computer: electronic machine capable of performing calculations and other manipulations of various types of data, under the control of a stored set of instructions. The machine itself is the hardware; the instructions are the program or software. Depending upon size, computers are called mainframes, minicomputers, and microcomputers. Microcomputers include desk-top and portable personal computers.

Finally, the Wikipedia proffers a relatively elegant definition that includes the three essential elements of machine, data and instructions[5]:

A computer is a machine for manipulating data according to a list of instructions known as a program.

For the purposes of this text, a computer can be defined in terms of a set of characteristics that illustrate how it functions, sometimes called an input-processing-output model:

(a)   it receives an *input* of some sort, by way of a disk file, mouse, keyboard or through a communication channel;
(b)   it *processes* the information;
(c)   it produces an *output* to a disk file or a printer, for instance;
(d)   it must be able to *store* information; and
(e)   it must be able to *control* what it does.

[1]   *Oxford English Dictionary* (*electronic edition*) (2nd edn, 1989 and Additions, 1993–7).
[2]   http://www.cs.panam.edu/cs1380/frames/define.html.
[3]   http://www.computerdictionary.info/computer-term-details/Computer.
[4]   http://www.casde.unl.edu/vn/glossary/earth_c.htm.
[5]   http://en.wikipedia.org/wiki/Computer.

The components of a computer system

1.03 To understand more fully the types of evidence that a computer is capable of creating, it is useful to be familiar with the basic components of a computer system. The main components of a computer include the following:

Hardware

1.04 The hardware forms the tangible part of the computer which, in turn, can comprise some or all of the following:

(a)   physical components that can be separate from the main computer or integrated, as for a laptop computer: keyboard, mouse, display screen, printer, external disks (floppy, CD, DVD and other forms of disk) and hard disk;
(b)   a processor, also called the central processing unit ('CPU'). This unit comprises a large number (typically millions) of electrical circuits, co-located, or integrated on to a single chip of silicon, also known as a computer chip; and
(c)   there is also a working memory, or dynamic random access memory ('RAM' or 'DRAM'). If the power to a computer is switched off, data in this memory will be lost.

THE PROCESSOR

1.05 The processor is the core constituent of every computer and is made up of a number of components. Each component listed below may also be made up of a number of separate parts and there may be more than one of them in a given processor:

(a)   an arithmetic logic unit ('ALU'). This unit is a calculator that performs logical and arithmetic operations;

(b)   a control unit ('CU'), which controls the processing of instructions by moving data between the different parts of the processor; and

(c)   an interface unit or processor bus. This component is a collection of conductive wires that connects components together, permitting values to be moved from one element to another.

Each of these components comprises conductive paths and semi-conductive switching elements, etched into the silicon and often bonded with metals.

STORAGE

1.06 No computer would be able to perform complex operations without a storage device that is capable of retaining programs and other data on which programs operate. The processor needs to obtain access to programs and other data in order to operate. A storage device typically takes the form of semiconductor memory. Semiconductor memory can be a separate functional unit, and is manufactured in a number of forms:

(a)   a storage chip known as random access memory ('RAM'). This form of chip can be both written to and read from repeatedly;

(b)   a storage chip that is capable of storing data once, but cannot be re-written to: once data has been put into it, it can only be read from. This is called read-only memory ('ROM');

(c)   a storage chip that can have data put into it and which behaves as a ROM during its normal operation, but can also be erased in such a way as to allow new data to be put into it. Where the method of erasing the data is electrical in nature, his form of device is known as erasable programmable read-only memory ('EPROM'). Early versions of this type of device were erased by exposing them to ultraviolet light, and these types of device are known as electrically erasable programmable read-only memory ('EEPROM's). A flash ROM is a type of EEPROM.

The storage capability of a memory device is measured by the number of memory locations and the length of the values stored in the chip. To understand more fully how these measurements are arrived at it is necessary to understand the rationale. Amongst other methods of representing data, computers use the binary number system that uses the digits '0' and '1'. A binary digit, either 0 or 1, is also called a 'bit'. A group of eight bits is known as a 'byte'. A collection of bytes handled as a whole unit for processing is called a 'word'. A memory chip can be made in various sizes, although the CPU determines the size of the memory unit. For instance, the description '4x16' means that the chip has four separate memory locations, and each location has a length of 16 bits. Similarly, the description '256x16' describes a chip that has 256 different memory locations, each of which is 16 bits long.

No matter how big the memory chip, many computers use a number of chips to make up the computer memory. As a result, it is necessary to have a 'memory map'. The memory map enables the computer to use storage space comprising a number of memory chips as if it were a single entity.

Software

1.07 Software consists of programs that give instructions to the computer. There are two main categories of software required to run a computer.

SYSTEM SOFTWARE

1.08 If a computer did not have system software most people would not be able to use a computer effectively, because the user would have to specify every operation that was required at a level that could be directly executed by the CPU. This software, which is large and complex, is comprised of many different components. The various system software programs that manage the computer are called the 'operating system'. The operating system controls the flow of data, allocates memory and manages the hardware components of the computer, such as the keyboard, mouse scanner, disk drive and printer. The software also permits the user to manage their files. The operating system acts as an interface between the hardware and the application software. It allows the user to use the computer effectively. Current operating systems include two main classes: Windows and UNIX. Windows, which is produced by the Microsoft Corporation, is available in a number of different versions, including Windows 98, 2000 and XP. UNIX has spawned a number of commercial systems, such as Sun Solaris, IBM AIX, HP-UX and Mac OS X, as well as a number of free systems such as Linux, OpenBSD and FreeBSD. Other operating systems include VAX VMS, IBM z/OS and, historically, MS-DOS. When instructing a forensic expert to examine a computer it is essential to ensure that they have sufficient knowledge of the operating system, otherwise mistakes may occur in the investigation of the computer.

APPLICATION SOFTWARE

1.09 The application software represents the user-facing side of a computer. This is software that enables the user to carry out useful work on the computer: examples include Microsoft Word, Netscape, Star Office and the wide range of other programs that enable us to use computers.

The clock

1.10 One further component must be discussed in relation to the operation of a computer: the clock. The clock serves two functions:

(a) it is a device that produces pulses of time to ensure that events are synchronised and occur in a predictable order. The clock coordinates all the components of the CPU. Each step in any operation must follow in order and some operations run at different speeds. The operations are synchronised to the pulses of an electronic clock, thus the clock acts as the master control. The frequency of pulses is controlled by a phase locked loop ('PLL') which, in turn, is regulated by a quartz crystal. The speed at which the crystal oscillates, the step-up ration of the PLL and the number of steps that each instruction requires will determine the speed at which the computer performs;

(b) the clock also serves to keep the time of day and date in a human sense. Larger server systems synchronise their clocks with a reliable time source, such as Network Time Protocol, available over the Internet.

The built-in clock is powered by a battery and runs continuously, even when the computer is switched off. Older computers may not 'boot up' when they are turned on because the battery has run down, causing the CPU to fail to recall the hardware settings. It should also be noted that the clock is rarely accurate, regardless of the device. This is a matter of grave importance because assumptions about the accuracy or otherwise of a clock can lead to misleading conclusions.

The clock features a great deal in digital evidence, as the case of Harold Shipman in 1999[1]. Detective Sergeant John Ashley of the Greater Manchester Police examined the computers in Shipman's office. In particular, he examined the patient records recorded on the Microdot program, which is designed as a computerised medical records database. He examined the records relating to a number of victims and demonstrated that a number of records were altered retrospectively. He was cross-examined on Wednesday, 10th November, 1999 by Mr Winter. Mr Winter demonstrated that it was possible to alter the information in the software and then change the date of the computer clock to hide the evidence relating to the change made in the software. However, as pointed out by Detective Sergeant Ashley, even if the computer clock had been changed this would have been obvious to any forensic examiner because the clocks on the other computers would have had to be re-set:

> Q. Now please analyse to see when the computer thinks that entry was made. The computer thinks that entry was made on the 10th December 1997. Do we understand therefore by that, by the simple changing of the internal computer clock at the outset of the programme, one can completely alter the effective operation of the computer?

> This data base was held on a separate server. The actual data base manipulation would take place at work stations throughout the surgery.

> Q. Although it has a central server?

> It could be done in the manner in which we have done it, but obviously all entries made thereafter would be incorrect. One would have to come back out of the data base and reenter the correct time for all the other entries then to pick up the right time. Quite in overall a lengthy operation.

Mr Wright, QC, prosecuting, then asked a number of questions in re-examination that illustrated the actions Shipman would have had to take if he altered the computer clock:

Q. What about if there are 3 successive late entries, each of different dates for example. How could that be done?

In an individual record?

Q. Yes?

It means that by that methodology one would have to go and change the clock 3 times.

Q. And then put it back to the correct time?

Yes.

Q. In other words, once you have put in 3 entries for December 97, September 97 or April 98, you would then have to return to the correct time being the 10th November 1999?

Yes.

The manual relating to this particular software was approximately 300 pages long. Even an experienced computer user might have had difficulties in reading through the manual and learning what the software was capable of doing. Although the internal audit trail, as it was described in the trial, was capable of being altered by the changes made to one computer, it would have required a complex procedure to alter the other computers on the network to hide the changes made retrospectively[2].

[1]   *R v Harold Frederick Shipman* (1999). The trial was held between Friday 8 October 1999 and Monday 31 January 2000 before Mr Justice Forbes in the Preston Crown Court, No. T982105. Transcript available at the time of writing from http://www.the-shipman-inquiry.org.uk.
[2]   Chet Hosmer, 'Proving the Integrity of Digital Evidence with Time' (2002) International Journal of Digital Evidence vol 1 issue 1, available online at http://www.ijde.org; Chris Boyd and Pete Forster 'Time and date issues in forensic computing—a case study' (2004) Digital Investigation vol 1, no 1, 18–23; Malcolm W Stevens 'Unification of relative time frames for digital forensics' (2004) Digital Investigation vol 1, no 3, 225–239.

Storage media and memory

1.11 The types of storage media vary. Some forms of storage are built into the computer. Other forms of storage, called offline storage, are kept outside, and sometimes well away from, the computer, except when they are being written-to or read-from by it. This is where data is transferred to separate storage devices, such as magnetic tape, optical and magneto-optical disks, floppy disks, write-once-read-many-times ('WORM'), DVD-Rom, CD-Rom and USB memory stick. Inside the computer, conventional memory is called 'primary memory'. Secondary memory may be considered as the hard disk. The hard disk and associated offline storage media tend to be the richest source of digital evidence on a computer. Another distinction to be aware of is the difference between volatile and non-volatile memory. Volatile or dynamic memory does not retain its content when power is switched off, whereas non-volatile or static memory retains its content when power is removed.

The forensic examiner may be able to detect a range of data on a hard disk:

(a)   where an individual intentionally marks portions of the hard disk as 'bad', they can then hide substantial amounts of data that would not be seen without the use of an appropriate disk diagnostic tool;

(b)   when the user deletes data it remains on the disk until the old file is overwritten by new data. Only the system's pointers in the filing system are deleted. Even where part of a file has been overwritten, it is still possible to recover part of the deleted file if the entire set of disk blocks containing the original file has not been overwritten.

Most of the digital evidence that can be recovered will be stored in some form of storage media. However, just because evidence is found does not automatically mean that that evidence is genuine or to be trusted. Errors abound in all forms of information technology systems, which means that the certainty of any evidence that is discovered should be considered. Examples include the corruption of data, loss of data, interference with data and errors in the interpretation and analysis of the evidence[1]. This is not to say that a system deliberately corrupts data, although the introduction of a 'Trojan horse' or other form of malicious software may cause data to be corrupted.

Further, it should be observed that the reliability of the evidence would also be affected by the way in which the examination is carried out by a digital investigator. If the actual process of investigation has affected the evidence then it will be less reliable.

[1]   Peter Sommer 'Downloads, Logs and Captures: Evidence from Cyberspace' [2002] C.T.L.R. issue 2, 33–42; Eoghan Casey 'Error, Uncertainty, and Loss in Digital Evidence' (2002) International Journal of Digital Evidence Summer vol 1, issue 2, available online at http://www.ijde.org; Caroline Allinson 'Audit Trails in Evidence—A Queensland Case Study' work in progress, (2002) The Journal of Information, Law and Technology (1) at http://elj.warwick.ac.uk/jilt/02–1/allinson.html; and 'Audit Trails in Evidence: Analysis of A Queensland Case Study' (2003) The Journal of Information, Law and Technology (2) at http://elj.warwick.ac.uk/jilt/03–2/allinson.html.

Data formats

1.12 Computer data may be broadly classified into binary data, where the information is handled as a number represented in binary form, and text data, including alphanumeric and punctuation data. Text can be entered into the computer by a range of methods:

(a)   the typing of letters, numbers and punctuation, mainly when using the keyboard;

(b)   scanning a page with an image scanner and converting the image into data by using optical character recognition ('OCR') software;

(c)   using a bar code. The bar code represents alphanumeric data. The bar code is read with an optical device called a wand. The scanned code is converted into binary signals, enabling a bar code translation component to read the data;

(d)   reading the magnetic stripe on the back of a credit card; or

(e)   voice data, where a person speaks into a speaker capable of recording the sounds. This form of data, as well as video data, is encoded in binary form.

To enable a user to read text and numbers, and to view images or hear sound, the binary form of the data must be translated using a code. Binary information can be represented using the binary (base 2) number system, although it is more common to represent computer numbers in octal (base 8) or, most commonly of all, hexadecimal (base 16). Other, more efficient, systems have also been defined for converting binary data into text such as Multipurpose Internet Mail Extensions ('MIME'). This is a specification for formatting the content of messages to enable them to be sent over the Internet as email. The standards which email systems adhere to are only able to deal with 7 bits per character, rather than 8. MIME encoding is able to reduce a sequence of 8-bit data to a slightly longer sequence of 7-bit text characters. Other codes are required for keyboards. When a key is hit on the keyboard, a binary code, called a scan code, is generated. When the key is released, a second scan code is generated. Each key generates two scan codes.

A range of codes exists for text data. Some of the codes that are in common use are known as Unicode, American Standard Code for Information Exchange ('ASCII'), Extended Binary Code Decimal Interchange Code ('EBCDIC') and Unicode Transformation Format-8 ('UTF8'), which is the standard character code used over the Internet. Most computers now use Unicode and ASCII.

Tools are available to display binary data used in computers to enable a digital investigator to view features that are normally invisible to the computer user. For instance, documents in Microsoft Word format contain data that are normally invisible. An investigator is able to view the data by using certain types of software program. Such data may reveal crucial information that may help an investigation.

Starting a computer

1.13 Every time a computer is switched on, various components must interact with each other for it to begin working. This is called the start-up process or 'booting' the computer. Most computer systems will have a program in the read-only memory ('ROM') called variously a boot loader, boot process, boot strapping or initial program load. It is this program that enables the computer to start. In general terms, this is how it works:

(a) the program is located permanently in the computer's ROM area, and is known as the basic input and output system ('BIOS'). When the computer is switched on, or when the reset button is pressed, control is transferred to the first address of the boot loader program. However, in most modern personal computers the BIOS is contained in the flash ROM, which can be overwritten. All other states of the boot process come from files held on the hard disk;

(b) the boot loader program then tests the various components of the computer, verifying that they are active and working (those components tested include, but are not limited to, detecting and testing the disk drives, monitor and keyboard). The results of the various tests it carries out appear on the monitor screen. It can also clear local primary memory of all historical data and metadata. It then passes control to an operating system boot loader program, located in a particular configured place on the hard disk;

(c) the boot loader takes control of the computer. This program also contains a loader which, in turn, is configured to test and load the application software;

(d) finally, a logon program is initiated and, if the user is authorised, the application software (such as Windows XP, for example) is displayed and the user takes control of the system.

It should be noted that computers made by Sun Microsystems, Apple and other UNIX and mainframe system vendors follow slightly different boot sequences. In addition, the terminology used is also different. Some ROM-based loader programs permit the user to set a password, which means the loader will not run until the password is typed into the computer. If a password has been set it may be more difficult to collect evidence from the computer. For instance, a computer can be booted from a floppy disk or by requesting a recovery expert to manually control the computer to overwrite the password. If such processes are used they can alter the settings in the computer, including the date and time stamps of files, which, in turn, may reduce the weight to be attached to any evidence obtained from the computer.

Types of evidence available on a computer

1.14 A range of digital evidence from a computer can be made available by a forensic investigator. This section provides an outline of some of the types of evidence that can be gleaned. Although the examples given above emphasise the types of evidence available on a Windows system, other operating systems have similar attributes that enable digital evidence to be revealed by means of a forensic examination. It must be stressed that a computer can yield a great deal of digital evidence even when files are hidden or deleted. It takes a highly skilled person to remove all traces of evidence on a computer and such skill is very rare. Some forensic techniques exist that can recover data even when it has been strictly overwritten on disk. However, where these techniques are used the disk will no longer be usable afterwards. Evidence can also be obtained from email, which is discussed in greater detail below.

Files and logs

1.15 A wide range of application software is used on a computer, including programs enabling a user to send facsimile transmissions, prepare spreadsheets, databases, text documents, graphic files, multimedia and presentations. The files themselves include digital evidence, as do system logs. A great deal of data is capable of being retrieved, depending on the method of storage, the media it is stored on and how the storage device allocates space to data as it is created and stored. Below is a simple outline of some of the main sources of digital evidence.

Documents and files used by the user

1.16 Files containing text can be searched for key words; forensic tools can then be used to view the 'metadata' (the data that describes or interprets the meaning of data). The metadata can include information such as the storage location of the file on the disk, the printer, and the date and time the file was originally created.

System and program files

1.17 Two types of log maintained by some Windows systems, application and system logs could contain information about events that have taken place on a computer or a system. This information can help to identify how an unauthorised computer user obtained access to a system with the intent of stealing information from the computer.

Logging mechanisms on UNIX systems vary between manufacturers. Almost all have 'syslog', a program that logs system events, such as application startup, and various classes of error messages. One feature of syslog is that it is able to send its log messages to another networked system as well as retaining them locally. As a result, if someone had root privileges on a system and wanted to erase something from the local logs they would not be able to erase the datum from the remote logs unless they had appropriate privileges on the remote machine as well.

The Windows system also includes a 'registry'. This is a store of data that contains a great deal of information, including a comprehensive database containing information on every program that is compatible with Windows that has been installed on the computer. It also includes information about the user of the computer, the preferences exercised by the user, about the hardware components, and about the network (if it is connect to one). The values stored in the registry are in hexadecimal format but can be converted to ASCII. An example of the type of information that the registry can provide to an investigator includes the data that Internet Explorer can replicate for a user when they visit a website with the AutoComplete feature turned on, such as their name, address, telephone number, email address and passwords. In addition, it is possible to establish when the user last downloaded a file from the Internet, including the first page the user logged into.

Temporary files and cache files

1.18 When a computer connects to the Internet a range of information is retained in different locations, including a list of the websites that have been visited, the contents that were viewed and any newsgroups that were visited. In addition, some Windows systems maintain a log of when the modem was used. Temporary files of websites that have been visited are stored in cache folders. The purpose of storing this information is to enable the computer to download a file faster if it is re-visited. These folders contain fragments of the web page, including images and text. Some versions of software will retain information about the websites visited in more than one location.

In addition to browser caches, UNIX systems also have 'swap space'. This is an area of disk that is used as virtual memory. In the event that the applications being run on the system require more memory than a system has available RAM, applications that are running and using RAM that have a low priority are copied on to the swap space. This enables RAM to be used by applications with a higher priority. Swap space is rarely cleaned during the normal operation of the system. This means that, when a system needs to be forensically analysed, it is often the case that useful data associated with applications, which may not even be running at the time, can be found by analysing the content of the swap space. This can also apply to data that is normally stored on the standard file system in an encrypted form. Depending on the application and the precise circumstances, some applications may allow unencrypted copies of data to be stored in the swap file.

Deleted files

1.19 File systems are used to record where data is located on a disk. The way data is stored will differ, depending on the operating software and the architecture of the method used to allocate blocks of storage for files. In simple terms, the location of data on a disk is controlled by a file system. For instance, the disk can be divided into partitions and, where this is the case, the information will be provided in a partition table. When a file is deleted, the instruction to delete effectively removes the pointer to the location of the file but does not delete the file. In the vast majority of cases it is possible to recover data that has been deleted, depending on the amount of disk-writing activity that has been performed between the deletion of the file and the forensic analysis[1].

[1]   Andy Jones and Christopher Meyler 'What evidence is left after disk cleaners?' (2004) Digital Investigation vol 1, no 3, 183–188.

Handheld devices

1.20 A range of handheld devices has become very popular recently, including the Blackberry, various forms of personal digital assistant ('PDA'), mobile telephones, cameras and music players. All of these devices are computers, with a CPU, memory, batteries, a lens, keypad or mouthpiece (input) and a screen or earpiece (output). Like computers, handheld devices can have two types of memory: read-only memory ('ROM') and random access memory ('RAM'). The ROM stores the operating system and any essential software required for the device to function. The RAM is used to store other forms of software and data that the user may wish to retain. More recently, these devices are being manufactured with a programmable ROM that is capable of being modified. The most common form of programmable ROM used in these devices is called 'flash'. This is a form of solid-state memory chip that is capable of retaining content without power. Data can be stored and erased on this type of memory many times.

It is possible to use additional storage space to back-up data or hide incriminating data, and it is possible to import a database with a false date and time stamp into such devices. Such devices, especially digital music players, have the capacity to use wireless technology to download large volumes of data from a computer without the user being aware the data is being stolen. These devices, including laptop computers, are increasingly being used by organisations as part of an overall information technology infrastructure. Devices may be connected to the infrastructure either by way of the Internet or with the use of wireless technology, 802.11 or 'Bluetooth'. Such devices can be investigated for digital evidence, although the amount of information that can be obtained will differ between each device. For instance, it may only be necessary to find a list of the most recent telephone numbers called from a mobile telephone, whilst a Blackberry will probably contain substantial amounts of data, especially emails and other data, from a network that might aid an investigation.

NETWORKS

1.21 Gone are the days when most computers stood alone on a desk. The vast majority of computers are now connected, at least intermittently, to some form of network. The trails left by the assortment of logs and files in computers can produce digital evidence in abundance, including use of email, connection to the Internet and viewing of websites, and the transfer of files between computers. Other sources of digital evidence can be obtained from server logs, the contents of devices connected to the network and the records of traffic activity. In some instances, evidence contained on a network might be the only evidence that will be available, because the perpetrator of a crime may have successfully persuaded the victim to destroy evidence by disposing of their hard drive and any other hardware before the wrongful act is committed.

Types of network

Internet

1.22 The development of the Internet was brought about because the military in the United States of America recognised the need to ensure military communication networks could continue to communicate, even when important parts of the infrastructure were damaged beyond repair. The world wide web was introduced in 1993, making it easier for people to use the Internet. Other networks also exist that operate at higher speeds, such as the Abilene network[1]. When a computer connects to the Internet it uses a set of protocols called Internet protocol ('IP'). This can be considered as a common language that enables various types of network to communicate with each other. When a computer is connected to a network, it is referred to as a 'host'. The computer uses a modem or a network interface card ('NIC') to send and receive information, although large and medium sized organisations will have a Local Area Network ('LAN') gateway to the Internet. A computer, or host, that is connected to two or more networks is called a 'router' if it mediates the passage of traffic between them, and if the networks have different addresses. Most networks use bespoke routers. Routers are a very important part of a network because they act to direct data from one network to another, filter traffic that is not sought after, and keep logs of activity. Some routers maintain system logs and others may generate NetFlow logs and Argus logs amongst others that contain more detailed data. A further component of the modern communication infrastructure is the server, often viewed as a very powerful computer that provides a service to a range of clients: for instance, allowing a user to connect to the Internet and to receive and send emails. Some servers permit anyone to obtain access to its resources without limitation, such as web servers. Other servers, such as email servers, only permit authorised users to obtain access to the service, usually by means of a password and a secondary form of identification. Sources of digital evidence from servers include logs recording when a user logs on to a server, whether to obtain access to the Internet or to download email.

1   At http://abilene.Internet2.edu.

Corporate intranets

1.23 An intranet, usually run by a large organisation, is a network that is based on Internet protocols. In theory, an intranet is only available to members, employees or others with authorisation to enter it and use the information contained on the intranet. The intranet looks like a smaller version of the Internet, providing websites, mail servers and time servers amongst other facilities, and being situated within a corporate firewall, which aims to keep unauthorised users from gaining access and usually protects it.

Wireless networking

1.24 One further recent development is the introduction of wireless technology. Wireless networking is also known as 'Wi-Fi', meaning 'wireless fidelity' (Wi-Fi is a mark used by the Wi-Fi Alliance, formerly known as the Wireless Ethernet Compatibility Alliance, to denote interoperability), and 802.11 networking. The number 802 is the name given to the interoperability standard developed by the Institute of Electrical and Electronic Engineers for Local Area Networks and Metropolitan Area Networks and Wi-Fi is based on 802.11, which is a sub-set of the 802 standard relating to wireless local area networks. This form of technology uses radio waves to carry data. Another wireless technology, known as Bluetooth, actively attempts to connect to devices within its (usually much shorter) range on a different radio frequency band. Various logs will record the use of the wireless network, enabling digital evidence of use to be uncovered if necessary.

Cellular networks

1.25 The technology that enables devices to transfer data between a computer and a cellular telephone, and between cellular telephones, is developing rapidly. A cellular network enables a computer to connect to the Internet by using a cellular telephone in a similar way that a modem is used to connect the computer using a telephone line. The network is made up of a number of cell sites within a defined geographical area. An individual connected to a cell site can make and receive calls over the network. Each cell site is connected to a central computing infrastructure, called a Class 5 switch. This infrastructure processes the calls by routing them to their destination and retains logs for the purpose of sending out bills, maintenance and, if necessary, to carry out investigation. The most recent developments in the technology include General Packet Radio Service ('GPRS') and Third Generation Mobile Telephones ('3G') over Universal Mobile Telephony Service ('UTMS'), developments that provide faster transmission rates and enable the transmission of music and video over a network. The most widely known form of cellular network is used by mobile telephones. These supplant, and will eventually replace, the Global System for Mobile Communication ('GSM') standard which, while incorporating encryption mechanisms, is now considered to have security flaws which are feasible, though complex, to exploit.

A mobile telephone has two numbers that identify the device. The manufacturer includes an Electronic Serial Number in the microchip when the item is produced, sometimes known as an IMSI or TIMSI, and the subscriber is given a Mobile Identification Number or telephone number (often referred to as an 'MSISDN'), when they enter into an agreement to subscribe to the network. The telephone company uses these numbers to direct calls to the telephone. In order to ensure the telephone company knows where to direct the call, the position of the telephone is constantly tracked when it is switched on, by reference to which hex it is located in. The range of digital evidence associated with the use of a mobile telephone includes where the telephone was located geographically and details of calls made and received. Where a telephone is capable of being used in other ways, such as making micro-payments, data relating to such services is also capable of being retrieved[1].

[1] Svein Yngvar Willassen 'Forensics and the GSM mobile telephone system' (2003) International Journal of Digital Evidence vol 2, issue 1, available online at http://www.ijde.org.

Dial-up

1.26 Many computers are connected to the Internet by means of the traditional copper telephone line. A dial-up modem in the computer only connects the computer to the Internet when the user specifically instructs the computer to make the connection.

Types of application that run on a network

Email

1.27 It is possible to state, without fear of contradiction, that the bulk of correspondence undertaken within and between organisations now takes the form of the exchange of email. Email is, essentially, an unstructured form of communication. As a result, it is the content that determines the purpose:

(a)   an email discussing official business between employees internally is an internal memorandum;

(b)   a similar email sent out to a third party relating to official business is an external communication and should be treated as official stationery, by being sent with the same corporate information that is contained on the stationery;

(c)   an extension of a telephone conversation, confirming something, for instance, is a note to be added to a file, whether it is sent to people within the organisation or to external addressees, or a mix of internal and external addressees;

(d)   a note to a friend to say you enjoyed the party last night, or to colleagues inviting them to join you in a glass of port and a slice of Dundee cake to celebrate your birthday, is an item of private correspondence using the organisation's resources. The use of email for this purpose may or may not be authorised by the organisation.

Email is an important source of digital evidence. However, emails should be treated with some discretion because a person can conceal their identity and hide behind a false email address with relative ease. It is very easy to send an email that appears to come from someone other than the real source. In spite of the ease by which emails may be forged, email has been used in a variety of cases, both criminal and civil. To obtain access to email it is normal to interact with two different services, one for outgoing mail and one for incoming. These services may or may not be provided by the same server. To read email, the individual must direct the email program to connect to a mail server using one of a number of protocols, the most common of which are:

(a)   Post Office Protocol ('POP');

(b)   Internet Mail Access Protocol ('IMAP');

(c)   a proprietary protocol by Microsoft, called Messaging Application Programming Interface ('MAPI').

The POP protocol (POP 3 is the most widely used version) permits the user to read their email by downloading it from a remote server and on to the hard disk of their local computer. Once the email has been downloaded from the server it is automatically deleted from the live server, but probably not from the back-up server that will invariably be used by an ISP for the purpose of recovering from a failure for any reason. By contrast, the IMAP protocol (IMAP4 being the most widely used) enables the user to leave all their email on the mail server. Keeping all the email on a single server can be an advantage for an organisation because the email for the entire organisation can be backed up from a central location. However, the problem with keeping all email communications on the server is that the server will eventually become overloaded due to the volume of data. These protocols require a user to have a username and a password before the user can obtain access to the mail download service. In addition, the protocol servers keep logs of who checked email and when it was checked. This enables an investigator to look for evidence of email traffic, even where a user has deleted all of their emails.

Outgoing email uses a different protocol, called Simple Mail Transfer Protocol ('SMTP'), although MAPI also includes outgoing email. The servers support-ing SMTP do not normally require a user to use a password. This makes it very easy for an individual to forge a message. However, the SMTP server may keep a log of the messages that pass through the system.

When an email is sent from a computer, it will pass on to one of a number of Message Transfer Agents ('MTA'). The MTAs act in the same way as the post office. A local MTA will receive the email. Upon receipt, it will add the current time and date, the name of the MTA, together with additional information, at the top of the message. The information is included in what is called the header of the email. As the message passes through MTAs, so each MTA will add further date and time stamps to the header. The most recent information will be at the top of the header. Another item of information that tends to be collected in the header is the Internet protocol ('IP') address of the computer or system connecting to the server. Technically astute users of email who may wish to hide their identity can send messages through anonymous or pseu-donymous remailing services. When email is sent through such a remailing agent, the header information may be stripped out before the message is sent on to its destination. However, some forms of digital evidence are transferred during such a process, and it is possible for forensic investigators to attempt to find evidence that may be useful[1].

[1] Craig Earnshaw and Sandeep Jadav 'Email Tracing' (2004) Computers and Law, June/July, pp 7–9 for an introduction.

Instant messaging

1.28 Instant messaging ('IM') is a form of software that enables the user to generate a variety of conversations with other individuals in order to commu-nicate in real time over the Internet. This form of communication is similar to a conversation over the telephone but the users communicate by typing messages into the software. The technology also permits the user to share files. Instant messaging has become popular because the software can be down-loaded at no cost and is easy to install and use. Depending on the type of software used, the program will, when a message is initiated, connect the two computers in a direct link through the computer ports. There are two significant problems: the instant message server does not necessarily log such messages, which means that such conversations can be considered conceptu-ally similar to a conversation over the telephone; and the program has a feature that allows messages to pass through legitimate open ports if others are not available. Whether such conversations are recorded will depend on the software used.

An earlier variant of IM exists which enables conversations to take place in a similar way to a conference call, as distinct from the computer-to-computer conversation with Instant Messaging. This technology is known as Internet Relay Chat ('IRC'), and frequently suffers from the same issues as IM, in that servers are not typically configured to log conversations.

Computer-to-computer

1.29 As personal computers have developed, so their capacity and power has increased. As a result, there is less of a dividing line between a client and a server. This is because any host can be made into a server by installing appropriate software into the computer. The software then permits other hosts to obtain access to the computer over the network. This is called peer-to-peer networking ('P2P') [1].

[1] Geoff Fellows 'Peer-to-peer networking issues—an overview' (2004) Digital Investigation vol 1, no 1, pp 3–6.

SOME PROBLEM AREAS

Malicious software

1.30 The range of tasks performed by such malicious software is probably only restricted to the imagination of the person that creates the program. A number of recent cases in the criminal courts, where people have been accused of being in possession of child pornography on their computer, have used the defence that some form of malicious software caused data to be downloaded to a computer or enabled a third party to obtain access to the computer without the permission of the owner of the computer[1]. In the case of *R v Caffrey*,[2] the defendant was charged with causing unauthorised modification of computer material under s 3(1) of the Computer Misuse Act 1990. The prosecution alleged that the defendant sent a deluge of electronic data from his computer to a computer server operated in the Port of Houston, Texas, Unites States of America, the effect of which was to cause the computer at the Port of Houston to shut down. He claimed, in his defence, that unknown hackers obtained control of his computer and then launched a number of programs to attack the computer at the Port of Houston. The forensic examiner for the prosecution could not find any evidence of a Trojan horse on the computer. The defence claimed that it was impossible for every file to have been tested and that the Trojan horse file might have had a facility to destroy itself, leaving no trace of having resided on his computer. The forensic examiner for the prosecution stated that a Trojan horse would leave a trace on the computer. The jury acquitted Mr Caffrey[3].

[1] *R v Schofield* (April 2003) Reading Crown Court and *R v Green* (October 2003) Exeter Crown Court.
[2] Southwark Crown Court, October 2003.
[3] Esther George 'Casenote' (2004) Digital Investigation vol 1, no 2, p 89.

1.31 It should be noted that just because an individual may have such materials on their computer, it does not follow that they were responsible for downloading it on to their computer. It is important for any forensic examiner to report their findings within the context of what the technology is capable of doing. For instance, it is possible to introduce malicious software on web pages without the permission of the website owner. When a person visits the website, the software will re-direct the computer to pornographic websites containing indecent material and the computer will automatically download the material on to the computer into the temporary cache file without the user's permission or knowledge[1].

[1]   Megan Carney and Marc Rogers 'The Trojan Made Me Do It: A First Step in Statistical Based Computer Forensics Event Reconstruction' (2004) International Journal of Digital Evidence (2004) vol 2, issue 4, available online at http://www.ijde.org.

The Trojan horse

1.32 A Trojan horse is a malicious software program containing hidden code that is designed to conceal itself in a computer as if it is a legitimate item of software. When activated, the software will perform an operation that is not authorised by the user. A Trojan horse program, when initiated, can cause the destruction of data (including the entire hard drive); collect data on a computer and send it to a third party without the user being aware of what is happening; counteract security measures installed on a computer; instruct the computer to perform tasks, such as take part in a denial of service attack, or permit the creator of the program to obtain access to the computer.

Viruses

1.33 A virus is a small piece of software that attaches itself to a program that reproduces itself when the program runs. A computer virus shares some of the traits of biological viruses, hence the name. The computer virus is designed to pass from computer to computer. It will load itself into memory and then affect other programs or documents in the computer. This process is also called 'infection'. A virus can destroy, change or alter data and can also be designed to slow down or hinder other operations of the system. Viruses can also be classified as email viruses when they are transported by way of email. This form of virus may replicate itself automatically, or it may require the intervention of an unwitting user to run it.

Encrypted data

1.34 Encryption (or enciphering) is the process by which a plaintext (or cleartext) message is disguised sufficiently to hide the substance of the content. As well as ordinary text, a plaintext message can be a stream of binary digits, a text file, a bitmap, a recording of sound in digital format, audio images of a video or film and any other information formed into digital bits. When a message has been encrypted, it is known as ciphertext. The opposite procedure, that of turning the ciphertext back into plaintext, is called decryption (or deciphering). Criminals and terrorists are using encryption to protect data stored on their computers and to hide their activities when using the Internet and email. The three methods of resolving the problem with data that is encrypted are to find the encrypted data in plain form; obtain the password that protects the encryption key; or attempt to guess what the password is[1]. It is probable that most suspects will not offer up the relevant password or key, so investigators have to try other means to determine the content of the encrypted files. Another way of obtaining the plain text is to examine the keys, as in the United States case of *United States of America v Hersh aka Mario*[2]. In his summary of the facts, Circuit Judge Marcus pointed out that a search of Hersh's residence uncovered evidence of computer images of juvenile males engaged in sexual activities. A number of files were encrypted, and the judge described, in footnote number four, how these were handled by the investigators:

> Several computer files containing child pornography were found in Hersh's residence: (1) three recovered computer files with viewable images found on the C-drive of Hersh's computer, and (2) encrypted files found on a high-capacity Zip disk. The images on the Zip disk had been encrypted by software known as F-Secure, which was found on Hersh's computer. When agents could not break the encryption code, they obtained a partial source code from the manufacturer that allowed them to interpret information on the file print outs. The Zip disk contained 1,090 computer files, each identified in the directory by a unique file name, such as 'sfuckmo2,' 'naked31,' 'boydoggy,' 'dvsex01, dvsex02, dvsex03,' etc., that was consistent with names of child pornography files. The list of encrypted files was compared with a government database of child pornography. Agents compared the 1,090 files on Hersh's Zip disk with the database and matched 120 file names. Twenty two of those had the same number of pre-encryption computer bytes as the pre-encrypted version of the files on Hersh's Zip disk.

In this instance, although the files could not be decrypted there was, nevertheless, a sufficient link between the names of the files and evidence of child pornography known to the police[3].

[1] Eoghan Casey 'Practical Approaches to Recovering Encrypted Digital Evidence' (2002) International Journal of Digital Evidence vol 1, issue 3; Jason Siegfied, Christine Siedsma, Bobbie-Jo Countryman and Chester D Hosmer 'Examining the Encryption Threat' (2004) International Journal of Digital Evidence vol 2, issue 3, online at http://www.ijde.org; Hank Wolfe 'Penetrating encrypted evidence' (2004) Digital Investigation vol 1, no 2, 102–105.
[2] United States Court of Appeals for the Eleventh Circuit No 00–14592 July 17, 2002 before Anderson and Marcus, Circuit Judges, and Middlebrooks, District Judge, available in electronic format at http://laws.lp.findlaw.com/11th/0014592opn.html.
[3] For some problems that encryption might have on the authentication of digital evidence, see Eric Thompson 'MD5 collisions and the impact on computer forensics' (2005) Digital Investigation vol 2, no 1, 36–40. For an example where an encoded message was sent by an accused whilst in a county jail awaiting trial and subsequently used to help prove guilt, see Dorn Vernessa Samuel 'Code Breaking in Law Enforcement: A 400-Year History' (2006) Forensic Science Communications vol 8, no 2, available online at http://www.fbi.gov/hq/lab/fsc/backissu/april2006/research/2006_04_research01.htm.

Steganography

1.35 Steganography is the method of hiding a message inside a digital object, such as graphic files, pictures, films or sounds. The sender is able to hide a message in a seemingly innocuous file, and the recipient can retrieve the message upon receipt. Methods used to hide data including writing data to slack space or space that has not been allocated a use; hiding data on a hard drive in a secret partition; and the transmission of data under the cover of transmission protocols. Various types of commercial and free software are available to perform steganography on data. It can be relatively difficult to detect hidden data within a file and the communication can be even more difficult to uncover if the message has been compressed and encrypted before being hidden in the carrier. At present, it is unlikely that many investigators undertake a routine examination for hidden data[1].

[1] Brent T McBride, Gilbert L Peterson and Steven C Gustafson 'A new blind method for detecting novel steganography' (2005) Digital Investigation vol 2, no 1, 50–70; a wide range of references on this topic is provided in Gary C Kessler 'An Overview of Steganography for the Computer Forensics Examiner' (2004) Forensic Science Communications vol 6, no 3, available online at http://www.fbi.gov/hq/lab/fsc/backissu/july2004/research/2004_03_research01.htm.

CONCLUDING REMARKS

1.36 Now that we live in the age of the computer and networked devices, the range of digital evidence that is capable of being investigated and disclosed in legal proceedings is very wide. From the files on a digital camera to the complex behaviour of a computer attached to the Internet, assessing digital evidence is becoming the staple of a lawyer's life.

Chapter 2

THE CHARACTERISTICS OF ELECTRONIC EVIDENCE

STEPHEN MASON

2.01 Documents that exist in a format other than on paper are commonly described as 'electronic documents' or 'digital documents'. Whether the terms are considered interchangeable or not, the word 'electronic' is a useful shorthand to describe the nature of the medium. Either term may be correct, but the reader should not be confused between analogue and digital.

Examples of evidence obtained from analogue devices include vinyl records, audio tape, photographic film and telephone calls made over the public switched telephone network. Analogue systems or products generate evidence in the form of data that is capable of being produced in a permanent form. For instance, a camera (depending on the type of camera: a camera that produces instant photographs does not have a negative) will create primary evidence, in the form of a negative transparency or plate, and secondary evidence, in the form of photographs taken from the film. Examples of digital data include anything that has been created or stored on a computer or is made available by way of the Internet, including CDs, DVDs, MP3s and digital broadcast radio. The term 'electronic' may be considered to be a generic term which encompasses all forms of data, whether produced by an analogue device, or in digital form.

Digital

2.02 Two definitions are offered for the word 'digital' by the Oxford English Dictionary[1], both of which help to explain the meaning of digital:

> Relating to or operating with signals or information represented by discrete numeric values of a physical quantity such as voltage or magnetic polarization (commonly representing the digits 0 and 1); designating a signal or information of this kind. Opposed to analogue.

> Relating to or involving the capture, storage, or manipulation of images by digital means; (of an image) stored or represented digitally; (of a device) capturing or generating such images. Also in Cinematogr.: utilizing this technology in film or television production.

The entry for digital in the Wikipedia includes the following[1]:

> A digital system is one that uses discrete numbers, especially binary numbers, or non-numeric symbols such as letters or icons, for input, processing, transmission, storage, or display, rather than a continuous spectrum of values (an analog system) ... The word digital is most commonly used in computing and

electronics, especially where real-world information is converted to binary numeric form as in digital audio and digital photography. Such data-carrying signals carry either one of two electronic or optical pulses, logic 1 (pulse present) or 0 (pulse absent). The term is often meant by the prefix 'e-', as in email and ebook, even though not all electronics systems are digital.

Although this definition specifically applies to the way in which a computer uses data, the definition of 'digital' is, nevertheless, sufficiently wide to encompass any hardware or software that can be included within the concept of information technology. The phrase 'information technology' is meant, in this context, to include any form of technology that utilises the building blocks included in a computer or any other device that uses the basic components of a computer.

1   *Oxford English Dictionary* (electronic edition) (2nd edn, 1989 and Additions, 1993–7).
2   http://en.wikipedia.org/wiki/Digital.

2.03 Other definitions of digital evidence include 'information of probative value stored or transmitted in binary form'[1] and 'information stored or transmitted in binary form that may be relied on in court'[2]. Both of these definitions have been criticised because they focus on the value of the information as evidence and whether it can be relied upon in court. In addition, the use of 'binary' is too restrictive because it only describes one form of data[3]. Casey defines digital evidence for the purpose of the text of his book, which specifically relates to crime, as[4]:

> any data stored or transmitted using a computer that support or refute a theory of how an offense occurred or that address critical elements of the offense such as intent or alibi.

The data referred to in this definition covers the combinations of numbers that represent information held in digital format, such as text, images, audio and video files. Also, it is to be assumed that the use of the word 'computer' is meant to be understood in its widest possible sense and incorporates any form of device that stores, manipulates or transmits data. Whilst this definition is wider than the previous examples, the emphasis is on digital evidence that applies to criminal investigations and not to digital evidence generally. In addition, it also implies that the evidence is relevant and admissible. A sound definition can be helpful to both practitioners and lawyers, if only to ensure that when the phrase is used both parties are aware of what it means. With the aim of attempting to offer a wider-ranging definition, that includes both civil and criminal cases, the following definition is proffered:

Electronic evidence: data (comprising the output of analogue devices or data in digital format) that is created, manipulated, stored or communicated by any device, computer or computer system or transmitted over a communication system, that is relevant to the process of adjudication.

This definition has three elements. First, it intends to include all forms of evidence that is created, manipulated or stored in a product that can, in its widest meaning, be considered a computer. Second, it aims to include the various forms of device by which data can be stored or transmitted, including analogue devices that produce an output. Ideally, this definition will include any form of device, whether it be a computer as we presently understand the meaning of a computer; telephone systems, wireless telecommunications systems and networks, such as the Internet; and computer systems that are embedded into a device, such as mobile telephones, smart cards and navigation systems. The third element restricts the data to information that is relevant to the process by which a dispute is decided by an adjudicator, whatever the nature of the disagreement and whatever the form and level the adjudication takes. This part of the definition does not cover the admissibility of the evidence because some evidence will be admissible but excluded by the adjudicator within the remit of their authority.

In summary, lawyers are required to offer appropriate advice to clients in relation to the disclosure or discovery of data in digital format. Conceivably, if lawyers fail in their duty to understand more fully the issues surrounding digital data they may find themselves subject to actions for negligence in the future.

[1]   'Best practices for digital evidence laboratory programs' v1.0, Scientific Working Group for Digital Evidence, Glossary, available in electronic format at http://ncfs.org/swgde/documents.html.

[2]   'G8 Proposed Principles for the Procedures Relating to Digital Evidence' International Organization on Computer Evidence, available in electronic format at http://www.ioce.org/G8_proposed_principles_for_forensic_evidence.html. This definition has been adopted by the US Department of Justice Officer of Justice Programs National Institute of Justice in both of its documents 'Electronic Crime Scene Investigation A Guide for First Responders' July 2001 and 'Forensic Examination of Digital Evidence: A Guide for Law Enforcement' Special Report April 2004, both available in electronic format at http://www.ncfs.org/digital_evd.html.

[3]   Eoghan Casey *Digital Evidence and Computer Crime Forensic Science, Computers and the Internet* (2nd edn, 2004) p 12.

[4]   *Casey* (2004) p 12.

CHARACTERISTICS OF DIGITAL EVIDENCE[1]

2.04 Documents in digital format have particular characteristics that affect both the test for authenticity or provenance should authenticity be in issue, and the way in which the evidence is secured and handled at the pre-trial stage. Arguably, evidence in digital format ought to be subject to a more rigorous mechanism than would normally be associated with a document extant on physical media. John D Gregory has observed that the integrity of physical documents is 'often protected fairly causally'[2], yet the same could be said of documents that are created, modified, communicated, stored and deleted in digital format. The two forms of document, physical and digital, cannot be compared like-for-like because the criteria by which a document in digital format must be tested will differ, by its very nature, to that of a physical document. Both forms of document may have similar tests, such as testimony of creation and signature, for instance. However, the nature of the different type of documents will determine the most appropriate tests for authenticity, should authenticity be in question. Similarly, the distinctive characteristics of evidence in digital format highlight the unique nature of the additional problems that parties to litigation must take cognisance of. One very simple feature of digital evidence illustrates the nature of the medium: the term 'ghosting' is used to include white letters on a white background, or black letters on a black background. Obviously there is nothing new in this technique, because forms of clear ink have been used to achieve the same effect on paper documents. This technique can be undertaken with ease on a digital document to hide text but, unless tests are undertaken to reveal whether a document has been subject to this technique, it is possible that evidence might be missed. Documents in digital format have a number of features that present particular challenges that a paper carrier does not in the physical world, as outlined below.

1 William Kent *Data and Reality* (2nd edn, 2000) for an interesting plunge into how humans perceive and process information, and how humans impose this outlook on data processing machines.
2 John D Gregory 'Authentication Rules and Electronic Records' (2002) Can BR vol 81, 533.

The dependency on machinery and software

2.05 Data in digital format is dependant on hardware and software. The data requires an interpreter to enable it to be rendered into a 'human readable' format. A user cannot create or manipulate digital data without appropriate hardware in the form of machines. The machines are useless unless the associated software is loaded on to the hardware. Both the hardware and the software produce evidence that includes, but is not limited to, metadata and logs that may be relevant to any given file or document in digital format. Thousands of software programmes that were common in the 1990s are now no longer available commercially and, even if application software were available, it might be impossible to load the software on to an up-to-date version of the operating system. An additional problem for older data is that it might be necessary to have a specific machine with specific software loaded on to it in order to read the data[1]. This can cause additional expense to a party, as in the case of *PHE, Incorporated dba Adam & Eve v Department of Justice*[2], where PHE were ordered to review information contained in a database, even though no program existed to enable them to obtain the information requested by the Department of Justice.

1 For instance, the jazz club Ronnie Scotts, based in Soho, London, was refurbished in 2005–2006. As each part of the club was renovated, so large numbers of recordings of jazz musicians and singers, such as Dizzy Gillespie, Ella Fitzgerald, Chet Baker, Sarah Vaughan and Buddy Rich, recorded during live performances, were discovered. Some of the recordings were made on tapes that required machines that were no longer in the possession of the club, so they will have to find a specialist company that has retained the relevant type of machine in order to re-play the tapes. Report by Bob Sherwood (2006) Financial Times, June 28, 2006, p 1.
2 139 F.R.D. 249 (D.D.C. 1991).

The mediation of technology

2.06 Data in electronic format must be rendered into human-readable form through the mediation of a set of technologies. This means differences occur in how the same source object is displayed in different situations. A good example, familiar to all users of the Internet, is that a website can look very different depending on, amongst other things, when it is viewed and what browser is used. As a result, there can be no concept of a single, definitive representation of a particular source digital object.

Speed of change

2.07 The technology used in the operating systems, application software and hardware changes rapidly. As a result, digital documents may reach a point where they cannot be read, understood or used. Technical obsolescence is a major problem that will affect disclosure or discovery, particularly because the rate of change has become so rapid. Another situation to take into account arises where a software company no longer produces software that is backward-compatible, also referred to as being downward-compatible. Backward compatibility occurs where new versions of software are able to operate with other products that were designed for an older product.

Volume and replication

2.08 Digital documents are easy to manipulate: they can be copied, altered, updated, deleted (deleted does not mean expunged) or intercepted, as in the English case of *Relf v Rifkind; Hibbert v Rifkind*[1] in which David Relf, a property developer, negotiated a commercial property investment for Network Housing Association in 1997. Network entered into two agreements with the developers,Charles Rifkind and Jonathan Levy and their company, Point Ventures Ltd, for the purchase and sub-sale of a development and to split the profits out of the development and sale of the property. In August 2000, Network began action against Point Ventures. It sought a declaration that the joint venture agreement of 17 October 1997 was valid and enforceable, and for damages for the failure of Point Ventures to obtain planning permission in accordance with the terms of the agreement. Point Ventures denied the existence of any enforceable contract. In 2001, Point Ventures raised a new issue that if there was an agreement, as alleged, it was not enforceable because, it was alleged, it had been procured by reason of a corrupt relationship between Mr Relf and Peter Hibbert, the Chief Executive of Network Housing Association. It transpired that Rifkind and Levy had been tapping the voicemail box of Mr Hibbert's mobile telephone for between two and three years. They alleged there was a corrupt relationship between Peter Hibbert and David Relf. The evidence they adduced was a series of messages that had been pieced together in an attempt to create the impression of a corrupt relationship around the time of the property transaction, 1997. When the evidence was provided to the lawyers for David Relf, it transpired that the messages had been tapped from 2000, years after the property transaction. A settlement was reached with a record reward of damages (£115,000) for breach of confidence.

A significant development took place in the latter quarter of the twentieth century that allowed data to be created and exchanged in far greater volumes than had been possible hitherto. This was the integration of telecommunications and computers to form computer networks. Computers that were physically seperate were linked by way of local area networks and computer networks. This development gave users the ability to communicate between computers in the same office or building. Local area networks were soon linked together through wide area networks, the most well known of which is the Internet. Once computers are networked together in this fashion, the user has the ability to create and transmit large volumes of data. For instance, one Word document can be sent to any number of people across the globe. If the creator of this document sends the file to 20 people, the number of copies will far exceed 20 when each person copies the file to another drive on their computer, and their organisations back up their email databases each day, then back up their main database each week, and copies are burnt on to CD-ROMs or copied on to external storage devices. This phenomenon is described as 'networked communications'. In essence, email, instant messaging and other forms of communication are a duplicate and distributed technology. As a result, the volumes of data that need to be identified to obtain relevant documents pertaining to litigation or the prosecution of a criminal offence have now become enormous[2]. In addition, there is the vexed question of the number of copies of a document that exist, which can affect the parties to litigation in determining which version of a document to rely upon. An email, for instance, will exist, at a minimum, on at least two computers or servers: those of the sender and the recipient. The metadata associated with the email that is sent will differ to the metadata to the email that has been received, even if nothing else in the email is altered. It is conceivable that the facts of case may turn on the content of the email in question and, if so, forensic evidence may be crucial in helping to determine the probability that the content of one email is to be trusted over the content of the other.

[1]   [2002] EWHC 2199 (Ch); 'Watch what you say in that voicemail' (2003) The Times, 25 February, p 10.
[2]   For an estimate of the volumes of data, see 'How much information?' a study produced by members of the faculty and students at the School of Information Management Systems at the University of California at Berkeley: 'this study is an attempt to estimate how much new information is created each year. Newly created information is distributed in four storage media: print, film, magnetic, and optical and seen or heard in four information flows: telephone, radio and TV, and the Internet.' Available online at http://www2.sims.berkeley.edu/research/projects/how-much-info/.

Metadata

2.09 Metadata is, essentially, data about data. In digital documents, metadata tends to be information that is hidden from the replication of the text as viewed on a screen. For instance, the metadata in relation to a piece of paper may be:

(a)   explicit from perusing the paper itself, such as the title of the document, the date, the name of the person that wrote it, who received it and where the document is located;
(b)   implicit, which includes such characteristics as the types of typeface used, such as bold, underline or italic; perhaps the document is located in a coloured storage file to denote a particular type of document; labels

may also act as pointers to allow the person using the document to deal with it in a particular manner, such as a file marked 'confidential', for instance.

Physical documents can be subject to intensive scrutiny, and the data contained on the document can be analysed in great detail. One example is document tav/149, which was adduced as evidence in the trial of Ivan Demjanjuk in the Special District Court of Jerusalem in 1986. The defendant was accused of being an accomplice to mass murder in the Treblinka concentration camp who, as a response to his alleged actions, was called by the prisoners of the camp 'Ivan Grozny' or 'Ivan the Terrible'. The document in question appeared to be a service certificate of the guard forces in the service of the SS and the police in the eastern territory, situated in the Trawniki training centre in the Lublin district of Poland. The certificate had the name of the defendant, together with further identifying particulars: date and place of birth, a photograph in SS uniform, which appeared to contain his image, and the name of his father. The prosecution went to great lengths to prove this document was genuine, and therefore authentic, particularly in the light of the defence claim that it was a forgery by the KGB. Ivan Demjanjuk was found guilty of the charges. He was subsequently released in 1993 after an appeal hearing which established that the document was not what it purported to be, and another person was identified as the notorious guard at Treblinka[1].

Implicit data needs to be made explicit if it is to be used to help interpret the purpose of electronic documents. All documents in digital format will contain metadata in one form or another, be they email communications, spreadsheets, websites or word-processing documents. Such data can be included by, and be taken automatically from, the originating application software, or supplied by the person that originally created the record. The list of information that is available includes, but is not limited to: when and how a document was created (time and date); the file type; the location from which the file was opened or where it was stored; when the file was last opened (time and date); when it was last modified; when the file was last saved; when it was last printed; the identity of the previous authors; the location of the file on each occasion it was stored; the details of who else may be able to obtain access to it, and, in the case of email, revealing blind carbon copy (bcc) addresses. The name of the author may also be available, although this will not necessarily be reliable where a document is revised on a number of occasions, on different computers or by different people: the name of the author may bear no resemblance to the document; the person originating a document may not use a new file, but create the document by opening an old file, deleting the majority of the text, then creating the genesis of the new text; and the name of the author may not be accurate if somebody other then the purported author logged on to a computer or system using the name of the person.

[1] *The State of Israel v Ivan (John) Demjanjuk*, Criminal Cases (Jerusalem) 373/86, a full transcript of which is published in *The Demjanjuk Trial* (1991); Yoram Sheftel *Show Trial* (1994) Victor Gollancz; Tom Teicholz *The Trial of Ivan the Terrible* (1990); Williem S Wagenaar *Identifying Ivan* (1988). See Dana M Wagner *Fouled Anchors: The 'Constellation' Question Answered* (1991) David Taylor Research Centre, Technical and Administrative Services Department, Research and Development Report DTRC-91/CT06, for details of the forgery of the physical documentation relating to the USS Constellation, anchored in Boston, available online at http://www.dt.navy.mil/cnsm/faq_13.html.

2.10 In broad terms, there are three main types of metadata:

(a)   descriptive metadata, which may describe a resource for a particular purpose, such as a disclosure or discovery exercise. The metadata may include such information as title, key words, abstract and the name of the person purporting to be the author. To more fully understand the history of the document it would be necessary to obtain the underlying information about how and when the system recorded the name of the purported author;

(b)   structural metadata, which will describe how a number of objects are brought together. Some examples of structural metadata include 'file identification' making it possible to identify an individual chapter that forms part of a book or report; 'file encoding', which identifies the codes that were used in relation to the file, including the data encoding standard used (ASCII, for instance), the method used to compress the file and the method of encryption, if used; 'file rendering', which serves to identify how the file was created and may include such information as the software application, operating system and hardware dependencies; 'content structure,' which defines the structure of the content of the record, such as a definition of the data set, the data dictionary, files setting out authority codes and such like; and 'source', which identifies the relevant circumstances that led to the capture of the data; and

(c)   administrative metadata, which provides information to help with the management of a resource. Administrative data is divided into further subsets that also may appear as discreet types of metadata. There are rights management metadata and preservation or record-keeping metadata.

The metadata can be fundamentally linked to a record in electronic format, included in the systems used to produce the record, contained within the electronic record, or linked from a separate system[1]. Metadata can be viewed in a variety of ways, one of which is to look at the 'properties' link in the application that created the document, such as in MS Word, or by using software written specifically for the purpose. Some metadata can also be removed with specialist software. This can be useful when sending files to third parties, but can attract additional expense if a court orders the data to be delivered up in its original format, as in the case of *Williams v Sprint/United Management Co*[2]. Sprint, before passing on documents in electronic format to the plaintiffs, modified MS Excel files by deleting certain adverse analyses, deleted social security numbers of employees mentioned in the spreadsheets, deleted metadata from the electronic files that included the spreadsheets and prevented the recipients from viewing certain data contained in spreadsheets by locking the value of the cells in the document. In this instance, Sprint was ordered to produce the spreadsheets in the manner in which they were maintained, including the metadata, although the adverse analyses and deleted social security numbers could be redacted, and was also ordered to produce unlocked versions of the spreadsheets. In his judgment, the learned judge discussed metadata and whether it forms part of a document in electronic format sufficiently for it to be given up to the other party[3].

---

[1]   See also the discussion by Waxse J in *Williams v Sprint/United Management Company* 230 F.R.D. 640 (D.Kan. 2005); 2005 WL 2401626 (D.Kan. 2005) at 646–647.

2   230 F.R.D. 640 (D.Kan. 2005); 2005 WL 2401626 (D.Kan. 2005).
3   230 F.R.D. 640 (D.Kan. 2005) at 646–648.

2.11 Two cases that have occurred in the United States of America serve to highlight how concerns relating to the preservation of data are viewed and the relevance of metadata. In the case of *Armstrong v Executive Office of the President, Office of Administration*[1], researchers and not-for-profit organisations challenged the proposed destruction of federal records. The Executive Office of the President, the Office of Administration, the National Security Council, the White House Communications Agency and Trudy Peterson, Acting Archivist of the United States, intended to require all employees to print out electronic communications on to paper in an attempt to discharge their obligations under the provisions of the Federal Records Act. The members of the United States Court of Appeals, District of Columbia Circuit, rejected this solution, because the hard-copy printed version 'may omit fundamental pieces of information which are an integral part of the original electronic records, such as the identity of the sender and/or recipient and the time of receipt' in the words of Mikva, CJ at 1277, although the judgment dealt with the technical issues in slightly greater detail.

By comparison, in the case of *Public Citizen v Carlin*[2] the plaintiffs, representing historians, researchers, journalists, and libraries, challenged the content of the General Records Schedule 20 (1995), which was issued by the federal Archivist that governed the disposal of electronic documents created by federal agencies. Advice was given in this Schedule that permitted agencies to retain records in hard-copy format, rather than in electronic format. It was this part of the Schedule that was in issue. The case was originally decided in favour of the plaintiffs, but the decision was reversed in 1999 when the United States Court of Appeals, District of Columbia Circuit rejected the notion that all records created in electronic format had to be archived in electronic format. Even though the appeal failed it is, nevertheless, of interest to observe a very important argument that was used by the plaintiffs in this case respecting the nature of email communications. It was argued that:

> Studies of electronic mail suggest that electronic communications are often the first, most candid, and most crucial communication of the information, see JA 542, and, as Iran-Contra investigators found, are particularly valuable because they provide 'first-hand, contemporaneous account of events.' Report of the President's Special Review Board [Tower Commission Report], at III-1 (Feb. 26, 1987). But defendants' guidelines encourage staff to discard such contemporaneous electronic records as nonrecord material if the 'information' appears elsewhere or will be 'reduced to' a formal, distilled paper document. As the district court found, 'this encourages staff to classify electronic materials as nonrecord, thus exempting them from preservation,' JA 75, and violates the FRA, which provides that two non-identical communications that record information on official business are both records, even if they record the same information.

> Indeed, the flaw in these instructions is underscored by defendants' admission that they equate electronic communications with 'telephone calls or face-to-face meetings'[3].

1   1 F.3d 1274 (D.C. Cir. 1993).
2   2 F.Supp.2d 1 (D.D.C. 1997); reversed 184 F.3d 900 (D.C. Cir. 1999).

3   Oral argument schedules for June 15, 1993 Nos. 93–5002, 93–5048. United States Court of Appeals for the District of Columbia Circuit, *Armstrong v Executive Office of the President*, on appeal from the United States District Court for the District of Columbia, Brief for the Appellees/Cross-Appellants dated May 3, 1993, available online at http:// listserv.muohio.edu/scripts/wa.exe?A2=ind9310e&L=archives&P=380.

2.12 As MacNeil makes clear, 'in making these assertions, the plaintiffs (and the courts) are ascribing a unique truth-value to electronic mail messages based on their superior candour and immediacy. Such ascription is perfectly consistent with the 'rule of zero' theory underpinning the selection of historical sources and with the 'ground-zero' theory underpinning the assessment of legal evidence. According to both the rule and the theory, a record is deemed to be true if it was produced close to the events that are in question'[1]. Although the first version of events described in a contemporaneous email is still subject to its own perspective, it does not detract from the value of the content, as illustrated in the English Employment Tribunal case of *Bower v Schroder Securities Ltd*[2]. During the mid-1990s, it was decided internally at Schroder Securities (now Schroder Saloman Smith Barney) that it was important to recruit a new drinks analyst who could cover the European market. In keeping with common practice within the industry, a group of senior people discussed the names of those they knew that they might approach to recruit for such a role. The name of Mrs Bower emerged as a potential candidate, partly because some had read her research and some knew her. Mrs Bower had nine years' experience of working in the City, she had previously worked for Credit Lyonnais and, from 1994, she worked for ABN-Amro, becoming a director in March 1996. Whilst at ABN-Ambro, she built up a team to analyse the two drinks sectors in the UK, covering alcoholic beverages and breweries, pubs and restaurants. Mrs Bower was interested in joining Schroder Securities and, after a series of meetings and discussions about contractual terms, she began working for Schroder on 1 April 1997, leaving on 8 October 1999. Although Mrs Bower's contract directed her to report to Patrick Wellington, Head of UK Research, it transpired that her immediate superior was Michael Crawshaw, Head of European Research. By October 1997, it became apparent that Mr Crawshaw preferred that Mrs Bower did not continue with her employment. Initial evidence for this conclusion was the existence of an email sent by Mr Crawshaw to Rachel Harry in personnel, as follows:

> Can you tell me what [Mrs Bower's] package is, when bonuses are paid out and what it would cost to pay her off if we need to (unfair dismissal, decided you aren't what we want etc.).

As time went by, disagreements between Mrs Bower and other people within Schroder occurred. For instance, during the course of April and June 1998 there was a debate, conducted largely by email, as to whether Mrs Bower or Caroline Levy in New York should cover Coca-Cola beverages. Barry Tarasoff was Caroline Levy's line manager. Mrs Bower was made the lead analyst for 12 months, to be reviewed thereafter, which resolved the matter. However, by early 1999 it appeared Mr Crawshaw was keen to remove Mrs Bower, evidence for which is demonstrated in an email from him to Mr Tarasoff in New York:

> I am now managing Julie out of the business. Although she has one or two fans at Schroder's and among the client base, she doesn't get on with many of the

people that count. In no particular order of importance: Leon Kalvaria, Rory Maw, Kieran Mahon, Andy Smith, Caroline Levy (me?).

If she were truly inspirational we might put up with the personality. However, her research is average at best, no target account rates her in their top three, commission figures are low, and her standing with the sales force is the lowest of any senior analyst.

I told her to buck up in her mid-year appraisal. In the end-year appraisal just gone I told her that she was dramatically under-performing the other analysts and that her relationships with colleagues were poor. Her bonus is getting slashed in a fortnight and then she will probably leave and/or I'll ask her to leave (I don't want to fire someone just before bonus round, and in any case, she does still deserve some small bonus.)

We shall then be looking to replace her and get Caroline involved in the process.

On the same day, Mr Crawshaw also sent an email to Philip Kay, Head of Japan, the content of which indicated Mrs Bower would not remain an employee of Schroder's for long: 'I wouldn't factor a global brewing piece into your plans'. A further dispute about what areas of stock Mrs Bower covered arose in August 1999 in connection with the coverage of Bass. Matters came to a head when Jean-Baptiste Delabare, the leisure analyst and Head of French Research, made an enquiry of Mrs Bower which she saw as an attack on what areas of stock she covered. As a result, she replied to Mr Delabare's request, which he had sent by email, and included the following: 'I have launched an official grievance against the management of Schroder's to uphold my contract, a situation with which the chairman of Schroder's is now involved. At this stage, therefore, my position is that the Paris office will not cover, write on, or meet with these companies (i.e. Bass, Compass and LVMH) until further notice.' Mrs Bower sent copies of this response to Mr Crawshaw, amongst others. Mr Crawshaw responded by sending a copy of a note to most of the people that received Mrs Bower's email, as follows: 'Julie has gone too far this time. I have prepared the pack of supporting evidence for Julie's dismissal and will circulate it later today.' This response was sent within three hours of Mrs Bower's email to Mr Delabare. As a result of this exchange of emails, Schroder's initiated a formal disciplinary procedure against Mrs Bower at the end of which she resigned, her notice expiring on 8 October 1999.

The members of the Tribunal concluded that Mrs Bower's claim for unfair dismissal succeeded. In respect to her claims for unlawful sex discrimination and equal pay, it was determined that the claim was successful in respect of the 1998 bonus and succeeded as a sex discrimination claim in respect of dismissal. The members of the Tribunal came to this decision party because of the evidence adduced in the form of the emails set out above. The members of the Tribunal said of the email Mr Crawshaw sent in response to Mrs Bower's email to Mr Delabare 'we agree with the Applicant [Mrs Bower] that he [Mr Crawshaw] must have been collecting evidence in support of her dismissal over the previous few months, which is why he was able to react so promptly.' An important aspect of the findings of the members of the Tribunal in this case is that they found from the evidence that they heard and read, that 'her [Mrs Bower's] tone in e-mails and other correspondence demonstrated increasing non-cooperation and anger as the plots which she perceived seemed to thicken around her. However, her fears, anxieties and suspicions were well-placed in respect of Mr Crawshaw and we are satisfied that she would have behaved differently if she had been nurtured and supported by him (as were the comparators) rather than undermined.' The claim failed with respect to the bonus for 1997, the failure to be promoted to director in April 1999 and as an equal pay claim in respect of a £1.5m bonus and potential entry to the partnership plan which became terms of the comparator's contracts in June 1999. Mrs Bower was awarded £740 net compensation for unfair dismissal and £1,414,619.65 net (inclusive of interest) in respect of unlawful acts of sex discrimination.

Another consideration in respect of email from an evidential point of view, is the propensity of people to continue corresponding by sending and returning the same email, thereby producing a long string of correspondence, perhaps with several subjects mentioned and discussed throughout the thread, with some of the correspondence copied in to different people at various times during the exchange, some as open copies and some as 'blind carbon copies'. Such exchanges also attest to the spontaneity of the evidence, which has a particular resonance that helps establish the authenticity of the documents, as well as the completeness of the evidence[3].

[1]   Heather MacNeil *Trusting Records Legal, Historical and Diplomatic Perspectives* (2000) p 82, see pp 77–85 for a full discussion of the two cases and the issues that were not discussed sufficiently.

[2]   London Central Employment Tribunal (Hearings throughout 2000, 2001 and 2002, Case No 3203104/99 and 3203104/99/S). For a list of cases where email has played a part in employment cases in England and Wales, see Stephen Mason *Email, networks and the internet: A concise guide to compliance with the law* (6th edn, 2006).

[3]   Mark D Robins 'Evidence at the electronic frontier: Introducing email at trial in commercial litigation' (2003) Rutgers Computer and Technology Law Journal vol 29, no 2, 219–315.

Storage media

2.13 The media upon which digital data is stored are fragile: they are inherently unstable and, unless they are stored correctly, can deteriorate quickly and without external signs of deterioration. They are also at risk from accidental or deliberate damage and accidental or deliberate deletion. Furthermore, the form of storage media also changes. The history of external floppy disk drives demonstrates the speed of change: the 8-inch disk gave way to the 5 1/4-inch, which was superseded by 3.5-inch floppy disks. A range of alternative storage products became available in the mid-1990s, including the Zip drive produced by Iomega. This had a capacity of 100 MB, with later versions that increased the capacity to 750 MB. Although this format became popular, it never replaced the 3.5-inch floppy disk. Most forms of floppy disk have now been superseded by flash-drive systems as well as rewritable CDs, CD-ROM and DVD (also known as 'Digital Versatile Disc' or 'Digital Video Disc') [1].

Computers and systems now operate largely in a networked environment. Networks run in parallel with the physical world. The networked world comprises products (MP3 files, computers, laptop computers, mobile telephones, personal digital assistants ('PDA's), the Blackberry and iPAQ) linked by means of applications (facsimile transmissions, voice over Internet protocol ('VoIP'), email, computer-to-computer, instant messaging) that run over networks (the Internet, intranets, wireless networking, cellular networks, dial-up). The nature of this structure means that almost everything anybody does on a device that is connected to a network is capable of being distributed and duplicated with ease. As a result, the same item of digital data can reside almost anywhere. The ramifications for lawyers and police officers are obvious: the relevant document may be available, but it might not be clear where it resides. This affects how a criminal investigation is conducted and how much effort a party to a civil case will have to devote to finding relevant documents for discovery or disclosure.

¹   For an interesting summary, see the entry in the Wikipedia at http://en.wikipedia.org/wiki/Floppy_disk.

2.14 Two examples from the United States of America serve to illustrate some of the problems faced by a large organisation in locating relevant documents in digital format, especially email correspondence, some of which might be on back-up tapes whilst others may be stored elsewhere. Laura Zubulake was employed in 1999 as a director and senior salesperson with UBS Warburg LLC and when offered the post it was suggested that she would be considered for the position of manager if it became vacant. In December 2000, the manager moved to the London office. Ms Zubulake was not considered for the job and Matthew Chapin was appointed. Ms Zubulake subsequently accused him of treating her differently from the time he took up the post. Ms Zubulake was dismissed in October, and in February 2002 she commenced legal proceedings for gender discrimination. The allegations were denied because it was claimed that Mr Chapin treated all employees equally badly. After a trial lasting three weeks, the jury found against UBS and awarded Ms Zubulake US$9.1 million in compensatory damages and almost US$20.2 million in punitive damages.

A number of preliminary hearings occurred before the trial took place. Of relevance are the decisions in May and July 2003 relating to the disclosure of email communications¹. The parties disagreed about the extent of the disclosure of emails, although it was not in dispute that email was an important means of communicating. Each salesperson received approximately 200 emails each day, and the Securities and Exchange Commission Regulations required UBS to store emails. Two storage methods were used: back-up tapes for the purpose of disaster recovery and optical disks. This meant that there were three possible places that relevant email communications could be found: in files that were in use by employees, emails archived on optical disks, and emails sent to and from a registered trader (internal emails were not captured) that were stored on optical storage devices. Ninety four back-up tapes were identified as being relevant for the purposes of disclosure. UBS used a back-up program that took a snapshot of all emails that existed on a given server at the time the back-up was taken: at the end of each day, on every Friday night and on the last business day of the month. Because emails were backed up intermittently, some emails were not stored, in particular where a user received or sent an email and deleted it on the same day. Scheindlin J determined that

Ms Zubulake was entitled to disclosure of the emails because they were relevant to her claim. UBS was ordered to produce all relevant emails that existed on the optical disks or its servers at its own expense, and from five back-up tapes selected by Ms Zubulake. Pinkerton Consulting restored and searched the tapes for US$11,524.63. Additional expenses included the time it took lawyers to review the emails, which brought the total cost to US$19,003.43. Some 1,541 relevant emails were discovered. Fewer than 20 relevant emails were found on the optical disks. In July, Ms Zubulake made a further application for the remaining back-up tapes to be restored and searched. UBS estimated that the cost would be US$273,649.39, and applied for the costs to be shifted to Ms Zubulake. In considering the seven-factor test (which is not relevant for the purposes of this particular discussion), the judge noted that a significant number of relevant emails existed on back-up tapes and that there was evidence that Matthew Chapin deleted relevant emails. Scheindlin J decided that Ms Zubulake should pay twenty-five per cent of the cost of restoring the back-up tapes. UBS were required to pay all other costs.

1   *Zubulake v UBS Warburg LLC* 217 F.R.D. 309 (S.D.N.Y. 2003); *Zubulake v UBS Warburg LLC* 216 F.R.D. 280 (S.D.N.Y. 2003).

2.15 The second example is the case of *Coleman (Parent) Holdings, Inc v Morgan Stanley & Co Inc*[1]. Coleman (Parent) Holdings ('Coleman') was induced by misrepresentations made by employees of Morgan Stanley relating to the financial condition of Sunbeam into accepting 14.1 million shares of Sunbeam stock when it sold its 82 per cent interest in the Coleman Company, Inc to Sunbeam on 30 March 1998. Morgan Stanley was also the sole underwriter for a debenture in the sum of US$750m, used by Sunbeam to finance part of the transaction. When the true financial position emerged after the sale, Coleman took action against Morgan Stanley. On 16 May 2005, the members of the jury entered a verdict against Morgan Stanley. The damages awarded to Coleman on 16 May 2005 amounted to US$604,334,000, and on 18 May 2005 the members of the jury awarded a further US$850m in punitive damages against Morgan Stanley. The verdict was subsequently reversed, including the amount of damages awarded. It was held on appeal that there was no proof presented at trial on the correct measure of damages, which meant the trial judge should have granted Morgan Stanley's motion for a directed verdict. The final judgment for compensatory damages was reversed and remanded for entry of a judgment for Morgan Stanley. For this reason, the award of punitive damages was also reversed[2].

A number of preliminary hearings took place relating to the extent of the discovery of documents, in particular email communications. Coleman accused Morgan Stanley of failing to provide relevant emails when requested. Eventually, Maass, J issued an adverse inference order on 23 March 2005[3]. Putting aside the allegations by Coleman that Morgan Stanley misled the court in relation to its state of knowledge respecting the whereabouts of relevant emails, a number of problems were raised by Morgan Stanley in attempting to identify and produce the materials requested. In November 2004, external counsel to Morgan Stanley discovered back-up tapes in various locations that had not been searched; the tapes were not clearly labelled as to their contents, nor were they found in locations where such tapes were customarily stored, and many of the back-up tapes were in a different format than other email back-up tapes. Additional issues identified during the renewed motion for entry of default judgment on 23 March 2005 before Maass J, included: as at 7 June 2004, only 120 out of 143 SDLT tapes had been processed into an archive; an analysis requested by the Securities and Exchange Commission indicated that, based on a representative sample, ten per cent of back-up tapes were overwritten after January 2001; a software error caused blind carbon copies not to be captured in the archiving process; a software error caused the searches to be case-sensitive which, in turn, meant not all relevant emails were captured; and a script error caused the archive to have problems pulling group email in Lotus Notes. Yet further problems were noted by Maass J: an additional 282 tapes were found on 23 and 25 February 2005; an additional 3,536 tapes were discovered on 23 February 2005 in a security room, and 2,718 tapes found at Recall, a third party off-site vendor on 3 March 2005; finally, a further 389 tapes were found between 2 and 5 March 2005.

The purpose of describing these examples is to illustrate the problems that multi-national organisations have in locating relevant evidence in digital format. These examples have focused on the difficulty in identifying relevant email communications, perhaps because email has now become the default method of communication. The nature of the distributed environment means that a range of practical problems have begun to emerge in determining what material needs to be disclosed or discovered to the other side. First, it is necessary to prevent the destruction of evidence, and then it is necessary to establish where the evidence is likely to be, before undertaking the exercise of sifting through the various sources to identify relevant documents. This will invariably require a party to locate where all back-up tapes are situated, whether on the premises or held with third parties in off-site remote storage, or held on individual computers, servers, in an archive or a disaster recovery system. The types of storage media that will need to be identified and located include tapes, disks, drives, UBS sticks, Ipods, laptops, PCs, PDAs, mobile telephones, pagers and audio systems (including voicemail) to name but a few.

1   For details of the issues Morgan Stanley were facing in connection with the SEC at the same time, see US Securities and Exchange Commission, Litigation Release No. 19693/ May 10, 2006 *SEC v Morgan Stanley & Co. Inc* Civil Action No. 06 CV 0882 (RCL) (D.D.C.), available online at http://www.sec.gov/litigation/litreleases/2006/lr19693.htm; for a related matter, see *Clare v Coleman (Parent) Holdings, Inc* 928 So.2d 1246 (Fla. App. 4 Dist. 2006); 2006 WL 1409137 (Fla. Ct. App.).

2   The District Court of Appeal of the State of Florida, 4th District, heard an appeal in the January Term of 2007, and the decision was published on 21 March 2007, *Morgan Stanley & Co., Inc. v Coleman (Parent) Holdings Inc.*, No. CA4D05–2606, Fla. Ct. App., 4th Dist. (March 21, 2007). Note the dissenting opinion of Farmer J.

3   2005 WL 674885 (Fla. Cir. Ct.); for an earlier hearing on March 1 2005, see 2005 WL 679071 (Fla. Cir. Ct.).

Deletion and destruction of evidence

2.16 Unlike a physical object or piece of paper that can be destroyed effectively, it is relatively difficult to obliterate a document in digital format. All a user does when they click the 'delete' icon on a computer, is, in general terms, remove the pointer to the data. The document or data remains, and it is possible to retrieve this data in certain circumstances, even if it is overwritten[1]. This attribute adds a great deal of complexity to both civil litigation and the investigation of alleged crimes. On occasions, a party may have a reasonable suspicion that the other party might intend to delete files, or has already deleted files. In *United States of America v Triumph Capital Group, Inc*[2] Frederick W. McCarthy, the CEO and controlling shareholder of Triumph, Charles B. Spadoni, Vice President and General Council of Triumph, together with number of others, were accused of a variety of offences relating to racketeering, including bribery, obstruction of justices and witness tampering, amongst other offences. It came to the notice of the government that Spadoni was alleged to have purchased a software program to purge his computer of incriminating evidence. Triumph was ordered to deliver up the relevant computer for forensic tests. The tests revealed that relevant data had been deleted, and files were recovered. A search of the deleted Internet cache files for relevant evidence revealed evidence of other offences. This caused the investigator to cease the search and obtain a further warrant to search and seize evidence of the further crime. In *L C Services v Brown*[3] the operating system on Andrew Brown's computer had been changed or re-installed at the time the claimants were pursuing disclosure of documents by the defendants, but a digital forensic specialist was able to recover the remains of email communications. More recently, Sanjay Kumar, the former chief executive of Computer Associates, Inc., pleaded guilty to a number of charges, including conspiracy to commit securities fraud and wire fraud; securities fraud; providing false filings to the Securities and Exchange Commission; conspiracy to obstruct justice; obstruction of justice and making false statements. Apparently, Mr Kumar reformatted his computer to run the Linux operating system to clear the memory, even though the prosecuting authorities had begun their investigations and, in response to the investigations, employees were ordered to retain any relevant evidence. He was sentenced on 2 November 2006 to 12 years' imprisonment and ordered to pay a fine of US$8 million, although the fine has been deferred until the court determines the scale of the restitution he will be required to make to the victims of the fraud, which is expected to be known by 2 February 2007. After serving the sentence, he will be supervised for three years.

Where there is a reasonable suspicion that a party might delete files, as in the proceedings leading up to divorce in the case of *Ranta v Ranta*[4], it may be possible to obtain an order to prevent a party from deleting, removing or uninstalling any programs, files or folders. Sanctions may follow for deleting files, depending on the seriousness of the action, where a party deliberately wipes hard drives after a court has ordered their production, as in *Electronic Funds Solutions v Murphy*[5]. Furthermore, it is not inconceivable for a court to order a party to search for relevant documents in back-up tapes, archives and to provide information about data that has been deleted[6].

---

[1] *Nucleus Information Systems v Palmer* [2003] EWHC 2013 (Ch) where employees used software in an attempt to overwrite the data on computers owned by the company before being returned; *R v Smith, R v Jayson* [2003] 1 Cr App R 212; [2002] Crim LR 659; [2002] EWCA Crim 683; 2002 WL 237226; (2002) Times, 23 April, CA, in which Jayson deleted a number of abusive images of children that were recovered.

[2] 211 F.R.D. 31 (D. Conn. 2002).

[3] [2003] EWHC 3024 (QB), [2003] All ER (D) 239 (Dec) at 53 and 54.

4   2004 WL 504588 (Conn. Super.).
5   36 Cal.Rptr.3d 663 (Cal. Ct. App. 2005); 2005 Cal. App. LEXIS 1910 (Cal. App. 4th Dist. Dec 14, 2005).
6   *Zhou v Pittsburg State University* 2003 WL 1905988 (D. Kan.).

2.17 Successful attempts have been made to delete files from a computer, as in the case of *Arista Records, LLC v Tschirhart*[1]. In this instance, the defendant used 'wiping' software to expunge evidence of downloading music files using iMesh and BearShare computer-to-computer software in defiance of a notice issued by a court to preserve such evidence. The plaintiff's motion for terminating sanctions was granted, and the judge ordered the plaintiffs to submit a proposed order of default judgment, setting out the damages in the case. Although difficult, it is not impossible to expunge data on a hard drive. However, the destruction of a computer, including the hard drive, does ensure the data is lost, as in *Strasser v Yalamanchi*[2]. It was claimed that a hard drive containing relevant data had been severely damaged by lightening, and an employee saw fit to dispose of the computer as a result. In response to the extensive pre-trial actions and the failure to provide an adequate reason for the destruction of the computer whilst litigation was under way, the trial judge subsequently instructed the members of the jury that the negligent destruction of evidence may be inferred from the failure of the appellant to preserve and maintain evidence. This decision was subsequently upheld by the appeal court.

In comparison to the deliberate attempt at destruction to prevent others from obtaining evidence, hard-copy files of underlying source documents may be destroyed for perfectly legitimate reasons and reliance might subsequently be made on the version held in digital format. This tends to occur when organisations attempt to reduce the cost of storage of paper documents, but tends to fail to consider the cost of electronic storage and the need to deal with old data when a system is upgraded. In the case of *Heveafil Sdn. Bdh v United States*[3], the Department of Commerce refused to accept a copy of a database containing a bill of materials stored on a computer diskette as a means of verifying cost information in an investigation into anti-dumping extruded rubber. Heveafil claimed the database held on the diskette had been taken from the mainframe and that it used the previous version in the course of normal business, and asserted that the database on the diskette contained an exact duplicate of the database developed on the mainframe computer. In an appeal from the United States Court of International Trade, the Court of Appeals for the Federal Circuit accepted the argument by the Department of Commerce that it could reject the data on the diskette as not having been properly authenticated and a finding of adverse inference was admissible in the circumstances. The assertions by Heveafil were not sufficient because it failed to provide evidence of the veracity of the contents of the diskette, such as explanations of how the copy was made. In this instance, the company merely copied data from the mainframe and then deleted the original digital files, as well as the underlying paper versions, without taking into account the need to provide a trail of evidence to demonstrate what procedures were undertaken to provide for the veracity of the copy.

1   2006 WL 2728927.
2   783 So.2d 1087 (Fla. App. 4 Dist. 2001).
3   58 Fed.Appx. 843, 2003 WL 1466193 (Fed.Cir.), 25 ITRD 1128.

Falsifying data

2.18 Lawyers are very familiar with the introduction of fraudulently manufactured evidence to support a claim, and such evidence, when introduced by a
client, is tested by their own lawyers immediately it becomes apparent that the
evidence may not be what it purports to be. The process of verifying the
authenticity of the evidence in civil cases is usually undertaken in the
preliminary stages, before action begins. Lawyers for both sides, if lawyers are
appointed, will elicit the facts and evidence their clients will reply upon, whilst
obtaining further evidence from the opponent that might go to show the
claims made by their client are correct or demonstrates the client has failed to
provide a full and frank disclosure of their true position.

The case of *Scholastic, Inc v Stouffer*[1] helps to illustrate the problems that
might arise in future. Nancy Stouffer made a number of claims against J K
Rowling, the author of the 'Harry Potter' books, one of which was the
infringement of her intellectual property rights in the words 'muggles' and
'Larry Potter'. She based her case on the submission of at least seven items of
falsified evidence. This included altered copies of an advertisement, the text in
a play and a book, drawings, a forged invoice and an altered draft of a
distribution agreement. Although this case may appear to be unusual, it
demonstrates that some people are willing to take extraordinary steps to
pursue a claim. Whilst Scholastic, J. K. Rowling and Time Warner had a good
case to defend, they had to go to the expense of proving Nancy Stouffer had
fabricated some of the evidence: for instance, an advertisement was adduced
as evidence to demonstrate Nancy Stouffer's rights over the word 'muggles'.
The advert submitted to the court included the 'TM' mark next to 'muggles'.
However, the 'TM' mark did not appear in the advertisement that was
actually printed. Scholastic demonstrated that the version submitted to the
court could not have been used for the original advert because the printing
technology used in producing the additional words in the forged version was
not invented when the advert was first designed and used. Similarly, Nancy
Stouffer submitted a draft copy of a distribution agreement to establish proof
of her claims. The agreement she provided to the court contained a list of the
booklets that were to be distributed, the third of which was 'RAH'. However,
Scholastic was able to obtain two original copies of this agreement from other
sources, and a comparison between these two and the copy put forward by
Nancy Stouffer indicated that the third item on the original documents was
'The Land of the Nother-One', not 'RAH,' and the words 'RAH' were not
aligned with the other words on the page, clearly indicating somebody had
altered the copy in Nancy Stouffer's possession. The judge concluded that
Nancy Stouffer had perpetrated a fraud on the court by submitting fraudulent
documents, as well as through her untruthful testimony. The motion for
summary judgment was granted, Nancy Stouffer's counterclaims and cross
claims were dismissed with prejudice, and she was ordered to pay US$50,000
in sanctions and legal costs.

[1]   221 F.Supp.2d 425 (S.D.N.Y. 2002); 2002 U.S. Dist. LEXIS 17531.

2.19 Such attempts to adduce fraudulent evidence before a court are rare[1].
However, it is conceivable, given the ease with which digital data is manipulated and altered, that attempts will be made in the future to falsify and alter

documents before a trial takes place. Even such mundane items as parking tickets have been subject to the alteration of digital evidence, as in the case of Kevin Maguire, who parked his car in Market Place in Bury town centre, Greater Manchester at 7.15 am on 31 August 2003. He returned at 5 pm to find he had been given a parking ticket at 9.15 am. Normally there were no restrictions on a Sunday and, when he parked his car, there were no signs to indicate there were any temporary restrictions in place. There were no signs because the NCP staff did put them up on the previous night because of the likelihood of the signs being pulled down or damaged by revellers overnight. The signs were put up after Mr Maguire parked his car. When Mr Maguire complained to NCP, it was asserted that he had parked illegally and he was sent a photograph of his parked car, which was dated 31 August 2003. Mr Maguire appealed against the parking fine. It transpired that Gavin Moses, a member of the NCP staff, changed the date on the digital photograph from 30 August to 31 August, so that it appeared Mr Maguire had parked illegally. Mr Maguire was cleared of parking illegally and he was awarded costs. Gavin Moses subsequently entered a plea of guilty when he was prosecuted for perverting the course of justice in early 2005. His Honour Judge Jonathan Geek subsequently sentenced Moses to 150 hours of community service[2].

Considerably more attention may have to be paid to demonstrating the integrity of digital data in the future which, in turn, will help substantiate the claim for authenticity which reflects on the reliability of the data.

[1] See *Premier Homes and Land Corporation v Cheswell, Inc* 240 F.Supp.2d 97 (D.Mass. 2002) for fabrication of an email; *People v Superior Court of Sacramento County* 2004 WL 1468698 (Cal.App. 3 Dist.) for fabrication of letters on a computer after the event.

[2] BBC News online news item ' "Fit up" parking warden sentenced' (2005) 28 January, online at http://news.bbc.co.uk/1/hi/england/manchester/4216539.stm. A further article was published by a Manchester website dated Thursday 27 January 2005 at http://www.manchesteronline.co.uk/news/s/144/144290_parking_attendant_cleared_.html, but the web page no longer appears to be active.

REVIEWING THE INTELLECTUAL FRAMEWORK

2.20 The conceptual differences between the physical world, with its familiar paper documents, and the digital world, which appears so alien to the uninitiated, is a divide that lawyers and judges must bridge. The familiarity of the record created in a ledger or a letter filed in a folder that is subsequently filed in a cabinet is rapidly receding. Data in digital format that is made visible to the human eye on a screen or a print-out is an illusion that must be understood more fully. In a digital record system, the components that make up the data are stored independently of one another. Different items of data are stored in different parts of the application system, and they are made manifest in human readable format when brought together on a screen as if an entire and complete record. The software brings together separate items of data and constructs them in a format that appears to indicate the file is a complete entity. The computer undertakes an exercise in the display of sequential logical relationships between various items of data that are retrieved by the operator for the benefit of the human. The files does not exist as it claims to exist on the screen and, in the same way, the individual components of the 'file' are not guaranteed to be preserved in the manner that will enable the file to be reconstructed over time.

Chapter 3

INVESTIGATION AND EXAMINATION OF DIGITAL EVIDENCE

STEPHEN MASON

3.01 The activities associated with the investigation and examination of digital evidence is relatively new compared to other forms of forensic analysis[1]. A number of respected commentators that also practice as expert investigators encourage their peers to advance the process of dealing with digital evidence as a separate discipline of forensic science[2]. In the UK, Jack Straw, the then Secretary of State for the Home Department, announced the establishment of a Forensic Science Registration Council in response to concerns expressed over a number of celebrated miscarriages of justice, stating[3]:

> The Council's aim will be to promote and maintain high standards of competence, practice, discipline and ethics amongst forensic science practitioners. It will be non-statutory, self-financing, self-regulating and independent, with input from users. The Council will operate on a three tier basis, comprising:
>> a Council, to include legal, lay and expert members, and incorporating a disciplinary panel;
>> an Executive/Registration Board, which would set the criteria for registration and operate the register; and
>> Assessment Panels, which would assess qualifications and competence for each specialism within the forensic science community.

[1]   Mark James *Expert Evidence: Law and Practice* (2nd edn, 2006); Sir Louis Blom-Cooper QC, ed *Experts in the Civil Courts*, (2006) and Neil Andrews *English Civil Procedure Fundamentals of the New Civil Justice System* (2003) ch 32 for a general introduction to the topic in the civil context.
[2]   Eoghan Casey *Digital Evidence and Computer Crime Forensic Science, Computers and the Internet*, (2nd edn, 2004), p 1; Sarah Mocas 'Building theoretical underpinnings for digital forensics research' Digital Investigation vol 1, no 1, pp 61–68; Carrie Morgan Whitcomb 'An Historical Perspective of Digital Evidence: A Forensic Scientist's View' (2002) International Journal of Digital Evidence vol 1, issue 1, online at http://www.ijde.org; Mark Reith, Clint Carr and Greggs Gunsch 'An Examination of Digital Forensic Models' (2002) International Journal of Digital Evidence vol 1, issue 3, online at http://www.ijde.org; Eoghan Casey 'The need for objective case review' (2004) Digital Investigation vol 1, no 2, pp 83–85; Nigel Jones 'Training and accreditation—who are the experts?' (2004) Digital Investigation vol 1, no 3, pp 189–194.
[3]   House of Commons, Hansard, col 449, 21 May 1998.

3.02 The Council for the Registration of Forensic Practitioners[1] was set up to undertake the tasks set out by the Home Secretary. The Council is a

41

professional regulatory body and a not-for-profit company limited by guarantee. Although the Council is independent of government, the Home Office provided the initial funding. The Council's main role is to initiate and manage a register of currently-competent forensic practitioners. This exercise has been conducted in phases, beginning with what are considered to be the mainstream forensic specialties: science, fingerprints and scene examination. The next phases will extend the register to include forensic medicine, transport investigation, information technology, accountancy and other professional areas. In early 2004, the Council initiated a pilot registration scheme for digital evidence in relation to civil court cases and tribunals. It also began a pilot project in the Northern circuit, Cheshire and North Wales, setting out what the register is and how it works, with a view to asking judges and prosecutors to begin using the register in connection with court proceedings[2]. The Council is well aware of the need to help set standards and it has taken the view that it should embrace all ranges of opinion from within the industry in order to ensure that the investigation and examination of digital evidence is considered as a valuable, discrete discipline of forensic science.

[1]   Website: http://www.crfp.org.uk/. Michael Turner 'Registered Forensic Practitioner: A New Breed of Expert' (2006) Computers and Law vol 17, issue 1, pp 17–18.
[2]   News from CRFP Newsletter no 13, June 2004, no longer available online.

3.03   International moves in relation to digital evidence began in 1995, when the International Organisation on Computer Evidence ('IOCE') was established to provide international law enforcement agencies with a forum to facilitate the exchange of information relating to computer crime investigations and other issues relating to digital forensic investigation[1]. This organisation, together with a number of other agencies, including the Association of Chief Police Officers and the National High-Tech Crime Unit, have produced a number of guidelines that influence the investigation and examination of digital evidence within a criminal context. Although various sets of guidelines have been produced specifically for criminal investigations the IOCE's guides provide significant help to practitioners and lawyers in civil matters.

[1]   See also N Dudley-Gough 'Digital Forensic Certification Board' (2006) Digital Investigation vol 3, no 1, pp 7–8; Amber Schroader and N Dudley-Gough 'The Institute of Computer Forensic Professionals' (2006) Digital Investigation vol 3, no 1, pp 9–10.

3.04   Until recently, experts in the field of information technology have tended to express their qualifications against their working experience, together with what they have learnt from books and other sources of information. The formation of the Council for the Registration of Forensic Practitioners, the provision of specialist courses by universities, and a generally recognised need for those practicing in the field to put the practice of the investigation and examination of digital evidence on to a more scientific basis, give grounds to expect that the number, and knowledge, of experts in the information technology field will increase[1].

[1]   For an indication of what is happening at the FBI, see Douglas A Schmitknecht 'Building FBI computer forensics capacity: one lab at a time' (2004) Digital Investigation vol 1 no 3, pp 177–182; Ryan Leigland and Axel W Krings 'A Formalization of Digital Forensics' (2004) International Journal of Digital Evidence vol 3, issue 2, at http://www.ijde.org; Matthew Meyers and Marc Rogers 'Computer Forensics: The Need for Standardization

and Certification' (2004) International Journal of Digital Evidence vol 3, issue 2, at http://www.ijde.org; Andrew Sheldon 'The future of forensic computing' (2005) Digital Investigation vol 2 no 1, pp 31–35; Nicole Lang Beebe and Jan Guynes Clark 'A hierarchical, objectives-based framework for the digital investigations process' (2005) Digital Investigation vol 2 no 2, pp 147–167.

SUBJECT AREAS OF EXPERTISE

3.05 There is a recognition within the field of the need to distinguish between the different roles that an investigator may have with respect to the investigation and examination of digital evidence. It has been suggested that there are three distinct groups, each of which require different levels of knowledge and training[1]:

> Digital Crime Scene Technicians: individuals responsible for gathering data at a crime scene should have basic training in evidence handling and documentation, as well as in basic crime reconstruction, to help them locate all available sources of evidence on a network;
> Digital Evidence Examiners: individuals responsible for processing particular kinds of digital evidence require specialised training and certification in their area;
> Digital investigators: individuals responsible for the overall investigation should receive a general training but do not need very specialised training or certification. Investigators are also responsible for reconstructing the actions relating to a crime using information from first responders and forensic examiners to create a more complete picture from investigators and attorneys.

[1] *Casey* (2004) p 1.

3.06 The Council for the Registration of Forensic Practitioners has also taken the view that a demarcation is required between the various skills and knowledge that are required when dealing with digital evidence, and have established the following categories:

(a)   data capture, which involves the retrieval of relevant data from the subject equipment by a forensically sound process and the creation of check data and logs to permit future verification.

(b)   data examination, which involves the identification and examination of data that may be relevant to a case and the production of information or exhibits to assist investigators or the court.

The Council for the Registration of Forensic Practitioners has used the term 'digital evidence specialist' to describe a person that is capable of investigating and examining digital evidence. Such specialists are required to make judgements about the appropriateness of the tools and techniques they use to carry out their work. They must also provide an analysis of their findings, setting out the basis upon which their judgment is formulated. In addition, it is necessary for a practitioner to identify any data that appears to be inconsistent with their assessment.

HANDLING DIGITAL EVIDENCE

3.07 As with any other form of evidence, there are a number of discrete elements that accompany the collection and handling of digital evidence. It is suggested that a digital evidence specialist should, ideally, undertake their duties against the highest standards propounded by their peers, regardless of whether they advise in a criminal or civil matter. To this extent, the various guidelines put forward as best practice by such organisations as the Association of Chief Police Officers and the National High-Tech Crime Unit, the Scientific Working Group on Digital Evidence ('SWGDE') and the International Organisation on Digital Evidence ('IOCE') provide sound advice and guidance when dealing with digital evidence. Although the guidelines issued by the police are directed towards criminal investigations, the standards set they out are useful for investigations in civil matters and can act, if followed, to counter allegations that the evidence has not been gathered or dealt with properly. Following proper evidence handling procedure is particularly important due to the unique nature of digital evidence, which is extremely volatile and can be altered with ease, even by the simple act of switching a computer on or off[1].

[1]   Police Scientific Development Branch 'Digital Imaging Procedure 02–02' (Version 1.0, March 2002), available online at: http://scienceandresearch.homeoffice.gov.uk/hosdb/publications-2/cctv-publications/02–02_DIP?view=Standard&pubID=356166;   SWGDE/ SWGIT *Guidelines & Recommendations for Training in Digital & Multimedia Evidence*, Version: 1.0 (November 15, 2004) available online at http://ncfs.org/swgde/documents.html; SWgde Best Practice for Computer Forensics (v 2.1, July 2006) available online at http://ncfs.org/swgde/documents/swgde2006/Best_Practices_for_Computer_Forensics%20July06.pdf; Interpol, *IT security and crime prevention methods*, (an introduction to what an investigator needs to know about Information Technology (IT) security measures in order to be able to carry out investigations in an IT environment and to give advice in crime prevention methods), available online at http://www.interpol.int/Public/TechnologyCrime/CrimePrev/ITSecurity.asp; *Searching and Seizing Computers and Obtaining Electronic Evidence in Criminal Investigations*, Computer Crime and Intellectual Property Section, Criminal Division, United States Department of Justice (July 2002), available online at http://www.cybercrime.gov/s&smanual2002.htm; Cyber Tools Online Search for Evidence, CTOSE 'Project Results,' available online at http://www.ctose.org/; IETF RFC 3227 *Guidelines for Evidence Collection and Archiving*, available online at http://www.rfc-archive.org/getrfc.php?rfc=3227.

Identifying digital evidence

3.08 Evidence discovered in a digital format may be the first sign that something is wrong. For instance, a security administrator in a bank might consider an investigation is needed where the intrusion detection system sets off an alarm, or where the email logs indicate that a particular member of staff is receiving an excessive number of emails during the course of a day or over an extended period. The case of *Miseroy v Barclays Bank plc*[1] illustrates the nature of the problems associated with the use of communication systems. Mr Hilary Miseroy was employed by Barclaycard in the Fraud Prevention Department between 14 March 1988 and 13 September 2002. The staff manual, dated 16 June 2000, included a policy in relation to the supply and trafficking of drugs and money laundering. In addition, the group IT security policies, dated July 2002, included instructions about the use of the corporate email facilities. Clear guidance was set out by Barclays in both these areas. In July 2002, Maureen Crane, a Senior Fraud Analyst, was informed that an individual within her team appeared to be receiving a disproportionate number of emails during the day. A formal investigation was subsequently initiated. The Information, Risk and Security Department carried out an audit of the emails sent and received by three employees. The audit indicated that Mr Miseroy sent a significant number of emails. As a result, he was also included in the investigation. After a series of investigatory meetings, it was concluded that Mr Miseroy had abused the email facilities, as follows:

(a)   he sent out an unwarranted number of personal emails. On some days eight or more exchanges had taken place in quick succession;

(b)   some of the emails he sent out included content that was derogatory, offensive and sexist. During his first interview, he accepted that the comments he made were not appropriate. Later, he contended that there was a great deal of social activity and laddish banter between employees working within the Fraud Department and he did not consider that anybody had been offended;

(c)   a number of emails were exchanged between him and Andrew West, a manager in a different department, between 26 April and 30 April 2002. The content of these emails referred to the purchase of cannabis from a friend of Mr Miseroy, who in turn passed the drug to Mr West. Similar emails had been passed between Mr Miseroy and Mr West between 15 February and 10 April 2002. In an email dated 15 February, Mr Miseroy wrote to Mr West: 'I've brought it in with me. Fag-break about 10.30?' In a further email sent on 18 February, Mr Miseroy asked 'quality ok?'; and

(d)   it was also determined that Mr Miseroy disclosed confidential information regarding Barclay's operations and customers.

Mr Miseroy was summarily dismissed for gross misconduct on 13 September 2002. The members of the Tribunal accepted that the dismissal of Mr Miseroy was within the range of reasonable responses of a reasonable employer in relation to the circumstances of the case.

[1]   (2003) Bedford employment tribunal, Case No 1201894/2002, 18 March.

3.09 In such a case, the source and reliability of the information needs to be assessed, which requires an investigation into the facts. At such an early stage, the actions of the investigator may cause changes to the digital evidence which is why it is essential to have an appropriate procedure in place to deal with the way an investigation is initiated and conducted. In a civil case, there is an obligation for each party to disclose documents relating to matters in question in the action under the provisions of the Civil Procedure Rules[1]. In criminal matters, the relevant investigating authorities have both common law and statutory powers to search and seize evidence. These matters are discussed in more detail elsewhere in this text, but it is useful to consider the nature of the procedures that a digital evidence specialist should consider adopting. In the criminal context, the investigating police officers will be expected to have conducted themselves in accordance with the recognised guides for their jurisdiction. In the United Kingdom, ACPO and NHTCU have produced the Good Practice Guide for Computer based Electronic Evidence ('ACPO Guide')

[2]. Although the ACPO Guide does not apply to disclosure in civil cases, a digital evidence specialist may consider it appropriate to follow procedures that are similar to or identical with the provisions of the ACPO Guide. It should be noted that the ACPO Guide sets out four main phases: collection, examination, analysis, and reporting, and concentrates on the collection phase[3].

The following discussion concentrates on discussing matters relating to digital evidence in the context of a criminal investigation. However, it is anticipated that the reader will readily acknowledge the relevance of the discussion in the context of a civil matter. As a result, it is anticipated that a digital evidence specialist, when undertaking work in the disclosure phase of a civil action, will be equally aware of the points that follow[4].

[1] For a discussion of some flaws in the legal and forensice process, see Vlasti Broucek, Paul Turner and Sandra Frings 'Music piracy, universities and the Australian Federal Court: Issues for forensic computing specialists' (2005) Computer Law & Security Report vol 21, no 1, pp 30–37.

[2] ACPO and NHTCU *Good Practice Guide for Computer based Electronic Evidence* (v3.0, 2003), available online at http://www.acpo.police.uk/asp/policies/Data/gpg_computer_based_evidence_v3.pdf.

[3] See also European Network of Forensic Science Institutes, Forensic Information Technology Working Group *Guidelines for Best Practice in the Forensic Examination of Digital Technology*, (v5, 28 July 2006) available online at http://www.enfsi.org/ewg/fitwg/.

[4] The tension between forensics and investigations is discussed, amongst other things, in Monique Mattei Ferraro and Andrew Russell 'Current issues confronting well-established computer-assisted child exploration and computer crime task forces' (2004) Digital Investigation vol 1, no 1, pp 7–15.

Gathering digital evidence

3.10 Once it has been established that it is necessary to seize or gather evidence in a digital format, a further set of procedures should be in place to guide the digital evidence specialist in respect to the scene itself, including the identification and seizure of the evidence, if necessary[1]. It is now well-established practice that the scene should be photographed and the layout of the hardware recorded. The investigator then needs to determine what, if any, physical evidence should be retained, such as computers, printers or facsimile machines, for instance. The ACPO Guide provides a list of the types of hardware and storage devices that are susceptible to being retained[2]. Clearly, it will be important not to permit anybody to disturb the hardware or the network, or data on a computer that is liable to being seized and retained[3]. The problem with digital evidence is the ease by which the evidence can be altered or destroyed. Digital devices are volatile instruments. For instance, the random access memory in a computer will contain a great deal of information relating to the state the computer, such as the processes that are running, whether the computer is connected to the Internet and what file systems are being used. Immediately a computer is switched off, a large part of this volatile data is lost. Depending on the circumstances of the case being investigated, such data may be very important to retain before the computer is switched off, or simply unplugged from the electricity supply. Whether a computer should be switched off or unplugged from the electricity supply will depend on the circumstances[4]. Indeed, there may be occasions when great care should be taken when arresting suspects caught physically at a computer, because it is possible that they might switch off the computer and disrupt or delete any incriminating files before any preventative action can be taken, This happened in the case of Aleksei Kostap, who was arrested by members of the Serious and Organised Crime Agency, who attached handcuffs to him, but with his hands in front of his body. According to a press report, he managed to take action that caused databases to be deleted. It was thought the databases might have contained records of his gang's activities. Apparently, the act by Kostap also initiated the use of intricate layers of encryption on the computer systems, which experts were not able to decrypt[5].

[1] For a brief discussion about gathering evidence and issues surrounding personal privacy, see María Verónica Péez Asinari 'Legal Constraints for the Protection of Privacy and Personal Data in Electronic Evidence Handling' (2004) International Review of Law, Computers & Technology vol 18, no 2, pp 231–250.

[2] The books listed at the end of this chapter discuss physical evidence at the scene in more detail. See also Brian Carrier and Eugene H Spafford 'Getting Physical with the Digital Evidence Process' (2003) International Journal of Digital Evidence vol 2, issue 2, online at http://www.ijde.org.

[3] Although failing to follow the relevant guidelines may not rule inadmissible any evidence subsequently found on a computer: *R v Good* [2005] DCR 804. For problems when investigating mainframes and very large systems, see Matthew Pemble 'Investigating around mainframes and other high-end systems: the revenge of big iron' (2004) Digital Investigation vol 1, no 2, pp 90–93.

[4] *Eoghan Casey* (2004) p 224.

[5] Tom Espiner 'Jailed ID thieves thwart cops with crypto' (2006) *ZEDNet UK* 19 December, online at http://news.com.com/Jailed+ID+thieves+thwart+cops+with+crypto/2100-7348_3-6144521.html.

3.11 The problem of what to seize and retain can be compounded where a computer, or an entire system of computers, is linked to a network and the sources of digital evidence exist in a number of separate geographical locations. In such circumstances it will be necessary to ascertain whether it is possible or feasible to shut the network down before taking any action. In most instances, this will not be an option. Consequently, the investigator will need to be aware of the range of information that might be required, should they be presented with such a situation. This will include establishing information about the network that is to be investigated, especially if a system administrator will not co-operate. For instance, it will probably be necessary to establish the numbers of computers on a network and the various types of network connections, such as Internet, email, cellular data networks and wireless connections. In addition, it may be also necessary to establish whether there are any third party services on the Internet that are used to store data remotely. Data can be deleted on the remote server before it can be captured[1].

[1] For a discussion on the complexities of recovering data from modern operating systems and file systems, see Geoff H. Fellows 'The joys of complexity and the deleted file' (2005) Digital Investigation vol 2, no 2, pp 89–93.

3.12 Throughout this phase of an investigation, the onus will be on the digital evidence specialist to make informed decisions as to what equipment to seize and retain in any given set of circumstances. It will be necessary to give reasons for seizing and retaining the property and it will also be essential to ensure the entire procedure is properly documented. The documentation relating to digital evidence is important. Standard operating procedures, such as those described in the ACPO Guide, should be followed. A record should be kept of every item seized and exhibit labels should be attached to every article retrieved.

There are occasions when the physical hardware cannot be seized, because it is too large or where it would cause an organisation to cease functioning. In such circumstances, the digital evidence will have to be copied exactly. Great care must be exercised when digital evidence is retrieved and copied in its original format. The range of digital evidence that might need to be copied includes audit trails, data logs (application, Internet and firewall to name but a few), biometric data, the metadata from applications, the file system[1], intrusion detection reports and the content of databases and files. Given the nature of the evidence to be copied, maintaining the evidential continuity and integrity of the evidence that is copied, and its subsequent history, is of paramount importance[2]. Such evidence is open to cross examination in relation to its integrity. As a result, the process of copying and handling such evidence should be carried out to the highest standards. To this extent, the four principles of computer-based electronic evidence as set out in the ACPO Guide[3] help to illustrate the importance of this phase of the process:

> Principle 1: No action taken by law enforcement agencies or their agents should change data held on a computer or storage media which may subsequently be relied upon in court.

> Principle 2: In exceptional circumstances, where a person finds it necessary to access original data held on a computer or on storage media, that person must be competent to do so and be able to give evidence explaining the relevance and the implications of their actions.

> Principle 3: An audit trail or other record of all processes applied to computer based electronic evidence should be created and preserved. An independent third party should be able to examine those processes and achieve the same result.

> Principle 4: The person in charge of the investigation (the case officer) has overall responsibility for ensuring that the law and these principles are adhered to.

[1] Florian Buchholz and Eugene Spafford 'On the role of file system metadata in digital forensics' (2004) Digital Investigation vol 1, no 4, pp 298–309.

[2] The volumes of digital evidence are causing problems respecting the methodologies around the collection of evidence, as discussed in the US context by Erin E. Kenneally and Christopher LT Brown 'Risk sensitive digital evidence collection' (2005) Digital Investigation vol 2, no 2, pp 101–119.

[3] ACPO and NHTCU Good Practice Guide for Computer based Electronic Evidence (v3.0, 2003), 6. See also *Casey, ed* (2002) ch 23 for a further discussion of digital evidence handling guidelines and a sample preservation form.

3.13 It will be necessary to take copies of digital evidence in a format that it will be acceptable to adduce in evidence[1]. It is possible to make an exact bit-for-bit copy of each medium to an identical or similar medium, or to create a bit-for-bit image of the original medium in one or more files[2]. A bit-for-bit copy captures all of the data from the original medium to the medium it is copied to, including hidden and residual data. As a result, the copy will include information that will enable a digital evidence specialist to reconstruct deleted files, for instance. There are two fundamental principles in relation to copying digital evidence that a digital evidence specialist should be aware of:

(a)   the process of making the image should not alter the original evidence. This means the appropriate steps should be taken to ensure that the process used to take the image should not write any data to the original medium; and

(b)   the process of copying data should produce an exact copy of the original. Such a reproduction should allow the specialist to investigate the files in the way they that existed on the original medium[3].

To ensure the original data and the copy are the same, the data should undergo a hashing process, described below. The reason for establishing hash values for data, including the time and date stamps of each file, is that this information will serve as a reference for checking the authenticity or veracity of the files after they have been copied.

[1]   Computers have different requirements and the expert should make sure the lawyer is aware of such issues, see Keith McDonald 'To image a Macintosh' (2005) Digital Investigation vol 2, no 3, pp 175–179.

[2]   *Casey, ed* (2002) p 32.

[3]   Troy Larson 'The other side of civil discovery: disclosure and production of electronic records' in *Casey, ed* (2002) p 35.

3.14   The quality of digital files that are copied can be crucial. In the case of *Gates Rubber Company v Bando Chemical Industries Ltd*[1] Schlatter, United States Magistrate Judge, commented on the evidence of two digital evidence experts. The judge was impressed by the 'credentials, experience and knowledge' of the expert for Bando, Robert Wedig, and indicated in his decision that he relied on his opinions. Much less weight was placed on the expert for Gates, who failed to obtain an expert in a timely fashion[2]. The expert for Gates, Robert Voorhees, failed to undertake appropriate measures to secure the evidence[3]:

> Gates argued that Voorhees did an adequate job of copying the Denver computer. Wedig persuaded me, however, that Voorhees lost, or failed to capture, important information because of an inadequate effort. In using Norton's Unerase, Voorhees unnecessarily copied this program onto the Denver computer first, and thereby overwrote 7 to 8 percent of the hard drive before commencing his efforts to copy the contents.
>
> Wedig noted that information which is introduced into a computer is distributed, in a random manner, to space which is not being used, or to space which contains a deleted file and is therefore available for use. To use Norton's Unerase, it was unnecessary for Voorhees to copy it onto the hard drive of the Denver computer. By doing so, however, the program obliterated, at random, 7 to 8 percent of the information which would otherwise have been available. No one can ever know what items were overwritten by the Unerase program.
>
> Additionally, Voorhees did not obtain the creation dates of certain of the files which overwrote deleted files. This information would have assisted in determining the deletion date of some files. If a deleted file has been overwritten by a file which was created prior to the Gates litigation, for example, Bando would be relieved of suspicion as to that file. Thus, failure to obtain the creation dates

49

of files represented a failure to preserve evidence which would have been important to Bando in its efforts to resist Gates' motions for default judgment.

Wedig pointed out that Voorhees should have done an 'image backup' of the hard drive, which would have collected every piece of information on the hard drive, whether the information was allocated as a file or not. Instead, Voorhees did a 'file by file' backup, which copies only existing, nondeleted files on the hard drive. The technology for an image backup was available at the time of these events, though rarely used by anyone. Wedig testified that Gates was collecting evidence for judicial purposes; therefore, Gates had a duty to utilize the method which would yield the most complete and accurate results. I agree with Wedig. In these circumstances, Gates failed to preserve evidence in the most appropriate manner. Gates' failure to obtain an image backup of the computer is a factor which I have weighed against Gates as I considered a number of the claims which Gates has asserted.

Although the tools and techniques used by digital evidence specialists are constantly changing and improving, the comments made by the judge in this case illustrate a very clear point: when digital evidence is copied, the techniques that are used must comply to the highest possible standards for the subsequent evidence to have any probative value in court[4].

1   167 F.R.D. 90 (D. Colo. 1996).
2   167 F.R.D. 90 (D. Colo. 1996) at 111(a).
3   167 F.R.D. 90 (D. Colo. 1996) at 112(a) and (b).
4   For a sample imaging procedure, see Troy Larson 'The other side of civil discovery: disclosure and production of electronic records' in *Casey, ed* (2002) pp 36–37.

3.15 This part of the exercise should include an examination of the surrounding area of the scene, including any materials that are likely to be relevant to disclosure or a criminal investigation. For instance, in the case of *Regina v Pecciarich*[1] the police seized a number of documents, catalogues and a scrapbook of newspaper articles concerning trials of sexual assault and proposed legislation dealing with child pornography. In this instance, the material constituted real evidence. It was also considered as a statement that Sparrow Prov.Div. J determined was circumstantial evidence to support the allegations that Pecciarich distributed child pornography. The relevance of materials found at the scene, including fingerprints and DNA samples taken directly from hardware devices, may become more obvious once the digital evidence specialist has examined the digital evidence in detail.

1   22 OR (3d) 748.

Preserving digital evidence

Validating digital evidence

3.16 Digital evidence in particular needs to be validated if it is to have any probative value. A digital evidence specialist will invariably copy the contents of a number of disks or storage devices, in both criminal and civil matters. To prove the digital evidence has not been altered, it is necessary to put in place checks and balances to prove the duplicate evidence in digital format has not been altered since it was copied. An electronic fingerprint is used to prove the integrity of data at the time the evidence was collected. The electronic fingerprint uses a cryptographic technique that is capable of being associated with a single file, a floppy disk or the entire contents of a hard drive. As digital evidence is copied, a digital evidence specialist will use software tools that are relevant to the task. The software tool used will invariably incorporate a program that causes a checksum operation, called a 'hash function' to be applied to the file or disk that is being copied. The result of applying a hash function to digital data is called a 'hash value'. The hash value has been calculated against the content of the data. This is a one-way function, containing the mathematical equivalent of a secret trapdoor. For the purposes of understanding the concept, this algorithm is easy to compute in one direction and difficult to compute in the opposite direction, unless you know the secret[1]. The hash function is used to verify that a file, or the copy of a file, has not changed. If the file has been altered in any way, the hash value will not be the same and the investigator will be alerted to the discrepancy. A digital signature can also be used in this way, by combining the hash value against some additional information, such as the time.

[1] It has yet to be proven that a mathematical function can have a one-way function, see Fred Piper, Simon Blake-Wilson and John Mitchell *Digital Signatures Security & Controls* (1999) p 16.

The chain of custody

3.17 For those experienced in criminal matters, the concept of the chain of custody is well established. However, the chain of custody, in both civil and criminal matters, should be considered very carefully with respect to digital evidence. The reason for taking particular care with digital evidence is that the nature of the evidence is such that it is easy to alter. It is necessary to demonstrate the integrity of the evidence and to show it cannot have been tampered with after being seized or copied. There is another reason for being meticulous about ensuring the chain of evidence is correctly recorded: in a case involving a number of items of hardware and more than one computer, it will be necessary to ensure there is a clear link between the hardware and the digital evidence copied from that hardware. In this respect, the record should address such issues as:

(a)   who collected the evidence;
(b)   how and where the evidence was collected;
(c)   the name of the person who took possession of the evidence;
(d)   how and where the evidence was stored;
(e)   the protection afforded to the evidence whilst in storage; and
(f)   the names of the people that removed the evidence from storage, including the reasons for removing the evidence from storage[1].

[1] Warren G Kruse and Jay G Heiser *Computer Forensics Incident Response Essentials,* (2002) pp 6–11.

Transporting and storing digital evidence

3.18 Consideration should be given to the methods by which any hardware and digital evidence is transported and stored[1]. Computers need to be protected from accidentally booting up; consideration should be made to ensure hardware is clearly marked to prevent people from using the equipment unwittingly; loose hard drives, modems, keyboards and other such materials should be placed in anti-static or aerated bags. Storage conditions should be appropriate: hardware and digital evidence should be protected from dirt, humidity, fluids, extremes of temperature and strong magnetic fields. It is possible for data to be rendered unreadable if the storage media upon which the digital evidence is contained is stored in a damp office or in an overheated vehicle during the summer.

1   Philip Turner 'Unification of digital evidence from disparate sources (Digital Evidence Bag)' (2005) Digital Investigation vol 2, no 3, pp 223–228.

ANALYSIS OF DIGITAL EVIDENCE

3.19 A digital evidence specialist is not only required to obtain and copy digital evidence that has a high probative value, but must also provide an analysis of the evidence. The analysis of the evidence will involve reviewing both the text of the data and the attributes of the data. This exercise may also include, but will not be limited to, looking for and recovering deleted files, and other data that may be hidden on the disk, checking logs for activity and checking unallocated and slack space for residual data. Casey suggests there are a number of sub-categories to this process[1]:

(a)   assessment (content and context)—digital evidence that is viewed or read by a human, with a view to considering issues such as means, motivation, and opportunity;

(b)   experimentation—This is where unorthodox or previously untried methods and techniques might be called for during an investigation. If new methods are used, it is important to document the experiment properly. By experimenting, a new technique will either accepted or rejected;

(c)   fusion and correlation—Bringing together the digital and non-digital evidence to help understand the full story. For instance, the timing might be in issue: the sources of digital data may be able to help piece together a sequence of events, such as telephone call records and email transcripts, and compare them against statements made by witnesses and the suspect; and

(d)   validation—this part of the analysis represents the finding of the digital evidence specialist, based on sound reasoning.

1   *Casey* (2004) p 111.

3.20 Failure to assess the digital evidence can lead to false assumptions, as the case of *Liser v Smith*[1]. Jason Lister was arrested for the murder of Vidalina Semino Door after being identified as a person that withdrew money from an automatic teller machine ('ATM') owned by the Bank of America on the night of the murder. The facts of the case were not in dispute. The victim was shot after leaving work on the night of 5 May 2000. Police attended the scene shortly after the murder. By Monday 8 May, it was known that the victim's bank card had been used to withdraw US$200 from a Bank of America

Branch in Anacostia, about twenty minutes after the murder, approximately one mile from where the body was found. According to the digital evidence, the withdrawal occurred at 1.47 am on 6 May. A further US$81 was taken out of another ATM machine owned by a Seven-Eleven store on Oxon Hill, Maryland at 2.17 am. The Bank of America ATM machine also had a video surveillance tape, which was subsequently retrieved by the police. The ATM machine at the Seven-Eleven store did not have a working video camera.

[1]   United States District Court for the District of Columbia No 00–2325 (ESH) March 26, 2003 before District Judge Ellen Segal Huvelle, available online at http://www.dcd.courts.gov/Opinions/2003/Huvelle/00–2325.pdf.

3.21 The bank manager informed the police that there would be a discrepancy of up to fifteen minutes between the time indicated on the surveillance tape and the actual time. When the tape was viewed, there was no ATM activity recorded at 1.47 am. The transaction occurring closest to 1.47 am was at 1.52 am, when a black male wearing a white t-shirt was recorded as standing before the machine. Whilst the evidence seemed to lead to the conclusion that the man recorded at 1.52 am was one of the killers, the evidence contained on the surveillance video did not warrant such an assumption. Other pictures from the videotape showed black males other than Liser using the ATM at 1.56 am and 2.05 am and a black female using the machine at 2.04 am. Copies of these pictures were provided to the court. All of them were grainy and poorly photocopied. However, of relevance is that both of the men in question appeared, like Jason Liser, to have been wearing white t-shirts and to be relatively young.

In August, it was decided to send out a press release and a copy of the photograph of the man recorded as standing at the ATM machine at 1.52 am. Mr Liser was subsequently recognised and arrested. He was held for less than a week because the police decided, at this late point in time, to carry out an experiment at the Anacostia branch. The result of the experiment led the police to conclude that the discrepancy was greater than the fifteen-minute gap they were led to believe. Mr Liser was subsequently released. It is instructive to note the comments made in the Memorandum Opinion by the judge[1]:

> While this issue is a close one, the Court is not ready to conclude that it was objectively reasonable under the circumstances of this investigation for the police to rely solely on the bank's representations about the time discrepancy without attempting to verify that information by empirical (or other) means. The crucial point here is that this was not a fast moving investigation in which the officers were called upon to make snap judgments based on limited information. Far from it. Detective Smith had the surveillance tapes within a week after the murder; at that early date he had been told by the branch manager that the time on the tape could be off by up to fifteen minutes. (Ex.12 [Smith Dep.] at 71–72.) Plaintiff was not, however, arrested until August, three months later. During this lengthy interval, neither Detective Smith nor anyone on his team made any further attempt to verify the estimation about the length of the gap. They had no further contact with anyone at Bank of America,

53

especially its security personnel, who might have had more accurate information about the camera's timer. (Ex.12 [Smith Dep.] at 59–60.) They did not
inspect the camera itself. Nor did they attempt use the ATM themselves to
compare real time against tape time.

In short, despite the fact that the tape was their central lead as to the identity of
the murderer, the investigators did nothing to pin down exactly how far off the
video clock was, at least not before plaintiff was arrested. (Footnote 3: The fact
that the police finally sought to verify the information—and quickly and readily
learned that it was inaccurate—*after* Liser's arrest certainly does not help their
cause. That such an simple test was not done in the three months preceding the
arrest, and if done would have cast serious doubt on the propriety of that
arrest, suggests an investigative sloppiness that at least casts doubt on whether
the initial arrest was actually supported by probable cause.) Instead, Detective
Smith and his team chose to rely solely on a single, untested statement from the
bank manager. Such reliance might well have been unassailable had the
investigators been making an on-the-spot determination as to whether probable
cause existed to arrest plaintiff in the first frantic days after the murder. But in
the circumstances of the deliberate, slowly unfolding investigation that ensued,
during which the officers should have had ample time to pursue leads and to
check facts, their failure to verify the length of the gap on the video stands in a
rather different light. Their conduct appears more sloppy than reasoned, the
product of carelessness rather than craft. The Court is thus unable to say with
certainty that this crucial mistake was ultimately a permissible one, or that
prudent investigators would necessarily have conducted themselves as defendants did here.

[1]   United States District Court for the District of Columbia No 00–2325 (ESH) March 26,
2003 before District Judge Ellen Segal Huvelle, 11–12.

3.22 Compare this case with the murder of Denise Mansfield, who was found
bound and strangled in her home in Prince George's County on 29 June 2002.
It was thought that she had been dead since 22 June. The police investigation
centred on a surveillance camera that recorded images of people using an
ATM machine, owned by the Sun Trust Bank in Mitchellville. This ATM
machine was used to withdraw US$200 from the victim's bank account at
2.30 pm, using her debit card. Three women, Virginia Shelton, her daughter
Shirley and one of her daughter's friends, Jennifer Starkey, were subsequently
arrested. They were identified as using the machine between 2.28 pm and
2.33 pm and the women did not dispute using this particular ATM machine.
They were subsequently released after three weeks. After they were arrested, it
came to light that it had been assumed the clocks on the transaction computer
and the ATM machine were synchronised. This was not correct: the women
used the ATM machine earlier than the time stamp on the video recording. It
is reported that police officer had these records in their possession on the day
they arrested the women, but it is not clear if they examined the records before
making the arrests. It was not until Mr Starkey obtained a copy of the relevant
records that the women were released[1].

[1]   Ruben Castaneda 'Mistaken Arrests Leave Pr. George's Murder Unsolved' washingtonpost-
.com Sunday June 22 2003 available online at http://www.washingtonpost.com/ac2/wp-
dyn?pagename=article&contentId=A19633–2003Jun21&notFound=true,   visited   on
16 July 2003, re-visited on 6 November 2006.

3.23 Another unfortunate example is that of *Virdi v Commissioner of Police of the Metropolis*[1]. Letters containing racist comments were sent through the internal mail system at Hanwell and Ealing police stations on 24 December 1997 and 19 January 1998, addressed to ethnic minority members of staff. Police Sergeant Virdi was arrested and charged with criminal offences relating to the production and dissemination of racist letters. He was suspended from duty and subsequently faced a disciplinary hearing. At his disciplinary hearing, expert evidence was given for the police that purported to identify how and when the racist letters were produced. The documents were reconstructed, then print runs were matched against evidence in the event logs, and the identity of the person logged on at the time the print run was working aimed to make it clear who the culprit was. The defence did not offer any expert evidence. Police Sergeant Virdi was found guilty on a number of counts, including producing and distributing the racist letters and impersonating a colleague by using her User ID and password. He was subsequently dismissed from the service.

[1] London (North) Employment Tribunal (July, August and December 2000, Case No 2202774/98); Michael Turner 'Beware: Computer Evidence Quicksand' (2001) Computers & Law, pp 36–38.

3.24 During a subsequent hearing before an Employment Tribunal, Police Sergeant Virdi had the benefit of expert help. The case for the police rested on the following interrelated assumptions[1]:

> It was assumed that there was only one way of creating a series of documents and that both sets of racist letters were:
> created and printed within the Ealing Division of MPS using MS Word
> printed as a consecutive sequence of unnamed MS Word documents.

All the evidence emanated from event logs on the MPS OTIS system servers. It was claimed that this system was secure; each user had a User ID and a password that was not meant to be disclosed to other users. Passwords had to be changed every 28 days and the same password could not be re-used within a 12-month period.

[1] Michael Turner 'Beware: Computer Evidence Quicksand' (2001) Computers & Law, p 37.

3.25 The document reconstruction technique was invented by the Assistant Systems Administrator for the Ealing Division. He thought that the January 1998 racist letters may have been produced in-house and to test this theory he set out to recreate the document. He produced a reconstructed document and noted the size of the print file (note that this is not the same as the file size) when it was printed. He then searched the event logs for a sequence of printed documents that matched that print file size and identified a sequence of documents printed at a specific time using a specific user ID. It was these event log entries that formed the basis of MPS' evidence.

The hearing established that the initial investigation of the computer at Hanwell police station was carried out in such a way as to destroy evidence; no attempt was made to secure and obtain an image of the relevant servers; evidence of the abuse of passwords was given by both the defence and prosecution witnesses; the reliability of the server log time-stamps was questioned on a number of grounds by the defence expert witnesses; the document reconstruction technique was, in the opinion of Turner, 'untested, unverified, untestable, unverifiable, unaccepted and unscientific. It was based on a false premise—that it was possible to precisely determine the size of a Windows print job file by examining only the information available on the face of a printed document'[1]. The techniques used were novel and, counsel for Police Sergeant Virdi argued, far from valid when taking into account the tests in *Daubert* and *Kumho Tire*[2]. It does not appear that any attempt was made to establish the reason why an ethnic minority Police Sergeant would want to send racist hate mail to himself and other ethnic employees. In this instance, the Metropolitan Police were required to pay Mr Virdi a total of £151,688 by order of the Employment Tribunal because he was subject of discrimination because of his race. He was subsequently re-instated. As pointed out by Turner[3]:

> The case clearly demonstrates the risks of over-reliance on expert interpretation of computer evidence. Experts giving evidence on computer evidence have a special responsibility to distinguish clearly between facts and speculation, assumption, inference and opinion. It appears that distinction was not always made in this case.

[1] Michael Turner 'Beware: Computer Evidence Quicksand' (2001) Computers & Law, p 38.
[2] *Daubert v Merrell Dow Pharmaceuticals, Inc* 509 U.S. 579 (1993); 125 L.Ed.2d 469; 113 S.Ct. 2786; *Kumho Tire Company Ltd v Carmichael*, 526 U.S. 137; 143 L.Ed.2d 238; 119 S.Ct. 1167 (1999).
[3] *Turner* (2001) p 38.

3.26 The case of *Liser v Smith* is a good example of the failure to test the digital evidence fully, as happened in the case of police constable Munden in 1992. After returning from holiday, he discovered there had been six withdrawals totalling £460 from his account. He complained to his bank and was duly accused of obtaining to money by deception. It appears that evidence at his trial demonstrated that the bank's system had been implemented and subsequently managed in an unsound way. In addition, it seems the bank claimed, without putting forward any evidence, that the ATM system did not suffer from problems. The conviction was overturned on appeal, but only after the prosecution provided a report from the auditors of the bank that the system was secure. When the bank refused to permit the defence expert to examine the banks' system, the court apparently disallowed the evidence in the case[1]. PC Munden was subsequently re-instated.

[1] Ross J Anderson *Security Engineering A Guide to Building Dependable Distributed Systems* (2001) pp 203–204; for further details of this case, see the chapter on evidentiary foundations.

3.27 These cases serve to illustrate the need to test the digital evidence rigorously. In discussing the certainty of computer evidence, Casey introduces a proposed scale for categorising levels of certainty in digital evidence[1]. This scale is well thought out and, if used with a Wigmorean analysis[2], could lead to more accurate examination of raw data, both digital and non-digital. The aim should be to test the accuracy of the evidence and to ask if the conclusions are correct, rather than making decisions based on an imperfect analysis of the available evidence. It should never be assumed that because evidence is in digital format it must therefore be correct and impervious to being tested to prove whether it is accurate or false. As an afterthought, it is to be wondered why a bank bothers goes to the length and expense of installing a surveillance camera adjacent to an ATM machine if the quality of the evidence is such that it has little or no probative value[3].

1   *Casey* (2004) p 176.
2   For an introduction, see William Twining *Rethinking Evidence Exploratory Essays* (1994) and Terence Anderson and William Twining *Analysis of Evidence* (1998).
3   For the importance of taking care about the clocks on computers, time zones and the idiosyncrasies of forensic software, see Chris Boyd and Peter Forster 'Time and date issues in forensic computing—a case study' (2004) Digital Investigation vol 1, no 1, pp 18–23.

Tools

3.28 A digital evidence specialist will not only require an in-depth knowledge of the operating system they are to investigate, but will also need to employ a number of proprietary tools in the performance of their investigation and analysis of digital evidence. The types of tool they use will depend on the operating system (Windows, Unix, Macintosh) they are required to look at, and whether they are investigating a network, handheld devices, embedded systems or wireless networks[1]. The specialist digital evidence textbooks consider these matters in depth and the reader is encouraged to familiarise themselves with the technology and techniques by referring to appropriate practitioner texts[2]. The tools used can be the subject of cross-examination and the underlying scientific methodology and structure of such tools can be questioned[3]. This section aims to illustrate why and how tools are used in the context of the Windows operating system, partly because it is so popular.

Automated tools are necessary to perform forensic examination of a computer economically. However, the digital evidence specialist should understand the process used by the tool to perform the relevant tasks. This is because it may be necessary to explain the process to a court, or to carry out the analysis without the aid of a tool, since the use of a tool in any given situation may not be appropriate. These are issues that lawyers may well need to take cognisance of in the future. For instance, it is not clear that practitioners themselves are familiar with some tools and question the worth of early versions[4]. This is because, it seems, such tools are tested rather than formally proven correct and it has been suggested that such tools should be tested formally[5].

1   W Jansen and R Ayers 'An overview and analysis of PDA forensic tools' (2005) Digital Investigation vol 2, no 2, pp 120–132.
2   Brian Carrier 'Defining Digital Forensic Examination and Analysis Tools Using Abstraction Layers' and James R Lyle 'NIST CFTT: Testing Disk Imaging Tools' (2003) International Journal of Digital Evidence vol 1, issue 4, online at http://www.ijde.org.
3   SWGDE Recommended Guidelines for Validation Testing (v1.0, July 2004) available online at fs.org/swgde/documents/swgde2004/SWGDE%20Validation%20Guidelines%20_July%202004_.pdf.
4   Eoghan Casey 'Network traffic as a source of evidence: tool strengths, weaknesses, and future needs' (2004) Digital Investigation vol 1, no 1, pp 28–43.

⁵   James R Lyle 'NIST CFTT: Testing Disk Imaging Tools' (2003) International Journal of Digital Evidence vol 1, issue 4, online at http://www.ijde.org; Matthew Gerber and John Leeson 'Formalization of computer input and output: the Hadley model' (2004) Digital Investigation vol 1, no 2, pp 214–224.

Copying the hard drive

3.29 Before entering a computer, it is essential that the investigator is familiar with the underlying operating systems, files systems and applications. By understanding the file systems, the digital evidence specialist will be aware of how information is arranged which, in turn, enables them to determine where information can be hidden, and how such information can be recovered and analysed. The digital evidence specialist should understand Windows NT accounts and the control mechanism that determines which files a user is permitted to gain access to once they are logged on to a system in order to establish answers to questions such as who might have had access to a computer or system; which files they would have been able to look at; and whether it was possible for an unauthorised outsider to obtain access to the computer from the Internet.

To avoid altering any evidence on a computer, it is necessary to bypass the operating system. When the power supply is switched on the basic input and output system ('BIOS') will carry out a power-on self test ('POST') before looking for the operating system. After the BIOS is activated and before the POST test has completed its cycle it is possible to interrupt the process. Most computers are programmed to expect the operating system to be found on a floppy disk, hard disk or compact disk. As a result, the system looks at these disks in the order set out in something called the Complimentary Metal Oxide Silicon ('CMOS') configuration tool. The CMOS RAM chip retains the date, time, hard drive parameters and other details relating to configuration whilst the main power is switched off. By looking at the CMOS tool between the POST test and the computer being fully powered up, the digital evidence specialist is able to determine where the computer will look for the operating system: whether on a floppy disk, hard disk or compact disk. By knowing where the computer is going to look for the operating system, the investigator is able to pre-empt the operating system on the computer and provide an alternate operating system from another disk. By interrupting the normal boot up process, the evidence on the hard drive remains intact and unaltered thereby permitting the content to be copied in the state it was in when the computer was switched off. Various techniques and tools, such as an evidence acquisition boot disk, can be used to intercept this process, the precise technique depending on the circumstances of a case.

Once the computer is booted from a suitable tool, the program can then copy the digital evidence sector-by-sector. Some tools will acquire the data and undertake an integrity check at regular intervals. There is a discussion in the digital evidence field regarding whether or not some of the tools that undertake these tasks take an exact copy of the disk, even though all of the information is copied from the disk. One reason is that the data will be arranged in a different manner in the proprietary file format. Casey suggests that this is not as important as ensuring that the integrity of the evidence is maintained. In addition, he also suggests that two copies are made with different tools[1].

¹   *Casey* (2004) pp 261–264.

Viewing the data

3.30 When the digital evidence has been copied, the data can be viewed physically or logically. To view data such as the files and the properties associated with the files physically, it is necessary to view the directory through a tool. This is because the files use ASCII or Unicode to set out data, and a human being needs this code to be interpreted before the data can be viewed and interrogated. The data can be viewed in hexadecimal form on one side of a screen and in plain text on the other side of the screen. Depending on the tool used, the data can be examined and analysed. For instance, a tool can recover slack or unallocated space and compare files to determine if there are any differences to be observed[1].

Viewing data in logical view enables the user to examine data as represented by the file system. This way of looking at the data permits the user to analyse the data in a different way, but it does not show the underlying information that is visible when using the physical method. Both forms of viewing data have their limitations and it is also important to be aware that data can be misinterpreted. There is some debate about the best way of examining digital evidence, but the emphasis should be on verifying the accuracy of the evidence by using different tools.

¹   Note also that the volume of images that need to be reviewed and searched are increasing and that tools are being developed for this purpose: Paul Sanderson 'Mass image classification' (2006) Digital Investigation vol 3 no 4, pp 190–195.

Recovering data

3.31 It is probably correct to imagine that there will be increasing numbers of people that delete the hard drives of their in computers in anticipation of legal action or after legal action has begun[1]. For instance, in the case of *L C Services Ltd v Andrew Brown*[2] Andrew Brown, the sales director of LC Services, was found to have broken the fiduciary duty he owed to LC Services. He also breached the terms of his services agreement and misused confidential information belonging to LC Services. It appeared that Mr Brown altered or re-installed the operating system on his computer on 1 October 2003, at the time the claimants were pursuing disclosure documents from the defendants. A digital evidence specialist was subsequently able to retrieve the residue of the text of the relevant database in dispute and the remains of a number of emails sent by Mr Brown. The content of these emails went to show that he was in breach of his fiduciary duties to LC Services. It is not difficult to envisage the time will come when it might become a regular requirement in litigation that the parties to an action will have to use a digital evidence specialist to recover hard drives that have been deleted or written over and, perhaps, to ensure hidden areas of a hard disk are also investigated as a matter of course[3].

There are several techniques that can be used to recover data that has been deleted. This can be done manually or using tools, depending on the complexity of the problem faced by the specialist. For instance, some tools use a bit-for-bit copy of a disk to display a reconstruction of the file system, including any deleted files. However, where files are fragmented, it will be necessary to recover files by hand. Another technique to recover deleted files involved searching unallocated space and swap files for such information as headers and footers. Although there are many types of file that can be recovered this way with an appropriate tool, such as graphic files, word processing and executable files, recovery is limited to those files that have headers that have not been deleted[4].

[1]   This is, in fact, already happening: Ewa Huebner, Derek Bren and Cheong Kai Wee 'Data hiding in the NTFS file system' (2006) Digital Investigation vol 3, no 4, pp 211–226.
[2]   [2003] EWHC 3024 (QB), [2003] All ER (D) 239 (Dec).
[3]   Bruce J Nikkel 'Forensic acquisition and analysis of magnetic tapes' (2005) Digital Investigation vol 2, no 1, pp 8–18; Mayank R Gupta, Michael D Hoeschele and Marcus K Rogers 'Hidden Disk Areas: HPA and DCO' (2006) International Journal of Digital Evidence vol 5, issue 1, online at http://www.ijde.org.
[4]   Paul Alvarez 'Using Extended File Information (EXIF) File Headers in Digital Evidence Examination' (2004) International Journal of Digital Evidence vol 2, issue 3, online at http://www.ijde.org.

Passwords and encryption

3.32   A number of tools are available that are capable of removing passwords, and bypassing or recovering passwords. Some tools are available to guess passwords, if the encryption keys are small enough, and where it is not possible to defeat a password it is sometimes possible to search for unencrypted versions of the data in other areas of the hard disk[1].

[1]   Eoghan Casey 'Practical Approaches to Recovering Encrypted Digital Evidence' (2002) International Journal of Digital Evidence vol 1, no 3, at http://www.ijde.org.

Traces of evidence

Network connections

3.33   One of the biggest difficulties with computers once they are connected to a network like the Internet, or where a series of computers are connected in an organisation, is the possibility that a hacker or malicious employee might enter the system without authority and undertake a series of actions that causes an innocent person to be accused of doing something they did not do[1]. This is where data logs can help. Two types of log, the application and system event logs, contain information about how users have used the computer. By scrutinising these logs, either using a tool or manually, can help to obtain a clear picture about the activities that took place on the system, although consideration must be given to the integrity of the logs themselves.

¹   Srinivas Mukkamala and Andrew H Sung 'Identifying Significant Features for Network Forensic Analysis Using Artificial Intelligence Techniques' (2003) International Journal of Digital Evidence vol 1, issue 4, online at http://www.ijde.org; Bruce J Nikkel 'Domain name forensics: a systematic approach to investigating an internet presence' (2004) Digital Investigation vol 1, no 4, pp 247–255; Bruce J Nikkel 'Improving evidence acquisition from live network sources' (2006) Digital Investigation vol 3, no 2, pp 89–96; Eoghan Casey and Aaron Stanley 'Tool review—remote forensic preservation and examination tools' (2004) Digital Investigation vol 1, no 4, pp 284–297.

Logs, files and printing

3.34 In addition, when a user uses their computer they leave traces of their actions across a range of data logs and files[1]. A data log is capable of containing any type of data, depending on what the system is programmed to capture[2]. For instance, if a file is downloaded from the Internet, a date and time stamp will be added to the file to demonstrate when the file was downloaded on to the computer. When the file is moved, opened or modified, the time and date stamps will be altered to reflect these changes. In addition, the metadata can also help provide more information about the file, such as the location to which it was stored on the disk, the printer and the original time and date the file was created. When a file is printed, the computer tends to store the print job in a temporary file and then sends the file to the printer when the printer has the capacity to print the document. Once the command to print has been passed to the temporary store the user can continue to work with the application, for instance they can continue to type a new document whilst the previous document is waiting to be printed. The temporary print store retains valuable information, such as the name of the file to be printed, the type of application used, the name of the printer, the name of the person whose file is to be printed, and the data itself. In addition, there is a date and time stamp added to these files to show when the file was printed. It should be noted, however, that the date and time stamp can be altered, which means it is important to ensure the time and date stamp is corroborated by other methods[3].

¹   In relation to intrusion detection systems, see Peter Sommer 'Intrusion Detection Systems As Evidence' [2002] CTLR 3, pp 67–76; Vlasti Broucek and Paul Turner 'Intrusion Detection: Issues and Challenges in Evidence Acquisition' International Review of Law, Computers & Technology (2004) vol 18, no 2, pp 149–164; Jean-Marc Dinant 'The Long Way from Electronic Traces to Electronic Evidence' (2004) International Review of Law, Computers & Technology vol 18, no 2, pp 173–183.
²   Erin E Kenneally 'Digital logs—proof matters' (2004) Digital Investigation vol 1, no 2, pp 94–101.
³   Karen Kent and Murugiah Souppaya *Guide to Computer Security Log Management* (2006) National Institute of Standards and Technology Special Publication 800–92, at 2.1.3, fourth bullet point. Online at http://csrc.nist.gov/publications/nistpubs/.

Use of the Internet

3.35 When a person obtains access to the Internet, a range of data is created and retained on a computer, including the websites that have been visited, the content a user has viewed and the newsgroups they obtained access to[1]. Some systems also include a log of the times and dates the modem was used. The types of information include:

1   Yeong Zee Kin 'Computer Misuse, Forensics and Evidence on the Internet' Communications Law (2000) vol 5, no 5, pp 153–170; Vivienne Mee, Theodore Tryfonas and Iain Sutherland 'The Windows Registry as a forensic artefact: Illustrating evidence collection for Internet usage' (2006) Digital Investigation vol 3, no 3, pp 166–173.

BROWSER CACHE

3.36 When viewing a page on the Internet, the browser retains an image of the page, called a cache. The computer gives the page a date and time stamp at the time the page was downloaded. The reason for doing this is that when the page is visited again, the cached file is used by the computer and subsequently updated. Another item of information created and logged in some browser history databases include the number of times a web page was visited. It must not be assumed, however, that just because the computer has recorded certain types of web page the user actually viewed such pages. This is because some websites, in particular those peddling pornography, will redirect a browser to different websites, and may even make changes to the computer that the user has not authorised. It is also possible to recover these files even if they are deleted. Recovered files can provide such information as when the computer was used to obtain access to web-based email, whether or not purchases were made or financial transactions undertaken.

COOKIES

3.37 Many websites seek to keep a track of the visit by individuals to their websites by placing information in 'cookie files' on the user's computer. If cookies have not been disabled, the information in the cookie directory can help with an investigation. As for websites included in the temporary cache file, it does not follow that because there is a cookie on the computer a user necessarily went to all of the websites included in the cookie directory. Some advertisements on a website may add a cookie, even though the user did not click on and view the particular website. Further, where the user's browser has been redirected without their permission, cookies can be added to the directory without their knowledge.

USENET USE

3.38 Where the user of a computer visits Usenet newsgroups, a record of this activity is usually stored in a specific file. The type of information that can be obtained from such files includes the name of the newsgroup, details of subscriptions, the articles that have been downloaded and the last time the user looked at the newsgroup. This information can be invaluable, especially when dealing with cases of child pornography.

EMAIL AND INSTANT MESSAGING

3.39 Email has now become the dominant method of communication for the vast majority of organisations and individuals. As a result, a great deal of evidence can be discovered from email correspondence. Some software programs store email in plain text files, whilst others use proprietary formats that will require the digital evidence specialist to use a number of tools in order to read the messages. It is sometimes possible to recover email messages that have been deleted but have not been removed from the email files. Where it is impossible or difficult to restore emails on a single computer, it might be possible to track email traffic through the network it has travelled[1]. Organisations are beginning to recognise the importance of their email correspondence and it is conceivable that, in future, many organisations will have archives of email communications that can be investigated. Also, instant messaging (a form of peer-to-peer or, more accurately, computer-to-computer communication) has become the default method of communication for many people, especially children, and presents problems for the investigator, particularly where they may need to view a home computer to help determine why a child might have left home, for instance[2]. Voice over Internet Protocol ('VoIP') is another computer-to-computer technology that has expanded rapidly and will need to be considered when conducting an investigation[3].

[1] Eoghan Casey, Troy Larson and H Morrow Long 'Network Analysis' in *Casey, ed* (2002) pp 234–239.
[2] Harlan Carvey 'Instant messaging investigations on a live Windows XP system' (2004) Digital Investigation vol 1, no 4, pp 256–260; Mike Dickson 'An examination into MSN Messenger 7.5 contact identification' (2006) Digital Investigation vol 3, no 2, pp 79–83; Mike Dickson 'An examination into Yahoo Messenger 7.0 contact identification' (2006) Digital Investigation vol 3, no 3, pp 159–165; Paul Sanderson 'Identifying an existing file KaZaA artefacts' (2006) Digital Investigation vol 3, no 3, pp 174–180; Mike Dickson 'An examination into AOL Instant Messenger 5.5 contact identification' (2006) Digital Investigation vol 3, no 4, pp 227–237; Jessica Reust 'Case study: AOL instant messenger trace evidence' (206) Digital Investigation vol 3, no 4, pp 238–243.
[3] Xinyuan Wang, Shiping Chen and Sushil Jajodia 'Tracking Anonymous Peer-to-Peer VoIP Calls on the Internet' available online at http://se.gmu.edu/~xwangc/Publications/CCS05-VoIPTracking.pdf.

REPORTING

3.40 The findings and any conclusions made by the digital evidence specialist will be set out in a report. Whether prepared for criminal or civil proceedings the report should include a range of information that is pertinent to the case, including, but not limited to:

(a)   notes prepared during the examination phase of the investigation;
(b)   details about the way in which the investigation was conducted;
(c)   details about the chain of custody;
(d)   the validity of the procedures used; and
(e)   details of what was discovered including, but not limited to:
    (i)   any specific files or data that were directly related to the investigation;
    (ii) any further files or data that may support the conclusions reached by the specialist. This will include the recovery of any deleted files and the analysis of any graphic files;
    (iii) the types of search conducted, such as key word searches, and the programs searched;

(iv)   any relevant evidence from the Internet, such as emails and the analysis of websites visited and log files;

(v)   indications of names that might demonstrate evidence of ownership of software, such as to whom software is registered; and

(vi)   whether there was any attempt to hide date in any way and, if so, what methods were used.

The report needs to reflect how the examination was conducted and what data was recovered. It may be that the digital evidence specialist will have to give evidence about their conduct of the examination and the validity of the procedures and tools they used. Essential to any report will be the conclusions reached by the specialist. Where an opinion is offered, that opinion should set out the basis of the evidence. An example is given by Casey, in which he sets out two examples in relation to the conclusions that might be offered by a digital evidence specialist relating to a particular item of evidence[1]:

1   Log entries from System 2 indicate that Suspect B was logged in at the time of the crime and is almost certainly the offender.

2   The wtmp log on trusted System 1 (C4) indicates that the offender logged in from System 2. The wtmp log on untrusted System 2 (C2) indicates that two potential suspects were logged in at the time of the crime. However, RADIUS logs (C4) relating to Suspect A's PPP connection show that she disconnected from the Internet long before the crime, indicating that the associated wtmp entry on untrusted System B was not terminated properly, probably due to an abrupt disconnection on her part. Therefore, only Suspect B was logged onto system 2 at the time of the crime. The pact logs on System 2 (C4) show that Suspect B was using Secure Shell (SSH) at the time of the crime. Although the pact entry does not indicate which system Suspect B was connecting to using SSH, an examination of his command history (C2) shows that he was connecting to System 1. Based on this evidence, it is *probable* that suspect B is the offender. [Italics in the original]

As Casey points out, the validity of the first conclusion cannot easily be assessed. However, the second example sets out the reasons for the conclusion based on the evidence that was uncovered. It may be that another digital evidence specialist might legitimately challenge some of the conclusions reached in the second example—but at least the challenge can be made on the basis of the evidence rather than a bald assertion, as set out in the first example.

Consideration should also be given to: rates of error; including the origin and timing of events that have been recorded; taking care when reaching conclusions where data is lost; being aware that digital evidence can be fabricated; and to consider evaluating the evidence based 'on the reliability of the system and process that generate the records'[2]. As pointed out by Sommer, it is important to be aware that digital evidence specialists have to use a variety of techniques to cope with the wide variety of hardware and software encountered. Reliability is one factor to take into account. Another factor is the degree of reliance on the conclusions reached by a digital evidence specialist. The digital evidence must be interpreted and care should be taken to ensure the underlying rationale is sustainable[3].

---

[1]   *Casey* (2004) p 177.

FUTURE CONSIDERATIONS

3.41 One of the major difficulties in investigating evidence in digital formats relates to the incompatibility of formats used to store digital data. The problems arise when an investigator has to deal with different disk image formats. The difficulty is compounded when dealing with different types of digital evidence, such as a network data log or the content of a mobile device[1]. As the website of the Common Digital Evidence Storage Format points out, 'converting between proprietary formats may result in incorrect data, missing metadata, and lost productivity'[2]. This is because raw data is copied from a disk drive or other storage device, but the raw format does not store metadata that might be important to the investigation. In addition, converting from proprietary formats can cause similar problems. To this end, an attempt is being made to define a standard format for storing and transmitting evidence in digital format by the Common Digital Evidence Storage Format Working Group.

Also, a word to the future that is already partly with us: consideration should be made in respect of 'trusted computing' and the effect this will have on investigations and the examination and cross-examination of digital evidence, especially because an increasing number of third parties will have access to computers in the future[3]. In addition, the methods used by attackers in the digital environment will mean it is increasingly necessary to take into consideration the use of rarer techniques to obtain evidence in the future[4].

1   Barrie Mellars 'Forensic examination of mobile phones' (2004) Digital Investigation vol 1, no 4, pp 266–272; Adam Laurie 'Digital detective—Bluetooth' (2006) Digital Investigation vol 3, no 1, pp 17–19; Wayne Jansen and Rick Ayers *Draft Guidelines on Cell Phone Forensics: Recommendations of the National Institute of Standards and Technology* (Computer Security Division, Information Technology Laboratory, National Institute of Standards and Technology, Special Publication 800–101 Sponsored by the Department of Homeland Security) available online at http:// csrc.nist.gov/publications/drafts/Draft-SP800–101.pdf.
2   Common Digital Evidence Storage Format, a working group of the Digital Forensic Research Workshop, more details available online at http://www.dfrws.org/CDESF/index.html.
3   Stephen Mason 'Trusted computing and forensic investigations' (2005) Digital Investigation vol 2, no 3, pp 189–192, this article is merely an introduction to the topic that includes relevant references, and see also 'Trusting your computer to be trusted' (2005) Computer Fraud & Security January, pp 7–11 with a number of additional references by the same author. Some people are waking up to the implications: Mark Rasch 'Vista's EULA Product Activation Worries' *Security Focus* 20 November 2006 online at http://www.securityfocus.com/columnists/423?ref=rss.
4   Kris Harms 'Forensic analysis of System Restore points in Microsoft Windows XP' (2006) Digital Investigation vol 3, no 3, pp 151–158.

Chapter 4

THE EVIDENTIAL FOUNDATIONS

STEPHEN MASON

4.01 It may be necessary to lay the evidential foundations of digital evidence before the evidence is accepted in legal proceedings; alternatively, the authenticity of digital evidence may be the subject of a challenge. In determining whether the burden has been discharged by a party adducing digital evidence that requires an evidential foundation, a range of factors will need to be taken into account, some of which will apply equally to each form of evidence, and some of which will be relevant to one or another, because of the nature of the evidence. Where the authenticity of digital evidence is the subject of a challenge in legal proceedings a range of evidence may be required, covering some or all of the technical attributes associated with the preservation of digital data. In preparing and presenting evidence of the authenticity of digital data, reference will undoubtedly be made to standards, both national and international. In addition, authoritative papers, such as those prepared by the National Archives in the United Kingdom, amongst others, will also be of help in establishing and testing the authenticity of the data in question[1]. The services of a digital evidence specialist may also be necessary, depending on the facts at issue. The nature of the evidence available to a court to determine the authenticity of digital data will differ from case to case, as indicated by Lord Griffith in *R v Shephard*[2]:

> Computers vary immensely in their complexity and in the operations they perform. The nature of the evidence to discharge the burden of showing that there has been no improper use of the computer and that it was operating properly will inevitably vary from case to case. I suspect that it will very rarely be necessary to call an expert and that in the vast majority of cases it will be possible to discharge the burden by calling a witness who is familiar with the operation of the computer in the sense of knowing what the computer is required to do and who can say that it is doing it properly[3].

Although Lord Griffiths was referring to the requirement to comply with s 69 of the Police and Criminal Evidence Act 1984 ('PACE 1984'), which has since been appealed, nevertheless the comment is a useful reminder that when there is a requirement to prove the reliability of a digital document it will be necessary to ensure the relevant witnesses are qualified to offer the requisite evidence.

[1] The National Archives:
Generic requirements for sustaining electronic information over time: 1 Defining the characteristics for authentic records;
Generic requirements for sustaining electronic information over time: 2 Sustaining authentic and reliable records: management requirements;
Generic requirements for sustaining electronic information over time: 3 Sustaining authentic and reliable records: technical requirements;
Generic requirements for sustaining electronic information over time: 4 Guidance for categorising records to identify sustainable requirements,

available online at http://www.nationalarchives.gov.uk/electronicrecords/reqs_sustain.htm.
2   [1993] AC 380, [1993] 1 All ER 225 (spelt Shepherd in All ER), [1993] Crim LR 295, HL.
3   [1993] AC 380 at 387. See *Connolly v Lancashire County Council* [1994] RTR 79, QBD,
     where the prosecution elected to produce evidence that a weighbridge was working
     properly, but failed to demonstrate the computer was functioning properly at the material
     time.

4.02 The comments and underlying assumptions made by some authors of
the technical literature appear to assume that the nature of the evidence builds
to form a cohesive whole. For instance, it is stated by the author of 'Generic
requirements for sustaining electronic information over time: 1 Defining the
characteristics for authentic records'[1] that authenticity can only exist if the
three characteristics set out in BS ISO 15489–1:2001 'Information and
documentation. Records management. General—reliability, integrity and
usability' are also present. The suggestion is that:

> As such authenticity is an implicit value derived or presumed from the presence
> of the explicit elements that characterise the other three characteristics. A
> presumption of authenticity is an inference that is drawn from known facts
> about the manner in which a record has been created, handled, and maintained.

This is an attractive proposition but, although the mass of evidence may
appear to have a cumulative effect, the failure in any single part of a technical
or organisational characteristic will serve to undermine the totality of the
evidence. According to the author of 'Admissibility Of Electronically Filed
Federal Records As Evidence'[2] in 1990, cross-examination in relation to the
integrity of computer stored or generated files include questioning the following: the source of the input data or information and the process for
transcribing it to machine-readable form; the computer programs that create,
edit and update the files; the computer programs that produce the output or
stored files; and the reliability of the hardware and vendor-supplied 'off-the-
shelf' software that systematically manages the internal processes of the
computer. In this respect, the lawyer whose duty it is to test the evidence is not
interested in the gradual build-up of the various layers of technical and
organisational characteristics that form the basis for the authenticity of data in
digital format. They are interested in exposing weaknesses and, if it can be
demonstrated that a sufficient number of weaknesses exist, the totality of the
cross-examination may mean that the party submitting the document has
failed the evidential burden of convincing the adjudicator to accept the
evidence[3].

1   The National Archives, undated, para 3.1.4.
2   IV. Conclusion, (US Department of Justice, October 1990) available online at http://
     www.lectlaw.com/files/crf03.htm.
3   For a discussion relating to email, see Chris Reed 'Authenticating electronic mail
     messages—some evidential problems' (1989) Modern Law Review vol 52, pp 649–660;
     Mark D. Robbins 'Evidence at the electronic frontier: introducing email at trial in
     commercial litigation' Rutgers Computer and Technology Law Journal, vol 29, no 2, pp
     219–315.

4.03 However, the guidance issued by various public record offices across the
world in relation to the authenticity of electronic records remains sound.
Procedures, process and technical measures such as audit logs, system security
and the use of digital signatures are all highly relevant in providing for the

authenticity of electronic documents. The development and provision of standards and guidelines is merely one part of the whole. The most significant issue in relation to this matter is how such standards or guidelines are actually implemented. The gap between what is stated in the standard or guideline and what actually occurs in reality will be a central focus of cross-examination in a court.

An example: the automated teller machine ('ATM')

4.04 By way of introduction, it will be useful to illustrate some of the practical issues that have occurred in the past in relation to digital evidence, in particular, cases referring to financial transactions. Where withdrawals have taken place from a bank account by way of an ATM, the actual fact of the withdrawal may not be at issue and, in any event, the bank under the relevant business records or the Bankers' Books exemptions can adduce the evidence. What may be at issue is whether the person who's personal identification number ('PIN') was used was the person that actually used the PIN to make withdrawals[1]. In 1980, Dorothy Judd discovered two withdrawals were made from her account by use of a cash card and PIN in the sum of US$800[2]. At the material time she was at her place of employment and her employer corroborated her evidence by writing a letter to confirm her presence at her place of work. Citibank produced computer print-outs setting out the details of the withdrawals at issue, the content of which was explained by the branch manager. It appears from the report that the bank merely asserted, by way of a statement in support, that the security measures in place to prevent the unauthorised use of cash cards was so stringent as to prevent the possibility of a PIN from being used other than by the person whose number it was. Marmarellis J indicated that the case turned on issues of evidence, burden and credibility. In his judgment, the learned judge referred to the lack of expert qualifications of the manager, but not the evidentiary foundations of the statement from the bank, in which the soundness of the security system in place was asserted. He determined the issue by considering whether the plaintiff had proven her case by a fair preponderance of the credible evidence. In this instance, the issue was whether to believe the person or the machine. In reaching a decision, Marmarellis J referred to the 1977 Report to the Congress 'EFT in the United States, Final Report of the National Commission on Electronic Fund Transfers'[3] and recommendation 5, which reads:

> If the depository institution denies the alleged error or its responsibility for the error or unauthorized use, the customer should have the burden of initiating any further proceeding, such as a lawsuit, to establish his right to have his account credited or recredited. Once a lawsuit has been initiated by a depositor, the depository institution has the burden to prove that there was no error or unauthorized use for which it was responsible.

The learned judge commented that the recommendations of the Commission were not law, and looked forward to legislation dealing with the issue[4]. He decided not to apply the recommendations of the Commission, but commented, at 212:

> ... this court is not prepared to go so far as to rule that where a credible witness is faced with the adverse "testimony" of a machine, he is as a matter of law

faced also with an unmeetable burden of proof. It is too commonplace in our society that when faced with the choice of man or machine we readily accept the 'word' of the machine everytime. This, despite the tales of computer malfunctions that we hear daily. Defendant's own witness testified to physical malfunction of the very system in issue.

The judge determined that the plaintiff proved her case 'by a fair preponderance of the credible evidence' and judgment was awarded in the amount of the loss plus interest and disbursements.

[1] See *McConville v Barclays Bank plc* 1993 WL 963563, (1993) *Times*, June 30, where a claim for distress was included in the action.
[2] *Judd v Citibank* N.Y.City Civ.Ct., 435 N.Y.S.2d 210.
[3] National Commission on Electronic Fund Transfers 'EFT in the United States, Final Report of the National Commission on Electronic Fund Transfers' (Washington DC, October 1977).
[4] The Electronic Fund Transfer Act (15 USC 1693) was passed in 1978 and the Electronic Code of Federal Regulations, Part 205—Electronic Fund Transfer (Regulation E) applies to cash cards.

4.05 In comparison to the civil actions taken over such unauthorised withdrawals, in England and Wales some banks make a complaint to the police and the matter is then dealt with through the criminal courts. For instance, in the case of *R v Cochrane*[1], which was decided before s 69 of PACE 1984 was repealed, the members of the Court of Appeal allowed the appeal of the defendant because the prosecution failed to adduce adequate evidence to properly rule that till rolls were admissible as evidence. In this instance, a building society inadvertently credited Cochrane's account with more than he had paid in. Shortly thereafter, a number of withdrawals were made in quick succession from ATM machines in different towns. The Crown wished to show that Cochrane made the withdrawals before the building society noticed the mistake. He was convicted of theft by fraudulent use of his cash card. At issue was whether or not each till roll recording the initial enquiry and the subsequent withdrawal could be produced by an official of the branch at which the transactions took place. In this instance, evidence was adduced to show that when a person used an ATM machine, the information typed in by the user was relayed to the branch computer, which retained a back-up copy. The information was then transmitted to the central mainframe computer. It appears that the prosecution attempted to establish an evidentiary foundation for the admission of the evidence but failed to provide satisfactory evidence of the link between the ATM machine and the mainframe computer. No witness was able to give evidence of the location of the mainframe computer and the prosecution failed to establish the link between the use of the card and PIN and the link to the relevant account, an action that was carried out between the ATM and the mainframe, not the local branch computer. In addition, none of the witnesses were able to offer affirmative information that the mainframe computer was operating correctly (which was required at the time). The members of the Court of Appeal indicated that it was necessary to adduce evidence to explain how each of the relevant pieces of information printed on the till roll came into existence. It was therefore necessary that appropriate evidence of sufficient authority must be called to describe the function and operation of the mainframe computer, including the process by which it validated a transaction. None of these matters were covered by any of the witnesses.

[1]   [1993] Crim LR 48, CA.

4.06 This case was followed shortly thereafter by the prosecution of PC John Munden at Mildenhall Magistrates' Court, Suffolk, in February 1994, after the trial had been adjourned in late 1993[1]. PC John Munden was charged with attempting to obtain money by deception after he protested that he was not responsible for making six transactions via ATM machines, all of which appeared on his statement in September 1992. He complained to the manager of the Halifax Building Society in Newmarket and made it clear that his bank card had been in his possession at all times. The Building Society claimed that is was satisfied that its computer systems were properly secure, and the Building Society concluded that PC Munden must have made these transactions, or suffered them to be made, and that his complaint was dishonest.

[1]   For a resume of the case by Ross Anderson, Professor of Security Engineering at the Computer Laboratory Research Group at Cambridge University, who appeared as an expert witness, see http://catless.ncl.ac.uk/Risks/15.54.html#subj8; for an update of the case, see http://www.doc.ic.ac.uk/~ids/dotdot/misc/titbits/phantom_ATM_withdrawals.html and http://catless.ncl.ac.uk/Risks/18.25.html.

4.07 The brief facts set out below are taken directly from the commentary by Professor Ross Anderson, who appeared as an expert witness. A Mr Beresford of the Halifax Building Society gave evidence for the Crown at the initial hearing. In essence, his evidence comprised the following: an admission that he had no expert knowledge of computer systems; that he did not carry out the investigation; he asserted that the society was satisfied that its systems were secure, which led the Halifax to believe the transactions must have been made with the card and the PIN issued to the customer; he further asserted that fraudulent transactions were rarely, if ever, made from ATMs situated in the lobby area of a building because of the visibility of closed-circuit cameras. After an adjournment, he subsequently admitted that there were between 150–200 transactions that had not been resolved over the previous 3–4 years, and that it would be possible for a third party to observe somebody type in their PIN at the ATM and then produce a card to use on the account. Further, he also confirmed that the person who investigated the incident had no technical qualifications and had acted under his authority, rather than under his direct supervision. The branch manager also gave evidence and he was recalled and examined on the balancing procedures. He described the process and how, as a matter of policy, the balancing records were kept for two years, although it transpired that the balancing records for the two machines in question could not be produced. A Mr Dawson, the technical support manager, also gave evidence and the reader is referred to the account of this evidence by Prof Anderson. A nuance to this case was revealed when PC Munden gave evidence. He gave evidence that when he complained of the withdrawals to the manager, the manager asked him about his holiday in Ireland. The branch manager was alleged to have observed to PC Munden that the transaction code for one of the ATM withdrawals corresponded to their branch in Omagh. Prof Anderson records that this was not apparent from the records eventually produced in court.

PC Munden was convicted, and appealed against his conviction before Turner J, sitting with two Magistrates at Bury St Edmunds Crown Court. It appears that the defence attempted to obtain information about the computer systems, records and operational procedures of Halifax Building Society, but the Halifax apparently refused to provide such evidence, except in the form of a report by a third party. The court decided that PC Munden's conviction could not stand, and he was acquitted. This case illustrates the need to ensure proper evidential foundations are laid before a court. In this instance, if the report of the case by Prof Anderson is to be accepted, it appears clear that the prosecution failed to satisfy itself that an offence was committed by PC Munden and failed to submit testimonial evidence from appropriate witnesses.

4.08 The facts of this case are very disturbing. A number of issues ought to be addressed in such cases, yet do not appear to have been considered: why did the bank make a complaint to the police? What evidence did the bank have that the customer was attempting to perpetrate a fraud so openly? Before contemplating legal action of any description, had the bank considered the likelihood that this particular customer was attempting to defraud the bank? This does not mean that because PC Munden was a police officer he could not have attempted to commit the fraud, but the questions is what evidence did the bank have of the propensity of the customer to make such an attempt to defraud the bank? For instance, did the bank look back on the history of the customer's dealing with the bank to ask whether this particular customer, given their history, was likely to attempt to defraud the bank? Did the bank ask if the customer used this particular bank account as their main account and, if so, why this particular customer should attempt to defraud the bank? In addition, banks have been operating for hundreds of years, so they undoubtedly have historical records that provide reasonably accurate risk profiles of categories of professions or jobs that customers fall into—if such a database exists (which, it seems to an outsider, it ought), then consideration might be given to comparing the historical profile against known methods of attempting to defraud. (Although the author might be exhibiting a naivety in this respect, in assuming such valuable historical evidence is available and acted upon by banks, which might not be the case). None of these questions relate to the digital evidence, but they ought to have been canvassed by the bank before it was decided to take such drastic action.

The reason for the police to agree to charge PC Munden also ought to be canvassed. Given the failure of the bank, it appears, to address any of the issues raised in the preceding paragraph, the question must be raised as to why the police took action without sufficient evidence or consideration of the issues raised above. Similarly, the question must be asked of the Crown Prosecution Service as to why such a prosecution was brought, given the paucity of evidence and the lack of any relevant expertise that could be offered by some of the witnesses.

4.09 In Germany, an appeal from a civil action[1] not too dissimilar to the cases noted above, was brought before the Bundesgerichtshof (the Federal Supreme Court) in 2004. The plaintiff's purse, containing her cash card, was stolen. One or two hours later, cash was withdrawn at two different ATMs using the correct PIN. The plaintiff insisted she had not written down the PIN and only recorded evidence of it as a telephone number in her mobile telephone, which had not been stolen. The plaintiff took action against her bank to recover the money debited to her account. The bank refused to reimburse the customer, asserting she had been negligent, which excluded the bank's liability under its general terms and conditions for the issue of cash cards. The court of first instance found for the plaintiff and a regional court reversed the decision on appeal. The plaintiff appealed to the Federal Supreme Court on a point of law. The sole issue before the Federal Supreme Court concerned the burden of proof. The judges confirmed the decision of the regional court. It was held that the rules on prima facie evidence applied. This was because the facts proved in the matter (the withdrawal of cash in conjunction with a stolen bank card and the use of the correct PIN) typically resulted from a different set of facts (the storage of PIN with the card). The court also held that, in order to prove her case, the plaintiff must show that the same result could occur in another way, to rebut the prima facie evidence. This requirement poses a very high evidential burden on a plaintiff in such cases and will require them to conduct extensive research into how ATMs are attacked to demonstrate the assertions of the bank that their security was so good as to preclude any failure.

In comparison, two judges in separate jurisdictions across the world have reached a different decision on similar facts. In the case of 5526/1999[2], on the 12 October 1995, the claimant returned to his parked car to discover it had been broken into and that a number of items had been stolen, including his bank cash card and other credit cards. The document setting out the PIN was not with the card. The claimant immediately informed the police and the bank but the bank failed to put a stop on the account in time and funds were subsequently removed from his account. The learned judge, D Gavalas, accepted it was possible for the thieves to withdraw money because they knew the PIN, although it was understood that the thieves could also obtain the PIN by other means. The learned judge determined that it was the responsibility of the bank to provide the appropriate security for ATMs, both from an organisational and professional point of view, because it was an activity undertaken by the bank. The bank attempted to enforce the terms and conditions that applied to the issuance of the card, relying on the strict liability of the customer where the card was used without authority. This term was considered unfair, first, because such a term was contrary to the main principle of fault allocation in Greek law and, second, because such terms are contrary to good faith. It was observed that bank could not transfer the risks of unauthorised transactions to the weakest party of the transaction, that is, the customer. It is not clear whether the decision reached by the learned judge was based on the failure of the bank to prove its case or based on the unfairness of the terms and conditions that applied to the card. Compare this decision to the South African case of *Diners Club SA (Pty) Ltd v Singh*[3] where Levinsohn J held, at 659, that a contract term by which the customer was liable, irrespective of who used the PIN, was not against public policy.

This is a very wide and sweeping decision that cannot, it is respectfully suggested, be maintained in the light of the relative ease by which a PIN can be obtained without the consent or authority of the cardholder.

1   BGH October 5, 2004, XI ZR 210/03. It is anticipated that this case will be translated into English and published in a future issue of the Digital Evidence Journal.
2   Court of First Instance of Athens constituted by one judge 5526/1999, a translation into English is to be published in the Digital Evidence Journal, vol 4, no 1.
3   2004 (3) SA 630 (D).

4.10 In the Papua New Guinea District Court, Seneka J found for Mathew Roni against the Bank of South Pacific[1]. Mr Roni discovered the loss of his Save Card and informed the bank immediately he knew of the loss. It was not in dispute that the bank put a stop to all withdrawals on 21 October 2002 at 10 am. It subsequently transpired that a number of transactions occurred after 10 am, and the bank looked to Mr Roni to compensate them for the withdrawals. The evidence demonstrated that a number of withdrawals took place simultaneously at different locations, as described by Seneka J:

> How could the person who stole complainant's Save Card on 18/10/02 withdraw K1000.00 from Mt. Hagen by 06:04 am on 21/10/04 and another K1000.00 from Goroka at 6:16 am same date. Then within 1 ½ hours later in Goroka at Bintangor and Best Buy used the card for K884.05. At about 8:30 am same date withdraw K1000.00 from BSP Mt. Hagen. Defendant has no explanation nor raised any to these transactions.

In this instance, the learned judge reached the conclusion that the bank was negligent. The report of the case does not indicate whether the card was lost with the PIN, but two separate ATMs were used to obtain access to, and remove cash from, the same account in two separate physical locations at roughly the same time. In comparison, the decision by the Federal Supreme Court in Germany is of some concern. The finding implies that the plaintiff was lying and that she actually made the cash withdrawals herself, just as in the case of PC Munden. The problem with cases of this nature is that the evidence provided by the banks tends to assert that their systems are perfect and, therefore, they are not at fault. The evidence does not support such assertions. For example, Maxwell Parsons used an MP3 player to obtain details of cards as they were used in free standing ATMs. He entered a plea of guilty at Minshull Street Crown Court in Manchester in November 2006 to possessing equipment to make a false instrument, deception and unlawful interception of a public telecommunication transmission. He was sentenced to 32 months in prison. He, together with others, stole up to £200,000 from free standing ATMs. Reports in the media explained how it worked: the cable linking the ATM to the main telephone line was disconnected and a two-way adaptor inserted. The MP3 player was then placed between the ATM output cable and the telephone socket. The MP3 player recorded the tones sent over the telephone line, and the data was subsequently converted to readable numbers using a separate computer program, and used to clone cards to be used to steal by buying goods using the legitimate data. The police were made aware of the scheme by accident when they stopped Parsons for a motoring offence in London. They found a false bank card in his possession and, after searching his home in Manchester, discovered technical equipment necessary to carry out the swindle, together with 26 bank cards, 18 of which were cloned[2]. As this prosecution indicates, it is clearly beyond the ability of the holder of a card to exercise any control over their card, whether the card remains in their possession or not.

The banks themselves are also to blame for the failure of their systems and an example of the lax controls that can become apparent with respect to ATMs is illustrated in the case of *Patty v Commonwealth Bank of Australia*[3]. In this instance, A$27,400 was stolen from an ATM machine. The police investigated the complaint made by the bank but reached the conclusion that there was insufficient evidence to prosecute[4]. The bank subsequently continued to investigate the theft, and eventually dismissed Mr Patty. Of relevance are the findings of fact by the Judicial Registrar, none of which were significantly challenged in the subsequent application to review the decision. The findings of fact illustrate the lax nature of the controls that can exist within one bank respecting the security of ATMs. First, it is helpful to describe how the ATMs were serviced. The learned Judicial Registrar described the system as follows[4]:

> ATM machines are usually accessed by removing two combinations, a top combination known as the 'A' combination or lock and the bottom combination known as the 'B' combination or lock. ATM service teams usually comprise two officers. The teams are rostered to attend to operational faults out of hours and especially to attend to these faults at weekends. Machine malfunction is common. Many operational faults are fixed by ATM service teams. The usual procedure involves each member of the team being responsible for calculating and removing either the A or B combination on the ATM. Each team member is issued with a sealed envelope which contains numbers which allow for the calculation of either the A or B combination.

1   *Roni v Kagure* [2004] PGDC 1, DC84 (1 January 2004).
2   Reports at http://www.out-law.com/page-7492 and Russell Jenkins 'Hole-in-wall thief used MP3 player' (2006) The Times, November 15 online at http://www.timesonline.co.uk/article/0,,29389-2453590,00.html. For excellent photographs of micro cameras and specially-designed covers for ATMs, see http://www.snopes.com/crime/warnings/atmcamera.asp. For information about different types of attack on ATMs, see Ann All 'ATM History Industry 2002: A year in view' 7 January 2003 online at http://www.atmmarketplace.com/article.php?id=3281.
3   Industrial Relations Court of Australia VI-2542 of 1996, [2000] FCA 1072.
4   Compare *Windebank v Pryce* [2001] NTSC 45, where the investigation was woefully inadequate.
5   There are neither page numbers nor paragraph numbers in the Internet version of this judgment.

4.11 The events that occurred before the theft, together with the nature of the controls put in place by the bank, are taken from the judgment and set out in detail below to illustrate the nature of the problem, and the issues that arise:

> At 13.43.39.04 (ie at 1.43 pm) Centofanti logged on with the Voice Response Unit (VRU) in Sydney. He did this by telephone from the Collingwood Service Centre at 150 Smith Street. Very soon thereafter, the applicant contacted the Security Monitoring Centre (SMC) and advised that the service team was in the branch and was about to deactivate the alarm system. There are log reports provided by SMC and Wormald Security Monitoring Service confirming these logging on calls.

> Centofanti attempted to obtain the B combination for the ATM by using a touch phone and keying in his staff number and (supposedly) the bank branch

number. At about 13.45.33.04 (ie at 1.45 pm) Centofanti keyed in an incorrect branch number and could not further access a series of numbers which, if obtained, and deducted from other numbers held by him in a sealed envelope, would have provided the correct combination for the B lock on the ATM machine.

At this stage, the applicant went downstairs. He has stated that he went downstairs to use the toilet. Meanwhile, Centofanti, having failed to obtain the B combination because of an invalid branch number, attempted to contact two other bank officers by phone with a view to obtaining the correct branch number and accessing it. He was unsuccessful in locating either bank officer and began searching desk drawers in the hope of locating the correct branch number. He located a grey key card wallet in the top drawer on the left hand side of a desk normally occupied by the second in charge of the bank. Centofanti described the wallet as 'old and tatty'. Within the wallet, on a 'Record of Account Details Card', two series of numbers were written. He assumed that the numbers might have been the actual combinations of the A and B locks for the ATM. He was correct in the assumption that one series of numbers represented the A combination. Using these numbers he removed the A combination. Using the other series of numbers, he unsuccessfully tried to remove the B combination. The applicant had by then returned from downstairs. Centofanti asked the applicant to try and remove the B combination using the numbers on the card. The applicant tried and was also unsuccessful.

The Court pauses to note that the recording of ATM combination numbers and the leaving of such numbers in any place where access might be obtained was a clear breach of the respondent's security procedures. This was only one of many breaches of security procedures which occurred at 150 Smith Street and which appear to have occurred frequently at many branches of the bank. On that day Centofanti was responsible for the B combination. His removal of the A combination was a breach of security procedure. The applicant was responsible for the A combination. His attempts to remove the B combination were also a breach of security procedure.

At this stage, Centofanti successfully contacted another ATM service member by telephone and obtained from her the correct branch number. While Centofanti was so engaged, the applicant continued to search desk drawers in the hope of locating the B combination.

Once Centofanti had obtained the branch number he logged on again with VRU by touch phone and was placed on hold. At weekends, service team members often have to wait to be provided with numbers which allow calculation of combination locks. Such relatively short delays appear to be an inevitable result of the volume of telephone calls made by service team members. While Centofanti was on hold, the applicant successfully 'solved' the ATM 'communication problem' by resetting a controller or rebooting a modem.

While the applicant was so engaged, Centofanti obtained the appropriate numbers from VRU and calculated the B combination which he wrote on 'a piece of paper'. Although the ATM communication problem appeared solved because of the applicant's resetting of a controller, Centofanti decided to open the ATM and confirm the machine was working by performing what is known as a 'COCO' test. To perform the COCO test, having earlier removed the A combination, he removed the B combination using the combination number on the piece of paper, partially opened the ATM security door and flicked a toggle switch located inside the ATM security area. The ATM then performed a self-test program which registered a 'COCO display' which indicated that the machine was once more in working order. Centofanti then secured the ATM door by spinning the combinations and telephoned VRU to log on for the next service call. At the same time, the applicant advised SMC that the alarm was about to be reactivated.

The banks, by various mechanisms, force their customers to use technology, yet the very systems upon which they rely are not always as robust as they could be[1]. As Anderson illustrates[2], the systems put in place by banks are not as secure as some maintain, also demonstrated by evidence of attacks on Internet bank sites through such means as social engineering, also called 'phishing'[3]. For instance, it has been demonstrated that it is possible for an attacker to discover approximately 7000 PINs in 30 minutes[4], and known weaknesses in standards that may be responsible for 'phantom' withdrawals have not been addressed by the banks. Additionally, the processing system used by banks is open to abuse. One method is to attack the translate function in switches and another makes use of the functions that are used to allow customers to select a new PIN online. In both instances, the flaws enable an attacker, if they have access to the online PIN verification facility or switching processes, to discover PINs, such as those entered by customers while withdrawing cash from an ATM[5]. Thefts also take place entirely from within the bank[6], although attempts at stealing large sums of money tend to be conducted with help from a mixture of the lax controls within the bank itself, together with somebody working on the inside of the bank[7], as illustrated in the cases of *Adeniyi Momodu Allison v Bow Street Magistrates' Court ex parte Adeniyi Momodu Allison*[8] in which it was alleged Joan Ojomo, a credit card analyst, supplied account information to her external co-conspirators, who were then able to obtain a PIN or replacement PIN to withdraw cash from ATMs, and *R v Stephen Edward Seaton*[9], the details of which are described by the Vice President:

> The applicant and the others conspired to obtain money from automated teller machines, referred to as ATMs, by the use of counterfeit credit and cash cards. They planned to enter British Telecom exchanges with the assistance of corrupted employees of that organisation, in order to gain access to lines passing from ATMs to the mainframe computers. Taps and memory boards were placed on those lines, and used to record details of the cards of account holders while they were being transmitted down the lines. Those details recorded in that way were then to be downloaded onto a computer, and decrypted.

> The information obtained by that means was then to be transferred, using a read/write machine, onto blank plastic cards obtained for the purpose. The blank cards thus informed could then be used at ATMs to withdraw money.

> The applicant played a major role in this conspiracy. He had a list of door code keys for every telephone exchange within the M25 area, and he said those had been obtained from a BT engineer. The coaccused, Moore, was in charge of the computer program. The coaccused, Haward, owned premises which constituted the main operational base for the conspirators.

[1] For instance, most banks in the UK will not permit, or make it very difficult for, customers to make cash withdrawals over the counter using a withdrawal slip in combination with a manuscript signature. See also Ross Anderson 'Growing epidemic of card cloning' 26 July 2006, online at http://www.lightbluetouchpaper.org/category/legal/page/2/; Mike Bond 'Chip and PIN (EMV) Point-of-Sale Terminal Interceptor' online at http://www.cl.cam.ac.uk/~mkb23/interceptor/; the Financial Crimes Task Force of Southwestern Pennsylvania 'Consumer Alert' has photographs of the equipment used to create a false

front for an ATM which electronically record and store the information from the user's card online at http://www.financialcrimestaskforce.com/atmfraud.html.

2 Ross Anderson *Security Engineering* (2001) ch 9.

3 For a description of an early form of social engineering which the bank was aware of, see the criminal scheme outlined in: *Robert Abrams v Citibank, NA,* 537 F.Supp. 1192 (1982) at 1193, and *Ognibene v Citibank, NA,* 112 Misc.2d 219, 446 N.Y.S.2D 845.

4 Mike Bond and Piotr Zielinski 'Decimalisation table attacks for PIN cracking' Technical Report Number 560 (February 2003) Computer Laboratory UCAM-CL-TR-560 available online at http://www.cl.cam.ac.uk/TechReports/UCAM-CL-TR-560.html; Ross Anderson, Mike Bond, and Steven J. Murdoch 'Chip and Spin' Computer Laboratory, University of Cambridge available online at http://www.chipandspin.co.uk/ and http://ww.cl.cam.ac.uk/~sjm217/papers/cl05chipandspin.pdf; John Leyden 'Online manuals enable ATM reprogramming scam' (2006) The Register, 22 September available online at http://www.theregister.co.uk/2006/09/22/atm_reprogram_scam/; Markus G. Khun 'Probability Theory for Pickpockets—ec-PIN Guessing' available online at http://www.cl.cam.ac.uk/~mgk25/ec-pin-prob.pdf. Also see Jolyon Clulow 'The design and analysis of cryptographic application programming interfaces for security devices' (v4.0, 17 January 2003) MSc dissertation, available online at http://www.cl.cam.ac.uk/~jc407/ and the references contained in these publications. Mike Bond runs a website dealing with phantom withdrawals for victims of ATM fraud at http://www.phantomwithdrawals.com/.

5 Omer Berkman and Odelia Moshe Ostrovsky 'The unbearable lightness of PIN cracking,' available online at http://www.arx.com/documents/The_Unbearable_Lightness_of_PIN_Cracking.pdf.

6 *United States of America v Bonallo,* 858 F.2d 1427 (9th Cir. 1988); *Kumar v Westpac Banking Corp* [2001] FJHC 159; *Sefo v R* [2004] TOSC 51; *R v Clarke* [2005] QCA 483; see *Windebank v Pryce* [2001] NTSC 45 for a discussion of 'Night and Day' cards, the inadequate safeguards in place within a bank branch respecting the PIN, and lax controls over logging on to computers by members of staff; the problem is not always the failure of the bank ATM system, but in the procedural system employed to issue cards of a similar nature, such as electronic benefit transfer cards issued by the Retirement and Disability unit of the Penrith office of Centrelink in *R v Thompson* [2002] NSWCCA 149; Charles Arthur 'How ATM fraud nearly brought down British banking Phantoms and rogue banks' (2005) The Register, Friday 21 October, online at http://www.theregister.com/2005/10/21/phantoms_and_rogues/print.html. Insider Threat Study: Illicit Cyber Activity in the Banking and Finance Sector (Carnegie Mellon Software Engineering Institute) August 2004, available online at http://www.cert.org/archive/pdf/bankfin040820.pdf and http://www.secretservice.gov/ntac_its.shtml; Insider Threat Study: Illicit Cyber Activity in the Banking and Finance Sector (Carnegie Mellon Software Engineering Institute) June 2005, available online at http://www.cert.org/insider_threat/insidercross.html.

7 *Anderson* p 192.

8 [1998] EWHC Admin 536.

9 [1998] EWCA Crim 754.

4.12 In another case, that of *R v Stubbs*[1], a clerk, a member of a password reset team (comprising two people), was involved in fraudulent money transfers from the HSBC Bank between 23 July and 27 July 2002. In this case, four attempts were made to transfer money from corporate clients of the bank using an online banking system called 'Hexagon', and a fifth attempt, against the account of AT&T Wireless, succeeded. Three money transfers, each of about £1.9m, were made from the AT&T account on 25 July to an account held with Barclays Bank in Leicester in the name of Advanced New Technologies Corp Ltd. The deposit was then converted into euros before being transferred to the account of a company registered in Spain, trading as Vasat Importacion SL in Madrid. A further transfer of £6.1m was effected on 26 July from the AT&T account to the same recipients. None of the money removed from the AT&T account was recovered.

Criminals also obtain the confidential data held on debit cards from unsuspecting individuals with the specific intention of transferring the data to false cards in order to use ATMs to withdraw funds. A variety of methods are used to obtain sufficient information from a card to use it to steal money, such as copying a card as it is used in the ATM, where small electronic camera is mounted above the keypad of the cash machine to record the PIN being used, and a card reader is placed over the legitimate slot for the card and the data is read simultaneously by the false reader[2]. This enables thieves to collect details on the card numbers and the PIN before producing cloned cards. The wide availability of small card scanners enables a card to be skimmed, which enables the thief to produce a cloned version of the card[3], especially in restaurants and retail outlets, although the attacker may obtain the PIN by just watching the victim type the numbers into a keypad before stealing the card when the opportunity arises[4]. Yet another method of attempting to obtain the PIN is to use a mobile telephone to take photographs or to use the video facility to capture the PIN being used on a keypad; or the use of x-ray film to trap the card in the ATM so that, after the victim fails to recover their card, the thief can quickly return to the ATM and recover the legitimate card, having obtained the PIN[5]. In any event, the crime can be lucrative[6], although not all problems with ATMs are the result of attacks by criminals: the banks themselves may be put into a position where they are required to admit that they have problems, such as the failure of ATMs to balance, as in *Porter v Citibank N.A.* [7], where an employee of the bank admitted that, on average, the cash machines were out of balance once or twice a week. Also, simple attacks can be equally as effective, such as theft of the card and PIN before it reaches the customer[8].

[1]   [2006] EWCA Crim 2312, [2006] All ER (D) 133 (Oct). See the Canadian case of *R v Brum* [1999] O.J. No. 4727, [2001] O.J. No. 1731 in which the appellant was alleged to be in possession of both the upper and lower combination sets of access codes used to service ATMs, but the members of the Court of Appeal agreed that the evidence was not sufficient and ordered a new trial.

[2]   Described in the following cases: England & Wales *R v Cenan (Sebastian)* [2004] ECWA Crim 3388, [2004] All ER (D) 85 (Nov), 2004 WL 3255240 (CA (Crim Div)); *R v Chirila (Remus Tenistocle)* [2004] EWCA Crim 2200, [2005] 1 Cr App Rep (S) 523; *R v Dabija (Catalin Ionut)* [2005] EWCA Crim 318, [2005] All ER (D) 109 (Feb), 2005 WL 588736 (CA (Crim Div)). Canada: *R v Ciocata* [2004] A.J. No. 207, 2004 ABPC 39. Another methodology is described in the Singapore case of *Public Prosecutor v Meng* [2006] SGDC 243 involving defendants of an organised syndicate based in West Malaysia. The Financial Crimes Task Force of Southwestern Pennsylvania 'Consumer Alert' has placed photographs of the equipment used to create a false front for an ATM which electronically record and store the information from the user's card online at http://www.financialcrimestaskforce.com/atmfraud.html. For more photographs of micro cameras and specially designed covers for ATMs, see http://www.snopes.com/crime/warnings/atmcamera.asp. In Ireland, see 'Romanians sentenced to four years for ATM scam' (2006) *The Irish Times*, 6 October, online at (subscription required) http://www.ireland.com/newspaper/ireland/2006/1006/1158591432447.html; Niall O'Connor 'Two men get five years each for credit card scam' (2006) *The Irish Times*, 25 November, online at (subscription required) http://www.ireland.com/newspaper/ireland/2006/1125/1164403415868.html.

[3]   Described *R v Taj, R v Gardner, R v Samuel* [2003] EWCA Crim 2633, 2003 WL 22257755; *R v Wong (Kok Kee)* [2004] EWCA Crim 1170, 2004 WL 1060608 (CA (Crim Div); *A-G's Reference No. 73 of 2003 (Umaharan Ranganathan)* [2004] 2 Cr App Rep (S) 337, [2004] EWCA Crim 183, 2004 WL 229130; *R v Din (Ameen)* [2005] 2 Cr App Rep (S) 40, [2004] EWCA Crim 3364, 2004 WL 3131381. Canada: *R v Coman* [2004] A.J. No 383, 2004 ABPC 18; *R v Naqvi* [2005] A.J. No 1593, 2005 ABPC 339; *R v Mayer* 2006 ABPC 30. Singapore: *Balasingam v Public Prosecutor* [2006] SGHC 228.

⁴ New Zealand case of *R v Telea* (Court of Appeal, CA396/00, 4 December 2000, Keith, Blanchard and Tipping JJ).

⁵ 'New Scam Warning RE: ATM's-Folk's Slipping into Your Bank Account' online at http://resources.alibaba.com/resources_profile/greg12750.htm for a slideshow illustrating how the scam works, see http://www.slideshare.net/Trivia/atm-thefts/.

⁶ *R v Mayer* 2006 ABCA 149 (CANLII) where a group of thieves stole over C$1m in undertaking such activities. Attacks on ATMs continue, see 'Cash machine fraud up, say banks' (2006) BBC News, 4 November, online at http://news.bbc.co.uk/1/hi/uk/ 6115974.stm; for other weaknesses (mostly UK illustrations, but these are common across the world), see John Leyden 'Chip and PIN fraud hits Lloyds TSB Foreign ATM fraud loophole exposed by crooks' (2006) The Register, 11 May, online at http://www.theregister.co.uk/2006/05/11/lloyds_tsb_chip_and_pin_fraud/; information can be decoded from the magnetic strip: it is reported that Alex Harvie lost nearly £2,000 after her card was stolen while she was sitting in a cafe. Her bank refused to pay the money back because the thief entered the PIN number correctly every time, despite the fact that she had never used the number herself. See 'Banks Pass Buck On Fraud' (2006) Sky News, 30 June, online at http://news.sky.com/skynews/article/0,,30000–13530753,00.html.

⁷ 123 Misc.2d 28, 472 N.Y.S.2D 582.

⁸ India: *Bharteeya v The State* 121(2005) DLT 369, 2005 (83) DRJ 299; England & Wales: *R v Molcher (Andrew Alan)* [2006] EWCA Crim 1522, 2006 WL 2049662.

4.13 Invariably, a bank can demonstrate, to a reasonable degree of probability, that a card was used in an ATM with the correct PIN. The South African case of *Diners Club SA (Pty) Ltd v Singh*[1] illustrates the nature of the problem for a card issuer. In this instance, £55,000 (R583,722.04) was withdrawn from ATMs in London using a Diners Club card with the correct PIN during the course of 190 separate transactions on 4 and 5 March 2000. Mr Singh, whose PIN was used, was in Durban at the material time. It was his case that he did not use the card or PIN in London, and he suggested that an 'insider' in the plaintiff's organisation was responsible for the withdrawals. The issue was whether it was the customer who authorised the withdrawals. The case for the Diners Club was circumstantial, in that it could prove the transactions took place but could not prove Mr Singh used the card, although the plaintiff clearly carried out further investigations, because Mr Singh was cross-examined a second time respecting a number of his acquaintances whose movements at the material time suggested they may have been responsible for the withdrawals and that Mr Singh was part of a scheme to de-fraud the plaintiff. The position was set out by Levinsohn J at 661:

> Now it is common cause that the first defendant did not leave South Africa over that weekend. Indeed he did not leave Durban. The question that arises is whether the evidence adduced by the plaintiff raises any probability that he had given his card to someone else who in turn accessed the transactions in London. Counsel for the plaintiff has asked me to find as a matter of probability that that is what occurred. The plaintiff's case is essentially a circumstantial one.

Levinsohn J went on to set out the facts relied upon by the plaintiffs and reached the conclusion that, taken together, they established a strong preponderance of probability that a clear method was used to withdraw cash from ATMs, using the cards with the permission of the account holder. Of interest was the extensive amount of expert evidence adduced before the court and the time the learned judge took to set out and review the evidence in the judgment. In this instance, Ross Anderson and Mike Bond, both from the Computer Laboratory Security Group at Cambridge University, gave evidence. Levinsohn J reached the conclusion that their evidence did not take the matter any further, primarily because their evidence was based merely on a possibility that an insider in the bank caused the withdrawals to take place. The technical evidence of the plaintiffs proved sufficient to demonstrate the improbability of such an attack. The learned judge referred to the defence theory at 669–670:

> The defendants have at all times, as I have reiterated on a number of occasions during this judgment, conducted the case on the basis that there is indeed a probability that someone else, a fraudster, probably in the employ of Standard Bank or Diners Club International, accessed these transactions.
>
> The defendants' case rests on one pillar. That is that Anderson and Bond have proved in a laboratory that API attacks can be performed against the HSMs. Anderson has pointed a finger at what he terms as a dishonest insider, probably a disgruntled employee sitting in Farnborough, UK, perpetrating these frauds. Now it is self-evident, before one concludes that a state of affairs is probable or not, that a firm, factual foundation must be laid before the Court. In my view, and I say this at once, that no such factual foundation for any of Dr Anderson's theories has been put before me. The weight of the evidence points in an opposite direction. The UK witnesses established that the transactions on 3 and 4 March 2000 at the various ATMs were all performed regularly and in every case a proper audit trail was left which bears this out. If I think my way through all the facts of this case I find that the probability or indeed a reasonable possibility that an insider would have targeted only the first defendant's card from among millions of others in the world to be fanciful in the extreme.

[1]   2004 (3) SA 630 (D).

4.14   The defence case was considered to be speculative in nature, partly because the proposition put forward that an insider was responsible for the transactions was rebutted by the evidence of the security in place, partly because of the circumstantial evidence about the movements of the defendants and their links to others alleged to be involved in using the card and PIN to withdraw cash from ATMs in London, and partly because the learned judge reached the conclusion that the evidence of the two defendants was not to be relied upon. His conclusion is set out at 671:

> The circumstantial evidence against the defendants in this case is very strong, so much so that I am able to draw an inference on a substantial preponderance of probability that the first defendant gave his card to Kallichurum, Ragavaloo, Rangila and Oudhram, who travelled to London on the days in question and accessed the transactions concerned. Undoubtedly the first defendant was to benefit from these nefarious activities. This probable inference is in no way disturbed by any of the defendants' expert evidence. The evidence in regard to the *modus operandi*, and especially Samuels' evidence, renders the theories and hypotheses highly speculative, indeed improbable.

The case was found for the plaintiffs and the defendants were ordered to repay R607,423.12 with accumulated interest. Counsel for the plaintiff requested costs to be awarded on a scale applicable to attorney and own client as a mark of the court's displeasure at the way in which the defendants conducted the case. Levinsohn J agreed to this application, commenting at 678 that 'This relates more particularly to the first defendant's dishonest, untruthful and misleading testimony. I agree with this submission. Also, in my view, the plaintiff is entitled to all costs that were previously reserved'.

The facts of this case illustrate the nature of the problems faced by both the card issuer and the customer in circumstances where the customer claims they are not responsible for cash transactions withdrawn from an ATM. It is suggested that there is sufficient technical literature available to demonstrate that a variety of factors enable thieves to successfully obtain the correct PIN from a card with relative ease. However, just because thieves can obtain a given PIN by means of any of the attacks that are presently known, as well as attacks that are presently unknown, it does not follow that the withdrawal of funds from an ATM are the result of a theoretical possibility. By comparing the facts of *Judd v Citibank*[1] to those of *Diners Club SA (Pty) Ltd v Singh*[2], it becomes apparent that the surrounding evidence can and does play a significant part in determining whether a PIN was used by the customer, or the use of the PIN (and, possibly, the card) was authorised by the customer. It is suggested that the technical evidence is capable of establishing the following:

(a)   withdrawals were made with the correct PIN;
(b)   security procedures were in place (the effectiveness of the security is a separate issue); and
(c)   PINs are capable of being obtained without the knowledge or consent of the customer.

4.15 In such cases, the burden of proof will depend on the pleadings. Where a card issuer claims a withdrawal was made by the customer, the card issuer has the persuasive burden of demonstrating the customer either made or authorised the withdrawal. Proving the correct PIN was used tends to be sufficient to discharge the evidential burden of passing the judge to go before the tribunal. Once the card issuer has met this burden, it is for the defence to rebut the claim that the customer used the PIN or authorised the use of the PIN. In the case of *Judd v Citibank*, the evidence adduced by Mrs Judd demonstrated, to the satisfaction of the court, that she was elsewhere when the funds were withdrawn. Implicit in the evidence put forward by Mrs Judd was the probability that a third party obtained her PIN, although how it was obtained was not an issue that seemed to have been explored: nor did it have to be. In *Diners Club SA (Pty) Ltd v Singh*, the plaintiff proved the withdrawals had taken place. The defence then sought to rebut the inference that Mr Singh, either by himself or through a third party, was responsible for effecting the withdrawals by suggesting an employee or other person connected to the plaintiffs was responsible for the withdrawals. In attempting to rebut the plaintiff's case, the defence were required to provide a firm factual foundation and in this instance the theories propounded by Anderson were not considered sufficient by Levinsohn J. In this case, the weight of the evidence pointed in the opposite direction, as Levinsohn J indicated at 669–670:

> The weight of the evidence points in an opposite direction. The UK witnesses established that the transactions on 3 and 4 March 2000 at the various ATMs were all performed regularly and in every case a proper audit trail was left which bears this out. If I think my way through all the facts of this case I find that the probability or indeed a reasonable possibility that an insider would have targeted only the first defendant's card from among millions of others in the world to be fanciful in the extreme. Why not many others as well? Dr Anderson says that fraudsters within the banking system often target

accounts that are in a state of suspension. As I understand the evidence as at 3 March 2000 the first defendant's card had not been suspended overseas so it appears unlikely that any insider at Diners Club International would have known this. The HSMs in question are situated in Germany and, according to the evidence, the facilities at which they are housed are subject to the most stringent security. The evidence as a whole satisfies me that a programmer in the UK or anywhere else would not have been able to access these ATMs, in the way that Bond and Anderson say this can be done, without leaving a distinct audit trail. Mr Bird, for example, said that, if an attempt was made to introduce what he termed 'extraneous bits of code', this would be found, as Diners Club International made a practice of looking for such bits of code that may have been introduced either in error or maliciously. To date they have not found such traces.

In this instance, in attempting to rebut the plaintiff's case, the defendants failed to provide any convincing evidence that an insider could have been responsible for the withdrawals. In addition to this, the evidence of Mr Singh was deemed untruthful and this untruthfulness was taken into account by the learned judge. The plaintiff provided sufficient evidence to undermine the claims made by the defence, which meant the learned judge was able to reach the conclusion that the defendant in this instance colluded with others to defraud the card issuer.

The ultimate issue is whether it was the customer who effected the withdrawal. It is suggested that there is sufficient technical literature available to demonstrate that a variety of factors enable thieves to successfully obtain the correct PIN from a card with relative ease. Given the abundance of the technical literature on this topic, it is suggested that where a bank claims a withdrawal was made by the customer, the evidential burden of demonstrating that this was the case should include a requirement for the bank to show that it is impossible for the PIN to be obtained by any of the known attacks used by criminals, as indicated in the technical literature.

[1] N.Y.City Civ.Ct., 435 N.Y.S.2d 210.
[2] 2004 (3) SA 630 (D).

Issues to be taken into account for the authenticity of electronic documents[1]

4.16 The tests of authenticity for digital data (more accurately, a digital object)[2] will vary, depending on the source and type of the data. Digital data exists in a variety of formats: applications such as word processing and databases; applications that enable a user to obtain access to the Internet and email; information about devices such as mobile telephones; and storage hardware, such as disks, tapes and drives. Other examples include electronic cash and digital bearer bonds. Lawyers must look to digital forensic specialists for guidance. For instance, the print-out from a mainframe computer will demand a different approach in comparison to the data held on a personal computer. The mainframe computer cannot be removed, so reliance must be placed on the print-outs and relevant expert evidence which, in turn raises the question of how the reliability of the mainframe is to be tested. In comparison, an image can be taken of the disk of a personal computer and the data on the copy can then be analysed without affecting the original disk. Further problems about the reliability of digital data that are far from resolved concern the data on local area networks, and whether there is a need to obtain an image of the complete network, if this is possible. Data from the Internet is also subject to problems, because reliance may be placed on data obtained from remote computers, the computer of an investigator, and perhaps intercepted evidence.

1 See also Gregory P Joseph *Modern Visual Evidence* (1984–2006) 7.01[3].
2 For an exploratory essay on 'data', see Lee A Bygrave 'The meaning of "data" and similar concepts' in C Magnusson Sjöberg and P Wahlgren, eds *Festskrift till Peter Seipel* (2006) pp 117–126.

4.17 The term 'authentic' is used to describe whether a document or data is genuine. However, it is, perhaps, misleading to use the term 'authentic' when referring to digital data or a digital document. This is because of the way a digital object is created and made visible. For digital data to be made intelligible to a human being, it must be interpreted. Digital data is processed through a sequences of commands, so a simple document containing written text, for example, will consist of a number of ASCII character codes that must be interpreted before the text is reproduced on a screen in human-readable format. However, digital data is not restricted to simple text documents. The format of the data can be of a more elaborate nature, including active components such as macros and scripting language, which means that the data might require more complex interpretation to read the text. Also, a file displayed on a different computer to the computer that originally created the file can, and often does, lead to a different font and different line breaks. This is why the format of a file of documents will differ between computers. There is also the difference of form between a document stored as a file on some types of storage media (the document may have a time stamp associated with it, a designated 'owner', parameters setting who may have access to the document and other metadata, and might be digitally signed or encrypted), and a document rendered on a screen from computer memory (for instance, the document may not exist wholly in physical random-access memory, because some of it may be 'swapped out' to 'swap space' on the disk) which does not have the same metadata. Also, the representations of characters may not map perfectly between different operating systems, and compatibilities between different applications may not be perfect; for example: Unix systems terminate a line of characters with a carriage return, whereas Microsoft Windows uses a carriage return and linefeed: this means a simple text file generated on a Microsoft Windows system is rendered on the screen of a Unix system with an additional 'M' at the end of each line; and where applications differ in their degree of completeness of conformity to some standard, different applications will render the same file differently: for example, OpenOffice (http://www.openoffice.org/) does not yet render complex animations in presentations created in Microsoft PowerPoint in the same manner as Microsoft PowerPoint does. Another factor that can affect a document in digital format includes the stylesheet used to render the text into human-readable format, which is an important issue in safety-critical systems, such as the electronic version of the British national formulary.

The definition of authenticity in respect of a physical document comprises such attributes as the state of being the original or, more appropriately, of being faithful to an original, uncorrupted and, perhaps, with a verified provenance (comprising the following attributes: unique, unambiguous, concise, repeatable and comprehensible)[1]. The term 'trustworthiness' is often used to describe that a thing deserves, or is entitled to, trust or confidence. There are two qualitative dimensions to the concept of trustworthiness: reliability and authenticity, where reliability is meant to demonstrate the record is capable of standing for the facts to which it attests, and authenticity means the record is what it claims to be[2]. In this respect, the purpose of best evidence rule is to increase the probability of the trustworthiness of the document by reducing the opportunity for the deliberate or inadvertent alteration of the document. In comparison, it is more difficult to be clear as to what is meant by an 'authentic' digital object. If, for instance, a particular macro (say a macro that is used to automate frequently used movements of the mouse) is missing from a computer upon which a copy of the digital document rests, the question that must be raised is whether the lack of the macro in the computer that the data now rests renders the document something other than the genuine document. This blurs the distinction between what might be considered as the document and the environment in which it exists.

[1]   Attributes suggested by Philip Turner 'Digital provenance—interpretation, verification and corroboration' (2005) Digital Investigation vol 2, no 1, pp 45–49.
[2]   Heather MacNeil *Trusting Records Legal, Historical and Diplomatic Perspectives* (2000), p xi; see Livia Iacovino *Recordkeeping, Ethics and Law* (2006) p 41, for further comments about 'trustworthiness'.

4.18   To a certain extent, the technical focus of proving the authenticity of a digital object is on having checks and balances in place to demonstrate the history of how the data has been managed, which leads to the assertion that the data has not been modified, replaced, or corrupted and must, therefore, be original. This proposition rests on two conditions: first, the data is subject to a chain of custody; and second, the data has not been modified without authority between the time it was created, or added to the depository, and the moment it was required. The problem with this is pointed out by Rothenberg:

> The first of these conditions is only a way of supplying indirect evidence for the second, which is the one that really matters. An unbroken chain of custodianship does not in itself prove that records have not been corrupted, whereas if we could prove that records had not been corrupted, there would be no logical need to establish that custodianship had been maintained. However, since it is difficult to obtain direct proof that records have not been corrupted, evidence of an unbroken chain of custodianship serves, at least for traditional records, as a surrogate for such proof[1].

[1]   Jeff Rothenberg 'Preserving Authentic Digital Information' in *Authenticity in a Digital Environment* (2000) Council on Library Information Resources, p 57.

4.19   The unique nature of digital data means that, although the data may be created in program memory, it might be saved on a number of different storage media formatted to different specifications. For instance, if a file is copied from a storage device formatted with Microsoft NTFS to one formatted with Solaris ZFS, the representation of the file in each medium will be significantly different, in the encoding of both data (especially if compression or encryption are enabled in the filesystem) and metadata. Further, each digital object may be replicated in a number of places, which means there is no single 'original', as happens when disk arrays are aggregated into resilient filesystem volumes using redundant arrays of independent disks ('RAID') management. This has implications for understanding the nature of digital data. In essence, there is a need to accept that the concept of 'original' and 'authentic' digital object is meaningless. Therefore, it is necessary to consider the meaning of 'authentic' in terms of a digital object in the relevant context. Rothenberg proposes the following[1]:

> ... we therefore define a digital original as any representation of a digital informational entity that has the maximum possible likelihood of retaining all meaningful and relevant aspects of the entity.

> This definition does not imply a single, unique *digital-original* for a given digital informational entity. All equivalent digital representations that share the defining property of having the maximum likelihood of retaining all meaningful and relevant aspects of the entity can equally be considered digital-originals of that entity. This lack of uniqueness implies that a digital-original of a given entity (not just a copy) may occur in multiple collections and contexts. This appears to be an inescapable aspect of digital informational entities and is analogous to the traditional case of a book that is an instance of a given edition: it is an original but not the original, since no single, unique original exists [italics in the original].

[1] *Rothenberg* p 66.

4.20 Conceptually, a digital object is authenticated by verifying the claims that are associated with the object, such as: the organisational criteria demonstrating the provenance of the digital object, including the documentation pertaining to the chain of custody (and to what extent this documentation is trusted) and the extent to which the custodians can be trusted; the object can be examined forensically to establish whether its characteristics and content are consistent with the claims made about it and the record of its provenance (although the methods used may also be subject to challenge—for instance, how a mainframe is tested for reliability; whether the imagining techniques are challenged when relying on the evidence from a personal computer); any signatures, seals and time stamps[1] that may be attached to the object can help test the claims to consistency and provenance. For instance, time stamps are used to indicate when a digital object was written, but the time stamp might not be accurate. Similarly, digital signatures are also used for the same purpose, but any confidence in the integrity (meaning the data has not been corrupted) of the object can only be as good as the authenticity and integrity of the hash digest and the processes and procedures surrounding the digital signature and the equipment which generates and applies it[2]. It can be argued that the process of demonstrating the authenticity of a digital object is 'a process of examining and assigning confidence to a collection of claims'[3]. In essence, the ability to prove the authenticity of a digital object is not proving that an original exists, especially when referring to something as dynamic as a database. The issue is about trust, or the lack of trust. Proving the authenticity of a digital object means providing sufficient evidence to convince an adjudicator that the object that has been retrieved is a faithful representation of what is claimed to be the 'original,' or a reliable representation of the object that was relied upon by the originator. Thus the learned authors of the Uniform Electronic Evidence Act Consultation Paper in Canada made it clear that the emphasis needs to shift to the integrity of the record-keeping system, and the emphasis needs to be placed on 'system':

[24] The 'function' of the best evidence rule is to ensure the reliability, that is to say the integrity, of the record to be produced in evidence. It is presumably easier to tell that an original paper record has been altered than to determine any alteration by viewing a copy. In the electronic world, there may or may not be any original paper version of the electronic record. Therefore, the search for integrity of an electronic record has to proceed in another way.

[25] As Ken Chasse said in his 1994 paper for the Conference, at para 46,

'... the law should move from "original" to "system", that is, from a dependence upon proof of the integrity of the original business document to a dependence on proof of the integrity of the record-keeping system. This means that the best evidence rule loses most or all of its application in this field ...'

[26] Stated another way, the integrity of the record-keeping system is the key to proving the integrity of the record, including any manifestation of the record created, maintained, displayed, reproduced or printed out by a computer system[4].

As a result, the Canadian Uniform Electronic Evidence Act offers sound guidance in relation to the evidentiary foundations of electronic evidence and, in article 6, provides for relevant standards to be considered, although they are not mandatory:

6 For the purpose of determining under any rule of law whether an electronic record is admissible, evidence may be presented [in any legal proceeding] in respect of any standard, procedure, usage or practice on how electronic records are to be recorded or stored, having regard to the type of business or endeavour that used, recorded or stored the electronic record and the nature and purpose of the electronic record.

Requests were made to provide for a statutory presumption of reliability based on a standard, but this was rejected on the grounds that it constituted a higher standard for admissibility than was necessary, and the use of a standard might prevent a proper scrutiny of digital evidence as to weight[5].

---

[1]   Malcolm W Stevens 'Unification of relative time frames for digital forensics' (2004) Digital Investigation vol 1, no 3, pp 225–239.
[2]   For a discussion about the use of terms and meanings, see Sarah Mocas 'Building theoretical underpinnings for digital forensics research' (2004) Digital Investigation vol 1, no 1, pp 61–68.
[3]   Clifford Lynch 'Authenticity and Integrity in the Digital Environment: An Exploratory Analysis of the Central Role of Trust' in *Authenticity in a Digital Environment* (2000) Council on Library Information Resources, p 40.
[4]   Uniform Electronic Evidence Act Consultation Paper (March, 1997) available online at http://www.ulcc.ca/en/poam2/index.cfm?sec=1997&sub=1997hka.
[5]   *MacNeil* p 53.

4.21 The United States case of *American Express Travel Related Services Company, Inc. v Vee Vinhnee*[1] dealt with a failure to introduce a sufficient evidentiary foundation for the introduction of digital business records. In this case, American Express claimed Vinhnee failed to pay credit card debts, and took action to recover the money. After a trial that occurred in the absence of the defendant, the trial judge determined that American Express failed to authenticate certain records in digital format. American Express appealed the verdict, and the decision of the trial judge was affirmed. In respect of the issues in this particular trial, Klein J, pointed out, at 444 [14] that:

> ... the focus is not on the circumstances of the creation of the record, but rather on the circumstances of the preservation of the record during the time it is in the file so as to assure that the document being proffered is the same as the document that originally was created.

The learned judge made the pertinent point that 'Ultimately, however, it all boils down to the same question of assurance that the record is what it purports to be'[2]. The learned judge continued to explain the issues involved in this process, at 445 [16]:

> The logical questions extend beyond the identification of the particular computer equipment and programs used. The entity's policies and procedures for the use of the equipment, database, and programs are important. How access to the pertinent database is controlled and, separately, how access to the specific program is controlled are important questions. How changes in the database are logged or recorded, as well as the structure and implementation of back-up systems and audit procedures for assuring the continuing integrity of the database, are pertinent to the question of whether records have been changed since their creation.

> There is little mystery to this. All of these questions are recognizable as analogous to similar questions that may be asked regarding paper files: policy and procedure for access and for making corrections, as well as the risk of tampering. But the increasing complexity of ever-developing computer technology necessitates more precise focus.

1 336 B.R. 437 (9th Cir. BAP 2005), compare *State of Washington v Ben-Neth* 663 P.2d 156 (Wash.App. 1983). For the technical details relating to computer searches and the nature of the legal analysis, see *United States of America v Moussaoui* United States District Court for the Eastern District of Virginia Alexandria Division No 01–455-A Governments Opposition to E-mail Evidence. Some of the documents in this case can be found at http://www.ca4.uscourts.gov/moussaoui/moussaoui.htm, and further information can be found at http://www.vaed.uscourts.gov/notablecases/moussaoui//index.html, docket information is available at http://notablecases.vaed.uscourts.gov/1:01-cr-00455/DocketSheet.html and trial exhibits can be found at http://www.vaed.uscourts.gov/notablecases/moussaoui/exhibits/. The defendant was sentenced on 4 May 2006 to life in prison without the possibility of release.

2 At 445 [15].

4.22 Klein J reached the conclusion that early attempts at establishing a foundation for electronic evidence were too cursory, whilst also accepting that judicial notice is commonly taken of the validity of the theory underlying the use of computers and the validity of the data generated generally. The learned judge then set out the tests described by Professor Imwinkelried when considering electronic records as a form of scientific evidence[1]:

(a)   the business uses a computer;

(b)   the computer is reliable;

(c)   the business has developed a procedure for inserting data into the computer;

(d)   the procedure has built-in safeguards to ensure accuracy and identify errors;

(e)   the business keeps the computer in a good state of repair;

(f)   the witness had the computer readout certain data;

(g)   the witness used the proper procedures to obtain the readout;

(h)   the computer was in working order at the time the witness obtained the readout;

(i)   the witness recognises the exhibit as the readout;

(j)   the witness explains how he or she recognises the readout; and

(k)   if the readout contains strange symbols or terms the witness explains the meaning of the symbols or terms for the trier of fact.

1   Edward J Imwinkelried *Evidentiary Foundations* (6th edn, 2005) 4.09[4][c].

4.23 The steps outlined by Imwinkelried are helpful, but items (b) and (e) are particularly prone to being undermined by the failure of an organisation to consider such issues when operating their computers, although it is debatable whether the concepts of a computer being reliable or in a good state of repair are helpful, or relevant, in understanding whether a computer was working properly. In addition, even moderately-sized organisations have systems in place, not single computers, and the reliability and repair (if these terms are to be used) of the system will differ markedly. To consider just one example, if the security patches are not kept up-to-date, which they rarely are, the reliability of the system can be seriously undermined. The learned judge amplified the fourth step to include additional factors that are highly relevant, at 446[16]:

> The 'built-in safeguards to ensure accuracy and identify errors' in the fourth step subsume details regarding computer policy and system control procedures, including control of access to the database, control of access to the program, recording and logging of changes, back-up practices, and audit procedures to assure the continuing integrity of the records.

The court then proceeded to evaluate the exhibits submitted by American Express using the tests set out by Imwinkelried. It was made clear that the evidence of the custodian of the records at American Express was far too vague to be accepted. The following problems were identified:

(a)   generally, the evidence was vague and unpersuasive;

(b)   the custodian did not have the requisite knowledge to provide the evidence;

(c)   the person providing evidence on behalf of American Express merely asserted that he was an employee of American Express and was personally familiar with the systems, both hardware and software;

(d)   he failed to inform the court of his job title or of his relevant experience and training that would provide an element of authority to his evidence; and

(e)   American Express failed to provide information about its computer policy and system control procedures, control of access to the relevant databases, control of access to the applicable programs, how changes to the data recorded or logged, what back-up practices were in place, and whether there were any audit procedures used to provide assurance of the continuing integrity of the records.

4.24 The nature of the testimony will differ according to the nature of the evidence, such as whether the source is analogue or digital, and the nature of the digital evidence that is to be authenticated: evidence of the use of an ATM or cash card, pages from Internet websites, email correspondence, chat rooms, instant messaging sessions, to mention a few of the more obvious forms of evidence in digital format. For instance, in 1969 Gillespie J set out criteria for testimony in relation to data stored on magnetic tapes in the case of *King v State of Mississippi for Use and Benefit of Murdock Acceptance Corp*[1]. Print-out sheets of business records stored on magnetic tapes were admissible in evidence if it is shown:

> (1) that the electronic computing equipment is recognized as standard equipment, (2) the entries are made in the regular course of a business at or reasonably near the time of the happening of the event recorded, (3) the foundation testimony satisfies the court that the sources of information, method and time of preparation were such as to indicate its trustworthiness and justify its admission[2].

Gillespie J continued, at para 10, to make it clear that he did not consider the evidence produced from a computer is always correct: 'We are not to be understood as indicating that computer evidence is infallible. Its probative value is the same as conventional books, and it is subject to refutation to the same extent'. Although it will not be relevant or necessary to provide such an in-depth analysis of digital data in every case brought before a court, nevertheless, the comments made by Klein J help to illustrate the nature of the evidence that should be gathered, if it is necessary to adduce such evidence.

[1] Miss., 222 So.2d 393.
[2] Miss., 222 So.2d 393 at para 9. See *United States of America v Weatherspoon* 581 F.2d 595 (7th Cir. 1978) and *Rosenberg v Collins* 624 F.2d 659 (1980) where sufficient testimonial evidence was adduced to lay the foundations for the admission of computer print-outs.

4.25 It is not always necessary to obtain intricate details of a computer or its operating system for evidence in digital format to be accepted into evidence, and the means by which a document is authenticated may not necessarily require the evidence of an expert. There is a great deal of misunderstanding, for instance, over the admissibility of email, to consider just one example. It is often asserted that because emails can be easily forged it is important to prove an email has not been forged before it is admitted into evidence. This proposition is nonsense. Documents on paper are forged or altered, as in the case of *Scholastic, Inc v Stouffer*[1] and letters are forged, as in the case of *Arrow Nominees, Inc v Blackledge*[2]. The forgery of evidence is nothing new and just because it is possible to forge an email it does not mean that email correspondence is required to undergo an extensive forensic analysis to prove it is not a forgery for it to be admitted into evidence[3]. The authenticity of a document in digital format can be tested in other ways that are equally as effective. For instance, in *R v Mawji*[4] the appellant was convicted of making a threat to kill, and part of the evidence included an email sent to the victim dated 31 July 2002, which read:

Hi Bitch,

Don't think you're safe in the UK. I'm going to kill you.

I will make sure I get my hands on you ... waiting for you.

Your loving husband.

Riz.

A witness for the defence gave evidence to demonstrate how relatively easy it was to produce a document that purported to be an email but which had nothing to do with the email account from which it purported to come. It was suggested that somebody else was responsible for sending the email in question. One of the grounds of appeal was that the email was secondary evidence if adduced in the form of a print-out (which is correct), and that it was necessary to provide evidence of the audit trail or similar to show the authenticity of the document. The members of the Court of Appeal rightly rejected this submission. The analysis offered by Kay LJ centred upon the evidence produced by the victim when she saw the email on the screen and then printed it off. However, the email did not have to be authenticated in the way suggested by the appellant because of the circumstances surrounding the events and the other evidence in the case. The internal evidence of the content of the email was similar to other evidence produced at trial, which went to show that the email was written and sent by the appellant, and the members of the jury had to consider whether, in all the circumstances, it was possible that somebody else might have produced the email. The content of the email demonstrated its authenticity on the face of the totality of the evidence[5]. If the email was fabricated, it had to be questioned as to why somebody should go to the length of forging the content of an email that was so obviously linked to the other evidence produced at trial.

[1]   221 F.Supp.2d 425 (S.D.N.Y. 2002), 2002 U.S. Dist. LEXIS 17531. See *Breezevale Ltd v Dickinson* 879 A.2d 957 (D.C. 2005) for submission of a range of forged evidence, including computer documents produced before Breezevale even had computers.

[2]   [2000] 1 BCLC 709, (1999) Times, 8 December, [1999] All ER (D) 1200; reversing [2000] BCLC 167, [2000] All ER (D) 854, CA.

[3]   Emails can, of course, be forged: *R v Debnath* [2005] EWCA Crim 3472, [2006] Cr App Rep (S) 169.

[4]   [2003] EWCA Crim 3067, [2003] All ER (D) 285 (Oct), 2003 WL 22477344 (CA (Crim Div)).

[5]   For example, see the Malayan case of *Petroliam Nasional Bhd v Khoo Nee Kiong* [2003] 4 M.L.J. 216.

4.26 The same arguments were used in the case of *Illinois v Downin*[1], where an expert testified that the only way of authenticating the origin of one of the emails in question was by investigating the IP address, which was not included on the exhibit. As in the case of *R v Mawji*, the relevant email contained admissions of guilt. However, it is not necessary to authenticate the email by providing evidence of the IP address and then linking the chain of evidence to the sender of the email, as pointed out by O'Brien J at 22:

A finding of authentication is merely a finding that there is sufficient evidence to justify presentation of the offered evidence to the trier of fact and does not preclude the opponent from contesting the genuineness of the writing after the basic authentication requirements are satisfied ... The prosecution need only prove a rational basis upon which the fact finder may conclude that the exhibit did in fact belong to the defendant.

A digital document may be authenticated by direct or circumstantial evidence, and circumstantial evidence includes a range of factors, including, but not limited to, the appearance and contents of the document. Where the content demonstrates knowledge of the circumstances of the facts such that only very few people in the world will be aware of them, the inference as to authenticity must be overwhelming in most cases. Proving of the authenticity of instant messages is also perfectly possible through the use of compelling circumstantial evidence. In the case of *FP, a minor*[2], Ford Elliott J offered some robust and realistic comments on this topic that bear repeating:

> Essentially, appellant would have us create a whole new body of law just to deal with emails or instant messages. The argument is that emails or text messages are inherently unreliable because of their relative anonymity and the fact that while an electronic message can be traced to a particular computer, it can rarely be connected to a specific author with any certainty. Unless the purported author is actually witnessed sending the email, there is always the possibility it is not from whom it claims. As appellant correctly points out, anybody with the right password can gain access to another's email account and send a message ostensibly from that person. However, the same uncertainties exist with traditional written documents. A signature can be forged; a letter can be typed on another's typewriter; distinct letterhead stationery can be copied or stolen. We believe that email messages and similar forms of electronic communication can be properly authenticated within the existing framework ... We see no justification for constructing unique rules for admissibility of electronic communications such as instant messages; they are to be evaluated on a case-by-case basis as any other document to determine whether or not there has been an adequate foundation showing of their relevance and authenticity.

The learned judge listed a number of cases involving the authentication of email communications[3], web pages[4], and chat room exchanges[5], all of which included circumstantial evidence that provided compelling evidence to prove the authenticity of the documents in question. There will be occasions, however, when it will be necessary to provide evidence that a digital document is authentic as a matter of law and circumstantial evidence will not be sufficient, as in *Roads and Traffic Authority of New South Wales v Timothy Adam Michell*[6]. In this instance, a speed measuring device took a photograph of a vehicle being driven by the defendant, which demonstrated he was driving at a speed greater than the speed limit in force. At the trial, the defence objected to the photograph being submitted into evidence because the security indicator had been struck through. The prosecution made it clear that it did not rely upon the security number that was struck through and the Magistrate ruled that the photograph was admissible in evidence. At the end of the prosecution case, the Magistrate ruled there was a case to answer. Mr Michell neither gave nor called any evidence, and the Magistrate then had to decide whether he was satisfied beyond reasonable doubt that the offence had been proved. He reached the conclusion that he could not be satisfied that the photograph had not been altered since it was taken, and he therefore acquitted Mr Michell. On appeal, Adams J agreed that the Magistrate was correct in admitting the photograph in evidence. In dealing with the security number, the learned judge was required to interpret the provisions of s 47 of the Road Transport (Safety and Traffic Management) Act 1999. The relevant provisions are as follows:

47 Photographic evidence of speeding offences

(1) In proceedings for an offence of driving at a speed in excess of a speed limit imposed by or under this Act or the regulations, evidence may be given of a measurement of speed obtained by the use of an approved speed measuring device and recorded by an approved camera recording device.

(2) In proceedings in which such evidence is given:

   (a)   the provisions of section 46 relating to the accuracy or reliability of the approved speed measuring device apply, and
   (b)   subsections (3)–(5) apply in relation to the approved camera recording device, and
   (c)   evidence that a photograph taken by an approved digital camera recording device bears a security indicator of a kind prescribed by the regulations is evidence (unless evidence to the contrary is adduced) that the photograph has not been altered since it was taken.

(3) A photograph tendered in evidence as a photograph taken by an approved camera recording device on a specified day at a specified location:

   (a)   is to be accepted as having been so taken (unless evidence to the contrary is adduced), and
   (b)   is evidence (unless evidence to the contrary is adduced) of the matters shown or recorded on the photograph.

It was held that the true construction of s 47(2)(c) meant that the legislature deemed it necessary to provide for the authenticity of the photograph, otherwise the provisions of the sub-section would be redundant. This there-fore required the prosecution to adduce evidence of the authenticity of the photograph in order to demonstrate it had not been altered from the moment it was taken, to the moment in time it was used to demonstrate an offence had taken place.

¹   357 Ill.App.3d 193, 828 N.E.2d 341, 2005 Ill.App. LEXIS 402, 293 Ill. Dec, 371.
²   *FP, a minor* 2005 PA Super 220, 878 A.2d 91, 2005 Pa. Super. LEXIS 1499.
³   *Massimo v The State of Texas*, 144 S.W.3d 210 (Tex.App.-Fort Worth 2004); *Kearley v State of Mississippi*, 843 So.2d 66 (Miss.App. 2002), certiorari denied, 842 So.2d 579 (Miss. 2003); *United States v Siddiqui* 235 F.3d 1318 (11th Cir. Ala. 2000), certiorari denied 533 U.S. 940, 150 L.Ed.2d 737, 121 S.Ct. 2573 (2001).
⁴   *Perfect 10, Inc v Cybernet Ventures, Inc*, 213 F.Supp.2d 1146 (C.D.Cal. 2002)
⁵   *United States of America v Tank*, 200 F.3d 627 (9th Cir. 2000).
⁶   [2006] NSWSC 194.

The following section sets out, in general terms, some of the issues that are relevant to the question of the authenticity of digital data.

General

4.27 A great deal of work has been undertaken in understanding the nature of an electronic record and the dynamics of ensuring trustworthiness, reliabil-ity, integrity and authenticity¹. Some of the work has led to the implementa-tion of standards, such as the Design Criteria Standard for Electronic Management Software Applications (DoD 5015–2-STD (June, 2002)) issued by the Assistant Secretary of Defense for Command, Control, Communication and Intelligence in the USA, replacing an earlier standard from 1997. The availability of such research may be of use to lawyers in the event that the authenticity of a document in digital format is tested in a court. In summary, the University of British Columbia project identified eight components of an electronic record:

(a)   the medium, being the storage medium upon which the data is stored;
(b)   content, referring to the message contained in the document, which may only be made manifest when assembled into a complete whole either by rendering the text on a screen or as a print-out. When not in use, the content consists of pointers to data that will be located in different places within a database or a series of databases;
(c)   the physical form, comprising a range of elements, such as
    (i)   the script (type of font, formatting, inserts, the use of colours, and such like);
    (ii)   the language used;
    (iii)   additional information, such as attachments, comments, time-tamps; the configuration and architecture of the operating system, records and operating system.
any change in these elements will affect the data, and may, in turn, create a different record;
(d)   intellectual form comprises three elements:
    (i)   'information configuration', referring to how the content is represented (text, graphics, images, sounds or any combination);
    (ii)   'content articulation', comprising date, salutation, exposition; and
    (iii)   'annotations', referring to any additional information made to the record in the execution of the document (such as the authentication of a digital signature), how the matter is handled (whether it has been designated as being urgent, together with the date and time of any action), any developments that have occurred (evidence of subsequent actions taken), and the management of the record, such as the classification of the document and registry number;
(e)   action comprises the record of the act or action that gave rise to the record. A geographical information system has the capacity to present data in different formats, perhaps geographically within and between departments;
(f)   people are the agents that can create the content of the data. Those responsible for the existence of the data include the author and addressee. The retention of this information is necessary for the preservation of the provenance of the data over time;
(g)   the archival bond in the digital environment required a link to be created and maintained when data is removed from a system and put into an archive. It is necessary to make explicit the relationship between the records and the actions of archiving to demonstrate the original data is not altered;
(h)   the context refers to the framework of the document. Four elements have been identified:
    (i)   the legal and administrative context (the legal and organisational status of the body, such as body corporate, human);
    (ii)   the provenance (the body that is responsible for creating the data, structure, functions);

(iii)   the procedural context (the procedures by which the record is created); and

(iv)   the documentary context (the internal structure of the archive) which, in turn, represents the totality of the bonds that make up the context. In the digital environment, the technological context is crucial, and is discussed more fully below[2].

---

[1]   *The Preservation of the Integrity of Electronic Records*, a research project conducted by Luciana Duranti, principal investigator, Terry Eastwood, Co-Investigator and Heather MacNeil, research assistant, at the School of Library, Archival and Information studies, University of British Columbia between April 1994–March 1997. The findings are available online at http://www.interpares.org/UBCProject/intro.htm; see also a project by the University of Pittsburgh School of Information Sciences, *The Functional Requirements for Evidence in Recordkeeping*. The University of Pittsburgh School of Information Sciences website has the following statement: 'The Functional Requirements for Evidence in Recordkeeping was a project administered out of the University of Pittsburgh School of Information Sciences between 1992 and 1996 and funded by the National Historical Publications and Records Commission. Due to a technical glitch at the School the Website with the working files of this project was destroyed, but since the Website has not been updated since 1996 when the Project ended individuals interested in the project and use of the site can access it through the Internet Archive'. Available online at http://www2.sis.pitt.edu/~rcox/FunReqs.htm.

[2]   MacNeil pp 90–96; Livia Iacovino *Recordkeeping, Ethics and Law*, pp 46–55.

4.28 Three terms are used in relation to the authentication of digital data, and a brief outline of each may be useful:

(a)   authentication: the capacity to prove the digital object is what it purports to be. The authenticity of a digital object is preserved by the use of techniques to prevent the data from being manipulated, altered or falsified deliberately or inadvertently. Such methods include providing audit trails of transmissions and maintaining records of encryption. A number of attributes, taken together, provide evidence of authenticity: the mode, statue and form of transmission, together with the way in which the data is preserved and how it is managed;

(b)   integrity: relates to how sound the data is, such as whether the data is damaged in some way, and whether it is complete, in that it possesses all the necessary parts and links. Integrity is not an absolute condition but a state of relationships, and whether the burden of proof will be achieved in any individual case will depend on the strength of the relationships to the data; and

(c)   reliability: the capacity of a digital object to stand for the facts to which it purports to attest, which, in turn, is linked to ensuring sufficient procedural and technical attributes (including a combination of preventative measures, such as to prevent unauthorised amendments and changes, and verification measures to provide for a degree of assurance as to the identity of users and the provision of audit trails to document when data is viewed and manipulated) are in place and working to provide for a degree of assurance that the digital object can be deemed to be reliable. In essence, reliability is associated with the degree of control exercised over the procedures that permit the data to be created. It is not absolute.

Technical

METHOD OF PRESERVATION

4.29 Several methods are used to preserve electronic data[1]. Risks attach to whichever method is used and it is important to ensure that whatever method is employed can be defended should the data be the subject of a legal challenge as to its authenticity.

(a) technology preservation: this is the creation of a methodology to conserve the environment in which the data files are set. This includes saving the software and hardware to enable a user to obtain access to and read the data. This is a short-term solution that assumes that people in the future will want to use old hardware and software.

(b) technology emulation: this can take different forms. In essence, this is a method to run the original data and software on a new or current platform, or emulating a virtual environment. This is achieved by running software on the new platform that emulates the original platform. Detailed information about the original environment must be stored alongside the digital data itself. Such methods are difficult to develop, and the authenticity of the data will depend on the links between the emulator to the emulated system. This method relates to the format in which the data is encoded. The data is copied to the latest form of storage medium. Data is converted from one file format (which can no longer be read using the current software) to another format (which is readable with current software). Where the document has been part of a software migration, evidence will be required setting out

   (i) why migration took place;

   (ii) the methods used to effect the migration; and

   (iii) how the quality of the document was validated after migration, and records will be required setting out the names of the people undertaking the exercise, what they did and when they did it.

(c) data refreshing: this is where data is copied from one set or copy of the digital media to another of the same kind. It can also involve the copying of the data between media of the same type, or to a different kind of media.

[1] See also Charles M Dollar *Authentic Electronic Records: Strategies for Long-Term Access*, pp 29–33 and ch 2.

ESSENTIAL TECHNICAL CHARACTERISTICS

4.30 Identity: the identity of a digital document will need to be established, such as the name of the purported author[1], the date it was created, the place of origin and the subject matter. It can be argued that this information forms part of the reliability of the document, meaning that if it can be identified correctly, there is a degree of certainty about the document that could be relied upon.

Integrity: integrity, as discussed in 'Generic requirements for sustaining electronic information over time: 1 Defining the characteristics for authentic records'[2] is considered to refer to the 'wholeness and soundness' of the document. This, in turn, is related to whether the document can be considered to be complete and uncorrupted '... in all its essential respects during the course of its existence', whilst BS ISO 15489 provides that 'integrity' refers to the record being complete and unaltered. While these definitions of 'integrity' might relate to the ability to verify that the content of a document has not been changed since it was written, finished and adopted by the author (if the author is known, or remains anonymous for good reasons), it might be necessary to consider other matters, including, but not limited to:

(a)   whether a time stamp was used, and if so, whether it can be considered to be accurate, and if in doubt, what standards were observed with the particular type of time stamp used;

(b)   whether it is a partially-written document;

(c)   whether the test for integrity of the document should only apply to the original version (whatever that may be);

(d)   whether any tracking regarding the document's subsequent circulation is necessary. Following from this, the integrity of the circulation metadata may be required;

(e)   whether the metadata can be accepted as reliable and meaningful[3].

The concept of integrity will be closely related to the organisation's control over the preservation of a document. Underlying the integrity of a document will be the use of digital signatures to provide evidence of verification that the document has not been altered, and the integrity of any digital signatures may also be questioned. It may also be necessary to consider the relevance of any data logs that might exist. Data logs are a complex topic, but they have the potential to support or undermine the truth of a claim as to the actions that were being carried out on a particular computer or system at a material time[4].

[1]   Determining the identity of an author is not necessarily a simple process: Gaurav Gupta, Chandan Mazumdar, MS Rao and RB Bhosale 'Paradigm shift in document related frauds: Characteristics identification for development of a non-destructive automated system for printed documents' (2006) Digital Investigation vol 3, no 1, pp 43–55; Carole E Chaski 'Who's At The Keyboard? Authorship Attribution in Digital Evidence Investigations' (2005) International Journal of Digital Evidence vol 4, issue 1, at http://www.ijde.org.

[2]   Para 3.1.7.

[3]   See papers produced by the Recordkeeping Metadata Project, Records Continuum Research Group, Monash University, available online at http://www.sims.monash.edu.au/ research/rcrg/about/index.html; Metadata at http://www.ukoln.ac.uk/metadata/; Dublin Core Metadata Initiative at http://dublincore.org/; Recordkeeping Metadata Standard for Commonwealth Agencies, Version 1.0, National Archives of Australia, 1999 at http:// www.naa.gov.au/recordkeeping/control/rkms/summary.htm; David Bearman and Ken Sochats 'Metadata Requirements for Evidence', available online at http:// www.archimuse.com/papers/nhprc/BACartic.html; Michael Day 'Metadata for digital preservation: an update' available online at http://www.ariadne.ac.uk/issue22/metadata/.

[4]   Karen Kent and Murugiah Souppaya *Guide to Computer Security Log Management*, (2006) National Institute of Standards and Technology, Special Publication 800–92 at 2.1.3 fourth bullet point, online at http://csrc.nist.gov/publications/nistpubs/, although it should be noted that the authors of this text repeat the assumption, which tends to be a problem with many technically literate people, that a data log has the capacity of identifying 'who has used the application and when each person has used it'. All the data is able to demonstrate is the probable use of an application or system by a person who used a password or authentication token. It does not follow that the person using the password or authentication token was the person that was issued with or identified by the password or token that was actually used.

Organisational characteristics

4.31 Procedural controls provide circumstantial evidence of the integrity of a document in digital format. Where policies and procedures are followed, a degree of trust is created that acts to reinforce the probability that a document can be trusted. However, the assumption of integrity cannot be sustained where the procedures are tested in a court and found wanting by the adjudicator[1]. This is why some or all of the following are relevant:

(a)   the controls in place to prevent the modification or editing of the record;

(b)   evidence of the controls to support the document is authentic by the production of credible metadata, audit trails[2] and relevant reports;

(c)   the procedures in place to assess and maintain the authenticity of the document over the period of time it has been preserved, including where the document was created, the reason it was created, the technical and procedural framework in which it was created, for whom it was intended, when and how it was received by the person to whom it was addressed, how it related to other records linked to the same matter; and

(d)   evidence is available to demonstrate policies were properly created, and that procedures were subsequently adopted and followed to ensure the policies were correctly implemented[3].

[1]   *Denco Ltd v Joinson* [1991] 1 WLR 330, [1992] 1 All ER 463, [1991] IRLR 63, [1991] ICR 172, EAT. In this case, Wood J observed that the members of the industrial tribunal were 'extremely critical of the security arrangements made by the employers in connection with the use of the computer' [1991] ICR 172 at 178—although the observation was made in the context of security, the evidence of a sloppy attitude towards something as important as security serves to indicate that other problems may exist that undermine the integrity, and thus authenticity, of data held on such computer systems.

[2]   Caroline Allinson 'Audit Trails in Evidence—A Queensland Case Study' work in progress, (2002) Journal of Information Law & Technology (1) online at http://www2.warwick.ac.uk/fac/soc/law/elj/jilt/2002_1/allinson/; Caroline Allinson 'Audit Trails in Evidence—Analysis of A Queensland Case Study' (2003) Journal of Information Law & Technology (2) online at http://www2.warwick.ac.uk/fac/soc/law/elj/jilt/2003_2/allinson/.

[3]   For a discussion about the use of digital signatures in this process, see Stefanie Fischer-Dieskau and Daniel Wilke 'Electronically signed documents: legal requirements and measures for their long-term conservation' (2006) Digital Evidence Journal vol 3, no 1, pp 38–42; *MacNeil* pp 97–104.

4.32 For a reminder of the importance of the mix of organisational and technical issues that combine to make up for the trustworthiness of evidence in digital format, the Report of the Somalia Commission of Inquiry in Canada offer some stark insights:

Document disclosure remained incomplete throughout the life of the Inquiry. It took the form of a slow trickle of information rather than an efficient handing over of material. Key documents were missing, altered, and even destroyed. Some came to our attention only by happenstance, such as when they were uncovered by a third-party access to information request. Some key documents were disclosed officially only after their existence was confirmed before the Inquiry by others. Representatives from SILT were reminded continuously of the slow pace and incomplete nature of disclosure. Following numerous meetings on the document transmittal process and private meetings with SILT officials at which we expressed frustration with the process, there were still few results. Finally, faced with altered Somalia-related documents, missing and destroyed field logs, and a missing National Defence Operations Centre computer hard drive, we were compelled to embark on a series of hearings devoted entirely to the issue of disclosure of documents by DND and the Canadian Forces through DND's Directorate General of Public Affairs, as well as to the issue of compliance with our orders for the production of documents[1].

[1]   'Dishonoured Legacy: The Lessons of the Somalia Affair' Report of the Commission of Inquiry into the Deployment of Canadian Forces to Somalia (Ottawa, Minister of Public Works and Government Services Canada, 1997), Executive Summary: Sources of Information, para 3, available online at http://www.dnd.ca/somalia/vol0/v0s3e.htm.

4.33

Of the recommendations published by the Commission, 39.1 required the Department of National Defence to ensure that the National Defence Operations Centre logs are properly maintained in future by implementing the following:

(a)   an audit procedure to ensure that standing operating procedures provide clear and sufficient guidelines on the type of information to be entered and how the information is to be entered;

(b)   an adequate database system, which includes software controls to ensure accurate data entry in each field and appropriate training for operators and users of this system; and

(c)   increased system security to an acceptable standard compatible with the objective of national security, including restricting access to authorised persons using only their own accounts and passwords and extending the use of secure (hidden) fields to identify persons entering or deleting data[1].

[1]   http://www.dnd.ca/somalia/vol0/v0s39e.htm.

4.34   Given the fact that public documents are increasingly being created and stored by bureaucracies across the world in digital format, there is now a degree of pressure upon the keepers of public records to have sufficiently robust systems in place to store documents in digital format. But it is also incumbent on lawyers to be aware of the difficulties surrounding evidence in digital format, because they may need to be more circumspect when agreeing to admit documents that can be admitted into evidence by virtue of their public nature, or because a statute provides for the admissibility of a document that purports to be authentic. One example may serve to illustrate the nature of the problem: health records are increasingly being put into digital format, and health professionals are increasingly being required to add information to the record electronically. The physical piece of paper is fast disappearing in the health world and a serious problem will undoubtedly become manifest in the future, relating to the proof of which nurse or doctor entered a particular entry into an electronic record. If the actual entry is in dispute, then proof will be required that a particular person made the entry. This is where the authentication method will be crucial. Many systems rely on the use of digital signatures stored on smart cards for this purpose but, unless different mechanisms are used to ensure the actual person with the digital signature is the person using the signature as a means of authentication, it cannot be assumed that the person who purported to make an entry was the person that actually made the entry[1]. This is because many people frequently use other people's usernames and passwords to log on to systems. Those agreeing, either explicitly or implicitly, to the use of their means of authentication by others fail to understand the importance of what they agree to; and if their details are used without their knowledge or permission (for instance, where the practice is generally accepted within an organisation or department), then the difficulties in establishing who was responsible for inputting text becomes manifest.

[1]   Simone van Esch 'The electronic prescription of medication in a Netherlands hospital' (2006) Digital Evidence Journal vol 3, no 2, pp 73–77.

In summary

4.35 Where the authenticity of a digital object is issue, the range of considerations to be taken into account will differ, according to the nature of the evidence to be authenticated and where the evidence is to be found. In the majority of cases, oral and circumstantial evidence will be sufficient to provide for the authenticity of most documents in digital format. However, where evidence of a system or the way a computer operated is required, the nature of the evidence will be more demanding. Testing reliability for a mainframe will differ to that of a personal computer: the mainframe cannot be seized or moved, which means there are problems relating to demonstrating the system is working properly (if this is a necessary pre-condition), ensuring the nature of the digital evidence is complete, and determining how the other party can test the evidence. The personal computer can be the subject of a seizure order or warrant, thereafter the quality of the inferences to be drawn from a forensic analysis will depend on the trust in the technology used to take an image of the disk, the techniques undertaken to search the disk, the procedures adopted by the investigator and the substance of any conclusions made by the investigator. The hardware forming a local area network or the Internet cannot be seized, which means other issues must be considered, such as how an investigator ensures they have searched thoroughly for evidence, whilst at the same time demonstrating the reliability of the data. Issues that may need to be covered and tested include demonstrating the provenance of the source of the data, how it is authenticated, indicating the process by which the data was acquired, and proving the continuity and reliability of the evidence[1]. In essence, the requirements for authentication can be reduced to the following:

(a)   the content of the data that a party relies upon has not changed, without proper authorisation, from the moment it was created to the moment it is submitted as evidence;

(b)   the data can be proven to be from the purported source; and

(c)   the technical and organisational evidence demonstrates the integrity of the data is trustworthy, and is therefore considered to be reliable.

[1]   Peter Sommer 'Intrusion Detection Systems as Evidence' [2002] C.T.L.R. 67–76; Peter Sommer 'Downloads, Logs and Captures: Evidence from Cyberspace' [2002] C.T.L.R. 33–42; Jean-Marc Dinant 'The Long Way from Electronic Traces to Electronic Evidence' (2004) International Review of Law Computers & Technology vol 18, no 2, pp 185–192;

Bertrand Lathoud 'Formalization of the processing of Electronic Traces' (2004) International Review of Law Computers & Technology vol 18, no 2, pp 173–183; IETF RFC 3227/RFC3227 Guidelines for Evidence Collection and Archiving (Internet Best Current Practices for the Internet Community) available online at http://www.rfc-archive.org/getrfc.php?rfc=3227.

Chapter 5

USING GRAPHICAL TECHNOLOGY
TO PRESENT EVIDENCE

DR DAMIAN SCHOFIELD AND LORNA GOODWIN

INTRODUCTION

5.01 Inevitably, the future will be digital: digital cameras and videos, electronic document storage, network commerce, Internet business, intelligent search agents, computer animations and virtual simulators are already in common use. Computer technology in everyday society has altered the way we view and interact with the world around us and has changed the way we perform certain day-to-day tasks. As computers become more powerful, users reassess their problems in order to maximise the potential offered by the ever-increasing capabilities of this pervasive technology.

5.02 The continuing digital revolution influences the way forensic evidence is collected, analysed and interpreted and has even led to the defining of new types of digital evidence (for example, the computer digital imagery and video, hard drives and digital storage devices). The technological advance has also led to new means of presenting evidence in court. Digital displays and computer-generated graphical presentations are becoming commonplace. These visual tools can be used to present evidence and illustrate hypotheses based on scientific data, or they may be used to depict the perception of a witness, such as what may have occurred during a particular event relating to a specific scene. Digital reconstruction technology may also be used to explore and illustrate 'what if' scenarios and questions, testing competing hypotheses and possibly exposing any inconsistencies and discrepancies within the evidence[1].

[1] A Burton, D Schofield and L Goodwin 'Gates of Global Perception: Forensic Graphics for Evidence Presentation' Proceedings of ACM Symposium on Virtual Reality Software and Technology (2005) Singapore, 6–12 November.

5.03 It is important to realise that the use of such computer-generated presentations in a court is only the current manifestation of graphical visualisation in a long history of using graphics in litigation. However, computer animation (often called forensic animation in the context of a court) and virtual reality technology are unparalleled in their capabilities for presenting evidence. This, in turn, can affect the manner in which evidence can be assimilated and correlated; in some instances, it can help make the evidence more relevant and easier to understand[1].

¹ J Mervis 'Court Views Engineers as Scientists' (1999) Science vol 284, issue 5411, 21 and *Burton et al* (2005).

5.04 At first glance, graphical reconstructions may be considered useful in any court, and they can be treated like any other form of evidence. However, they warrant special care and attention due to their inherently persuasive nature and the undue reliance that the viewer may place on the evidence presented in the visualisation (often called the 'seeing is believing' tendency). This chapter aims to describe some of the presentation technology available, provide a number of examples of its use and highlight some of the issues surrounding the use of such technology.

BASIC COURT TECHNOLOGY

5.05 It is beyond the remit of this chapter to detail extensively all aspects of technology employed and utilised in modern courts. This has been undertaken by many other authors. For example, Brown¹ gives a comprehensive review of technology used in courts up to the end of the 20th century, and Goodwin² also gives details of many current applications.

¹ M Brown 'Criminal Justice Discovers Information Technology' (2000) Criminal Justice, vol 1, pp 219–259.
² L Goodwin 'Visualising Vehicle Accidents: Evidence Uncertainty, Presentation and Admissibility' PhD Thesis (2007) University of Nottingham.

5.06 For the purposes of this text, technology used in courts and chambers is defined as including any technology built into the court, and any technology used in court procedure. In 1997 it was estimated that there were between 10 and 50 high-technology courts around the world¹. It has been estimated more recently that there are now between 300 and 500 high-technology courtrooms in the United States of America and Australia alone². In the US, companies such as Doar Communications are setting up hundreds of courts with high-technology visual presentation systems. This experience is being slowly mirrored in the United Kingdom by companies such as Courtcom³. Although many of these currently cost around US$250,000, it is estimated that by 2010 such upgrades will cost half this amount⁴.

¹ FI Lederer 'An Introduction to Technologically Augmented Litigation' available online at: http://www.courtroom21.net/reference/articles/litigation.pdf, 1997 viewed on 27 August 2006.
² DI Hopper 'High-Tech Courtroom Comes to Life—Glitches and All' (2001) *East Valley Tribune* B10, 3 April.
³ J Barnett and P Dew 'IT Enhanced Dispute Resolution' Second International Online Dispute Resolution Workshop (2005) pp 1–10.
⁴ P Trexler 'High-Tech Court Gets a Trial Run; $250,000 Worth of Gizmos Bring Judge Cosgrove's Workplace Up-to-Date' (2003) *Akron (OH) Beacon Journal*, B1, June.

5.07 The existing high-technology courts contain different levels of technology, but many include options for the following¹:

(a)   electronic filing (potentially with document display capability);

(b)   foreign language translation (potentially simultaneous—with audio or visual and textual presentation);

(c)   multimedia court records captured using stenographic real-time electronic transcripts accompanied by digital audio and video;

(d)   information and evidence retrieval using imaged documents available from CD-ROM storage and retrievable by computer network;

(e)   access to legal materials and case-specific information from CD-ROM, Digital Versatile Disk (DVD), or the Internet;

(f)   high-technology information and evidence display systems (often multimedia screen capability);

(g)   teleconferencing and videoconferencing (which may include remote appearance, remote hearing or remote testimony); and

(h)   public access to court information via the World Wide Web.

[1]   See *Lederer* (2006) and *Goodwin* (2007).

5.08 Commercially available technology used to display and present evidence in the court can be categorised in one of two ways:

(a)   those relying on standard software packages; and
(b)   those which rely on dedicated or bespoke software packages.

5.09 The most pervasive form of commercially available presentation software is PowerPoint, part of the Office Suite from Microsoft. There are many articles on creating effective presentations within Microsoft PowerPoint, something that is not as straightforward as many people assume. An interesting discussion of how people learn and comprehend when faced with PowerPoint presentations and similar technology is given by Pence[1]. Parks[2] gives many examples of poor uses of PowerPoint.

[1]   HE Pence 'What is the Role of Lectures in High-Tech Education?' (1997) Journal of Educational Technology Systems vol 25, pp 91–96.
[2]   RP Parks 'Macro Principles, PowerPoint, and the Internet: Four Years of the Good, the Bad, and the Ugly' (1999) Journal of Economic Education, vol 30, no 3, pp 200–209.

5.10 Other software may be used for presentations in court. For example, word processors may be used to display text documents, image manipulation software may be used to display digital photographs or other imagery, and multi-media players can be used to play back digital video and audio content. Web browsers may be used to display Internet content, and packages such as Flash from Adobe may be used to generate simplistic two-dimensional animated content[1]. These commercially available software packages differ in the types of data formats that they can display. These differences could potentially affect how they are used and, therefore, how successful they can be at displaying data in a court. In order to convey data accurately the method of presentation needs to be appropriate for the particular context. The selection of particular software packages may effect the interpretation of the data being presented[2].

[1]   S Huskinson 'The Role of Usability in the Design of Forensic Data Interfaces' MSc Dissertation, (2006) University of Nottingham.

2   SM Alessi and SR Trollip *Multimedia for Learning: Methods and Development* (3rd edn, 2001).

5.11   There are also a number of commercially available software packages that can be used to display evidence in courts[1]. These include packages such as Director Suite, Sanction, Summation, Trialbook 32, TrialPro and Visionary. All of these packages provide a framework for the organisation and presentation of evidence in court, including transcripts, documents and often audio and video data. A few of the software packages provide a barcode system that allows a barcode reader to find and exhibit data on large screens in court and such systems also enable the technology to be used whilst witnesses are giving evidence. Most, however, provide a simple filing-cabinet-type interface which allows a user to drag and drop files once they have been stored within the system[2].

1   I Daniel *Going to Trial* (2nd edn, 1999).
2   *Huskinson* (2006).

5.12   While most of these commercially available evidence management and presentation systems are relatively easy to use, the very fact that so many variations exist can lead to some confusion and possibly, in extreme cases, varying interpretations of the evidence presented.

THE EFFECT OF USING VISUAL EVIDENCE

5.13   Our culture is dominated with images whose value may be simultaneously over-determined and indeterminate, whose layers of significance can only be teased apart with difficulty. Different academic disciplines (including critical theory, psychology, education, media studies, art history, semiotics, etc) have been developed to help explain how audiences interpret visual imagery[1].

1   CO Spiesel, RK Sherwin, and N Feigenson 'Law in the Age of Images: The Challenges of Visual Literacy' in Wagner, Summerfield, and Benavides, eds *Contemporary Issues of the Semiotics of Law* (2005) Onati International Series in Law and Society, Number 13.

5.14   However, the precise effect that visual imagery has on members of a jury, witnesses and other viewers in the court is not known and concerns are beginning to be articulated that the use of modern computer-generated visualisation technology can distort perceptions, memories, attitudes and decision-making in the court. Some research undertaken in the USA has examined how different forms of evidence effect how members of a jury retain details in their memory:

(a)   one study showed that the average person retains 87 per cent of information presented visually, but only 10 per cent of information presented orally[1];

(b)   another study showed that the average person retains 65 per cent of information presented visually and 15 per cent for when presented orally[2]; and

(c)   a further survey showed that members of a jury will retain twice the amount of information when using a visual presentation, as distinct from an oral presentation[3].

1   RF Seltzer 'Evidence and Exhibits at Trial' (1990) 387 PLI/Lit 371.
2   R Cobo 'An Approach to Demonstrative Exhibits' (1990) 3 PLI/Lit 359.
3   R Krieger 'Sophisticated Computer Graphics Come of Age—and Evidence Will Never Be the Same' (1992) Journal of the American Bar Association, December.

5.15   When the evidence is animated the improvement in memory retention is even more apparent: another survey revealed that members of a jury will retain 650 per cent more information when presented with presentations using a form of computer animation[1].

1   R Thomas 'Computer Re-Enactment' available online at: http://www.pimall.com/nais/n.reenact.html, 1997 viewed on 27 August 2006.

5.16   Recently, the Visual Persuasion Project, run by the New York School of Law, identified a number of issues and problems with the use of visual technology[1]. However, at present there is little or no research work covering these areas, such as the effect that visual evidence has on memory, attitudes and decision-making and their interrelationship in the court.

1   RK Sherwin *When Law Goes Pop: The Vanishing Line between Law and Popular Culture* (2nd edn, 2002) and RK Sherwin 'The Visual Persuasion Project' web pages hosted at the New York School of Law, available online at: http://www.nyls.edu/pages/2734.asp, viewed on 27 August 2006.

5.17   Improvements in forensic science and the introduction of new digital technology have led to an ever increasing amount of complex, technical evidence that is presented in court. The issues in question can be extremely complicated and difficult to explain without some form of graphical representation. A survey by the American Bar Association found that members of a jury are often confused, bored, frustrated and overwhelmed by technical issues or complex facts[1]. Other research has indicated that the attention span of an average member of a jury in a court is only seven minutes[2].

1   PF Kuehn 'Maximising your Persuasiveness: Effective Computer Generated Exhibits' (1999) Journal of the DuPage Country Bar Association, available online at: http://www.dcba.org/brief/octissue/1999/art41099.htm, viewed on 27 August 2006.
2   KJ Schroder 'Computer Animation: The Litigator's Legal Ally', Computers and Law Final Paper (1997) available online at: http://wings.buffalo.edu/law/CompLaw/CompLawPapers/schroder.html, viewed on 27 August 2006.

5.18   Any visualisation or graphic can be a valuable aid to help construe and convey a large amount of complex information. An American judge, C.B. Rubin[1] highlighted the problem of retaining the interest of the jurors when he stated:

It isn't difficult to tell when jurors have lost interest ... Such wandering attention is much less likely in a paperless trial, because the evidence is presented in a format jurors are used to watching ... I have noticed repeatedly that when a document is displayed on the monitors, the jurors sit up and pay attention. Such attention is far greater than that given to a document which they cannot see as it is being discussed by the attorney and the witnesses ...

This comment illustrates the perceived need to reduce lengthy verbal explanations and increase the use of visual tools which, in turn, can act to improve the ability to retain the evidence, maintain an interest in the proceedings and understand more fully the nature of the case.

[1]   CB Rubin 'A Paperless Trial' (1993) Litigation vol 19, no 3.

5.19 Static images such as diagrams and charts have, historically, been used to explain the testimony of an expert witness. It is now possible to use computer-generated animated technology to illustrate the passing of time. This extra dimension is extremely useful when explaining a chronological sequence of events, such as the reconstruction of a vehicle accident, where the movement of the vehicles may be dependent on a complicated engineering principle or theory. Computer-generated animations can also be used to take advantage of their lack of physical restrictions, which may allow the viewer to be placed in a position where it is physically impossible to be with a normal camera (such as inside an engine or a human body), or to show a witness views of a crime or accident from previously unseen points of view[1].

[1]   IS Jones, DW Muir and SW Groo 'Computer Animation—Admissibility in the Courtroom' in *Accident Reconstruction: Technology and Animation 1*, Society of Automotive Engineers, Warrendale, USA, pp 143–151.

Technology

5.20 'Computer Graphics' or 'CG' refers to a suite of computer applications that can be used to produce images and animations. CG utilise numerical three-dimensional ('3D') models of physical objects to create artificial environments. Rendering and shading algorithms are employed to build an animation or film from these environments frame-by-frame (in a series of still images) so that, when they are played back in quick succession, they create an experience of space, motion and time.

5.21 Objects such as equipment, vehicles, human figures, environment details, landscape features and other relevant items of evidence can be positioned accurately within the 3D environment, the evidence of which is often obtained from crime or accident scene survey data. The objects are inserted to scale and can be overlaid with relevant images to produce a credible, lifelike appearance. The facility to visualise, and then explore, a forensic scene provides the viewer with the potential to increase their comprehension of the important and underlying issues within that scene[1].

[1]   *Burton, et al* (2005).

5.22 'Virtual Reality' or 'VR' involves interactive real-time 3D graphical environments that respond to manipulation by the user, such as moving around in the virtual world or operating virtual equipment. Important aspects of VR are the underlying processes, simulations, behaviour and reactions, and the way users interact with objects within the world. A virtual reality user can, for example, sit in a virtual vehicle and drive it around an environment. The virtual vehicle will respond to the driver's input and behaviour, causing other vehicles in the virtual world to respond to those inputs—as in the case of a collision, for instance.

5.23 Many novel applications have emerged because of recent and rapid developments in personal computer technology, especially for desktop VR. The home computer games market has encouraged the development of software tools together with specialist 3D graphics accelerator boards and peripherals. Whilst much of the development is aimed at the leisure industry, there are many industrial applications in the process of being developed for a range of industry sectors. This has had a consequent effect on the legal profession as this technology has been slowly introduced into courts around the world over the past few years. These types of CG and VR display systems can offer major advantages over other visualisation media because of the interactive nature of the experience they create[1].

[1] D Schofield, J Noond, L Goodwin and K Fowle 'Accident Scenarios: Using Computer-generated Forensic Animations' (2001) Journal of Occupational Health and Safety (Aus NZ) vol 17, no 2, pp 163–173.

Advantages of computer-generated visual images in court

5.24 In court, computer-generated displays are either substantive evidence (scientific or forensic animations, or simulation) or illustrative (a visual aid). As technology advances, such displays will become more prevalent, due to a number of perceived benefits[1]:

(a) such displays can provide an effective means of conveying complex evidence to the judge and jury. Visual memory has been found to be highly detailed and almost limitless, in contrast with memory for verbal material[2]. Electronic media can also be regarded as a change in the way a case is presented in court as members of a jury readily engage with audio-visual forms of communication, rather than relying solely on verbal modes of discourse[3];

(b) displays can be a tool to help persuade members of a jury. Studies comparing oral, textual, and static visual presentation to computer animated presentations containing the same information, found the animations to be more memorable[4]. This has implications not only for the retention of information but also for the weight given to the evidence by the member of a jury or other trier of fact[5]. Evidence has also shown that members of a jury are twice as likely to be persuaded if the arguments are supported by such visual aids[6]. Furthermore, visual, rather than verbal, information activates more readily the formation of an impression[7];

(c) digital displays provide the presenter with a better illustration of their arguments: evidence can be retrieved instantaneously during a presentation and the display can be manipulated for better vantage points.

The person using the display can 'zoom in' to an item of evidence, pull apart a piece of machinery or see a crime scene from the point of view of a key witness[8]; and

(d)   such computer-generated displays may increase speed and efficiency in the court, thus saving court time, as arguments and complex information are understood at a faster rate. This saving of court time can, of course, lead to a reduction in costs.

[1]   *Burton et al* (2005).
[2]   P Chapman 'Remembering What We've Seen: Predicting Recollective Experience from Eye Movements When Viewing Everyday Scenes' in G. Underwood, ed *Cognitive Processes in Eye Guidance* (2005) pp 237–258.
[3]   J Simons 'Popular Culture and Mediated Politics' in J Corner and D Pels, eds *Media and the Restyling of Politics* (2003) pp 171–89.
[4]   *Seltzer* (1990), *Cobo* (1990), *Krieger* (1992) and *Thomas* (1997).
[5]   D Yale 'Computers on the Witness Stand: Expert testimony that relies on data generated by computers in the age of Daubert' (1996) available online at: http://www.iconn.net/dcyale/daubert.html, viewed on 27 August 2006.
[6]   FI Lederer 'Technology Comes to the Courtroom' *Emory Law Journal*, Volume 43, pp 1095–1113, 1994.
[7]   MB Brewer 'A Dual Process Model of Impression Formation' in TK Srull and RS Wyer, eds *Advances in Social Cognition* (1998) vol 1, pp 1–36.
[8]   *Schofield et al* (2001).

Disadvantages of computer-generated visual images in court

5.25   Despite the many benefits of using computer-generated visualisations in court, there are a number of potential dangers and disadvantages[1]:

(a)   the very fact that computer-generated visualisations impress themselves on the memory, and are persuasive and convincing, is also their greatest disadvantage: they leave a strong impression on viewers, they tend to mesmerise and they can relax an individual's natural critical faculties. This means that viewers are inclined towards a 'seeing is believing' attitude, as they do with television[2], potentially reducing the standards expected of legal evidence[3]. Simulations can assume a 'hyper-real' character that eclipses the significance of the reality[4]. Small alterations to a computer-generated representation can have a substantial effect on the impression it gives[5]. For example, judgments of speed and recklessness are critical in determining responsibility for road accidents[6]. A driver traveling at speed will seem to be reckless if the animation includes young children near the road, but reasonable if adults are represented. Thus, apparently innocuous decisions about representation are often critical[7];

(b)   similarly, the appearance (and visual effect) of the environment in a reconstruction depends largely on small details such as textures, foliage, and litter amongst other items[8]. Without guidelines or knowledge of the relevant factors it can be surprisingly easy for a forensic modeler or animator to present a location as either a likely or unlikely location for a crime or accident based on small, seemingly insignificant details. Atmosphere, lighting, colour saturation and the camera configuration (lens, camera angle) will also have an effect on the viewer[9];

(c)   another possible disadvantage of such visualisations is the potentially prejudicial effect of not using the technology. A party deciding to present a traditional case may be prejudiced by the use of the technology by the other side. Computer-generated displays may assist in achieving early settlement, thus avoiding the time and expense of a drawn-out court hearing. By 1992, where the technology had been used in many US courts all except 15 out of 858 civil cases using computer-generated displays were settled out of court and in all the 15 that went to trial, the party using computer-generated displays won the case[10];

(d)   it is often difficult to represent uncertainty in computer-generated evidence. Viewers often wrongly believe there is little or no margin of error in evidence thus presented[11]. Research at the University of Nottingham has examined how to visualise the uncertainty that is inherent in vehicle speeds when calculated for traffic accident reconstructions[12]. These provide good examples of uncertain evidence as the police calculate vehicle speed ranges, drivers remember their own speed and witnesses may report a different speed, yet only one speed value will usually be shown in any animated or virtual reconstruction[13]; and

(e)   finally, the flexibility of a computer-generated display also implies an inherent potential for tampering. The ability to change the perspective, the use of slow motion and stop-action in displays (for example, in a computer simulation or animation) enables the potential to portray the events in a particular light. A party may intentionally create an animation that provides a favourable perspective, or unintentionally choose a perspective that alters the appearance of the animation. This could create bias in the trier of the fact[14].

1   *Burton et al* (2005).
2   D O'Flaherty 'CG displays in the Courtroom: for Better or Worse?' Web Journal of Current Legal Issues (1996) issue 4, available online at: http://webjcli.ncl.ac.uk/1996/issue4/oflah4.html viewed on 27 August 2006.
3   J Habermas *The Structural Transformation of the Public Sphere*, (1996).
4   J Baudrillard *Simulacra and Simulation* (1994).
5   R Girvan 'An Overview of the Use of Computer-Generated Displays in the Courtroom' Web Journal of Current Legal Issues (2001) issue 1, available online at: http://webjcli.ncl.ac.uk/2001/issue1/girvan1.html, viewed on 27 August 2006 and *O'Flaherty*, 1996.
6   *Chapman et al* (2005) and C Lawrence and J Richardson 'Gender Based Judgements of Traffic Violations: The Moderating Impact of Car Type' Journal of Applied Social Psychology (2005) vol 33, no 9, pp 1796–1817.
7   SC Nichols, C Haldane & JR Wilson 'Measurement of Presence and Side Effects in Virtual Environments' International Journal of Human-Computer Studies (2000) vol 52, no 3, pp 471–491.
8   *Lawrence and Richardson* (2005).
9   *Nichols et al* (2000).and *Schofield et al* (2001).
10 *O'Flaherty* (1996).
11 L Goodwin and D Schofield 'Visualising Uncertainty: Combining Evidence with Statistics' Proceedings of Conference on Expert Evidence: Causation, Proof and Presentation, Prato, Italy, July 2002 and N Hussin, D Schofield and MT Shalaby 'Visualising Information: Evidence Analysis for Computer-Generated Animation (CGA)' Proceedings of 8th International Conference on Information Visualisation (IV04), London, 14–16th July 2004.
12 *Goodwin* (2007).
13 *Goodwin and Schofield* (2002).
14 A Billias 'The Role of Computer Simulations in Contemporary Litigation' Computers and Law Final Paper (1999), available online at: http://wings.buffalo.edu/law/Complaw/CompLawPapers/e.html, viewed on 27 August 2006.

Analysis of computer-generated visuals in court

5.26 Analyses of computer-generated displays show that they can be extremely advantageous in the court and other legal scenarios providing they are used appropriately. Such displays may be used in different ways in the court: as substantive evidence or to illustrate a point. However, a number of difficulties can occur when applying this technology in a court. The consequences of these problems cannot be underestimated: misuse, tampering or bias within visualisations could easily lead to miscarriages of justice[1].

1   TL Bohan 'Computer Aided Reconstruction: Its Role in Court, Accident Reconstruction: Technology and Animation 1' *Society of Automotive Engineers* (1991) Warrendale, USA, pp 179–186 and BJ Colandreo 'Computer-Generated Evidence: Purveyor of the Truth or Exploiter of the Under-Funded?' (1997) available online at: http://www.iandiorio.com/cge.htm, viewed on 27 August 2006.

5.27 A number of concerns relating to the viewer's understanding of the visual evidence can be identified and classified. These are areas that should be considered whenever a computer-generated visualisation is to be used in court[1]:

(a)   memory: the memory of a witness and members of the jury can be biased by a wide variety of seemingly inconsequential factors[2]. The results of Loftus' work can be extrapolated to predict that computer-generated visualisations are likely to lead to similar biases. Critical variables in such visualisations may include the representation of depth, speed, colour and distance. One question is to decide how much detail or realism is needed in order for a visualisation to be effective (ie believable). Object recognition studies have shown outline drawings can often be just as effective as full-colour photographs[3], but in other circumstances the interpretation of small details can be critical, such as the difference between an object being perceived as a gun or a stick, as was demonstrated in the case of Harry Stanley[4].

(b)   attitudes: research has found that when people believe they have a sufficient volume of evidence they feel more confident about making judgments, even when the information is irrelevant[5]. Computer-generated visualisations can provide just such an illusion of sufficiency. Members of the public are often more comfortable with visual simulations over legal discourse and hence the visualisations are considered more believable. Many factors also influence the credibility of witnesses' testimony, such as the gender of a witness, their race, appearance, and socio-economic circumstances[6]. A computer-generated visualisation based on witness testimony has the potential to cause members of the public to discount such factors. The anonymous and abstract nature of a computer generated reconstruction may help to remove any such bias or prejudice, or it may serve to emphasise any such differences[7].

(c)   decision-making: research on group decision-making has found that once a group starts a communal discussion many social and linguistic biases are exhibited, such as group polarisation, production losses, Grice's maxims[8]. Computer-generated visualisations can provide a shared memory or representation for a group of decision makers, such as members of a jury. Although this reduces some social and linguistic biases, it is likely to increase others (for example, production loss). There is a need to determine if the technology undermines critical reasoning; in other words, if the display that is to be used supports or hinders decision-making and whether it affects the way in which members of a jury or witnesses interact. A reconstruction often contains uncertain or inferred data which may need to be represented so it can be understood by the viewer[9]. The communication and collaborative process between individuals will also be affected by the type and extent of the display and will determine content in as much as it might affect the way groups reach decisions[10].

[1]   *Burton et al*, 2005 and L Leader and D Schofield 'Madness in the Method? Potential Pitfalls in Handling Expert Evidence' (2006) Journal of Personal Injury Law vol 6, no 1, pp 68–86.

[2]   EF Loftus *Eyewitness Testimony* (revised edn, 1996) and EF Loftus 'Our Changeable Memories: Legal and Practical Implications' (2003) Nature Reviews Neuroscience vol 4, pp 231–234.

[3]   I Biederman, and G Ju 'Surface vs Edge-Based Determinants of Visual Recognition' (1998) Cognitive Psychology vol 20, pp 38–64.

[4]   Crown Prosecution Service, 2001.

[5]   JM Darley and PH Gross 'A Hypothesis-Confirming Bias in Labeling Effects' (1983) Journal of Personality and Social Psychology vol 44, no 1, pp 20–33.

[6]   N Nunez, ML McCoy, HL Clark and LA Shaw 'The Testimony of Elderly Victim/Witnesses and their Impact on Juror Decisions: The Importance of Examining Multiple Stereotypes' (1999) Law and Human Behavior vol 23, no 4, pp 413–423; RA Schuller, D Terry, B McKimmie 'The Impact of Expert Testimony on Jurors' Decisions: Gender of the Expert and Testimony Complexity' (2005) Journal of Applied Social Psychology vol 35, no 6, pp 1266–1280; and KL Wuensch, MW Campbell, FC Kesler and CH Moore 'Racial Bias in Decisions Made by Mock Jurors Evaluating a Case of Sexual Harassment' (2002) Journal of Social Psychology vol 142, no 5, pp 587–600.

[7]   *Burton et al* (2005).

[8]   HP Grice 'Logic and Conversation' in P Cole and Morgan, eds *Speech Acts (Syntax and Semantics 3)* (1975) pp 41–58.

[9]   *Goodwin and Schofield* (2002).

[10] G Klein 'Recognition-Primed Decisions' (1985) Advances in Man-Machine Systems Research vol 5, pp 47–92.

CREATING AND USING VIRTUAL RECONSTRUCTIONS

5.28 Any forensic investigation begins with data collection. Accuracy is crucial because this data serves as the foundation for the evidence. At a physical scene an investigator makes field measurements, produces rough scene sketches, takes sets of photographs and then, at a later stage, drafts up accurate plans of the scene and collates the information. The evidence from the scene should be analysed by experienced and suitably qualified investigators. Finally, the investigators present their findings to a mixed audience of experts and lay people in a court. The evidence must reflect accurately the scientific data available and should augment the testimony of the witnesses. However, to be effective the evidence must not only tell 'the story' but also be understood easily. To that end, forensic scientists and technologists must strive continuously to develop new and creative ways to present complex evidence[1].

[1]   D Schofield, J Noond, L Goodwin and K Fowle 'When Does A Reconstruction Become Reality?' Proceedings of WREX2000 Conference, Dallas Texas (USA), September 2000.

5.29 The technology used for data collection and measurement ranges from tape measures and traditional surveying tools (widely used by private accident investigators), to Electronic Distance Measurement ('EDM') technology (widely used by the police), to full three-dimensional ('3D') laser scanners (such as those used by many large organisations and government agencies). Digital data collection allows the automatic generation of 3D co-ordinate information that will allow the data to be imported directly into the drafting software. These co-ordinates provide a reliable numerical data set for the creation of the geometry that is the foundation of any credible computer model of a scene.

5.30 The environment surrounding the scene may be included within the model. For example, a model may not only show the location of items or objects that may form part of the evidence, but also the position of such items in relation to nearby buildings or other features, and place these items within a time frame. As seen in the CG used for film and television, the realism in these 'virtual' environments is improving. As computer-processing power increases and software tools develop, it is natural to assume that it will be possible to achieve a similar level of realism within the computer-generated environments used in a court.

5.31 The virtual environments created by parties to litigation may be used to test hypotheses, such as to verify the location of a witness, especially where lines of sight around obstructions or hazards present in the environment may call into question the physical location of the witness. Other forensic data may be included within the virtual environment: location-based statistical or analytical data may be displayed, calculation and test results put into visual format, and original documents and photographs linked to 3D objects.

5.32 A recent reconstruction developed for the West Midlands Police in the United Kingdom by the author, for instance, uses real-time VR technology. The user can pass the mouse over any relevant item to receive textual data about that item and, by clicking on any particular item (in this case, mainly items of vehicle debris), relevant crime scene photographs and data will be displayed[1].

[1]   *Burton et al* (2005).

5.33 Before discussing the use of these virtual environments as evidence in a court or inquest, it is necessary to clarify the terms used to describe such technology. The standard form of evidence from such virtual environments usually consists of a series of still images and animations. In this context, the term 'computer animation' is often misused to describe an animation from a virtual environment that is not based on the laws of physics, but is still represented as 'simulating' a given event. The terms 'animation', 'scientific animation' and 'simulation' have specific definitions in the reconstruction community[1].

¹   WD Grimes 'Classifying the Elements in a Scientific Animation' in Accident Reconstruction: Technology and Animation 4 (1994) Warrendale, USA, Society of Automotive Engineers, pp 397–404.

5.34 'Animation' is a general term describing 'any presentation which consists of a series of graphical images being sequentially displayed, representing objects in different positions from one image to the next, which implies motion' This term may be used to describe a technical, science-based presentation or a presentation consisting of artist renditions, sometimes referred to as a 'cartoon animation'.

5.35 The phrase 'scientific animation' is, consequently, used to describe a more technically based presentation, and is defined as 'a computer animation that is based on the laws of physics and the appropriate equations of motion'. Velocities and positions are time integrals of the acceleration data and the objects and environment in a scientific animation are properly and consistently scaled.

5.36 In the reconstruction community, a 'simulation' is defined as being based on the laws of physics and containing specific underlying equations. A simulation goes further than a scientific animation, and can be further defined as 'a model that predicts an outcome. The model may be a physical or a mathematical model, but the significant property is that a simulation predicts a future result'.

5.37 In summary, an 'animation' may only be illustrative evidence whereas a 'scientific animation' is more technical and relies upon scientific laws and thus may be categorised as substantive evidence. A 'simulation' is more predictive in nature and consists of data or forecasts which are usually created via a computer program. The admissibility of a simulation depends on the category of the program used to create it and thus may either be classed as illustrative or substantive evidence.

5.38 When scientific evidence is submitted to a court or inquiry part of the procedural requirements involves the checking of any methodology, including programs and processes used. Depending on the type of software used and the method of creating the reconstruction, the evidence may be difficult or relatively straightforward to admit.

5.39 Legislation and case law exists in most countries that govern the admissibility of computer-generated displays (and, in fact, any visual or scientific evidence or display) in court in order to ensure fair, unbiased and appropriate use of this evidence. Digital visualisations have been used widely in American courts for the last 20 years. The technology has only begun to be introduced into the United Kingdom and Australian courts relatively recently. Accordingly, the vast majority of the research undertaken into their use, and most of the applicable case law, is from the United States. Although this means that the computer-generated evidence will often have been used at jury trials, it is suggested that many of the same advantages and concerns raised when showing computer-generated displays to members of a jury apply to judges or any other trier of fact[1].

[1]   *Goodwin* (2007).

EXAMPLES OF COMPUTER-GENERATED VISUALISATIONS IN THE US

5.40 Computer-generated displays and, more specifically, scientific animations or simulations must meet certain criteria before being admitted as evidence in court due to potential bias and unfairness. The legal requirements are dealt with elsewhere in this text and a number of examples are set out below to illustrate the nature of what can be achieved.

Computer-generated evidence in the US: civil case

5.41 Computer-generated evidence in the US has primarily been used in civil cases. One of the first major uses of computer-generated animations in court took place in the federal civil case for the Delta flight 191 crash. In August 1985 the Delta aeroplane with 163 people aboard was caught in a wind vortex and crashed while attempting to land at Dallas-Fort Worth Airport, a mile from the runway[1].

[1]   P Marcotte 'Animated Evidence: Delta 191 Crash Re-Created Through Computer Simulations at Trial' (1989) Am BAJ vol 75, no 12, pp 52–56.

5.42 During the crash 128 passengers, 8 crewmembers and 1 person on the ground were killed and there was extensive property damage. In the subsequent litigation computer-generated animations were used to explain the complex issues and technical matters to the members of the jury, without intending to overwhelm them with the complexities of the evidence. The US Government offered a 55-minute computer-generated presentation, including forensic animations, to the court to explain the details of each item of evidence. The animations that were created were based on ground-radar data and the design capabilities of the radar used by Delta 191[1].

[1]   S Gold 'Forensic Animation—Its Origins, Creation, Limitations and Future' (2001) available online at http://www.365video.com/editorial/features/forensic/forensic.shtml, viewed on 27 August 2006 and *Marcotte*, 1989. *Re Air Crash at Dallas/Fort Worth Airport on August 2, 1985*, 720 F.Supp 1258 (N.D. Tex. 1989), aff'd, 919 F.2d 1079 (5th Cir. 1991), cert. denied *sub nom Connors v United States*, 112 S. Ct. 276 (1991).

Computer-generated evidence in the US: criminal case

5.43 The use of computer-generated evidence in criminal cases can often be more problematic. The simple benefits and disadvantages of using computer-generated evidence in court can become magnified by the importance of the result of the trial. Admittance of computer-generated evidence to a civil trial may mean an award or loss of money, whereas in a criminal case loss of liberty may result[1].

1   EJ Bardelli 'The Use of Computer Simulations in Criminal Prosecutions' (1994) Wayne Law Review pp 1357–1377.

5.44 Computer animations and simulations may be used by the prosecution, but also by the defence to show that the prosecutor's version of events could not possibly have happened. An example of the latter is the state case of *People v McHugh*[1], which involved one of the first uses of a computer-generated simulation in a criminal trial. McHugh was driving his vehicle in New York City when he was alleged to have killed several people. He was charged with their deaths but argued he had not been criminally negligent. The defence claimed the accident occurred because the weather conditions caused the vehicle to leave the road and to hit an electrical box that was open at ground level. This, in turn, caused a tyre to rupture which caused the vehicle to spin into a concrete abutment[2].

1   124 Misc.2d 559, 476 N.Y.S.2d 721 (Sup. 1984).
2   SM Kassin and MA Dunn 'Computer-Animated Displays and the Jury: Facilitative and Prejudicial Effects' (1997) Law and Human Behavior vol 21, no 3, pp 269–281 available online at http://www.springerlink.com/content/k835363q2h2q6767/.

5.45 On behalf of the defence, a specialist in reconstructing accidents introduced a simple simulation illustrating the defence theory relating to the path the vehicle took. The prosecution moved for a pre-trial conference to evaluate the admissibility of the computer-generated evidence. After the court reviewed the expert's report outlining the construction of the computer simulation, it was ruled that there would be no need for a pre-trial hearing on the issue. Collins J classified the computer-generated evidence as demonstrative, at 722:

> The evidence sought to be introduced here is more akin to a chart or diagram than a scientific device. Whether a diagram is hand drawn or mechanically drawn by means of a computer is of no importance.

The judge ruled that the expert could use the simulation, provided the defence laid the proper foundations and qualifications of the expert[1].

1   TL Bohan and AC Damask *Forensic Accident Investigation: Motor Vehicles* (1995) and C D'Angelo 'The Snoop Doggy Dogg Trial: A Look at How Computer Animation will Impact Litigation in the Next Century' (1998) University of San Francisco Law Review pp 561–585.

5.46 As a result of the possible loss of an individual's freedom, and sometimes life, the use of computer animations and simulations in criminal cases must be analysed carefully. This is particularly true for scientific computer evidence since scientific evidence is far more difficult to admit than illustrative evidence, as previously mentioned. There is a high risk in a criminal trial that the members of the jury can be overwhelmed by the scientific techniques or devices employed.

Virtual reality technology in US courts

5.47 The case of *Stephenson v Honda Motors Ltd of America*[1] saw the first use of an interactive real-time simulator (based on real time VR technology) in US courts. After an accident on her motorcycle, Ms Stephenson claimed that the ground she was traveling on was smooth and her vehicle inherently unstable because it caused her to fall. Rain had eroded the road by the time of trial so it was impossible to determine the condition of the road. Honda argued that it was too dangerous to drive safely upon the terrain. Honda produced a virtual reconstruction of the terrain, which members of the jury could view by using VR headsets and a demonstration motorcycle simulator. Honda claimed that this method of viewing the environment was more realistic and relevant than photographs and videos since it gave the jury a better idea of the nature of the terrain. The VR evidence was admitted[2].

[1]   No. 81067 (Cal. Sup. Placer County, June 25, 1992).
[2]   JA Dunn 'Virtual Reality Evidence' (1999) available online at: http://www.lectlaw.com/files/lit04.htm, viewed on 27 August 2006.

EXAMPLES OF COMPUTER-GENERATED VISUALISATIONS IN ENGLAND AND WALES

5.48 There is extensive precedent concerning the use of computer-generated evidence in the United States, but comparatively little in England and Wales. Consequently, judges in England and Wales may look to the US for guidance in considering the issues of admissibility. This is particularly true for computer-generated animations and virtual simulations.

Computer-generated evidence in England and Wales: civil case

5.49 An early occurrence of the use of computer-generated evidence is seen in the civil case of *Owners of the Ship Pelopidas v Owners of the Ship TRSL Concord*. In 1996 a collision took place in the access channel to Buenos Aires between two vessels: the Pelopidas and TRSL Concord. The issue for the court to decide was the liability for the collision and the apportionment of that liability.

[1]   [1999] 2 Lloyd's Rep 675.

5.50 The items of computer-generated evidence submitted were two-dimensional computer-generated simulations of both vessels trajectories. A 'black box' on the *Concord* recorded various positioning, speed and heading data at 15-second intervals for the relevant collision time period. Thus both sides accepted the accuracy of the plot. David Steel J concluded that a fair apportionment of liability was 60:40 in favour of *Pelopidas*, and stated[1]

> ... there is a danger of losing sight of the true value of reconstructions. Of course they enable the Court and the parties to have a broad bird's eye view of

the events leading up to collision. But their true probative value is that they may sometimes enable the Court to determine, not what may have happened, but what could not possibly have happened.

¹   [1999] 2 Lloyd's Rep 675 at 682.

5.51 In stating the above, David Steel J was remarking on his accumulated experience of the usefulness of computer-generated reconstruction evidence. Although not familiar with the other possible benefits of computer-generated reconstructions, David Steel J highlighted the other side of the coin, so to speak, and illustrated another situation where this type of evidence can be relevant and necessary[1].

¹   *Goodwin* (2007).

Computer-generated evidence in England and Wales: criminal cases

5.52 An increasing number of jury members are likely to have some experience in the use of computers, so it is conceivable that the jury can be left to decide on the weight given to the computer evidence. It is also reasonable to assume that the opposing party could point out any problems with the computer or raise suspicion about the evidence. The judge could then make a decision on admissibility and appropriately warn the jury if the evidence is admitted[1].

¹   D Bainbridge *An Introduction to Computer Law* (3rd ed, 1996).

5.53 Due to the critical nature of criminal trials it is crucial that any computer-generated evidence put forward is thoroughly examined. The use of a jury in criminal cases is another important reason for assessing the prejudicial effect, accuracy and relevance of computer-generated evidence carefully. Juries are particularly vulnerable, often more so than judges and coroners, to any prejudicial effect and inaccuracy of scientific animations. Perhaps this is because juries do not have the same level of cynicism that years of experience of analysing evidence has given judges and, to a lesser degree, coroners[1].

¹   *Goodwin* (2007).

5.54 In the case of *R v Ore*, Tucker J stated the defence's apprehension for the admissibility of a computer-generated animation[1]:

> The concern which is expressed by [the defence]… is as to the impact which this evidence will have upon the jury and I understand that concern. [The defence] fears that the weight which the jury may place upon the graphic animation will be disproportionate to its value in the case. [The defence] fears that they may be distracted from concentrating as they ought to do upon the evidence to be given by the expert witnesses on either side and is concerned, naturally, that the graphic animation reproduces simply one particular side of the coin.

[1] Birmingham Crown Court, 1998, not reported. The editor tried to obtain a copy of the transcript of the case but the tapes were destroyed, in accordance with the retention and disposal policy (correspondence with Michael Ives, Marten Walsh Cherer Ltd). Sir Richard Tucker has confirmed, in a letter to the editor, that he no longer has the notes of this trial but confirms the remarks that are attributed to him as quoted in this text.

5.55 The concerns stated above are highly relevant and illustrate real fears about any computer-generated evidence. This is especially true for forensic reconstructions, hence any computer-generated reconstructions should be made as precisely and in as unbiased a way as possible, and their use proven to be necessary. Thus their probative value should outweigh any potential prejudicial effect.

5.56 The case of *Ore* introduced one of the first forensic computer-generated animations to an English criminal trial. The Crash Investigation and Training Unit of the West Midlands Police Service produced the animation. The case involved a collision between two vehicles at a junction; one of the drivers was killed as he pulled out in front of an oncoming vehicle. The views of both drivers were partially obscured by large hedges and walls around the junction[1].

[1] M Doyle 'Working Model: Helping the Police with Their Enquiries' (1997) *CAD User*, October.

5.57 Tucker J, who presided over this case, further stated in his ruling on 25 November 1998:

> I am told that this is the first time in which it has been suggested that a jury in a trial such as this should be shown a computer aided animation which pictorially represents a reconstruction of a road traffic accident. It may be that in years to come such displays will be commonplace and that lawyers will marvel that anyone should ever have questioned their admissibility.

> ... I am satisfied that it would be right to admit this evidence and, indeed, wrong to refuse so to do, provided, as I shall try to do, that I give the jury proper directions as to their approach to this evidence and provided I ensure, so far as I can, that they do not place disproportionate weight upon it. Accordingly, I rule that the evidence is admissible.

5.58 An example from Northern Ireland introduced an important reconstruction that has been highly relevant, unbiased and accurate[1]. Computer-generated evidence has been used at the Bloody Sunday Inquiry[2]. In 1972, thirteen people were killed in a peaceful demonstration that went awry. The original inquiry produced a report within 11 weeks of the incident and acquitted the soldiers involved. In 1998, a Tribunal of Inquiry was established to reassess the events[3]. Lord Saville, the chair of the tribunal, took full advantage of technology, and a computer software system was designed especially for use in the Inquiry to amplify the testimony of witnesses.

[1] See http://www.bloody-sunday-inquiry.org/index2.asp?p=7.
[2] See http://www.bloody-sunday-inquiry.org/.
[3] Statement by Tony Blair, Prime Minister, in the House of Commons, HC Official Report, col 501, 29 January 1998.

5.59 The Northern Ireland Centre for Learning and Resources produced the computer-generated virtual models. The system reconstructed a large area of Londonderry, which was extensively altered since 1972. The user was able to compare the same scene as it appeared both recently and in 1972. There were 80 locations which could be explored stored in the system, with any point of view recalled when switching between the representations. The system could also store oral evidence about location and movement and export scenes to a mark-up system so that witnesses could draw on top of images. The computer software system that was admitted was proven to be unbiased and accurate.

5.60 Although the Bloody Sunday Inquiry computer system was reputed to be a VR interactive simulation, it was not interactive in three dimensions. VR, by definition, is an interactive computer-generated simulated environment with which users can interact using a computer monitor or specialised hardware such as data gloves. The computer system used for the Bloody Sunday Inquiry was interactive in the sense that viewers were able to view images of different scenes at varied times. However, the viewer was not able to move around a full 3D virtual environment of Londonderry itself, as there was not one available.

5.61 Recently, full interactive 3D VR crime scene environments used during investigations have been introduced into courts across the UK and into a number of criminal courts in high profile cases[1].

[1]   *Burton et al* (2005).

COMPUTER-GENERATED VISUALISATIONS IN AUSTRALIA

Computer-generated evidence in Australian cases

5.62 There are a few examples of the use of computer-generated animations in Australian courts. One example is the *R v King* where three men allegedly raped a young woman in November 1995. Christopher John Bull, Rodney William King and James Luis Marotta each pleaded not guilty to deprivation of liberty and six counts of sexual penetration without consent[1].

[1]   *R v King* [1998] WASCA 3.

5.63 A reconstruction was admitted on behalf of the defence to illustrate how measurements of the crime scene were taken and that it was impossible to re-enact the crime without removing certain parameters, such as obstructing objects and wall geometry. In the animation that was produced it was demonstrated that the perpetrator's frame had to protrude through the shower wall, which demonstrated the crime could not have occurred as described by the prosecutor.

5.64 The case of *Brambles Australia Ltd v AM and JP Keune Pty Ltd*[1] involved the collision of two heavily-laden road trains on the Brand Highway, near Regans Ford. On 2 December 1991, the road train, owned by Brambles

Australia Ltd ('Brambles') was travelling south, and being driven by Mr Steven Lee, who died in the collision. The road train owned by AM and JP Keune Pty Ltd ('Keune') was travelling north from Perth to Tom Price, driven by Mr Ian Jones, who was injured in the collision.

[1]   *Brambles Australia Ltd v AM and JP Keune Pty Ltd* [1998] WASC 57.

5.65 Mr Jones' evidence was tested before the trial, both practically and theoretically. The practical test involved the reconstruction of the movements of the Brambles road train, as described by Mr Jones, by an experienced vehicle accident consultant. A video recording of this reconstruction was introduced as evidence. A further computer-generated reconstruction was created to simulate the collision from Mr Jones' point of view. Another qualified vehicle accident consultant carried out this simulation, in conjunction with ARRB Transport Research Ltd.

5.66 Although the simulations demonstrated that it would have been possible for both road trains to have moved in the way described by Mr Jones, the simulations did not concur fully with the other evidence. The simulation showing Mr Jones' version of events was not in full accordance with the video recording and the ARRB report findings on times of lane changes and the limit of stability of the road trains. Therefore, testing Mr Jones' evidence using the methods described illustrated that, although Mr Jones' account was seemingly possible, it did not provide a satisfactory explanation. Templeman J concluded that the version of events put forward by Brambles was more probable, and that Mr Lee was not responsible for the collision. The judge stated that Mr Jones was a competent driver and did not intentionally allow his vehicle to drift to the wrong lane, but that he had fallen asleep at the wheel.

CONCLUSIONS

5.67 Criminal trials are more critical due to the defendant's potential loss of freedom, compared to a possible loss or gain of money in civil cases. As a result of this, perhaps, there is less motivation to use computer-generated evidence in civil litigation and thus there are fewer instances of its use in civil cases. However, as large sums of money are often at stake in civil cases it may make good economic sense to use computer-generated animations and simulations as part of an argument, due to the apparent benefits of using such technology in court.

5.68 The use of computer-generated evidence in the United Kingdom is slowly changing. There are currently a number of companies producing this type of evidence, including scientific animations, for use in court.

5.69 The unavoidable future for courts across the world is the introduction of technology, whether this technology is merely electronic filing and teleconferencing or takes the form of computer-generated evidence presentations, such as virtual forensic reconstructions. Given the benefits of the use of information technology and computer-generated evidence shown in US courts, it is inevitable that the use of digital technology and evidence will increase.

5.70 As a specific technology for displaying computer-generated evidence, Virtual Reality has the potential to have an important effect on many future cases as the technology and the forensic community develops. Landmark opportunities exist within the legal system, which could benefit enormously from accurate and interactive Virtual Reality environments that jury members and other triers of fact would trust.

Chapter 6

AUSTRALIA

PHILIP N ARGY

LAW OF EVIDENCE

Relevance and admissibility

6.01 The admissibility of evidence in Australia is governed by both statute and common law. Australia is organised as a federal system. This means that there are eight different State and Territory Evidence Acts as well as a Federal (Commonwealth) Evidence Act. New South Wales ('NSW'), the Australian Capital Territory ('ACT') and Tasmania have adopted Evidence Acts that mirror the Commonwealth Act ('the Uniform Evidence Acts'). The remaining jurisdictions have their own Acts: Evidence Act 1958 (Victoria); Evidence Act 1977 (Queensland); Evidence Act 1906 (Western Australia); Evidence Act 1929 (South Australia); Evidence Act 1939 (Northern Territory). This chapter will deal mainly with the Uniform Evidence Acts. Where there are significant differences to the Uniform Evidence Acts in other jurisdictions, they will be discussed.

6.02 In order to be admissible, evidence must be sufficiently relevant to the facts at issue. Under s 55 of the Uniform Evidence Acts, evidence is considered relevant if it is capable of affecting the rational assessment of the probability of a fact at issue in the proceedings.

6.03 According to the Uniform Evidence Acts, anything from which writing can be produced with or without the aid of anything else is a document. Typically, therefore, electronic evidence such as information contained on the hard drive of a computer is subject to the same rules of evidence as any other type of document. However, the Uniform Evidence Acts do incorporate certain provisions which relate exclusively to electronic evidence.

6.04 In Victoria ('Vic'), Queensland ('Qld') and South Australia ('SA') the legislation specifically states that evidence derived from computer records will be admissible, subject to certain conditions of reliability. Although there are no express provisions regarding computer records in the remaining jurisdictions, each of them recognises a copy of an original document as equivalent to an original document[1]. Providing a copy is identical to the original in all relevant respects, it will be admissible. For example, where colour is not a relevant aspect of a document a black and white hardcopy version of a colour electronic record will be acceptable. Section 146 of the Uniform Evidence Acts provides for a rebuttable presumption that allows a photocopy, facsimile or electronic copy of a document to be taken as a true copy of the original document. If appropriate anti-tampering processes are in place, it will be difficult to rebut the presumption that an electronic copy of a document is accurate. This may include measures such as electronic logs of all access and modifications to documents, providing read-only access to everyone other than specified individuals, and the use of encryption to provide for integrity.

1   Uniform Evidence Acts, s 48.

6.05 The hearsay rule renders 'a previous representation made by a person' inadmissible for a hearsay purpose, that is, for the purpose of proving the existence of the fact the person intended to assert[1]. There are various exceptions to this rule, but a full discussion of the concept of hearsay is beyond the scope of this chapter. One particular exception that is of relevance, especially when deciding to store evidence electronically. Section 69 of the Uniform Evidence Acts provides an exception to the hearsay rule for business records. Business records are documents that form part of a record by a person, body or organisation in the course of, or for the purposes of, a business. A representation in a business record is admissible if the representation was made or recorded in the course of, or for the purposes of, the business. Section 147 provides a presumption similar to that contained in s 146 (see above). It allows a party tendering a copy of a business record to rely on a presumption that the copy is an accurate reproduction of the original. Due to this presumption, the party tendering copies of business records will not need to call evidence to prove the accuracy of the electronic device or process that has produced the record, unless the opposing party impugns it by adducing evidence to rebut the presumption.

1   Uniform Evidence Acts, s 59.

6.06 Although the Uniform Evidence Acts contain a presumption that copies of original documents are admissible, there is no presumption that such evidence is reliable. The rules of evidence can operate in a way that copies of the original document or an electronically stored version of the original, even if introduced in evidence, are given a lower weight. For example, a document which has been stored electronically may be admissible in court but a judge may attach little weight to it, as there may be no evidence to counter an allegation that the content of the document has been tampered with.

6.07 As a result, when dealing with electronically-stored records, there is a far greater focus on the integrity of the process by which information is captured, stored and reproduced in electronically stored records. Therefore, when storing documents or information electronically, audit trails, access and other logs, and metadata need to be retained to provide evidence of the integrity of the content of the record. Total Quality Management and other standard process methodologies improve the probability that documents will be accepted as having been captured or processed correctly.

The 'best evidence' rule

6.08 Traditionally, the common law in Australia recognised the 'best evidence' rule. This rule operated to exclude secondary evidence of the contents of a document unless primary evidence was not available. This meant that the original document had to be tendered in evidence and a copy of such a document would not be admissible unless the absence of the original could be adequately explained, such as that the original had been lost, it would be impractical or unduly burdensome to produce it, or the original was in the possession of another party. The best evidence rule has been abolished by statute in the Federal, New South Wales, Australia Capital Territory and Tasmanian jurisdictions[1]. Section 48 specifically allows for proof of the contents of documents by evidence that would formerly have been inadmissible as secondary evidence, including tendering of an extract, copy or transcript of a document. However, failure to produce an original document is still relevant to the probative value that will be accorded to secondary evidence of its contents.

[1]   Uniform Evidence Acts, ss 48 and 51.

6.09 The best evidence rule remains operative in South Australia, Western Australia, Northern Territory, Victoria and Queensland. Under the rule, the contents of a document can be proved by secondary evidence if:

(a)   the original is in the possession or control of the opposing party and that party fails to produce it after receipt of a notice to produce;

(b)   the original is in the possession of a stranger to the litigation who lawfully refuses to produce it pursuant to a subpoena;

(c)   the original has been lost. Secondary evidence is admissible even where the original document has been deliberately destroyed by the person seeking to adduce such evidence, though its weight will be affected by the circumstances of the destruction; or

(d)   production of the original is impossible—for example production is physically impossible or the original is in the hands of a person outside the jurisdiction, who cannot be compelled to produce it.

Role of experts

Admissibility of expert evidence under the Evidence Act

6.10 Section 79 of the Uniform Evidence Acts provides for expert opinion evidence. A person who has specialised knowledge based on his or her training, study or experience may give opinion evidence that is wholly or substantially based on that knowledge.

6.11 It must be established that there is a field of specialised knowledge and there must be an identified area of that field in which the witness demonstrates that they are an expert as a result of specified training, study or experience. Therefore, although s 80 of the Uniform Evidence Acts abolishes the 'common knowledge' rule, it is still relevant to consider whether the knowledge possessed by the expert witness is general knowledge, because then it cannot be specialised knowledge within the meaning of s 79. It is for the judge to determine whether the witness has undergone sufficient study and training or has sufficient experience to be rendered an expert in the given specialised field. It is not necessary for the expertise to have been acquired professionally.

6.12 The expert's opinion must be wholly or substantially based on his or her expert knowledge. This means that experts cannot give opinion evidence outside their area of expertise. The expert witness must identify the area of expertise he can bring to bear and his opinions must be related to that expertise[1]. The facts on which an expert's opinion is based must be available for scrutiny by a tribunal of fact. Hence, insofar as the opinion is based on facts observed by the expert, they must be identified and proved by the expert; and insofar as it is based on assumed facts, these must be identified and proved in some other way. It must be established that the facts on which the opinion is based form a proper foundation for it, and the expert's evidence must demonstrate how his or her field of specialised knowledge applies to the facts so as to produce the opinion propounded.

1   *HG v R* (1999) 197 CLR 414, (1999) 160 ALR 554 at [39].

6.13 Under s 59 of the Uniform Evidence Acts, hearsay evidence is inadmissible if it is adduced for a hearsay purpose. Evidence of representations made to an expert would be admissible, if it is relevant, for the *non-hearsay* purpose of proving the factual basis or foundation for the expert's opinion. The fact that a representation was made to an expert is generally relevant irrespective of the truth of the representation because it gives the fact-finder a basis to assess the expert's conclusions.

Court Rules regarding expert evidence

6.14 In some states parties must exchange expert witness statements or reports prior to trial[1]. The statement or report should include the name, address and qualifications of the expert and the substance of the evidence to be adduced. Usually, evidence that is not covered in substance by the statement or report may not be adduced at trial. However, the court has the discretion to allow such evidence to be adduced provided the other party is not prejudiced.

1   NT Supreme Court Rules r 44.3; Tas Supreme Court Rules r 516; WA Rules of the Supreme Court r 36.2(3); Vic Supreme Court (General Civil Procedure) Rules r 44.03(1); QLD Uniform Civil Procedure Rules 1999 r 429; NSW Uniform Civil Procedure Rules 2005 r 31.18.

6.15 There are also provisions for the court to direct that the expert witnesses of opposing parties confer in order to endeavour to reach agreement on outstanding matters and to provide the court with a joint report specifying matters agreed and not agreed upon and the reasons for any failure to reach agreement[1].

[1]   NSW Uniform Civil Procedure Rules 2005 r 31.25; Cth Federal Court Rules r 34A.3; Vic Supreme Court (General Civil Procedure) Rules r 44.06; Tas Supreme Court Rules r 541; WA Rules of the Supreme Court 29A.3(l).

6.16 Court rules permit the court to appoint an expert to report to the court, however court experts are rarely appointed[1].

[1]   Federal Court Rules O 34 r 2; Uniform Civil Procedure Rules 2005 (NSW); Supreme Court Rules (SA) 1987, r 82.1; Rules of the Supreme Court 1971 (WA) O 40 r2.

Electronic transactions and electronic signatures

6.17 The Electronic Transactions Act 1999 (Cwlth) and corresponding State Acts[1] were introduced to remove legal impediments to recognition of electronic documents and digital signatures as meeting legal requirements for documents to be in writing and signed. Under the Electronic Transactions Acts, a transaction is not invalid merely because it took place by means of one or more electronic communications[2]. The Act allows legal requirements to give information in writing[3], to produce a document[4], to record information[5] or to retain a document[6] to be satisfied in electronic form.

[1]   Electronic Transactions Act 2001 (ACT); Electronic Transactions Act 2000 (NSW); Electronic Transactions (Northern Territory) Act 2000 (NT); Electronic Transactions (Queensland) Act 2001 (QLD); Electronic Transactions Act 2000 (SA); Electronic Transactions Act 2000 (Tas); Electronic Transactions (Victoria) Act 2000 (Vic); Electronic Transactions Bill 2001 (WA)—together the 'Electronic Transactions Acts'.
[2]   Electronic Transactions Act 1999 (Cwlth), s 8.
[3]   Electronic Transactions Act 1999 (Cwlth), s 9.
[4]   Electronic Transactions Act 1999 (Cwlth), s 10.
[5]   Electronic Transactions Act 1999 (Cwlth), s 11.
[6]   Electronic Transactions Act 1999 (Cwlth), s 12.

6.18 Where a person is required to given information in writing, this requirement is taken to have been met if the person gives the information by means of an electronic communication if:

(a)   it was reasonable to expect the information contained in the electronic form of the document would be readily accessible so as to be usable for subsequent reference;

(b)   the person to whom the information is required to be given consents to the information being given by way of electronic communication; and

(c)   if the information is required to be given to a Commonwealth or State entity, Commonwealth or State requirements for verification of receipt and information technology requirements have been met.

6.19 Where a person's signature is legally required, this requirement is taken to have been met in relation to an electronic communication if:

(a)   the method used to identity the person and to indicate the person's approval of the information communicated was as reliable as was appropriate for the purposes for which the information was communicated;

(b) the person to whom the signature is required to be given consents to the requirement being met electronically; and

(c) if the signature is required to be given to a Commonwealth or State entity, Commonwealth or State information technology requirements are also met.

6.20 Where a person is legally required or permitted to produce a paper document, the requirement is taken to have been met if the person produces an electronic form of the document[1] where:

(a) the method of generating the electronic form of the document provides a reliable means of assuring the integrity of the information contained in the document;

(b) it was reasonable to expect the information contained in the electronic form of the document would be readily accessible so as to be usable for subsequent reference;

(c) the person to whom the document is to be produced consents to the production by means of an electronic communication, or an electronic form of the document; and

(d) if the document is required to be produced to a Commonwealth or State entity, Commonwealth or State requirements for verification of receipt and information technology requirements are also met.

[1] Electronic Transactions Act 1999 (Cwlth), s 11.

6.21 Where a person is legally required to retain a record of a 'paper document', this requirement will be met if the person retains an electronic form of the document[1] where:

(a) the method of generating the electronic form of the document provided a reliable means of assuring the integrity of the information contained in the document; and

(b) it was reasonable to expect the information contained in the electronic form of the document would be readily accessible so as to be usable for subsequent reference.

[1] Electronic Transactions Act 1999 (Cwlth), s 12.

6.22 Where a person is legally required to retain a record of an 'electronic communication', this requirement will be satisfied where:

(a) if a particular kind of storage device is required by regulations, that requirement has been met;

(b) if additional information to identify the origin of the electronic communication, the destination of the electronic communication and the times at which it was sent and received is also to be kept, that requirement has been met.

6.23 Under the Electronic Transactions Acts, the integrity of information contained in a document is maintained if, and only if, the information has remained complete and unaltered, apart from the addition of any endorsement or any immaterial change which arise in the normal course of communication, storage or display[1].

[1]   Electronic Transactions Act 1999 (Cwlth), ss 11(3) and 12(3).

6.24 There is a risk that there will be a loss of essential attributes when storing information in electronic form. For example, the depth of the impression made by a signature on a cheque is an attribute lost by two dimensional scanning. If the third dimension of the signature is material, for instance if there is a dispute about the authenticity of the signature, the two-dimensional stored image will not be acceptable to a handwriting expert called upon to advise, and therefore the value of the electronic 'copy' of the record is seriously diminished compared to the original.

6.25 The Electronic Transactions Acts provide that the time of dispatch of an electronic communication is the time at which it first enters an information system outside the control of the originator[1]. The time of receipt of an electronic communication is the time at which it enters the information system designated by the addressee for the purpose of receiving such communications. If no information system has been designated, the time of receipt is when the communication comes to the attention of the addressee.

[1]   Electronic Transactions Act 1999 (Cwlth), s 14.

CRIMINAL LAW

Search warrants

6.26 A search warrant allows the search and seizure of those items which are reasonably expected to be connected with a crime and fall within the terms of the warrant. Evidence may be seized if the person conducting the search and seizure reasonably believes at the time of seizure that there are grounds for suspecting the material seized would afford evidence of the commission of one or more of the offences listed in the warrant[1].

[1]   *Harts Australian Ltd v Commissioner, Australia Federal Police* (2002) 74 ALD 637.

6.27 Search warrants may be obtained under a number of Commonwealth, State and Territory Acts. This chapter focuses on the Crimes Act 1914 (Cwlth). However, similar principles apply to search warrants granted under corresponding State and Territory legislation[1].

[1]   Crimes Act 1990 (ACT); Summary Offences Act 1953 (SA); Magistrates Court Act 1989 (Vic); Law Enforcement (Powers and Responsibilities) Act 2002 (NSW); Police Administration Act (NT); Search Warrants Act 1997 (Tas); Criminal Code (WA); Criminal Code (QLD).

Taking photographic or video evidence

6.28 Section 3J(1) of the Crimes Act 1914 (Cwlth) allows an officer executing a search warrant to take photographs, including video recording, of the premises or of things at the premises for a purpose incidental to the execution of a warrant, or if the occupier consents in writing.

Seizing electronic evidence from a computer at the premises

6.29 Under s 3K(1) of the Crimes Act 1914 (Cwlth), an executing officer may bring on to the premises any equipment reasonably necessary for the examination or processing of a thing found at the premises in order to determine whether it may be seized under the warrant. In order to do this, there can be a break during the execution of the warrant of an hour or longer if the occupier consents in writing[1].

[1] Crimes Act 1914 (Cwlth), ss 3J(2)(a)–(b).

6.30 Under s 3L of the Crimes Act 1914 (Cwlth), the officer executing the search warrant may operate electronic equipment at the premises to obtain access to data, including data not held at the premises, if he or she believes on reasonable grounds that the operation of the equipment can be carried out without damaging the equipment. The executing officer may also obtain an order from a magistrate requiring a person with knowledge of a computer or computer system to provide assistance in obtaining access to data held in, or accessible from, a computer, copying the data to a data storage device or to convert the data into documentary form[1]. If the executing officer believes on reasonable grounds that any data viewed by operating the electronic equipment might constitute evidentiary material, they may copy an image of the data to a disk, tape or other associated device[2].

[1] Crimes Act 1914 (Cwlth), s 3LA.
[2] Crimes Act 1914 (Cwlth), s 3L(1A).

6.31 Further, the officer has the power to 'secure' computer equipment on-site for 24 hours or more, so that an expert can attend to operate the equipment[1]. However, the Act is silent as to any power to re-enter the property. In *R v Coco* [2] it was held that once a warrant is executed, there is no right of re-entry unless expressly provided for by statute. In light of this decision, it is arguable that officers would need to make a fresh application for a search warrant before they re-enter the premises with an expert to inspect and search equipment that was previously secured. Accordingly, it might be expected that, wherever practicable, offices are more likely to remove equipment from the premises under s 3K (see below).

[1] Crimes Act (Cwlth), ss 3L(4)–(8).
[2] (1994) 179 CLR 427.

6.32 Before an officer secures a computer for later use, they must hold a belief on reasonable grounds that if they do not secure the equipment the material contained in the equipment or accessible via the computer may be destroyed, altered or otherwise interfered with[1].

¹   Crimes Act 1914 (Cwlth), s 3L(4)(c).

Seizing electronic equipment

6.33 In circumstances where it is not practicable to copy material at the premises, sections 3K(2) and (3) of the Crimes Act 1914 (Cwlth) authorise the lawful removal of computers for examination away from the premises in certain circumstances. A computer or other electronic device may be removed from the premises if it is significantly more practicable to do so, having regard to the timeliness and cost of examination or processing of the thing at another place, and the availability of expert assistance. If a computer or other electronic device is moved to another place for examination or processing, the executing officer must inform the occupier of the premises of the address of the place and the time at which the examination or processing will be carried out and allow the occupier or his or her legal representative to be present during the examination[1]. Any electronic device removed from the premises must only be removed for a reasonable time. Since computer software can be copied in a very short period of time, it is unlikely that computer equipment can ordinarily be seized for more than 72 hours. However, this limitation would not apply if the possession of the equipment itself could constitute an offence, such as the possession of stolen equipment.

¹   Crimes Act 1914 (Cwlth), s 3K(3).

Evidence that may be taken from a computer

6.34 Officers are entitled to copy evidentiary material from computers that have been seized, but do not have authority to download the entire content of the hard drives or servers of computer systems. This limitation is based on the fact that the officer executing the search warrant could not reasonably believe that the entire contents of the material stored on the computer would be covered by the warrant[1]. In *Bartlett v Weir*[2], a computer expert accompanied by officers in the execution of a search warrant seized a very large number of floppy disks and computer hardware, although neither the expert nor the officer knew what the disks and hardware contained. As a result, the execution of the warrant was rendered unlawful, since the officer and expert could have had no reasonable basis to believe that the items seized contained evidence of the commission of the offences specified in the warrant, or of any other offence. The seizure of the items was so random as to indicate that a reasonable belief was not held in relation to each of the items.

¹   *George v Rockett* (1990) 170 CLR 104; *Williams v Keelty* (2001) 111 FCR 175; *Harts Australian Ltd v Commissioner, Australia Federal Police* (2002) 74 ALD 637.
²   (1994) 72 Crim R 511.

6.35 The question of propriety in relation to seizure is whether in relation to each item, such as each file, disc or other document, the officer had reasonable cause to believe that it would contain evidence as to the commission of a crime. Ideally, given the practicalities involved with the gathering of evidence in electronic format, a search warrant ought to cover whole disks so that an image of the entire disk may be taken, but care will then need to be taken to ensure that only those parts of the image that are germane to the enquiry are examined.

Electronic evidence that is seized

6.36 If electronic equipment is seized under a warrant, or is removed from the premises for the purpose of examination or processing, the executing officer must provide the occupier of the premises with a receipt[1]. Additionally, if a document, film, computer file or any electronic storage device that can be easily copied is seized, a copy must be made for the occupier of the premises as soon as practicable after the seizure if a request is made by the owner[2]. This will not apply if the possession of the document, film, computer file or information could constitute an offence (such as copyright infringement).

[1] Crimes Act 1914 (Cwlth), s 3Q.
[2] Crimes Act 1914 (Cwlth), s 3N.

Damage to electronic equipment

6.37 If damage is caused to the equipment through its use by the officer, and the damage is caused as a result of insufficient care being exercised in selecting the person to operate the equipment, or by the person operating the equipment, it is expressly provided that compensation for the damage is payable to the owner of the equipment[1].

[1] Crimes Act 1914 (Cwlth), s 3M(1).

Warrants to enter

6.38 Warrants may be granted in order to collect evidence electronically, such as warrants to intercept telephone calls or to record conversations. These warrants allow an officer to enter specified premises where necessary, but do not allow them to conduct a search.

6.39 The Telecommunications (Interception and Access) Act 1979 (Cwlth) prohibits interception of a communication 'passing over' a telecommunications system[1], that is, a 'real time' communication. It is also prohibits authorising or enabling a person to intercept such a communication[2]. A communication is not limited to voice communication but includes other forms of data such as SMS, instant messaging and email. A 'telecommunications system' is a telecommunications network within Australia or that part of an international network that is within Australia. It includes any equipment, lines or facilities connected to the network. A recording made by a microphone external to the telephone *after* the sound of the speaker's voice has left the telecommunications system does not amount to an interception[3]. Instead, this would fall under the 'listening devices' jurisdiction of the States and Territories. Such offences are discussed below.

[1] Telecommunications (Interception and Access) Act 1979 (Cwlth), s 7(1)(a).
[2] Telecommunications (Interception and Access) Act 1979 (Cwlth), s 7(1)(b) and (c).
[3] *R v Oliver* (1984) 57 ALR 543 at 548; *Clyne v Bowman* (1987) 11 NSWLR 341 at 345–6.

6.40 Information obtained by intercepting telecommunications is inadmissible in a legal proceeding[1] and it is an offence to communicate, use, make a record of or give evidence of such information[2]. Where communications are intercepted pursuant to a valid warrant, an officer of the relevant agency may communicate the intercepted information for a purpose connected with an investigation, a proceeding, the keeping of records or any other permitted purpose[3]. There are certain 'exempt proceedings' in which it is lawful to give intercepted information as evidence[4]. In these circumstances the information is admissible as evidence[5].

[1] Telecommunications (Interception and Access) Act 1979 (Cwlth), s 77.
[2] Telecommunications (Interception and Access) Act 1979 (Cwlth), s 63.
[3] Telecommunications (Interception and Access) Act 1979 (Cwlth), ss 67 and 73.
[4] Telecommunications (Interception and Access) Act 1979 (Cwlth), ss 5(1), 5(B).
[5] Telecommunications (Interception and Access) Act 1979 (Cwlth), ss 77(1)(a) and 77(3).

6.41 A person issued with a warrant to intercept telecommunications is under an obligation to take all reasonable steps to protect the secrecy of information obtained under the warrant and to ensure the information is not disclosed except as expressly permitted by legislation[1]. Where the chief officer of an agency is satisfied that information obtained by interception that is in the possession of the agency is not likely to be required for a purpose connected with an investigation, a proceeding, the keeping of records or other permitted purposes, he or she must ensure that records of the information are destroyed[2].

[1] *Brown v Cmr of Australian Federal Police* (1988) 15 ALD 318.
[2] Telecommunications (Interception and Access) Act 1979 (Cwlth), s 79.

6.42 The Telecommunications (Interception and Access) Act 1979 (Cwlth) also prohibits accessing a 'stored communication', or authorising or permitting another person to do so without the knowledge of either the receiver or the sender of the communication[1]. A stored communication is one that is not passing over a telecommunications system but is held on equipment in the possession of a carrier. Officers of law enforcement agencies may apply for warrants to access stored communications[2]. A warrant in respect of a person will be granted if there are reasonable grounds for suspecting that a particular carrier holds stored communications that the person has made, or that another person has made, and for which that person is the intended recipient, and the information likely to be obtained by accessing the stored communications would be likely to assist in the investigation of a serious criminal offence. In exercising the discretion to issue a warrant, a judicial officer must consider the privacy implications, the gravity of the criminal offence involved, how useful the information will be and the extent to which alternative methods of investigation are available[3].

[1] Telecommunications (Interception and Access) Act 1979 (Cwlth), s 108.
[2] Telecommunications (Interception and Access) Act 1979 (Cwlth), s 110 and 117.
[3] Telecommunications (Interception and Access) Act 1979 (Cwlth), s 116.

6.43 It is an offence to communicate, make a record of, make use of or give evidence of information obtained by accessing a stored communication, whether in contravention of s 108 or pursuant to a stored communications warrant[1]. However, there are exceptions to this general provision; for example, employees of carriers may communicate information gained by obtaining access to stored communications to officers executing warrants[2] and law enforcement officers may communicate such information in connection with the investigation of serious offences[3]. Stored communications are only admissible as evidence in criminal proceedings for certain offences[4]. If the chief officer of an enforcement agency is satisfied that information or a record that was obtained by obtaining access to stored communications is not likely to be required for criminal investigation or proceedings, he or she must order the information or record to be destroyed[5].

[1] Telecommunications (Interception and Access) Act 1979 (Cwlth), s 133.
[2] Telecommunications (Interception and Access) Act 1979 (Cwlth), s 135.
[3] Telecommunications (Interception and Access) Act 1979 (Cwlth), s 139.
[4] Telecommunications (Interception and Access) Act 1979 (Cwlth), s 147.
[5] Telecommunications (Interception and Access) Act 1979 (Cwlth), s 150.

6.44 The Review of the Regulation of Access to Communications ('Blunn Report')[1] found that sound policy reasons exist for maintaining the distinction between interception of 'real time' communications and access to stored data. The Blunn Report's recommendations resulted in the enactment of the Telecommunications (Interception) Amendment Bill 2006, which inserted provisions regarding stored communications into the Telecommunications (Interception and Access) Act 1979. Prior to this, the Act only dealt with interception of real-time communications.

[1] Anthony S Blunn AO *Report of the Review of the Regulation of Access to Communications* (2005).

6.45 Under the Telecommunications Act 1997 (Cwlth), it is an offence for carriers, carriage service providers or their employees to disclose or use the contents or substance of a communication that is, or has been, carried by a carrier or carriage service provider which comes to their knowledge or into their possession in the course of business[1]. The exceptions to this are:

(a)   where disclosure occurs in the performance of a person's duties as an employee;

(b)   where a person is summoned as witness in proceedings;

(c)   where an authorised officer of a law enforcement agency has certified that the disclosure or use is reasonably necessary for the enforcement of the criminal law, enforcement of a pecuniary penalty or the protection of public revenue;

(d)   disclosure to the Australian Security Intelligence Organisation in connection with the performance of its functions;

(e)   disclosure to the Australian Communications and Media Authority or the Australian Competition and Consumer Commission;

(f)   disclosure in circumstances where the sender and recipient of the communication might reasonably be expected to would consent and disclosure by carriers and service providers to each other for business purposes[2].

[1]   Telecommunications Act 1997 (Cwlth), s 276.
[2]   Telecommunications Act 1997 (Cwlth), ss 279, 281–284, 290 and 291.

6.46 State legislation prohibits the use of listening devices to record or listen to a private conversation by people who are not parties to the conversation[1]. A private conversation is a conversation that occurs in circumstances that may reasonably be taken to indicate that any of the parties to it desires it to be heard only by themselves. A party to a private conversation may not record it except with the express or implied consent of all the principal parties to the conversation (except in Victoria, Queensland and Tasmania, where a party to a private conversation may record it without consent).

[1]   Listening Devices Act 1984 (NSW); Listening Devices Act 1992 (ACT); Surveillance Devices Act 1999 (Vic); Listening Devices Act 1991 (Tas); Listening and Surveillance Act 1972 (SA); Surveillance Devices Act 1998 (WA); Surveillance Devices Act 2000 (NT); Invasion of Privacy Act 1971 (Qld).

6.47 It is an offence to possess recordings of private conversations that a person knows have been obtained by the use of a listening device in contravention of the legislation, except with the consent of the parties to the conversation. It is also an offence to communicate or publish a record of a private conversation that the publisher knows was made using a listening device except with the consent of the parties. A party to a private conversation may publish the contents of a private conversation to another party to that conversation. The legislation provides for warrants authorising the recording of private conversations. Unlawfully obtained evidence of private conversations is inadmissible in all civil and criminal proceedings.

6.48 Since the abolition of the 'best evidence' rule, evidence of the contents of tape recordings may be given in at least two ways:

(a)   by tendering a document that is a copy of the document in question and which has been produced by a device that reproduces the contents of a document[1]; or

(b)   by tendering a document which is a transcript of the words[2].

The tape recording may be used as evidence of the conversations or other sounds recorded.

[1]   Evidence Act (Cwlth), s 48(1)(b).
[2]   Evidence Act (Cwlth), s 48(1)(c).

Admissibility

6.49 The Crimes Act 1914 (Cwlth) does not establish any evidentiary consequences for failure to comply with the Act when executing a search warrant. Evidence collected during the improper execution of a search warrant, or without a search warrant, may be excluded under common law principles or under the statutory power to exclude improperly or illegally obtained evidence. Under s 138 of the Uniform Evidence Acts, evidence which is collected improperly or illegally may be rendered inadmissible and excluded as evidence. The matters which a court may take into account when determining if evidence should be excluded include (but are not limited to):

(a) the probative value of the evidence;

(b) the importance of the evidence in the proceedings;

(c) the nature of the relevant offence;

(d) the gravity of the impropriety or contravention;

(e) whether the impropriety or contravention was deliberate or reckless;

(f) whether the impropriety or contravention was contrary to, or inconsistent with, a right of the person recognised by the International Covenant on Civil and Political Rights;

(g) whether any other proceedings have been or are likely to be take in relation to the impropriety or contravention; and

(h) the difficulty (if any) of obtaining evidence without impropriety or contravention of Australian law.

The Court must also refuse to admit prosecution evidence if the probative value of that evidence is outweighed by the danger of unfair prejudice to the defendant[1].

[1] Uniform Evidence Acts, s 137.

6.50 Additionally, public interest immunity may be pleaded in order to exclude evidence collected in relation to a search warrant. Section 130 of the Uniform Evidence Acts provides that evidence may be excluded if the public interest in admitting the evidence is outweighed by the public interest in preserving secrecy or confidentiality. In *Marinovich v DPP*[1], public interest immunity was successfully pleaded. It was held that the applicant and his legal representative could not inspect the affidavit of a police officer produced to the judge who had issued the warrant authorising the use of a listening device, as this would have revealed highly confidential information such as police methods of investigation.

[1] (1987) 14 ALD 315 at 316–317.

Defects in warrant

6.51 In some circumstances, a defect in a search warrant may make the warrant invalid. However, a search warrant is not invalidated by a defect, other than a defect which affects the substance of the warrant in a material particular. A material particular means 'no more or no less than that the defect must be of moment or of significance, not merely trivial or inconsequential'[1].

[1]   *Minister for Immigration v Dela Cruz* (1992) 34 FCR 348.

6.52 Thus, where a warrant is formally defective because it is unsigned, undated, executed after it has expired, executed at the wrong place or wrong time, fails to specify the thing to be searched, a court will be required to determine whether the defect affected the substance of the warrant in any material particular in order to make a determination as to whether the warrant was invalid. In *Ousley v R*[1] the court accepted that a search warrant may be invalid if it is so vaguely worded that a person affected by it cannot know the object of the search.

[1]   (1997) 192 CLR 69.

Seizure of evidence relating to other offences

6.53 Section 3F(1)(d) of the Crimes Act 1914 (Cwlth) allows an executing officer to seize things or items found at the premises during the search which he or she believes to be evidential material in relation to an offence to which the warrant relates or evidential material in relation to another offence that is an indictable offence. This means that evidence in relation to another offence, not specified in the search warrant, can be properly seized and will be admissible evidence of the commission of that offence, providing the search is confined in kind and scope to that which is necessary to find the items for which the search is authorised[1].

[1]   Crimes Act 1914 (Cwlth), s 3F(1)(c).

6.54 This means that if an officer executing a warrant in relation to tax offences searches data contained on, or accessible from, a computer to locate evidence in relation to that offence, they may also collect evidence in relation to another (usually limited to an indictable) offence. This evidence, although not evidence relating to the search warrant, may be used as evidence in prosecuting the further charge.

Disclosure obligations

6.55 Under the Crimes Act 1914 (Cwlth) any person may apply for a warrant. However, a search warrant may only be executed by a constable[1]. Under the State and Territory legislation, usually only a constable can apply for a search warrant. In an application, the person applying for the warrant must give information relating to the warrant under oath or in a sworn form if the application is via telephone. A search warrant will be issued if information is provided by the applicant which demonstrates that there exists reasonable grounds for suspecting that there is, or there will be within the next 72 hours, any evidentiary materials at the premises[2]. 'Evidentiary material' is any thing relevant to an indictable or summary offence[3]. Therefore, the test for the issue of a search warrant is an objective one and the applicant will need to show that there are reasonable grounds for suspecting that there is or will be material on the premises which relates to a indictable or summary offence.

1   Crimes Act 1914 (Cwlth), s 3E(4).
2   Crimes Act 1914 (Cwlth), s 3E(1).
3   Crimes Act 1914 (Cwlth), s 3C.

6.56 The person applying for the warrant must also disclose whether they have previously applied for a warrant in relation to the same person or premises and the result of that application[1].

1   Crimes Act 1914 (Cwlth), s 3E(4).

Consequences of non-disclosure

6.57 It is an offence in an application for a warrant to make a statement which the person knows is false or misleading in a material particular[1]. Such an offence carries a maximum penalty of two years' imprisonment.

1   Crimes Act 1914 (Cwlth), s 3Z.

Criminal offences relating specifically to electronic equipment

Computer hacking

6.58 Part 10.7 of the Criminal Code 1995 (Cwth) creates several computer offences. A person commits an offence if he or she knowingly causes unauthorised access or modification of data held in a computer, or unauthorised impairment of electronic communication to or from a computer, intending to commit or facilitate commission of a serious offence against any State, Territory or Commonwealth law by so doing[1]. It is an offence to use the Internet to cause an unauthorised modification of computer data where the person knows the modification is unauthorised and is reckless as to whether the modification will impair access to the data or the reliability, security or operation of the data[2].

1   Criminal Code 1995 (Cwlth), s 477.1.
2   Criminal Code 1995 (Cwlth), s 477.2.

6.59 It is also an offence to have possession or control of data with the intent that the data be used to commit one of these offences[1].

1   Criminal Code 1995 (Cwlth), s 478.3.

6.60 It is an offence to intentionally cause unauthorised access to, or modification of, restricted data if the restricted data is held on a Commonwealth computer or is held on behalf of the Commonwealth, or if the access or modification occurs via the Internet[1]. Restricted data means computer data to which access is restricted by means of an access control system.

[1] Criminal Code 1995 (Cwlth), s 478.1.

6.61 It is an offence to intentionally cause unauthorised impairment of the reliability, security or operation of data held on an electronic storage device if the device is owned or leased by a Commonwealth entity[1].

[1] Criminal Code 1995 (Cwlth), s 478.2.

6.62 State legislation also criminalises various forms of computer hacking and misuse[1].

[1] QLD Criminal Code, s 409D; VIC Crimes Act 1958, ss 247A–247(I); WA Criminal Code, s 440A; NSW Crimes Act 1900, ss 308–308I.

Child pornography and paedophilia

6.63 State legislation also criminalises the use of computers to produce, obtain access to, or store child pornography[1] or to procure minors for sexual activities[2].

[1] VIC Crimes Act 1958, s 68; NSW Crimes Act 1900, s 91G.
[2] QLD Criminal Code, s 218A; WA Criminal Code, s 204B.

Spam

6.64 The Spam Act 2003 (Cwth) prohibits the sending of 'unsolicited commercial electronic messaging'. This includes email, SMS (short message service) and other forms of electronic messaging, but not facsimile transmissions. Commercial electronic messages must not be sent without the express or inferred consent of the recipient. The Spam Act requires all commercial electronic messages to contain accurate information about the person or organisation that authorised the message as well as a functional 'unsubscribe' facility to allow people to opt out of receiving future messages. The Act also prohibits the supply, acquisition or use of address lists and software that harvests electronic addresses from the Internet.

Threats

6.65 Legislation prohibits the use of computers and the Internet to threaten[1].

[1] NSW Crimes Act 1900, s 93IH; Cwlth Criminal Code, s 474.15.

Possession of prohibited devices

6.66 Section 189 of the Radiocommunications Act 1992 (Cwth) makes it an offence to operate, supply or possess for the purposes of operation or supply, a prohibited device without reasonable excuse. The penalty is two years' imprisonment for an individual or 200 penalty units (currently A$220,000) for a corporation. Section 190 of the Radiocommunications Act 1992 (Cwth) confers power on the Australian Communications and Media Authority (ACMA) to prohibit certain radiocommunications devices and equipment pursuant to the Act. In 2004 ACMA made a declaration prohibiting mobile telephone jammers. Consequently, the use or possession of such devices is illegal[1].

[1]   Radiocommunications Act 1992 (Cwth), s 189.

CIVIL LAW

Pre-commencement powers

Identity discovery

6.67 Where an applicant is unable, after making reasonable inquiries, to sufficiently ascertain the identity or whereabouts of a prospective defendant for the purpose of commencing proceedings, Federal and most State court rules provide that a court may order a third party who may have information or documents which would assist in obtaining this information, to attend court to give evidence and (or) to give discovery to the applicant of all documents in their possession that relate to the identity or whereabouts of the prospective defendant[1]. A potential litigant would be able to utilise these rules to obtain information from an Internet Services Provider or Internet content host. The rules may be used against a 'mere witness' or bystander, hence they facilitate preliminary discovery against any entity on the Internet that is in a position to identify the prospective defendant. The applicant is not required to show a prime facie case against the prospective respondent[2].

[1]   NSW Uniform Civil Procedure Rules 2005, r 5.2; Vic General Rules of Procedure in Civil Proceedings 1996, r 32.03; Federal Court Rules, r 15A.3; ACT Court Procedures Rules 2006, r 650; WA Supreme Court Rules 1971, r 26A.3; SA Supreme Court Civil Rules 2006, r 146.
[2]   *Levis v McDonald* (1997) 75 FCR 36 at 41.

Discovery from a prospective respondent

6.68 Where there is reasonable cause to believe that an applicant has or may have the right to obtain relief against an identified prospective defendant, and after having made reasonable inquiries is unable to obtain sufficient information to decide whether or not to commence proceedings against that person, court rules also provide for an order that the prospective defendant give discovery of all documents in his or her possession that relate to this question[1].

[1]   NSW Uniform Civil Procedure Rules 2005, r 5.3; Vic General Rules of Procedure in Civil Proceedings 1996, r 32.05; Federal Court Rules, r 15A.6; ACT Court Procedures Rules 2006, r 651; WA Supreme Court Rules 1971, r 26A.4; SA Supreme Court Civil Rules 2006, r 146.

6.69 The 'reasonable cause to believe' requirement does not require an applicant to demonstrate a prima facie case but the applicant must do more than merely assert that there is a case against the prospective defendant[1]. An order may be made when a defendant has already established a prima facie case but still lacks information regarding whether to proceed[2]. It is not sufficient that the applicant genuinely believes the right exists, as the court may determine that this belief is unfounded, an 'objective foundation' that takes the existence of a right to relief beyond a mere allegation, suspicion or assertion[3]. The cases demonstrate that the threshold is set at a 'low level'[4]. In *Sony Music Entertainment (Australia) Ltd v University of Tasmania*, the existence, on a respondent's servers, of computer files in a form commonly used by computer pirates and with names matching those of well-known recordings was sufficient to ground a successful application, even though no direct evidence of piracy existed[5].

1   *Hooper v Kirella Pty Ltd* (1999) 96 FCR 1 at 11–12.
2   *Alphapharm Pty Ltd v Eli Lilly Australia Pty Ltd* [1996] FCA 391.
3   *Minister for Health & Aged Care v Harrington Associates Ltd* [1999] FCA 549; *C7 Pty Ltd v Foxtel Management Pty Ltd* [2001] FCA 1864.
4   *Gull Petroleum (WA) Ltd v Tah Land Pty Ltd* [2001] FCA 1531.
5   [2003] FCA 532.

6.70 These rules are generally only available against the prospective defendant, but will also be against a third party that has secondary liability for an infringement (for example, by allegedly facilitating or authorising the infringement). In such a case, information on the activities of Internet users will be discoverable where this information is known by the third party or passes through its network[1].

1   *Sony Music Entertainment (Australia) Ltd v University of Tasmania* [2003] FCA 532.

Destruction of evidence

6.71 Destruction of evidence that a party knows may be relevant to a potential litigation will usually constitute contempt of court or an attempt to pervert the course of justice if the destruction is attributable to a deliberate strategy to render the documents unavailable for litigation rather than a genuine document management policy. If this is proved at trial, adverse inferences may be drawn against a defendant or pleadings may be struck out. However the Victorian Court of Appeal has recognised that 'there must be some balance struck between the right of any company to manage its own documents, whether by retaining them or destroying them, and the right of the litigant to have resort to the documents of the other side'[1]. In Victoria there is now specific legislation prohibiting the destruction of evidence[2].

1   *British American Tobacco Australia Services Ltd v Cowell (representing the Estate of McCabe (decd))* [2002] VSCA 197 at 173.
2   Crimes (Document Destruction) Act (2006) VIC.

Urgent search and seizure orders ('Anton Piller orders')

6.72 Anton Piller orders are a form of preliminary discovery. They allow applicants to search and seize property in order to preserve vital evidence which may otherwise be destroyed by the other party.

6.73 The jurisdiction of State Supreme Courts to grant Anton Piller orders derives from their inherent jurisdiction as superior courts of record[1]. The jurisdiction of the Federal Court and courts of limited statutory jurisdiction derives from implied jurisdiction. In addition, the power to grant Anton Piller orders (alternatively called 'search orders' in the legislation) has been provided by statute in Queensland, South Australia, Tasmania, New South Wales, the Australian Capital Territory and the Commonwealth[2].

[1]   *Simsek v MacPhee* (1982) 148 CLR 636.
[2]   Uniform Civil Procedure Rules 1999 (QLD), r 261; Supreme Court Rules 1987 (SA), r 68.4; Federal Court Rules 1979 (Cth), Ord 25B; Uniform Civil Procedure Rules 2005 (NSW), r 25.18–25.24; Supreme Court Rules 2000 (Tas), r 937 I–O; Court Procedures Rules 2006 (ACT) rr 751–753.

6.74 The three essential preconditions for granting Anton Piller orders were described in *Piller (Anton) KG v Manufacturing Processes Ltd* [1976] Ch 55 CA. The preconditions are that the applicant has a very strong prima facie case, that the potential or actual damage to the applicant if the order is not made will be very serious, and that clear evidence exists that the respondent possesses important evidentiary material and there is a real possibility that they will destroy it prior to the proceedings. These common law requirements are mirrored in the statutory formulations of search orders.

6.75 An Anton Piller order will be more readily granted in respect of electronic evidence than if the evidence were in hard-copy, due to the particularly fragile nature of electronically stored evidence. In *Liberty Financial Pty Ltd v Scott* it was held that 'the relative ease with which electronic evidence can be destroyed or deleted' combined with 'the powerful incentive on the part of those who may have misappropriated confidential and commercially sensitive information to conceal evidence of their wrongdoing' was persuasive in finding that a real likelihood of removal or destruction of the evidence existed.

[1]   [2002] FCA 345 at [78].

6.76 The unique nature of dynamic electronic information was considered by the Federal Court in *Universal Music Australia Pty Ltd v Sharman License Holdings Ltd*. It was suggested that where evidence is of a transient or highly perishable nature Anton Piller orders may be made to preserve or record it even if there is no evidence that it is likely to be deliberately destroyed. Wilcox J noted 'it is one thing to expect parties to litigation not to destroy existing evidence; it is another to expect them conscientiously to co-operate in the creation and recording of evidence useful to their opponents'.

[1]   (2004) 205 ALR 319 at 336.

6.77 The Court Rules also provide that a solicitor independent of the applicant's firm of solicitors must be appointed to supervise the execution of the search order[1]. The Federal Court and some State Supreme Courts have issued practice notes outlining their usual practice in making Anton Piller orders[2]. These aim to safeguard the respondent's rights in view of the fact that the Anton Piller order 'is an extraordinary remedy in that it is intrusive, potentially disruptive and made ex-parte and prior to judgment'[3]. The practice notes specify that the independent solicitor should be experienced in commercial litigation and, preferably, in the execution of search orders. The responsibilities of the independent solicitor include explaining the terms of the search order to the respondent, supervising the carrying out of the order, taking custody of all the items removed from the premises pending further orders of the court and, if the independent solicitor considers it necessary to remove a computer from the premises, to return the computer to the premises within the time prescribed by the order with a list of any documents that have been copied or printed out. The practice notes also provide that:

(a)   ordinarily the search party should not include the applicant or the applicant's directors, officers, employees or partners or anyone else associated with the applicant (except the applicant's solicitor);

(b)   the applicant's solicitor must undertake to the court to pay the reasonable costs of the independent solicitor and computer expert. The applicant's solicitor must also undertake not to disclose to the applicant, without leave of the court, any information the solicitor has acquired during or as a result of execution of the search order;

(c)   if the respondent's computers need to be searched by a specialised computer expert or imaged this may only be done by an independent computer expert that is bound to give undertakings to the court; and

(d)   the applicant is not permitted, without the court's leave, to inspect things removed from the premises (or copies thereof) or to be given any information about them by members of the search party.

[1]   Federal Court Rules 1979 (Cwlth), r 25B.6.
[2]   Federal Court Practice Note No 24: Search Orders (also known as 'Anton Piller orders') issued 5 May 2006; Supreme Court of NSW Practice Note SC Gen 13: Search Orders (also known as 'Anton Piller orders') issued 14 June 2006; Supreme Court of Tasmania Practice Direction Search Orders (also known as 'Anton Piller orders') issued 19 July 2006.
[3]   Federal Court Practice Note No 24: Search Orders (also known as 'Anton Piller orders') issued 5 May 2006.

Discovery

6.78 A court can require parties to litigation to discover all relevant documents that are in their possession, custody or control. The term 'documents' has been interpreted very widely by the courts to encompass electronic files and databases as well as the physical media on which they are stored (eg hard drives, CD-ROMs or back-up tapes)[1]. Traditionally, the obligations of parties subject to a discovery process have involved the production of a hardcopy document or an identical copy of that document. Therefore, the rules governing discovery can sometimes produce anomalies in the context of electronically stored materials. As electronic information is practically impossible to eliminate entirely, parties may be unaware of electronic documents that are in their possession, custody or control. For example, emails that have been deleted may still remain on a hard drive or servers. In order to give complete discovery, a computer expert may have to be engaged to retrieve information in the form of digital footprints.

[1]   *Sony Music Entertainment (Australia) Ltd v University of Tasmania* [2003] FCA 532.

6.79 Because of the large amount of data capable of being stored electronically, the scope of discovery of electronic documents can be extremely broad. In *Sony Music Entertainment (Australia) Ltd v University of Tasmania*[1], Sony sought discovery of information from the University's computers to help identify individuals who had breached copyright by downloading music files. The University offered to conduct 140 targeted searches over the data using specific keywords such as 'mp3'. The court accepted Sony's argument that this approach would not catch all relevant material. It allowed Sony's computer expert to take possession of the CD-ROMs and back-up tapes to conduct a more rigorous search. The retrieved data was then to be handed over to the University so it could assess relevance and make confidentiality or privilege claims prior to making discovery. This approach reflects the fact that a single computer storage device can contain many discrete files. While the device is a single 'document' within the definition of the Uniform Evidence Acts, only some portions of the information contained in that document (that is, the files recorded on the device) may be relevant. An order limiting the scope of discovery to relevant files is analogous to ordering discovery of a physical document masked to conceal irrelevant or confidential material.

[1]   [2003] FCA 532.

6.80 Courts have been reluctant to use their discretion to relieve parties of their obligation to discover electronic documents merely because the task would prove costly and time consuming. In *BT (Australasia) Pty Ltd v State of New South Wales & Anor (no 9)*[1], a party to discovery was required to restore up to 970 back-up tapes in order to recover deleted emails and their attachments because some of the documents 'may have contained relevant information.' Despite finding that the 'purpose of making and retaining the [back-up] tapes was essentially disaster recovery and not archival' the court rejected the submission that this task would be too burdensome due to the vast amount of information kept on back-up tapes. Sackville J stated 'I do not think that technical sophistication is a prerequisite to a litigant or its advisors making inquiries to ascertain whether discoverable electronic communications or documents have been recorded and retained in retrievable form'.

[1]   [1998] FCA 363.

6.81 In *NT Power Generation Pty Ltd v Power & Water Authority*[1] the court required a party to proceedings to discover emails which had been deleted but still existed on back-up tapes stored for the purpose of disaster recovery. The court held that despite the time, effort and expense involved in retrieving the emails the interests of justice dictated this be done.

[1]   [1999] FCA 1623.

Solicitors' obligations

6.82 A solicitor has a professional duty to ensure that a client gives complete discovery and must be personally satisfied with the adequacy of the list of discoverable documents produced by a client[1]. Statutory provisions in some jurisdictions require a solicitor to fully explain the disclosure requirements involved in discovery to a client and certify that this has been done[2].

1   *Ferguson v Mackaness Produce Pty Ltd* [1970] 2 NSWLR 66 at 68.
2   Court Procedures Rules 2006 (ACT) r 672; Uniform Civil Procedure Rules (1999) (QLD) r 226.

Non-compliance with discovery orders

6.83 Failure to comply with a court order to give discovery may result in the proceedings or defence being struck out[1].

1   QLD Uniform Civil Procedure Rules 1999 r 225(2); SA Supreme Court Rules 1987 r 59.06(1); Vic Supreme Court (General Civil Procedure) Rules 2005 r 24.02; WA Rules of the Supreme Court Order 26 r 15(1); Tas Supreme Court Rules 2000 r 372; NT Supreme Court Rules r 24.02; ACT Court Procedures Rules 2006 r 671.

Electronic Discovery

6.84 The Federal Court and State Supreme Courts have issued practice notes advising parties involved in civil litigation to utilise electronic discovery[1]. Parties to civil litigation are encouraged to use electronic data or databases to create lists of their discoverable documents, to undertake discovery by exchanging electronic data or databases created in compliance with an agreed protocol, exchange electronic versions of court documents such as pleadings and affidavits, to arrange for inspection of discovered documents by means of images if appropriate and to consider and make submissions regarding the use of information technology during the hearing itself.

1   NSW Supreme Court Practice Note No. 7; Vic Supreme Court Practice Note No 1 of 2002; Federal Court Practice Note No 17; Qld Supreme Court Practice Direction No 8 of 2004; SA Supreme Court Practice Direction No 52; NT Supreme Court Practice Direction No 2 of 2002.

Confidentiality

6.85 There is an implied undertaking by the recipient of discovered material not to use the discovered documents, or material contained in them, for any ulterior purpose other than the proceedings in relation to which they were produced. A breach of this duty will be punishable as contempt of court. If discovered documents contain commercially sensitive or confidential information the court may require the party seeking inspection to give express confidentiality undertakings and may limit the persons authorised to inspect the documents (most commonly to outside legal advisors)[1].

1   For example, *ABC v Parish* (1980) 43 FLR 129; *Magellen Petroleum Australia Ltd v Sagasco Amedeus Pty Ltd* [1994] Qd R 37.

6.86 The court may allow a party, upon application, to use discovered documents for a purpose other than conduct of the proceedings in which they were discovered if there are 'circumstances which take the matter out of the ordinary course' which make such an exercise of the court's discretion in the interests of justice[1]. The same implied undertaking not to use documents for a collateral purpose applies to 'wherever the coercive power of the court has been employed to enable a person to obtain the documents of another'[2] including in relation to witness statements, answers to interrogatories, affidavits, subpoenaed documents and documents obtained pursuant to Anton Piller orders.

[1] *Holpittt Pty Ltd v Varium Pty Ltd* (1991) 29 FCR 576.
[2] *Duke Group Ltd (in liq) v Plimer* (1993) 60 SASR 29 at 34.

Electronic document management systems (parties and the courts)

6.87 Federal Court and State Supreme Court practice notes provide that a party served with court documents such as interrogatories, pleadings or affidavits may ask the other party to provide a copy of that document in electronic format[1].

[1] NSW Supreme Court Practice Note No. 7; Vic Supreme Court Practice Note No. 1 of 2002; Federal Court Practice Note No. 17; Qld Supreme Court Practice Direction No. 8 of 2004; SA Supreme Court Practice Direction No. 52; NT Supreme Court Practice Direction No. 2 of 2002.

Electronic Filing

6.88 Order 1 rule 5AC of the Federal Court Rules allows documents to be filed and lodged electronically. Documents may be filed through the court's homepage in a range of formats including rtf, pdf, gif, jpeg and doc, and fees may be paid online by credit card. Under rule 3.4 of the Uniform Civil Procedure Rules (NSW), electronic filing of documents is also available in the NSW Supreme Court. The County Court of Victoria, Magistrates Courts in Queensland and Victoria, the New South Wales Land and Environment Court and the Victorian Civil and Administrative Tribunal also utilise electronic filing.

Electronic Courts

6.89 The Federal Court's online forum is a virtual court that assists in management of pre-trial matters by allowing directions and interlocutory orders to be made online via the court's website.

6.90 In May 2007 NSW Courts will introduce CourtLink eServices, This will include the following services:

(a) e-filing: electronic filing of documents;
(b) ecmCourt: a bulletin board where parties can post submissions seeking directions or documents for perusal by other parties and the presiding judicial officer, and orders can be made by the judicial officer;
(c) eListing: a facility allowing parties to select available listing dates;

(d)   eInformation: parties may view online any details that are not suppressed, including any electronic documents lodged in the case;

(e)   eTranscripts: a facility allowing people to order, pay for and download a transcript of a hearing.

PRIVACY

6.91 Organisations frequently wish to retain electronic records of documents pursuant to statutory requirements or in anticipation of potential litigation. However, privacy legislation imposes legal obligations to destroy information or documents relating to the personal information of individuals.

6.92 Section 16A of the Privacy Act 1988 (Cwlth) mandates organisations to comply with the National Privacy Principles ('NPPs') set out in Schedule 3 to the Act. The NPPs regulate the collection and subsequent use of personal information that is stored in a record by an organisation. Organisations may need to comply with these obligations if they:

(a)   have an annual turnover of more than A\$3 million (or are related to another business, for example, its holding company or a subsidiary, that has an annual turn over of more then A\$3 million); or

(b)   collect, disclose or use credit information.

6.93 Under the NPPs, organisations are required to:

(a)   take reasonable steps to make sure that the personal information they collect, uses and disclose is accurate, complete and up-to-date (NPP 3);

(b)   take reasonable steps to protect the personal information they hold from misuse and from unauthorised access, modification and disclosure (NPP 4.1);

(c)   take reasonable steps to destroy or permanently de-identify personal information if it is no longer required for any authorised purpose (NPP 4.2); and

(d)   provide the individual in respect of whom they hold personal information with access to the information on request (NPP 6.1, refer to the Act for several important exceptions).

6.94 Personal information is defined broadly as information or an opinion (including information or an opinion forming part of a database), whether true or not, about an individual whose identity is apparent, or can reasonably be ascertained, from the information or opinion[1].

[1]   Privacy Act 1988 (Cwlth), s 6.

6.95 An organisation must not collect personal information unless the information is necessary for one or more of its functions and activities[1]. A company can only collect personal information about individuals by 'lawful and fair means'[2] and not in an unreasonably intrusive way. At or before the time (or, if that is not practicable, as soon as practicable after) an organisation collects personal information about an individual, the organisation must take reasonable steps to ensure that the individual is aware of:

(a)   the identity of the organisation and how to contact it;
(b)   the fact that he or she is able to gain access to the information; and
(c)   the purposes for which the information is collected and the organisation (or types of organisations) to which information of that kind is usually disclosed. Where the purpose for which the information is collected is obvious it need not be disclosed. However, any other purpose should be disclosed whether it is related or unrelated.

[1]   NPP 1.1.
[2]   NPP 1.2.

6.96 If personal information that is required to be destroyed is stored electronically it is important that the 'destroyed' information cannot be easily retrieved from digital footprints or that back-up tapes containing the information do not still exist.

Chapter 7

CANADA

ROBERT J CURRIE AND STEVE COUGHLAN[1]

INTRODUCTION

7.01 This chapter will survey briefly the state of the law regarding the gathering, discovery and admissibility of electronic evidence in Canada. As a general comment, it is offered that Canada is a comparatively wealthy and technologically-developed Western country and, in terms of the creation and use of electronic data, it is probably abreast of most other OECD member states. Perhaps because of its relatively small population (approximately 32 million) the amount of litigation is much smaller compared to other countries, particularly the United States. As a result, while both the legislatures and the common law are grappling with the new legal frontiers created by the need to deal with electronic evidence, the law is more well-developed in some areas than in others.

7.02 A key feature that should be noted for the foreign reader is Canada's jurisdictional structure, which is much more segmented than some[2]. Canada is a federal state, and the constitution divides jurisdiction over legislative matters between the 'federal' or central government and the governments of the ten provinces and three territories. There is, therefore, a regulatory jurisdiction inherent in each level of government. The most important distinction for present purposes is that the federal government has jurisdiction over criminal law while jurisdiction over civil and property matters rests with the provinces and territories. Canada is a constitutional monarchy and member of the Commonwealth; the monarch of England is formally the head of state for Canada, and both the federal and provincial governments are each often referred to as the 'Crown'.

---

[1]   Robert J Currie and Steve Coughlan thank Pat Canning (LLB Dalhousie, 2006) for his very able research assistance and John D Gregory (Ministry of the Attorney General, Ontario) for his comments.

[2]   An authoritative general resource on Canadian constitutional law is Peter Hogg *Constitutional Law of Canada* (looseleaf edn, 1992).

7.03 Each province has a court structure that can be roughly broken into inferior, superior and appellate courts. All three levels of court can administer both federal and provincial or territorial law. Operating parallel to the provincial courts is the Federal Court of Canada, which has concurrent jurisdiction with the provincial courts in civil cases where the Federal Crown is a litigant, and also has jurisdiction over cases in some specialised areas within federal legislative jurisdiction (tax, admiralty, immigration, intellectual property)[1]. Appeals from both the provincial appellate courts and the Federal Court of Appeal are heard by the Supreme Court of Canada, which is the highest appellate court.

[1] There are also federally and provincially-constituted administrative tribunals, appeals from which generally go to the Federal Court of Canada or the provincial appellate courts, respectively.

CANADIAN EVIDENCE LAW[1]

Essential information

7.04 As in most common law jurisdictions[2], Canadian evidence law emerges primarily from the common law. The common law of evidence does not vary between jurisdictions so each court will apply essentially the same evidence law regardless of whether it is hearing a case based in federal or provincial competence. However, the common law is modified and supplemented by evidence statutes in each jurisdiction, each of which modifies the law of evidence within that legislative realm. Criminal and federal regulatory matters come under the *Canada Evidence Act*[3], while each of the provinces and territories has its own evidence statute[4].

[1] The standard reference works on Canadian evidence law are David Paciocco & Lee Stuesser *The Law of Evidence* (4th edn, 2005) and J Sopinka, S Lederman and A Bryant *The Law of Evidence in Canada* (2nd edn, 1999). On this specific topic see Alan M Gahtan *Electronic Evidence* (1999).
[2] The province of Québec is primarily a 'civil law' (in the European sense) jurisdiction and areas of provincial legislative competence come under this civil law regime. Book VII of the Civil Code of Quebec functions as that province's equivalent to the other provincial evidence statutes. Most matters peculiar to Québec law will not be given specific attention in this chapter.
[3] *Canada Evidence Act*, R.S.C. 1985, c. C-5.
[4] Eg Nova Scotia *Evidence Act*, R.S.N.S. 1989, c. 154; Ontario *Evidence Act*, R.S.O. 1990, c. E.23.

7.05 The interrelation of law and jurisdiction can be confusing. For clarity, the following may be helpful: in the province of Nova Scotia, the Supreme Court of Nova Scotia is the province's superior court. On Monday it might hear a criminal murder trial, in which it would apply the criminal law (federal, under the *Criminal Code of Canada*[1]) and in which it would adhere to the common law of evidence as modified by the *Canada Evidence Act*. On Tuesday, it might hear a civil negligence case (provincial, since it is a civil matter) in which it would adhere to the common law of evidence as modified by the Nova Scotia *Evidence Act*[2].

[1] *Criminal Code*, R.S.C. 1985, c. C-46.
[2] Nova Scotia *Evidence Act*, R.S.N.S. 1989, c 154.

7.06 Canadian litigation is adversarial in nature and maintains the traditional distinction between trier of law and trier of fact. Juries are available to function as trier of fact in both criminal and civil cases, though they are more common in the former than in the latter (and not terribly common in either).

7.07 The basic concepts which underpin Canadian evidence law will be familiar to most readers. At trial the judge, as trier of law, decides whether each item of evidence offered by any party is admissible, ie whether it can be placed before the trier of fact for consideration in its decisions as to what the facts are. For evidence to be admissible it must be relevant to a fact that is material. This is to say, the item of evidence must have some tendency to make the existence of a fact more or less probable, and that fact must be one that is at issue in the case[1].

1   For an excellent synopsis of these basic concepts see David Paciocco ' "Truth and Proof": The Basics of the Law of Evidence in a "Guilt-Based" System' (2000) 6 Can Crim L Rev 71.

7.08 Canadian evidence law also maintains the distinction between primary and secondary relevance. Evidence 'is primarily material when it is about a question of fact that is put into issue by a rule of law that has application in the case, and ... is secondarily material when it is about the value or credibility of other evidence that has been called in the case'[1]. As an example, an email from one party to another offering a sale of goods will be primarily relevant since it goes to the material issue of whether there was a contract. The testimony of the company's records-keeper regarding the technical specifications of their email storage system, by contrast, would be secondarily relevant since it goes to the integrity of the email and whether it is reliable enough to be admissible.

1   *Paciocco* (2000), p 97.

7.09 Beyond the basic relevance threshold, Canadian evidence law contains many of the traditional canons of exclusion, eg those regarding character, opinion, hearsay and so on. Over the last 30 years or so, the Supreme Court of Canada has incorporated a very pro-admissibility or 'inclusionary' tone to the law of evidence, by which all relevant and material evidence should be admitted presumptively unless legal or policy grounds clearly point to its exclusion[1]. The Court has buttressed this approach with an explicit effort to replace formalism and categorisation in evidence law with principled flexibility and discretion on the part of the trial judge. This 'principled approach' is encapsulated by the phrase 'evidence may be excluded where its probative value is outweighed by its prejudicial effect,' and of late the Court has sought to re-cast much of traditional evidence law as being applications of this principle[2].

1   *R v Corbett* [1988] 1 S.C.R. 670 at 691. See also *R v Seaboyer* (1991), 66 C.C.C. (3d) 321 at 399.
2   See J Sopinka, S Lederman and A Bryant *The Law of Evidence in Canada* (2nd edn Supplement, 2004), pp 1–6.

7.10 Two other substantive evidence laws important to this chapter should be quickly canvassed:

(a)   expert opinion: there is a distinct admissibility regime for the use of expert opinion testimony at trial. To be admissible, the expert opinion must be:

    (i)   relevant (ie both logically relevant and reliable enough to justify its admission);

    (ii)   necessary (meaning that it must provide information or inferences which the trier of fact could not reach on its own);

    (iii) given by a properly qualified expert; and

    (iv) not excluded by another rule of evidence[1].

(b)   privilege: various rules of privilege attach to evidence in certain circumstances and exempt them from disclosure in either pre-trial proceedings or at trial. Most important for litigation purposes are solicitor-client privilege and litigation privilege[2]. Solicitor-client privilege protects as confidential all communications between a lawyer and any person regarding the provision of legal advice by the lawyer to that person. Litigation privilege protects all communications, including documents, generated by a party and its solicitor which are made in contemplation of litigation including, for example, communications with experts.

[1]   *R v Mohan* (1994), 29 C.R. (4th) 243 (S.C.C.).

[2]   *Paciocco & Stuesser*, pp 208–228. See also *Blank v Canada (Minister of Justice)*, 2006 SCC 39; *General Accident Assurance Company v Chrusz* (1999), 45 O.R. (3d) 321, (1999), 180 D.L.R. (4th) 241 (Ont. C.A.).

7.11 Finally, as noted above, the common law of evidence is replaced or modified by the evidence statutes that govern trial proceedings. Similar modification can be done by the procedural rules that govern proceedings in each jurisdiction, which might abridge privilege, compel disclosure, etc. These rules, where relevant, will be covered under the sections entitled 'Criminal Litigation' and 'Civil Litigation' at paras 7.53 and 7.70, below.

Admissibility of electronic evidence

7.12 This subsection will survey some current developments regarding the admissibility of electronic evidence in Canada. Particular focus will be placed on recent statutory amendments which have entrenched rules for use by courts in making admissibility decisions. Evidentiary and procedural points which are very specific to either civil or criminal litigation will be made in the relevant sections below.

7.13 A key to understanding the Canadian approach to electronic evidence is the recognition among policy and law makers that this kind of evidence, while it is new in form and nature, can in substance be treated as documentary evidence—a kind of evidence with which the courts are well-acquainted. While this is not universally true, it is applicable to most kinds of electronic data that will be submitted by the parties in litigation: 'pure' electronic data will not usually be sought to be admitted but is more likely to underpin an expert's report. Otherwise most electronic evidence is most usefully assimilated to traditional documentary evidence for the purposes of admissibility in court, and this tends to be what Canadian courts have done[1]. Naturally, however, this needs to be done with careful attention to the unique issues involved.

[1]   See *Gahtan*, ch 9.

7.14 This point is, arguably, demonstrated by the work done on the issue by the Uniform Law Conference of Canada ('ULCC') which adopted the Uniform Electronic Evidence Act in 1998[1]. In 1997 the ULCC's working group on electronic evidence noted[2] that evidence law was in need of reform vis-à-vis electronic documents due in no small part to the tendency of courts to blur the lines between three aspects of the admissibility of documents:

(a)   the hearsay rule: documents adduced for the truth of their contents will be classified as hearsay;

(b)   authentication: to admit a document there must be evidence adduced that the document is what it is purported to be; and

(c)   the best evidence rule: the preference at common law was for a party relying on a document to provide the original of that document, or to satisfy the court that it would be reasonable to accept a copy.

[1]   Hereafter the 'Uniform Act' available, with detailed commentary, online at: http://www.ulcc.ca/en/us/index.cfm?sec=1&sub=1u2 (last visited August 21, 2006).

[2]   Uniform Law Conference of Canada, Uniform Electronic Evidence Act: Consultation Paper, March 1997, available online at: http://www.ulcc.ca/en/poam2/index.cfm?sec=1997&sub=1997hka.

7.15 Each of these evidentiary rules raises unique issues where electronic documents are concerned and the Uniform Act was formulated in an attempt to encourage coherent law reform in this regard. The Uniform Act has been adopted, either completely or in modified form, in nine Canadian jurisdictions[1]. Accordingly, it is worth exploring in some detail, using the relevant *Canada Evidence Act* provision as the focus[2] for discussion[3].

[1]   Including the *Canada Evidence Act*, ss 31.1–31.8 and the *Ontario Evidence Act*, R.S.O. 1990, c. E.23, s 34.1. See chart online at: http://www.ulcc.ca/en/cls/index.cfm?sec=4&sub=4b, under 'Electronic Evidence Amendments'.

[2]   There are very few reported decisions on the application of these legislative provisions, and those which do exist are all on the CEA provisions. We think this is not due to under-use of the provisions but, rather, because trial judges are simply applying them as a matter of course, and seriously-fought motions that would result in a reported decision are few and far between. Another contributing factor is that the civil procedure rules which govern civil cases often contain rules requiring parties to object to the 'integrity' of a document in the pre-trial phase, which settles in advance many objections that might otherwise be made at trial.

[3]   This section relies on the excellent scholarship on this point by John D Gregory 'Canadian Electronic Commerce Legislation' (2002) 17 B.F.L.R. 277, particularly pp 327–338.

7.16 While 'electronic documents' are sometimes electronic versions of paper documents (eg a scan of an existing paper document that is saved on a computer hard drive) much of the evidence required in litigation will be generated on a computer and will only see the light of day as a printout of that data. The definition of 'electronic document' in the Uniform Act is broad enough to prevent much court time being wasted on the topic, as it includes both data 'recorded or stored' on a computer system as well as 'a display, printout or other output of that data'[1].

[1]   *Canada Evidence Act*, R.S.C. 1985, c. C-46, s 31.8.

7.17 In terms of authentication of electronic documents, the Uniform Act codifies the common law rule which places the burden on the party adducing the document to provide 'evidence capable of supporting a finding that the electronic document is that which it is purported to be'[1]. Given the use of the words 'capable of supporting a finding,' this is best read as a strictly evidential burden: whether the document actually is what it purports to be will ultimately be decided by the trier of fact[2].

[1] *Canada Evidence Act*, R.S.C. 1985, c. C-46, s 31.1
[2] John D Gregory 'Canadian Electronic Commerce Legislation' (2002) 17 B.F.L.R. 277, p 331.

7.18 The other functional hurdle to the admissibility of a document is the best evidence rule. Traditionally, this rule was designed to compel a party to demonstrate the integrity of a document by either providing the original or by demonstrating that the copy adduced was sufficiently trustworthy for use by the court. The rule maps poorly on to electronic documents, which often cannot be traced down to an 'original', particularly in a networked environment. In addition, the distinction between 'original' and 'copy' is not of much use because there is usually, in practice, no discernible difference between the original and the copy. Thus, the original is not likely to be more clearly reliable than a copy.

7.19 The Uniform Act provisions provide the courts with an alternative means of assessing the integrity of electronic documents. They permit the adducing party to satisfy the best evidence rule for an electronic document by providing evidence as to 'the integrity of the electronic documents system by or in which the electronic document was recorded or stored'[1]. Several presumptions are set up to allow efficient proof of integrity, which can be established through:

(a)   proof that the storage medium was operating properly[2];
(b)   proof that the document was recorded or stored, or recorded and stored by an adverse party[3]; or
(c)   proof that the document was recorded or stored in the ordinary course of business by a party outside the litigation[4].

This integrity can be proven by way of affidavit[5], though depending on the nature of the technology, expert evidence may be required[6].

[1] *Canada Evidence Act*, R.S.C. 1985, c. C-46, s 31.2(1)(a). Note also the special provision regarding printouts of documents, which are deemed to satisfy the best evidence rule 'if the printout has been manifestly or consistently acted on, relied on or used as a record' (s 31.2(2)). For a case where neither was satisfied, see *R v Bellingham* 2002 ABPC 41.
[2] *Canada Evidence Act*, R.S.C. 1985, c. C-46, s 31.3(a).
[3] *Canada Evidence Act*, R.S.C. 1985, c. C-46, s 31.3(b).
[4] *Canada Evidence Act*, R.S.C. 1985, c. C-46, s 31.3(c).
[5] *Canada Evidence Act*, R.S.C. 1985, c. C-46, s 31.6(1). See *R v Morgan*, [2002] N.J. No. 15.
[6] See, eg *R v Gratton*, 2003 A.B.Q.B. 728 (CanLII), (2003), 23 Alta. L.R. (4th) 214.

7.20 The provisions also allow for evidence to be provided of current standards, procedures and practices with regard to the integrity of the recording or storing system[1]. This evidence can go to the integrity of the electronic document system but is also directed at 'determining under any rule of law whether an electronic document is admissible' and thus could also be used as a source of evidence of the 'reliability' of a document for hearsay purposes[2]. The provision seems to allow parties to test the current industry standards such as the Standard on Electronic Records as Documentary Evidence generated by the Canadian General Standards Board[3] or analogous standards from the International Standards Organization, for example. Such standards are not binding on the court, but will no doubt be persuasive.

[1]   *Canada Evidence Act*, R.S.C. 1985, c. C-46, s 31.5.
[2]   In Canadian evidence law the key to the admissibility of hearsay is whether the evidence is 'necessary' and 'reliable.' See, generally, *Paciocco & Stuesser* pp 111–120.
[3]   Available by purchase at: http://www.techstreet.com/cgi-bin/detail?product_id=1252845.

7.21 It is worth emphasising that the Uniform Act scheme is not a complete package for the admissibility of electronic documents. Rather, it confirms the application of the common law of authentication to electronic documents and provides a means by which parties may satisfy the best evidence rule[1]. The documents will still have to satisfy any other applicable rules of evidence in order to be admitted, such as exceptions to the hearsay rule[2].

[1]   It has been opined that, due to the onslaught of electronic copying mechanisms in the twentieth century, the best evidence rule was fading into obscurity; eg *Sopinka et al*, pp 1013–1014. Recognition that electronic document generation and storage raises its own issues has motivated, correctly in our view, this apparent revival of the rule.
[2]   See, eg, *R v Jiao* 2005 BCPC 12 (CanLII).

Web-based evidence

7.22 The issue of admissibility of web-based evidence is a unique one which had not attracted a great deal of judicial attention in Canada until very recently. In *ITV Television Inc v WIC Television Ltd*[1], a trademark dispute, the plaintiff ITV sought leave to use the Internet in court in order to demonstrate certain website mechanisms, such as hyperlinking and interactive streaming, and also to prove what the content of various websites had been at specific times in the past. The court, while accepting that any use of the Internet for truth of contents of the web pages would be hearsay, found that the 'Way Back Machine' at www.archive.org was a reliable means by which the previous content of websites could be proven[2].

[1]   2003 FC 1056 (CanLII), (2003), 29 C.P.R. (4th) 182, (2003) F.T.R. 203.
[2]   2003 FC 1056 (CanLII), (2003), 29 C.P.R. (4th) 182, (2003) F.T.R. 203 at paras 13–15. The Federal Court of Appeal affirmed the decision (2005) FCA 96 but expressly declined to rule on this issue; Pelletier J.A. commented 'the record is not sufficiently developed to provide an adequate factual underpinning for an informed consideration of the legal issues raised by the use of the Internet as a source of documentary evidence' para 30.

7.23 The court also opined in obiter dicta that 'official' websites, such as those of governments and well-known organisations, could 'provide reliable evidence that would be admissible as evidence'[1]. An 'unofficial' website, by contrast, would have to be assessed with regard to:

its sources, independent corroboration, consideration as to whether it might have been modified from what was originally available and assessment of the objectivity of the person placing the information online. When these factors cannot be ascertained, little or no weight should be given to the information obtained from an unofficial website[2].

In principle, use of the web itself as a means of proving web content at a given point in time should be uncontroversial, so long as the means by which the proof is given is sufficiently reliable. This may create problems at the disclosure stage, but the issues are mostly technological rather than legal, and not insurmountable if the parties are able to devote sufficient resources to solving them.

[1]   2003 FC 1056 (CanLII), (2003), 29 C.P.R. (4th) 182, (2003) F.T.R. 203 at para 17.
[2]   2003 FC 1056 (CanLII), (2003), 29 C.P.R. (4th) 182, (2003) F.T.R. 203 at para 18.

7.24 As to the hearsay content of websites, while one can be sympathetic to the desire to have 'official' websites considered to be reliable enough to escape the full rigour of the hearsay rule, there would need to be set criteria as to how such reliability should be established—a task perhaps best accomplished by amendment of the relevant evidence statutes.

Computer-generated demonstrative evidence

7.25 An issue emerging in Canadian case law is the admissibility of computer-generated images, usually digital animation, as a means of helping to explain or contextualise expert or lay witness testimony—in short, as demonstrative evidence. Canadian courts have been dealing with more general issues surrounding the power and potential prejudice of demonstrative evidence for some time and have paid attention to the distorting effect such evidence can have on the trier of fact[1]. However, there have to date been very few cases dealing directly with the admissibility of digitally-generated evidence[2].

[1]   See *R v MacDonald* (2000), 35 C.R. (5th) 130 (Ont. C.A.).
[2]   See *McCutcheon v Chrysler Canada Ltd* [1998] O.J. No. 5818 (Gen. Div.); *Sovani v Jin* 2005 BCSC 1852.

7.26 Those cases which have arisen, generally in jury trials, have tended to apply the same test commonly used for disputed demonstrative evidence: does it pass a cost-benefit analysis in terms of its probative value being outweighed by its prejudicial effect? To wit, will it help the jury to understand the evidence without creating undue sympathy towards the party proffering the evidence? In making this determination, trial judges have focused on how closely the digital images match the subject matter they are intended to represent and whether they are overly one-sided on hotly-contested factual issues[1]. Demonstrative evidence that uses a computer also tends to require expert testimony and thus the expert opinion rules will usually need to be applied.

[1]   For a solid, albeit American, source, see BS Fiedler 'Are Your Eyes Deceiving You? The Evidentiary Crisis Regarding the Admissibility of Computer Generated Evidence' (2004) 79 New York Law School Law Review 295.

7.27 We are not convinced that this test needs any further development, since it is consistent with the Supreme Court of Canada's policy of encouraging trial judge discretion in evidentiary matters. Nonetheless, the issue remains open and is likely to see more consideration in the near future.

ELECTRONIC EVIDENCE-GATHERING IN CRIMINAL MATTERS

7.28 In Canada today most laws of criminal procedure are derived from the *Canadian Charter of Rights and Freedoms*, which was enacted in 1982. These rights have constitutional status with the result that all other laws, including those governing police investigative techniques, must comply with *Charter* standards. To fully understand today's situation, however, it is necessary to understand the pre-*Charter* rules with regard to the gathering and admission of evidence.

7.29 Prior to 1982, there were effectively no rules in Canada preventing the use of illegally-obtained evidence. Evidence had to comply with the rules of admissibility, discussed above, but the fact that it might have been obtained through illegal means was effectively irrelevant. As a result, there was really no limit on the techniques police could use to gather evidence short of actions such as beating an accused and, even then, any statements would only be inadmissible because they were not reliable.

7.30 The one pre-*Charter* exception to this rule concerned electronic surveillance. When legislation governing wiretapping was introduced in 1974 it was recognised that it posed a far greater threat to privacy than other investigative methods of the time. The details of the scheme will be reviewed later but, in general terms, the *Criminal Code* made the interception of private communications illegal, with exceptions for certain police investigative techniques. In addition, a rule was added making wiretap evidence inadmissible unless it was gathered in accordance with the provisions of the *Code*[1].

[1]   Note that this latter rule no longer exists: see the discussion under 'Criminal Litigation' at 7.53.

7.31 The pre-*Charter* situation, then, was that there were some rules governing police investigative techniques but if the police did not comply with those rules any evidence gathered was likely to be admissible nonetheless, except in the case of electronic surveillance.

7.32 When the *Charter* was enacted in 1982 it created a number of individual rights that affected police investigative techniques. The most important for this discussion are set out in s 8, which guarantees the right to be free from unreasonable search and seizure, and s 24(2), which provides a potential remedy of exclusion of evidence. Most of the rest of this part will be devoted to s 8, while s 24(2) will be discussed under 'Criminal Litigation' at 7.53.

7.33 Several key facts must be noted in order to understand electronic (or other) evidence-gathering in Canada today. First, the Supreme Court of Canada has decided that an 'unreasonable' search in s 8 means an illegal search: one not authorised by statute or common law[1]. Therefore, any search for which no legal authority can be pointed to will violate the *Charter*. Second, a 'search' is defined as anything which impinges on a person's reasonable expectation of privacy[2]. The concept of 'reasonable expectation of privacy' will be discussed at greater length below but this definition means that 'search' includes not only techniques such as searching the pockets of an accused, but also listening in to a telephone conversation or placing a device on a car to track its movements. Third, a warrantless search is prima facie an unreasonable search and a *Charter* violation[3].

[1]   *R v Kokesch* [1990] 3 S.C.R. 3.
[2]   *R v Wise* [1992] 1 S.C.R. 527 at p 533.
[3]   *Hunter v Southam Inc* [1984] 2 S.C.R. 145.

7.34 Further, in *Hunter v Southam*[1], one of the earliest *Charter* decisions, the Court laid down rules regarding the issuing of warrants. A warrant must be issued by a person capable of acting judicially, typically a judge or justice of the peace, and must be issued prior to the search. The warrant must be based on reasonable grounds to believe that an offence has been committed and that the search will produce evidence relating to that offence, both of which must be proven on balance of probabilities, on oath, to the person issuing the warrant.

[1]   [1984] 2 S.C.R. 145.

7.35 In sum, the *Charter* states that any search conducted without a warrant prima facie violates an accused's s 8 rights and that warrants should only be issued in compliance with the *Hunter* standards. Those standards, though, are not absolute requirements: they are a benchmark for the appropriate balance between the privacy interests of the individual and the interests of the state. As either factor takes on greater or lesser importance, the warrant requirements might become more or less stringent.

7.36 Against that background, the Court has assessed various police investigative techniques, including various electronic methods of evidence gathering. Among the early methods reviewed were the statutory schemes governing the use of wiretaps to intercept telephone calls or other private communications, which conformed to the *Charter*[1], and the use of bodypacks to surreptitiously record conversations between a police informant and others, which did not[2].

[1]   *R v Garofoli* [1990] 2 S.C.R. 1421.
[2]   *R v Duarte* [1990] 1 S.C.R. 30.

7.37 Canadian wiretap law is set out in a portion of the *Code* entitled 'Invasion of Privacy'. In broad terms the *Code* makes the electronic interception of private communications[1] illegal, but then makes exceptions for some police investigative techniques. In particular, the police can apply for a warrant—referred to as an authorisation—to intercept the private communications of particular persons[2]. These requirements for authorisations not only comply with the *Hunter* standards noted above, they include additional restrictions making them less available than most other types of warrants[3].

1   Note that the definition of 'private communication' includes cell telephone calls if they are scrambled, but not otherwise: s 183.
2   Electronic surveillance case law in Canada is very complex and there has been a great deal of litigation over issues such as whether a particular person was or was not a 'known' person who should have been named in the authorisation (*R v Chow* 2005 SCC 24), specifying the places to which the subject 'resorts' (*R v Thompson* [1990] 2 S.C.R. 1111), the limits involved in tapping pay telephones (*Thompson*), interception of privileged communications (*R v Robillard* (2000), 151 C.C.C. (3d) 296 (Que.C.A.) and many others. The statutory scheme also contains many details not mentioned here, such as the warrantless use of interception in emergency situations. Those details are beyond the scope of this chapter and the interested reader should consult a specialist work, such as the looseleaf volume by Robert W Hubbard, Peter M Brauti and Scott K Fenton *Wiretapping and Other Electronic Surveillance: Law and Procedure* (2000).
3   It is important to note that, despite these restrictions, electronic surveillance is—or at least has been—quite common in Canada. A study by the Law Reform Commission of Canada found that police in Canada applied for authorisations at *twenty* times the rate of police in the United States (Law Reform Commission of Canada *Electronic Surveillance* (1986) p 10). However, that study predated many of the *Charter* cases discussed in this section so it is possible that the actual rate of use in Canada is lower now.

7.38 First, an application for an authorisation must be made to a judge: a justice of the peace has no jurisdiction. Also, authorisations can only be used in the investigation of certain relatively serious listed offences. These offences are not limited to ones in the *Criminal Code*, but also include some offences in the *Bankruptcy Act*, the *Competition Act*, the *Export and Import Permits Act*, the *Security of Information Act* and others. Limiting this investigative technique to listed offences does restrict its use to some extent, though the list of offences has steadily increased since the provisions were first introduced.

7.39 In addition, there are two pre-conditions to the granting of an authorisation beyond the *Hunter* standards. First, the judge must be satisfied that granting the application is in the interests of justice[1]. Second, 'investigative necessity' must be shown. This criterion is not an absolute 'last resort' requirement, but does require that there be 'practically speaking, no other reasonable alternative method of investigation, in the circumstances of the particular criminal inquiry'[2].

1   *Criminal Code*, R.S.C. 1985, c. C-46, s 186(1)(a).
2   *R v Araujo* 2000 SCC 65, para 29.

7.40 The bodypack provisions in the Invasion of Privacy section, on the other hand, were found to violate the *Charter* as they stood. The notion behind the provisions had been that, as long as one of the parties to a private conversation agreed to the recording, the taping was by consent and no warrant was needed. In practice, of course, this meant that police could audiotape private communications whenever they used an informant or undercover officer, without judicial pre-authorisation. In *R v Duarte*, the Court held that this scheme therefore fell short of the minimum standards required by *Hunter*, and so violated the *Charter*. The court below had held that consent tapings were acceptable, on the theory that anyone talking to another always risked that that person would repeat the conversation to the police: the tape did not increase that risk, it merely made the record of the conversation more reliable. The Supreme Court held that that reasoning missed the real issue:

The very efficacy of electronic surveillance is such that it has the potential, if left unregulated, to annihilate any expectation that our communications will remain private. A society which exposed us, at the whim of the state, to the risk of having a permanent electronic recording made of our words every time we opened our mouths might be superbly equipped to fight crime, but would be one in which privacy no longer had any meaning[1].

The issue was not use of this technique at all, but use of it by the police at their sole discretion. As a consequence, even 'consent' wiretaps now also require that the police obtain an authorisation from a judge.

1   [1990] 1 S.C.R. 30, para 22.

7.41 Following *Duarte*, the next real issue which arose for the Court was the use of surreptitious video recording. The invasion of privacy provisions in the *Code* did not touch on this issue at all—neither to make it illegal nor to provide authorisations allowing police to do it. In *Wong*[1], the police were investigating illegal gambling conducted in a hotel room. Deciding that they could not investigate through undercover officers, the police installed a camera in an adjoining room and videotaped the gambling: since no warrants were available to authorise this, they did not obtain one. The Crown argued that as there was no statutory prohibition on video surveillance, the police were entitled to use it at will, an approach which the Court said 'wholly misunderstands *Duarte*'[2]. The correct conclusion, the Court held, was that in the absence of judicial pre-authorisation, the search failed to comply with the *Hunter* standard and violated the *Charter*. If there was no method of judicial pre-authorisation, then the police could not use the technique at all, rather than use it at will.

1   *R v Wong* [1990] 3 S.C.R. 36.
2   [1990] 3 S.C.R. 36, para 28.

7.42 Shortly thereafter, the Court decided *Wise*[1], in which the police had, without a warrant, placed a tracking device on the accused's car in order to follow its movements. The Court concluded with no difficulty that this was an unconstitutional search. Of interest, though, was that the Court also observed that the privacy interest at stake with regard to tracking devices was low, on the basis that there is a reduced expectation of privacy in a vehicle, and that the search was less intrusive than electronic audio or video surveillance. Justice Cory for the majority therefore expressed the view that if there were to be legislation authorising tracking devices it could be based on a lower standard than the *Hunter* requirement of reasonable grounds.

1   *R v Wise* [1992] 1 S.C.R. 527.

7.43 In the wake of these decisions, new warrant provisions were introduced, which can conveniently be considered in four categories. First, the *Code* now permits the police to place a tracking device on a vehicle: rather than requiring reasonable belief to do this, the warrant is available on the lower standard of reasonable suspicion[1]. Second, the *Code* permits the police to place a dial number recorder ('DNR') on a suspect's telephone. This device will not intercept communications, but will record the activity occurring on the telephone keypad: this warrant, too, is available on the lower reasonable suspicion standard[2]. Thirdly, warrants for video surveillance are available: although these provisions are not in the 'Invasion of Privacy' section the video surveillance warrants incorporate the rules governing audio surveillance, including those limiting the offences which can be investigated in this way[3].

1   *Criminal Code*, R.S.C. 1985, c. C-46, s 492.1
2   *Criminal Code*, R.S.C. 1985, c. C-46, s 492.2
3   *Criminal Code*, R.S.C. 1985, c. C-46, s 487.01(4) and (5).

7.44 Finally, Parliament also introduced the 'general warrant' provisions into the *Code*, a provision which is true to the letter of *Duarte* and *Wong* but contrary to its spirit. Those cases held that in the absence of specific authorisation, police should not use particular investigative techniques: it was a message of restraint. The effect of the general warrant provisions is to remove those restraints and permit judges to authorise literally any investigative technique: the provision allows police to seek a warrant to 'use any device or investigative technique or procedure or do any thing'[1]. General warrants are only available on criteria slightly stricter than the *Hunter* standards: only a judge has jurisdiction to issue the warrant, and it must be in the interests of justice to do so.

1   *Criminal Code*, R.S.C. 1985, c. C-46, s 487.01(1).

7.45 The current situation in Canada with regard to electronic investigative techniques, then, is that warrantless searches will, subject to the issue of reasonable expectation of privacy, (to be discussed below) violate the *Charter*, but with a warrant anything is permissible. Two final points should be made, however.

7.46 The first is that the array of warrant provisions creates much potential for confusion since some are available from justices of the peace and some are not, some require reasonable belief while for others reasonable suspicion is sufficient, and some impose additional requirements—the 'interests of justice' and investigative necessity for video and audio surveillance, just the 'interests of justice' for general warrants—beyond the *Hunter* standards which apply to ordinary search warrants. The result is that police and others can be confused over which warrant to seek in which situation[1]. Consider a cell telephone, for example: police wishing to intercept communications through it must proceed under a wiretap authorisation, which is only available if investigative necessity is satisfied, but could obtain a dial number recorder warrant on mere reasonable suspicion. On the other hand if the goal is to determine when an accused made telephone calls and which towers the calls were routed through (to locate the telephone at the scene of a crime) then an ordinary search warrant is sufficient[2]. Similar issues arise over email: an ordinary search warrant is sufficient to seize and examine a computer. Indeed, the *Code* specifically notes that anyone with a warrant to search a computer is entitled to use the computer to search any data available to the system[3]. Search warrants can also be used to obtain the records of an Internet Service Provider, which might give access to email communication. This raises a number of questions, such as whether these messages should be seen as more akin to private communications like those protected by the Invasion of Privacy provisions. Similarly, what if a webcam or voice operated Internet protocol ('VOIP') communication is made over the computer? Is an ordinary search warrant the proper method to monitor or discover after the fact that data?[4]

1   See, for example, *R v Gerrard* [2003] Carswell Ont 421 (Ont.S.C.) where the police obtained a tracking warrant under s 492.1, which is available on standards lower than the *Hunter* ones, but also felt they needed a higher standard general warrant to have authority to remove the accused's car and place the tracking device in it.
2   *R v Cole* [2006] O.J. No. 1402.
3   *Criminal Code*, R.S.C. 1985, c. C-46, s 487(2.1) also explicitly permits printing out and seizing copies of anything contained on the computer.
4   See the discussion in James A Fontana *The Law of Search and Seizure in Canada* (6th ed, 2005) noting that case law concerning the use of warrants for computers has not clearly distinguished between whether the computer is the repository of information, the means by which the crime was created, or an instrument of communication. See also Department of Justice *Emails: Considerations for Criminal Law Policy* (Ottawa: Department of Justice, 2005) online: http://www.cippic.ca/en/projects-cases/lawful-access/doj_-_email.ppt #312,14, and Dominique Valiquet *Telecommunications and Lawful Access: I. The Legislative Situation in Canada* (Ottawa: Parliamentary Information and Research Service, 2006) available online at http://www.parl.gc.ca/information/library/PRBpubs/prb0565-e.html.

7.47 Secondly, this legislative mix includes some very particular provisions, such as tracking warrants, and very general ones, like general warrants. This raises the question of which approach is best equipped to protect society and individual liberty while keeping pace with technological change. The general warrants provide a more flexible approach, but one must have some concern about a provision which literally authorises 'any thing'. On the other hand, more specific provisions risk being left behind. In *Wise*[1], for example, an important rationale for the lower authorisation standard was that tracking devices were unsophisticated and could not track the movement of the vehicle. With the advent of Global Positioning System ('GPS') and laptop computer mapping software that is exactly what tracking devices today accomplish, but they are still authorised on the lower standard of reasonable suspicion[2].

1   *R v Wise* [1992] 1 S.C.R. 527.
2   Note as well that since 1992, when DNR warrants were created, the types of activities performed on telephone keypads have increased dramatically: entering credit card numbers, PINs, etc. See the discussion in Steve Coughlan and Marc Gorbet 'Nothing Plus Nothing Equals ... Something?: A Proposal for FLIR Warrants on Reasonable Suspicion' (2005), 23 C.R. (6th) 239.

7.48 There is one final issue about which a bit more should be said: reasonable expectation of privacy. It has already been noted that reasonable expectation of privacy enters into the Court's analysis of what level of protection individuals should receive: the lower expectation of privacy in a vehicle leads to tracking device warrants on a lower standard but, for example, the particularly high privacy interest in one's own DNA leads to extra protections being incorporated into the *Code*'s DNA warrant provisions[1]. There is a conceptually prior way in which the concept also arises, though, which is worth observing in the context of electronic evidence.

1   *Criminal Code*, R.S.C. 1985, c. C-46, see ss 487.04–487.091 as well as *R v S.A.B.* [2003] 2 S.C.R. 678 and *R v Rodgers* 2006 SCC 15.

7.49 A search is any investigative technique which impinges on a reasonable expectation of privacy: conversely, therefore, if an accused had no reasonable expectation of privacy then any investigative technique used was not a search, and so was not an unreasonable search. Courts have from time-to-time used this method of reasoning as a way of avoiding finding a *Charter* violation.

7.50 This was one of the Crown's arguments in *Wong*, the video surveillance case: since the accused had invited others into his hotel room to gamble he had no reasonable expectation of privacy. The Court rejected the argument in that case and, importantly, noted that a 'risk assessment' was the wrong approach to take. If the issue was whether privacy as a practical matter was at risk, advancing technology would mean that individuals would only have a reasonable expectation of privacy when sitting silently in the dark in the cellar. The question, the Court said, was what level of privacy the individual is entitled to expect[1]. Over a series of cases the Court distinguished between territorial, informational and personal privacy, though more than one can be relevant in a single situation; DNA testing involves both informational and personal privacy, for example. This is still very much a developing area of law in Canada and the interplay between the various types of privacy has not yet been clearly worked out.

[1] The argument failed as well in *Duarte* [1990] 1 S.C.R. 30, where the Court rejected the claim that bodypack recording was no different from the risk that the informant might repeat the conversation.

7.51 Once or twice the 'no search since no privacy' argument has succeeded. The Court has decided that police are entitled to obtain the power consumption records of an accused without a warrant, since no privacy interest is at stake[1]. More recently, they have decided that police can train a Forward Looking Infrared Scanner ('FLIR') at the home of a suspect without the need for a warrant, since there is no privacy interest in the pattern of heat escaping from one's house[2]. This latter decision has created some confusion in lower courts as to whether other investigative techniques require a warrant or not, including Digital Recorder Ammeters which are attached to the power lines leading into a house to track the cycling pattern of electricity use and, somewhat surprisingly, drug sniffing dogs.

[1] *R v Plant* [1993] 3 S.C.R. 281.
[2] *R v Tessling* [2004] 3 S.C.R. 432.

7.52 Oddly, then, given the current legislative scheme, novel electronic methods of investigation either are not searches at all, and so are completely unregulated, or are searches which can only be authorised under the stricter-than-usual standards for general warrants.

CRIMINAL LITIGATION

7.53 This portion of the chapter will deal with issues potentially arising at the trial stage of a criminal matter. In particular, three issues most likely to be relevant to issues of electronic evidence will be considered:

(a)   the disclosure obligation of the Crown with regards to electronic surveillance and other evidence;

(b)   reviewing the basis upon which a wiretap authorisation or other warrant was issued and;

(c)   the effect on admissibility of a finding that evidence was gathered illegally.

Disclosure

7.54 As in many other areas of criminal law, the rules about disclosure of evidence are governed by the *Charter*. The Crown has an obligation to disclose to an accused all relevant evidence in its hands, whether the Crown intends to use the evidence or not. This obligation arises from the accused's right to a fair trial, which is contained within s 7 of the *Charter*. This rule supersedes any individual rules which might otherwise apply to electronic evidence. The wiretap provisions in the *Code*, for example, were initially drafted to provide that all materials relied upon to grant an authorisation would be sealed and would not normally be given to the accused. Now, the opposite is true and the ordinary rule for wiretaps is the same *Charter* presumption of full disclosure that applies to all other evidence[1].

[1]   See *Garofoli* [1990] 2 S.C.R. 1421; *R v Durette* [1994] 1 S.C.R. 469 and s 187 of the *Criminal Code*.

7.55 Nonetheless, the duty to disclose does not extend to privileged material and, in the case of warrants, the police might have relied upon information obtained from confidential informants. Informer privilege is recognised in Canadian law and so the materials disclosed to the accused are first edited by the prosecutor to remove information which might identify a confidential informant. The *Code* legislates this rule for wiretaps as well as allowing editing to protect ongoing investigations, undercover officers or techniques, and innocent persons[1]. If too much information is edited from the supporting material, however, the accused might be entitled to a remedy based on a breach of the right to disclosure. This is independent of the question of reviewing a warrant, discussed below, and the remedy might be granted even if the material disclosed was sufficient to justify the issuance of the authorisation[2].

[1]   *Criminal Code*, R.S.C. 1985, c. C-46, s 187(4).
[2]   *Durette* [1994] 1 S.C.R. 469.

7.56 The disclosure obligation is also limited to relevant material. Accordingly, an accused charged with an offence is not entitled to know whether he or she has been a target in wiretaps other than that relating to the particular offence charged[1].

[1]   *R v Chaplin* [1995] 1 S.C.R. 727.

7.57 There are also some special rules regarding electronic evidence. First, by statute, there might be an obligation to disclose some methods of investigation even if no charges have been laid. Section 196 of the *Code* requires that the person whose communications were intercepted must be notified of the interception at most 90 days after the authorisation expires, though this period can be extended by periods of up to three years where the investigation is continuing[1]. A similar rule applies in the case of general warrants[2] though, somewhat surprisingly, there is no similar rule for DNR or tracking warrants.

[1] *Criminal Code*, R.S.C. 1985, c. C-46, s 196.
[2] *Criminal Code*, R.S.C. 1985, c. C-46, s 487.01(5.1).

7.58 There can also be technical issues around disclosure of electronic evidence. In *R v Cassidy*[1], for example, the accused was charged with possession of child pornography and the police had seized his computer hard drives. They examined the hard drives with two software programs, one of which was available only to the police the other of which was commercially available but cost (including training) CN$4500.00. In that particular case the court concluded the proper method of disclosure was to provide the accused with a copy of the hard drive and allow the accused's expert to use the programs in private at the police station. They left open the possibility that on some facts disclosure might require providing the accused with the software and training.

[1] (2004), 182 C.C.C. (3d) 294 (Ont.C.A.).

7.59 Exactly what result will flow if the Crown fails to disclose evidence which it should is a complex question in Canadian law, since the issue depends on what *Charter* remedy is appropriate and just in the circumstances. If the non-disclosure is discovered at a pre-trial stage, the only remedy will likely be an order for disclosure. Mid-trial the remedy might also include an adjournment, though a new trial is also a possibility. If the non-disclosure does not come to light until post-trial then an appeal court might do anything from deciding that a conviction must be overturned and a stay of any further proceedings ordered, to deciding that no remedy at all is necessary[1].

[1] The rules around *Charter* remedies for non-disclosure are quite complex and inconsistent in some ways, even over the fundamental question of whether there is an independent right to disclosure or whether it is just an aspect of the right to a fair trial. The most important cases have not concerned electronic evidence, but since those cases fall within the general regime of *Charter* violations and *Charter* remedies, the principles apply in that context. More information concerning remedies for non-disclosure can be found in Don Stuart *Charter Justice in Canadian Criminal Law* (4th edn, 2005) under 'Right to a Fair Trial (Right to Make Full Answer and Defence)'.

Review of warrants

7.60 Warrants are normally granted on an ex parte basis[1], which means that it will not usually be until trial that the accused has a chance to challenge the basis upon which the warrant or wiretap authorisation was issued[2]. If it is found that the warrant ought not to have been issued that will render whatever search was made a warrantless one which, as noted above, makes it prima facie an unreasonable search violating s 8 of the *Charter* and potentially entitling the accused to a remedy.

1   The SCC noted in *R v S.A.B.* [2003] 2 S.C.R. 678; 2003 SCC 60, dealing with DNA warrants, that judges have the discretion to conduct an inter partes hearing in an application for such a warrant, but no warrant provisions in Canada *require* inter partes hearings.

2   In principle it might be open to seek a review before a judge other than the trial judge, but the Supreme Court has said the preferred course is to make the challenge at trial: see *Garofoli* [1990] 2 S.C.R. 1421.

7.61 The standard on review is whether there was any basis upon which the authorising judge could have granted the warrant: the reviewing judge does not substitute his or her discretion on the question of whether the warrant should have been issued. It is neither necessary nor sufficient for an accused to show fraud or misrepresentation on the part of the police in obtaining the warrant or authorisation in order to have the warrant quashed. If fraud or misrepresentation is shown, however, that material is excised and the question is whether the remaining material provided a basis to issue the warrant[1]. On the other hand, where errors in the affidavit are minor technical ones made in good faith—but only then—the affiant is permitted to 'amplify' the affidavit in cross-examination: that is, the errors can be corrected and the new information can be relied upon in the review[2]. The Court has held that this is the appropriate balance between requiring pre-authorisation but not permitting form to triumph over substance. This rule was handed down in the particular context of electronic surveillance but it has been taken to apply to warrant provisions generally and, therefore, should apply to any other potentially electronic searches, such as DNRs, tracking devices or general warrants and, indeed, to ordinary search warrants.

1   *Garofoli* [1990] 2 S.C.R. 1421.
2   *Araujo* 2000 SCC 65.

7.62 In challenging a wiretap authorisation, an accused does not have an automatic right to cross-examine the affiant: rather, leave to cross-examine must be obtained from the trial judge. The trial judge has discretion but should allow cross-examination when it is necessary to enable the accused to make full answer and defence. In particular, the accused must show a reasonable likelihood that cross-examination will tend to discredit the existence of one of the preconditions to the authorisation. When cross-examination is permitted it is limited to questions directed to establish that there was no basis for granting the authorisation[1].

1   *Garofoli* [1990] 2 S.C.R. 1421, and recently re-affirmed in *R v Pires*; *R v Lising* 2005 SCC 66.

Admissibility of illegally obtained evidence

7.63 As noted above, the pre-*Charter* situation in Canada essentially allowed no exclusion of evidence based on the fact that it had been illegally obtained. The only exception to that rule was in the case of evidence gathered through the electronic surveillance provisions in the *Code*. In that case, if the police had not complied with the law for wiretaps the evidence was automatically excluded. Since the *Charter*, both of those situations have changed. The provision in the *Code*, which previously provided for the inadmissibility of illegally obtained wiretap evidence, was repealed in 1993. As a result, the possible exclusion of all illegally obtained evidence is now a *Charter* question[1].

---

1   The Court has recently suggested in *R v Buhay* 2003 SCC 30 that there is some possibility of excluding evidence other than under s 24(2), and that this power predated the *Charter*. The power has been little in evidence prior to, or since, the *Charter*.

7.64 When the *Charter* was introduced, it was recognised that if the rights guaranteed within it were to have real meaning then remedies for breach of those rights had to be available. Although it was agreed that those remedies needed to include the exclusion of evidence, it was also seen as important that automatic exclusion of evidence should not follow from a *Charter* breach. Accordingly, a special provision was incorporated in addition to the more general remedy provision discussed above under 'Disclosure'. Section 24(2) of the *Charter* provides for exclusion of evidence gathered in violation of a *Charter* right where 'the admission of it in the proceedings would bring the administration of justice into disrepute'. The onus is on the applicant to show that the evidence should be excluded.

7.65 Over a number of years the Supreme Court of Canada has developed a test for exclusion of evidence under s 24(2), usually referred to as the *Stillman* test. It can be quite complex in application but, for purposes of this discussion, a less detailed discussion will be sufficient.

7.66 The *Stillman* test considers the possible exclusion of evidence through three questions, the first two of which are reasons to exclude evidence and the last of which is a reason for not excluding. First, if admission of the evidence would affect the fairness of the trial, then the evidence ought to be excluded. Evidence will affect the fairness of the trial if it is 'conscriptive' or is derived from conscriptive evidence. For example, if an accused were to confess as a result of a *Charter* violation then that confession would be conscriptive, since it consisted of the state causing the accused to bring into being evidence which would not have existed without the accused's involvement[1]. If, in the confession, the accused tells the police the location of a murder weapon, then that weapon will also be excluded as conscriptive evidence, subject to the 'discoverability' exception. That is, if the location of the murder weapon was a place the police were bound to search in any case then it is not unfair to use that evidence and so the fairness of the trial is not affected.

---

1   Evidence other than statements can be conscriptive: taking part in a police line-up, for example (*R v Ross* [1989] 1 S.C.R. 3) or taking a breathalyser test (*R v Bartle* [1994] 3 S.C.R. 173; *R v Pozniak* [1994] 3 S.C.R. 310) both produce conscriptive evidence.

7.67 Generally speaking, this first basis for exclusion is unlikely to affect illegally-obtained electronic evidence. The very fact that such investigative techniques impinge on privacy and (potentially) violate s 8 of the *Charter* makes it unlikely that the accused is being made to produce evidence which would not otherwise exist, rather, pre-existing information, whether documents already on a computer or statements already being made, is being discovered[1]. If the authorisation to surreptitiously record is later determined to have been improperly issued[2], or even if the police surreptitiously record a conversation without having sought an authorisation at all[3], trial fairness will not lead to exclusion of the evidence.

[1]   See for example the discussion in *R v Mooring* 2003 BCCA 199. See also *R v Wise* [1992] 1 S.C.R. 527, noting that evidence obtained by illegally placing a 'beeper' in the accused's car to track its location was not conscriptive and did not go to trial fairness.
[2]   See *R v Fliss* 2002 SCC 16.
[3]   See *R v Wijesinha* [1995] 3 S.C.R. 422.

7.68 If illegally-obtained electronic evidence is excluded, it is more likely to be due to the second basis for exclusion, the seriousness of the breach. In this branch of the test courts consider a number of factors, including

(a)   whether the breach was flagrant and deliberate or, alternatively, committed in good faith; the nature of the interest violated by the breach;
(b)   whether the violation was merely technical;
(c)   whether there was urgency to the situation; and
(d)   whether the police ignored a legal method by which they could have proceeded.

Balancing these factors is a more subjective exercise. Where police act on a wiretap authorisation which is later found to have been invalidly issued it is likely that the evidence will not be excluded, on the basis that they relied on the authorisation in good faith[1]. On the other hand, if the police engaged in deliberate deception to obtain the authorisation such a good faith claim will likely not succeed. The importance of the accused's interest will also be relevant: privacy concerns are generally seen as important, so that a violation of them is likely to be serious. However, there is a reduced expectation of privacy in a vehicle and so intruding on that aspect of privacy might not matter much[2]. This aspect of the test is difficult to predict. In *Tessling*, as noted above, the Supreme Court found no expectation of privacy and no *Charter* breach from using a FLIR to detect heat emanations. The Ontario Court of Appeal, however, had found a *Charter* breach serious enough to warrant exclusion. They held that the intrusion was into the home, 'the most protected physical zone of privacy'[3], and that the difference between surveillance possible with the device and without it created a 'subtle but almost Orwellian' intrusion[4].

[1]   *Fliss* 2002 SCC 16.
[2]   *Wise* [1992] 1 S.C.R. 527.
[3]   *Tessling* [2004] 3 S.C.R. 432 at 76.
[4]   *Tessling* [2004] 3 S.C.R. 432 at 79.

7.69 The final consideration is the effect on the reputation of the justice system if the evidence is excluded. This factor generally relates more to the nature of the offence and the importance of the evidence rather than to the nature, electronic or not, of the evidence. Simply put, evidence is less likely to be excluded if it is crucial evidence regarding a serious offence.

CIVIL LITIGATION[1]

7.70 Civil cases in Canada are conducted under civil procedure rules (or 'rules of court')[2], which exist for every court which has jurisdiction over civil matters. The vast bulk of civil cases occur in the provincial superior courts while certain specialised civil cases in federal jurisdiction are heard in the Federal Court of Canada. While the procedural rules vary, sometimes widely, from jurisdiction to jurisdiction, one can see a reasonably coherent and generalised body of procedural law at play in the country at large.

[1]   A general resource and casebook for Canadian civil procedure is Janet Walker et al *The Civil Litigation Process: Cases and Materials* (6th edn, 2005).
[2]   Eg the Ontario *Rules of Civil Procedure*, Made under the *Courts of Justice Act*, R.R.O. 1990, Reg. 194, available online at: http://www.e-laws.gov.on.ca/DBLaws/Regs/English/900194a_e.htm; the Nova Scotia *Civil Procedure Rules*, Made by the Judges of the Nova Scotia Court of Appeal and the Supreme Court of Nova Scotia, available online at: http://www.courts.ns.ca/Rules/toc.htm; and the Federal Court Rules.

7.71 The civil procedure rules in each jurisdiction govern every aspect of a civil case, from initiating proceedings through to appeals. While electronic evidence issues may arise at many stages they are most pressing at the stage of documentary discovery, on which this very brief overview will focus[1].

[1]   For a broad overview of electronic discovery issues see Dan Pinnington 'Needle in a haystack' (2006) 15/4 *National* 42.

General mechanics of discovery

7.72 Under each set of procedural rules, all parties to a civil action are obliged to disclose and produce documents which are relevant and not privileged. This is a unilateral obligation, with which each party must comply on its own initiative, and is typically completed after the close of pleadings. Documentary discovery generally comprises two steps. First, the party prepares a list of all relevant documents which the party has, or at one time had, in its control or possession[1], and provide this list to the other parties as well as filing it with the court. Second, the opposing parties are formally entitled to inspect and obtain copies of the relevant and non-privileged documents, though, in practice, copies are delivered between and among the parties within specified time frames. Most civil procedure rules also provide for documentary discovery from non-parties[2].

[1]   In some jurisdictions the list is just that, a list (eg Nova Scotia Rule 20), while in other jurisdictions the 'list' takes the form of an affidavit or sworn statement by the party to the effect that the list contains all known relevant documents (eg Ontario Rule 30.03). The latter type of rule often imposes the additional requirement that counsel swear that he/she has explained the discovery obligation to his/her client.
[2]   Eg Nova Scotia Rule 20.06, Ontario Rule 30.10.

7.73 The definition of 'document' or 'record' is invariably very broad, and the rules' drafters have clearly intended that the term catch virtually everything that might be considered 'electronic evidence,' including the contents of computers, Blackberries, Palm Pilots, Personal Digital Assistants ('PDA's), and the like[1]. Courts have also shown a willingness to order the production of metadata where it is demonstrably relevant[2].

[1] See, eg *CIBC World Markets Inc v Genuity Capital Markets* [2005] O.J. No. 614 (Ont. S.C.J.); *Re Portus Alternative Asset Management Inc* (2005), 28 O.S.C.B. 2670 (Ont. Sec. Comm.); *Desgagne v Yuen* 2006 BCSC 955.

[2] *Desgagne* 2006 BCSC 955 at 26–34.

Electronic discovery

7.74 The unique issues associated with the discovery of electronic documents, as well as differing levels of familiarity with technological issues among the bar and judiciary, has made electronic discovery (or 'ediscovery') a topic of great interest in Canada in the recent past[1]. It has been commented regarding Canada that 'judicial reasoning exploring the obligations of the parties to produce electronic evidence remains in its infancy'[2]. For the moment, the battle for coherence is being fought in the procedural trenches. However, the litigation bar has moved ahead with developing this area of practice and in 2005 the Ontario Bar Association's Discovery Task Force[3] developed and issued the Electronic Discovery Guidelines[4], drawing on similar work done in the US[5].

[1] For a wide-ranging reading list and links to substantial electronic resources, see the practicePRO website at: http://www.practicepro.ca/practice/eDiscovery_Rlist.asp.

[2] Susan Wortzman 'Spoliation, preservation and other "gotchas": The US & Canadian Jurisprudence' (2005) 4/2 LawPRO 7 at 8.

[3] The Ontario Bar Association ('OBA') is a provincial branch of the Canadian Bar Association, a voluntary membership organisation which provides support to the legal profession through legal education and 'representation to government on topics of current concern' (see www.oba.org/en/admin/about_en/). The OBA's 'Discovery Task Force E-Discovery Guidelines and Resources Page' can be found online at: http://www.oba.org/en/main/ediscovery_en/default.aspx. The reader will note in particular the 'Canadian Common Law E-Discovery Case Law Digest,' which is happily acknowledged as a significant research source for this section. The Canadian Judicial Council has also begun a project on both ediscovery and the presentation of electronic evidence in court. The beginning portion of their work can be found at: http://150.101.156.34/pdcanada.

[4] Available online at: http://www.oba.org/en/pdf_newsletter/E-DiscoveryGuidelines.pdf.

[5] Most notably by the Sedona Conference; see www.thesedonaconference.org.

7.75 The goal of the Electronic Discovery Guidelines is to develop a set of 'best practices' for counsel involved in ediscovery and, specifically, to:

(a)   prevent and resolve discovery disputes;
(b)   provide for efficient and cost-effective means of meeting discovery obligations; and
(c)   suggest technology options that may ease the process[1].

The Guidelines are intended to have no binding effect but simply to 'provide an appropriate framework to address how to conduct e-discovery, based on norms that the bench and bar can adopt and develop over time as a matter of practice'[2]. They are one of the more authoritative sources of current thinking and practices in an area otherwise in its litigation 'infancy' and are likely, in the future, to affect the various ediscovery issues canvassed below[3].

1   Electronic   Discovery   Guidelines,   http://www.oba.org/en/pdf_newsletter/E-Discovery
    Guidelines.pdf, at pp 1–2.
2   Electronic   Discovery   Guidelines,   http://www.oba.org/en/pdf_newsletter/E-Discovery
    Guidelines.pdf.
3   The Guidelines are already beginning to appear in the case reports; see *Sycor Tehcnol-
    ogy Inc v Kiaer* 2005 CanLII 46736 (Ont. S.C.); *Air Canada v WestJet Airlines Ltd* 2006
    CanLII 14966 (Ont. Sup. Ct. Jus.).

Pre-action discovery

7.76 Canadian law and procedure provide that in some circumstances
discovery may take place prior to litigation commencing. Authorisation for
pre-action discovery is found either in specific civil procedure rules, in those
provinces which have a reception date prior to the development of equitable
pre-action discovery in English law, or in the inherent jurisdiction of the court,
for those provinces with later reception dates or where it is specifically
provided for in the rules[1].

1   See, generally, *Glaxo Wellcome plc v Minister of National Revenue* (1998), 162 D.L.R.
    (4th) 433 (Fed. C.A.).

7.77 Two noteworthy brands of effectively pre-action discovery have emerged
of late. One is the 'John Doe' or 'rolling Anton Piller' order[1], essentially an
Anton Piller order issued in intellectual property cases where the plaintiff is
aware that copyright or trademark is being infringed but does not know the
identity of the infringers. The order is issued ex parte and executed on the
infringer's premises or property once its identity is known to the plaintiff. The
second is the Norwich order, which allows a potential plaintiff to 'demand
disclosure of full information from wrongdoers or third parties that are mixed
up in the wrongdoing' prior to beginning an action[2].

1   See generally D Drapeau, J Cullen 'Anton Piller Orders and the Federal Court of Canada'
    (2004) 17 I.P.J. 301.
2   R Block et al 'Sealed *Ex Parte Norwich* Orders: Safeguarding Against Abuse of the
    Pre-Action Disclosure Remedy' in T Archibald and M Cochrane, eds *Annual Review of
    Civil Litigation* (2003) at p 231.

Scope and cost

7.78 While it varies slightly between jurisdictions 'the general scope of
documentary discovery [in Canada] is extremely broad'[1]. The general tendency is for the courts to adhere to the traditional *Peruvian Guano* standard[2],
and require the disclosure of documents which tend to have a 'semblance of
relevancy'[3] or any bearing on any question which is or might be at play
between the parties.

1   *Walker et al*, p 709.
2   *Compagnie Financiere et Commerciale du Pacifique v Peruvian Guano Co* (1882), 11
    Q.B.D. 55 (C.A.).
3   *Eastern Canadian Coal Gas Venture Ltd v Cape Breton Development Corp* (1995), 141
    N.S.R. (2d) 180 (N.S.C.A.).

7.79 Though there is nothing new about litigation that may require massive and onerous documentary production[1], electronic data accumulates in huge quantities that may be difficult to search, let alone disclose, and may also be functionally collected and stored within specialised software. In general terms, Canadian courts have sought to uphold the breadth of the discovery obligation, applying the broad definition of 'document' so as to include all manner of electronic data[2], and making determinations as to whether production should extend to data or to the technical machinery which contains it[3].

[1] See *Peter Kiewit Sons Co of Canada Ltd v British Columbia Hydro and Power Authority* (1982), 134 D.L.R. (3d) 154 (B.C.S.C.).
[2] Eg *Robak Industries Ltd v Gardner* 2005 BCSC 1133 (Master).
[3] In *Sourian v Sporting Exchange Ltd* 2005 CanLII 4938 (Ont. S.C., Master), for example, the court held that the proper way of disclosing the relevant contents of a database was to require the party to generate a report containing 'the subset of relevant information in usable form', even though this meant that the party would actually have to create a document—an order 'significantly more intrusive than ordinary documents production' (para 12). On this issue, see the *E-Discovery Guidelines* p 7, fn 7.

7.80 If there is a trend, it has been for courts to utilise more frequently their discretion to decline to order production of documents where to do so would be needlessly costly or oppressive[1], or where the information sought is of tangential relevance[2]. For example, in *Baldwin Janzen Insurance Services (2004) Ltd v Janzen*[3], the plaintiff sought production of mirror image copies of the defendant's hard drives for forensic analysis. Humphries J ruled that '[w]ithout some indication that the application of the interesting technology might result in relevant and previously undisclosed documents, the privacy interests of the third parties and the avoidance of unnecessary and onerous expense militate against allowing such a search merely because it can be done'[4]. It may be that the sheer volume of work and expense required to complete some kinds of electronic disclosure is indirectly compelling the courts to tighten-up slightly the scope of the production obligation, though whether this will be true in the long term remains to be seen.

[1] *Dulong v Consumers Packaging Inc* [2000] O.J. No. 161 (Ont. Sup. Ct. Jus., Comm. List, Master) (QL). On cost-shifting, see Karen Groulx 'The issue of costs' (2005) 4/2 LawPRO 9.
[2] *Park v Mullen* 2005 BCSC 1813.
[3] 2006 BCSC 554.
[4] 2006 BCSC 554 at 36.

Failure to produce, obligation to preserve and spoliation

7.81 The procedural regime in each jurisdiction provides for penalties or remedies for failure by a party to produce relevant evidence. A good example is found in Ontario Rule 30.08, which provides that failure to produce a document could result in loss of ability to use the document at trial, revocation or suspension of the party's right to discover, or dismissal of the action. Canadian courts are also slowly recognising a duty to preserve evidence, which appears to arise once a party knows of, or should reasonably anticipate, litigation[1].

[1] *Doust v Schatz* 2002 SKCA 129. See also *Gahtan*, pp 122–23.

7.82 All of the procedural rules give courts the discretion to order parties to preserve evidence where necessary[1], along with appropriate remedies for failure to comply[2] that may include a contempt order[3]. Beyond the latter, however, the doctrine of spoliation is taking on new prominence. Spoliation is well-established in Canada as an evidentiary doctrine that creates a presumption that the destroyed evidence would have operated unfavourably against the spoliating party[4]. However, the law is currently uncertain as to whether spoliation is simply the mirror image of a duty to preserve[5], or whether there is an independent tort of spoliation[6]. The 'leading' decision is that of the Ontario Court of Appeal in *Spasic (Estate) v Imperial Tobacco Ltd*[7], which affirmed the possible existence of a tort of spoliation. However, the elements of such a tort have not been laid out authoritatively.

[1]   Eg *HSBC Bank Canada v Creative Building Maintenance Inc* 2006 CanLII 18361 (Ont. S.C.). Similar powers may, of course, be exercised under an Anton Piller or Mareva injunction.
[2]   *Cheung (Litigation Guardian of) v Toyota Canada Inc* (2003), 29 C.P.C. (5th) 267 (Ont. S.C.J.), disallowing reliance on expert reports regarding the missing evidence.
[3]   *iTrade Finance Inc v Webworx Inc* 2005 CanLII 9196 (Ont. S.C.).
[4]   *St. Louis v Canada* [1896] S.C.R. 649.
[5]   *North American Road Ltd v Hitachi Construction Machinery Company, Ltd* 2005 ABQB 847 at para 16.
[6]   See generally British Columbia Law Institute *Report on Spoliation of Evidence* B.C.L.I. Report No. 34 (November 2004), available online at: http://www.bcli.org/pages/projects/evidence/spoliation/Spoliation_of_Evidence_Rep.pdf.
[7]   (2000), 49 O.R. (3d) 699 (C.A.) at paras 18–22, leave to appeal to S.C.C. denied at (2001), 269 N.R. 394 (note).

7.83 In any event, parties who destroy or materially alter evidence will have an array of procedural relief, at least, available against them. While Canadian courts have shown no inclination to impose the kinds of obligations and sanctions which emerged from recent and prominent US decisions[1], developments are still at an early stage.

[1]   Notably *Zubulake v UBS Warburg LLC* 217 F.R.D. 309 (S.D.N.Y. 2003), *Zubulake v UBS Warburg, LLC* 216 F.R.D. 280 (S.D.N.Y. 2003), *Zubulake v UBS Warburg, LLC* 220 F.R.D. 212 (S.D.N.Y. 2003) and *Coleman v Morgan Stanley* 2005 WL 679071 (Fla. Cir. Ct., March 1, 2005).

Privilege

7.84 Privilege concerns are a live matter in any civil case, but Canadian case law is beginning to reflect some of the particular issues that arise with electronic evidence. Some are simple evidentiary issues, such as whether the opening of an email from a third party's email account amounts to waiver of privilege[1]. In one case, a court applied the absolute privilege attaching to pleadings (ie privilege as against defamation claims) and ruled that the privilege applied to metadata in the pleadings[2].

[1]   *Dublin v Montessori Jewish Day School of Toronto* 2006 CanLII 7510 (Ont. S.C., Master).
[2]   *Big Pond Communications 2000 Inc v Kennedy* 2004 CanLII 18758 (Ont. S.C.).

7.85 A common problem arises from hard drives or networks which are full of inter-mingled communications, usually via email, that might contain a mix of communications between solicitor and client, and discussions between the employees of a corporate party that might contain communications protected by litigation privilege. While the problem is not unique to the electronic context, 'ediscovery does, in some circumstances, involve a heightened or special risk of inadvertent or unintended disclosure of privileged information'[1].

[1] *Electronic Discovery Guidelines*, at p 16.

7.86 Designing means by which disclosure can be accomplished, while avoiding inadvertent release of privileged material, can be challenging. For that matter, combing voluminous electronic files for relevant material, possibly including drafts and metadata, can be costly and expensive. In *Air Canada v WestJet*[1], the plaintiff argued that continuing with a previously-agreed mode of electronic document review was too costly and onerous, and requested that it be permitted to deliver documents without review for relevance or privilege. Any 'inadvertent' production of privileged document was requested not to constitute waiver[2]. The court was 'unmoved'[3] by the plaintiff's cost concerns and dismissed the motion on the basis that solicitor-client privilege should not be 'readily sacrificed to the interests of expediency or economics'[4].

[1] 2006 CanLII 14966 (Ont. Sup. Ct. Jus.).
[2] 2006 CanLII 14966 (Ont. Sup. Ct. Jus.), para 1.
[3] 2006 CanLII 14966 (Ont. Sup. Ct. Jus.), para 16.
[4] 2006 CanLII 14966 (Ont. Sup. Ct. Jus.), para 15.

7.87 What is clear is that the courts will guard the privilege of litigants assiduously and provide significant relief where violations are found. In one case[1], the plaintiff seized the contents of a computer server belonging to the defendants. The court found that the only effective remedy was to stay the action. In another[2], servers formerly belonging to a defendant were purchased by a third party and came into the possession of solicitors for the plaintiff. One of the solicitors reviewed various emails on the server, and realised that a number of them were likely subject to solicitor-client privilege. The court found the solicitors had, in fact, seen some of the privileged emails and removed several of the solicitors from the record as a remedy.

[1] *Autosurvey Inc v Prevost* 2005 CanLII 36255 (Ont. S.C.).
[2] *National Bank Financial Ltd v Daniel Potter* 2005 NSSC 113.

Pre-discovery discussions

7.88 The Electronic Discovery Guidelines encourage parties to confer with each other prior to discovery beginning in order to attempt to resolve technical issues and agree on a scope and format for production, among other things[1]. The courts have endorsed this idea, and decisions are beginning to appear in which chambers judges encourage[2] or order[3] parties to at least attempt to reach agreement on these issues.

[1] *E-Discovery Guidelines*, pp 12–16.

2   *Logan v Harper* 2003 CanLII 15592 (Ont. S.C., Master).
3   *Sycor Technology* 2005 CanLII 46736 (Ont. S.C.); *CIBC World Markets Inc v Genuity Capital Markets* 2005 CanLII 3944 (Ont. S.C.).

Chapter 8

ENGLAND & WALES

STEPHEN MASON

8.01 The aim of this chapter is to set out the principle factors relating to evidence in electronic format in civil and criminal proceedings. The intention is to supplement the standard practitioner and academic texts on the topics of evidence, disclosure and procedure. For this reason, the work of the Law Commission that led to the passing of the Criminal Justice Act 2003 is not referred to in detail, because it is fully covered in the standard texts on evidence[1].

[1] Law Commission, Evidence in Criminal Proceedings: Hearsay and related topics (LC 245, 19.06.97).

TYPES OF EVIDENCE

8.02 Broadly, the types of evidence fit into two categories: direct and indirect evidence.

Direct and indirect evidence[1]

8.03 The existence of a physical object constitutes direct evidence. The object can be proven by its production or by the testimony or declaration, which must be admissible, of a person who actually perceived the object—hence the human perception of a screen print-out is admissible. In terms of evidence in electronic format, judges have admitted a record of the product of mechanical devices and automatic recordings, including photographs[2], tape recordings[3] the movements of a ship as traced by radar and automatically recorded on film,[3] the print-out of the results of a test undertaken on a breath-test machine[5], video recordings[6] and computer print-outs[7], although there is a distinction between the content of the print-out and the metadata logically associated with the document in digital format: the metadata may be relevant, in which case it will need to be rendered into human-readable format. Another form of direct evidence is the existence of a fact. A fact can only be asserted by the testimony of a person.

[1] Hodge M Malek, gen ed *Phipson on Evidence* (16th edn, 2005) paras 1–10 to 1–16.
[2] *R v Tolson* (1864) 4 F & F 103, (1864) 176 ER 488, where a photograph was admitted in a case of alleged bigamy. Willes J commented in his summing up to the members of the jury: 'The photograph was admissible because it is only a visible representation of the image or impression made upon the minds of the witnesses by the sight of the person or the object it represents; and, therefore, is, in reality, only another species of the evidence which persons give of identity, when they speak merely from memory'. The jury subsequently entered a verdict of not guilty.

3   *R v Burr and Sullivan* [1956] Crim LR 442, (1956) *Times*, May 11; *R v Ali (Maqsud); R v Hussain (Ashiq)* [1966] 1 QB 688, [1965] 3 WLR 229, [1965] 2 All ER 464, (1965) 49 Cr App Rep 230, 129 J.P. 396, 109 Sol Jo 331, CA; for an example in Scotland, see *Hopes and Lavery v Advocate (HM)* [1960] Crim LR 566, 1960 SC(J) 104, (1960) SLT 264.

4   *Statute of Liberty, The, Sapporo Maru M/S (Owners) v Steam Tanker Statute of Liberty (Owners)* [1968] 1 WLR 739, [1968] 2 All ER 195, [1968] 1 Lloyd's Rep 429, (1968) 112 Sol Jo 380, P.D and Admlty.

5   *Castle v Cross* [1984] 1 WLR 1372, [1985] 1 All ER 87, [1985] RTR 62, [1984] Crim LR 682, (1984) 81 LSG 2596, (1984) 128 Sol Jo 855, DC.

6   *Kajala v Noble* (1982) 75 Cr App Rep 149, [1982] Crim LR 433, CA, *R v Grimer* [1982] Crim LR 674, (1982) 126 SJ 641, CA; *R v Thomas (Steven)* [1986] Crim LR 682; *XXX v YYY and ZZZ* EAT/0729/01 and EAT/0413/02 ILB.

7   *Wood (Stanley William)* (1983) 76 Cr App Rep 23, [1982] Crim LR 667, CA, the results of an automated analysis.

8.04   Once a fact is proven, indirect evidence, which stems from the proof of the initial fact, can be introduced. Indirect evidence comprises facts that can be logically inferred from the initial fact. Most of the digital evidence tendered into courts comprises indirect evidence. The most significant inference made for digital evidence consists of the assertion that the evidence tendered is accurate, and can therefore be trusted[1].

1   The challenge of proving that evidence in digital format is authentic was the subject of *R v Cochrane* [1993] Crim LR 48, CA and, more recently, a case in the United States of America: *American Express Travel Related Services Co Inc v Vee Vinhnee* 336 B.R. 437 (9th Cir. BAP), (2005) WL 3609376.

Real evidence

8.05   The term 'real evidence' tends not to be used in practice, and is best described as 'Material objects other than documents, produced for inspection of the court'[1], a proposition that Professor Tapper agrees with. In respect of evidence in electronic format, in *Statute of Liberty, The, Sapporo Maru M/S (Owners) v Steam Tanker Statute of Liberty (Owners)*[2] Sir Jocelyn Simon P determined that the film recording of a radar set of echoes of ships within its range was real evidence, even though it was recorded from a mechanical instrument. The film comprised real evidence because it merely recorded the information given out by the radar set, and he rejected the submission that the evidence was hearsay, at 196:

> In my view the evidence in question in the present case has nothing to do with the hearsay rule and does not depend on the Evidence Act 1938. It is in the nature of real evidence, which is conveniently defined in *Cockle's Cases And Statutes On Evidence* (10th edn, 1963) at p 348: 'Real evidence is evidence afforded by the production of physical objects for inspection or other examination by the court.' If tape recordings are admissible, it seems equally a photograph of radar reception is admissible—as, indeed, any other type of photograph. It would be an absurd distinction that a photograph should be admissible if the camera were operated manually by a photographer, but not if it were operated by a trip or clock mechanism. Similarly, if evidence of weather conditions were relevant, the law would affront common sense if it were to say that those could be proved by a person who looked at a barometer from time to time, but not by producing a barograph record. So too with other types of dial recordings. Again, cards from clocking-in and out machines are frequently

admitted in accident cases. The law is bound these days to take cognisance of the fact that mechanical means replace human effort.

¹ *Malek* (2005) para 1–14.
² [1968] 2 All ER 195 at 196.

8.06 By comparison, the decision of the Court of Appeal in *R v Pettigrew*¹ held that a print-out from a computer operated by an employee of the Bank of England was a hearsay statement. The operator fed bundles of bank notes with consecutive serial numbers into the machine, and the machine automatically rejected any notes in the bundle that were defective. The machine also recorded the first and last serial numbers of each bundle of 100 notes. As the operator fed the bundles into the machine, he noted the first serial numbers in the bundle on a card. The purpose of adducing the evidence was to permit the prosecution to trace the issuance of the notes, and to link bank notes found in the possession of Pettigrew to a particular bundle of notes that had been stolen in a burglary. Counsel for the prosecution argued that the print-out was admissible under the provisions of the Criminal Evidence Act 1965 as a business record. However, s 1(1)(a) required that, for such a record to be admissible as evidence of the truth of any matter dealt with in the record, the information would have to be supplied by a person who had, or may reasonably be supposed to have, personal knowledge of the matters. The members of the Court of Appeal reached the conclusion that the operator did not have personal knowledge of the numbers of the notes that were rejected, because they were compiled automatically by the computer. This was an accurate application of the hearsay rule but omitted any consideration that the print-out might be considered real evidence².

¹ (1980) 71 Cr App Rep 39.
² Colin Tapper *Computer Law* (4th edn, 1989) p 375; JC Smith, 'The Admissibility of Statements by Computer' [1981] Crim LR 387; print-outs were admitted under the provisions of s 1(1) of the Criminal Evidence Act 1965 in *R v Ewing* [1983] QB 1039, [1983] 3 WLR 1, [1983] 2 All ER 645, (1983) 77 Cr App Rep 47, [1984] E.C.C. 234, [1983] Crim LR 472, (1983) 127 Sol Jo 390, (1983) *Times* March 15, CA.

8.07 Compare this decision to the assessment in *Wood (Stanley William)*¹. In this case, it was determined that a computer print-out was a piece of real evidence. The computer was considered as a tool and the print-out an item of real evidence which, in turn, had to be proved by the testimony of witnesses, including an expert witness. The basis of admitting a print-out of an output as an item of real evidence is explained by Tapper: 'Evidence derived from a computer constitutes real evidence when it is used circumstantially rather than testimonially, that is to say that the fact that it takes one form rather than another is what it makes it relevant, rather than the truth of some assertion which it contains'². One explanation to reinforce the point is to consider how a print-out is brought about. If the print-out is from a computer, the computer will have held the output of the data in memory. The print-out is a record, in human-readable form, of the result of the computation made by the computer. Arguably, the item of real evidence, as with any computer, comprises the hard drive or the equivalent of the hard drive, and the print-out. If real evidence is considered to be a material object other than a document, the hard drive is the item that comprises the material object and the data stored on the hard drive can be classified as a document[3]. However, although the computer containing the hard drive might be admitted into evidence, the content of the hard drive would need to be provided to the court in human-readable format. As a result, the print-out of the hard drive is adduced as real evidence, although the print-out is not necessarily the primary source of evidence. It is secondary evidence of the content of the hard drive. This is because the data printed on the print-out only represents a part of the data relating to the document that is printed. Other data that is not printed on the print-out includes the metadata and the historical changes made to the document. However, it does not follow that a print-out is not acceptable because it is secondary evidence and therefore may not be the best evidence available. It will only be necessary to consider adducing the hard disk, the actual computer itself or an authentic copy of the hard disk into evidence, if the metadata or the history of the document, are in issue.

1   (1983) 76 Cr App Rep 23. See also the earlier case of *R v McCarthy (Colin Paul), R v Warren (Mark Stephen), R v Lloyd (Leigh Cedric), R v Warren (Robert John)* [1998] RTR 374, CA.
2   *Tapper* (1989) p 373.
3   *Derby v Weldon (No 9)* [1991] 1 WLR 652, [1991] 2 All ER 901, (1990) *Times*, November 9, CA, Vinelott J suggested a document stored on a computer was similar to the carbon copy of a letter that was stored in a file.

8.08 This can be compared to the analysis offered by Kennedy J in *Castle v Cross*[1] at common law, where he indicated that a police sergeant could give evidence of his perceptions as he observed an Intoximeter 3000 when it was working. The Intoximeter 3000 appears to be an analogue device that measures breath alcohol values[2]. In this case, it was determined that the print-out is an item of real evidence and was compared it to a speedometer, calculator, or a sophisticated tool. Of interest, Kennedy J made a perceptive remark in relation to computers with a memory function:

> Of course, where a computer is used in respect of its memory function, it is possible to envisage where it might fall foul of the rule against hearsay[3].

In this instance, the print-out comprised information that was produced by the Intoximeter, because the data had not passed through a human mind. In such a case, the content of the print-out is not hearsay, but amounted to real evidence. This point is reinforced by the comments of Taylor LJ at 192 in *R v Spiby (John Eric)*[4]:

> This was not a print-out which depended on its contents for anything that has passed through the human mind. All that had happened was that when someone in one of the rooms in the hotel had lifted the receiver from the telephone and, with his finger, pressed certain buttons, the machine had made a record of what was done and printed that out. The situation would have been quite different if a telephone operator in the hotel had had herself to gather the information, then type it into a computer bank, and there came then a print-out from that computer.

Taylor LJ adopted the explanation provided by Professor Smith[5], that the distinction is whether the content of the print-out can be considered a mere recording of a fact, such as when data is processed by a computer without any human input of any description (in this instance, a computerised machine called a 'Norex' monitored the telephone calls of hotel guests in order to work out how much to charge for the use of the telephone) and whether the content of the print-out has been processed in some way by a human being, in which case it is hearsay.

1   [1984] 1 WLR 1372 at 1380.
2   The discussion in the case of *DPP v McKeown; DPP v Jones* [1997] 2 Cr App Rep 155, [1997] 1 All ER 737, HL does not provide a satisfactory answer as to whether the Intoximeter is an analogue device or a computer.
3   [1984] 1 WLR 1372 at 1380.
4   (1990) 91 Cr App Rep 186, [1991] Crim LR 199, (1990) *Times*, March 16, (1990) *Independent*, April 2, (1990) *Daily Telegraph*, March 30, CA.
5   JC Smith 'The Admissibility of Statements by Computer' [1981] Crim LR 387.

8.09 Lord Hoffmann provided a useful discussion about whether the accuracy of a clock on a device was relevant in *DPP v McKeown; DPP v Jones*[1]. In the two cases brought together in this appeal, the clocks on the Intoximeter 3000 used to measure the breath alcohol values were not accurate. In addressing whether the accuracy of the clocks were relevant to the accuracy of the reading, he indicated that, for the purposes of s 69 of the Police and Criminal Evidence Act 1984, a malfunction was irrelevant unless it affected the way in which the computer processes, stores or retrieves the information used to generate the statement[2]. Regrettably, Lord Hoffmann went on to make a remark that was not quite accurate in relation to clocks on computers:

> I have considered the matter on the assumption that the error in the clock display showed that the computer was not operating properly. I should say, however, that I am not satisfied that this conclusion should have been drawn. Computer clocks, like any others, have to be set to the correct time and the most obvious explanation for the 15 minute discrepancy was that someone had made a mistake when he last set the clock[3].

It might have been correct that the clock was one hour out because of the difference in time zone, but clocks in computers are not always accurate[4]. Smart AJ also commented on the accuracy or otherwise of clocks in the case of *R v Ross Magoulias*[5], where the identity of the appellant centred on the recordings made by an ATM and a security video:

> It is a notorious matter of fact that reliable clocks or timing devices may show slightly different times. A clock may gain or lose ever so slightly and it may be some days before the difference becomes noticeable. When setting a clock or timing device there might be a very small error. Perhaps the clock from which the timing device is set is slightly astray. It is exceedingly well known that the timing of differing clocks needs to be synchronised if pinpoint accuracy is required. It is beyond argument that both KB and the appellant attended the service station on 7 July 2001. She can be seen on the video tape for about three minutes (18.37.18 to 18.40.25 according to the video tape timing device). That cannot be disputed. Nor can it be disputed that the appellant attended at the ATM and withdrew $50 (18.40.59 according to the ATM timing device). As earlier pointed out there was no direct evidence available to the jury that the timing mechanisms were not synchronised. If there had been the video tape would have recorded a person (the appellant) withdrawing $50 from the appellant's account at 18.40.59 (bank record time). The video does not show anybody near the ATM at that time. Thus there was no room for any presumption to operate in any useful way.

1   [1997] 2 Cr App Rep 155, [1997] 1 All ER 737, HL.

2   [1997] 1 All ER 737 at 744. A study later demonstrated that breath alcohol values measured on the Lion Intoximeter 3000 are not affected if the machine clock is incorrect by more than four minutes: RC Denny 'The Intoximeter 3000 and the four minute fallacy', Medical Science Law, April 1998, 38(2):163–4. Minor typographical errors on a print-out do not alter the validity of the results, either: *Reid v DPP* (1998) *Times*, March 6.

3   [1997] 1 All ER 737 at 745. See also the presumption in *R v Reynard* [2005] EWCA Crim 550 where the clocks on a computer were presumed to be in working order: on the facts of this case, the accuracy or otherwise of the clocks it seemed immaterial, bearing in mind there did not seem to be any question of testing the authenticity of the evidence from the computer.

4   Clocks on facsimile machines may also be far from accurate, and the comments by Burton J (President) at 14 imply that the data recorded by the logs at the offices of the Employment Appeals Tribunal are accurate as a matter of 'common sense,' which cannot be right: '... it must make common sense to accept the accuracy, as I believe there to be, of the record of receipt in the fax log of the EAT, and not to accept either uncertain evidence about the accuracy of the sender's machine or some kind of speculation as to electronic receipt short of the record in the EAT fax log' *Woodward v Abbey National plc; J P Garrett Electrical Limited v Cotton* [2005] ICR 1702, [2005] IRLR 782. The accuracy of the clocks are a separate matter, however, in refining a procedural rule, as in this case, that the log of the facsimile machine in the offices of the Employment Appeals Tribunal is to govern the timing of receipt of a facsimile transmission. In *R v Good* [2005] DCR 804, the clock in the computer was running 42 minutes and 30 seconds behind the actual time.

5   [2003] NSWCCA 143 at 41.

8.10 The accuracy of a clock can cause serious problems, especially for the financial sector. The computers in a bank, for instance, must ensure the accuracy of the clocks in the computer to provide for the accuracy of the records created for each transaction. Similarly, where a system is required to deal with synchronous communications, such as the software controlling the manufacturing process in a factory, the accuracy of the clock is paramount. This is why a great deal of attention is given to the accuracy of the clock in such systems. There are a number of reasons why a software clock does not maintain accurate time: where a computer is left switched on for long periods of time, the software clock might become inaccurate; conversely, when a computer is switched off, the software clock stops running, which means it must synchronise with the hardware clock when the power is switched on, but the hardware clock in turn relies on a battery, which means it will in turn fail to maintain accuracy over time; however, a well-written software clock should synchronise with the hardware clock periodically, so the drift would never become too serious. The batteries used for hardware clocks are designed to last for five years; this means the main reasons for frequency error are the changes in temperature, air pressure and magnetic fields[1].

1   Michael Lombardi 'Computer Time Synchronization' (Time and Frequency Division, National Institute of Standards and Technology), available online at http:// tf.nist.gov/ service/pdf/computertime.pdf; Bradley Schatz, George Mohay and Andrew Clark 'A correlation method for establishing provenance of timestamps in digital evidence' The Proceedings of the Digital Forensic Research Workshop 2006, (2006) Digital Investigation, vol 3S, pp S98–S107.

8.11 Computers are designed to undertake a wide range of tasks. This means that the evidence available as an output of a computer is equally as varied. Two popular uses of computers include the formation of records and where the computer records the credits and debits of an account. This means the print-out of records of computer payment transactions are considered to be real evidence, as the members of the House of Lords made clear in *R v Governor of Brixton Prison, Ex p Levin; sub nom Levin (Application for a Writ of Habeas Corpus), Re*[1]. In this appeal against extradition, it was alleged that Vladimir Levin used a computer terminal in St Petersburg to gain unauthorised access to a Citibank terminal in Parsipanny, New Jersey to make 40 fraudulent transfers of funds to the value of US$10.7m from the accounts of clients of the bank to accounts which he or his associates controlled-.·Lord Hoffmann took the opportunity of distinguishing between real evidence and hearsay with respect to digital evidence that is printed on paper. Print-outs of screen displays of the historical records of computer payment transactions were adduced before the magistrate in the extradition proceedings. A witness gave evidence to illustrate how the records were created. Lord Hoffmann took the opportunity of making clear the difference between a hearsay statement and evidence of a record of a transaction:

> The print-outs are tendered to prove that such transfers took place. They record the transfers themselves, created by the interaction between whoever purported to request the transfers and the computer program in Parsipanny. The evidential status of the print-outs is no different from that of a photocopy of a forged cheque[2].

It is now clear that print-outs are considered a form of real evidence, although the truth of the content of the print-out will be a matter of further testimony[3]. It is important, therefore, to ensure the proper testimonial foundations of digital evidence are presented to a court to demonstrate the truth of the statement included in a print-out of digital evidence.

[1]   [1997] AC 741, [1997] 3 WLR 117, [1997] 3 All ER 289, [1998] 1 Cr App Rep 22, [1997] Crim LR 891, (1997) 94(30) LS Gaz 28, (1997) 147 NLJ 1990, (1997) 141 Sol Jo LB 148, (1997) *Times*, June 21, (1997) *Independent* July 2, HL.
[2]   [1997] AC 741 at 746.
[3]   A point made by Gage J in *O'Shea v City of Coventry Magistrates' Court* [2004] EWHC 905 (Admin) at 25.

Best evidence

8.12 The meaning of 'best evidence' has been used in different senses, as pointed out in Phipson[1]: the nature of the fact admitted, or the best evidence that the circumstances would allow, or the best evidence the party could produce. Used in the sense of an original document, if the location of the original document could not be ascertained the plaintiff failed in their action, although equity might, in such circumstances, have offered relief[2]. On this topic, Lord Hardwicke commented that the 'The judges and sages of the law have laid it down that there is but one general rule of evidence, *the best that the nature of the case will admit*' [italics in the original][3]. However, it is pertinent to observe the other remarks he offered on the subject, which illustrate the positive and negative aspects of the rule. He made it clear that the best evidence was not always readily available, although reliance upon the memory of a witness was something to be avoided if possible:

> The first ground judges have gone upon in departing from strict rules, is an absolute strict necessity. *Secondly*, a presumed necessity. In the case of writings subscribed by witnesses, if all are dead, the proof of one of their hands is

sufficient to establish the deed: where an original is lost, a copy may be admitted; if no copy, then a proof by witnesses who have heard the deed, and yet it is a thing the law abhors to admit by the memory of man for evidence [italics in the original][4].

1 *Malek* (2005) para 7–38.
2 *Anon. Case 58* (1740) 2 Atk 61, 26 ER 435; *Sugden v St Leonards* (1876) 1 PD 154; *Malek* (2005) para 7–42.
3 *Omychund v Barker* 1 Atk 21 at 49, 26 ER 15.
4 *Omychund v Barker* 1 Atk 21 at 49.

8.13 The best evidence rule can be considered from two points of view. It can be regarded as an inclusionary rule under which whatever is the best evidence is admissible, thus overcoming exclusionary rules such as the hearsay rule. Alternatively, it can be regarded as an exclusionary rule, so that anything which is not the best evidence is inadmissible. In *Omychund v Barker*, the evidence was from a non-Christian at a time when a Christian oath was required. In this instance, Lord Hardwicke used the rule as an inclusionary rule because it was the best evidence, as the only persons who had direct knowledge of the relevant event were all non-Christians. In the majority of cases that followed, the rule was used in an exclusionary way to deny the use of copies of documents when the absence of the original was not satisfactorily accounted for. Reaction against the rule began in the nineteenth century[1], and by the latter part of the twentieth century, it was recognised that the best evidence rule was no longer as relevant as it once was. Lord Denning MR added his robust comments to this effect in *Garton v Hunter (Valuation Officer)*[2]:

> It is plain that Scott LJ had in mind the old rule that a party must produce the best evidence that the nature of the case will allow, and that any less good evidence is to be excluded. That old rule has gone by the board long ago. The only remaining instance of it that I know is that if an original document is available in your hands, you must produce it. You cannot give secondary evidence by producing a copy. Nowadays we do not confine ourselves to the best evidence. We admit all relevant evidence. The goodness or badness of it only goes to weight, not to admissibility.

1 *Malek* (2005) paras 7–38 and 7–39.
2 [1969] 2 QB 37 at 44, [1968] 2 WLR 86, [1969] 1 All ER 451, 133 J.P. 162, 67 L.G.R. 229, 15 R.R.C. 145, (1968) Sol Jo 924, (1962) *Times*, November 15, CA.

8.14 In a limited way, the rule is now confined to written documents in the strictest sense of the term, not having any relevance to tapes or films[1]. Ackner LJ made this clear in *Kajala v Noble* at 152:

> The old rule, that a party must produce the best evidence that the nature of the case will allow, and that any less good evidence is to be excluded, has gone by the board long ago. The only remaining instance of it is that, if an original document is available in one's hands, one must produce it; that one cannot give secondary evidence by producing a copy. Nowadays we do not confine ourselves to the best evidence. We admit all relevant evidence. The goodness or badness of it goes only to weight, and not to admissibility ... In our judgment, the old rule is limited and confined to written documents in the strict sense of the term, and has no relevance to tapes or films.

In this instance, the BBC offered an authentic copy of the original tape to the court to view, which was supported by appropriate evidence from Derek McCallister, an Assistant Editor with the BBC. Two interesting points were argued by counsel for the defendant: first, the failure to call the cameramen meant the date of the filming could not be ascertained accurately; and second, the film shown was an edited version of the total amount of filming that took place, which meant that, in the absence of the evidence from the cameramen, it was not possible to tell whether the film showed the events in their true sequence. These concerns were quickly dismissed by Ackner LJ. He indicated that the examination of the material was sufficient to ascertain the date of the filming. In response to the second issue, Ackner LJ indicated that the defendant did not challenge the integrity of the film in that, by editing the films, the finished product might have distorted the activities of the defendant. The pertinent observation made by Ackner LJ was that, even if the events were not shown in their true sequence, what mattered was whether the film accurately illustrated the activities of the defendant.

[1]   *Kajala v Noble* (1982) 75 Cr App Rep 149, DC.

8.15 In 1990, Lloyd LJ observed that the best evidence rule had become a rule of practice or procedure[1]. He also made the following remarks about the rule:

> ... this court would be more than happy to say goodbye to the best evidence rule. We accept that it served an important purpose in the days of parchment and quill pens[2]. But since the invention of carbon paper and, still more, the photocopier and the telefascimile machine, that purpose has largely gone. Where there is an allegation of forgery the court will obviously attach little, if any, weight to anything other than the original; so also if the copy produced in court is illegible. But to maintain a general exclusionary rule for these limited purposes is, in our view, hardly justifiable[3].

More recently, the inadvertent destruction of evidence has not prevented the admission of testimony by a witness in respect of evidence in analogue format. In the case of *Taylor v Chief Constable of Cheshire*[4], the appellant was convicted of stealing one packet of Duracell batteries to the value of £1.89 from WHSmith. There were two remote cameras located in the store, the images of which were viewed by a security officer on two monitors. The security officer was also able to manoeuvre the cameras remotely. One of the screens was linked to a video recorder. The recorder was switched on and a recording was made of a person, who, with their back to the camera, picked up the batteries and slipped them inside his jacket. The person then turned, glanced up at the camera, offering a full view of his face, and walked out of range of the camera. The images recorded on the video recorder were later seen by the manager of the store, three police officers, and the lawyer for the accused. The recording was stored by WHSmith for safe keeping. When the case was heard, it transpired that the recording had been erased from the video cassette by new security officers. The magistrates permitted the witnesses to give evidence of what they saw on the video recording. An appeal was rejected. Counsel for the prosecution, Jane Hayward, submitted that, once it was proved that a video recording has been made of the incident, the evidence offered by the witnesses who viewed the images that were recorded was no different from evidence of witnesses who claim to have seen the events by being physically present at the time the incident took place. This proposition was accepted by Ralph Gibson LJ:

> In substance I accept the contention made for the prosecutor. For my part I can see no effective distinction so far as concerns admissibility between a direct view of the action of an alleged shoplifter by a security officer and a view of those activities by the officer on the video display unit of a camera, or a view of these activities on a recording of what the camera recorded[5].

Although the best evidence in this instance was the video recording of the incident, nevertheless the absence of that evidence did not preclude the admission into evidence of the testimony of those witnesses that viewed the recording. The recollections of the witnesses ought not to be precluded because the best evidence is not available. The evidence offered by the witnesses is, as pointed out by Ralph Gibson LJ, 'direct evidence of what was seen to be happening in a particular place at a particular time' and it is for the trier of the facts to assess its weight, credibility and reliability[6].

1   *R v Governor of Pentonville Prison ex p Osman (No 1) sub nom Osman (No 1), Re* [1990] 1 WLR 277, [1989] 3 All ER 701, (1990) 90 Cr App Rep 281, [1988] Crim LR 611, (1990) 87(7) LSG 32, (1990) 134 Sol Jo 458, (1988) *Times*, April 13, (1988) *Independent*, April 15, (1988) *Guardian*, April 19, (1988) *Daily Telegraph*, April 21, DC.
2   It will be interesting to know how many ancient documents were previously admitted into evidence that were actually copies: A Guide to Seals in the Public Record Office (2nd edn, 1968) p 30.
3   [1990] 1 WLR 277 at 308.
4   [1986] 1 WLR 1479, [1987] 1 All ER 225, (1987) 84 Cr App Rep 191, (1987) 151 JP 103, [1987] Crim LR 119, (1987) 151 JPN 110, (1987) LS Gaz 412, (1986) 130 Sol Jo 953, QBD.
5   [1987] 1 All ER 225 at 230.
6   [1987] 1 All ER 225 at 230.

8.16 With rare exceptions[1], the rule no longer dominates the admission of evidence into proceedings. The practical effects of not submitting best evidence was illustrated by Lloyd LJ:

> What is meant by a party having a document available in his hands? We would say that it means a party who has the original of the document with him in court, or could have it in court without any difficulty. In such a case, if he refuses to produce the original and can give no reasonable explanation, the court would infer the worst. The copy should be excluded. If, taking that view, we are cutting down still further what remains of the best evidence rule, we are content[2].

The members of the Court of Appeal have made it clear that the best evidence rule is no longer of any relevance. In *Springsteen v Masquerade Music Ltd*[3], Mr Springsteen claimed damages and injunctive relief against the appellants in relation to the manufacture, importation and supply of compact discs containing recordings and performances by him in the early 1970s of 19 songs, which he had written and composed. At the trial, the appellants required Mr Springsteen to prove his title to the copyrights, and denied infringement. Mr Springsteen was required to prove the links in the chain of title dating back to 1972. Unfortunately, he did not have some of the relevant documents and relied on secondary evidence as to the existence of various items of evidence. It was claimed by the appellants that Mr Springsteen failed to discharge the burden of proof because the secondary evidence was not admissible of the contents of a written document, especially secondary evidence of the assignments of the relevant intellectual property. The trial judge, Ferris J, considered the secondary evidence and decided, on the balance of probabilities, that the copyrights had been effectively assigned[4]. The members of the Court of Appeal concluded that the judge was fully justified to admit secondary evidence of the assignments. In his judgment, Jonathan Parker LJ considered the best evidence rule in detail and reviewed the case law extensively[5], and he went on to state:

> For my part, I would not even recognise the continuing existence of that 'remaining instance' of the application of 'the old rule'. In my judgment, the 'obligation' of a party who has a document to produce the original in evidence is founded not on any rule of law but is simply a reflection of the fact that a party to whom a document is available will by reason of that very fact be unable to account to the satisfaction of the court for his non-production of it when inviting the court to admit secondary evidence of its contents, with the practical consequence that the court will attach no weight to the secondary evidence[6].

After discussing a number of further authorities, he made the position clear with respect to the best evidence rule in the twenty-first century:

> In my judgment, the time has now come when it can be said with confidence that the best evidence rule, long on its deathbed, has finally expired. In every case where a party seeks to adduce secondary evidence of the contents of a document, it is a matter for the court to decide, in the light of all the circumstances of the case, what (if any) weight to attach to that evidence. Where the party seeking to adduce the secondary evidence could readily produce the document, it may be expected that (absent some special circumstances) the court will decline to admit the secondary evidence on the ground that it is worthless. At the other extreme, where the party seeking to adduce the secondary evidence genuinely cannot produce the document, it may be expected that (absent some special circumstances) the court will admit the secondary evidence and attach such weight to it as it considers appropriate in all the circumstances. In cases falling between those two extremes, it is for the court to make a judgment as to whether in all the circumstances any weight should be attached to the secondary evidence. Thus, the 'admissibility' of secondary evidence of the contents of documents is, in my judgment, entirely dependent upon whether or not any weight is to be attached to that evidence. And whether or not any weight is to be attached to such secondary evidence is a matter for the court to decide, taking into account all the circumstances of the particular case[7].

Waller and Laws LJJ both agreed with the decision. The unanimous decision in this case makes it clear that it will be rare for the best evidence rule to be considered an issue in the future. As a result, the best evidence rule is now tightly confined, and applies to both civil and criminal cases[8]. The ramifications for evidence in electronic format are significant. Evidence in analogue format will continue to rely either on a recording of the operation of a device, or the testimony of an individual that physically observes the device working. Evidence in digital format should be treated in a slightly different manner. The item of real evidence is the physical product that stores the data, if the data is actually stored[9]. However, the physical production of a device in court as an item of evidence is of no help to the finder of fact. The production of a computer only serves to assure the court that the item exists: it has no further value as an item of evidence unless, perhaps, it is introduced to demonstrate a link to a fact in issue. An example would be if a computer screen was used as a weapon or if the device contained traces of DNA that demonstrated a person was using the keyboard at a material time. The submission of secondary evidence has always been the norm for electronic evidence and will continue to be. The form that the secondary evidence takes will continue to comprise data in the form of documents that are printed on to paper, or data that is loaded into a server and then viewed on screen. Proving the integrity of the data will be important in such circumstances where the authenticity is in issue. Integrity goes to show the data has not been corrupted and is one facet of a number of issues that may need to be considered in determining the authenticity of the data.

1   *R v Wayte* (1982) 76 Cr App Rep 110, CA where photostat copies of two letters were not admissible in circumstances where the party seeking to reply on the documents refused to produce the original letters.
2   [1990] 1 WLR 277 at 308.
3   [2001] EMLR 654, [2001] All ER (D) 101 (Apr), [2001] EWCA Civ 513.
4   *Springsteen v Flute International Ltd* [1999] EMLR 180, [1998] EWHC Patents 277.
5   [2001] EMLR 654 at 64–85.
6   [2001] EMLR 654 at 80.
7   [2001] EMLR 654 at 85.
8   *R v Wayte* (1982) 76 Cr App Rep 110.
9   Vinelott J postulated that the 'memory or database of the word-processor is the original document' in *Derby & Co Ltd v Weldon (No. 9)* [1991] 2 All ER 901 at 906. Instant messaging is an example of evidence that might not be stored, which means it becomes analogous to an oral conversation.

Primary and secondary evidence

8.17 In the physical world, the distinction between primary and secondary evidence lies in the difference between the production of an original document to prove the content in question and the submission of inferior evidence, such as a copy of a document, termed secondary evidence. The concepts of 'primary' and 'secondary' evidence take a different shape when applied to material objects that must be processed to be viewed. Consider, for instance, a photograph taken with a camera containing film, or a plate. The negative or the plate consists of the image in reverse. It is the negative or plate that comprise the primary evidence. However, few people will be satisfied by looking at the primary image, if only because it is not easy to view and may not have been intended to be viewed in this format, unless by means of a projector. This means the printed image is secondary evidence. Any number of copies of the primary object can be made, although no printed copy will be an exact copy of the film or plate. This is because the processes followed, and the mix of chemicals used in transforming the negative into a print, will determine how accurately the photograph reflects the image, in particular the degree of contrast (that is the range of gray tones) captured on the negative. For example, the degree of contrast will affect how bruising is reproduced on the photograph: a high contrast makes the bruising appear darker and more dramatic, whilst a low contrast will lessen the effect of the visual image, making the bruise seem somewhat less consequential.

8.18 The primary evidence of a document in digital format differs from the primary evidence of a physical document. The original of a physical document, such as a commercial contract between two parties, signed by the authorised representatives of both parties and acknowledged as the original document, is primary evidence of the content of the contract. If the contract was created on a computer, the physical document will be the original document where it is signed and adopted by both parties[1]. However, should the contract, which was subsequently acted upon by both parties, only exist on a computer, the next consideration (if the content of the document is in issue) will be to determine whether there is primary evidence of the document and, if so, where it is located. The primary evidence will comprise the hard drive or storage media upon which the document resides. If the parties can agree that the contract is stored on a particular hard drive, then printing the document out on paper will provide copies in a human readable format and this, in turn, will comprise secondary evidence of the document.

[1] The physical document might have a digital counterpart, as in Austria: Friedrich Schwank 'CyberDOC and e-Government: the electronic archive of Austrian notaries' (2004) e-Signature Law Journal, vol 1, no 1, pp 28–30.

8.19 Even if the hard drive or storage device is correctly identified as the primary evidence, the physical item is of no value unless a person testifies to its relevance and the qualities that make it pertinent, such as an assertion that the stored data is germane to the proceedings. In practice, primary evidence containing digital data is not tendered into evidence. Courts rely on the production of the output of digital data in human-readable format and printed on paper, which can be considered as secondary evidence of the digital data. Where the credibility of the data is in question, foundation testimony will have to be introduced and tested to determine whether it can be accepted into evidence. Given the ease by which digital data is replicated, copied, altered and disseminated, it may be difficult to establish the precise document that both parties relied upon. However, it is also relevant to remark that, in the event the hard drive or storage medium is considered to be the original and the print-out a copy, it is conceivable that an authentic print-out of a document of the material data at a time in the past may be a better form of evidence than the state of the internal memory at a later time. This inversion of the concept of best evidence provides a good illustration of the danger of assuming that the print-out may not be the best evidence in any given situation. It must also be made clear that the range of evidence in digital format will not just comprise print-outs of what might be termed conventional files, such as copies of letters, contracts or spreadsheets. Other forms include reports from databases, the records of transactions and the reproduction of images that are stored, such as the scanned image of an original paper document.

Civil proceedings

8.20 In responding to this issue, consideration first can be given to the provisions of s 8 of the Civil Evidence Act 1995, which permits the introduction of copies of documents into evidence for the purpose of proving the statement contained in the document:

8.—(1)   Where a statement contained in a document is admissible as evidence in civil proceedings, it may be proved—

- (a)   by the production of that document, or
- (b)   whether or not that document is still in existence, by the production of a copy of that document or of the material part of it, authenticated in such manner as the court may approve.

(2)   It is immaterial for this purpose how many removes there are between a copy and the original.

It is relevant to note that it is the statement that is important, not the document[1]. The original document from an analogue device is the record of the measurements of a device, which comprises the statement, such as the film in *The Statute of Liberty* or the print-out from an Intoximeter. Determining what is meant by an original document created in digital format on a computer can be slightly more complex. Consider drafting a simple contract. Assume the document is created on a single computer and the file stored in the hard disk of the computer is the only form of the contract that exists. In such circumstances, the print-out is capable of being identified precisely. The print-out can be compared to the digital text and, if both are identical, then the print-out is admissible as secondary evidence of the digital file and is also considered real evidence. In such circumstances, the print-out is a copy of the original and the statement contained in the document can be considered to be authentic. Now consider the matter one stage further. Assume the original digital file is opened and closed on a number of occasions after the contract is completed, but the content of the file is not altered: perhaps particular clauses are copied for other reasons. It is possible that the metadata will have changed, perhaps to record the action of opening and closing the file, especially if the user accepts the changes, even if no changes are made. Although the metadata might have been altered, it has not affected the content of the file in question. In these circumstances, it might be considered that the integrity of the original digital data is compromised. Given such a simple example, it will be readily observed that, because the content of the print-out is identical to the digital data, the digital document remains the primary evidence, and the print-out is a faithful copy of the original. The metadata merely records when the file was opened and viewed. The record of the metadata can be compared to a register in the physical world that records the name of the person to whom the file was given, the date and time they obtained the file, and the date and time it was returned: this information does not alter the content of the statements made on the documents contained in the file (unless, that is, a person alters the contents recorded on a document). In such circumstances, the information conveyed by the metadata does not affect the integrity of the digital data which, in turn, does not affect the authenticity of the original document stored on the hard drive of the computer, which also means the secondary evidence of the file in the form of the print-out remains a reliable reproduction of the original file and, therefore, the statement contained in the document is to be trusted.

[1]   The reader is referred to the standard textbooks for the presumptions that apply to public documents and requirements relating to private documents.

8.21 Undoubtedly, there are many instances where the original digital data can be ascertained reasonably readily and a faithful print-out of the file can be obtained to provide evidence of the statement recorded in the file. However, the development of technology, and the way technology is now used, has meant the working environment is more complex. Consider another example: the drafting of a contract by an external lawyer for a multinational company. The task will comprise a number of stages, including liaising with a number of people internally with different responsibilities to produce an initial draft of the contract; it will be passed to the other contracting party for their comments before, after many weeks, if not months, of negotiation, a final version is produced to the satisfaction of both parties. In all probability, various versions of the contract will exist in several hard drives on several computers, perhaps across the world. In addition, copies of versions may also exist on an unknown number of back-up tapes in various locations, and copies may even exist on private computers of employees, including laptop computers and hand-held devices. If the contract is then printed out and signed with manuscript signatures by the appropriate representatives of the two parties, the actual document will comprise the printed version, and copies of this physical document will be admissible in evidence to prove the statements recorded in the document. The version in digital format will no longer be of any value. The physical document will contain the authoritative text: unless, that is, the physical document ceases to exist or is lost. However, should the contract never be signed but both parties fulfil their obligations under the terms of the contract, one issue that might arise in the event of a dispute is how to determine which version of the contract governed the agreement. It might be that each party relied on different versions of the document, containing different text. If this is the case, and neither party disputes the authenticity of the print-outs, then it will not be a matter of determining which version was the original, but a question of interpretation in the light of the relevant substantive law. Consider the matter further. Assume the contract was not printed out and signed, but the obligations were performed and the consideration paid; that it was a contract for the purchase of a product that subsequently failed to operate correctly and caused damage; that the range of evidence available to both parties comprised exchanges of email communications and documents in digital format, some of which were attached to a number of the emails exchanged between the parties. Establishing what might be termed the original document held in the form of digital data may more difficult in such circumstances. If the precise wording of the warranties were in dispute, it might be that various versions of the relevant clauses exist in different files, diverse places and on different platforms. If neither party disputes the provenance of any of the documents that are printed out and included in the trial bundle, it may, again, be a matter of construction as to which version governs the contract: the authenticity of the documents will not be in issue. However, if one of the parties allege that a document has been altered, or the authenticity of the document is called into question, then it may be necessary to prove the provenance of the document. In all probability it will be rare for a party to be required to provide evidence of the authenticity of a document in digital format[1]. However, if the authenticity of the content of a digital document is challenged then appropriate evidentiary foundations must be adduced by the party relying on the document.

1   Three defendants were asked to pay for items bought in Internet auctions. The defendants
     denied taking part in the bidding process. The cases were dismissed because each of the
     claimants failed to prove that the declarations were sent by the defendants and, conse-
     quently, that a contract had been concluded: see Michael Knopp, Case Note: OLG Köln,
     19 U 16/02; LG Konstanz, 2 O 141/01 A; AG Erfurt, 28 C 2354/01 (2005) e-Signature
     Law Journal, vol 2, no 2, pp 119–120.

8.22 Where the authenticity of a document is questioned, the party raising
the issue is required to do so at an early stage of the proceedings, thereby
providing the party submitting the document the opportunity of gathering
evidence to prove the veracity of the document. The issues relating to proving
the authenticity of documents in digital format are dealt with elsewhere in this
chapter.

Criminal proceedings

8.23 The standard of proof is set at a higher bar than for civil proceedings,
which generally means that more care is taken over the production of digital
evidence in criminal proceedings. Generally, investigating authorities will take
great care to ensure that an exact copy of the original data is taken from a
computer and that the copy is obtained in such a way as to exclude the
possibility that the original data, including the metadata, is altered. The digital
copy can then be printed out, should it be considered necessary, or it can
remain in digital format if there is no need for the data to be printed, such as
images of children being abused in a sexual manner. If a file is produced as a
print-out, the print-out is secondary evidence once removed from the original
data. This does not represent any difficulties, as reflected in the provisions of
s 27 of the Criminal Justice Act 1988, as follows:

27.   Where a statement contained in a document is admissible as evidence in criminal
proceedings, it may be proved—

(a)   by the production of that document; or
(b)   (whether or not that document is still in existence) by the production of a
      copy of that document, or of the material part of it,

authenticated in such manner as the court may approve; and it is immaterial for the
purposes of this subsection how many removes there are between a copy and the
original.

Section 133 of the Criminal Justice Act 2003, has similar provisions:

133 Proof of statements in documents

Where a statement in a document is admissible as evidence in criminal proceedings, the
statement may be proved by producing either—

(a)   the document, or
(b)   (whether or not the document exists) a copy of the document or of the
      material part of it,

authenticated in whatever way the court may approve.

There is a slight change in nuance in that, in s 133, there is no longer a
mention of the number of times a copy is removed from the original. It is
important to note that it is the content that is important, not the actual

document. Naturally, the original, if available, should be adduced into evidence, whether it is a physical document or a digital file. However, as already discussed, digital data tends to be adduced as secondary evidence and may be at least two removes from the original. This should not matter, providing the copy of a file in digital format has been copied in a way that captures the files in its entirety, including all its attributes such as the metadata, without altering the original file. In *R v Neville*[1], the prosecution introduced a copy of a print-out. The evidence in question comprised the records of the use of a mobile telephone. As the telephone was used, a computer recorded the date, time and duration of each call. The details were then sent to another computer (although it is not clear if the data was transferred over a network digitally) and the second computer used this information to produce an itemised bill to the person hiring the telephone. Once the bill was paid, the print-out was copied on to microfiche. The members of the Court of Appeal noted the accused did not query the accuracy of the bill when it was paid and there was no suggestion that there was anything wrong with the computer. The Crown adduced oral evidence by way of a witness, rather than produce a certificate asserting the computer was working properly. The members of the court held that the evidence of the witness was admissible if s 69 of the Police and Criminal Evidence 1984 did not apply. Unfortunately, as pointed out by JC Smith, at 290, no authority was offered for receiving the hearsay if s 69 did not apply.

[1]   [1991] Crim LR 288.

8.24 To a certain extent, it might be convenient to change the conceptual framework concerning digital data. Rather than question whether a document in digital format is an original or a copy, it might be more useful and relevant to refer to the proof of authenticity, or provenance, or reliability of a digital file. This, in turn, encapsulates proof of the integrity of the content of the data. This is proffered because, unlike a document in physical format, a document in digital format may not be readily replicated as it was originally created. A physical document will be stored and retrieved when necessary. The document remains as a physical document even though, through the ravages of time and the handling it receives, it may accumulate coffee stains, fingerprints, rips, items stapled to it, and the addition of manuscript text applied by humans. A digital document, in contrast, may be migrated from one form of software to another and from one form of storage device to another. The data will also undergo changes but, unlike its physical counter-part, the changes the data is subject to will need to be documented in such a way as to preserve the integrity and authenticity of the data. Thus it might be more relevant, when referring to digital data, to concentrate on establishing which version of the data is required and then to provide evidence, if such is necessary, of the authenticity of the history of the data to establish reliability, rather than debate about whether digital data is a copy of an original.

Video-recorded and tape-recorded evidence

8.25 Evidence may be given in civil cases by means of a video link or any other means, providing leave is obtained from the court, as provided for in

CPR 32.3 which is supplemented by Practice Direction 32—Evidence Annex 3[1]. In criminal matters, it is possible to record the initial interview with children[2]. The recording is admissible in evidence, subject to leave of the court and any editing that the court decides is necessary[3]. Leave is required to adduce a video recording of testimony of a witness in accordance with the provisions of s 27 of the Youth Justice and Criminal Evidence Act 1999, and the procedure is set out in the Crown Court (Special Measures Directions and Directions prohibiting Cross-Examination) Rules 2002, SI 2002/1688[4].

[1] See also the Admiralty and Commercial Courts Guide, Appendix 14 and the Chancery Court Guide, ch 14.
[2] s 35A of the Criminal Justice Act 1988 was added by s 54 of the Criminal Justice Act 1991.
[3] Criminal Justice Act 1988, s 35A(2).
[4] For further detail, see *Malek* (2005) paras 10–37 to 10–42; Archbold *Criminal pleading, evidence and practice* (Sweet & Maxwell); *Blackstone's Criminal Practice*; Archbold *Magistrates' Court Criminal Practice*.

ADMISSIBILITY

8.26 Evidence is admitted into legal proceedings if it is relevant to an issue in dispute, subject to a number of exceptions[1]. It is a matter of law for a judge to determine whether evidence is admissible. Generally, judges are required to determine whether evidence is to be excluded in criminal trials far more frequently than in civil matters, especially where admitting the evidence might not be in the interests of justice[2]. For instance, in *R v Fowden and White*[3] the Court of Appeal concluded that the admission of a video film showing activities that were consistent with the acts of theft was held to have been improperly admitted. The prejudicial value outweighed its probative effect because the witnesses that identified the accused knew them from a similar case of theft that occurred a week after the events recorded in the video film, and the defence were therefore not able to test the accuracy of the identification without causing prejudice and embarrassment.

[1] For a more detailed discussion, see *Malek* (2005) ch 2 and paras 7–01 to 7–16; Colin Tapper *Cross and Tapper on Evidence* pp 70–81; for a brief consideration of a number of jurisdictions, see Olivier Leroux 'Legal Admissibility of Electronic Evidence' International Review of Law Computers & Technology, July 2004, vol 18, no 2, 193–220.
[2] Police and Evidence Act 1984, s 78; Criminal Justice Act 2003, s 114(1)(d).
[3] [1982] Crim LR 588.

8.27 In civil cases, evidence that is admissible can be excluded in accordance with the provisions of CPR 32.1(2), which provides a judge with the explicit general power to exclude evidence when in the role of managing a case:

32.1 (1)   The court may control the evidence by giving directions as to—

(a)   the issues on which it requires evidence;
(b)   the nature of the evidence which it requires to decide those issues; and
(c)   the way in which the evidence is to be placed before the court.

(2)   The court may use its power under this rule to exclude evidence that would otherwise be admissible.

However, the power, as pointed out by Arden LJ, in adopting the argument of the appellants in *Great Future International Ltd v Sealand Housing Corpn*, 'must be used with great circumspection for the purpose of achieving the overriding objective'[1]. Tapper notes that the modern tendency is to admit evidence then to consider its weight, as illustrated by the comment of Cockburn CJ in *R v Churchwardens, Overseers and Guardians of the Poor of the Parish of Birmingham*: 'People were formerly frightened out of their wits about admitting evidence lest juries should go wrong. In modern times we admit the evidence and discuss its weight'[2].

[1]   [2002] EWCA Civ 1183 , [2002] All ER (D) 391 (Jul) at 24.
[2]   (1861) 1 B & B 763 at 767; 121 ER 897; *Cross and Tapper on Evidence* p 81.

WEIGHT

8.28 The questions of weight, credibility and sufficiency of the evidence are decisions for the members of a jury, and for the judge where a case is tried without a jury. There are no fixed rules to determine what weight to give to any item of evidence. In *R v Madhub Chunder Giri Mohunt*, Birch J observed 'For weighing evidence and drawing inferences from it, there can be no canon. Each case represents its own peculiarities and in each common sense and shrewdness must be brought to bear upon the facts elicited'[1] and Lord Blackburn commented in *Lord Advocate v Lord Blantyre* that 'The weight of evidence depends on rules of common sense'[2].

[1]   (1874) 21 WRCr 13 at 19.
[2]   (1879) 4 App Cas 770 at 792.

8.29 When conducting a trial with members of a jury, the judge may withdraw an issue because the proponent has failed to adduce sufficient evidence in support of the claim. Furthermore, in summing up to the members of the jury at the end of the trial, the judge is required to provide directions on a range of issues including, but not limited to, who has the burden of proof; what presumptions, if any, apply; when supporting evidence should be considered before putting weight on certain types of evidence; and to offer comments on matters including the weight of the evidence, although it must be made explicit that such comments are meant to help the members of the jury, because they must reach their own decision[1]. In addition, there are a number of factors set out in s 114(2) of the Criminal Justice Act 2003 that deal with the assessment of weight of hearsay in criminal proceedings.

[1]   The Specimen Directions issued by the Judicial Studies Board are available online at http://www.jsboard.co.uk/criminal_law/cbb/index.htm.

DOCUMENT

8.30 The meaning of 'document' has been construed widely, thus the court in *Lyell v Kennedy (No. 3)*[1] admitted photographs of tombstones and houses as documents for the purposes of discovery and, in *R v Daye (Arthur John)*[2], Darling J suggested that the meaning of a document should not be defined in a narrow way:

> I think that it is perfectly plain that the sealed envelope itself might be a document. Nothing but the sealed envelope itself might be a document. But I should myself say that any written thing capable of being evidence is properly described as a document and that it is immaterial on what the writing may be inscribed. It might be inscribed not on paper, but on parchment; and long before that it was on stone, marble, or clay, and it might be, and often was, on metal. So I should desire to guard myself against being supposed to assent to the argument that a thing is not a document unless it be a paper writing. I should say it is a document no matter upon what material it be, provided it is writing or printing and capable of being evidence[3].

Although the meaning of 'document', as the discussion below indicates, has been construed widely, nevertheless it was held by the court in *Darby (Yvonne Beatrice) v DPP*[4] that a visual reading cannot be a document. This must be correct. A visual reading conveys information and the person perceiving this information is capable of giving evidence of their perception. Unless the reading is stored in some way that enables it to be read at a later date, the reading is merely a transitory phenomenon that can only be captured by a person, who can give evidence about what they saw[5].

1   (1884) 50 LT 730.
2   [1908] 2 KB 333 KBD.
3   [1908] 2 KB 333 at 340. See *Malek* (2005) para 41–02 for a more detailed discussion of documents within the rule.
4   [1995] RTR 294; (1995) 159 J.P. 533, (1994) The Times Law Reports November 4, 555, DC.
5   *Owen v Chesters* [1985] RTR 191 where a police officer gave evidence of the reading from a breath test machine.

8.31   Audio tapes were also accepted as a discoverable document in *Grant v Southwestern and Country Properties Ltd*[1], in which the meaning of a document was defined by its quality to convey information, as determined by Walton J at 198: 'I conclude that a tape recording, provided of course that what is recorded is indeed information—relevant sounds of some description—is a document'. Television film is also considered a document[2], as is the output of facsimile transmissions[3], data stored on a computer (in this instance a database) is a document for the purposes of the obligation to discover under the provisions of Ord 24 of the Rules of the Supreme Court[4], and a label on a bottle containing a specimen of blood provided by the accused[5]. The material may sometimes determine the admissibility of the evidence, but the definition is considered wide enough to bring any medium into its ambit without causing difficulties[6]. The term 'document' is something upon which information is stored. This must be correct because if information is not stored the content is not available and, therefore, remains oral evidence.

1   [1975] Ch 185, [1974] 3 WLR 221, [1974] 2 All ER 465, 118 Sol Jo 548, 232 E.G. 333, Ch D. See also *R v Senat, R v Sin* (1968) 52 Cr App Rep 282; *R v Stevenson* [1971] 1 WLR 1, [1971] 1 All ER 678; *R v Robson (Bernard Jack); R v Harris (Gordon Federick)* [1972] 1 WLR 651, [1972] 2 All ER 699, (1972) 56 Cr App Rep 450, [1972] Crim LR 316, 116 SJ 313, CCC.

[2] *Senior v Holdsworth ex p Independent Television News* [1976] QB 23, [1975] 2 WLR 987, [1975] 2 All ER 1009, 119 Sol Jo 393, CA.
[3] *Hastie and Jenkerson v McMahon* [1990] 1 WLR 1575, [1991] 1 All ER 255, [1990] RVR 172, (1990) 134 Sol Jo 725, CA.
[4] *Derby v Weldon (No. 9)* [1991] 1 WLR 652, [1991] 2 All ER 901, (1990) *Times*, November 9, CA.
[5] *Khatibi v DPP* [2004] EWHC 83 (Admin), (2004) 168 JP 361.
[6] Charles Hollander QC and Tom Adam *Documentary Evidence* (2000) p 79.

8.32 The meaning of 'document' in the context of data stored on a computer, in an instance where the burden of proof was set at the criminal standard (that is, beyond reasonable doubt) was the subject of *Alliance & Leicester Building Society v Ghahremani* [1] in which a solicitor, Naresh Chopra, was alleged to have deliberately deleted part of a file stored on his computer in contempt of court. The Alliance & Leicester Building Society was investigating a possible mortgage fraud by Mr and Mrs Ghahremani. Mr Chopra was a partner in a firm of solicitors, which was dissolved on 3 June 1991, who acted for Mr and Mrs Ghahremani and the building society. The building society alleged that the solicitors were negligent and instructed new solicitors, who subsequently attempted to obtain the conveyancing file from Mr Chopra. Having failed to obtain the files, an application was made to Knox J who subsequently issued a preservation order on 4 July 1991 against Mr Chopra and his partner, restraining them from destroying or altering any document relating to the transaction and requiring him to deliver up all such documents in his control to the society's solicitors. When representatives of the solicitors attended the offices of Mr Chopra, he showed them a file on his computer that gave details of a completion statement. The first page indicated a consideration of £6,000,000 and the disbursements were set out on the second page. Later that day a computer expert attended Mr Chopra's office to examine the computer and when the same file was called up on to the screen the first page of the document was missing. The evidence was that Mr Chopra had been sitting at the computer shortly before the IT expert took control of the computer and the relevant file had last been saved at the time Mr Chopra was using the computer. The solicitors had reason to believe Mr Chopra had deleted part of the document, contrary to the order. They subsequently began proceedings to commit Mr Chopra for contempt. At the hearing, counsel for Mr Chopra argued that the word 'document' required there to be some form of visible writing on paper or other material and, because there was no physical document, the order had not been breached. Hoffmann J mentioned the comments of Vinelott J in *Derby v Weldon (No. 9)* [2] and concluded that the word 'document' would bear the same meaning in the order issued by Knox J, which was for advance discovery. In respect of the alleged contempt, Hoffmann J was not convinced by any of the conflicting explanations offered by Mr Chopra in his defence, especially when a complete version of the document was produced which, in turn, was a copy taken by Mr Chopra from the computer on 14 April 1991. Mr Chopra also tendered further evidence in an attempt to show that the computer record had not been altered at the material time. Taking into account the expert evidence, which contradicted Mr Chopra's evidence, the learned judge reached the conclusion that the document was forged. Hoffmann J concluded that it was proved beyond reasonable doubt that Mr Chopra did alter or destroy part of the document and, therefore, committed a contempt. The motion for committal to prison for contempt of court was granted, although he was eventually fined in the sum of £1,000[3].

1   [1992] RVR 198, [1992] NLJR 313, Ch D.
2   [1991] 1 WLR 652, [1991] 2 All ER 901, (1990) *Times*, November 9, CA.
3   Email communication between Nicholas Leviseur, counsel for Mr Chopra, and the author.

8.33   The tenor of judicial comments indicate very clearly that technology will not prevent the definition of a document from being expanded. This was emphasised by Buxton LJ in *Victor Chandler International v Customs and Excise Comrs* [1] where he observed, in respect of distributed technology, that '... the word "document" is not constrained by the physical nature that documents took in 1952, so we are entitled, and indeed bound, to consider the appropriate application of the concept of circulation, etc, of a document in the light of current practice and technology'. In essence, the term 'document' is construed in terms of a item upon which information is stored, which must be right, as illustrated by Lord Milligan in *Rollo (William) v HM Advocate*[2] when he made it clear that the information stored in a Sharp Memomaster 500 hand held device was a document:

> Unsurprisingly, the word 'document' in normal usage is most frequently used in relation to written, typed or printed paper documents. Where information is stored by other means on other surfaces we accept that the storing item concerned is more readily referred to by reference to the means of storage or surface for storage concerned rather than as a 'document'. Hence reference to, for example, machines or tapes. However, terminological emphasis in description in such cases on the means or surface for recording information does not deprive such alternative stores of information from qualifying as 'documents' any more so than, for example, a tombstone, which is expressly included in the dictionary definition referred to. It seems to us that the essential essence of a document is that it is something concerning recorded information of some sort. It does not matter if, to be meaningful, the information requires to be processed in some way such as translation, decoding or electrical retrieval[3].

As is made abundantly clear from the discussion above, the meaning of 'document' is so widely defined as to include any data held in digital format. No doubt future challenges to the definition will be dealt with in the same robust fashion that has prevailed hitherto.

1   [2000] 2 All ER 315 at 329.
2   1997 JC 23, 1997 SLT 958; 1996 SCCR 874, HCJ.
3   1997 SLT 958 at 960 F–G.

INSTRUMENT

8.34   Of the references Reed found when researching his book where the word 'instrument' was used in a statute, only one statute, s 8(1) of the Forgery and Counterfeiting Act 1981, specifically referred to digital information, whilst other definitions that refer to 'document' do not necessarily exclude digital information[1]. The meaning given to the word 'instrument' was discussed in *R v Riley*[2] where the prisoner sent a telegram to a bookmaker after he knew the winner of the Newcastle Handicap run at 2.45pm on 27 June

1895 was named Lord of Dale. He contrived to make it appear that the telegram was sent from a sub-post office, which would mean the telegram would not arrive with the bookmaker until some time after the race was run. However, he actually sent the telegram from the head office after the news arrived in the office that Lord of Dale had won the race. The court held that a telegram amounted to an instrument for the purposes of s 38 of the Forgery Act 1861. In his judgment, Hawkins J suggested the word should be interpreted according to its ordinary meaning and quoted a number of dictionary meanings before concluding that they covered an 'infinite variety of meanings'[3]. In his judgment, Willis J concurred, and went on to offer the following comment:

> I cannot see anything in the nature of such a section which should make it necessary or desirable to restrict the application of the word 'instrument' to writings of a formal character, and I think it is meant to include writings of every description if false and known to be false by the person who makes use of them for the purpose indicated[4].

Lord Russell of Killowen CJ and Vaughan Williams J had reservations about the meaning of the word in the context of the Act, although Vaughan Williams J accepted the word had been used in a narrow, restrictive meaning that referred to the formation of a legal document, not to the wider meaning adopted by Hawkins and Willis JJ. Reed's comment on this case, 'However, it must be recognised that in 1896 a non-written document would be abnormal, and the case cannot be considered as a very strong authority for the proposition that an electronic record cannot be an instrument'[5] must be correct, although there is a good reason to suggest that there is a reason why this case may appear to be helpful in the context of electronic data. This is relates to the method by which the telegram came into being to begin with. As discussed above, the sending party may write down the message on a form or dictate it to an operator. The operator would then send a series of electronic pulses to the receiving operator, who in turn would interpret the code and write the text down by hand. This carrier forms the 'document' or 'instrument'. No consideration in this case was given to the transmission of the original text to the receiving operator, yet the telegram received by the bookmaker was considered to be a document. It could be argued that information in digital format is identical in concept to the pulses passed over a telegraph wire, with the exception that technology can now store the message, which was not possible with the telegraph.

[1]   Chris Reed *Digital Information Law Electronic Documents and Requirements of Form* ch 4.
[2]   [1896] 1 QB 309, 65 LJMC 74, 74 LT 254, 44 WR 318, 18 Cox 285, 60 JP 519.
[3]   [1896] 1 QB 309 at 314.
[4]   [1896] 1 QB 309 at 321.
[5]   *Reed* p 186.

WRITING

8.35   Writing is defined in Sch 1 to the Interpretation Act 1978, and includes

> typing, printing, lithography, photography and other modes of representing or reproducing words in visible form, and expressions referring to writing are construed accordingly.

This definition emphasises the need for the writing to be in visible form, which appears to exclude information in electronic format, although microfilm and fiche are in writing even though a machine is required to read the content recorded. This means that information in digital format will only come within this definition if it comes within the method set out in the definition: '... and other modes of representing or reproducing words ...'[1]. In his conclusion of whether information in electronic format will amount to writing, Professor Reed suggested there were two possible approaches to this problem:

> The distinction is not between information affixed to a carrier or not, but between informal speech and formally recorded information, in the same way that the content of a message was recorded by means of telegraph, although the problem with this analysis is that there is no distinction between the use of the technology in a formal or informal capacity.
>
> The second possibility is to suggest that the requirement of 'writing' is merely evidential in nature, although the courts continue to maintain the position that tendering oral evidence cannot rectify the lack of formality[2].

It is useful to note the range of functions that writing performs in relation to a physical carrier, as considered in the UNCITRAL Model Law on Electronic Commerce[3]:

> ... the following non-exhaustive list indicates reasons why national laws require the use of 'writings': (1) to ensure that there would be tangible evidence of the existence and nature of the intent of the parties to bind themselves; (2) to help the parties be aware of the consequences of their entering into a contract; (3) to provide that a document would be legible by all; (4) to provide that a document would remain unaltered over time and provide a permanent record of a transaction; (5) to allow for the reproduction of a document so that each party would hold a copy of the same data; (6) to allow for the authentication of data by means of a signature; (7) to provide that a document would be in a form acceptable to public authorities and courts; (8) to finalize the intent of the author of the 'writing' and provide a record of that intent; (9) to allow for the easy storage of data in a tangible form; (10) to facilitate control and subsequent audit for accounting, tax or regulatory purposes; and (11) to bring legal rights and obligations into existence in those cases where a 'writing' was required for validity purposes[4].

[1] Chris Reed *Digital Information Law Electronic Documents and Requirements of Form* pp 83–84 for other statutory definitions and further comments.
[2] *Reed* pp 94–102.
[3] The Model Law on Electronic Commerce was adopted by the Commission on 12 June 1996, following its 605th meeting, which, in turn, was adopted by the General Assembly in Resolution 51/162 at its 85th plenary meeting on 16 December 1996, and includes an additional article 5 bis as adopted by the Commission at its 31st meeting in June 1998.
[4] Guide to Enactment, para 48.

RECORD

8.36 The need to define a record is of relatively recent origin. A definition is provided in s 13 of the Civil Evidence Act 1995 as 'anything in which information of any description is recorded' and this definition is also adopted in CPR Pt 31.4. In respect to the use of 'record' in statute, the majority of provisions bring information in electronic format within the ambit of a record, although a number of statutes may make assumptions that records are retained in hard-copy. The case law illustrates that the meaning of 'record' is discussed in relation to the admissibility of a body of evidence and the purpose for which the record has been made[1].

[1] The reader is directed to a very helpful discussion by Chris Reed *Digital Information Law Electronic Documents and Requirements of Form* pp 136–147, and referred to ISO 15489 Information and documentation—Records Management and the definitions cited therein.

ELECTRONIC SIGNATURES

8.37 The European Union, in the context of electronic signatures, has provided that signatures cannot be denied legal effectiveness solely on the grounds that they are in electronic format. Under the provisions of art 5 of Directive 1999/93/EC of the European Parliament and of the Council of 13 December 1999 on a Community framework for electronic signatures[1], provision has been made to ensure that advanced electronic signatures are admissible as evidence in legal proceedings, and other forms of electronic signature are also admissible:

Legal effects of electronic signatures

(1)   Member States shall ensure that advanced electronic signatures which are based on a qualified certificate and which are created by a secure signature-creation device:

(a) satisfy the legal requirements of a signature in relation to data in electronic form in the same manner as a handwritten signature satisfies those requirements in relation to paper-based data; and

(b) are admissible as evidence in legal proceedings.

(2)   Member States shall ensure that an electronic signature is not denied legal effectiveness and admissibility as evidence in legal proceedings solely on the grounds that it is:

— in electronic form, or
— not based upon a qualified certificate, or
— not based upon a qualified certificate issued by an accredited certification-service-provider, or
— not created by a secure signature-creation device.

There was no requirement to provide for the general admissibility of electronic signatures under either US or English law, as demonstrated in the United States case of *Wilkens v Iowa Insurance Comr, Wilkens v Allstate Insurance*[2] and in England by the Industrial Tribunal case of *Hall v Cognos Ltd*[3]. However, Parliament subsequently passed the Electronic Communications Act 2000 and, to correct a failure to incorporate the entire provisions of the EU Directive into the Act, followed this with the Electronic Signatures Regulations (SI 2002/318) two years later[4]. The Act received the Royal Assent on 25 May 2000, and extends to Northern Ireland[5]. The Act provides, in s 7(2), the following definition of an electronic signature, which incorporates additional features that are not included in the definition set out in the Directive:

(2) For the purposes of this section an electronic signature is so much of anything in electronic form as—

is incorporated into or otherwise logically associated with any electronic communication or electronic data; and

purports to be so incorporated or associated for the purpose of being used in establishing the authenticity of the communication or data, the integrity of the communication or data, or both.

1   (OJ L13/12 19.1.2000).
2   457 N.W.2d (Iowa App. 1990).
3   Case No 1803325/97.
4   Stephen Mason *Electronic Signatures in Law* (2nd edn, 2007); Dennis Campbell, ed *E-Commerce and the Law of Digital Signatures* (2005); MHM Schellenkens *Electronic Signatures Authentication Technology from a Legal Perspective* (2004); Lorna Brazell *Electronic Signatures Law and Regulation* (2004); for translations of electronic signature cases from Europe, Brazil, China and Colombia into English, see past issues of the e-Signature Law Journal, the precursor to the Digital Evidence Journal.
5   s 16(5).

8.38 The term 'authentication' has two meanings in the context of information security, which is pertinent in the context of electronic signatures[1]. One refers to the authentication of the origin of the data, whilst the other verifies the identity of a person or entity. In the context of the Act, the meaning of authenticity relates to the single issue of verifying the person or entity, as provided for in s 15(2). This definition relates to the evidential issues regarding the authentication of the communication or data. Whichever party has the burden of proof will be required to submit evidence in response to the guidance set out in s 15(2), together with any other extrinsic evidence that may be necessary to support the evidential burden.

Section 7(1) of the Act provides for the admissibility of the electronic signature in two ways:

7(1)   In any legal proceedings—

(a)   an electronic signature incorporated into or logically associated with a particular electronic communication or particular electronic data, and

(b)   the certification by any person of such a signature,

shall each be admissible in evidence in relation to any question as to the authenticity of the communication or data or as to the integrity of the communication or data.

First, an electronic signature is admissible under the provisions of s 7(1)(a) where it is incorporated into, or logically associated with, a particular electronic communication or data. Alternatively, in accordance with the provisions of s 7(1)(b), the authenticity or the integrity of the communication or data can be admissible where any person certifies the signature. The certificate would normally be provided by an entity such as a trusted third party, although it does not follow that such a certificate has to be provided by a trusted third party.

There is no specific provision for the concept of an advanced electronic signature in the Act. However, the government has set out the extent of the liability that a certification-service-provider faces when they issue a key pair that conforms to the criteria of an advanced electronic signature under the provisions of the Electronic Signatures Regulations 2002, which came into force on 8 March 2002[2]. There are various types of signature, all of which can demonstrate the intent of the signing party to authenticate the document. The act of the person writing a manuscript signature or applying the impression of the seal is the act of intent and the evidence of the act is the physical manifestation of the signature by the application of ink on to paper, or the wax placed on to the surface of the material. In the same way, a signature in electronic format is the act of the person peforming an act, or series of acts, which may compromise more than one act at different times, which is subsequently manifest in human-readable format. The different types are outlined below.

[1]   Fred Piper and Sean Murphy *Cryptography: A Very Short Introduction* (2002) p 92.
[2]   SI 2002/318.

Typing a name into a document

8.39 This method was accepted in the UK, before the passing of the Electronic Communications Act 2000, in the Industrial Tribunal case of *Hall v Cognos Ltd*[1]. A series of emails between Mr Hall, his line manager and personnel were held to be signed when printed, and varied the terms of the written contract of employment. Case law in the United States of America also indicates the acceptance of this form of electronic signature[2].

[1]   Case No 1803325/97. For an earlier decision in the United States of America, see *Wilkens v Iowa Insurance Commissioner, Wilkens v Allstate Insurance* 457 N.W.2d (Iowa App. 1990); see also the German cases of *OLG Köln* 19 U 16/02; *LG Konstanz* 2 O 141/01 A; *AG Erfurt* 28 C 2354/01, where the party relying on emails failed to prove that the emails were sent by the purported senders, Michael Knopp, Case Note, (2005) e-Signature Law Journal, vol 2 no 2, 119–120.
[2]   *Sea-Land Service, Inc v Lozen International, LLC* 285 F.3d 808 (9th Cir. 2002); *Cloud Corporation v Hasbro, Inc* 314 F.3d 289 (7th Cir. 2002) although compare the position in Missouri: *Toghiyany v Amerigas Propane, Inc* 309 F.3d 1088 (8th Cir. 2002); *Roger Edwards, LLC v Fiddes & Son Ltd* 245 F.Supp.2d 251 (D.Me. 2003).

The name in an email address

8.40 The name in an email address can be a form of electronic signature and has been so held in the United States of America[1], Greece[2], Australia[3], Italy[4] and Singapore.[5] A recent decision in England and Wales on the same question[6] reached a contrary conclusion that cannot be reconciled with the international cases, long-standing English case law (especially taking into account the comments recorded in the case of *Lobb and Knight v Stanley*)[7], or the provisions of s 7 of the Electronic Communications Act 2000. Two of the most notable English cases, *Lobb and Knight v Stanley* (1844) 5 QB 574, 114 ER 1366 and *Tourret v Cripps* (1879) 48 LJ Ch 567, 27 WR 706 were neither cited or discussed and no relevant cases from other jurisdictions were cited. The learned judge made observations about the technicalities of email in the absence of expert evidence at 897, as did P. Lyberopoulos, the learned President of the court in the Greek case *1327/2001—Payment Order*. The assumptions made by the learned judge with respect to email software and how it works led him to determine that the appearance of the email address was divorced from the main body of the message. He concluded, in the absence of any evidence to the contrary, that the email address could not, therefore, be intended as a signature. No consideration was given to the provisions of s 7 of the Electronic Communications Act 2000, which clearly bring an email address within the ambit of the Act as a form of electronic signature. The learned judge also stated, at 900, that it was his understanding that the Electronic Communications Act 2000 was enacted to give effect to Directive 2000/31/EC on certain legal aspects of information society services, in particular electronic commerce, in the Internal Market (Directive on electronic commerce) (OJ L 187/1, 17.7.2000). This is incorrect. The aim of the Act was to implement the provisions of Directive 1999/93/EC of the European Parliament and of the Council of 13 December 1999 on a Community framework for electronic signatures (OJ 19.1.2000 L13/12), as set out in Note 19 of the Explanatory Notes to the Act.

1   *United States of America v Siddiqui* 235 F.3d 1318 (11th Cir. 2000) where emails were correctly authenticated under the requirements of Fed.R.Evid. 901(a) because a number of internal factors supported the authenticity of the email, including the email address, nickname of the sender and pertinent content.

2   *1327/2001—Payment Order*, an email address in combination with the use of a password held to be a signature under the provisions of arts 444(3) and 445 of the Civil Procedure Code. For an English translation by Michael G Rachavelias, see (2006) Digital Evidence Journal, vol 3, no 1, 57–60.

3   *McGuren v Simpson* [2004] NSWSC 35, the name in an email address held to be a signature for the purpose of the Limitation Act 1969, s 54(4).

4   *Tribunale Mondovì*, 7 giugno 2004, n. 375 (decr.), Giur. It. 2005, 1026, the combination of an email address and a user password of the Internet Service Provider was held to be an electronic signature for the purposes of a summary judgment. See (2007) Digital Evidence Journal, vol 4, no 1, (forthcoming) for a translation.

5   *SM Integrated Transware Ltd v Schenker Singapore (Pte) Ltd* [2005] 2 SLR 651, [2005] SGHC 58, the name in an email address held to be a signature for the purposes of the Civil Law Act (Cap 43, 1994 Rev Ed) s 6(d).

6   *J Pereira Fernandes SA v Mehta* [2006] 1 WLR 1543, [2006] 2 All ER 891, [2006] 1 All ER (Comm) 885, [2006] All ER (D) 264 (Apr), [2006] IP & T 546, (2006) *Times*, 16 May, [2006] EWHC 813, Ch, in respect of the Statute of Frauds 1677, s 4.

7   (1844) 5 QB 574, 114 ER 1366.

Clicking the 'I accept' icon

8.41 The 'click wrap' method of indicating intent, namely clicking the 'I accept' icon to confirm the intention to enter a contract when buying goods or services electronically.

Personal Identification Number ('PIN')

8.42 A Personal Identification Number ('PIN'), used to obtain money from cash machines or to 'sign' a credit card with a PIN number[1].

1   The banks have led the way in the use of PINs and now rely on technology to a great extent. However, there are serious concerns about the use of the PIN, discussed in further detail elsewhere in this text.

Biodynamic signature

8.43 A biodynamic version of a manuscript signature: a special pen and pad measure and record the actions of the person as they sign. This creates a digital version of the manuscript signature. This file can then be attached to electronic documents. Another variation of this type of signature is the measurement of an attribute, such as a fingerprint, iris scan or other measurement of the human body. A scan is taken of the attribute, such as a fingerprint, then the fingerprint, when presented to the reading device, is used to determine the probability that the finger presented is similar to the scanned version of the fingerprint on the database. There are a number of problems associated with this form of technology, including the false positive rate, although the most serious is where fingerprints are used to protect items or to obtain access to ATMs, because ruthless thieves will cut off fingers and thumbs to gain their despicable ends[1].

[1] Citibank have announced that it will set up a network of biometric ATMs in India. It is intended that thumbprints will be scanned to enable a customer to obtain access to their account. The report of this initiative does not indicate how the bank is going to deal with customers who have thumbs cut off by thieves: Joe Leahy 'Citigroup gives Indian poor a hand with thumbprint ATMs' (2006) *Financial Times*, 2/3 December, p 15. See the example of Mr Kumaran, who had the tip of his index finger chopped off because the security system installed in his S-Class Mercedes Benz utilised the measurements of both the index fingers and thumbs of the owner. The immobiliser system caused the engine in the vehicle to cut out after a few minutes unless the owner pressed their finger or thumb on to the sensor. See a report at 'His finger for his car' (2005) *New Straits Times* 31 March, archived at Persatuan Insurans Am Malaysia (General Insurance Association of Malaysia), Insurance News, online at http://www.piam.org.my/news/insnews/ins_news.asp.

Scanned signature

8.44 A scanned manuscript signature: a manuscript signature is scanned and transformed into digital format, which can then be attached to an electronic document.

Digital signature

8.45 The digital signature uses cryptography. Within a Public Key Infrastructure, using asymmetric keys, the signing party uses a key pair (private and public key). The sender affixes the signature using their private key and the recipient checks the signature with the public key.

Despite the provisions of the EU Directive, electronic signatures have not been universally recognised in Europe for a variety of reasons. For instance, a restrictive approach was taken by the French courts before the introduction of the French law on electronic signatures. In the case of *Société Chalets Boisson v M. X*[1], the council of the Society Chalets Boisson entered an appeal before the Cour d'Appel of Besançon against a decision of a Conseil de prud'hommes (employment tribunal). The notice of appeal was sent to the office of the clerk of the court by email, bearing an electronic signature. The defendant sought to have this appeal declared invalid because the electronic signature was deemed not to identify the signatory. The Cour d'appel of Besançon accepted this argument and then declared this appeal inadmissible. The Cour de Cassation approved the Cour de Besançon decision. For an order to be valid, an appeal must be signed by its author and an electronic signature, before the 13 March 2000 Act[2], was not sufficient to identify the author. The comments by Philippe Bazin bear repeating:

> ... judges at the time (and unfortunately still today) did not have any technical understanding about what these notions concretely represent. These that they know, they have practiced for a long time, and they have to do with paper, not the electronic environment.

> In the 30th April 2003 decision, the Court adopted a systematic position of mistrust with respect to the electronic signature. It confirms that—culturally—it is the paper, and only the paper, that constitutes the only solid legal guarantee[3].

Clashes stemming from the requirements of procedural rules that have not been amended to take into account the relevant electronic signature legislation have occurred. An example in which the provisions relating to electronic signatures do not conform to procedural rules is illustrated in the case of 2572-2573-2002 of the Regeringsrätten (Swedish Supreme Administrative Court). An appeal submission against a decision by the tax authorities in Malmö at first instance was filed by email to the competent court of second instance, the Gothenburg Administrative Court of Appeal. The appeal was dismissed on the grounds that the Förvaltningsprocesslagen (Swedish Act on Administrative Procedure) requires the appeal submission to be signed with a handwritten signature, which it was not. A further appeal to the Swedish Supreme Administrative Court failed on the grounds that the Swedish Act on Administrative Procedure requires an appeal to be signed with a handwritten signature, even though the appeal was signed with an electronic signature[4].

[1] Case No 00–46467 Cour de Cassation, chambre civile 2 30 April 2003 available in electronic format at http:// www.juriscom.net/jpt/visu.php?ID=239. See Philippe Bazin 'Case Note' (2004) e-Signature Law Journal, vol 1, no 2, pp 93–94.
[2] Loi No 2000–230 du 13 mars 2000 portant adaptation du droit de la preuve aux technologies de l'information et relative á la signature électronique.
[3] Philippe Bazin 'Case note' (2004) e-Signature Law Journal, vol 1, no 2, p 94.
[4] Anna Nordén 'Case note' (2004) e-Signature Law Journal, vol 1, no 1, p 40.

8.46 Compare the Swedish decision to the Estonian case of *AS Valga Külmutusvagunite Depoo (in bankruptcy)*[1]. In a similar manner, it was alleged that the appellant failed to respond to a matter being dealt with by the Tallin Administrative Court, in that the response was sent to the court with a digital signature attached. The court of first instance did not accept the digital signature on the basis that the procedural rules required a manuscript signature. This was overturned by the members of the Administrative Chamber of the Tallin Circuit Court on the basis that the provisions of Digitaalallkirja seadus Vastu võetud 8. märtsil 2000. a. (RT I 2000, 26, 150) jõustunud 15. detsembril 2000 (Digital Signature Act) acted to permit the use of digital signatures regardless of the procedural requirements[2].

[1] Administrative matter no 2–3/466/03.
[2] Viive Näslund 'Case Report' (2004) e-Signature Law Journal, vol 1, no 1, pp 35–39.

HEARSAY

8.47 The hearsay rule has long been considered a complex and confusing exclusionary rule of evidence. For a discussion of the rule in its present format, the reader is directed to the standard textbooks on evidence[1]. This section restricts discussion of the rule in relation to evidence in electronic format. Before the virtual abolition of the hearsay rule in civil proceedings, one of the concerns relating to computer evidence had been whether such evidence constituted original evidence or hearsay. Although the hearsay rule has been amended in both civil and criminal proceedings, the same problem regarding the reliability of evidence in digital format is of concern now, as much as it was in respect of oral testimony. One reason for adopting the hearsay rule was to provide for the reliability of the perceptions of a witness. Introduced inconsistently and within a mainly oral tradition, the aim of the hearsay rule was to enhance the reliability of the evidence before the members of a jury[2]. Bearing in mind that the special rules which previously applied to the output of a computer have been repealed[3], where the reliability of digital evidence is in dispute it might have to be authenticated before it can be accepted into evidence. This may be the case whether a dispute is heard by a single adjudicator or more than one adjudicator that decide both facts and law, or whether evidence is adduced before a judge and jury.

[1]   For a detailed treatment of the rationale, history of reform, critical analysis and present status of hearsay in civil and criminal proceedings, see Hodge M Malek, gen ed *Phipson on Evidence* chs 28, 29 and 30; Colin Tapper *Cross and Tapper on Evidence* chs XII, XIII and XIV.
[2]   *Tapper* (1989) pp 366–367; *Cross and Tapper on Evidence* p 579.
[3]   In the case of civil proceedings, Sch 2 to the Civil Evidence Act 1995 and, in criminal proceedings, by s 60 of the Youth Justice and Criminal Evidence Act 1999.

Exception to the hearsay rule: Bankers' Books

8.48 The exclusionary rules of the common law were relaxed at an early stage by the Bankers' Books Act 1879. This Act provided that copies of entries in bankers' books, that is ledgers, day books, cash books, account books and all other books kept in the ordinary business of the bank, are considered as prima facie evidence of the matters recorded, subject to a number of requirements before they can be admitted into evidence. As Tapper remarks, the primary purpose was to prevent the business from being disrupted by the need to produce the original books in court[1]. The technology used by banks altered considerably during the twentieth century, but this did not prevent judges from providing a wide construction to the statute, as in the (criminal) case of *Barker v Wilson*[2]. The Divisional Court was requested to provide an opinion by way of case stated from North Yorkshire Justices sitting at York. The question was whether the justices reached the correct decision that microfilm was included within the definition of 'bankers' books' in accordance with s 9 of the Act. Caulfield and Bridge LJJ were both of the opinion that this was correct. Caulfield J said:

> The justices came to the conclusion—and they put their conclusions in these terms: that they adopted some robust common sense—that section 9 does include microfilm, which is a modern process of producing banker's records. It is probable that no modern bank in this country now maintains the old-fashioned books which were maintained at the time of the passing of the 1879 Act and possibly maintained for many years after 1879[3].

Bridge LJ also made some robust comments that reinforced the point:

The Bankers' Books Evidence Act 1879 was enacted with the practice of bankers in 1879 in mind. It must be construed in 1980 in relation to the practice of bankers as we now understand it. So construing the definition of 'bankers' book' it seems to me that clearly both phrases are apt to include any form of permanent record kept by the bank of transactions relating to the banks' business, made by any of the methods which modern technology makes available, including, in particular, microfilm[4].

The flexibility of the judiciary to amend a statutory rule in such circumstances was commended by Tapper[5]. Section 9 has been amended by various enactments and the relevant section, s 9(2), now reads as follows:

(2) Expressions in this Act relating to 'bankers' books' include ledgers, day books, cash books, account books and other records used in the ordinary business of the bank, whether those records are in written form or are kept on microfilm, magnetic tape or any other form of mechanical or electronic data retrieval mechanism.

Other statutory exceptions to the hearsay rule are covered in depth in the standard practitioner text on the subject[6].

1   *Tapper* (1989) p 407.
2   [1980] 1 WLR 884, [1980] 2 All ER 81, (1980) 70 Cr App Rep 283, [1980] Crim LR 373, 124 Sol Jo 326, DC.
3   (1980) 70 Cr App Rep 283 at 286.
4   (1980) 70 Cr App Rep 283 at 287.
5   *Tapper* (1989) p 408. See also the decision in *Victor Chandler International v Customs and Excise Commissioners* [2000] 1 WLR 1296, [2000] 2 All ER 315, (2000) 97(11) LS Gaz 36, (2000) 150 NLJ 341, (2000) Sol Jo LB 127, (2000) *Times*, March 8, (2000) *Independent*, March 10, CA, in which the Court of Appeal adopted an 'always speaking' construction to a statute, taking into account developments that had taken place since the provision was first enacted, even though it created a criminal offence.
6   *Malek* (2005) ch 32.

Civil proceedings

8.49 The hearsay rule provides that only a witness giving evidence could testify to the truth of the assertions they made in evidence. The hearsay rule excluded assertions made by a person other than the witness about the truth of a claim. Hearsay was abolished for civil proceedings by s1(1) of the Civil Evidence Act 1995, which reads:

1.—(1) In civil proceedings evidence shall not be excluded on the ground that it is hearsay.

(2) In this Act—

(a) 'hearsay' means a statement made otherwise than by a person while giving oral evidence in the proceedings which is tendered as evidence of the matters stated; and

(b) references to hearsay include hearsay of whatever degree.

The Act applies to all civil proceedings[1], including proceedings in the magistrates' court[2]. A party that intends to adduce hearsay evidence in civil proceedings is required to give the other party or parties notice of their intention and, should it be requested, particulars of the evidence[3]. Although in *Sunley v Gowland White (Surveyors & Estate Agents) Ltd*[4], a report was seen and used by both parties but the requisite notice had not been given under s 2(1)(a) or CPR 33.2(1). However, para 27.2 of Practice Direction—Evidence (supplementing CPR 32) provides that, where bundles of documents are agreed for use in a hearing, the documents shall be admissible as to their contents unless the court orders otherwise or a party gives written notice of objection of the admissibility of particular documents.

¹ s 11.
² The Magistrates' Courts (Hearsay Evidence in Civil Proceedings) Rules 1999, (SI 1999/681) (L.3).
³ Civil Evidence Act 1995, s 2.
⁴ [2003] EWCA Civ 240, [2004] PNLR 15.

8.50 The Act has retained a number of relevant exceptions to the hearsay rule that are particularly relevant to documents in digital format. Published works, public documents and public records are all admissible under the provisions of s 7(2). In addition, where a document can be shown to be part of the records of a business or public authority then the document, not the statements recorded in the document or any facts asserted by the wording contained in the document, can be received into evidence in civil proceedings without further proof, in accordance with s 9, which provides:

9.—(1) A document which is shown to form part of the records of a business or public authority may be received in evidence in civil proceedings without further proof.

(2) A document shall be taken to form part of the records of a business or public authority if there is produced to the court a certificate to that effect signed by an officer of the business or authority to which the records belong.

For this purpose—

(a) a document purporting to be a certificate signed by an officer of a business or public authority shall be deemed to have been duly given by such an officer and signed by him; and

(b) a certificate shall be treated as signed by a person if it purports to bear a facsimile of his signature.

(3) The absence of an entry in the records of a business or public authority may be proved in civil proceedings by affidavit of an officer of the business or authority to which the records belong.

(4) In this section—

'records' means records in whatever form;
'business' includes any activity regularly carried on over a period of time, whether for profit or not, by any body (whether corporate or not) or by an individual;
'officer' includes any person occupying a responsible position in relation to the relevant activities of the business or public authority or in relation to its records; and
'public authority' includes any public or statutory undertaking, any government department and any person holding office under Her Majesty.

(5) The court may, having regard to the circumstances of the case, direct that all or any of the above provisions of this section do not apply in relation to a particular document or record, or description of documents or records.

The meanings of 'document' and 'copy' are set out in s 13 as follows, and are replicated in CPR 31.4:

13. In this Act—

'document' means anything in which information of any description is recorded, and 'copy', in relation to a document, means anything onto which information recorded in the document has been copied, by whatever means and whether directly or indirectly;

The combined force of the provisions of the Act and the procedural rules ensure that the form a technology takes will not prevent the admission into evidence of data stored in digital format. For discussion of the meaning of 'document' generally, see the wider discussion above.

Criminal proceedings

8.51 The Criminal Justice Act 2003 repealed the provisions relating to hearsay in the Criminal Justice Act 1988, as well as abrogating most of the common law of hearsay[1]. The changes and the implications for criminal proceedings are fully covered in the main texts on evidence[2]. The provisions of s 114(1) act to exclude hearsay, although a number of common law exceptions are retained by virtue of s 118 (however, the exceptions relate to a set of exclusionary rules that are differently defined, which means the implications of the retention of the exceptions is not clear). Hearsay evidence is permitted in criminal proceedings, subject to the provisions of s 114(1), whilst the qualifying provisions of s 114(2) set out the limitations of admitting such evidence. Section 121 provides for additional requirements for the admissibility of multiple hearsay and s 126 provides for the general discretion to exclude evidence. Section 114(1) provides:

114   Admissibility of hearsay evidence

In criminal proceedings a statement not made in oral evidence in the proceedings is admissible as evidence of any matter stated if, but only if—

(a)   any provision of this Chapter or any other statutory provision makes it admissible,
(b)   any rule of law preserved by section 118 makes it admissible,
(c)   all parties to the proceedings agree to it being admissible, or
(d)   the court is satisfied that it is in the interests of justice for it to be admissible.

The interpretation of the provisions of s 114(1)(d) appear to indicate that the nuances of the more detailed provisions contained in s 114(2) may be softened in favour of admitting evidence because it is in the interests of justice to admit the evidence[3].

---

[1]   Previously, where a computer recorded the numbers of various components that were fitted to motor cars, the print-out was a hearsay statement where it was offered in evidence to prove that a number of components were fitted to a specific motor car: *Myers (James William) v DPP* [1965] AC 1001, [1964] 3 WLR 145, [1964] 2 All ER 881, (1964) 48 Cr App Rep 348, 128 JP 481, 108 Sol Jo 519, HL.
[2]   *Malek* (2005) ch 30; *Tapper* (2004) ch XIV.
[3]   *R v Xhabri* [2006] 1 All ER 776, [2006] 1 Cr Ap R 413, [2005] EWCA Crim 3135, 20 BHRC 233, 2005 WL 3353257, (2006) *Times*, January 10.

8.52 Of relevance for this text are the provisions of s 117, which provide a statutory exception for documents created in the course of a trade, business, profession or other occupation. The full text of the section is set out below:

117 Business and other documents

(1) In criminal proceedings a statement contained in a document is admissible as evidence of any matter stated if—

   (a) oral evidence given in the proceedings would be admissible as evidence of that matter,

   (b) the requirements of subsection (2) are satisfied, and

   (c) the requirements of subsection (5) are satisfied, in a case where subsection (4) requires them to be.

(2) The requirements of this subsection are satisfied if—

   (a) the document or the part containing the statement was created or received by a person in the course of a trade, business, profession or other occupation, or as the holder of a paid or unpaid office,

   (b) the person who supplied the information contained in the statement (the relevant person) had or may reasonably be supposed to have had personal knowledge of the matters dealt with, and

   (c) each person (if any) through whom the information was supplied from the relevant person to the person mentioned in paragraph (a) received the information in the course of a trade, business, profession or other occupation, or as the holder of a paid or unpaid office.

(3) The persons mentioned in paragraphs (a) and (b) of subsection (2) may be the same person.

(4) The additional requirements of subsection (5) must be satisfied if the statement—

   (a) was prepared for the purposes of pending or contemplated criminal proceedings, or for a criminal investigation, but

   (b) was not obtained pursuant to a request under section 7 of the Crime (International Co-operation) Act 2003 (c. 32) or an order under paragraph 6 of Schedule 13 to the Criminal Justice Act 1988 (c. 33) (which relate to overseas evidence).

(5) The requirements of this subsection are satisfied if—

   (a) any of the five conditions mentioned in section 116(2) is satisfied (absence of relevant person etc), or

   (b) the relevant person cannot reasonably be expected to have any recollection of the matters dealt with in the statement (having regard to the length of time since he supplied the information and all other circumstances).

(6) A statement is not admissible under this section if the court makes a direction to that effect under subsection (7).

(7) The court may make a direction under this subsection if satisfied that the statement's reliability as evidence for the purpose for which it is tendered is doubtful in view of—

   (a) its contents,

   (b) the source of the information contained in it,

   (c) the way in which or the circumstances in which the information was supplied or received, or

   (d) the way in which or the circumstances in which the document concerned was created or received.

The provisions of ss 117(2) and (5) set out the criteria by which the document can be admitted; s 117(6) provides a discretion to the court to refuse to admit evidence under this section, and s 117(7) provides the judge with the authority to make a direction if there is any doubt about the reliability of the statement in view of the criteria set out in s 117(7)(a)–(d). There was a requirement that such a statement could only be admitted with leave in accordance with s 26 of the Criminal Justice Act 1988, but leave is no longer required under s 117 if the document is prepared in the court of a criminal investigation or for criminal proceedings. Section 134 provides that a ' "copy", in relation to a document, means anything on to which information recorded in the document has been copied, by whatever means and whether directly or indirectly' and a ' "document" means anything in which information of any description is recorded.'

The provisions of s 117 are very wide and permit the admission into evidence of multiple hearsay, although the judge retains the discretion to make a direction in relation to reliability of the statement, which is an important safeguard in respect of digital documents[1]. A judge also has the ability to refuse to admit a statement in accordance with s 126(1)(b) where 'the court is satisfied that the case for excluding the statement, taking account of the danger that to admit it would result in undue waste of time, substantially outweighs the case for admitting it, taking account of the value of the evidence.'

[1]   For a general discussion about the European Convention on Human Rights in the context of hearsay evidence in criminal proceedings, see *Malek* (2005) at 30–59 to 30–67; *Cross and Tapper on Evidence* pp 654–656.

PRESUMPTIONS

8.53   The aim of a presumption, which allocates the burden of proof[1], is to alleviate the need prove every item of evidence adduced in court or to reduce the need for evidence in relation to some issues. In relation to digital evidence in criminal proceedings, there is a presumption that a mechanical device has been properly set or calibrated[2]. The rationale for this presumption stems from the distinction between the cases of *R v Wood*[3] and *R v Coventry Justices, ex p Bullard*[4]. In *Wood*, the evidence of the analysis of the tests carried out and produced by a computer was not hearsay because the chemists gave oral evidence of the results of the tests. In comparison, the computer print-out in *R v Coventry Justices, ex p Bullard* included a statement that a person was in arrears with their poll tax. This was correctly held to be inadmissible hearsay because the content of the print-out contained information that had been put into the computer by a human, and the print-out had not been properly proved. The Law Commission considered this distinction was correct and should be preserved[5].

[1]   *Cross and Tapper on Evidence* p 146.
[2]   Criminal Justice Act 2003, s 129(2).
[3]   (1983) 76 Cr App Rep 23, [1982] Crim LR 667, CA.
[4]   (1992) 95 Cr App Rep 175, [1992] RA 79, [1992] COD 285, (1992) NLJR 383, (1992) 136 Sol Jo LB 96, (1992) *Times*, February 24, (1992) *Independent* February 26, (1992) *Guardian* March 11, QBD.
[5]   Evidence in Criminal Proceedings: Hearsay and related topics, (LC 245, 19.06.97), 7.48.

8.54   In the absence of evidence to the contrary, it has been presumed that stopwatches and speedometers[1] were working properly at the material time, as with traffic lights[2]. The comments of Stephen Brown LJ in *Castle v Cross*[3] indicate that the courts will presume that a mechanical instrument is working accurately in the absence of evidence to the contrary. In fact Stephen Brown LJ quoted a passage from *Cross on Evidence* and omitted the qualification that 'the instrument must be one of a kind as to which it is common knowledge that they are more often than not in working order'[4]. It is pertinent to note the observation by Lord Griffiths in *Cracknell v Willis*[5] that ' "trial by machine" is an entirely novel concept and should be introduced with a degree of caution' and that he went on to make it clear that it would be unthinkable that somebody should be convicted by a machine that is not reliable.

[1]   *Nicholas v Penny, sub nom Penny v Nicholas* [1950] 2 KB 466, [1950] 2 All ER 89, 66 TLR (Pt 1) 1122, 114 JP 335, 48 LGR 535, 21 ALR2d 1193, 94 Sol Jo 437, DC.
[2]   *Tingle Jacobs & Co v Kennedy* [1964] 1 WLR 638n, [1964] 1 All ER 888n, 108 Sol Jo 196, CA.
[3]   [1984] 1 WLR 1372 at 1377.
[4]   *Cross and Tapper on Evidence* p 41.
[5]   [1988] AC 450 at 459, [1987] 3 All ER 801 at 806, HL.

8.55 However, various challenges have been made in criminal proceedings, especially in relation to the accuracy of speed-measuring devices and breath-analysis machines[1]. With rare exceptions, challenges have failed. In many instances, as in the case of *Darby (Yvonne Beatrice) v DPP*[2], the assertions of a police officer familiar with the use of such a device tends to held to be sufficient evidence to support the finding that the device was working correctly.

[1]   The following is not an exhaustive list of case law, but aims to offer an indication of some of the cases. Breath measuring machines: *Hughes v McConnell* [1986] 1 All ER 268, [1985] RTR 244; *Greenaway v DPP* [1994] RTR 17, 158 JP 27, DC; *Gunn v Brown* 1986 SCCR 179, 1986 SLT 94 (Scotland case); *Haggis v DPP* [2004] 2 All ER 382, [2003] EWHC 2481 (Admin), [2003] All ER (D) 113 (Oct). Speed measuring machines: *DPP v Memery* [2002] All ER (D) 64 (Jul), WL 1310940 (QBD (Admin Ct)), (2003) 167 JP 238, (2003) 167 JPN 431, [2003] RTR 18, [2002] EWHC 1720 (Admin), (2002) *Times*, September 9, in which it was made clear that the device used by the police was authorised by the Secretary of State and such authorisation was neither irrational nor unreasonable.
[2]   [1995] RTR 294, (1995) 159 JP 533, TLR November 4, 1994, 555, DC.

8.56 Professor Tapper has suggested that the presumption that a machine, such as a computer, is presumed to have been working, can be considered a somewhat 'rash assumption in relation to such sophisticated devices, with so much potential for error, as computers'[1]. One of the problems with computers is that lay people are not aware of the inherent design faults and trust to their personal experience to reassure themselves that computers are reliable machines[2]. However, the presumption only acts to place an evidential burden on the party opposing the presumption and, if they succeed, then the relying party is required to discharge the legal burden in relation to the reliability of the machine and, therefore, the evidence.

[1]   Stephen Saxby, ed *Encyclopedia of Information Technology* para 11.404.
[2]   David Harel *Computers Ltd. What they really can't do* (2003); see also a list of comments available on the Internet (please note, this is just one reference as a starting point: http://www.csl.sri.com/users/neumann/insiderisks.html).

COMPUTER-GENERATED ANIMATIONS AND SIMULATIONS[1]

8.57 The technical details of this topic are dealt with in detail elsewhere in this text. In criminal cases, s 31 of the Criminal Justice Act 1988 permits, with leave of the court, the use of evidence in any form for the purpose of helping members of a jury understand complicated issues of fact or technical terms. One example of such a use in a criminal prosecution was in *R v Ore*[2], in which the Crash Investigation and Training Unit of the West Midlands Police Service produced a computer generated animation based on the evidence of a collision between two vehicles at a junction where one of the drivers was killed. In the civil context, the trajectories of the two vessels were projected in a two-dimensional computer-generated simulation in *Owners of the Ship Pelopidas v Owners of the Ship TRSL Concord*[3]. The *Concord* had a device on board that recorded the position, speed and heading data at 15-second intervals covering the relevant period up to the collision, and it was this data that was used to provide the underlying data for the simulation.

1   Gregory P Joseph *Modern Visual Evidence* (Law Journal Press, 1984–2006) ch 7 for greater discussion and reference to relevant US case law.
2   Birmingham Crown Court, 1998, not reported.
3   [1999] 2 Lloyd's Rep 675.

8.58 It is a matter for the trial judge to decide whether to admit such evidence and, in reaching a decision, a number of matters will have to be canvassed:

(a)   An animation is a sequence of illustrations that create the illusion that the objects are in motion. A computer-generated animation is admissible where it can be demonstrated that the illusion portrays the evidence fairly and accurately, and that the events it portrays are significantly similar in all material respects to the underlying evidence.

(b)   Simulations can comprise reconstructions and re-creations of events. They are based on a model, comprising a number of operating assumptions that aim to represent a set of facts in mathematical terms. The accuracy of the simulation depends on how well the relevant elements and possible actions that occur in the physical world are matched in the assumptions included in the model of the simulation. If the simulation is effective, it is possible to illustrate the probable consequences of any theory of a case.

Although mention is made of animations and simulations above, it is, nevertheless, pertinent to make the observation that the distinction will not always be clear-cut, as observed by Katz J in *State of Connecticut v Swinton*[1]: 'Not only can we not anticipate what forms this evidence will take, but also common sense dictates that the line between one type of computer generated evidence and another will not always be obvious'. Gregory offers a checklist of factors for the trial judge to consider before admitting computer-generated evidence into the proceedings[2]. They include the factual foundation; the underlying scientific or technical theory; authenticity of the simulation; and prejudicial effect.

1   847 A.2d 921, (Conn. 2004) at 938 [11].
2   *Joseph* at 7.01[4][c], 8.03 and 8.05.

The factual foundation

8.59 The factual foundation comprises three aspects:

(a)   admissibility;

(b)   the provision to use such evidence either by virtue of the relevant procedural rules or as provided for in statute, or both; and

(c)   demonstrating the suitability of the animation or simulation by reference to the underlying evidence from witnesses and whether there is sufficient witness testimony to admit the animation or simulation which, in turn, will depend on the certainty or otherwise of the witness statements.

The underlying scientific or technical theory

8.60 There are no tests that are used to consider the underlying scientific or technical theory of a new form of technology or area of expertise in England and Wales and Tapper has remarked, in the context of evidence from a witness with the requisite degree of specialist knowledge, that

> The better, and now more widely accepted, view is that so long as a field is sufficiently well-established to pass ordinary tests or relevance and reliability, then no enhanced test of admissibility should be applied, but the weight of the evidence should be established by the same adversarial forensic techniques applicable elsewhere'[1].

The proponent wishing to adduce evidence of a computer animation or simulation will be required to provide evidence of the underlying mathematical model used in preparing the illusion together with the factual premise upon which the illusion is predicated. In addition, it will be necessary for the expert introducing the evidence to explain their opinion at the preliminary stage in order for the trial judge to decide whether the evidence of the animation or simulation, together with the opinion of the expert, embraces the ultimate issue to be decided[2]. Consideration also ought to be given where the animation or simulation is accompanied with the recording of a narrative. Such a recording is an extrajudicial statement and it must be determined whether the narration is to remain or whether the narration is to be excluded.

1   *Cross and Tapper on Evidence* p 571.
2   See the comments of the Lord Chief Justice in relation to experts offering an opinion on the ultimate issue in *R v Stockwell* (1993) 97 Cr App Rep 260 at 265–266; *Malek* (2005) paras 33–12 to 33–15.

Authenticity of the simulation

8.61 The main difference between simulations and other forms of evidence generated by computers is the simulation model used, which means it is important to pay attention to demonstrating or undermining, whichever the case may be, the reliability and trustworthiness of the model. Apart from the normal considerations that are relevant to the authentication of computer evidence generally, Gregory has listed a number of issues that ought to be the subject of testimony[1]:

(1)   that the model appropriately measures the factors that have been selected to represent the real life system;
(2)   that those factors are relevant and inclusive of all important aspects of the system;
(3)   that the mathematical techniques selected for constructing the model are appropriate so that the model actually performs the functions it was intended to perform;
(4)   that the mathematical tools are appropriately applied; and
(5)   that the problem at issue was appropriately translated into mathematical symbols comprising the model.

The degree of reliability has been the subject of comment in the United States and a variable degree of reliability that is consistent with the current state of the art in the modeling techniques used has been applied[2]. In practical terms, where a simulation of a road traffic accident is presented, for instance, consideration ought to be given to the authenticity of the representations of physical objects, such as the road surface. Some models do not include references to pot holes, the curb on a pavement, other impediments on the side of the road, and perhaps, if relevant, the camber of the road.

1   Gregory P Joseph *Modern Visual Evidence* at 8.03[2][b].
2   *Joseph* at 8.03[2][b] for cases, 8.03[3] for a list of the types of illustrative simulations that have been used and some of the problems identified.

Prejudicial effect

8.62   In criminal cases in particular, the trial judge will, during the trial within a trial, be required to balance the probative value against the prejudicial effect of the evidence proffered. It was observed by Steyn LJ in *R v Clarke*[1] on the matter of probative value in the context of facial mapping (but is relevant to all forms of digital manipulation) that 'the probative value of such evidence depends on the reliability of the scientific technique (and that is a matter of fact), and it is one fit for debate and for exploration in evidence'. There is always a concern that the simulation may have the effect of being overly persuasive to the members of a jury[2].

The use of computer-generated simulations and animations can be very effective in helping the trier of the facts reach a decision. The matters set out in this section also apply to other forms of digital evidence, such as computer-enhanced photographic images, the product of digital photography and enhanced videotapes. Whatever the form of the computer-generated evidence that a party seeks to adduce, careful consideration ought to be addressed with respect to the underlying authenticity and reliability of the techniques used to generate the evidence. Finally, an assertion by the opposing party about the ease by which digital evidence can be altered or manipulated is not a sufficient claim to cause the proponent of the evidence from adducing it. If the opponent cannot offer an objection of substance that acts to undermine the methods by which the authenticity of the evidence has been preserved, it is questionable as to whether the objections of the opponent are meritorious.

1   [1995] 2 Cr App Rep 425 at 431F.
2   For a critical analysis of video tape evidence, see: DW Elliott 'Video Tape Evidence: The Risk of Over-Persuasion' [1998] Crim LR 159.

VIDEO TAPE AND SECURITY CAMERA EVIDENCE

8.63 Surveillance cameras, the prominence of which began in the latter decades of the twentieth century, are very much part of life in the twenty first century. Evidence of images from security cameras can be very helpful in identifying the perpetrators of crimes and the enhancement of the images, together with the use of more advanced techniques such as facial mapping, can help to identify parties to an offence. Such evidence has been admitted in English courts, mainly in criminal cases[1].

The technique of facial mapping is relatively new, and careful attention should be given to how the technique has been used by an expert witness before admitting the evidence[2]. It is for this reason that the conclusions set out by Gregory in relation to the use of enhanced digital imagery, are very helpful[3]:

(a)   the original image needs to be properly authenticated;
(b)   the original image must remain intact to enable the original to be compared with the enhanced version;
(c)   the original image should be preserved in such a way that its integrity cannot be impugned;
(d)   the process of enhancement should be fully documented;
(e)   the process of enhancement should be carried out in such a way that the process can be repeated by the other party; and
(f)   the enhanced images should be preserved in such a way that prevents them from being manipulated and thereby preserves their integrity.

The outline above goes some way to the satisfy the remarks by Steyn LJ in *Clarke (Robert Lee)*[4], where he commented that the evidence should be scrutinised because such evidence could be flawed in the same way that fingerprint evidence can be flawed.

1   A non-exhaustive list includes: *McShane* (1978) 66 Cr App Rep 97; *R v Fowden and White* [1982] Crim LR 588, CA; *R v Grimer* [1982] Crim LR 674, 126 Sol Jo 641, CA; *R v Dodson (Patrick); R v Williams Danny Fitzalbert Williams)* [1984] 1 WLR 971, (1984) 79 Cr App Rep 220; *R v Stockwell (Christopher James)* (1993) 97 Cr App Rep 260; *R v Clarke (Robert Lee)* [1995] 2 Cr App Rep 425; *Clare (Richard), Peach (Nicholas William)* [1995] 2 Cr App Rep 333; *R v Feltis (Jeremy)* [1996] EWCA Crim 776; *R v Hookway* [1999] Crim LR 750; *R v Briddick* [2001] EWCA Crim 984, 2001 WL 513023 (CA (Crim Div)), (2001) *Independent*, May 21; *Loveridge (William)* [2001] 2 Cr App Rep 29, [2001] EWCA Crim 973—in this instance, the accused were recorded by video in the court, an act which was prohibited by s 41 of the Criminal Justice Act 1925, and the recording was also held to have infringed the rights of the accused under art 8 of the Human Rights Act 1998. However, neither infringement was held to have interfered with the right to a fair trial. Elliott Goldstein 'Photographic and Videotape Evidence in the Criminal Courts of England and Canada' [1987] Crim LR 384.
2   Michael C Bromby 'At face value?' (2003) NLJ Expert Witness Supplement, February 28, 302 and 304; *R v Jung* [2006] NSWSC 658.

215

3   *Joseph* at 8.04[4].
4   [1995] 2 Cr App Rep 425 at 430 F.

DATA PROTECTION

8.64 Although data in digital format is protected under the provisions of the Data Protection Act 1998, s 35(1) provides that personal data are exempt from the non-disclosure provisions where disclosure is required by or under any enactment, rule of law or by order of a court[1]. Exemptions that will affect the advice offered to clients are the provisions of para 7 of Sch 7 to the Act, which reads as follows:

> Personal data which consist of records of the intentions of the data controller in relation to any negotiations with the data subject are exempt from the subject information provisions in any case to the extent to which the application of those provisions would likely to prejudice those negotiations.

The provisions of this paragraph indicate that the data controller is not required to deliver up personal data that set out the data controller's intentions towards settling any dispute with the data subject. Of practical relevance is the point in time when negotiations to settle a dispute alter from being merely negotiations and escalate into litigation. It is suggested that care must be taken to ensure that the provisions of this paragraph are not used to prevent the disclosure of documents in circumstances where it becomes obvious that negotiations have broken down between the parties.

1   *Rowley v Liverpool City Council* (1989) *Times*, October 26, CA; see also *Johnson v Medical Defence Union Ltd* [2004] EWHC 2509 (Ch), (2004) *Times*, November 25, where an individual may seek to obtain access to data by making an application for disclosure in the course of proceedings where there are allegations of breach of the Data Protection Act 1998.

FREEDOM OF INFORMATION

8.65 The Freedom of Information Act 2000 grants a right of access to information held by public authorities. The Act provides for the establishment of an Information Tribunal and appeals from the Information Commissioner are directed to this Tribunal, which has jurisdiction to hear appeals under the Data Protection Act 1998 and the Freedom of Information Act 2000. In the appeal of *Harper v Royal Mail Group plc*[1], the members of the Tribunal considered the question of whether data that had been deleted was subject to the provisions of the Act and whether a public authority will be obliged to attempt to recover data that had been deleted. The members of the Tribunal considered the provisions of s 1(4), which reads:

(4)   The information—

   (a)   in respect of which the applicant is to be informed under subsection (1)(a), or
   (b)   which is to be communicated under subsection (1)(b),

is the information in question held at the time when the request is received, except that account may be taken of any amendment or deletion made between that time and the time when the information is to be communicated under subsection (1)(b), being an amendment or deletion that would have been made regardless of the receipt of the request.

8.66

The provisions of this section envisage circumstances where information may have been held at one time, but not held at the time the request is received. The members of the Tribunal concluded that where data is deleted in the normal course of events it need not be recovered. However, where a request is received and the data is deleted during the period of 20 working days within which a response must be made, the deletion will not be in the ordinary course of business and therefore the deletion will be unlawful. However, the point was made in the decision that it was not a question of whether an account 'must' be made of any amendment or deletion, but that it 'may' be taken into account. In respect of the need to search for deleted materials, the members of the Tribunal offered the following interpretation at 18:

> 'The Tribunal interprets this as meaning that where the deleted or unamended information is still readily accessible and this is the information that the applicant wants, then the deleted or original version of the information should be recovered and that is what should be communicated to the applicant, with perhaps an explanation of what has happened to the information since the request was received.'

The members of the Tribunal went into some detail as to how data could be recovered that is not germane to the decision, but reached the conclusion, at 21, that

> it may be incumbent on a Public Authority to make attempts to retrieve deleted information. Accordingly, the authority should establish whether information is completely eliminated, or merely deleted. In the latter case, the authority should consider whether the information can be recovered and if so by what means.

8.67 Whether data can be retrieved will be a matter of fact and degree, depending on the circumstances of the individual case. Further guidance was given in relation to the extent that an authority should search for deleted data at 27:

> The extent of the measures that could reasonably be taken by a Public Authority to recover deleted data will be a matter of fact and degree in each individual case. Simple restoration from a trash can or recycle bin folder, or from a back-up tape, should normally be attempted, as the Tribunal considers that such information continues to be held. Any attempted restoration that would involve the use of specialist staff time, or the use of specialist software, would have cost implications, which could be significant. In that event, the exemption arising from exceeding the appropriate limit, set from time to time under section 12 of the Act, might be relied upon by an authority. Also it is relevant that the 20 day time limit itself gives an indication of the period for which an authority should strive diligently to comply with a request.

This decision illustrates that the information, once deleted, may still be regarded as being in existence, which illustrates the need for public authorities to have provisions in place to suspend the automatic deletion of data until a request has been fulfilled. Finally, the members of the Tribunal indicated that where data had been deleted but not expunged, and a version remained on the system, it will be necessary to determine which version is subject to disclosure. In such circumstances, where two versions of a document exist, it is suggested that, in determining which version should be disclosed, it will be necessary to decide which of the versions is the relevant document in relation to the nature of the request.

1   EA/2005/0001; 'Freedom of information and deleted electronic records' (2005) Communications Law, vol 10, no 6, 226–227.

ENTERPRISE ACT

8.68 Part 9 of the Enterprise Act 2002 provides statutory authority for the disclosure of information relating to the affairs of an individual or a business by a public authority[1] for specific purposes, covering civil investigations, criminal proceedings and proceedings overseas. Before the provisions of Pt 9 entered into force, in June 2003, disclosure was restricted to particular statutes. The aim of Pt 9 was to provide for a single disclosure regime. More recently, the Enterprise Act 2002 has been amended with the insertion of s 241A[2]. The provisions of the new section widen the scope of disclosure for information to which s 237 applies:

241A   Civil proceedings

(1)   A public authority which holds prescribed information to which section 237 applies may disclose that information to any person—

    (a)   for the purposes of, or in connection with, prescribed civil proceedings (including prospective proceedings) in the United Kingdom or elsewhere, or

    (b)   for the purposes of obtaining legal advice in relation to such proceedings, or

    (c)   otherwise for the purposes of establishing, enforcing or defending legal rights that are or may be the subject of such proceedings.

For the provisions of s 241A to enter into force, secondary legislation is required. At the time of writing, a draft Statutory Instrument enabling disclosure of information for civil proceedings under the Enterprise Act 2002 was prepared by the Department of Trade and Industry[3] and was the subject of consultation. It was anticipated that the draft Statutory Instrument would enter into force at the October 2007 common commencement date. It is expected that a summary of the responses received, together with a Government response, will be published by 1 April. Regulation 3 of the draft Statutory Instrument provides the matters for which disclosure may be made, covering the following: consumer credit, the subject matter of the Property Misdescriptions Act 1991, personal injury, product liability, sale and supply of goods and services to consumers, safety of consumer goods and services, time share and package travel, intellectual property rights.

Given the probability that public authorities will be in possession of reasonable amounts of evidence in digital format in relation to the matters for which disclosure is made, it is foreseeable that disputes may occur over who pays the cost of providing the evidence: providing the authority actually retains the digital evidence, and does not delete it (either deliberately—for instance, by an automatic process—or inadvertently). In addition, courts may have to consider what responsibility, if any, an authority has for failing to handle the evidence appropriately such that it undermines its authenticity and integrity, and perhaps rendering it useless in legal proceedings.

¹ A public authority is to be construed in accordance with s 6 of the Human Rights Act 1998: Enterprise Act 2002, s 238(3).
² Inserted by s 1281 of the Companies Act 2006.
³ The Enterprise Act 2002 (Disclosure of Information for Civil Proceedings) Order 2007.

CIVIL PROCEEDINGS

8.69 The law relating to civil procedure and disclosure is dealt with at length in the standard texts, to which the reader is referred for further reference[1]. The narrow aim of this discussion is to explore the issues that affect disclosure in relation to electronic documents. The purposes of disclosure are noted by Matthews and Malek as follows:

(a)   the extraction of 'all relevant documents and other information from others';
(b)   to enable a party 'to obtain the best possible evidence or admissions from his opponent';
(c)   to enable a party to 'evaluate the strength of the opponent's case'; and
(d)   to decrease the time taken in litigation, which in turn hopefully reduces the cost of taking legal action[2].

Disclosure is intended to ensure the process of litigation is fair to both sides, and to make it clear what issues are in dispute between the parties. The aim is to prevent surprises at trial and to encourage the parties to reach a resolution of their differences before inviting an adjudicator to reach a decision based on the evidence adduced at trial. However, it does not follow that the advantages of disclosure are clear to every party participating in the judicial process. The process can be both expensive and onerous. In the world of paper documents, a party can be overwhelmed by the sheer volume of paper, which also takes up a significant amount of physical space. When electronic documents are disclosed, the disadvantages can be even more significant, because the quantity of electronic documents can reach enormous proportions.

¹ Paul Matthews and Hodge M Malek *Disclosure* (2nd edn, 2001); Neil Andrews *English Civil Procedure Fundamentals of the New Civil Justice System* (2003); *Civil Procedure*; *Blackstone's Civil Practice*; *The Civil Court Practice*; *Civil Court Practice*.
² *Matthews and Malek* (2001) at 1.02; *Andrews* at 26.04.

8.70 Significant changes occurred to civil litigation when the Civil Procedure Rules took effect, on 26 April 1999, as a result of the report by Lord Woolf[1]. Lord Woolf identified the following problems:

> Our present system is:
> too *unequal*: there is a lack of equality between the powerful, wealthy litigant and the under-resourced litigant;
> too *expensive*: the costs often exceed the value of the claim;
> too *uncertain*: the difficulty of forecasting what litigation will cost and how long it will last induces fear of the unknown;

slow in bringing cases to a conclusion;

too *complicated*: both the law and procedure can be incomprehensible to many litigants;

too *fragmented* in the way it is organised: there is no-one with clear overall responsibility for the administration of civil justice;

too *adversarial*: cases are run by the parties, not by the courts. The rules of court are, all too often, ignored by the parties and not enforced by the court[2].

1   Lord Woolf, Access to Justice: Final Report (July 1996) available online at http://www.dca.gov.uk/civil/final/index.htm. For a discussion of the reforms, including the background, see Neil Andrews *English Civil Procedure Fundamentals of the New Civil Justice System* ch 2.
2   Lord Woolf, Interim Report to the Lord Chancellor on the civil justice system in England and Wales, a summary set out on the website at http://www.dca.gov.uk/civil/interfr.htm.

8.71 The new code has served to revise the relationship between the parties, their lawyers and the judges. The shift is marked. The judges now control the proceedings, not the parties. Judges are required to give effect to the overriding objective when they exercise the powers set out in the Rules[1]. The overriding objective is set out in CPR 1:

1(1)   These Rules are a new procedural code with the overriding objective of enabling the court to deal with cases justly.

(2)   Dealing with a case justly includes, so far as is practicable—

(a)   ensuring that the parties are on an equal footing;
(b)   saving expense;
(c)   dealing with the case in ways which are proportionate—
      (i)   to the amount of money involved;
      (ii)   to the importance of the case;
      (iii)   to the complexity of the issues; and
      (iv)   to the financial position of each party;
(d)   ensuring that it is dealt with expeditiously and fairly; and
(e)   allotting to it an appropriate share of the court's resources, while taking into account the need to allot resources to other cases.

1   CPR 1.2.

8.72 Judging by the amount of reported hearings in the United States of America respecting the costs of discovery and documents in digital format, the search for digital documents can be a long and expensive process. No doubt similar arguments rage between lawyers and their clients in England and Wales, although the lack of any case law may well be because the lawyers for each side generally undertake to 'meet and confer' in order to resolve any differences. There is no question that most lawyers are fully alive to the requirements of the disclosure of electronic evidence and the main issue is the question of what is considered to be a reasonable search. A second reason for the absence of case law on the subject may rest with the judges and masters, who are resolving disputes about the reasonableness or otherwise of searching for digital documents, together with the costs associated with the entire process (searching, reviewing, producing lists, documenting and preparing for trial), within the provisions of the overriding objective and the relevant procedural rules and without the need to create precedents. When considering the reasonableness or otherwise of the search for documents in electronic format, consideration must be given to the possible location of electronic documents—at trial, judges will only see a tiny proportion of the documents that were considered to be relevant. Well before trial, instructing solicitors will have advised the client to conduct searches across a wide range of devices to ensure a reasonable search has been carried out of the likely places to find relevant documents, as well as shifting through the documents found. Invariably, differences of opinion will occur at this early stage of litigation and it will be important for a judge to take cognisance of this part of the process when deciding disputes about the extent and reasonableness of searches for documents in electronic format. Such arguments, if any, will mainly be held before the judge or master appointed to manage the case, which is a distinctive feature of the new regime, as provided by CPR 1.4:

(1)   The court must further the overriding objective by actively managing cases.

(2)   Active case management includes—

(a)   encouraging the parties to co-operate with each other in the conduct of the proceedings;
(b)   identifying the issues at an early stage;
(c)   deciding promptly which issues need full investigation and trial and accordingly disposing summarily of the others;
(d)   deciding the order in which issues are to be resolved;
(e)   encouraging the parties to use an alternative dispute resolution procedure if the court considers that appropriate and facilitating the use of such procedure;
(f)   helping the parties to settle the whole or part of the case;
(g)   fixing timetables or otherwise controlling the progress of the case;
(h)   considering whether the likely benefits of taking a particular step justify the cost of taking it;
(i)   dealing with as many aspects of the case as it can on the same occasion;
(j)   dealing with the case without the parties needing to attend at court;
(k)   making use of technology; and
(l)   giving directions to ensure that the trial of a case proceeds quickly and efficiently.

The parties are also required to help the court further the overriding object in accordance with the provisions of CPR 1.3.

Pre-trial

8.73 A search order, previously known as an Anton Piller order[1], is a mandatory interlocutory injunction issued under the provisions of s 7 of the Civil Evidence Act 1997, CPR 25.1(1)(h) and Practice Direction—Interim Injunctions, under which the court can make an order for:

(a)   the preservation of evidence which is or may be relevant, or
(b)   the preservation of property which is or may be the subject-matter of the proceedings or as to which any question arises or may arise in the proceedings[2].

Section 7(3)(a) of the Act provides for the authority to enter any premises in England and Wales for the purposes of carrying out a search for or inspection of anything described in the order, and to make or obtain a copy, photograph,

sample or other record of anything described in the order[3]. The provisions of
s 7(5) may also direct the person to whom the order is addressed to provide
any information or article described in the order, or to allow the person
described in the order to retain for safe keeping anything described in the
order. A penal notice is included on the Search Order, making it clear that it is
a contempt of court to disobey the order[4]. A search order cannot be used to
determine whether there is a cause of action[5]; there must be very strong
evidence in relation to the main complaint[6]; there must also be a serious risk
that the applicant's interests will be damaged if the order is not granted[7]; there
must be a need to prevent a denial of justice and an order for delivering up the
materials will not be sufficient[8]; it must be demonstrated that the respondent
possesses the evidence and there is a danger that it will be destroyed unless
there is a surprise search[9], and the harm caused to the respondent in executing
the order must not be excessive or out of proportion to the object of the order,
which means restrictions may be imposed on the circumstances in which
search orders will be made[10].

[1]   *Piller (Anton) KG v Manufacturing Processes Ltd* [1976] Ch 55, CA.
[2]   Civil Evidence Act 1997, s 7(1).
[3]   Civil Evidence Act 1997, s 7(4).
[4]   This is regardless of whether a Managing Director of a company takes the view that he is
      'upset and angry that the plaintiffs were entitled to take' such action: *Chanel Ltd v 3 Pears
      Wholesale Cash & Carry Co* [1979] FSR 393.
[5]   *Hy-trac v Conveyors International* [1983] 1 WLR 44, CA.
[6]   *Piller (Anton) KG v Manufacturing Processes Ltd* [1976] Ch 55 at 62 per Ormrod LJ.
[7]   *Piller (Anton) KG v Manufacturing Processes Ltd* [1976] Ch 55 at 62 per Ormrod LJ.
[8]   *Lock International plc v Beswick* [1989] 1 WLR 1268, [1989] 3 All ER 373, [1989] IRLR
      481, (1989) Sol Jo 1297, (1980) 139 NLJ 644, [1989] LSG November 1, 36.
[9]   *Piller (Anton) KG v Manufacturing Processes Ltd* [1976] Ch 55 at 59–60 per Lord Den-
      ning; there is no infringement of a right to a fair trial where the order is issued as a result
      of affidavit evidence that shows there is a probability that relevant materials would no
      longer be available if the order were not made: *Hermès International (a partnership limited
      by shares) v FHT Marketing Choice BV* (Case C-53/96), ECJ.
[10] *Columbia Picture Industries v Robinson* [1987] Ch 38, [1986] 3 WLR 542, [1986]
      3 All ER 338, [1986] FSR 367, (1986) 130 Sol Jo 766, (1986) 83 LSG 3424.

European Convention on Human Rights

8.74   The making of a search order, providing it is appropriate, is not a breach
of art 8 of the European Convention on Human Rights. In the case of
Chappell v United Kingdom[1] the court did not find a breach where a civil
search order was granted in respect of a domestic dwelling. However, the
procedural rules relating to search orders, together with the provisions of
search and freezing orders, are aimed at ensuring sufficient control is exercised
over such orders as to prevent breach of the Convention. Such controls
include, but are not limited to, the inability to issue a civil search warrant and
criminal search warrant at the same time[2]; provisions aimed at controlling the
way an order is processed[3]; the opportunity for the respondent to obtain legal
advice[4], and the timing of the search[5]. The rule against self-incrimination in
relation to search orders has not affected the general position in English law[6].

[1]   (1989) 12 EHRR 1, [1989] FSR 617, EHCR.
[2]   Practice Direction—Interim Injunctions, Search Order para 8.
[3]   Practice Direction—Interim Injunctions, para 7.5.

4   Practice Direction—Interim Injunctions, para 7.4(4).
5   Practice Direction—Interim Injunctions, para 7.4(6).
6   *Matthews and Malek* (2001) 2.54–2.59.

Computer evidence

8.75 The search and seizure of computers are dealt with in paras 16 and 17 of the Search Order:

> 16.The Respondent must immediately hand over to the Applicant's solicitors any of the listed items, which are in his possession or under his control, save for any computer or hard disk integral to any computer. Any items the subject of a dispute as to whether they are listed items must immediately be handed over to the Supervising Solicitor for safe keeping pending resolution of the dispute or further order of the court.

> 17.The Respondent must immediately give the search party effective access to the computers on the premises, with all necessary passwords, to enable the computers to be searched. If they contain any listed items the Respondent must cause the listed items to be displayed so that they can be read and copied[1]. The Respondent must provide the Applicant's solicitors with copies of all listed items contained in the computers. All reasonable steps shall be taken by the Applicant and the Applicant's solicitors to ensure that no damage is done to any computer or data. The Applicant and his representatives may not themselves search the Respondent's computers unless they have sufficient expertise to do so without damaging the Respondent's system.

The practical effects of the search order will differ for each search undertaken. However, it is conceivable that, unless there are very good reasons for seizing and removing a computer or any other similar device, it will be sufficient to take a forensic image of any relevant hard drives, although this will be difficult for a large system. This method was used in *Admiral Management Services Ltd v Para-Protect Europe Ltd*[2] where images of hard drives were taken during a search[3].

1   Footnote 8 at this point of the text reads as follows: 'If it is envisaged that the Respondent's computers are to be imaged (i.e. the hard drives are to be copied wholesale, thereby reproducing listed items and other items indiscriminately), special provision needs to be made and independent computer specialists need to be appointed, who should be required to give undertakings to the court'.
2   [2003] 2 All ER 1017, [2002] EWHC 233 (Ch).
3   For the role of the expert in this process, see Craig Earnshaw 'Search and Seize Orders—The Role and Responsibility of the Forensic Computing Specialist' (2003) Computers & Law, February/March, 11–13.

8.76 Search orders are expensive to enforce and are, rightly, open to challenge if the search fails to yield the evidence claimed. An alternative procedure has been suggested by Peter Susman QC. It has two main stages: first, the claimant applies to the court, without notice, for an order by way of injunction requiring the defendant to lodge information and data stored on computers with its own solicitors, together with a directory of all files and the size (in bytes) of each file (to prevent changes being made); if the order is granted, it is served on the defendant with a notice of a further application. The second stage begins with the further application, starting with an application on notice, for the information to be disclosed on a confidential basis to an expert engaged by the claimant. The claimant will then need to apply for the information to be disclosed to the claimant itself[1]. He reports that so far as he knows, in every case in which this procedure has been tried, the dispute has been resolved before an order has been made at the second stage.

[1]   Peter Susman QC 'Court Orders for the Preservation of Computer Data' (2001) Computers & Law, June/July, 20–23; see also (2001) Computers & Law, August/September, 39.

Disclosure

8.77   The main form of disclosure concerns documents, and the meaning of a document is discussed elsewhere in this chapter. Disclosure is dealt with under the provisions of CPR 31, which applies to all claims but small claims. Disclosure is limited to standard disclosure under CPR 31.6 unless the court dispenses with or limits standard disclosure, or the parties agree in writing to dispense with or to limit standard disclosure under CPR 31.5, or vary the technicalities of disclosure or its legal effect under CPR 31.10(8), 31.13 and 31.22(1)(c). Standard disclosure is set out in CPR 31.6, as follows:

31.6   Standard disclosure requires a party to disclose only—

(a)   the documents on which he relies; and

(b)   the documents which—

(i)   adversely affect his own case;
(ii)   adversely affect another party's case; or
(iii)   support another party's case; and

(c)   the documents which he is required to disclose by a relevant practice direction.

The duty of disclosure continues until the proceedings are concluded[1], although inspection and searching for documents must not be disproportionate[2]. Each party has the obligation to comply with five central duties:

(a)   to preserve documents;
(b)   to conduct a reasonable search in accordance with the provisions of CPR 31.7;
(c)   to disclose documents and allow them to be inspected (CPR 31.10 and CPR 31.14) [3];
(d)   to serve a list of documents and make a disclosure statement certifying that the duties have been undertaken, also explaining the way in which the search was carried out (CPR 31.10(5)–(9); and
(e)   the 'implied undertaking': the recipient must comply with the 'implied undertaking', that is only to use the documentary information provided for the purpose of the present proceedings[4].

As an observation, it should be noted that source code is disclosable, and it may be necessary to include the source code in the list of documents[5]. The disclosure of the source code is more relevant to intellectual property matters and, where it is disclosed, it is recommended that a great deal of care is given to protecting how the code will be dealt with by the recipient, because the source code is capable of forming the basis of alternative software products.

[1]   CPR 31.11.
[2]   CPR 31.3(2).

³   See *Punjab National Bank v Jain* [2004] EWCA Civ 589, [2004] All ER (D) 1 (May); and
    Marion Smith 'Not a shred of evidence' (2006) New Law Journal, 24 February at 317–318
    where the defendants claimed that the claimant's disclosure of documents was deliberately
    selective, or that documents had been deliberately destroyed.
⁴   *Andrews* at 26.45–26.56.
⁵   *Format Communications MFG Ltd v ITT (United Kingdom) Ltd* [1983] FSR 473, CA.

Preservation of data

8.78   A meeting with the company secretary, if the client is a company, should
be held as a matter of course. The company secretary, not the IT department,
has the legal responsibility for the retention and disposal of documents, and is
the first person that must be appraised of the need to suspend the routine
disposal of documents and data and to ensure adequate notices have been
given to members of staff to prevent the further disposal and alteration of
documents and data[1].

1   *Rockwell Machine Tool Co Ltd v E P Barrus (Concessionaires) Ltd* (Practice Note) [1968]
    1 WLR 693, [1968] 2 All ER 98, Ch D.

8.79   Depending on the number of employees and size of the client, a meeting
must be arranged with the client's head of information technology, preferably
somebody at board level, together with the company secretary. The meeting
should occur as a matter of urgency and a clear understanding must be
reached immediately respecting the channels of communication between the
lead solicitor and the person with ultimate responsibility for implementing the
requirements of the procedural rules. In addition, time should be taken to
obtain a thorough grasp of the communications infrastructure, together with
the relevant document retention and disposal policies that might be in place
that affect the retention and disposal of electronic data.

The standard of proof in civil litigation is lower than that of prosecutions in
criminal courts and there is less of a need to consider the quality of the
evidence in electronic format. However, if it is thought appropriate, it may be
considered a prudent measure where, for instance, allegations of deliberate
destruction of documents can be foreseen, to engage an independent digital
evidence specialist to take an image of all relevant hard drives and servers.

Conduct a reasonable search

8.80   Concern over the issues relating to electronic evidence brought about the
formation of a working party chaired by Mr Justice Cresswell in 2004[1]. As a
result of this working party's Report, amendments were made to the Commercial and Admiralty Court Guide. Although the members of the committee had
no remit to advise the Rules Committee, the members of the Rules Committee
nevertheless adopted the guidance with minor changes. The Practice
Direction—Disclosure and Inspection (which supplements CPR 31) was
subsequently amended to deal with electronic evidence, and the additional
rules are set out below:

2A.1 Rule 31.4 contains a broad definition of a document. This extends to electronic documents, including email and other electronic communications, word processed documents and databases. In addition to documents that are readily accessible from computer systems and other electronic devices and media, the definition covers those documents that are stored on servers and back-up systems and electronic documents that have been 'deleted'. It also extends to additional information stored and associated with electronic documents known as metadata.

2A.2 The parties should, prior to the first Case Management Conference, discuss any issues that may arise regarding searches for and the preservation of electronic documents. This may involve the parties providing information about the categories of electronic documents within their control, the computer systems, electronic devices and media on which any relevant documents may be held, the storage systems maintained by the parties and their document retention policies. In the case of difficulty or disagreement, the matter should be referred to a judge for directions at the earliest practical date, if possible at the first Case Management Conference.

2A.3 The parties should co-operate at an early stage as to the format in which electronic copy documents are to be provided on inspection. In the case of difficulty or disagreement, the matter should be referred to a Judge for directions at the earliest practical date, if possible at the first Case Management Conference.

2A.4 The existence of electronic documents impacts upon the extent of the reasonable search required by Rule 31.7 for the purposes of standard disclosure. The factors that may be relevant in deciding the reasonableness of a search for electronic documents include (but are not limited to) the following:—

   (a)   The number of documents involved.
   (b)   The nature and complexity of the proceedings.
   (c)   The ease and expense of retrieval of any particular document. This includes:
      (i)   The accessibility of electronic documents or data including email communications on computer systems, servers, back-up systems and other electronic devices or media that may contain such documents taking into account alterations or developments in hardware or software systems used by the disclosing party and/or available to enable access to such documents.
     (ii)   The location of relevant electronic documents, data, computer systems, servers, back-up systems and other electronic devices or media that may contain such documents.
    (iii)   The likelihood of locating relevant data.
    (iv)   The cost of recovering any electronic documents.
     (v)   The cost of disclosing and providing inspection of any relevant electronic documents.
    (vi)   The likelihood that electronic documents will be materially altered in the course of recovery, disclosure or inspection.
   (d)   The significance of any document which is likely to be located during the search.

2A.5 It may be reasonable to search some or all of the parties' electronic storage systems. In some circumstances, it may be reasonable to search for electronic documents by means of keyword searches (agreed as far as possible between the parties) even where a full review of each and every document would be unreasonable. There may be other forms of electronic search that may be appropriate in particular circumstances.

The new provisions make it clear that it is intended that parties are required to conduct reasonable searches across live systems and storage media[2]. This does not necessarily mean an exhaustive search is necessary, but any search must be proportionate. For instance, the main people involved in the facts leading up to the disputed facts should be identified and then it must be established what types of device they used to disseminate relevant, or potentially relevant, information. All forms of hardware are covered, including PDAs, Blackberry communication devices, CD-ROMs stored in the back of a cupboard or on a laptop located in a private dwelling. In appropriate cases, it may be necessary for parties to meet and confer in order to more fully understand how a business was run and how the networked communications system operated, in order to more fully understand where documents were likely to be. A balance will have to be struck between the cost of such a search and the likelihood of finding relevant data but, bearing in mind the extensive use of various forms of hardware devices, it will probably be reasonable for a party to insist that the main personnel involved in a case must be required to search all relevant hardware devices, wherever they may be located[3].

[1]   Mr Justice Cresswell 'Electronic Disclosure, A Report of a Working Party of the Commercial Court Users Committee'. For a brief discussion relevant to the comments about back-up tapes in the report, see Victoria Cooper 'Redefining the Rules of Engagement' (2005) Computers & Law, vol 16, issue 4, October/November, 7–8.

[2]   *Marlton v Tectronix UK Holdings* [2003] EWHC 383 Ch, [2003] Info TLR 258, 2003 WL 1610255, Ch D where the inadequate disclosure of email communications (where the date of receipt of email communications was an issue) meant the only solution was an order for the inspection and imaging of a hard disk by a digital forensic specialist. Although this case pre-dates the amended rules, nevertheless, the reason for the application appears to demonstrate the nature of the problem of what is meant by reasonable and Pumfrey J was required to hear evidence of the issues before he could make an order; Tom Hopkinson 'Filtering Electronic Evidence' Computers & Law, December 2003/January 2004, 16–20.

[3]   Although the case of *Hands v Morrison Construction Services Ltd* [2006] EWHC 2018 (Ch), [2006] All ER (D) 186 (Jun) related to pre-action disclosure, Mr Briggs QC, sitting as Deputy Judge in the Technology and Construction Court, considered the volume of electronic documents held on a server when exercising his discretion as to whether to make a pre-action disclosure order. In this instance, he considered a number of the factors that are relevant to the determination of the reasonableness of a search for disclosure of electronic documents, as set out in the Practice Direction. See also the comments of Sir Philip Bailhache, Bailiff, in which he indicated the geographical location of evidence on computers should not cause a problem in producing the data where the litigation is to be held: *Koonmen v Bender* 5 ITELR 247.

8.81 It will be necessary to ascertain where relevant data may be located and to identify all relevant items of hardware and other devices that may contain data. The lists contained in the Disclosure Statement provide an initial guide to the possible sources of data[1]. The search for data will have to be undertaken in accordance with the requirements of the criteria set out in the Practice Direction to CPR 31 and all relevant data will probably need to be copied on to other forms of storage media. In the process, the integrity of the data must not be compromised otherwise the authenticity of the data may be called into question. The Cresswell Report indicated, in para 2.18, some of the sources of data that will need to be considered:

> Active or online data: this is data which is directly accessible on the desktop computer. Online storage is used in the very active steps of an electronic record's life, when it is being created or received and processed, as well as when the access frequency is high and the required speed of access of fast. Examples of such data include material held on hard drives, filed documents and inbox and sent items in an email system.

Embedded data: this is data which is not normally visible when a document is printed, although can be viewed on the screen. Word programs usually store information about when data files are created, when edited, by whom, and who has accessed them. Other examples are formulae for spreadsheets and calculations which are programmed into a system, but are not visible on printed out documents.

Replicant data (otherwise known as 'temporary files' or 'file clones'): this is automatically created by the desktop computer. Many programs have an automatic back-up feature which creates and periodically saves copies of a file as the user works on it. These are intended to assist recovery of data caused by computer malfunction, power failure or when the computer is turned-off without the user saving the data. Examples of such data include automatic saves of draft documents, temporary copies of opened email attachments and recovered files automatically available following a computer malfunction.

Back-up data: this is data held in a storage system. On the most basic level it can consist of offline storage in the form of a removable optical disk or magnetic tape media, which can be labelled and stored in a shelf (in contrast with near line data which is directly accessible from the computer and is readily accessible). Most organisations use back-up data to preserve information in case of a disaster. This can take various forms ranging from copying information stored on the system to a back-up system in the form of magnetic tapes or by sending files over the Internet to a third party's computer (some companies even offer computer users free storage space on their websites). The disadvantage with back-up systems is that usually the data is compressed and can be difficult and costly to retrieve.

Residual data: this is material deleted from the user's active data and stored elsewhere on the database. Deleting a file or email removes it from the user's active data, instead the data is stored elsewhere on the database and can become fragmented. The data can usually be retrieved with sufficient expertise and time.

[1]   One of the difficulties faced by lawyers is the failure of a client to produce or admit to having relevant data, especially email communications: *Phones4u Ltd v Phone4u.co.uk Internet Ltd* [2006] EWCA Civ 244, [2005] EWHC 334, Ch.

8.82 Arrangements will also need to be put in train to provide disclosure to the other party. In addition, the Disclosure Statement relating to electronic data was also introduced as an Annex to the supplementary Practice Direction—Disclosure and Inspection to CPR31:

I, the above named claimant [or defendant] [if party making disclosure is a company, firm or other organisation identify here who the person making the disclosure statement is and why he is the appropriate person to make it] state that I have carried out a reasonable and proportionate search to locate all the documents which I am required to disclose under the order made by the court on day of ..... I did not search:

for documents predating ....,

for documents located elsewhere than ....,

for documents in categories other than ....

for electronic documents

I carried out a search for electronic documents contained on or created by the following:

[list what was searched and extent of search]

I did not search for the following:

documents created before ....,

documents contained on or created by the Claimant's/Defendant's PCs/portable data storage media/databases/servers/back-up tapes/off-site storage/mobile phones/laptops/notebooks/handheld devices/PDA devices (delete as appropriate),

documents contained on or created by the Claimant's/Defendant's mail files/document files/calendar files/spreadsheet files/graphic and presentation files/web-based applications (delete as appropriate),

documents other than by reference to the following keyword(s)/concepts .... (delete if your search was not confined to specific keywords or concepts).

I certify that I understand the duty of disclosure and to the best of my knowledge I have carried out that duty. I certify that the list above is a complete list of all documents which are or have been in my control and which I am obliged under the said order to disclose.

8.83 It is not clear that all of the problems relating to digital evidence have been resolved by these amendments, but they may have gone some way to resolving some of the issues—especially where opposing parties meet and confer to resolve issues before making an application to a judge or master[1]. From a practical point of view, lawyers will increasingly be required to have a template of relevant actions and advice to offer clients in relation to electronic evidence, regardless of the size of firm, whether a sole trader or a major partnership[2]. The nature and complexity of the guidance will depend on the nature of the proposed litigation and the intricacy of the client's IT infrastructure. In *Derby v Weldon (No. 9)*, Vinelott J illustrated the problems in detail in 1991[3]:

> ... when information is stored in the memory or database of a word-processor or computer, the inspection and copying of the 'document' gives rise to problems which the courts have not previously encountered. Some of the difficulties which have arisen in this case and which are likely to occur with increasing frequency in the future are as follows.
>
> A. Even when the relevant material is online and capable of being shown on screen or printed out, some means will have to be found of screening out irrelevant or privileged material. The party seeking discovery cannot be allowed simply to seat himself at his opponent's computer console and be provided with all necessary access keys.
>
> B. There may be material on the computer which is not accessible by current programs but which can be retrieved by reprogramming. Prima facie the powers of the court would extend to requiring that the computer be reprogrammed so as to enable the relevant information to be retrievable. Otherwise an unscrupulous litigant would be able to escape discovery by maintaining his records in computerized form and altering current programs when litigation was in prospect so that

information previously retrievable could not be retrieved without reprogramming. Of course questions may then arise as to who bears the cost
of any necessary reprogramming and whether it can be done without
affecting current programs.

C.   If, as will often be the case, the computer is in daily use, the question
       may arise—it arose actually in the instance case—whether access can be
       arranged, in particular whether any necessary reprogramming can be
       done or whether information stored in the retrieval or history files can
       be retrieved without unduly interrupting the necessary everyday use of
       the computer.

D.   Safeguards may have to be embodied in order to ensure that tapes or
       discs which may have deteriorated in storage are not damaged by use
       and that the use of them does not damage the computer's reader. In the
       instant case, the condition of some discs was such that read once they
       would be unreadable or only partially readable a second time and the
       use of some old discs in fact caused damage to the computer's reader.

E.   In some cases it may be possible for the database to be copied by
       transfer onto a disc or tape directly onto another computer. If that is
       done the material may be capable of being analysed in ways which were
       not originally contemplated. Provision may have to be made for the
       results of any such analysis, any print-outs made, to be made available
       to the other party in good time so that he is not taken by surprise at the
       trial. In the instant case agreement was recently reached for the
       provision of further experts' reports dealing with information gleaned
       from parts of the plaintiffs' computer database which was transferred to
       Coopers' computer.

Although the landscape has changed somewhat since Vinelott J made these
remarks, the central thrust of his comments remains relevant.

[1]   Katerina Maidment 'United Kingdom: New guidance on disclosure of electronic docu-
      ments' (2006) Computer Law & Security Report, vol 22, no 2, pp 176–177; Janet Lambert
      'Electronic disclosure in England & Wales' (2006) Digital Evidence Journal, vol 3, no 2, pp
      91–94.
[2]   For general guidance, see the LiST Group, Data Exchange Protocol: Part 1: the exchange of
      Electronic Disclosure Documents, (v. 1.1, 4 May 2006), Part 2 Exchange of electronic
      Disclosure Data; available online at http://www.listgroup.org/; The Sedona Conference,
      Best Practices Recommendations & Principles for Addressing Electronic Document Pro-
      duction, A Project of The Sedona Conference Working Group on Best Practices for
      Electronic Document Retention & Production (WG1) (July 2005 Version) and Draft issues
      for Multi-National Organisations Relating to E-Disclosure/E-Discovery (3 May 2006),
      available online at http://www.thesedonaconference.org/; the Electronic Discovery Refer-
      ence Model (EDRM) Project addresses standards and guidelines in relation to electronic
      discovery, available online at http://edrm.net/index.php/Main_Page.
[3]   [1991] 2 All ER 901 at 906–907.

Meet and confer

8.84 Solicitors are required to co-operate under the terms of the Practice
Direction—Disclosure and Inspection (which supplements CPR 31), 2A.2 and
2.A3. In practice, meetings are agreed by both sides to discuss and agree as
many of the matters relating to electronic searches as possible. It may be that
firms have also instructed a specialist company to on these matters. The
relevant practice directions require both parties to resolve as many practical
differences as possible before the first Case Management Conference.

Reviewing and disclosing data

8.85 There will, invariably, be a large amount of data that is irrelevant to the issues in the case. This means action will need to be taken to reduce the data, such as eliminating duplicate data, removing data that does not fall within the agreed date ranges and removing data that is not identified by word searches[1]. In preparation for the disclosure exchange, the data will have to be reviewed for data that is to be disclosed, privileged or irrelevant. The format in which the disclosure exercise is undertaken will invariably be agreed between the lawyers. It may be thought that the exchange can be by way of printed materials if the volume of materials is manageable in paper format. Alternatively, the exchange of data in electronic format is becoming far more frequent. Where data is exchanged in electronic format, it is necessary to agree the precise format. The data can be published into pdf or tif formats, allowing the text to be searched. Alternatively, the data can be transferred in native format, thus retaining the metadata providing, that is, that it has not been stripped out, intentionally or otherwise. The Practice Direction does not offer any specific guidance as to how electronic documents should be presented to the other side, or how a list of the data can be provided with any ease. In any event, the format of disclosure will probably be agreed between the lawyers. Where agreement cannot be reached, matters may need to be adjudicated through the case management process.

1 Tom Hopkinson and Michele C S Lange 'Filtering Electronic Evidence' Computers & Law, December 2003/January 2004, pp 18–20.

8.86 The size of the task involved with searching, indexing and reviewing data in complex cases can be illustrated by the remarks made by Lloyd J in *Morris v Bank of America National Trust & Savings Association*[1] in which the sheer size of the task was one of the reasons for the case taking so long to prepare.

1 [2002] EWCA Civ 425, [2003] C.P.L.R. 251, CA.

8.87 Judges retain a wide discretion in respect of the cost of disclosure. CPR 44.3 provides guidance to judges when allocating costs and further considerations are reflected in CPR 31.7 and the overriding objective in CPR 1.1. The Cresswell Report offered some further comments on this topic, at para 3.24:

> ... where substantial costs have been incurred in dealing with electronic disclosure, we consider that in appropriate cases, at the conclusion of the trial (or earlier if appropriate), Judges should give separate consideration as to the costs incurred in relation to electronic disclosure and who should pay those costs, having regard to the reasonableness and proportionality of the disclosure requested and given, the relevance of the disclosure given or ordered to be given to the issues in the case presented at trial, and the conduct of the parties generally in relation to disclosure.

It may be the case that where a party has failed to meet and confer before the case management conference, where the circumstances were such that it was manifestly necessary to do so, that an order for costs will be difficult to oppose, especially if the other party made strenuous efforts to effect such a meeting.

Failure to comply with obligation of disclosure[1]

8.88 Data in digital format can be deleted and, if a serious attempt is made, it is possible to expunge data to such a degree that recovering any residual data will be disproportionately time-consuming and expensive. It is much easier to delete digital data, at least superficially, and it is possible, in most instances, for almost anybody within an organisation to delete data, unless it is protected. A number of instances have already occurred where digital data has been deleted once litigation has begun[2] and the content of some emails have been shown to demonstrate evidence had probably been forged in preparation for a trial, although the forgery of evidence is not new[3].

[1]   *Matthews and Malek* (2001) ch 11; Neil Andrews *English Civil Procedure Fundamentals of the New Civil Justice System* ch 26.
[2]   *L C Services v Brown* [2003] EWHC 3024 (QB), [2003] All ER (D) 239 (Dec) at 68, where the operating system on Andrew Brown's computer had been changed or re-installed at the time the claimants were pursuing disclosure of documents by the defendants; *Crown Dilmun v Sutton* [2004] EWHC 52 (Ch), [2004] 1 BCLC 468 where Nicholas Sutton only disclosed relevant emails at trial (134) and deleted the contents of the C drive on his laptop; *Douglas v Hello! Ltd* [2003] 1 All ER 1087, [2003] EWHC 55 (Ch) where emails had been deleted; *Takenaka (UK) Ltd and Corfe v Frankl* [2001] EWCA Civ 348 where a forensic analysis of the computer revealed extensive evidence of corruption of the hard drive in a deliberate attempt to destroy material.
[3]   *Istil Group Inc v Zahoor* [2003] All ER (D) 210 (Feb), [2003] EWHC 165 (Ch) in which Lawrence Collins J stated at 106 '… in this case the relevant emails show … that they knew that there had been a forgery of the bogus Appendix 1 by an unknown person or persons'. He went on to say, at 111, 'I am satisfied that the strong probability is that the bogus Appendix 1 was created for the purpose of this litigation, and that no credible alternative has been put forward'.

The duty of the client to preserve documents

8.89 The client is required to preserve documents, as illustrated in the case of *Infabrics Ltd v Jaytex Ltd*[1]. In this instance, most of the relevant invoices, stock records and similar documents relating to the goods in question that were in the possession of the defendants had been lost or destroyed after the action was commenced. The learned judge made adverse findings against the defendants for failing to preserve documents affecting the quantum of damages, even though the onus primarily rested on the plaintiffs to prove their loss. In discussing the evidence submitted in respect of the missing documents, Deputy Judge Jeffs QC commented, at 79:

> Mr Butler (a director of the defendant company) gave evidence to the effect that his company's records were not knowingly destroyed but were not there when he came to look for them in 1978, despite the fact that he had given instructions that they were to be preserved. It is not enough simply to give instructions. It is essential that the court should have access to the relevant documents and that effective steps should be taken to preserve them. In the absence of the documents which are missing, Mr Butler's evidence fell far short of what the

court could reasonably expect. Although he spoke to the general trade practices of his company (evidence which I did not find very convincing and to which I shall have to return shortly) he was unable to help on specific deliveries and delivery dates, which are essential matters.

The destruction of documents can have an adverse consequence on the party guilty of destroying or permitting documents to be destroyed, as indicated by Sir Arthur Channell in *The Ophelia*[2]:

> If any one by a deliberate act destroys a document which, according to what its contents may have been, would have told strongly either for him or against him, the strongest possible presumption arises that if it had been produced it would have told against him; and even if the document is destroyed by his own act, but under circumstances in which intention to destroy evidence may fairly be considered to be rebutted, still he has to suffer. He is in a position that he is without the corroboration which might have been expected in his case.

The time the duty arises is very important, and the Cresswell Report[3] made the following comments at para 2.33 on this point:

> As to when the obligation not to destroy documents arises, the situation at the extremes is fairly easy to state. Before any litigation is contemplated there are no disclosure obligations requiring a person to retain documents or data. Once an order for disclosure has been made, a party must preserve the documents ordered to be disclosed. It is a contempt of court intentionally to destroy documents the subject of a disclosure order.

In addition, it was also observed, at para 2.36, that:

> Despite the current uncertainty as to when the obligation arises on a party to anticipated litigation to preserve potentially relevant documents, it is the experience of the Working Party that the general practice of solicitors practising in the Commercial Court is that they advise clients to preserve documents which may be relevant once litigation is contemplated.

1 [1985] FSR 75, aff'd [1987] FSR 529, CA.
2 [1916] 2 AC 206, HL at 229–230.
3 Mr Justice Cresswell 'Electronic Disclosure, A Report of a Working Party of the Commercial Court Users Committee' 6 October 2004.

8.90 In the light of the comments made in the Cresswell Report, the members of which are highly regarded in their respective areas of expertise, the client is arguably required not to dispose of any document that might possibly be considered material:

(a)   once litigation is contemplated; and
(b)   once an order for disclosure has been made.

Clearly the state of client's knowledge will be relevant when determining whether litigation is contemplated and the solicitor will undoubtedly advise their client upon this matter immediately they are instructed. The deliberate suppression of a material document is a serious abuse of process and might merit the exclusion of the offender from further participation in a trial, but striking out a defence or dismissing an action should only be undertaken where 'there remained a real risk that justice could not be done'[1]. In *Logicrose Ltd v Southend United Football Club Ltd*[2] the plaintiff failed to comply with the requirements for discovery under the former Ord 24, r 16 of the Rules of the Supreme Court. The allegation, which could not be proved, was that Mr Harriss, the principle director and shareholder of the plaintiff, failed to disclose the existence of a crucial document in his possession or control and, having obtained the document during the trial, not only proceeded to deliberately suppress it but also concealed its existence from the court for a period of time. The defendants sought an order that the action be dismissed, the defence to the counterclaim be struck out and judgment entered for the defendant. Millett J made it clear that, if contempt was proven, preventing the offender from taking any further part in the proceedings and to give judgment against him was not an appropriate response by the court to contempt. Such a response might be appropriate for failure to comply with the rules relating to discovery, even in the absence of a specific order of the court. Such a response would be appropriate:

> ... not because that conduct was deserving of punishment but because the failure had rendered it impossible to conduct a fair trial and would make any judgment in favour of the offender unsafe. Before the court took that serious step it needed to be satisfied that there was a real risk of that happening.

Millett J considered that the conduct of the proceedings was paramount[3]:

> It would not be right to drive a litigant from the judgment seat, without a determination of the issues, as a punishment for his conduct, however deplorable, unless there was a real risk that the conduct would render the further conduct of proceedings unsatisfactory.

Minor breaches of rules will not justify the striking out of a claim but where there is evidence of the creation of false documents and lies it will be appropriate to strike out a defence, as in *Arrow Nominees, Inc v Blackledge*[4]. Of recent, there have been two cases that have dealt with the matter of destruction of documents before a trial, one in the State of Victoria, Australia, and one in the United States of America.

1   *Logicrose Ltd v Southend United Football Club Ltd* (1988) *Times*, March 5, per Millett J.
2   (1988) *Times*, March 5.
3   *Logicrose Ltd v Southend United Football Club Ltd* (1988) *Times*, March 5.
4   [2000] All ER (D) 854, [2000] 2 BCLC 167, [2001] BCC 591 revsd [1999] All ER (D) 1200, [2000] 1 BCLC 709.

THE VICTORIA TEST

8.91   In *McCabe v British American Tobacco Australia Services Ltd*[1] Rolah McCabe initiated legal action against British American in Australia in 2001 for damages for having contracted lung cancer from smoking. Both sides consented to a speedy trial because Mrs McCabe had a life expectancy of months, possibly weeks. The date of the trial was set for 18 February 2002 but a range of pre-trial issues had to be resolved before the trial commenced, in particular the discovery and admissibility of relevant documents from British American, who were reluctant to deliver up certain documents to the other side. The lawyers for Mrs McCabe applied to the judge for British American's defence to be struck out and judgment be entered for her because it was argued that there was no possibility of a fair trial taking place. For this reason, a hearing concerning these issues started on 30 January 2002 and continued to 1 March 2002. During the course of this hearing, the judge was provided with volumes of witness statements, given copies of letters and other documents relating to the legal advice offered by a number of firms of lawyers in Australia and England in relation to the British American document retention policy, and listened to the evidence of a number of lawyers, senior managers and directors of British American. The judge held that the test was whether Mrs McCabe was able to receive a fair trial. If she could not receive a fair trial, he then had to decide whether judgment be entered against British American. Having heard the evidence, the judge decided that British American had a document retention and disposal policy; that the original policy and subsequent versions of the policy were intended to permit the destruction of documents relating to British American's knowledge of the health risks of smoking, the addictive qualities of cigarettes and their response to such knowledge; that British American knew there was a possibility of legal action being taken against them at the time the destruction of documents were authorised, but destroyed the documents anyway; and destroyed material contained in electronic format on CD-ROMs, together with evidence of the contents of each CD-ROM (which meant it could not be determined what records had been destroyed), even though it would have been possible to retain such records because of the minimal space required for storage purposes. The judge concluded that British American subverted the process of discovery with the deliberate intention of denying a fair trial to Mrs McCabe, in that most of the relevant documents were no longer available. He ordered their defence to be struck out and judgment was entered for Mrs McCabe. Damages were later assessed at A$700,000.

1   [2002] VSC 73; *British American Tobacco Australia Services Ltd v Cowell (representing the estate of McCabe (decd))* [2002] VSCA 197, (2002) 7 VR 524.

8.92 British American subsequently appealed the decision and members of the Court of Appeal heard the appeal during August and September 2002. Their decision was handed down on 6 December 2002. The members of the Court of Appeal approved the trial judge's approach but concluded that the evidence did not support the view of the trial judge that the document retention and disposal policy (including the amended versions) represented a deliberate attempt by British American to destroy documents relating to its knowledge of the health risks of smoking, the addictive qualities of cigarettes and their response to such knowledge. Every effort had been made to devise a policy that was appropriate. There was no evidence to show that the destruction of documents was carried out in the knowledge that legal action may be taken against British American at some time in the future. Proper enquiries were made before disposing of documents and it was irrelevant that material stored in electronic format on CD-ROM was destroyed, given the fact that the original manuscript documents had been destroyed in accordance with the document retention and disposal policy. It was held that striking out the defence was out of proportion to the issues brought before the judge. The members of the Court of Appeal allowed the appeal by British American. The order striking out the defence was set aside and the judgment given for damages was also set aside. The proceedings as a whole were remitted to the Trial Division of the Supreme Court of Victoria for a new trial. The Court of Appeal held that where documents are destroyed before the commencement of litigation they may attract a sanction (other than the drawing of adverse inferences) if that conduct amounts to an attempt to pervert the course of justice, or (if open) contempt of court, meaning criminal contempt.

This test has been criticised. The issue of intent will, in practice, be very difficult to prove and it also leaves open the timing of when the duty arises. It has been suggested that the proper test should be whether the destruction of documents made a fair trial impossible, which must be right[1]. However, the State of Victoria have subsequently passed the Crimes (Document Destruction) Act 2006, which provides for a new criminal offence of destruction of evidence into the Victorian Crimes Act 1958. New s 254 provides as follows:

254. Destruction of evidence

(1) A person who—

    (a) knows that a document or other thing of any kind is, or is reasonably likely to be, required in evidence in a legal proceedings; and

    (b) either—

        (i) destroys or conceals it or renders it illegible, undecipherable or incapable of identification; or

        (ii) expressly, tacitly or impliedly authorises or permits another person to destroy or conceal it or render it illegible, undecipherable or incapable of identification and that other person does so; and

    (c) acts as described in paragraph (b) with the intention of preventing it from being used in evidence in a legal proceeding—

is guilty of an indictable offence and liable to level 6 imprisonment (5 years maximum) or a level 6 fine or both.

The person that destroys the document may not necessarily be the person that has committed the crime, so if a junior employee is directed by another to destroy documents in the knowledge that the documents may be, or are, required for legal proceedings, it is the person giving the instruction that is guilty if the offence. The meaning of 'reasonably likely' will undoubtedly be a focus of attention in the future.

[1] Camille Cameron and Jonathan Liberman 'Destruction of Documents before Proceedings Commence: What is a Court to Do?' (2003) Melbourne University Law Review, vol 27, no 273, pp 273–307. See also the report by Professor Peter A Sallman 'Document Destruction and Civil Litigation' (May 2004), available online at http:// www.iim.org.au/national/ resource/200733482_1_Document%20Destruction%20for%20IIM.pdf.

THE US TEST

8.93 More recently, the US Supreme Court has also had the opportunity to determine a test in the appeal of *Arthur Andersen, LLP v United States*[1], in which the accounting firm Arthur Andersen appealed against the conviction and fine of US$500,000 of criminal charges during June 2002 for destroying documents in the knowledge that an investigation had been initiated against Enron. In June 2004, the federal Court of Appeals for the Fifth Circuit rejected an appeal, but the Supreme Court overturned the conviction on 31 May 2005. Rehnquist CJ gave the decision of the court, which held that the judge's instruction to the members of the jury failed to convey the need for the jury to find the requisite consciousness of wrongdoing for a conviction and that there was also a failure to require a nexus between the persuasion to destroy the documents and a particular set of proceedings that were in motion at the time the deletions took place. Thus, in the United States there is a requirement for consciousness of wrongdoing and a nexus between a persuasion to destroy documents and a particular proceedings. A person cannot knowingly persuade others to shred documents under a document retention policy when they do not have in contemplation any particular official proceeding in which those documents might be material.

1   *Arthur Andersen LLP v United States* 374 F.3d 281; conviction overturned 544 US 1; 125 S.Ct. 2129 (U.S. 2005).

ENGLAND AND WALES

8.94 In England and Wales, Sir Andrew Morritt VC, in the case of *Douglas v Hello! Ltd*[1], followed the decision in the Court of Appeal of Victoria in the *McCabe* case. In this instance, it was not in dispute that various files, including email correspondence, had been deleted by the defendants before the proceedings began. The Vice-Chancellor made clear the distinction, at 86:

> There is, however a distinction to be drawn between those which were destroyed or disposed of before these proceedings were commenced and those which were destroyed or disposed of thereafter. With regard to the former category it is established in the very recent decision of the Court of Appeal for the State of Victoria in *British American Tobacco Australia Services Ltd v Cowell (representing the Estate of McCabe (decd))* [2002] VSCA 197 paras 173 and 175 that the criterion for the Court's intervention of the type sought on this application is whether that destruction or disposal amounts to an attempt to pervert the course of justice. There being no English authority on this point I propose to apply that principle, not only because the decision of the Court of Appeal for the State of Victoria is persuasive authority but because I respectfully consider it to be right.

Unfortunately, this decision by the Vice-Chancellor approves the test in *McCabe* without considering the provisions of CPR 3.9(1). The test should not be state of mind of the party who destroys documents, but the effect that the destruction might have on the fairness of the trial, as illustrated in *Logicrose Ltd v Southend United Football Club Ltd*[2].

1   [2003] 1 All ER 1087, [2003] EWHC 55 (Ch).
2   *Matthews and Malek* (2001) (Third Supplement) 11.07.

The duty of the solicitor

8.95 The duty of preservation does not extend to the solicitor but the solicitor is required to provide help and advice to their client in such matters, which means it is important to ensure the solicitor provides sufficient explanation of the client's obligations. The comments of Megarry J in *Rockwell Machine Tool Co Ltd v E P Barrus (Concessionaires) Ltd* at 694 sum up the duty[1]:

> ... it seems to me necessary for solicitors to take positive steps to ensure that their clients appreciate at an early stage of the litigation, promptly after writ issued, not only the duty of discovery and its width but also the importance of

237

not destroying documents which might by possibility have to be disclosed. This burden extends, in my judgment, to taking steps to ensure that in any corporate organisation knowledge of this burden is passed on to any who might be affected by it.

The provisions of CPR 31 Practice Direction—Disclosure and Inspection at 4.4 also makes this duty evident:

If the disclosing party has a legal representative acting for him, the legal representative must endeavour to ensure that the person making the disclosure statement (whether the disclosing party or, in a case to which rule 31.10(7) applies, some other person) understands the duty of disclosure under Part 31.

1   Practice Note [1968] 1 WLR 693, [1968] 2 All ER 98, Ch D.

Sanctions

8.96 Where a party either refuses to provide documents at the discovery phase or continues to decline to provide discovery, the other party is at liberty to apply for a specific order for disclosure. Where specific disclosure has been ordered by a judge, the main options open to the court are as follows:

(a)   to permit an extension of time to allow the defaulting party to comply with the rule or order;

(b)   to permit an extension of time with an 'unless' or conditional order, setting out the consequences to the defaulting party if it fails to comply with the order. The conditions may include striking out the statement of case of the party in default unless the defaulting party complies with the order within the specified time frame; or

(c)   an immediate order striking out the statement of case of the defaulting party. This power is only exercised in exceptional circumstances[1].

Other sanctions that are available for failing to comply with an order for discovery or the production of documents include committal for contempt of court[2]; the ability of the party not in default to cross-examine the witnesses of the defaulting party for the failure to provide documents; the restriction of the use of documents that are disclosed at trial, or the refusal to permit the documents to be admitted in trial; the drawing of adverse inferences at trial in the absence of documents; the dismissal of the action at trial; the ordering of a re-trial, and an order to pay costs[3]. The Civil Procedural Rules requires the court to take into account a number of factors when deciding how to deal with a party that has failed to comply with a rule, as set out in CPR 3.9(1)[4]:

3.9 (1)   On an application for relief from any sanction imposed for a failure to comply with any rule, practice direction or court order the court will consider all the circumstances including—

(a)   the interests of the administration of justice;
(b)   whether the application for relief has been made promptly;
(c)   whether the failure to comply was intentional;
(d)   whether there is a good explanation for the failure;
(e)   the extent to which the party in default has complied with other rules, practice directions, court orders and any relevant preaction protocol;
(f)   whether the failure to comply was caused by the party or his legal representative;

(g) whether the trial date or the likely trial date can still be met if relief is granted;

(h) the effect which the failure to comply had on each party; and

(i) the effect which the granting of relief would have on each party.

For evidence in electronic format, the Cresswell Report (at para 2.31) also offered further comments that might be considered relevant by a court when deciding what sanction, if any to impose:

> Where relevant information has been destroyed the sanction (if any) will depend on various factors including the following:
>
> (1) When the document (or data) was destroyed. Was it before litigation was contemplated, was it after the action began or was it after an order for disclosure was made?
>
> (2) Why and in what circumstances the document (or data) was destroyed? Was it pursuant to a policy to destroy out of date information, was it inadvertent or was it done to prevent it being disclosed in litigation?
>
> (3) How relevant is the information that has been lost?
>
> (4) Is a fair trial of the action still possible?

1 *Landauer Ltd v Comins & Co (a Firm)* [1991] TLR 382; *Logicrose Ltd v Southend United Football Club Ltd* (1988) *Times*, March 5.

2 *Marks & Spencer plc v Cottrell* [2001] All ER (D) 385 (Feb), [2001] IP & T 668, in which Lightman J committed Mr Cottrell to prison for twelve months for failing to comply with orders for the swearing of affidavits, providing relevant information and documents, disclosure of relevant data on his computer and copies of relevant email correspondence; *LTE Scientific Ltd v Thomas* [2005] EWHC 7 (QB), [2005] All ER (D) 09 (Jan) in which Richards J considered committing Mr Thomas for contempt of court for deleting files from his computer and failing to deliver up his computer, and an order for costs on an indemnity basis was deemed a sufficient sanction against Mrs Thomas for failing to deliver up the home computer and failure to provide her husband's mobile telephone number.

3 *Mahon v Air New Zealand Ltd* [1984] AC 808 where the Chief Executive ordered the deliberate destruction of evidence, the concealment and denial of evidence by senior management.

4 Neil Andrews *English Civil Procedure Fundamentals of the New Civil Justice System* 14.05 note 11 for cases applying the criteria.

Obtaining disclosure from third parties

8.97 The time of disclosure can vary but covers the time before proceedings commence, at the time proceedings have begun, after judgment has been given, disclosure where there are no English proceedings in existence or contemplated, and foreign disclosure for English proceedings[1]. It is possible to apply to a court to order pre-action disclosure. The courts have the power to order pre-action disclosure under the provisions of s 3 of the Supreme Court Act 1981[2], s 52 of the County Courts Act 1984 and CPR 31.16, where both the respondent and the applicant are likely to be parties to the proceedings. Pre-action disclosure is also possible against third parties under the provisions of s 34 of the Supreme Court Act 1981, s 53 of the County Courts Act 1984 and CPR 31.17. Where pre-action disclosure has been ordered, the general rule is that the court will award the person against whom the order is sought his costs of the application and the reasonable costs of complying with any order made on the application[3]. The court may make a different order in the light of the particular circumstances of the case, including:

(a) the extent to which it was reasonable for the person against whom the order was sought to oppose the application; and

(b) whether the parties to the application have complied with any relevant pre-action protocol[4].

The new rule was reviewed in the case of *Black v Sumitomo Corp*[5], in which Rix LJ set out a number of factors that judges should consider when exercising the discretion to allow pre-action disclosure[6].

1   *Matthews and Malek* (2001) ch 2; Neil Andrews *English Civil Procedure Fundamentals of the New Civil Justice System* ch 26.
2   Previously, s 33 of the Supreme Court Act 1981 only applied to pre-action disclosure relating to personal injury claims. This section was amended to cover all types of civil claim by art 5(a) Civil Procedure (Modification of Enactments) Order 1998 (Statutory Instrument 1998 No 2940), which in turn was passed pursuant to s 8 of the Civil Procedure Act 1997.
3   CPR 48.1(2).
4   CPR 48.1(3).
5   [2002] 1 WLR 1562, [2002] 1 Lloyd's Rep. 693, [2001] EWCA Civ 1819, (2002) *Times*, January 25, (2001) *Independent*, December 13, CA.
6   For a detailed discussion of the topic and any analysis of the *Sumitomo* case, see *Matthews and Malek* (2001) paras 2.25–2.30 (and third supplement); *Andrews* paras 26.57–26.128.

8.98 Given that the networked world operates in parallel with the physical world, and given the extent of the activities that take place in the networked world, it is inevitable that evidence in digital form relating to a cause of action will be in the hands of third parties. This means that it may become more commonplace for a party to seek disclosure from third parties in the future. One example that has been used in this context is the Chancery procedure that was previously used in common law actions, known as the 'bill of recovery'. Now called a 'Norwich Pharmacal order'[1], an application can be made to require third parties to disclose the identity and address of a particular person, being a person that is alleged to have committed the wrong or who possesses property relating to the action. In the case of *Totalise plc v Motley Fool Ltd*[2] the defendant operated a website including a number of discussion boards upon which users could post information and opinions about particular companies. Before posting a comment, a user was required to agree to the terms of use, one clause of which provided that the operator would not reveal the identity of the user. The complainant complained to the operator of the website about a number of comments posted on its website that contained content that was alleged to be defamatory by a person using the name 'Zeddust'. Totalise requested the operator to reveal the identity and registration details of Zeddust. This information was refused. Totalise applied to the court for an order that the operator provide this information and it was granted by Owen J[3] because he considered a clear message had to be given out to users of the Internet that they could not use the ability to be anonymous to act improperly:

> I have no hesitation in finding that the balance weights heavily in favour of granting the relief sought. To find otherwise would be to give the clearest indication to those who wish to defame that they can do so with impunity behind the screen of anonymity made possible by the use of websites on the Internet. It follows that I propose to make an order against both defendants in the terms sought by the complainant.

Other information that a party may ask of a third party under the provisions of this order include to determine if a wrong has been committed against the applicant; to identify the wrongdoer when a wrong has been committed or is highly likely to have been committed; to establish whether the person that committed the act has assets that the applicant has a claim over and must be traced, and to identify assets as part of the process of execution following judgment.

1   *Norwich Pharmacal Co v Comrs of Customs & Excise* [1974] AC 133, [1973] 3 WLR 164, [1973] 2 All ER 943, HL.

2   [2001] IP & T 764.

3   The defendant was also ordered to pay the costs of the application, in the sum of £4,817. It was held in the Court of Appeal that where an application was granted requiring an innocent third party to disclose the identity of an alleged malefactor, the applicant should pay the costs of the disclosing party, including the costs of making the disclosure (see para 30 of the judgment of Aldous LJ for the factors to be taken into account when making a different order for costs): *Totalise plc v Motley Fool Ltd* [2002] 1 WLR 1233, [2003] 2 All ER 872, [2001] EWCA Civ 1897, [2002] CP Rep 22, [2002] EMLR 358, (2002) 99(9) LSG 28, (2002) 146 Sol Jo 35; 151 NLJ 644, (2002) *Times*, January 10, CA.

8.99 It is possible to obtain disclosure abroad for the purposes of English proceedings, providing such an application complies with the local law. The Hague Convention on the Taking of Evidence Abroad in Civil or Commercial Matters[1] is one method to adopt for the obtaining disclosure from foreign third parties who are parties to the Convention. Where a country is not a party to the Hague Convention or a member of the European Union[2], the government may have entered into a bilateral convention for taking evidence abroad[3]. Alternatively, a request for disclosure in aid of English proceedings can be made direct to a court where the local law permits such an application and other mechanisms of obtaining disclosure are set out in Matthews and Malek[4]. A significant difficulty that parties have in obtaining evidence from some European countries centres on claims that the evidence is not available because of data protection laws. Such a claim was made in the recent case of *Reino de Espana v American Bureau of Shipping*[5]. In November 2002, the tanker *Prestige* broke apart off the coast of Spain. This caused one of the worst oil spills in maritime history. The Kingdom of Spain brought an action in the United States federal court against the American Bureau of Shipping, ABS Group of Companies, Inc, and ABS Consulting, Inc, to recover damages and costs associated with the process of cleaning up the spillage. In January 2004, Spain was served with a document request seeking records about the handling of the *Prestige*, especially email correspondence from thirteen government ministries. After prevaricating, Spain eventually produced 62 emails, supplementing the production some months later with a further 300 emails, only a handful of which were dated within the period of the disaster.

1   Concluded on 18 March 1970 and entered into force 7 October 1972; see also Hague Convention of 15 November 1965 on the Service Abroad of Judicial and Extrajudicial Documents in Civil or Commercial Matters, concluded 15 November 1965 and entered into force 10 February 1969.

2   Council Regulation (EC) No 1348/2000 of 29 May 2000 on the service in the Member States of judicial and extrajudicial documents in civil or commercial matters, (OJ L160, 30.06.2000 pp 37–52), which entered into force on 31 May 2001; for EU Member States other than Denmark, see Council Regulation (EC) No 1206/2001 of 28 May 2001 on co-operation between the courts of the Member States in the taking of evidence in civil or commercial matters, (OJ L174, 27.06.2001 P. 0001–0024), which entered into force on 1 July 2001.

3 The following states have concluded bilateral conventions with the United Kingdom: Austria, Bahamas, Belgium, Czech Republic, Denmark, Finland, France, Germany, Greece, Hungary, Iraq, Israel, Italy, Lebanon, Netherlands, Norway, Poland, Portugal, Romania, Spain, Sweden, Switzerland, Turkey, Yugoslavia (which continues to apply between the United Kingdom and Bosnia & Herzegovina, Croatia and Slovenia).
4 *Matthews and Malek* (2001) paras 2.86–2.87.
5 No. 03 Civ. 3573 (S.D.N.Y. November 2, 2006), a decision for a motion by American Bureau of Shipping before Magistrate Judge Ellis to compel Spain to disclose records concerning email communications.

8.100 Spain objected to any further production, claiming the requests by the American Bureau of Shipping were overbroad, unduly burdensome and violated privacy laws. Privilege was also claimed for certain records. A two-day evidentiary hearing was held between 9 and 10 February 2006. Several expert witnesses and three Spanish government officials gave evidence. Magistrate Judge Ellis did not find the testimony of David Alonso-Mencia, the technical advisor to the General Director of the Merchant Marine, to be credible: this led the judge to determine that the efforts to locate relevant email correspondence and records were inadequate and he reached the conclusion that there was no systematic method for preserving email, which undermined the Spanish position and indicated that evidence relating to the *Prestige* was probably lost. Fernando Bregon, the director of telecommunications and computers at the State Society of Salvage and Marine Safety, also gave evidence. Mr Bregon asserted that the records were preserved because officials knew they had an obligation to preserve records without being reminded or directed to do so, but the record did not support his evidence. A notice directing individuals to voluntarily preserve records relating to the *Prestige* was not issued until over a year after the incident. The learned judge determined that this notice was late in being issued, which also meant relevant documents were lost. Alonso Prades, who worked in email and Internet services management at the Ministry of Development, testified and claimed that individual computers could not be searched without the user's consent because of privacy concerns. Magistrate Judge Ellis commented, at p 9, that a warrant or court order appeared to be necessary to search individual computers, but went on to observe that Spain failed to indicate any specific court order, legislative act or directive of the executive branch to sustain its claim respecting this matter.

It was determined by the judge that the requests were neither burdensome nor overbroad; that the notices issued to prevent the deletion of documents by the Spanish government were late, which meant evidence was lost; that the objections relating to privacy laws were vague; and that whatever privilege that might have attached to the records was waived when related records were produced to the International Maritime Organisation and the International Oil Pollution Compensation Fund. The defendant's Motion to Compel Further Production was granted, and the defendant was invited to file an application for appropriate relief and sanctions against Spain by 12 December 2006.

Confidentiality and legal professional privilege[1]

8.101 The very nature of evidence in digital format creates a significant problem for lawyers, especially when dealing with large volumes of documents in digital format. There is a greater possibility of inadvertently passing privileged or confidential information to the other side in the disclosure exercise. For this reason, lawyers must exercise a great deal of care on behalf of their clients when conducting the review prior to the exchange of documents at the disclosure phase. Two forms of privilege exist: legal advice privilege and litigation privilege. In both instances, the privilege is that of the client, not the lawyer. Legal advice privilege refers to confidential communications between the client and the lawyer, and such communications are privileged against compulsion to disclose with the exception of advice sought or given for the purpose of furthering a crime, fraud or any other form of wickedness. Litigation privilege provides the same protection to communications between a client and a third party, a lawyer and a third party, and to internal communications within the organisation that are predominantly directed towards the preparation and support of pending or contemplated litigation, whether civil or criminal[2].

[1] Colin Passmore *Privilege* (2nd edn, 2006); Bankim Thanki QC, ed *The Law of Privilege* (2006).
[1] *Passmore* (2006) chs 2 and 3; *Matthews and Malek* (2001) ch 10; *Andrews* chs 27 and 28.

8.102 Privilege can be deliberately waived, but the central concern for lawyers and their clients when disclosing electronic documents is to ensure that no information is handed over to the other side that contains privileged material[1]. The Civil Procedure Rules provides for such circumstance in CPR 31.20, in that such material may not be used without permission of the court:

Where a party inadvertently allows a privileged document to be inspected, the party who has inspected the document may use it or its contents only with the permission of the court.

It should be noted that the rule refers to privileged documents, which incorporates legal advice and litigation privilege as well as other forms of privilege[2]. Evidence of metadata will also be relevant in such instances and consideration ought to be given to whether metadata has been removed from a digital document and, if so, the purpose for which it was removed.

[1] For two cases relating to privileged materials in the context of electronic disclosure, see *ISTIL Group Inc v Zahoor* [2003] 2 All ER 252, [2003] All ER (D) 210 (Feb), [2003] EWHC 165 (Ch) and *USP Strategies plc v London General Holdings Ltd* [2004] EWHC 373 (Ch), [2004] All ER (D) 132 (Mar).
[2] *Andrews* para 28.19.

Role of experts[1]

8.103 The tradition in England and Wales was to leave the appointment of experts to the parties but, since the Woolf reforms, the Civil Procedure Rules have altered the landscape somewhat towards the appointment of a single joint expert, unless the issues are complex. The regulation of expert witnesses is governed by CPR 35, Practice Direction—Experts and Assessors, and the 'Protocol for the Instruction of Experts to give Evidence in Civil Claims' (June 2005). In essence, the CPR provides for the following:

(a) CPR 35.3 makes it plain that the expert has a duty to help out the court 'within his expertise' and this duty overrides any obligation to the person from whom he has received instructions or by whom he is paid.'

(b) The court controls the admission of expert evidence under the provisions of CPR 35.4 and the court may also limit the fees to be paid to an expert.

(c) The court may direct that a single expert is to be appointed under CPR 35.7 and, where the parties cannot agree on a joint expert, the court can select the expert from a list prepared or identified by the instructing parties, or direct that the expert be selected in such other manner as the court may direct.

(d) Where a joint expert is appointed, both parties may give instructions to the expert (CPR 35.8).

(e) In the event two experts are appointed, the court has the power under CPR 35.12 to require the experts to identify and discuss the expert issues in the proceedings and, where possible, reach an agreed opinion on those issues. The court may also determine the issues that the experts must discuss.

8.104 The Practice Direction expands on the duties of the expert, including the occasions when the expert may alter their opinion for any reason:

1.1 It is the duty of an expert to help the court on matters within his own expertise: rule 35.3(1). This duty is paramount and overrides any obligation to the person from whom the expert has received instructions or by whom he is paid: rule 35.3(2).

1.2 Expert evidence should be the independent product of the expert uninfluenced by the pressures of litigation.

1.3 An expert should assist the court by providing objective, unbiased opinion on matters within his expertise, and should not assume the role of an advocate.

1.4 An expert should consider all material facts, including those which might detract from his opinion.

1.5 An expert should make it clear:

(a) when a question or issue falls outside his expertise; and
(b) when he is not able to reach a definite opinion, for example because he has insufficient information.

1.6 If, after producing a report, an expert changes his view on any material matter, such change of view should be communicated to all the parties without delay, and when appropriate to the court.

The Protocol provides guidance to experts, and to those instructing them, and is intended to help interpret the provisions of CPR 35 and the Practice Direction. The Protocol offers guidance respecting the test of 'independence' in para 4.3, by commenting: 'that the expert would express the same opinion if given the same instructions by an opposing party'. Further guidance is provided, amongst other things, in respect of the appointment of experts, the instructions to be given to experts, the acceptance of instructions by the expert, withdrawal by the expert, and the right of the expert to ask for directions from the court.

[1] Mark James *Expert Evidence: Law and Practice* (2nd edn, 2006); Sir Louis Blom-Cooper QC, ed *Experts in the Civil Courts* (2006); *Andrews* ch 32 and fn 1 for further references; Ian Freckelton and Hugh Selby *Expert Evidence: Law, Practice, Procedure and Advocacy* (2nd edn, 2002); *Malek* (2005) ch 33.

8.105 Expert reports can be highly relevant to evidence in digital format, especially where the authenticity of a document may be in issue. It is highly improbable that a judge would order a single expert to provide a report in such circumstances but, where such an order is made, the parties may apply to a court to appoint their own expert. In the case of *Cosgrove v Pattison*[1], Neuberger J, as he then was, provided a list of nine factors to be taken into account in circumstances where a party could instruct their own expert where a disagreement existed with the joint expert:

> First, the nature of the issue or issues; secondly, the number of issues between the parties; thirdly, the reason the new expert is wanted; fourthly, the amount at stake and, if it is not purely money, the nature of the issues at stake and their importance; fifthly, the effect of permitting one party to call further expert evidence on the conduct of the trial; sixthly, the delay, if any, in making the application, seventhly, any delay that instructing and calling of the new expert will cause; eighthly, any other special features of the case; and, finally, the overall justice to the parties in the context of the litigation[2].

[1] [2001] CP Rep 68, [2001] 2 CPLR 177, 2000 WL 1841601 (Ch D), (2001) *Times*, February 13.
[2] 2000 WL 1841601 (Ch D) at 3.

8.106 The independence of the expert was the subject of an appeal in *Helical Bar plc v Armchair Passenger Transport Ltd*[1]. Nelson J reviewed the authorities relating to the independence of the expert witness, and indicated, at 29, the following principles the emerged from these authorities:

(i) It is always desirable that an expert should have no actual or apparent interest in the outcome of the proceedings.

(ii) The existence of such an interest, whether as an employee of one of the parties or otherwise, does not automatically render the evidence of the proposed expert inadmissible. It is the nature and extent of the interest or connection which matters, not the mere fact of the interest or connection.

(iii) Where the expert has an interest of one kind or another in the outcome of the case, the question of whether he should be permitted to give evidence should be determined as soon as possible in the course of case management.

(iv) The decision as to whether an expert should be permitted to give evidence in such circumstances is a matter of fact and degree. The test of apparent bias is not relevant to the question of whether or not an expert witness should be permitted to give evidence.

(v) The questions which have to be determined are whether:
   (i) the person has relevant expertise and
   (ii) he or she is aware of their primary duty to the Court if they give expert evidence, and willing and able, despite the interest or connection with the litigation or a party thereto, to carry out that duty.

(vi) The Judge will have to weigh the alternative choices open if the expert's evidence is excluded, having regard to the overriding objective of the Civil Procedure Rules.

(vii) If the expert has an interest which is not sufficient to preclude him from giving evidence the interest may nevertheless affect the weight of his evidence.

The appointment of a digital evidence specialist may be relatively rare in civil litigation, although they are increasing being used in a consultancy role. For instance, many lawyers are not certain or do not have sufficient knowledge to fill in the forms for submission to the court, or they may need somebody to recover deleted files. In this respect, digital evidence specialists are able to provide assistance and help to lawyers, even though their services are not required in the form of expert testimony, and an increasing number of companies provide evidence gathering services, by which they will prepare the electronic documents for the client, ensuring the relevant documents are prepared in systems that allow for searching and manipulation of the data when necessary. The use of such specialist services may have an effect on costs. It may be necessary to determine whether such services are necessary and, if so, what is reasonable and proportionate, although this is a problem that affects most litigants now and it could be argued that, where a party uses computers and computer systems in the course of their business, it becomes axiomatic that they must also recognise there is a cost to using computers. Finally, when lawyers determine expert evidence is necessary they will be required to have sufficient knowledge to ask the right questions of the expert.

[1]   [2003] EWHC 367 (QB), [2003] All ER (D) 436 (Feb).

CRIMINAL LAW[1]

8.107 It is unquestionably the case that agencies responsible for the prevention and investigation of crime across the globe already tackle, and will continue to face, an increasing number of obstacles as technology improves and those intent on committing criminal acts use the technology of computers and the Internet to achieve their nefarious aims. A range of factors cause considerable problems to police forces, including the size of a case, the extent and volume of the malicious software that is often found on computers[2], and the need to consider obtaining evidence remotely, whilst balancing the data protection and human rights issues against the need to obtain the evidence[3]. More complex considerations also have to be considered, such as the use of professionals from other disciplines to help with investigations[4]. Digital evidence can be very useful. For example, the evidence of ATM receipts have helped to track down a criminal responsible for kidnapping children and holding them for a ransom[5], photographs taken at ATMs have helped to identify the perpetrator of a manslaughter[6], and the assailant in a case of assault[7].

[1]   Archbold, *Criminal pleading, evidence and practice*; *Blackstone's Criminal Practice*; Archbold, *Magistrates' Court Criminal Practice*.
[2]   Clive Carmichael-Jones 'Trojan Horse Complexities' Computers & Law, December 2003/ January 2004, 33; Megan Carney and Marc Rogers 'The Trojan Made Me Do It: A First Step in Statistical Based Computer Forensics Event Reconstruction' (2004) International Journal of Digital Evidence, Spring, vol 2, issue 4, at http://www.ijde.org; Esther George 'UK Computer Misuse Act—the Trojan virus defence Regina v Aaron Caffrey, Southwark Crown Court, 17 October 2003' (2004)Digital Investigation, vol 1, no 2, p 89; Susan Brenner and Brian Carrier with Jef Henninger 'The Trojan Horse Defense in Cybercrime Cases' 21 Santa Clara Computer and High Technology Law Journal 1 (2005); Dan Haagman and Byrne Ghavalas 'Trojan defence: A forensic view' (2005) Digital Investigation, vol 2, no 1, pp 23–30, and (2005) Digital Investigation, vol 2, no 2, pp 133–136.

³ Philip Sealey 'Remote forensics' (2004) Digital Investigation, vol 1, no 4, pp 261–265, although human rights and privacy issues are not discussed in this paper; see also Andy Johnston and Jessica Reust 'Network intrusion investigation—Preparation an challenges' (2006) Digital Investigation, vol 3, no 3, pp 118–126.

⁴ Eric D Shaw 'The role of behavioural research and profiling in malicious cyber insider investigations' (2006) Digital Investigation, vol 3, no 1, pp 20–31.

⁵ *HKSAR v Hon* [2002] HKCA 42.

⁶ *R v Cooney* 1995 CanLII 707 (ON C.A.).

⁷ *R v Ross Magoulias* [2003] NSWCCA 143.

Pre-trial

8.108 The initial stages of criminal proceedings are dominated by the requirements of the police to investigate an alleged crime. The process is controlled by a statutory regime that appears to change with increasing rapidity, especially in line with the increased risk associated with terrorist activities, and the use of the digital environment by people intent on committing criminal acts of one description or another. The rights of investigators are balanced against the restraint of abuse of power and the preservation of the rights of the subject[1].

¹ Problems in reconciling the provisions of different statutes to technology, and the balancing act of securing access to email correspondence whilst protecting privacy, is not always easy to reconcile, as in *R (on the application of NTL Group Ltd) v Ipswich Crown Court* [2003] QB 131, [2002] 3 WLR 1173, [2003] 1 Cr App Rep 14, [2002] EWHC 1585 (Admin), (2002) 99(31) LSG 33, (23002) 152 NLJ 1434, (2002) 146 Sol Jo LB 193, (2002) *Times*, August 6, (2002) *Independent*, October 28 (CS), QBD (Admin).

Search and seizure[1]

8.109 Although the main use of the powers of search and entry will by the police, many of the matters discussed herein will also apply to other agencies, such as the Serious Fraud Office, HM Revenue & Customs and the National High-Tech Crime Unit, amongst others. The investigation of an alleged offence is provided for in general powers at common law, the Police and Criminal Evidence Act 1984 (as amended and supplemented) ('PACE'), the Codes of Practice made under the provisions of s 66 of PACE[2] and a number of other statutes that will be considered in brief below. There are very few powers of entry without a warrant under the common law[3], although the police have a power to enter and search premises following an arrest[4]. By comparison, PACE has, to a great extent, acted to consolidate the police powers in England and Wales.

¹ Richard Stone *The Law of Entry, Search, and Seizure* (4th edn, 2005); for a discussion about the need for protocols in the US, see Susan W. Brenner 'Requiring protocols in computer search warrants' (2005) Digital Investigation, vol 2, no 3, pp 180–188.

² Contravention of the provisions contained in the Codes will not give rise to any criminal or civil liability in accordance with s 67(10) of PACE, although a court may take account of any breach of the Codes in determining any proceedings to which the breach is relevant: s 67(11) PACE.

³ *Stone* (2005) paras 3.03–3.13.

⁴ *R (on the application of Rottman) v Comr of Police for the Metropolis* [2002] UKHL 20, [2002] 2 All ER 865; *Ghani v Jones* [1970] 1 QB 693, CA.

WARRANTS

8.110 Provisions for warrants to enter and search premises are covered by ss 15 and 16 of PACE, together with the directions set out in Code B of the Codes of Practice. They apply to all warrants issued under any enactment issued to constables, although the provisions have been extended to include others[1]. A warrant to enter and inspect, or an arrest warrant used to obtain entry, is not covered by these provisions[2]. An entry or search that is subject to the provisions of ss 15 and 16 and any entry or search that does not comply with them is unlawful[3]. An application is made to a Justice of the Peace, or a judge, in writing and the constable is required to answer any questions put by the judge or justice on oath[4]. The grounds upon which the application is made must be clear, together with the enactment under which the warrant is to be issued, the identity of the premises to be entered and searched and the articles or persons sought. Section 19(1) enables a constable to seize items where they are lawfully on the premises, and s 19(4)[5] provides the constable with powers in relation to data in digital format:

The constable may require any information which is stored in any electronic form and is accessible from the premises to be produced in a form in which it can be taken away and which it is visible and legible or from which it can readily be produced in a visible and legible form if he has reasonable grounds for believing—

   (a)   that—
          (i)   it is evidence in relation to an offence which he is investigating or any other offence; or
          (ii) it has been obtained in the commission of an offence; and
   (b)   that it is necessary to do so in order to prevent it being concealed, lost, tampered with, or destroyed.

Stone observes that this might include data held anywhere in the world[6] and the practical problems relating to this become obvious for a constable, who may be exposed to a civil action for trespass against items that were seized and later shown to be exempt from seizure[7]. This particular problem has now been addressed in ss 50–52 of the Criminal Justice and Police Act 2001 (supplemented by paras 7.7–7.13 to Code B of the Codes of Conduct) [8]. Section 50(2) deals with property on any premises:

(2)   Where—

   (a)   a person who is lawfully on any premises finds anything on those premises ('the seizable property') which he would be entitled to seize but for its being comprised in something else that he has (apart from this subsection) no power to seize,
   (b)   the power under which that person would have power to seize the seizable property is a power to which this section applies, and
   (c)   in all the circumstances it is not reasonably practicable for the seizable property to be separated, on those premises, from that in which it is comprised,

that person's powers of seizure shall include power under this section to seize both the seizable property and that from which it is not reasonably practicable to separate it.

(3)   The factors to be taken into account in considering, for the purposes of this section, whether or not it is reasonably practicable on particular premises for something to be determined, or for something to be separated from something else, shall be confined to the following—

(a) how long it would take to carry out the determination or separation on those premises;

(b) the number of persons that would be required to carry out that determination or separation on those premises within a reasonable period;

(c) whether the determination or separation would (or would if carried out on those premises) involve damage to property;

(d) the apparatus or equipment that it would be necessary or appropriate to use for the carrying out of the determination or separation; and

(e) in the case of separation, whether the separation—

    (i) would be likely, or

    (ii) if carried out by the only means that are reasonably practicable on those premises, would be likely,

to prejudice the use of some or all of the separated seizable property for a purpose for which something seized under the power in question is capable of being used.[9]

Section 51 also provides for similar, additional, powers of seizure from a person where existing powers already exist to carry out a search of the person. Paragraph 165 of the Explanatory Notes explain the need for this additional provision: 'This section gives additional powers of seizure from the person where there is an existing power to search that person. It is almost identical to section 50. It is necessary because, for example, individuals might have on them handheld computers or computer disks which might contain items of electronic data which the police would wish to seize. Alternatively, they could be carrying a suitcase containing a bulk of correspondence which could not be examined in the street.'

[1]   *Stone* (2005) para 3.16.

[2]   s 17(1)(a).

[3]   s 15(1). The requirements should be applied stringently: *R v Central Criminal Court, ex p AJD Holdings* [1992] Crim LR 669 and, if the exercise of power complies with the provisions, there is no scope for a submission based on Art 8 of the Human Rights Act: *Kent Pharmaceuticals Ltd v Director of the Serious Fraud Office* [2002] EWHC 3023.

[4]   s 15(4).

[5]   As amended by the Criminal Justice and Police Act 2001, Sch 2, para 13(2).

[6]   *Stone* (2005) 3.60.

[7]   *R v Chesterfield Justices ex p Bramley* [2000] QB 576, [2000] 2 WLR 409, [2000] 1 All ER 411, [2000] 1 Cr App Rep 486, [2000] Crim LR 385, [1999] 45 L S Gaz R 34, 143 Sol Jo LB 282, DC.

[8]   Explanatory Notes to the Act, paras 156–164.

[9]   *Stone* (2005) paras 3.120–3.139.

8.111 Taken together, these provisions undoubtedly cover the use of imaging technology to obtain copies of data held on a computer, as accepted in the case of *R (on the application of Paul Da Costa & Co (a firm)) v Thames Magistrates Court*[1] where images of hard drives were taken by Customs and Excise during a search[2]. The comments by Kennedy LJ, in response to the complaint that a great deal of information that was not covered by the order was included in the copies of the hard disks, are relevant to the problems that will inevitably be caused in such cases:

Imaging was much less intrusive than seizing the hard disks. It was apparently agreed to by a partner, who I accept did not have authority to waive professional privilege on behalf of clients. If the result was that the Customs and Excise obtained amongst other things information in relation to clients of the accountancy practice that is no more objectionable than if they had for good reason taken possession of a leather bound ledger much of which contained information of a similar kind[3].

Documents containing legally privileged material are excluded from being seized by s 19(6) and, although the provisions of s 50(1) do not enable a constable to seize items which they reasonably believe to be legally privileged, nevertheless it does give the power to remove and examine material which is not thought to be legally privileged but which might or might not be within the terms of the power to conduct the search:

(1) Where—

    (a) a person who is lawfully on any premises finds anything on those premises that he has reasonable grounds for believing may be or may contain something for which he is authorised to search on those premises,

    (b) a power of seizure to which this section applies or the power conferred by subsection (2) would entitle him, if he found it, to seize whatever it is that he has grounds for believing that thing to be or to contain, and

    (c) in all the circumstances, it is not reasonably practicable for it to be determined, on those premises—

        (i) whether what he has found is something that he is entitled to seize, or

        (ii) the extent to which what he has found contains something that he is entitled to seize,

that person's powers of seizure shall include power under this section to seize so much of what he has found as it is necessary to remove from the premises to enable that to be determined.

There is a specific power under s 14 of the Computer Misuse Act 1990 for a constable to obtain a search warrant in connection with the investigation of offences created under s 1 of the Act[4]. The provisions read as follows:

14.—(1) Where a circuit judge is satisfied by information on oath given by a constable that there are reasonable grounds for believing—

    (a) that an offence under section 1 above has been or is about to be committed in any premises; and

    (b) that evidence that such an offence has been or is about to be committed is in those premises;

he may issue a warrant authorising a constable to enter and search the premises, using such reasonable force as is necessary.

The application must be made to a circuit judge and a warrant cannot be obtained in respect of material that is legally privileged, excluded or is special procedure material, as defined in PACE, s 14(2). In addition, care must be taken to ensure that there is no discrepancy between the content of the information sworn by the officer and the warrant issued by the judge[5]. Additional persons may be authorised to accompany the constable executing the warrant[6], which remains in force for 28 days from the date of issue[7]. When the constable has gained access to the premises, the general powers of seizure under PACE, s 19 will apply, together with the additional power that the constable 'may seize an article if he reasonably believes that it is evidence that an offence under section 1 above has been or is about to be committed', s 14(4). A constable also has the powers under the provision of PACE, s 19(4), discussed above. The Proceeds of Crime Act 2002 sets out further powers of search and seizure, but are not dealt with in this text[8].

1   [2002] EWHC 40 (Admin), [2002] STC 267.
2   In respect of Commissioners of the Inland Revenue, see *R (on the application of H) v IRC* [2002] EWHC 2164 (Admin), [2002] STC 1354.
3   [2002] EWHC 40 (Admin), [2002] STC 267 at para 20.
4   A person is guilty of an offence under s 1(1) if they cause a computer to perform a function with the intention of obtaining unauthorised access to any program or data held in any computer. Sections 33–36 of the Police and Justice Act 2006 have expanded the provisions on the unauthorised modification of computer material in the Computer Misuse Act 1990 to make it an offence where a person does an unauthorised act in relation to a computer with 'the requisite intent' and 'the requisite knowledge', which includes the intent to do the act and, by so doing, to impair the operation of any computer, to prevent or hinder access to any program or data held in any computer, or to impair the operation of any program or data held in any computer. It is not necessary for the intent to be directed at any particular computer or any particular program or data. Yaman Akdeniz 'Section 3 of the Computer Misuse Act 1990: an Antidote for Computer Viruses!' [1996] 3 Web JCLI; Indira Carr and Katherine S Williams 'Securing the e-commerce environment' (2000) Computer Law & Security Report, vol 16, no 5, pp 295–310; Kelly Stein ' "Unauthorised Access" and the U.K. Computer Misuse Act 1990: House of Lords "leaves no room" for ambiguity' (2000) Computer and Telecommunications Law Review, vol 6, issue 3, pp 63–66; Anne Flanagan 'Cybercrime and the UK' (2005) Computers and Law, June/July, pp 33–36.
5   *R v Central Criminal Court, ex p AJD Holdings* [1992] Crim LR 669.
6   Computer Misuse Act 1990, s 14(3)(a).
7   Computer Misuse Act 1990, s 14(3)(b).
8   *Stone* (2005) paras 3.175–3.205; and for specific powers under various Acts, see ch 4.

Powers to conduct surveillance[1]

8.112 In the past, English law has been found wanting in relation to the provisions of art 8 of the European Convention on Human Rights[2]. Successive governments have responded by putting statutory regimes into place to govern surveillance, principally the Police Act 1997[3], which governs the bugging of premises (on-site or remotely) and the Regulation of Investigatory Powers Act 2000[4], covering the interception of communications. The legislation does not cover the use of a device placed in a location that is only capable of listening to one side of a conversation[5].

1   Michael Cousens *Surveillance Law* (2004); *Stone* (2005) paras 3.140–3.174; Yaman Akdeniz, Nick Taylor and Clive Walker 'Regulation of Investigatory Powers Act 2000 (1): Big Brother.gov.uk: State surveillance in the age of information rights' [2001] Crim LR 73.
2   For interception of telephone calls, see *Malone v United Kingdom* (1984) 7 EHRR 14. For a bugging device used to transmit sounds, see *R v Khan (Sultan)* [1997] AC 558, [1996] 3 All ER 289; and *Khan v United Kingdom* (2001) 31 EHRR 45. The Interception of Communications Act 1985 (replaced by the Regulations of Investigatory Powers Act 2000) was considered by the members of the House of Lords in *R v Preston* [1994] 2 AC 130, [1993] 4 All ER 638; *R v Effik* [1995] 1 AC 309, [1994] 3 All ER 458; *Morgans v DPP* [2001] 1 AC 315, [2000] 2 All ER 522; *R v P* [2002] 1 AC 146, [2001] 2 All ER 58; *R v Sargent* [2001] UKHL 54, [2003] 1 AC 347, [2002] 1 All ER 161.
3   Extending to the United Kingdom with some exceptions, s 137.
4   Extending to Northern Ireland, s 83.
5   *R v E* [2004] 1 WLR 3279, [2004] 2 Cr App Rep 29, [2004] EWCA Crim 1243.

8.113 The Police Act 1997 permits an authorising officer[1] to issue an authorisation under the Act[2]. The officer authorising the act must believe, in accordance with s 93(2)(a), 'that it is necessary for the action specified to be taken on the ground that it is likely to be of substantial value in the prevention or detection of serious crime' and, in making a decision, the officer is required to consider whether it is possible to achieve the object by other means[3]. The requirement for proportionality is necessary because any action taken under the terms of the Act will impinge upon the rights of respect for privacy under art 8 of the European Convention on Human Rights and the Human Rights Act 1998. Section 97 sets out the circumstances where authority must be obtained from a Commissioner before surveillance can be begun[4], relating to the nature of the premises and the type of information that is likely to be obtained:

(2) Subject to subsection (3), this section applies to an authorisation if, at the time it is given, the person who gives it believes—

> (a) that any of the property specified in the authorisation—
>> (i) is used wholly or mainly as a dwelling or as a bedroom in a hotel, or
>> (ii) constitutes office premises, or
> (b) that the action authorised by it is likely to result in any person acquiring knowledge of-
>> (i) matters subject to legal privilege,
>> (ii) confidential personal information, or
>> (iii) confidential journalistic material.

The categories are defined in ss 98–100 and the relevant Code of Practice relating to Pt III of the Police Act 1997 and issued by the Home Office 'Covert Human Intelligence Sources, Code of Practice' make it clear that care should be taken when there is a possibility that such material might be involved, especially over the issue of 'collateral intrusion'.

[1] s 93(5).
[2] An authorisation must be in writing, and notice of it must be given to a Commissioner: s 96 and the Police Act 1997 (Notification of Authorisations, etc,) Order 1998 (SI 1998/3241), but in an emergency the authority can be given orally, s 95(1). Authorisations are not under the control of Justices of the Peace or judges, but are subject to the supervision of Surveillance Commissioners appointed by the First Lord of the Treasury (also known as the 'Prime Minister') and from the members of the senior judiciary, s 91. The Commissioner has the power to quash or cancel an authorisation, s 103. The Office of Surveillance Commissioner has a website at http://www.surveillancecommissioners.gov.uk/.
[3] s 93(2)(b).
[4] The lawfulness of the approval forms signed by the Surveillance Commissioners need not be questioned and disclosure of the materials underlying the approval does not need to be provided to the defence: *R v GS* [2005] EWCA Crim 887.

8.114 The interception of communications is dealt with by Pt I of the Regulation of Investigatory Powers Act 2000 (RIPA). The Home Office issued a Code of Practice under the provisions of s 71 which also covers Pt III of the Police Act 1997. Section 1 provides that the interception of any communication over any public telecommunication system is unlawful unless authorised, and s 1(2) prevents unlawful interception within private systems[1]. Interception is possible without a warrant where the person intercepting the communication reasonably believes that the sender and recipient consented to the intercept[2]; the intercept was authorised under the provisions of Pt II of RIPA[3]; the intercept is undertaken by or on behalf of a person who provides the service, and 'it takes place for purposes connected with the provision or operation of that service or with the enforcement, in relation to that service, of any enactment relating to the use of postal services or telecommunications services'[4] or, where the interception is of a communication by wireless telegraphy undertaken by a designated person under s 5 of the Wireless Telegraphy Act 1949 and for the purposes set out in ss 3(4) and (5). Section 4 of the Act also provides for authorised interceptions to be dealt with by regulations. The only regulations currently in place are the Telecommunications (Lawful Business Practice)(Interception of Communications) Regulations 2000 (SI 2000/2699). Regulation 3 provides the authority to people carrying on a business, government departments and 'any public authority or of any person or office holder on whom functions are conferred by or under any enactment'[5] to intercept communications carried over the telecommunications system of the organisation for the following purposes:

(a) to establish the existence of facts relevant to a business (3(1)(a)(i)(aa));

(b) to ascertain compliance with regulatory or self-regulatory practices or procedures relevant to the business (3(1)(a)(i)(bb));

(c) to ascertain or demonstrate standards which are, or ought to be, achieved by persons using the system (3(1)(a)(i)(cc));

(d) in the interests of national security (3(1)(a)(ii));

(e) to prevent or detect crime (3(1)(a)(iii));

(f) to investigate or detect the unauthorised use of telecommunications systems (3(1)(a)(iv));

(g) to ensure the effective operation of the system (3(1)(a)(v));

(h) for the purpose of determining whether or not the communications are relevant to the business (regulation 3(1)(b)); and

(i) for the purpose of monitoring communications to a confidential anonymous counselling or support helpline (regulation 3(1)(c)).

The conduct is only authorised under the provisions of para 1 of the Regulation if the interception is solely for the purpose of monitoring or, where appropriate, keeping a record of communications that are relevant to the business of the controller[6]; the telecommunication system upon which the interception takes place is provided for use wholly or partly in connection with the business[7]; and reasonable efforts are made to inform those using the systems that their communications may be intercepted[8].

[1] *Halford v United Kingdom* (1997) 24 EHRR 523, [1997] IRLR 471, 3 BHRC 31, [1998] Crim LR 753, (1997) 94(27) LS Gaz 24, (1997) *Times*, July 3.
[2] s 3(1).
[3] s 3(2).
[4] s 3(3).
[5] Reg 2(a).
[6] Reg 3(2)(a).
[7] Reg 3(2)(b).
[8] Reg 3(2)(c).

8.115 Interception can also be authorised by means of a warrant, which is governed by ss 5–16 of RIPA. The Secretary of State for the Home Department (also known as the 'Home Secretary') has the power to issue a warrant and should sign the warrant personally[1]. The list of officials that have the power to apply for a warrant is set out in s 6(1) and the Home Secretary is only permitted to issue a warrant if it is necessary so to do for one of the purposes set out in s 5(3):

(a) in the interests of national security;

(b) for the purpose of preventing or detecting serious crime[2];

(c) for the purpose of safeguarding the economic well-being of the United Kingdom; or

(d) for the purpose, in circumstances appearing to the Secretary of State to be equivalent to those in which he would issue a warrant by virtue of paragraph (b), of giving effect to the provisions of any international mutual assistance agreement.

The Secretary of State should not issue an interception warrant unless the interception is proportionate[3]. The aim is to ensure that the power is capable of being defended against claims made under the Human Rights Act 1998, and the Code of Practice also offers comments in relation to the test of proportionality:

2.4 Obtaining a warrant under the Act will only ensure that the interception authorised is a justifiable interference with an individual's rights under art 8 of the European Convention of Human Rights (the right to privacy) if it is necessary and proportionate for the interception to take place. The Act recognises this by first requiring that the Secretary of State believes that the authorisation is necessary on one or more of the statutory grounds set out in s 5(3) of the Act. This requires him to believe that it is necessary to undertake the interception which is to be authorised for a particular purpose falling within the relevant statutory ground.

2.5 Then, if the interception is necessary, the Secretary of State must also believe that it is proportionate to what is sought to be achieved by carrying it out. This involves balancing the intrusiveness of the interference against the need for it in operational terms. Interception of communications will not be proportionate if it is excessive in the circumstances of the case or if the information which is sought could reasonably be obtained by other means. Further, all interception should be carefully managed to meet the objective in question and must not be arbitrary or unfair.

The content and duration of warrants are dealt with by ss 8 and 9, and the Code of Practice. The implementation of a warrant will invariably require the co-operation of a telephone company or Internet service provider and s 11 imposes a duty on a person to whom the warrant is served to assist in implementing the interception so far as is reasonably practicable, although failure to do so may be an offence under the provisions of s 11(7). The results of any interception are not disclosed beyond those that need to know[4] and there is no disclosure in legal proceedings of any evidence relating to the use of an interception warrant[5], with the exception that the results may be disclosed to a prosecutor[6] and a judge if it is necessary to ensure fairness in the proceedings[7]. Neither the intercepted materials nor the fact that interception has taken place is to be disclosed to the defence[8]. Legally privileged materials are dealt with in paras 3.3–3.11 of the Code of Practice and, if such materials are to be intercepted, the Secretary of State is required to determine whether it is necessary and proportionate to intercept such materials, and may impose additional conditions if such materials are the subject of interception[9].

---

[1] s 7(1).

[2] A serious crime is defined in s 81(3), and is similar to the definition in Pt III of the Police Act 1997.

3   s 5(2)(b).
4   s 15. Also, material that has been intercepted is destroyed once retention is no longer necessary, s 15(3), although see s15(4) for exceptions.
5   s 17.
6   Code of Practice, paras 7.5–7.10.
7   Code of Practice, paras 7.11–7.14.
8   Code of Practice, para 7.14.
9   Code of Practice, para 3.6.

8.116 Challenges to the interception of communications are highly unlikely, given the fact that the subject of the interception will not become aware of the fact until after the event, if at all, although an application can be made to the Investigatory Powers Tribunal established under the provisions of RIPA, s 65 and Sch 3. There is an independent Interception of Communications Commissioner who produces an annual report which goes to the Prime Minister, is received by Parliament and subsequently published[1].

1   The Investigatory Powers Tribunal website, where the annual reports are available, is at http://www.ipt-uk.com/.

Improper interception

8.117 At common law, evidence that is intercepted is not automatically inadmissible, as in *R v Derrington*[1]. The prisoner asked the turnkey if he would post a letter to his father but, contrary to the promise made, the turnkey handed the letter over to the visiting magistrates at the gaol, who in turn sent it to the prosecutor. Curwood for the prisoner objected to the letter being admitted into evidence. Garrow, B admitted the letter into evidence, and pointed out that there were only two instances where evidence may be inadmissible, at 419:

> 1st, where the prisoner is induced to make any confession in consequence of the prosecutor, &c. holding out any threat or promise to induce him to confess: and 2dly, where the communication is privileged, as being made to his counsel or attorney.

The method by which the communications have been recorded is irrelevant, as in *R v Khan (Sultan)*[2] where a listening device had been installed on the outside of a house to enable the police to listen to and record conversations that took place inside the dwelling. In one conversation recorded by the police, the defendant said things that clearly indicated that he had been involved with the importation of heroin. The Crown conceded the installation of the device to the outside of the house involved a civil trespass and, if the recording of the conversation was ruled inadmissible, the defendant had no case to answer. The trial judge declined to rule the evidence inadmissible and the defendant entered a plea of guilty. The matter was appealed to the Court of Appeal and the House of Lords, in which it was held that, although the evidence constituted a breach of the European Convention for the Protection of Human Rights and Fundamental Freedoms, the circumstances of the case were such that the trespass and damage were slight and were outweighed by the public interest in the detection of crime. However, the European Court of Human Rights took a different view. It was accepted that the admissibility of the tape recording in evidence did not breach art 6(1) of the Convention, which guarantees a fair trial, but it took the view that articles 8[3] and 13[4] of the Convention had been violated because there were no statutory provisions in place to regulate the use of covert listening devices. A distinction was made between the admissibility of evidence and the requirements of a fair trial. Admissibility was a matter governed by domestic law:

> While Article 6 guarantees the right to a fair hearing, it does not lay down any rules on the admissibility of evidence as such, which is therefore primarily a matter for regulation under national law. It is not the role of the Court to determine, as a matter of principle, whether particular types of evidence—for example, unlawfully obtained evidence—may be admissible or, indeed, whether the applicant was guilty or not. The question which must be answered is whether the proceedings as a whole, including the way in which the evidence was obtained, were fair[5].

The Police Act 1997 was passed as a direct result of this case, although the Act was put in place before the case was heard by the European Court of Human Rights. It may be argued that this case caused the government to consider the additional problems that would inevitably occur in relation to evidence in digital format, especially the ease by which data can be encrypted to prevent third parties from reading the content of messages or files sent over the Internet or stored on computers, ultimately leading to the passing of the Regulation of Investigatory Powers Act 2000[6].

1   (1826) 2 C & P 418; 172 ER 189.
2   [1997] AC 558; [1996] 3 All ER 289; and *Khan v United Kingdom* (2001) 31 E.H.R.R. 45. See more detailed discussions and reference to relevant case law in Colin Tapper, *Computer Law* pp 546–549 and *Malek* (2005) paras 35–10 to 35–14.
3   Guaranteeing personal privacy.
4   Guaranteeing the right to an effective remedy for breach of the provisions of the Convention.
5   *Khan v United Kingdom* (2001) 31 EHRR 45 at 34.
6   For an interesting critique, see David Ormerod and Simon McKay 'Telephone intercepts and their admissibility' [2004] Crim LR 15; see also Peter Mirfield 'Regulation of Investigatory powers Act 2000 (2): Evidential Aspects' [2001] Crim LR 91; *PG and JH v United Kingdom* [2002] Crim LR 308, and the commentary in *R v Lawrence, Hope, Stapleton (Senior), Stapleton (Junior), Bravard and May* [2002] Crim LR 584.

Disclosure

8.118   For matters pertaining to committal proceedings generally, the reader is referred to the standard texts[1]. This section only considers the general duties to disclose evidence, although it should be noted that the provisions of s 1(1)(a) of the Criminal Procedure and Investigations Act 1996 also apply to offences tried in the Magistrates' courts[2], as do the Criminal Procedure Rules[3]. There is no requirement under the Criminal Procedure and Investigations Act 1996 or art 6 of the European Convention on Human Rights of advanced disclosure in summary proceedings, although disclosure ought to be given by the prosecution if the defence makes a request[4]. In any event, it would be difficult for the defence to serve a defence case statement on the prosecution without advance disclosure.

1   Archbold, *Criminal pleading, evidence and practice*; *Blackstone's Criminal Practice*; Archbold, *Magistrates' Court Criminal Practice*; *Hodge M Malek* (2005) paras 10–16 to 10–36; see also a critical analysis by Mike Redmayne 'Criminal Justice Act 2003 (1) Disclosure and its Discontents' [2004] Crim LR 441.

2   For greater detail, see *Malek* (2005) paras 10–43 to 10–56.
3   The Criminal Procedure Rules 2005 (SI 2005/384 (L.4)).
4   *R v Stratford Justices ex p Imbert* [1999] 2 Cr App Rep 276.

8.119 The comments in this section mainly refer to disclosure in the Crown Court, although the majority of cases are tried in the Magistrates' courts in England and Wales. The police provide the relevant evidence to the prosecution and the disclosure officer appointed to a case is responsible for providing disclosure to the prosecutor, under the provisions of the Code of Practice issued under Pt II of the Act, which can be on a computer disk[1]. The Attorney General issued a revised set of Guidelines on Disclosure[2] and, although these do not have the force of law, they should be given due weight[3]. The provisions of para 57 apply to summary trials:

> The prosecutor should, in addition to complying with the obligations under the Act, provide to the defence all evidence upon which the Crown proposes to rely in a summary trial. Such provision should allow the accused and their legal advisers sufficient time properly to consider the evidence before it is called.

It is probable that any failure to disclose material in summary proceedings may breach art 6(1) of the European Convention on Human Rights, discussed below. If this is the case, then the prosecution may face a significant duty towards the accused in cases involving evidence in digital format where the defence raise reasonable questions concerning the authenticity of the evidence. Where digital evidence is challenged by the defence, it will require advanced disclosure of materials and the time to instruct an expert witness.

1   Code of Practice, 4.1.
2   April 2005, available online at http://www.lslo.gov.uk/guidelines.htm; see also 'Disclosure: A protocol for the Control and Management of Unused Material in the Crown Court' (Department of Constitutional Affairs, 20 February 2006), available online at http:// www.dca.gov.uk/criminal/procrules_fin/contents/pd_protocol/pd_protocol_disclosure.htm.
3   *R v Winston Brown* [1994] 1 WLR 1599, [1995] 1 Cr App Rep 191.

8.120 Pre-trial disclosure is governed by the Criminal Procedure and Investigations Act 1996, as amended, and the Criminal Procedure Rules. The police are required to record and retain relevant materials, together with any material which 'might reasonably be considered capable of undermining' the prosecution case[1]. The prosecutor has a duty to provide primary disclosure to the accused of any prosecution material 'which has not previously been disclosed to the accused and which might reasonably be considered capable of undermining the case for the prosecution against the accused or of assisting the case for the accused'[2] or to provide the accused with a statement in writing, confirming there is no material to disclose[3]. This includes forensic tests conducted by an expert witness[4]. The defence are, in turn, required to disclose the nature of the defence by means of a written statement, together with the details of any witnesses it intends to call to testify[5]. The defence is not required to provide details of the evidence which it proposes to use, although it is required to inform the prosecution of its intention to call expert evidence and to disclose its basis[6]. The prosecution and defence are both under a continuing duty to keep their respective disclosures under review and to provide supplementary disclosure as required under the Act[7]. The prosecution may apply to a court for an order that disclosure should not take place on the basis the materials are subject to public interest immunity and, where an application is made in the absence of the accused, it appears there is no violation of art 6(1) of the European Convention on Human Rights[8].

[1]   Words (new s 5A) inserted to s 5 of the Criminal Procedure and Investigations Act 1996 by s 33(1)(a) of the Criminal Justice Act 2003.

[2]   s 3(1)(a) Criminal Procedure and Investigations Act 1996; additional words added by s 32 of the Criminal Justice Act 2003. This includes disclosure of defence statements by the prosecutor made by a co-defendant: *R v Cairns* [2003] 1 WLR 796, [2002] EWCA Crim 2838.

[3]   s 3(1)(b) Criminal Procedure and Investigations Act 1996. For evidence that has been destroyed and is no longer available, see *R (Ebrahim) v Feltham Magistrates' Court, Mouat v DPP* [2001] 2 Cr App Rep 427, [2001] EWHC Admin 130.

[4]   *R v Maguire* [1992] QB 936, [1992] 2 WLR 767, [1992] 2 All ER 433, (1992) 94 Cr App Rep 133, (1991) *Times*, June 28, (1991) *Independent*, June 27, 1991, (1991) *Guardian*, June 27, 1991, CA.

[5]   New s 6A requires a defence from the accused, s 6B requires updated disclosure by the accused, s 6C requires notification of intention to call defence witnesses and s 6D requires the defence to provide to the court and the prosecutor with a notice specifying the person's name and address, inserted to s 6 of the Criminal Procedure and Investigations Act 1996 by ss 33, 34 and 35 of the Criminal Justice Act 2003.

[6]   The Crown Court (Advance Notice of Expert Evidence) Rules 1987 (SI 1987/716 (L.2)); Criminal Procedure and Investigations Act 1996, s 20(3) and s 6D inserted by s 35 of the Criminal Justice Act 2003.

[7]   Prosecution—s 7A inserted by s 37 of the of the Criminal Justice Act 2003; defence—s 6B inserted by s 33(3) of the of the Criminal Justice Act 2003. In addition, the defendant may apply to the court for an order for further secondary disclosure: Criminal Procedure and Investigations Act 1996, 8(1) and (2), substituted by s 38 of the Criminal Justice Act 2003, also r 7 of the Crown Court (Criminal Procedure and Investigations Act 1996) (Disclosure) Rules 1997 (SI 1997/698 (L. 4))

[8]   Pt 25 of the Criminal Procedure Rules 2005 (SI 2005/384 (L.4)); *Malek* (2005) paras 10–53 to 10–54.

8.121   The obligations of disclosure by the prosecution ought to be viewed in the light of the ACPO and NHTCU *Good Practice Guide for Computer based Electronic Evidence* (v3.0, 2003), although these have, in fact, no legal authority. The ACPO guidelines are silent in relation to providing access to evidence in relation to the provisions of art 6 of the European Convention on Human Rights[1], as follows:

Article 6

1 In the determination of his civil rights and obligations or of any criminal charge against him, everyone is entitled to a fair and public hearing within a reasonable time by an independent and impartial tribunal established by law. Judgement shall be pronounced publicly by the press and public may be excluded from all or part of the trial in the interest of morals, public order or national security in a democratic society, where the interests of juveniles or the protection of the private life of the parties so require, or the extent strictly necessary in the opinion of the court in special circumstances where publicity would prejudice the interests of justice.

2   Everyone charged with a criminal offence shall be presumed innocent until proved guilty according to law.

3   Everyone charged with a criminal offence has the following minimum rights:

   (a)   to be informed promptly, in a language which he understands and in detail, of the nature and cause of the accusation against him;
   (b)   to have adequate time and the facilities for the preparation of his defence;

(c)   to defend himself in person or through legal assistance of his own choosing or, if he has not sufficient means to pay for legal assistance, to be given it free when the interests of justice so require;

(d)   to examine or have examined witnesses against him and to obtain the attendance and examination of witnesses on his behalf under the same conditions as witnesses against him;

(e)   to have the free assistance of an interpreter if he cannot understand or speak the language used in court.

In terms of the advanced disclosure of evidence by the prosecution, arts 6(1) and (3)(a)–(d) are highly relevant, particularly to the preparation of a defence case when digital evidence forms part, or the majority, of the evidence. For the most part, it is predominantly pertinent in cases where abusive images of children are found on computers because the expert for the accused is faced with significant difficulties in gaining access to the data seized by the police to investigate the digital evidence on behalf of the accused. The possession and distribution of abusive images of children is an offence under the provisions of s 1 of the Criminal Justice Act 1988, which includes 'pseudo photographs' (an image created by a computer)[2]. The defences to the possession of abusive images of children comprise: having a legitimate reason for possessing or distributing the images; not having seen the images or knowing them to be indecent; and, where the images were sent to the accused without their knowledge, and the accused did not keep them for an unreasonable length of time.

[1]   Incorporated into law by means of s 1(2) of the Human Rights Act 1998. The provisions of Art 6 are similar to Art 14 of the International Covenant on Civil and Political Rights (adopted and opened for signature, ratification and accession by General Assembly resolution 2200A (XXI) of 16 December 1966, entered into force on 23 March 1976, in accordance with Art 49).

[2]   s 84 of the Criminal Justice and Public Order Act 1994 as amended the Protection of Children Act 1978 by providing for a pseudo-photograph. For cases of pornography and cyber crimes, see Rupert Battcock 'Prosecutions under the Computer Misuse Act 1990' (1996) Computers and Law, vol 6, issue 6, pp 22–26; Dr Yaman Akdeniz 'Case Report' (2002) Computer Law & Security Report, vol 18, no 6, pp 433–435; Kit Burden and Creole Palmer 'Cyber Crime—A new breed of criminal?' (2003) Computer Law & Security Report, vol 19, no 3, pp 222–227.

8.122 The ACPO guidelines set out the conditions for the control of paedophile images on pp 26–28. For obvious reasons, great care has been taken to provide for the security of any images seized by the police and it is made clear that the images that have been transferred to a disk 'must remain in the possession of the case office (in Scotland the Forensic Computer Units)'[1]. The Guide provides that the only time the accused, or their lawyers, are permitted to obtain access to the images is by arrangement with the police, and viewing will only be conducted in premises controlled by law enforcement officers. It is made clear that further copies of the materials will not be permitted by the police unless by order of the trial judge or a magistrate. The Code does consider how to deal with a defence request to obtain a copy of the relevant materials in order to conduct their own analysis of the seized materials and, where neither side can agree how to resolve the matter, it is acknowledged that it is a matter for the court to determine upon a suitable application. However, despite the provisions set out in the Code, some digital evidence specialists have faced serious difficulties in obtaining a copy of the relevant evidence to undertake an analysis of the data. In most instances, the digital evidence specialist does not need to view the images but to examine the location of data files, how data fragments are distributed and other evidence that demonstrates the history of the use of the computer and of determining the process that is responsible for the presence of files on the computer seized by the police. This is a crucial part of the exercise for the defence and can take hours of patient work[2].

1   ACPO and NHTCU Good Practice Guide for Computer based Electronic Evidence (v3.0, 2003) p 26.
2   Dr D Hamilton Wallis 'It is far harder to stay clean in a dirty world than it is to get dirty in a clean one' (2004) *The Barrister*, no 19, 12 January, pp 15–16. In this article, Dr Wallis was able to demonstrate that the abusive images of children found on a computer were actually placed there by the police as part of a police operation to catch paedophiles using the Internet. The computer was used for this purpose after it was seized and before it was handed over for forensic analysis. This instance illustrates the lack of any control in the chain of custody by the police and could have led to the conviction of a man that appeared to be innocent of such a crime.

8.123 The reluctance of the police to hand over such materials is understandable. However, the argument that by so doing they would be breaking the law by copying the original does not stand up to scrutiny, given the police make copies of the materials themselves: first, a forensic image is taken of the disk, then a copy is made to optical disk, and each time the images are viewed on a computer monitor, another image is made. Further, if images are printed, a further making of the image occurs. In essence, it can be argued, as does Dr Wallis, that the provisions of the Protection of Children Act is written in such a way as to make it unlawful to undertake any activity that is necessary to prepare a prosecution or provide a defence in such cases[1]. The practical problem is to devise a system or procedure by which the defence can have access to the materials to enable a thorough investigation by a digital evidence specialist, but in conditions that reassure the police that the images are safe from any further copying or distribution.

1   *Wallis* (2004) p 16. See also Philip Bowles 'Trends in digital evidence handling' (2004) *The Barrister*, no 19, 12 January, pp 27–28.

8.124 In the case of *Rowe and Davis v United Kingdom*[1], where evidence was withheld from the defence by the prosecution without notifying or applying to a judge, the European Court of Human Rights held unanimously that such an action breached the provisions of art 6(1) of the Convention. This judgment raises the question as to whether the provisions for criminal disclosure fully comply with art 6. In their judgment, the members of the court made the following observations:

(a)   The prosecuting authorities should disclose to the defence all material evidence in their possession for or against the accused (para 60).

(b)   The entitlement to disclosure of relevant evidence is not an absolute right. Competing interests (national security, protection of witnesses, the need to keep secret police methods of investigation of crime, to preserve the fundamental rights of another individual or to safeguard an important public interest) must be weighed against the rights of the accused (para 61).

(c)   Only such measures restricting the rights of the defence that are strictly necessary are permissible under art 6(1) (para 61).

(d)   To ensure the accused receives a fair trial, any difficulties caused to the defence by a limitation on its rights must be sufficiently counterbalanced by the procedures followed by the judicial authorities (para 61).

(e)   The decision-making procedure should comply, as far as possible, with the requirements of adversarial proceedings and equality of arms and incorporate adequate safeguards to protect the interests of the accused (para 62).

Whale comments[2] that the first two points, above, follow the common law test set out in *R v Keane (Stephen John)*[3], although they do not adopt the more restrictive duties, set out under the 1996 Act, of primary and secondary disclosure and the cases of *Maan v HM Advocate*[4] and *Sinclair v HM Advocate*[5] indicate that the defence has an entitlement to be provided with information that directly affects the issue of guilt or innocence, but also information that tends to undermine the prosecution case[6].

1   30 EHRR 1.
2   Stephen Whale in *Malek* (2005) para 10–49.
3   [1994] 1 WLR 746, [1994] 2 All ER 478, (1994) 99 Cr App Rep 1, [1995] Crim LR 225, (1994) 144 NLJ 391, (1994) 138 Sol Jo LB 75; *Times*, March 15, 1994, *Independent*, March 16, 1994, CA.
4   2001 SLT 408, 2001 SCCR 172.
5   [2005] UKPL D2, 2005 SCCR 446, (2005) *Times*, June 1.
6   Martin Wasik 'Legislating in the Shadow of the Human Rights Act: The Criminal Justice and Police Act 2001' [2001] Crim LR 931 for critical comments on the extensions of state power and the erosion of liberty, and the observation that a Ministerial statement of compatibility under the Human Rights Act only applies to a Bill as introduced and not to the Act and any of the subsequent amendments added to the Bill during its course through Parliament.

8.125 In cases where the authenticity of the digital data is in issue or is likely to be important, the investigator may have to give thought to additional considerations in the investigation process. Given the unique nature of digital evidence, and the probability that very large numbers of computers across the globe have data on them that the owner is not only not aware of but will not be able to explain how it got there, more consideration ought to be given to ensuring the police undertake a more in-depth analysis of the disk to establish how materials found their way on to the system and to providing appropriate facilities or procedures, or both, to the digital evidence specialist appointed by the defence. This is particularly important, given the overriding objective of Pt 1.1(1) of the Criminal Procedure Rules, which requires criminal cases to be dealt with justly. In achieving this aim, it is necessary to acquit the innocent and convict the guilty (1.1(2)(a)); deal with the prosecution and the defence fairly (1.1(2)(b)) and recognise the rights of a defendant, particularly those under art 6 of the European Convention on Human Rights (1.1(2)(c)), and cases must be dealt with in a way that takes into account 1.1(2)(g):

(i)   the gravity of the offence alleged;
(ii) the complexity of what is in issue; and
(iii) the severity of the consequences for the defendant and others affected.

Clearly the interrogation of embedded data on computers is expensive and is often extremely time consuming. However, the defendant may sometimes be in custody awaiting trial and undue delay may equally affect the administration of justice. Care needs to be taken to establish that any request for disclosure by the defence is genuinely justified by the issues in the case. There are concerns that the complexities of technology might give rise to disclosure requests that are simply not objectively justifiable. There have been cases at first instance where this has been shown to be the case. It is at this stage that a careful interaction between official disclosure protocols and judicial intervention is likely to become increasingly important.

Evidence from other jurisdictions

8.126 The obtaining of evidence from other jurisdictions, as well as the provision of evidence for other jurisdictions, is governed by the provisions of ss 7–9 of the Crime (International Co-operation) Act 2003. A judicial authority, prosecuting authority or a person charged may make a request for evidence for use in the investigation or proceedings. Section 51(1) defines evidence to include 'information in any form and articles, and giving evidence includes answering a question or producing any information or article' which undoubtedly includes evidence in digital format. In respect of obtaining evidence from members of the European Union, the European Arrest Warrant[1] has been adopted by the United Kingdom under the provisions of the Extradition Act 2003[2]. The Home Office have produced a guide entitled 'The UK's operation of the European Arrest Warrant'[3] which is designed to assist other European Union Member States by explaining how the United Kingdom has given effect to the Framework Decision on the European Arrest Warrant and how they go about seeking the surrender of a person from the United Kingdom using the European Arrest Warrant procedures.

[1] Council Framework Decision 2002/584/JHA of 13 June 2002 on the European arrest warrant and the surrender procedures between Member States (OJ L 190 of 18.07.2002), replacing the 1957 European Extradition Convention; 1978 European Convention on the suppression of terrorism as regards extradition; agreement of 26 May 1989 between 12 Member States on simplifying the transmission of extradition requests; 1995 Simplified extradition procedure between Member States; 1996 Convention on extradition between Member States, and the relevant provisions of the Schengen agreement.
[2] Judge Rob Blekxtoon, editor in chief, *Handbook on the European Arrest Warrant* (2005).
[3] Available online at http://police.homeoffice.gov.uk/news-and-publications/publication/operational-policing/uk-operation-eaw.

Trial

8.127 The previous requirements relating to the authentication of computer evidence have been removed, and the current position is now governed by s 133 of the Criminal Justice Act 2003, which provides as follows:

133   Proof of statements in documents

Where a statement in a document is admissible as evidence in criminal proceedings, the statement may be proved by producing either—

    (a)   the document, or
    (b)   (whether or not the document exists) a copy of the document or of the material part of it, authenticated in whatever way the court may approve.

The Explanatory Notes to the Act state, at para 436, that s 133 'corresponds to the position under s 27 of the Criminal Justice Act 1988, whereby a statement in a document can be proved by producing either the original document or an authenticated copy' and continues 'It is intended to cover all forms of copying including the use of imaging technology'. Interestingly, the document must be an original or an authentic copy, which illustrates the need to pay careful attention to the means by which a document in digital format is authenticated before the court. The use of imaging technology is also a mechanism for obtaining a copy of the original data, although the actual technology that is used to image data may be challenged. The number of removes a copy may be from the original is dealt with indirectly by reference to the meaning of 'copy' which, 'in relation to a document, means anything on to which information recorded in the document has been copied, by whatever means and whether directly or indirectly'[1]. This requires the trial judge to determine how a digital document is authenticated, which is why guidance on the mechanisms by which authenticity is tested can be so important. In essence, the move has been towards assessing the weight to be given to digital evidence.

[1] s 134(1) Interpretation of Chapter 2.

8.128 However, the assumptions about the underlying reliability of 'machines' that create evidence in digital format appear to remain. The presumption that a mechanical device has been properly set or calibrated remains in s 129(2) of the Criminal Justice Act 2003. Of interest is what is meant by 'properly set or calibrated' when referring to a computer (however small or large it might be). There seems to be no guidance about what this means in relation to a computer. The case law centres around whether the provisions of s 69 of the Police and Criminal Evidence Act 1984 were satisfied. It was deemed unnecessary for a computer expert to provide evidence that a till roll connected to a computer was working properly in *R v Shephard*[1], under the provisions of s 69 of the Police and Criminal Evidence Act 1984. The oral evidence of a store detective, who demonstrated how the prices of goods were added to the till roll, was considered sufficient by the members of the House of Lords. In rejecting the need for a computer expert to sign a certificate where oral evidence has been given that was open to cross-examination, Lord Griffiths offered the following comments:

> Documents produced by computers are an increasingly common feature of all business and more and more people are becoming familiar with their uses and operation. Computers vary immensely in their complexity and in the operations they perform. The nature of the evidence to discharge the burden of showing that there has been no improper use of the computer and that it was operating properly will inevitably vary from case to case. The evidence must be tailored to suit the needs of the case. I suspect that it will very rarely be necessary to call an expert and that in the vast majority of cases it will be possible to discharge the burden by calling a witness who is familiar with the operation of the computer in the sense of knowing what the computer is required to do and who can say that it is doing it properly.

This comment by Lord Griffiths and the view that an expert is not always required to attest to the proper working of a computer is reinforced by *Darby v DPP*[2], where a police constable operating a speed-measuring device testified to the proper operation of the device—even though the device acted to corroborate his own testimony. Similarly, in *R v Dean and Bolden*[3], Lt Cdr Quigley, a Maritime Law Enforcement and Liaison Officer at the Department of State, contacted the Coast Guard Command Centre at US Coast Guard headquarters in Washington, D.C. to request a search for the vessel 'Battlestar.' A search was made of the Marine Safety Information System, a computer database containing information on all US vessels. The Command Centre also searched the databases of four coast States and no record of this vessel was found. One ground of appeal centred on the submission that there was no evidence from the people who carried out the searches that the computers were operating properly and, as a result, the evidence was not admissible under s 69 of PACE. The members of the Court of Appeal disagreed. It was considered that Lt Cdr Quigley could give evidence of the reliability of the computers because there were no reported problems with the databases and searches for the same name on three separate occasions failed to bring up the name of the vessel. Dyson J gave the judgment in this case and commented, at 178E, that 'the fact that searches on three separate occasions produced the same result provided strong support for the conclusion that the computers were operating properly on each occasion'. This conclusion needs to be reconsidered: the proposition should be that the database was searched on three occasions and the failure to find an entry for the vessel enables the conclusion to be reached that the name of the vessel was not on the database. This is a different issue as to whether the computer was working properly: the computer may not have been working completely to the expectation of the user because it might have had any number of problems with it that did not necessarily affect the effectiveness of the search facility. The computer might not have had the latest security upgrade or the latest anti-virus update. The lack of such items might affect the reliability of the computer generally but, equally, their absence might not affect the ability of the search engine to conduct an efficient search of the database. The effectiveness of the search of the database can be independent of the reliability of the computer. If the reliability of the computer is challenged, it must be necessary to provide a reasonable basis upon which the claim is made and there ought to be some evidence proffered to demonstrate that the computer might be so unreliable as to affect the output used in evidence. Mere assertions that all computers are prone to being attacked in some way, or are subject to manipulation by one means or another, cannot, it is submitted, be sufficient to overcome the evidential burden to provide at least a scintilla of evidence upon which the challenge is made.

1   [1993] AC 380, [1993] 1 All ER 225 (spelt Shepherd in All ER), [1993] Crim LR 295, HL.
2   [1995] RTR 294, (1995) 159 JP 533, (Times) November 4, 1994, DC.
3   [1998] 2 Cr App Rep 171, CA.

8.129 Although it is debatable that the comments by Lord Hoffman in *DPP v McKeown; DPP v Jones*[1], in which he opined that 'It is notorious that one needs no expertise in electronics to be able to know whether a computer is working properly'[2], can be considered to be the extreme view that will not be shared by many computer experts, it is noticeable that para 432 of the Explanatory Notes to the Criminal Justice Act 2003 indicated that, in respect of testimony under s 129(1):

This section provides where a statement generated by a machine is based on information implanted into the machine by a human, the output of the device will only be admissible where it is proved that the information was accurate.

Here the emphasis is on the accuracy of the information as an input to the computer, not whether the computer was working properly or, to put it another way, whether the system was not working in accordance with an expectation. For instance, key-logging software may be placed on a computer, either physically or by way of a malicious code sent over a network, as occurred in the case of attempted theft of £220m against the Sumitomo Bank in London during March 2005, where it was reported that cleaners inserted hardware bugs into the sockets of keyboards at the back of various computers, then reconnected the keyboards so the hardware bug was not visible. It is reported that investigators working for the bank found some of the devices[3].

¹ [1997] 2 Cr App Rep 155, [1997] 1 All ER 737 HL.
² [1997] 1 All ER 737 at 743b.
³ Paul Marks 'Attempted cyber-heist raises keylogging fears' (2005) *NewScientistTech* 18 March, available online at http://www.newscientisttech.com/channel/tech/electronic-threats/dn7168; Peter Warren and Michael Street 'Mission Impossible at the Sumitomo Bank: Key loggers, blank tapes and a cold trail' *The Register*, 13 April 2005 available online at http://www.theregister.co.uk/2005/04/13/sumitomu_bank/.

8.130 Alternatively, a root kit can embed itself into the operating system kernel in such a way that there is practically no way of detecting it. Depending on the nature of the code, it may then attempt to maintain its own integrity by preventing the user from detecting it. Such malicious codes may then send data to an unknown third party when the computer is connected to a network. In all probability, such codes will undertake this activity without the authority of the computer owner. The presumption is that owners use a computer to carry out specific tasks, but it is not anticipated that the computer will carry out the instructions of an unknown third party at the same time. Where malicious code has been surreptitiously sidled into the computer by some means, the computer cannot be trusted because the malevolent code causes the computer to work in a way that is not in accordance with the expectations of the owner. The problem is that Lord Griffiths considers the issue from the opposite perspective: an assumption that the computer is working because of what the user can see, not what an unknown third party does not want them to see or prevents them from seeing, and does not consider what else the computer may be doing without the knowledge of the owner. It is debatable whether a computer operating with such a parasite within its system can be considered to be working properly, although it is conceivable to consider a computer working in parallel: the definition of 'working properly' may include situations where a computer will operate properly, in accordance with the requirements of the owner, whilst simultaneously undertaking unrelated tasks for an unknown third party and neither activity will impinge on the accuracy of the other. The addition of malicious code is not the only problem. In the ATM cases, it is clearly the infrastructure of the ATM system that is at fault and consideration must be made to enable the defence to raise the valid charge that the ATM system is open to attack, thus laying the burden on the prosecution to prove that a particular ATM system was not at fault: a heavy burden, but not one that should be ignored.

Challenging the authenticity of digital documents

8.131 Laying the evidentiary foundations for the authenticity of digital evidence is discussed elsewhere in this text but, if the authenticity of evidence is raised by one of the parties, it is appropriate to deal with it in a trial within a trial. In *R v Stevenson*[1], Kilner Brown J was required to establish whether audio tapes were originals. After a lengthy and careful examination of the evidence held in a trial within a trial, it became clear that there was an opportunity for someone to have interfered with the original tape and there was clear evidence that some interference might have taken place. Given the nature of the evidence before him, he said:

> Once the original is impugned and sufficient details as to certain peculiarities in the proffered evidence have been examined in court, and once the situation is reached that it is likely that the proffered evidence is not the original, is not the primary and best evidence, that seems to be to create a situation in which, whether on reasonable doubt or whether on a prima facie basis, the judge is left with no alternative but to reject the evidence[2].

In the case of *R v Robson (Bernard Jack); R v Harris (Gordon Federick)*[3] the defence raised the issue of the admissibility of the evidence of 13 tape recordings. The judge decided to consider whether, on the face of it, the tapes were authentic in the absence of the members of the jury. In this instance, Shaw J heard evidence in a trial within a trial from a number of witnesses that gave evidence of the history of the tapes from the actual process of recording to the time they were produced in court. He also listened to four experts, called on behalf of the defence, whose examination of the tapes led them to question their originality and authenticity. The prosecution called a separate witness in rebuttal. After hearing the evidence, Shaw J decided that the tape recordings were originals and authentic, commenting that:

> My own view is that in considering that limited question [the primary issue of admissibility] the judge is required to do no more than to satisfy himself that a prima facie case or originality has been made out by evidence which defines and describes the provenance and history of the recording up to the moment of production in court[4].

Tapper expressed the view that this exercise should be conducted first by the judge and if, on the balance of probabilities, the judge determined the evidence could go before the jury, it would then be necessary to cover the ground again, in the same way as any other question of fact that must be decided at trial[5]. On the standard of proof to be used by the judge, O'Connor LJ indicated the criminal standard of proof is to be used in the context of handwriting[6], and in the case of *R v Minors (Craig); R v Harper (Giselle Gaile)*[7] Steyn J, as he then was, set out the opinion of the Court of Appeal on this matter in relation to a computer print-out:

> The course adopted by the judge in one of the two appeals before us prompts us to refer to the procedure which ought to be adopted in a case where there is a disputed issue as to the admissibility of a computer printout. It is clear that in such a case a judge ought to adopt the procedure of embarking on a trial within a trial[8].

He went on further to indicate that the judge should apply the ordinary standard of criminal proof in reaching a decision and, in the case of *R v*

Neville[9], the members of the Court of Appeal also noted, at 289, that trial judges 'should examine critically any suggestion that a prior computer malfunction has any relevance to the particular computer record tendered in evidence'. The decision of the Court of Appeal *R v Minors (Craig); R v Harper (Giselle Gaile)* to require a judge to apply the ordinary standard of criminal proof in reaching a decision when hearing evidence in a trial within a trial overrules the decision of Shaw J in *R v Robson (Bernard Jack); R v Harris (Gordon Federick)* in which he reached an opinion on the basis of the balance of probabilities[10], although there is much to commend the view of Shaw J when he suggested that the prosecution need do no more than set up a prima facie case in favour of the authenticity of the evidence:

> It may be difficult if not impossible to draw the philosophical or theoretical boundary between matters going to admissibility and matters going properly to weight and cogency; but, as I have already said, it is simple enough to make a practical demarcation and set practical limited to an inquiry as to admissibility if the correct principle is that the prosecution are required to do no more than set up a prima facie case in favour of it. If they should do so, the questioned evidence remains subject to the more stringent test the jury must apply in the context of the whole case, namely, that they must be sure of the authenticity of that evidence before they take any account of its content[11].

1   [1971] 1 WLR 1, [1971] 1 All ER 678.
2   [1971] 1 WLR 1 at 3G.
3   [1972] 1 WLR 651, [1972] 2 All ER 699, (1972) 56 Cr App Rep 450, [1972] Crim LR 316, 116 Sol Jo 313, CCC.
4   [1972] 1 WLR 651 at 653H.
5   *Tapper* (1989) p 370.
6   *R v Ewing* [1983] QB 1039, [1983] 3 WLR 1, [1983] 2 All ER 645, (1983) 77 Cr App Rep 47, [1984] ECC 234, [1983] Crim LR 472, (1983) 127 Sol Jo. 390, (1983) *Times*, March 15, CA.
7   [1989] 1 WLR 441, [1989] 2 All ER 208, (1989) 89 Cr App Rep 102; [1989] Crim LR 360; (1989) 133 Sol Jo 420, CA.
8   [1989] 1 WLR 441 at 448.
9   [1991] Crim LR 288.
10 [1972] 1 WLR 651 at 656C; this standard was agreed by counsel on both sides at 653E.
11 [1972] 1 WLR 651 at 655H–656A.

8.132 If the burden of proof of a trial within a trial is the criminal standard it can be argued that the prosecution are required to prove their case twice: once to the trial judge and a second time before the members of the jury. Arguably, the duty of the trial judge is to sift the evidence sufficiently to establish whether the evidence is to go before the members of the jury, in cases where the authenticity of the evidence is questioned by the defence. Should it become the norm for the defence to challenge the authenticity of evidence in digital format in the future, consideration, it is suggested, might be given to the development of a protocol to deal with such challenges. First, it might be necessary for the defence to warn the trial judge in advance that they question the authenticity of identified aspects of the evidence and outline the grounds upon which the challenge is made. Such an approach would be entirely consistent with effective trial management procedures set out in r 1 of the Criminal Procedure Rules 2005. This could be effected at the time when notice of expert witnesses is served under Pt 24 of the Criminal Procedure Rules. If this first hurdle is overcome, it will be for the trial judge to decide whether a trial within a trial is necessary and, if so, to set out the parameters, including the standard of proof, for which a ruling is required.

8.133 As all judges are only too well aware, there is a danger that the trial judge may be seen to be usurping the functions of the members of the jury in reaching preliminary decisions on authenticity when conducting a trial within a trial. Marshall J, in delivering the judgment of the Court of Appeal in the case of *R v Ali (Maqsud); R v Hussain (Ashiq)*[1], indicated that conducting a trial within a trial should be a rare occurrence:

> In the view of this court the cases must be rare where the judge is justified in undertaking his own investigation into the weight of the evidence, which, subject to proper directions from the judge, is really the province of the jury, but the court sees that there can be cases—but they must be rare—where the issues of admissibility and weight can overlay each other[2].

This restricted view was reinforced by the comments *of Kilner Brown J in R v Stevenson*[3]:

> ... as a general rule it seems to me to be highly undesirable, and indeed wrong for such an investigation to take place before the judge. If it is regarded as a general practice it would lead to the ludicrous situation that in every case where an accused person said that the prosecution evidence is fabricated the judge would be called upon to usurp the functions of the jury.

However, where the matter of authentication is raised the trial judge is required to decide whether to conduct a trial within a trial. Where the decision is made to hold a trial within a trial it will be useful for the judge to set out the scope of the hearing. Shaw J made it clear in *R v Robson (Bernard Jack); R v Harris (Gordon Federick)* at 655H that where such a hearing takes place it should be defined narrowly. This must be right.

[1]   [1966] 1 QB 688, [1965] 3 WLR 229, [1965] 2 All ER 464, (1965) 49 Cr App Rep 230, 129 JP 396, 109 Sol Jo 331, CA.
[2]   [1966] 1 QB 688 at 703C.
[3]   [1971] 1 WLR 1 at 4E.

8.134 In any event, when collecting digital evidence the investigator needs to pay careful attention to the process by which the evidence was captured and to demonstrate the provenance of the evidence. In *R v Skinner (Philip)*[1], the defence called into question certain evidence obtained by a police constable when conducting an investigation into indecent photographs of children. In the trial within a trial, the police officer was not able to offer evidence as to the source of some of the materials he sought to adduce that were captured from the Internet, and could only provide limited information about the provenance of the material he produced for the purposes of the investigation, namely images that appeared on screen that were produced in the form of a print-out. It was held by the members of the Court of Appeal that the trial judge wrongly admitted the evidence. First, the members of the Court accepted that it was probable that the screen images were real evidence, because their content did not require any computer input, and likened the image to somebody switching on a television set. However, the print-outs were not authenticated properly under the provisions of s 27 of the Criminal Justice Act 1988 and, for that reason, the trial judge should not have admitted them because there was no proper evidence for the evidence to be admitted. Second, there was no public interest immunity hearing to enable the judge to decide whether the prosecution need not disclose or need not give evidence as to the process by which the screen image reached the police officer or, in the absence of a proper explanation, how the screen image came to be on the police officer's computer. It was conceded that a public interest immunity hearing should have been requested and, in such circumstances, the trial judge was wrong to admit the evidence.

1   [2005] EWCA Crim 1439, [2005] All ER (D) 324 (May), [2006] Crim LR 56.

Qualifications of witnesses

8.135 Concern is sometimes expressed over the qualifications of the witness giving evidence of the reliability of a computer. This concern is illustrated in the case of *Sophocleous v Ringer*[1], where the defence questioned the admissibility of evidence from a computer used to analyse the alcohol content in a blood sample. The defence argued that s 69 of the Police and Criminal Evidence Act 1984 applied in this instance and, in the absence of any evidence as to the operation and accuracy of the computer, the evidence of the witness respecting the graph produced from the computer was inadmissible. The court decided that if the prosecution put the evidence of the computer record to the justices as containing a statement then the requirements of s 69 would indeed need to be addressed. However, the prosecution decided to prove its case by calling a witness, a scientist, to give evidence of the process by which she reached her conclusions. Macpherson J indicated that the defence could have cross-examined the witness about the computer and how it worked, but did not do so[2]. The case of *Wood (Stanley William)*[3] was raised by counsel for the appellant and Macpherson J pointed out that the proposition submitted by the defence was not supported by the judgment. In *Wood (Stanley William)*, the Lord Chief Justice described the difficulties with proving the reliability of a computer:

> This computer was rightly described as a calculating tool. It did not contribute its own knowledge. It merely did a sophisticated calculation which could have been done manually by the chemist and was in fact done by the chemists using the computer programmed by Mr Kellie whom the Crown called as a witness. The fact that the efficiency of a device is dependent on more than one person does not make any difference in kind. Virtually every device will involve the persons who made it, the persons who calibrated, programmed or set it up (for example with a clock the person who set it to the right time in the first place) and the person who uses or observes the device. In each particular case how many of these people it is appropriate to call must depend on the facts of, and the issues raised and concessions made in that case[4].

1   [1988] RTR 52, 151 JP 564, [1987] Crim LR 422.
2   Although s 69 has been appealed, nevertheless see the commentary by Professor Smith in *R v Neville* [1991] Crim LR 288 at 289–290 relating to s 69.
3   (1983) 76 Cr App Rep 23, [1982] Crim LR 667, CA.
4   (1983) 76 Cr App Rep 23 at 27.

8.136 The complexity of a computer, whatever the nature of the device (whether a hand-held personal assistant or a mainframe computer), may give rise to issues of authenticity, but a wider range of challenges may also be raised:

(a)   First, there may be a question about the accuracy or otherwise of the human input. Where the accuracy of the information is challenged, two factors will be pertinent: whether the human beings responsible for inputting the information entered the correct information; and, regardless of the conclusions reached in answering the first point, whether the computer harboured an item of malicious software that acted to change the information that was entered by humans. In the first instance, evidence from those that were responsible for entering the data, if they can be found, will need to be called. In the second instance, the evidence of either an outside expert or a suitable technician that is highly familiar with the system will be necessary. In both cases, it is unlikely that the 'reliability' of the computer will be in question so much as whether the information can be considered to be accurate or is not subject to manipulation other than as intended by the owner of the computer for the purposes to which it is put.

(b)   Second, the reliability of the underlying operating system and application software may be at issue. This is a separate question to the first type of challenge and will require a witness with different skills to the witnesses required in the first example. Here, it may be necessary to call the manufacturer of the hardware or the writer of any relevant software or, failing that, an expert in the specific operating or application software.

(c)   Third, the reliability or accuracy of the information may not be questioned, but the mechanisms developed to ensure a system operates properly and efficiently may be at issue. The prime example is that of bank ATMs, because the operating system is very complex, it is a notorious fact that attacks on ATMs are successful without the use of the correct card, and the PIN can be deduced in the absence of knowing what the PIN is. The range of experts will be wider when challenges of this nature are made, and will include experts that work in a bank as well as experts that are familiar with the weaknesses of bank ATM systems.

Thus the precise nature of the evidence to be given will be governed by the nature of the challenge by the defence in any one case. The observations made by the Lord Chief Justice in *Wood (Stanley William)* were later elaborated by Steyn J, as he then was:

> The law of evidence must be adapted to the realities of contemporary business practice. Mainframe computers, minicomputers and microcomputers play a pervasive role in our society. Often the only record of a transaction, which nobody can be expected to remember, will be in the memory of a computer. The versatility, power and frequency of use of computers will increase. If computer output cannot relatively readily be used as evidence in criminal cases, much crime (and notably offences involving dishonesty) will in practice be immune from prosecution. On the other hand, computers are not infallible. They do occasionally malfunction. Software systems often have 'bugs.' Unauthorised alteration of information stored on a computer is possible. The phenomenon of a 'virus' attacking computer systems is also well established. Realistically, therefore, computers must be regarded as imperfect devices[1].

1   *R v Minors (Craig); R v Harper (Giselle Gaile)* [1989] 1 WLR 441 at 443.

8.137 In the case of *Minors*, the appellant tendered a passbook with false entries purporting to show there was more money held in the account than the £1 that was actually recorded. An auditor on the audit investigation department of the Alliance and Leicester Building Society, who had 14 years' relevant experience and regularly worked with the particular computer, produced the computer record of the complete history of the appellant's account. The last four (forged) entries in the account book were not recorded in the computer print-out. The evidence of the computer print-out was relevant to the question whether there was, in fact, only a balance of £1 in the account. For technical reasons that no longer apply, it was held that the evidence of the building society auditor was wrongly admitted under the provisions of the Police and Criminal Evidence Act 1984 which prevailed at the time. It is pertinent to indicate that it was made clear that the auditor was properly qualified to testify as to the reliability of the computer. However, it is suggested that the reliability of the computer was not in issue in this case. The issue was whether the information entered into the computer was accurate and, if so, how the accuracy or otherwise of the information could be proved. The reliability of the computer is a separate issue. All the auditor would be doing in such circumstances is to provide evidence as to how the information was transcribed from the passbook to the computer and whether the methods used by the building society were capable of providing the assurance that the information was accurate.

8.138 In the case of *Harper*, it was alleged that the appellant presented a Capital Card when travelling on a London Transport bus. A revenue inspection protection official identified the number as one noted on a list of cards that had been stolen. The prosecution had to prove the card was stolen. The relevant sequence of events were as follows: in February 1985 a batch of cards were stolen at Alexandra Palace railway station; appropriate entries were made by an employee in the 'lost book' at the station; the relevant entries were transferred to a computer belonging to British Rail at King's Cross railway station; and the entries were further transferred from this computer to a computer at Waterloo railway station owned by London Regional Transport. At trial, the prosecution relied on a computer print-out from the final computer. The print-out was produced by a revenue protection official who worked at Baker Street station. The judge admitted the evidence, but it was held on appeal that it was incorrect to admit the evidence because the witness could not, from her own knowledge, testify to the reliability of the computer. However, the reliability of the computer was not relevant, given this set of facts. The fatal problem in this instance was a break in the chain of evidence, since the 'lost book' held at Alexandra Palace railway station was missing at the time of the trial. The Court of Appeal ruled the print-out was not admissible because the requirements of s 68 of the Police and Criminal Evidence Act 1984 were not satisfied. The witness may have been an appropriate person to give evidence of the procedures used to register and disseminate the knowledge of the loss of Capital Cards. However, on these facts, because there were so many separate connections in the chain, the prosecution ought to have obtained evidence from each person responsible for the process by which lost or stolen cards were brought to the attention of the relevant authority and by which the information was disseminated.

8.139 In the case of *R v Spiby (John Eric)*[1], the defence argued, unsuccessfully, that the sub-manager of a hotel could not discharge the burden under s 69 of the Police and Criminal Evidence Act 1984 to show that the computer was working properly. It was submitted that only a service engineer or an expert on the use of the particular computer system would have been able to say whether the machine was working correctly. Taylor LJ agreed with the decision of the trial judge and considered that the positive evidence of the sub-manager that the device was working was sufficient in this instance. With respect, this cannot be correct. Whether the computer in question was working properly can only be determined by a service engineer or an expert with knowledge of the particular computer system. The sub-manager was only competent to give evidence of his reliance on the output of the device for the purpose of submitting a record of the telephone calls made from particular extensions in the hotel and recorded by the machine for purpose of billing customers for the calls made. An assertion that the output is considered reliable because the hotel relies on the output of the device does not prove that the device is reliable. These are separate questions. Compare this case with the decision in *United States of America v Linn*[2]. A computer print-out of telephone calls was admitted into evidence. The appellant argued that the print-out was not admissible because it was an untrustworthy record generated by a computer. The appellant suggested, at 216, that the Director of Communications of the Sheraton hotel:

> did not understand the distinctions between 'menus', 'data bases', and computer 'code', she was 'confused and inadequately trained', and thus without personal knowledge of the way in which the computer printout was generated.

No evidence was offered to indicate why the content of the print-out was considered to be unreliable or why it was relevant that the witness failed to understand how the print-out was generated. Beezer, CJ rightly rejected the submission as frivolous. He pointed out that the telephone record was generated automatically and it was retained in the ordinary course of business, thus such records were considered business records under the relevant federal rules of evidence. In this case, the appellant appeared to conflate two separate issues in the submission: first, the witness was not an expert witness and therefore not qualified to give the evidence and, second, the witness failed to understand the underlying working of the computer that produced the print-out. If the reliability of the computer was in issue, the appellant ought to have alleged the content of the print-out could not be trusted and given sufficient reasons for the burden to fall to the prosecution to demonstrate that the computer was working correctly. Where there is a reason that the content of the computer print-out cannot be trusted the qualifications of the witness will be relevant, because of the nature of the evidence they will be required to give and be cross-examined upon.

[1]   (1990) 91 Cr App Rep 186, [1991] Crim LR 199, (1990) *Times*, March 16, (1990) *Independent*, April 2, (C.S.), (1990) *Daily Telegraph*, March 30, CA.
[2]   880 F.2d 209 (9th Cir. 1989).

8.140 The two issues are further illustrated in *R v Neville*[1], where the Crown sought to adduce evidence of a computer print-out showing telephone calls made on Neville's mobile telephone in connection with the hiring of a tractor unit and the employment of a driver to transport a large quantity of stolen hi-fi equipment. The mobile telephone was hired from Talkland, a subsidiary of ICL. A different company, Racal, undertook the telephone operations. The date, time and duration of each call were automatically recorded by the Racal computer and these details were passed on to Talkland. The computer belonging to Talkland produced an itemised bill for their customers. When the bill was paid, the print-out was stored on microfiche (it would, presumably, be scanned first). The Crown sought to adduce the microfiche (or, presumably, a print-out of the contents recorded on the microfiche) and the judge admitted it after a trial within a trial. The Crown then called a witness, an employee of Talkland with no apparent qualifications, to give evidence that she checked all relevant records and had no reason to believe that the telephone bill was inaccurate because of any improper use of either of the computers involved, including the Racal computer. She also stated that the computer at her place of work was working properly so far as her enquiries led. This cannot be correct. The witness might have had the competence to give evidence of the procedures within her knowledge to provide for the accuracy of billing information at Talkland[2], but was in no position (not being competent) to offer evidence of any material substance that the computer at Talkland was working properly and certainly not in a position to offer the same evidence relating to the procedures at Racal, nor as to whether the computer belonging to Racal (of which she had no knowledge, never mind expert knowledge) was working properly.

[1]   [1991] Crim LR 288.
[2]   The evidence can be admitted under the provisions of s 117 of the Criminal Justice Act 2003.

The expert witness

8.141 In brief, the rules relating to expert evidence in criminal cases are governed by amendments to the Police and Criminal Evidence Act 1984 and the Criminal Justice Act 1988. It appears there are no general duties to make advance disclosure by either the prosecution or the defence in summary proceedings[1], although the Criminal Procedure Rules provide for the disclosure of expert reports in relation to trials on indictment[2]. A further change was made under the provisions of s 30 of the Criminal Justice Act 1988, s 30(1) of which provides that hearsay evidence of the opinion of an expert is admissible, whether the expert is called to give oral evidence or not, although, where it is intended to put the report into evidence without calling the maker of the report, leave is required[3]. In reaching a decision, the judge is required to have regard to the matters set out in s 30(3):

(3)   For the purpose of determining whether to give leave the court shall have regard—

   (a)   to the contents of the report;
   (b)   to the reasons why it is proposed that the person making the report shall not give oral evidece;
   (c)   to any risk, having regard in particular to whether it is likely to be possible to controvert statements in the report if the person making it does not attend to

give oral evidence in the proceedings, that its admission or exclusion will result in unfairness to the accused or, if there is more than one, to any of them; and

(d) to any other circumstances that appear to the court to be relevant.

1   *Malek* (2005) pp 33–43; *Cross and Tapper on Evidence* pp 568–573.
2   s 35 of the Criminal Justice Act 2003 inserted s 6D into the Criminal Procedure and Investigations Act 1996, which requires the accused to provide to the court and the prosecutor a notice specifying the person's name and address if they decided to provide any expert opinion for possible use as evidence at the trial. See also Criminal Procedure Rules Pts 24 and 33, although no rules have been made under Pt 33 as at November 2007.
3   Criminal Justice Act 1988, s 30(2).

8.142 Whether an expert is competent is a preliminary matter for the judge and 'is one, upon which, in practice, considerable laxity prevails' as observed by Malek[1]. In trials on indictment, the trial judge has a discretion whether to hold a trial within a trial to determine the expertise of the witness, although the court expressed the view that the judge should avoid unnecessary satellite litigation and exercise the discretion sparingly[2]. The test of admissibility followed in England is the test set out by King CJ in the case of *R v Bonython*[3]and *R v Clarke (Robert Lee)*[4]. The South Australian Supreme Court concluded there were two tests for the trial judge to decide:

> Before admitting the opinion of a witness into evidence as expert testimony, the judge must consider and decide two questions. The first is whether the subject matter of the opinion falls within the class of subjects upon which expert testimony is permissible. This first question may be divided into two parts: (a) whether the subject matter of the opinion is such that a person without instruction or experience in the area of knowledge or human experience would be able to form a sound judgment on the matter without the assistance of witnesses possessing special knowledge or experience in the area, and (b) whether the subject matter of the opinion forms part of a body of knowledge or experience which is sufficiently organized or recognized to be accepted as a reliable body of knowledge or experience, a special acquaintance with which by the witness would render his opinion of assistance to the court. The second question is whether the witness has acquired by study or experience sufficient knowledge of the subject to render his opinion of value in resolving the issues before the court[5].

Where the expert has acquired their knowledge other than by special study or experience goes to weight, not admissibility[6]. Knowledge that is obtained from experience at work, in the absence of formal qualifications, is also acceptable[7]. The degree of expertise required in a witness was the subject of the appeal in *R v Stubbs*[8]. The appellant was convicted of conspiracy to defraud, in that he was involved in the fraudulent money transfers from the HSBC Bank of around £11.8m. The fraudulent activities were carried out using an online banking system called 'Hexagon'. The appellant was a member of password reset team, responsible for resetting customer passwords. The prosecution called Mr Richard Roddy, an employee of HSBC, to give evidence of the Hexagon system. Mr Roddy was not the only witness called to provide evidence of an expert nature. The defence objected at trial to the admissibility of parts of Mr Roddy's evidence on the basis that he lacked the expertise and independence to give expert opinion on the matters in question. It was accepted that he could give evidence about the processes within HSBC and the manner in which the system was designed to operate. However, it was contended that his detailed account of the actual activity within the system at the material times amounted to inadmissible opinion evidence. Following a trial within a trial, the judge ruled Mr Roddy's evidence to be admissible and declined to exclude it under s 78 of the Police and Criminal Evidence Act 1984 or art6 of the European Convention on Human Rights. The grounds of objection are set out in the judgment of Richards LJ at paras 48, 49 and 50:

> 48. Of particular importance was Mr Roddy's evidence that the activity reports all related to the same session, which had the reference number 'CC000051' and had been registered to the staff delegate identification PWRD on the morning of 24 July 2002. A session number would be allocated upon a user's log-on at a particular terminal. If all the transactions took place within one continuous session and there were legitimate transactions admittedly carried out by the appellant during that session just before and just after the illegitimate transactions, the prosecution could argue with force that the illegitimate transactions must have been carried out from the same terminal; and this also provided strong support for the argument that they must have been carried out by the appellant.

> 49. Mr Winter submitted that Mr Roddy did not have the expertise to give such evidence that the activity reports all related to a single session. The fact that they had the same number did not mean that it was a single session. There was evidence from the admitted expert, Mr Danbury, that *concurrent* log-ons (so as to target and hijack a live session) were not possible; but that left open the possibility of *non-concurrent* log-ons to the system under the same session number. This was something that Mr Roddy had not investigated and did not have the technical qualifications to investigate or to answer questions about.

> 50. Among the various points made by Mr Winter were these:
> (i) The activity reports themselves do not show when log-ons and log-offs occurred. For example, they do not show the undoubted log-off by the appellant at about 17.20. This leaves open the possibility that he had previously logged off at about 17.00, just before the illegitimate activity.
> (ii) There was no evidence about the appellant's log-on in the morning. Further, although Mr Roddy said that the computer timed out if the session was idle for a period, the evidence was not clear as to how long it needed before a timed log-off occurred. One would have expected a timed log-off when the appellant left at lunchtime, but there was nothing to show whether there had been a log-off followed by a fresh log-on by the appellant after lunch. In short, there was simply no evidence about when or how the appellant's CC000051 session was created.
> (iii) Mr Roddy gave evidence that, once a session ended, the next session would not be given the same number again: the number reverted to a pool of numbers available to be allocated by the computer to new sessions. He said in cross-examination that there was a 1 in 100,000 chance of it being reallocated to a different session on the same day. Yet there was evidence of three instances the previous day in which session numbers had been reallocated to other sessions after discontinuance of the session to which they were originally allocated. Mr Roddy was unable to say how this could have happened.
> (iv) There were other pointers to the illegitimate activity having been carried out by someone other than the appellant. The illegitimate activity involved a random attack on five companies beginning with the letter 'A', whereas the appellant would have known or could have discovered

the primary delegate identification for all the companies and would not have needed to do things in this way. Moreover, on two occasions in the course of the illegitimate activity the user deployed a shortcut that was never used by the appellant in the course of his legitimate transactions. The vulnerability of the system to attack by members of staff was illustrated by the fraud perpetrated by Mr Kareer earlier the same year, involving as it did the use of other people's terminals in their absence.

1   *Malek* (2005) pp 33–46.
2   *R v G* [2004] 2 Cr App Rep 638, [2004] EWCA Crim 1240.
3   (1984) 38 SASR 45; see also *R v O'Doherty* [2002] NI 263, [2003] 1 Cr App Rep 5, [2002] Crim LR 761; *R v Dallagher* [2003] 1 Cr App Rep 12, [2002] EWCA Crim 1903, [2002] Crim LR 821, (2002) *Times*, August 21, CA and *R v G* [2004] 2 Cr App Rep 638, [2004] EWCA Crim 1240 with further English references.
4   [1995] 2 Cr App Rep 425 (facial mapping), reiterated in *R v Harris* [2006] 1 Cr App Rep 55, (2005) 85 BMLR 75, [2005] EWCA Crim 1980 per Gage LJ.
5   (1984) 38 SASR 45 at 46–47.
6   *R v Silverlock* [1894] 2 QB 766 handwriting compared by a police superintendent; *R v Somers* [1963] 1 WLR 1306, [1963] 3 All ER 808, (1964) 48 Cr App Rep 11, 128 JP 20, 61 LGR 598, 107 Sol Jo 813, CA medical doctor interpreting a report; *R v Davies* [1962] 1 WLR 1111, [1962] 3 All ER 97, (1962) 46 Cr App Rep 292, 126 JP 455, 106 Sol Jo. 393, C-MAC a witness can state the impression they formed as to the condition of the accused at the time they saw the accused.
7   *R v Oakley* (1980) 70 Cr App Rep 7, [1979] RTR 417, [1979] Crim LR 657, CA police officer, with 15 years' experience in the traffic division, attended and passed a course as an accident investigator and having attended over 400 fatal road traffic accidents; *R v Murphy* [1980] QB 434, [1980] 2 WLR 743, [1980] 2 All ER 325, (1980) 71 Cr App Rep 33, [1980] RTR 145, [1980] Crim LR 309, 124 Sol Jo 189, CA police officer offering an opinion as to the nature of a collision.
8   [2006] EWCA Crim 2312, [2000] All ER (D) 133 (Oct).

8.143 In reaching the decision to admit the evidence, the trial judge applied the tests in *R v Bonython*[1]. Richards LJ agreed that it was not in dispute that the first test was satisfied, because the Hexagon system was a subject for expert testimony, and he went on to say, of the second question at para 55:

> In our judgment he was also right to give an affirmative answer to the second question, holding that Mr Roddy had acquired sufficient knowledge of the subject to render his opinion of value in resolving the issues before the court concerning the operation of the Hexagon system. This was an assessment properly made after hearing Mr Roddy's evidence on the voir dire. The extent of Mr Roddy's experience of the Hexagon system, as summarised above, enabled him to give valuable assistance on the interpretation of the data taken from the central computer and set out in the activity reports. It was accepted that he was not an IT specialist in any wider sense and that his technical knowledge of the system was limited. But this did not preclude his being regarded as an expert to the extent indicated by the judge.

The members of the jury were informed of the limitations in the evidence that Mr Roddy was able to give and it was a matter for them to determine whether they should accept and place weight on his evidence. It was submitted that Mr Roddy's evidence went to admissibility because he was an employee of HSBC and represented the victim of the fraud and, therefore, he was not an independent witness. The court rejected this submission. Expertise and independence are separate issues and it was pointed out that, although he made a concession to his lack of objectivity, no attention was given to any feature of his evidence that would support a case of conscious or lack of objectivity. Richard LJ indicated, at para 59, that

> In any event it was a matter for the jury to determine whether there was any conscious or unconscious bias or lack of objectivity that might render his evidence unreliable. This was, as the judge said, a matter going to weight rather than admissibility. The circumstances did not warrant a refusal by the judge to admit the relevant parts of Mr Roddy's evidence at all.

The technical evidence offered by Mr Roddy was not the only evidence of relevance that was led by the prosecution. There was supporting evidence for the prosecution case, for instance: the appellant left the building sometime after 17.00, and returned at 17.27. He claimed he returned to collect his umbrella and that it had been raining, yet the evidence from a CCTV camera located outside an office a few minutes away from the entrance revealed it was bright and sunny at the material time. The appellant also failed to produce relevant paperwork authorising the change in passwords, lied during his internal interviews, and the evidence he gave to the police when questioned was also inconsistent.

In addition to the evidence of Mr Roddy, the prosecution also called a Mr Alan Danbury, a computer expert who had been responsible for introducing the system into the United Kingdom in the early 1990s and the manager of the support team until he retired in 2004. During the trial within a trial, the judge also heard evidence from a witness for the defence, a Mr Michael Turner. Mr Turner was not able to provide a report because of a lack of information, for a variety of reasons, as set out by Richards LJ at 44: 'the appellant's workstation had not been retained or imaged; there was no computer running the 2002 version of the Hexagon system which could be analysed; he had been provided with no information as to how the HSBC computers operated or produced the audit logs relied on by Mr Roddy; and he did not have the underlying data from which he could safely reach any conclusion.' These comments highlight the problems faced by the defence in attempting to elicit co-operation from the victim when legitimate questions need to be investigated to cross-examine and undermine the evidence of prosecution witnesses. This is a particular problem when challenging such a victim as a bank, because the defence has a legitimate interest in challenging the ability of a particular system to withstand an attack or an attempt at subversion. Conversely, the bank cannot, when confronted with evidence that fraud may have taken place, suspend the operation of the system or disrupt it in such a way as to cause it to stop working, no matter how short a time it would take. If a bank were required to pay more attention to the gathering of forensic evidence at a sufficient standard to satisfy criminal proceedings then they, together with other organisations that may suffer similar attempts, will be either obliged to train employees or call in suitably qualified experts to conduct an investigation at the time the suspicion is raised. Apart from the added cost and the marginal utility of taking such steps, the victim must decide, at the time suspicion was raised, whether the integrity of the system will be at issue which, in turn, requires the victim to have hindsight of the future challenges.

In this instance, a balance had to be struck between adducing evidence of the system, and how it operated within the knowledge of the person responsible for the system at the bank, and whether it was necessary to require a more in-depth analysis from a person expert in the relevant system itself. The dividing line between the need for an expert in the operation of the computer system to give evidence and the evidence of someone who is familiar with the day-to-day operation of the system is a fine one, and the nature of the case will determine whether one expert is to be preferred over another[2]. In many cases, as this particular prosecution illustrates, the expert evidence, both internal and external, will not be conclusive. The members of the jury can be appraised of the conflicting technical evidence and will then be required to consider the technical evidence against the other evidence in reaching their decision. In this instance it can be argued that the technical evidence, which was not conclusive, was supported by the inconsistencies in the appellant's behaviour.

[1]   (1984) 38 SASR 45.
[2]   In *RTA v McNaughton* [2006] NSWSC 115, a witness was not permitted or sufficiently expert to give evidence of the position a vehicle was in at the material time.

The duties of the expert witness

8.144   The duties of the expert witness in criminal cases are laid down in common law, and Cresswell J set out guidance in *National Justice Compania Naviera S.A. v Prudential Assurance Co Ltd, The Ikarian Reefer*[1]:

> The duties and responsibilities of expert witnesses in civil cases include the following:
>
> (1)   Expert evidence presented to the Court should be, and should be seen to be, the independent product of the expert uninfluenced as to form or content by the exigencies of litigation[2].
>
> (2)   An expert witness should provide independent assistance to the Court by way of objective unbiased opinion in relation to matters within his expertise[3]. An expert witness in the High Court should never assume the role of advocate.
>
> (3)   An expert witness should state the facts or assumptions on which his opinion is based. He should not omit to consider material facts which detract from his concluded opinion[4].
>
> (4)   An expert witness should make it clear when a particular question or issue falls outside his expertise.
>
> (5)   If an expert's opinion is not properly researched because he considers that insufficient data is available, then this must be stated with an indication that the opinion is no more than a provisional one[5]. In cases where an expert witness who has prepared a report could not assert that the report contained the truth, the whole truth and nothing but the truth without some qualification, that qualification should be stated in the report[6].
>
> (6)   If, after exchange of reports, an expert witness changes his view on a material matter having read the other side's expert's report or for any other reason, such change of view should be communicated (through legal representatives) to the other side without delay and when appropriate to the Court.

(7)   Where expert evidence refers to photographs, plans, calculations, analyses, measurements, survey reports or other similar documents, these must be provided to the opposite party at the same time as the exchange of reports.

¹   [1993] 2 Lloyd's Rep 68, 81–82 (revsd [1995] 1 Lloyd's Rep 455, CA).
²   *Whitehouse v Jordan* [1981] 1 WLR 246 at 256 per Lord Wilberforce.
³   *Polivitte Ltd v Commercial Union Assurance Co plc* [1987] 1 Lloyd's Rep 379 at 386 per Garland J; and *Re J* [1990] FCR 193 per Cazalet, J.
⁴   *Re J* [1990] FCR 193 per Cazalet, J.
⁵   *Re J* [1990] FCR 193 per Cazalet, J.
⁶   *Derby & Co Ltd v Weldon (No 9)* (1990) *Times*, November 9, per Staughton LJ.

8.145 The members of the Court of Appeal in the case of *R v Harris*[1] approved the tests set out by Cresswell J, and Gage LJ went on to adopt guidance from the context of family law in respect of experts giving evidence involving children[2] and adopted the test set (at 192) out by Wall J, as he then was, regarding cases in which there is a genuine disagreement on a scientific or medical issue, or where it is necessary for a party to advance a particular hypothesis to explain a given set of facts:

> Where that occurs, the jury will have to resolve the issue which is raised. Two points must be made. In my view, the expert who advances such a hypothesis owes a very heavy duty to explain to the court that what he is advancing is a hypothesis, that it is controversial (if it is) and placed before the court all material which contradicts the hypothesis. Secondly, he must make all his material available to the other experts in the case. It is the common experience of the courts that the better the experts the more limited their areas of disagreement, and in the forensic context of a contested case relating to children, the objective of the lawyers and the experts should always be to limit the ambit of disagreement on medical issues to the minimum.

We have substituted the word jury for judge in the above passage.

Gage LJ went on[3]:

> In our judgment the guidance given by both Cresswell J and Wall J are very relevant to criminal proceedings and should be kept well in mind by both prosecution and defence. The new Criminal Procedure Rules provide wide powers of case management to the Court. Rule 24 and Paragraph 15 of the Plea and Case Management form make provision for experts to consult together and, if possible, agree points of agreement or disagreement with a summary of reasons.

More recently, in the case of *R v Bowman (Thomas)*[4], Gage LJ reiterated the tests set out by Cresswell J and summarised in *R v Harris*[5] and went on, at 176, to reiterate that the duties of the expert witness 'are owed to the court and override any obligation to the person from whom the expert has received instructions or by whom the expert is paid. It is hardly necessary to say that experts should maintain professional objectivity and impartiality at all times'. The learned judge continued, at 177, by adding a number of additional items of detail that are to be included in an expert report:

1.   Details of the expert's academic and professional qualifications, experience and accreditation relevant to the opinions expressed in the report and the range and extent of the expertise and any limitations upon the expertise.

2. A statement setting out the substance of all the instructions received (with written or oral), questions upon which an opinion is sought, the materials provided and considered, and the documents, statements, evidence, information or assumptions which are material to the opinions expressed or upon which those opinions are based.

3. Information relating to who has carried out measurements, examinations, tests etc and the methodology used, and whether or not such measurements etc were carried out under the expert's supervision.

4. Where there is a range of opinion in the matters dealt with in the report a summary of the range of opinion and the reasons for the opinion given. In this connection any material facts or matters which detract from the expert's opinions and any points which should fairly be made against any opinions expressed should be set out.

5. Relevant extracts of literature or any other material which might assist the court.

6. A statement to the effect that the expert has complied with his/her duty to the court to provide independent assistance by way of objective unbiased opinion in relation to matters within his or her expertise and an acknowledgment that the expert will inform all parties and where appropriate the court in the event that his/her opinion changes on any material issues.

7. Where on an exchange of experts' reports matters arise which require a further or supplemental report the above guidelines should, of course, be complied with.

The additional criteria set out by Gage LJ are particularly essential, especially when dealing with digital evidence, mainly because the specialist is often asked to offer an opinion on the evidence and, where this is the case, it is incumbent on the witness to set out the basis upon which they offer their opinion[6]. It might be usefully noted at this point that Malek has observed that the first proposition set out by Cresswell J 'cannot be read too literally'[7] because evidence that has no direction is useless. This applies particularly to the evidence of a digital evidence specialist. A report ought not to contain lists of possible attacks on computers and other devices, all or any of which the device may be subject to in theory. The report should concentrate on offering an explanation, citing relevant evidence, of the probable cause of why and how a particular action occurred.

[1]   [2006] 1 Cr App Rep 55, (2005) 85 BMLR 75, [2005] EWCA Crim 1980.
[2]   *Re AB (Child Abuse: Expert Witnesses)* [1995] 1 FLR 181.
[3]   [2005] EWCA Crim 1980 at 272 and 273.
[4]   [2006] EWCA Crim 417, [2006] 2 Cr App Rep 22.
[5]   [2006] 1 Cr App Rep 55, (2005) 85 BMLR 75, [2005] EWCA Crim 1980.
[6]   Eoghan Casey *Digital Evidence and Computer Crime Forensic Science, Computers and the Internet* (2nd edn, 2004) p 177.
[7]   *Malek* (2005) pp 33–41.

ELECTRONIC DOCUMENT MANAGEMENT SYSTEMS

8.146 The Joint-Judicial Steering Group on IT and Court Modernisation at the Department of Constitutional Affairs commissioned a feasibility study into the potential to introduce electronic filing and document management for the civil and family courts in England and Wales[1]. It is recognised that electronic filing needs to be undertaken in a secure fashion that also provides a high level of authentication. The aim would be to have document management facilities in place to allow courts to have electronic case files, thus enabling them to process and manage cases electronically. There is a potential for the electronic case file to become the official court file of record. If it is decided to introduce a form of electronic filing and document management, a phased introduction is the most likely and sensible approach. The Department of Constitutional Affairs website indicates the phased introduction may begin in 2008 or 2009 after an appropriate period of procurement takes place.

[1] The report is available online at http://www.hmcourts-service.gov.uk/publications/ policy_strategy/filing_doc_mgmt.htm. Practical problems will need to be addressed, however, such as providing for rules about the receipt of a document in electronic format, as in *Initial Electronic Security Systems Ltd v Avdic* [2005] IRLR 671, and making the sure the back-office does not cause problems for applicants over the timing of receipt of digital documents, as in *Tyne and Wear Autistic Society v Smith* [2005] IRLR 336.

8.147 Money Claims Online[1] is an Internet-based service run by HM Courts Service for claimants to submit their claims online, rather than attending a local court. A claimant can file a claim online and has the ability to observe the status of their claim, any judgment and any warrant issued. In the same way, a defendant can view the status of the claim against them and they can complete and send their defence or acknowledgement of service online. Apparently 6,000 cases apply to make claims each month[2]. Another service, Possession Claims Online, has been developed[3] and is now operational[4]. Practice Direction—Possession Claims Online (supplementing CPR 55.10A) applies to this form of claim, which enables an individual to make, or respond to, certain types of possession claim over the Internet.

[1] https://www.moneyclaim.gov.uk/csmco2/index.jsp.
[2] Delivering justice, rights and democracy DCA Departmental Report 2005/6, ch 8, online at http://www.dca.gov.uk/dept/report2006/ pdf/dca2006_chapter8_b.pdf.
[3] http://www.hmcourts-service.gov.uk/cms/2554.htm.
[4] https://www.possessionclaim.gov.uk/pcol/.

8.148 A system permitting the exhibition of information in the Crown Courts called the XHIBIT Portal, was developed by the Department for Constitutional Affairs. It provides information of the progress of cases to members of staff in the Crown Court, members of the public and approved members of the wider criminal justice community[1]. It is designed to display court lists and the progression of cases. In addition, witnesses can be contacted by mobile telephone, facsimile or land telephone.

[1] http://www.cjit.gov.uk/how-it-all-works/joining-up/xhibit-and-the-cjs-exchange-xhibit-portal/.

8.149 The secure email programme ('SeM') is designed to provide for secure methods of communication between various criminal justice agencies (CPS, police, magistrates' courts, Crown Court, Prison Service and Probation Service) and selected practitioners (defence practitioners, court witness services and the judiciary). The programme is designed to enable users to exchange electronic information up to the 'restricted' level of security securely[1]. In addition, the new Libra system will replace the existing IT systems in the magistrates' courts with a single national infrastructure and case management system[2].

[1] http://www.cjit.gov.uk/how-it-all-works/joining-up/secure-email/.
[2] http://www.cjit.gov.uk/how-it-all-works/case-management/libra/.

Chapter 9

HONG KONG SPECIAL ADMINISTRATIVE REGION ('HKSAR'), PEOPLE'S REPUBLIC OF CHINA

DAVID LEUNG[1]

LAW OF EVIDENCE IN GENERAL

Sources of law

9.01 Before reunification to the People's Republic of China on 1 July 1997, Hong Kong used to be a colony of the United Kingdom. By virtue of the Basic Law, the laws as applied to Hong Kong and the common law were parts of the laws of Hong Kong. Pursuant to article 8 of the Basic Law, the sources of law are:

The laws previously in force in Hong Kong, that is, the common law, rules of equity, ordinances, subordinate legislation and customary law shall be maintained, except for any that contravene this Law, and subject to any amendment by the legislature of the Hong Kong Special Administrative Region.

Article 18 of the Basic Law provides:

The laws in force in the Hong Kong Special Administrative Region shall be this Law, the laws previously in force in Hong Kong as provided for in article 8 of this Law, and the laws enacted by the legislature of the Region.

National laws shall not be applied in the Hong Kong Special Administrative Region except for those listed in Annex III to this Law. The laws listed therein shall be applied locally by way of promulgation or legislation by the Region.

The Standing Committee of the National People's Congress may add to or delete from the list of laws in Annex III after consulting its Committee for the Basic Law of the Hong Kong Special Administrative Region and the government of the Region. Laws listed in Annex III to this Law shall be confined to those relating to defence and foreign affairs as well as other matters outside the limits of the autonomy of the Region as specified by this Law.

In the event that the Standing Committee of the National People's Congress decides to declare a state of war or, by reason of turmoil within the Hong Kong Special Administrative Region which endangers national unity or security and is beyond the control of the government of the Region, decides that the Region is in a state of emergency, the Central People's Government may issue an order applying the relevant national laws in the Region.

Article 84 of the Basic Law reads:

The courts of the Hong Kong Special Administrative Region shall adjudicate cases in accordance with the laws applicable in the Region as prescribed in Article 18 of this Law and may refer to precedents of other common law jurisdictions.

[1]   The views of this chapter are that of the author only and do not represent those of the Department of Justice or the Government of the HKSAR.

EVIDENCE IN GENERAL

Relevance

9.02 The test for admissibility of a piece of evidence must be its relevance. The test of relevance for a piece of evidence in Hong Kong is the same as in the UK. As Colin Tapper indicates[1], the test for relevance could not be better put than in the Digest of the Law of Evidence[2]

> Any two facts to which it is applied are so related to each other that according to the common course of events one either taken by itself or in connection with other facts proves or renders probable the past, present or future existence or non-existence of the other.

Relevance has to be viewed in context of a case, namely, the issues involved. For example, if a particular fact has been admitted in the pleadings then, even if a piece of evidence will advance the existence of the fact in issue, given that the same fact in issue has been admitted, that piece of evidence is not relevant to any issue and hence not admissible in the proceedings.

[1]   Colin Tapper *Cross and Tapper on Evidence* (10th edn, 2004) p 71.
[2]   (12th edn) art 1.

Exceptions

9.03 There are a number of exceptions excluding relevant evidence to be tendered at trial.

Hearsay

9.04 Under common law, hearsay evidence is inadmissible. In civil cases, the position is governed by Pt IV of the Evidence Ordinance, Cap. 8. Under s 47 of the Evidence Ordinance, hearsay evidence is generally admissible 'unless the court is satisfied, having regard to the circumstances of the case, that the exclusion of the evidence is not prejudicial to the interests of justice'[1]. In criminal cases, the common position remains the same. Hearsay evidence is generally inadmissible unless there are other inclusionary rules admitting the hearsay evidence, for example, an oral admission of an accused under caution.

[1]   Evidence Ordinance, s 47(1)(b).

Opinion

9.05 Evidence of opinion from a witness is, in general, inadmissible unless

(a)   it is on age, height, speed, temperature and, possibly, handwriting; or
(b)   the witness is giving an opinion as an expert.

Role of experts

9.06 Experts are the second exception regarding a witness giving opinion evidence. Common experience is a party calling a medical officer, such as a doctor, to give evidence on the injuries suffered by a witness. Experts offer an opinion on matters which are not within the common experience or knowledge of the average man on the street. They impart the specialised knowledge they possess and give opinion to assist the judge or the jury to understand the evidence and reach a decision of the case. The common law rules governing the use of experts and their ability to give his opinion on the 'ultimate issue' in Hong Kong are the same as in England and Wales.

The only statutory provision governing the exchange of expert reports prior to trial in criminal cases is provided for in s 65DA of the Criminal Procedure Ordinance, Cap 221. It is the prosecution's duty to make disclosure in advance of the trial so, in practice, s 65DA governs the time for the defence to disclose their expert report. The defence should, as soon as practicable after the committal to the Court of First Instance or transfer to the District Court, disclose their expert report. For cases in the Magistrates' Courts, section 65DA does not apply and so there is no statutory time limit for an accused to do so.

In civil cases, experts may be called by either party or by the court pursuant to order 40 of the Rules of the High Court.

Character

9.07 The character of a witness is generally not relevant in civil case, unless that witness has previous criminal convictions which cast doubt on his honesty and integrity: for example, conviction of theft or a case in which the witness pleaded not guilty, elected to testify and was disbelieved by the court.

For the accused in a criminal trial, evidence of bad character, such as any previous convictions, is generally inadmissible unless in the limited circumstances of, for example, proving knowledge that goods which he handled were stolen[1]. As to good character of the accused, this is admissible to support credibility of testimony or propensity to commit a crime[2].

---

[1]   Theft Ordinance, s 29(3).
[2]   *Tang Siu Man v HKSAR* FACC 1/1997, [1997–1998] 1 HKCFAR 107, [1998] 1 HKLRD 350.

General exclusion

9.08   In criminal cases, a trial judge retains the common law power to exclude a piece of evidence, even if relevant, on the ground that its prejudicial value outweighs its probative value.

Primary and secondary concept of evidence

9.09   The rule of evidence in HKSAR is derived from the common law, hence the rules governing the primary and secondary concept of evidence are the same as in England and Wales.

RULES OF PRODUCTION OF ELECTRONIC EVIDENCE

9.10   As a general rule, and as with other forms of evidence, if the document in question is not in dispute and will be tendered by consent then the form of production is not important; the original or a copy of the document will be accepted by the court.

For records kept by licensed banks[1], irrespective of whether they have been kept physically or electronically, they are admissible in both civil and criminal cases by production of the original or a copy (for physical records). If the records are kept on computer, then a print-out will suffice[2]. For banks that have ceased business, the same principles apply[3].

In criminal cases, records stored on a computer may be produced in the form of a computer certificate made under s 22A of the Evidence Ordinance, Cap 8. Whether a combination of computers are used, different computers are used in succession or a combination of computers are used in succession, all are treated as a single computer for the purposes of s 22A[4].

There are two ways in which records from a computer can be admitted in criminal proceedings as prima facie evidence of a fact stated in the record under s 22A. The first is for evidence to be adduced, either orally or by consent, that:

(a)   the computer in question was used to store, process or retrieve information for the purposes of any activities carried on by any body or individual;

(b)   the information contained in the statement reproduces or is derived from information supplied to the computer in the course of those activities; and

(c)   while the computer was used in the course of those activities

    (i)   appropriate measures were in force for preventing unauthorised interference with the computer; and

    (ii)   the computer was operating properly or, if not, that any respect in which it was not operating properly or was out of operation was not such as to affect the production of the document or the accuracy of its contents[5].

The condition precedent is that direct oral evidence of that fact has to be admissible.

Condition (c)(i) uses the word 'appropriate' measures as opposed to 'reasonable' measures. It is suggested that appropriate measures are slightly less rigourous than reasonable measures. Use of login names and passwords and the installation of some form of antivirus software may suffice. This point has not yet been decided by the Hong Kong courts. Condition (c)(ii) provides for a situation where the computer was not functioning properly in some non-material aspect. Providing the data in question has been backed up, it is most unlikely that any malfunction will affect the accuracy of the records. The fact that all the information supplied to the computer was free from human intervention shall be treated as information supplied to the computer within the meaning of s 22A[6].

1   Meaning a bank with a valid banking licence granted by the Monetary Authority, see ss 2 and 16 of the Banking Ordinance, Cap 155.
2   Evidence Ordinance, s 20.
3   Evidence Ordinance, s 20A.
4   Evidence Ordinance, s 22A(4).
5   Evidence Ordinance, s 22A(1)(b) and (2)
6   Evidence Ordinance, s 22A(9)(a).

9.11 The first method requires, to a large extent, the oral evidence of a witness testifying on conditions (a) to (c) above, unless the defence agrees to such evidence. The second method, on the other hand, does not require a witness. It only requires a document produced from a computer. Such a document shall be prima facie of any fact stated within the document if it is shown that:

(a)   the computer in question was used over any period to store, process or retrieve information for the purposes of any activities ('the relevant activities') carried on over that period;

(b)   it is shown that no person (other than the accused) who occupied a responsible position during that period in relation to the operation of the computer or the management of the relevant activities

(i)   can be found; or
(ii) if such a person is found, is willing and able to give evidence relating to the operation of the computer during that period;

(c)   the document was produced under the direction of a person having practical knowledge of, and experience in, the use of computers as a means of storing, processing or retrieving information; and

(d)   at the time the document was produced the computer was operating properly or, if not, any respect in which it was not operating properly or was out of operation was not such as to affect the production of the document or the accuracy of its contents, but a statement contained in any such document which is tendered in evidence in criminal proceedings by or on behalf of any person charged with an offence to which such statement relates shall not be admissible under this subsection if that person occupied a responsible position during that period in relation to the operation of the computer or the management of the relevant activities[1].

Likewise, the condition precedent is that direct oral evidence of that fact has to be admissible in the proceedings[2], and that the computer was at the material time operating properly or, if not, any respect in which it was not operating properly or was out of operation was not such as to affect the production of the document or the accuracy of its contents[3].

A number of important points emerge from this subsection. First, subsection (b) covers the situation where the computer was operated by the accused alone. He would have been a person occupying a responsible position in relation to the operation of the computer. However, it is trite law that the accused would not be a compellable witness for the prosecution. Without the phrase 'other than the accused', sub-s (3) would be rendered otiose for a computer seized from an accused operating a business as a sole proprietor.

[1] Evidence Ordinance, s 22A(3).
[2] Evidence Ordinance, s 22A(3)(a).
[3] Evidence Ordinance, s 22A(3)(d).

9.12 Second, the document needs to be produced by a person 'having practical knowledge of and experience in the use of computers as a means of storing, processing or retrieving information'. It does not require this person to have knowledge and experience in the use of the computer in question; knowledge and experience of computers, in general, as a means of storing, processing or retrieving information is sufficient. In practice, such a person is usually a police officer of the Hong Kong police who has attended seminars and training in computer forensics. The capacity of such police officers in producing a document from the computer in question has not yet been challenged in the courts of Hong Kong.

Finally, sub-s 3(d) provides that the accused may not make use of sub-s 3 to produce a document from a computer to prove a statement in the document as part of the defence case. This is to avoid the accused making use of this subsection to render an otherwise inadmissible item of self-serving evidence admissible.

Under the second method, sub-s (5) dispenses with the evidence from the person having 'practical knowledge of and experience in the use of computers as a means of storing, processing or retrieving information' to testify in court provided that he signs a certificate, generally known as a computer certificate. The computer certificate should:

(a) identify the document containing the statement and describing the manner in which it was produced, explaining the nature and contents of the document. This document is usually annexed to the computer certificate;

(b) give the particulars of any device involved in the production of that document as may be appropriate for the purpose of showing that the document was produced by a computer. Essentially this involves identifying a cloned hard disk, a computer and a printer;

(c) demonstrate that appropriate measures were in force to prevent unauthorised access to the computer and that the computer was at the material times operating properly (matters in sub-s (2)); and

(d) purport to be signed by a person occupying a responsible position in relation to the operation of the relevant device or the management of the relevant activities. In practical terms, it is signed by the police officer who handled the hard disk, computer and printer.

The person signing the certificate is only required to state the matter in the computer certificate to the best of his knowledge and belief. The computer certificate will then be prima facie evidence of the statement.

Unless the person cannot be found or, if found, is not willing and able to testify (as in sub-s (3)), the Court may require the person who makes the computer certificate to attend court and give oral evidence on any of the matters referred to in sub-s (5) [1].

The computer certificate has to be served on the opposite party 14 days before the commencement of the trial unless the opposite party does not take issue in time[2]. The production of a copy, if the original document is not available, is permissible[3]. With regard to computer print-outs, the term 'original' is misleading as the computer can print out 10 copies, all of which are 'originals'.

[1]   Evidence Ordinance, s 22A(7).
[2]   Evidence Ordinance, s 22A(6).
[3]   Evidence Ordinance, s 22B(1).

9.13 Section 22A concerns proving the veracity of a statement contained in a document produced by a computer. If a computer record is tendered otherwise than to prove the truth of a statement contained in the document, then there is no need to follow strictly the requirements of s 22A. For example, where the production of a computer record is intended to prove that something did not happen (for example, an accused did not pay for goods), this can be achieved by proving a system has been followed in which a person acting under a duty has compiled a record of the occurrence of all events in question. Evidence that there is no record that the event in question occurred shall be admitted as prima facie evidence to prove that the event did not happen[1]. Applying these provisions to this example, a member of staff may give evidence regarding the payment system, for instance evidence that the bar code on items to be purchsed are scanned and the cost and payment details are recorded on a computer. This, taken together with absence of payment for a particular type of goods found in the possession of the accused at the material time documented in the computer payment records, will be prima facie evidence that the accused has not paid for the goods.

In *Secretary for Justice v Lui Kin Hong*[2], the Hong Kong Court of Final Appeal stressed that the failure to comply with the provisions of s 22A will only affect the admissibility of computer-generated records if the purpose of tendering the document is to prove the truth of its contents. If the computer-generated document is tendered for a purpose other than proving the truth of its contents, the requirements under s 22A need not be complied with.

[1]   Evidence Ordinance, s 17A(1).
[2]   FACC 3/1999, [2000] 1 HKC 95.

Civil cases

9.14 In civil cases, the rules for production of electronic evidence are much more relaxed than in criminal cases. Clearly, subject to relevance, the court will more readily accept a piece of electronic evidence submitted by consent. The records of a business or public body are admissible in civil proceedings without further proof if there is a certificate signed by an officer of that business or public body[1]. The definition of 'officer' includes any person occupying a responsible position in relation to the relevant activities of the business or public body or in relation to its records[2]. In simple terms, if the record concerns the personal details of the employees, then a member of staff of the human resources department can sign the certificate. For the purposes of this section, 'records' include computer-generated records.

Whilst records are admissible under s 54 of the Evidence Ordinance, under s 54(5), the court may, having regard to the circumstances of the case, direct that all or any of the provisions of this section do not apply in relation to a particular document or record. In *Preamble Properties Finance Ltd v Italian Motors (Sales and Service) Ltd*[3], the plaintiff, in proving its losses arising from loss of use of a car, put forward a number of documents. Defence counsel argued that s 54(5) should be applied, as there were numerous discrepancies contained within the documents regarding the age of the car and the amount of losses involved. The judge agreed to the defence submissions, treated the documents as hearsay documents rather than records and applied the criteria in s 49 of the Evidence Ordinance in assessing its weight[4]. Although in *Preamble*, the documents were physical ones, there is no reason why the principles involved are not applicable to computer-generated records.

1 Evidence Ordinance, s 54(1) and (2).
2 Evidence Ordinance, s 54(4).
3 HCA 2135/2000.
4 At para 38.

Weight of electronic evidence

9.15 Computer-generated documents may not only be hearsay in nature, depending on whether the document has been created by an automated process or has had some form of human intervention, but there will be instances where no one has personal knowledge of the contents. If they are records of business, s 54 applies and the contents are admitted without further proof. No question of weight arises in respect of the document itself. To attack the weight of such business records, other evidence is necessary.

On the other hand, if they are not business records, then s 49 of the Evidence Ordinance becomes relevant respecting the weight. Section 49 reads:

(1) In estimating the weight, if any, to be given to hearsay evidence in civil proceedings the court shall have regard to any circumstances from which any inference can reasonably be drawn as to the reliability or otherwise of the evidence.

(2) For the purposes of subsection (1), regard may be had, in particular, to the following—

(a) whether it would have been reasonable and practicable for the party by whom the evidence was adduced to have produced the maker of the original statement as a witness;

(b) whether the original statement was made contemporaneously with the occurrence or existence of the matters stated;

(c) whether the evidence involves multiple hearsay;

(d) whether any person involved had any motive to conceal or misrepresent matters;

(e) whether the original statement was an edited account, or was made in collaboration with another or for a particular purpose;

(f) whether the circumstances in which the evidence is adduced as hearsay are such as to suggest an attempt to prevent proper evaluation of its weight;

(g) whether or not the evidence adduced by the party is consistent with any evidence previously adduced by the party.

These factors can all be considered common sense in assessing the weight of electronic evidence. In a great many instances of computer-generated documents it will be difficult, perhaps impossible, to identify the originator of the document and, as a result, they cannot be called to give evidence. Much will depend on the nature of the document and the number of people that can be identified as being associated with the creation of the document.

In criminal cases, in considering the weight to be attached to a computer record admitted under s 22A, the court shall have regard to all the circumstances from which any inference can reasonably be drawn as to the accuracy or otherwise of the statement and in particular:

(a) whether or not the information contained in the statement was recorded or supplied to the computer contemporaneously with the occurrence or existence of the facts dealt with in that information; and

(b) whether or not any person concerned with the supply of information to that computer, or with the operation of that computer or any equipment by means of which the document containing the statement was produced by it, had any incentive to conceal or misrepresent the facts[1].

[1] Evidence Ordinance, s 22B(3)(b).

Electronic Transactions

9.16 Given the increase in the use electronic signatures and the growth in e-commerce globally, the Electronic Transactions Ordinance ('ETO'), Cap. 553 came into operation on 7 January 2000. The ETO was enacted to provide statutory recognition to transactions carried out electronically. ETO is not applicable to the following classes of documents: wills, trusts, power of attorney, stampable instruments (for example, contract for sale of shares and conveyancing instruments) oaths and affidavits, statutory declarations, judgments or orders of the court, negotiable instruments and warrants issued by a magistrate or a judge[1]. The ETO gives statutory recognition to contracts entered into by offer and acceptance by way of electronic means, without disturbing the common law right of the offeror specifying the method of communication of acceptance[2]. The ETO treats electronic transactions in the same way as physical ones in the following way: if an electronic record is accessible for future reference, then the information contained in the record satisfies a rule of law requiring or permitting information to be given in writing[3].

Similarly, retaining a document in the form of an electronic record satisfies a rule of law requiring that certain information be presented or retained in its original form, provided that there is a reliable assurance as to the integrity of the information from the time at which it was first generated in its final form to the time at which that information is presented, and that the information is capable of being displayed in a legible form[4]. Factors such as whether the information has remained complete and unaltered, except for the addition or change which arises in the normal course of communication, storage (for example, data backup procedures changing the time on which the file was saved) or display will determine the integrity of the information[5]. As to the standard of reliability of the assurance of the integrity of the information, that is determined by the purpose for which the information was generated and all other relevant circumstances[6].

Where a rule of law requires certain information to be retained, in writing or otherwise, retaining electronic records satisfies this requirement if

(i) the information contained in the electronic record remains accessible for subsequent reference; and

(ii) the relevant electronic record is retained in the format in which it was originally generated, sent or received, or in a format which can be demonstrated to represent accurately the information originally generated, sent or received; and

(iii) the information identifying the origin and destination of the electronic record, and the date and time at which it was sent or received, is retained[7].

A final sweeping power is that, without prejudice to any rules of evidence[8], an electronic record shall not be denied admissibility as evidence in any legal proceedings on the sole ground that it is an electronic record[9]. For almost all court proceedings in Hong Kong[10], the retention, signing and sending of documents by electronic means is unacceptable[11]. In other words, pleadings, affirmations and the service and filing of these documents still have to be done in the traditional way.

[1] Electronic Transactions Ordinance, Sch 1.
[2] Electronic Transactions Ordinance, s 17.
[3] Electronic Transactions Ordinance, s 5.
[4] Electronic Transactions Ordinance, s 7.
[5] Electronic Transactions Ordinance, s 7(2)(a)
[6] Electronic Transactions Ordinance, s 7(2)(b).
[7] Electronic Transactions Ordinance, s 8(1).
[8] For example, relevance of the evidence or requirements under ss 22A or 54 of the Evidence Ordinance.
[9] Electronic Transactions Ordinance, s 9.
[10] Electronic Transactions Ordinance, Sch 2.
[11] Electronic Transactions Ordinance, s 13 excluding the applications of ss 5, 5A, 6, 7 and 8.

Electronic signatures

9.17 The term 'electronic signature' is defined in s 2 to mean 'any letters, characters, numbers or other symbols in digital form attached to or logically associated with an electronic record, and executed or adopted for the purpose of authenticating or approving the electronic record', and 'digital signature' is defined in relation to an electronic record as:

an electronic signature of the signer generated by the transformation of the electronic record using an asymmetric cryptosystem and a hash function such that a person having the initial untransformed electronic record and the signer's public key can determine—

    (a)   whether the transformation was generated using the private key that corresponds to the signer's public key; and

    (b)   whether the initial electronic record has been altered since the transformation was generated.

For private citizens, if one party signs a document with an electronic signature and the other party consents to such mode of signing, then the electronic signature satisfies a rule of law requiring the signature of a party on a document[1]. If one of the parties signs on behalf of the government, then a digital signature is required[2].

[1]   Electronic Transactions Ordinance, s 6(1).
[2]   Electronic Transactions Ordinance, s 6(1A).

Service of documents

9.18 For the limited purposes of the proceedings specified in Sch 3 (that is, landlord and tenant related, government rent and rates) service of documents by electronic means shall be treated satisfying the requirement of personal service or service by post[1].

[1]   Electronic Transactions Ordinance, s 5A.

Criminal law

9.19 There is no single computer crime ordinance in Hong Kong. All the relevant sections governing computer crime or high technology crime are scattered amongst various ordinances. The first offence is criminal damage under s 60 of the Crimes Ordinance, Cap 200. Section 60 reads:

A person who without lawful excuse destroys or damages any property belonging to another intending to destroy or damage any such property or being reckless as to whether any such property would be destroyed or damaged shall be guilty of an offence.

Section 59 of the Crimes Ordinance, Cap 200 provides:

In this Part, 'property' means—

(1)(b) any program, or data, held in a computer or in a computer storage medium, whether or not the program or data is property of a tangible nature.

(1A) In this Part, 'to destroy or damage any property' in relation to a computer includes the misuse of a computer.

In this subsection, 'misuse of a computer' means—

    (a)   to cause a computer to function other than as it has been established to function by or on behalf of its owner, notwithstanding that the misuse may not impair the operation of the computer or a program held in the computer or the reliability of data held in the computer;

    (b)   to alter or erase any program or data held in a computer or in a computer storage medium;

    (c)   to add any program or data to the contents of a computer or of a computer storage medium,

and any act which contributes towards causing the misuse of a kind referred to in paragraph (a), (b) or (c) shall be regarded as causing it.

The combined effect of ss 59 and 60 of the Crimes Ordinance, Cap 200 deems the following activities to be offences:

(a)   a hacker that sends 'spyware' to a computer to cause the computer to send to the hacker, unknown to its owner, information of any kind (s 59(1A)(a));

(b)   to change or delete a program or data in the victim's computer. For example, to delete a word document, or make changes to entries to an accounting document (such as an Excel file) (s 59(1A)(b));

(c)   to introduce a virus to the victim's computer even if the virus is not operative;

(d)   a denial of service attack, where massive volumes of data are sent to the victim's computer (s 59(1A)(c)).

9.20 The second type of offence is obtaining access to a computer with a criminal or dishonest intent. Section 161 of the Crimes Ordinance reads:

Any person who obtains access to a computer—

    (a)   with intent to commit an offence;
    (b)   with a dishonest intent to deceive;
    (c)   with a view to dishonest gain for himself or another; or
    (d)   with a dishonest intent to cause loss to another,

whether on the same occasion as he obtains such access or on any future occasion, commits an offence and is liable on conviction upon indictment to imprisonment for 5 years.

(2)   For the purposes of subsection (1) 'gain' and 'loss' are to be construed as extending not only to gain or loss in money or other property, but as extending to any such gain or loss whether temporary or permanent; and—

    (a)   'gain' includes a gain by keeping what one has, as well as a gain by getting what one has not; and

    (b)   'loss' includes a loss by not getting what one might get, as well as a loss by parting with what one has.

An example of the offence described in s 161(1)(a) is where the culprit obtains access to his own computer with the intention to carry out a denial of service attack or with a view to summon other Internet users, say on a newsgroup, to commit a crime jointly. In *HKSAR v Chan Shek Ming*[1], the defendant posted two messages on a website to invite people to team up for a 'flash mob' rape, ie to encourage a group of strangers to gather in order to gang rape a woman. The defendant was charged with two counts of committing an act outraging public decency, a common law offence with two alternative charges of access to a computer with intent to commit a criminal offence. The judge found that the defendant did not have a real intent to commit gang rape when he posted the invitation, but said that the defendant's behaviour could still bring about dangerous consequences. The judge commented that the posting was not just a bad joke or a matter of poor taste and that there was a real risk of some viewers of the messages being tempted to commit such a crime. The defendant was sentenced to 160 hours of community service[2].

The concept of dishonesty, as required under s 161(b), is the same as dishonesty in other offences, for example, theft-related offences. This concept was considered in the classic case of *R v Ghosh*[3].

[1] DCCC 196/2006.
[2] See Community Service Order Ordinance, Cap 378.
[3] [1982] QB 1053, [1982] 2 All ER 689, [1982] 3 WLR 110.

9.21 The two offences under s 161(1)(c) and (1)(d) are most frequently used and are mirror images of each other. Section 161(1)(c) was first used to cover offences in which hackers, using the login name and passwords of other legitimate Internet users, gain access to the Internet and have the bill charged to the victim. Such an offence can be charged under either s 161(1)(c) (dishonest gain on the part of the accused) or under s 161(1)(d) (a dishonest intent to cause loss to the victim).

Section 161(1)(c) catches the acts preparatory to the commission of a crime or fraud. However, it is not restricted to such acts. It is the intent or purpose of the offender at the time of the access which must be considered, not his intent or purpose at some later stage[1]. 'Gain' is defined in s 161(2) in terms wider than just monetary gain: it includes intangible benefits and benefits which are transient. The word 'gain' in s 161(2) clearly includes the obtaining of information which the person obtaining access to the computer did not have before this access. The gain need not be something which can be utilised or used by the offender[2].

Another offence is provided under s 27A of the Telecommunications Ordinance, Cap 106 which is seldom used in practice. Section 27A reads:

> (1)Any person who, by telecommunications, knowingly causes a computer to perform any function to obtain unauthorized access to any program or data held in a computer commits an offence and is liable on conviction to a fine of $20,000.

'Telecommunications' is defined in s 2 as:

> any transmission, emission or reception of communication by means of guided or unguided electromagnetic energy or both, other than any transmission or emission intended to be received or perceived directly by the human eye.

This section is rarely used for two reasons. Firstly, the maximum penalty for this offence is only HK$20,000 (approximately US$2,500). A fine is rarely appropriate for hacking. If the offence can equally be laid under s 161 of the Crimes Ordinance, the offence under the Crimes Ordinance will always be laid. Secondly, the unauthorised access has to be by way of 'telecommunications'. For example, if the accused hacks into the victim's computer using his computer through the Internet, then it is by way of telecommunications and is chargeable under s 27A. However, if the accused physically entered into a restricted place and then gained access to the computer there, he did not gain access to the target computer by way of telecommunications and hence is not chargeable under s 27A. In practice, as most of the instances of unauthorised access to a computer are chargeable, and indeed charged, under s 161, s 27A has gradually been rendered otiose.

1   Per Chan CJHC, as he then was, in *HKSAR v Tsun Shui Lun* HCMA 723/1998, [1999] 2 HKC 747 at 19 and 20.
2   *HKSAR v Tsun Shui Lun* HCMA 723/1998, [1999] 2 HKC 747 at 25.

Sentence

9.22 In *HKSAR v Tam Hei Lun*[1], the Court of Appeal considered that it was inappropriate to lay down guidelines for sentencing, as there were very few prosecutions under s 161 and so the full range of crimes under s 161 would not be known or appreciated. However, Mr Justice Rogers VP commented that obtaining access to the computer of another person can in many respects be likened to burglary[2]. Matters such as the loss and damage which was caused to the victims, the gravity of the offence to the victim, the purpose for obtaining access and any gain, financial or otherwise, to the person perpetrating the access are all relevant to the question of sentence[3]. The court concluded by saying that, unless there are most unusual circumstances, a non-custodial sentence would be inappropriate.

A number of cases decided after *Tam* fell into one of two broad categories. They were either denial of services attack on victim's computers, the same type as in *Tam*, that is, using the log-in name and passwords of other Internet users to avoid paying the cost of obtaining access to the Internet. Most of these cases involved young defendants who were still in secondary school. Usually, a community service order was imposed on such defendants. The second category involves more mature defendants hacking into a computer either to obtain trade secrets or information for personal or financial gain. In *HKSAR v Ho Pak Sang*[4], the defendant, a police officer, was responsible for carrying out research into organised crime syndicates. As part of his official duties, he was authorised to gain access to information about the particulars of vehicles and drivers through the police computers. The defendant abused these powers by obtaining access to information the ex-husband of his girlfriend. He helped his girlfriend to check the address and whereabouts of her ex-husband, because the ex-husband had failed to pay maintenance. The defendant was charged with 17 counts of obtaining access to a computer with a view to dishonest gain under s 161(1)(c) of the Crimes Ordinance. He pleaded guilty to six counts and was sentenced to six months' imprisonment.

In *HKSAR v Alistair Currie* HCMA 795/2004, the appellant was at the material time a Chief Inspector of Police attached to the Marine Regional Command and Control Centre ('MRCCC'). The Control Centre has a computer system called 'Enhanced Computer Assisted Command and Control System' ('ECACCS'), which contains personal particulars of persons, whether related to crimes or not. Police officers attached to the MRCCC are authorised to obtain access to the computer to obtain information. On the day in question, the appellant requested a subordinate to obtain access to the computer by checking a person's details against an identity card number he had supplied. Information relating to that person, Leung, and his residential address appeared on the screen. The appellant asked the subordinate whether the address could be printed, and was told it was not. The appellant then wrote the identity card number and the police file reference number on a piece of paper. Leung was a former tenant of domestic premises let by the appellant as landlord. That tenancy was terminated by the tenant about two years prior to this incident. The appellant was convicted after trial on a single charge of obtaining access to a computer with a view to dishonest gain for himself, contrary to s 161(1)(c) of the Crimes Ordinance. He was sentenced to two months' imprisonment, suspended for two years. His appeals to the Court of First Instance and to the Appeal Committee of the Hong Kong Court of Final Appeal were dismissed[5].

[1]   HCMA 385/2000.
[2]   At para 19.
[3]   At para 18.
[4]   ESCC 2043/2001.
[5]   FAMC 57/2004.

9.23 In *HKSAR v Tsu Pai Ling* DCCC 231/2002, the defendant was employed for a period of one year by a private company as a manager in the marketing information and development department. Towards the end of the term of his employment contract, the defendant downloaded customer information from the company's computer. He then attempted to sell the information to a competitor of the company, at a price of HK$600,000. The matter was reported to the police. An undercover operation was carried out and the defendant was subsequently arrested. Shortly before his arrest, the defendant asked to see his employment contract, which was usually kept in a locked cabinet. That contract was subsequently lost in the office. On searching the defendant's home, the original employment contract was found. The defendant was charged with one count of 'Access to a computer with a view to dishonest gain' and one count of 'theft' (of the employment contract). The defendant pleaded not guilty to both charges and suggested that there was no restriction in the employment contract to prevent staff from downloading information from the office computer, and that he had downloaded the data and brought it home for work. The difficulty that the prosecution faced was that there was no express stipulation in the employment contract that members of staff could not download information, or a particular type of information, from the company's computer. Furthermore, it was difficult to establish the time and date at which the defendant downloaded the information.

Amongst property seized from the defendant's home, there were a number of CD-Roms. One of the CD-Roms was found to contain information of an order placed by a client of the company, which had been created after a certain date (close to the defendant's resignation). The prosecution argued that the defendant must have obtained access to the company's computer on or after that date. With reference to that date, the judge found that the defendant was dishonest when he downloaded the information of the company's client and sentenced the defendant to concurrent sentences of fifteen months' imprisonment on charge 1 (s 161(1)(c)) and three months' imprisonment on charge 2.

In *HKSAR v Kung Hang Ming*[1], the complainant was a company with its core business in locating properties for lease to large corporate clients. Each employee of the complainant was allocated an email address to facilitate the company's business by enabling the employee to correspond with the clients via email. Each member of staff was given a personal password for the purpose of obtaining access to the computer system. Employees were allowed to obtain access to the computer system for business purposes only. The defendant was a property agent employed by the complainant company and was responsible for assisting an associate director in negotiating tenancy agreements for major corporate clients. The associate director was on maternity leave between July and September 2000. Before she went on leave, the director provided the defendant with her password so that the defendant could communicate with clients via email. In October 2001, the defendant resigned from the complaint company and joined a competitor company as senior negotiator. In February 2002, the director discovered she had not received any emails for about two weeks. The technician employed by the company discovered somebody had been obtaining access to the computer system of the company and deleting emails from the director's account. The matter was reported to the police.

The defendant was arrested at her home whilst in the process of deleting emails from the director's email account. Under caution, the defendant admitted that she obtained access to the director's email account from her home, as she was curious about the activities of her former employer. A search of the defendant's computer revealed that it contained emails from clients to the director, and the company's internal emails to employees regarding a number of sensitive marketing information and strategies. The defendant was charged with ten counts of criminal damage and twenty counts of access to a computer with dishonest intent (sample counts). The defendant pleaded guilty to all charges and was sentenced to a total term of imprisonment of three months.

In *Liu Wai Shun v HKSAR*[2], Mr Justice Ribeiro PJ said *obiter* on sentencing of this type of offence:

> We would make one comment regarding sentence. Deliberate damage to computer software and data may of course result in very substantial economic and other harm to organisations using that software and data. The applicant may count himself lucky that the damage inflicted here was remediable largely

because of the preventive measures taken by his former employer. The seriousness of the damage inflicted in such a case should properly be reflected in the sentences handed down. If more serious damage had ensued, a fine would not have been a sufficient sentence. We were told that the Court of Appeal has, quite properly in our view, indicated that such cases should ordinarily attract a custodial sentence.

[1]   ESCC 2832/2002.
[2]   FAMC 30/2004.

Amendment in the statutes in relation to computer or Internet

Spamming

9.24 As at 1 December 2006, spamming is not an offence under the laws of Hong Kong. In practice, most of the spam and junk emails encountered are commercially-motivated. One of the reasons why spamming has not been criminalised is because, if an unsolicited email of a substantial size has been sent to a recipient, it may amount to 'adding data to a computer or a computer storage medium' within the meaning of s 59(1A)(c) of the Crimes Ordinance, Cap. 200, and hence be considered misuse of a computer, resulting in the commission of an offence of criminal damage under s 60.

The second reason is that a recipient of an email may make use of the provisions of the Personal Data (Privacy) Ordinance, Cap 486. Under s 34 of the Ordinance, a data user[1] who uses personal data of a data subject[2] for directing marketing purposes[3] shall inform the data subject that the data user is required to cease to so use those data if the data subject so requests, without any charge to the data subject. In other words, the recipient of a commercial email can inform the sender that he does not wish to receive further such promotional or commercial emails in the future: an opt-out exercise. If, after the opt-out, the sender still sends email to the recipient, the sender commits an offence under s 64(10) of the Ordinance, the maximum penalty for which is a fine at level 3[4].

The Government of the HKSAR has decided to regulate unsolicited electronic messages ('UEM's). According to the industry in Hong Kong, over 60 per cent of all the emails received in Hong Kong are UEMs[5]. In balancing the business interests of e-commerce and e-marketing against the rights of consumers and individuals not to be disturbed by UEM, the legislature proposes to use the Unsolicited Electronic Messages Bill to cover UEMs originated from Hong Kong and those sent from overseas to an electronic address in Hong Kong. As to the nature of the messages, the Bill will only cover those of a commercial nature, that is, those offering or promoting goods or services for furtherance of business[6]. The Bill will be technology-neutral, that is, all forms of electronic messages, such as emails, facsimile transmissions, SMS, voice or video calls will be covered. However, person-to-person voice or video messages are excluded from the scope of the Bill[7]. The proposed penalty is a fine up to HK$100,000 for a first conviction and up to HK$500,000 for second and subsequent convictions.

In cases of supply, acquisition or use of electronic address-harvesting software or harvested lists of email addresses for sending commercial electronic messages to recipients without their consent, the proposed penalty is a fine of HK$1,000,000 and imprisonment for five years[8]. For fraud and related activities in connection with spamming, the proposed maximum penalty is 10 years[9]. The rights of victims of UEMS to lodge civil claims for damages suffered are provided for under the Bill. At the time of writing, the Unsolicited Electronic Messages Bill[10] was with the Bills Committee. The Unsolicited Electronic Messages Ordinance should come into operation in 2007 or 2008 at the latest.

There has been a suggestion to include the offences under ss 59, 60 and 161 of the Crimes Ordinance and s 27A of the Telecommunications Ordinance in the Criminal Jurisdiction Ordinance, Cap. 461[11]. If these offences are included in the Criminal Jurisdiction Ordinance, then the Hong Kong Courts will have jurisdiction if a Hong Kong victim is attacked by an overseas hacker or a Hong Kong offender launches attacks against an overseas victim[12]. The proposed amendments are yet to be implemented.

[1] In relation to personal data, means a person who, either alone or jointly or in common with other persons, controls the collection, holding, processing or use of the data. See s 2 of Cap 486.
[2] In relation to personal data, this means the individual who is the subject of the data. See s 2 of Cap 486.
[3] This is defined under s 34(2) as 'the offering of goods, facilities or services, the advertisements of the availability of goods, facilities or services, the solicitation of donations or contribution' by a number of means, including by way of email.
[4] HK$10,000. See Sch 8 to the Criminal Procedure Ordinance, Cap 221.
[5] Legislative Council Brief on Unsolicited Electronic Messages Bill, para 2, available online at http://www.citb.gov.hk/ctb/eng/legco/pdf/LegCo_message.pdf
[6] Legislative Council Brief on Unsolicited Electronic Messages Bill, para 8.
[7] Legislative Council Brief on Unsolicited Electronic Messages Bill, para 9.
[8] Legislative Council Brief on Unsolicited Electronic Messages Bill, para 14.
[9] Legislative Council Brief on Unsolicited Electronic Messages Bill, para 15.
[10] http://www.legco.gov.hk/yr05–06/english/bills/b0607071.pdf.
[11] http://www.info.gov.hk/gia/general/200211/27/1127312.htm.
[12] Criminal Jurisdiction Ordinance, Cap 461 ss 3(1) and (3).

Chapter 10

INDIA

MANISHA T KARIA AND TEJAS D KARIA

10.01 The Indian Supreme Court has recognised that if the law fails to respond to the needs of a changing society either it will stifle the growth of society and choke its progress or, if that society is vigorous enough, it will cast aside a law which stands in the way of its growth. Law must, therefore, be constantly adapted to the speed of change in society and not lag behind[1]. The expanding horizon of science and technology has thrown new challenges to lawyers and judges dealing with proof of facts in disputes where advanced techniques in technology have been used. Storage, processing and transmission of data on magnetic and silicon media has become cost-effective and easy to handle. Conventional means of keeping records and data processing have become outdated and rules relating to admissibility of electronic evidence and its proof have been incorporated into Indian laws[2].

[1] *National Textile Workers' Union v PR Ramakrishnan* AIR SC 1983 at 75.
[2] *State v Mohd Afzal* (2003) DLT 385 at 278.

LAW OF EVIDENCE IN INDIA

10.02 India has shown dynamism in responding to the challenges presented by developments in information technology in relation to electronic evidence. The Information Technology Act 2000 ('IT Act'), discussed below, amending the Evidence Act 1872 ('Evidence Act') has made electronic records admissible as evidence in a court of law.

The principles of the law of evidence in India are contained in the Evidence Act. The Evidence Act is a branch of the adjective law and, accordingly, all questions of evidence must be decided by the laws of forum or court in which the action is tried. The application of the law of evidence is that of the law of the forum. Whether a witness is competent or whether certain evidence proves a certain fact is to be determined by the law of the country wherein the question arises or where the remedy is sought to be enforced.

The Evidence Act is, as it was intended to be, a complete code of the law of Evidence[1]. However, the Evidence Act is not exhaustive and it is possible to refer to the decisions of other countries, but only if the legislation uses expressions the same as, or similar to, those contained in the Evidence Act[2]. The court can also look to English common law in case of doubt or ambiguity over the interpretation of any of the provision of the Evidence Act[3]. As the law of evidence is a law of procedure, changes to this branch of the law are, like

changes in other rules of procedure, retrospective[4]. To meet with the requirement of the IT Act, the definition of 'evidence' has been amended to the effect
that all documents, including electronic records, produced for the inspection
of the court are called documentary evidence[5].

1   *HH Advani v State of Maharashtra* AIR 1971 SC 44.
2   *State of Madras v Sayed Abdul Rahman* AIR 1954 Mad 926.
3   *State of Punjab v SS Singh* AIR 1961 SC 493.
4   *Paras Ram v Mewa Kunwar* 125 IC 754.
5   Evidence Act, s 3.

TYPES OF EVIDENCE

10.03 Under s 3 of the Indian Evidence Act, the term 'evidence' means and
includes:

(a)   all statement which court permits or requires to be made before it by witness,
in relation to matters of fact under inquiry, such statements are called oral
evidence;

(b)   all documents including electronic records produced for the inspection of the
court, such documents are called documentary evidence.

The parties may rely on oral evidence as well as documentary evidence. In the
event of either party relying upon any documentary evidence, a number of
civil and criminal procedural rules must be followed. To that purpose, Indian
civil and criminal procedural laws provide that it is essential for parties to
produce all evidence that they wish to rely upon at the earliest possible
opportunity. The originals ought to be brought on record and the other party
has an opportunity to inspect and challenge them, if so desired. The basic
purpose is to ensure that the best possible evidence reaches the court to enable
the court to decide the matter before it and to give finality to the trial of all
issues between the parties.

Evidence can be classified under various headings, such as oral and documentary evidence, direct and indirect evidence, primary and secondary evidence,
hearsay and circumstantial evidence, scientific and expert evidence, real and
digital evidence. Any form of evidence may be sufficient to have a fact proved
before the court, depending upon the facts and circumstances of the case.

Oral and documentary evidence

10.04 'Oral evidence' means a statement which the court permits or requires
to be made before it by witnesses in relation to matter of fact under inquiry[1].
'Oral' ordinarily means 'words spoken by mouth', but a witness who is unable
to speak may give their evidence in any manner by which they can make it
intelligible, such as by writing or by signs[2]. Documentary evidence, on the
other hand, is evidence produced in the form of documents. A document
means 'any matter expressed or described upon any substance by means of
letters, figures or marks or by more than one of those means intended to be
used or which may be used for the purpose of recoding of matter'[3].

The Supreme Court of India observed in *State of Maharashtra v Praful B. Desai*[4], that:

> Section 273 [of the Criminal Procedure Code] provides for dispensation from personal attendance. In such cases evidence can be recorded in the presence of the pleader. The presence of the pleader is thus deemed to be presence of the Accused. Thus section 273 contemplates constructive presence. This shows that actual physical presence is not a must. This indicates that the terms 'presence', as used in this section, is not used in the sense of actual physical presence. A plain reading of section 273 does not support the restrictive meaning sought to be placed by the Respondent on the word 'presence'. One must also take note of the definition of the term 'Evidence' as defined in the Indian Evidence Act. Thus evidence can be both oral and documentary and electronic records can be produced as evidence. This means that evidence, even in criminal matters, can also be by way of electronic records. This would include video conferencing. Recording the evidence by video conferencing also satisfies the object of providing, in section 273, that evidence be recorded in the presence of the Accused. The Accused and his pleader can see the witness as clearly as if the witness was actually sitting before them. In fact the Accused may be able to see the witness better than he may have been able to if he was sitting in the dock in a crowded court room. They can observe his or her demeanour. In fact the facility to play back would enable better observation of demeanour. They can hear and rehear the deposition of the witness. The accused would be able to instruct his pleader immediately and thus cross-examination of the witness is as effective if not better.

It was observed by the High Court of Calcutta in *Amitabh Bagchi v Ena Bagchi*[5] that the rationale of the Supreme Court judgment in the above case is that 'presence' does not necessarily mean actual physical presence in the court. Thus, the physical presence of person in court may not be required for the purpose of adducing evidence. Sections 65A and 65B of the Evidence Act provide for evidence relating to electronic records and admissibility of electronic records, and electronic records includes video conferencing, therefore there is no bar to the examination of witnesses by way of video conferencing.

The potential for ensuring the safety of victims and witnesses through the use of information technology was recognised by the Supreme Court of India in the recent case of *Sakshi v Union of India*[6] in which the Supreme Court observed that:

> The whole inquiry before a court being to elicit the truth, it is absolutely necessary that the victim or the witnesses are able to depose about the entire incident in a free atmosphere without any embarrassment. Section 273 Cr PC merely requires the evidence to be taken in the presence of the accused. The section, however, does not say that the evidence should be recorded in such a manner that the accused should have full view of the victim or the witnesses. Recording of evidence by video conferencing has already been upheld. Moreover, there is a major difference between substantive provisions defining crimes and providing punishment for the same and procedural enactment laying down the procedure of trial of such offences. Rules of procedure are the handmaiden of justice and are meant to advance and not to obstruct the cause of justice. It is, therefore, permissible for the court to expand or enlarge the meanings of such provisions in order to elicit the truth and do justice with the parties. Thus, in holding trial of child sex abuse or rape a screen or some arrangements may

be made where the victim or witness (who may be equally vulnerable like the victim) do not see the body or face of the accused. Recording of evidence by way of video conferencing vis-à-vis section 273 Cr PC is permissible.

The Supreme Court of India in the case of *Ziyauddin Burhanuddin Bukhari v Brijmohan Ramdass Mehra*[7] has also observed that tape-recorded speeches consitiute a 'document', as defined by s 3 of the Evidence Act, which stand on the same footing as photographs, and they are admissible in evidence on satisfying the following conditions:

(a)   the voice of the person alleged to be speaking must be duly identified by the maker of the record or by others who knew it;

(b)   accuracy of what was actually recorded had to be proved by the maker of the record and satisfactory evidence, direct or circumstantial, to rule out possibilities of tampering with the record had to be presented;

(c)   the subject matter recorded had to be shown to be relevant according to rules of relevancy found in the Evidence Act.

[1]   Evidence Act, s 3.
[2]   Evidence Act, s 119.
[3]   Evidence Act, s 3, see definition of 'document'.
[4]   AIR 2003 SC 2053 at 12 and 19.
[5]   AIR 2005 Cal 11 (notes).
[6]   AIR 2004 SC 3566 at para 31.
[7]   AIR 1975 SC 1788 at para 19.

Direct and indirect evidence

10.05 Evidence is either direct or indirect. Direct evidence is that which proves the fact in dispute directly, without any interference or presumption, and which itself is a true and conclusively-established fact. Oral evidence must be direct evidence. If evidence is to be led about a fact, which can be heard or seen or perceived by any other sense, a witness must be produced who heard, saw or perceived that fact. Where evidence is to be given about an opinion, or as to the grounds on which opinion is held, the witness must state the opinion and the grounds upon which the opinion is held[1].

Indirect evidence is that which tends to establish the fact in dispute by proving another and which, though true, is not of itself conclusive.

[1]   Evidence Act, s 60.

Primary and secondary evidence

10.06 Primary evidence is called as the best evidence or that kind of proof which, under any possible circumstances, affords the greatest certainty of the facts in question. The primary evidence means the document itself produced for the inspection of the court[1].

The general principle is that if the original document exists, and is available, it must be produced because it is the best evidence. However, if the original is lost, destroyed or detained by an opponent or third person who does not produce it after notice, or it is physically irremovable, secondary evidence is admissible[2].

1   Evidence Act, s 62.
2   Evidence Act, s 63.

Hearsay evidence

10.07 The term 'hearsay' has various meanings. It can mean whatever a person is heard to say or it can mean whatever a person declares on information given by someone else[1]. Hearsay evidence is used with reference to written as well as spoken information and denotes evidence which does not derive its value solely from the witness himself, but depends in part on the competency of other persons. Essentially, it is evidence which is given by a person who has not perceived the events described themselves, but who has gleaned the information from some other source.

1   *JD Jain v Management, State Bank of India* AIR 1982 SC 673.

Circumstantial evidence

10.08 Where evidence is of a circumstantial nature, the circumstances from which the conclusion of guilt is to be drawn, should, in the first instance, be fully established and all the facts so established should be consistent only with the hypothesis of the guilt of the accused. The circumstances should be of a conclusive nature and tendency, and should be such as to exclude every hypothesis but the one to be proved. This evidence is another indirect type of the evidence that accrues out of the peculiar facts or circumstances of a particular situation or case and is relevant in proving a fact in dispute.

Scientific and expert evidence

10.09 An expert witness is one who has devoted time and study to a special branch of learning and is thus especially skilled with regard to the points upon which they are asked to state their opinion. Expert evidence is admissible to enable the tribunal to arrive at satisfactory conclusion. Section 45 of the Evidence Act defines an expert as one who has acquired special knowledge, skill or experience in any science, art, trade or profession; such knowledge may have been acquired by practice or careful studies. The terms 'science' and 'art' are to be construed widely[1]. An expert witness is to be treated like any other witness. Expert evidence tends to be considered a weak type of evidence, especially when it is demonstrated that the expert does not have sufficient knowledge of their subject[2]. Expert evidence cannot be as conclusive as opinion evidence. The court may refuse to rely on the evidence of an expert where it is not supported by reasoning.

Expert evidence has two aspects: data evidence and opinion evidence. Data evidence cannot be rejected if it is inconsistent with oral evidence, but opinion evidence is only an inference drawn from the data and does not have precedence over direct eye-witness testimony, unless the inconsistency between the two is so great as to obviously falsify the oral evidence[3]. Once the expert opinion is accepted by the court, it ceases to be the opinion of the expert and becomes the opinion of the court.

1   *Mahadeo Dewanna v Uyankammbai* AIR 1948 Nag 287.
2   *Melappa v Guramma* AIR 1956 Bom 129.
3   *Arshad v State of AP* 1996 Cr. LJ 2893.

Real and digital evidence

10.10 Real evidence is any material evidence which is objectively or externally demonstrable and is perceivable in nature. The proliferation of computers and the influence of information technology in human lives has raised the need for the admission of digital evidence in judicial proceedings. Real evidence relating to digital transactions is not available, and the only alternative is the admissibility of digital evidence in Indian courts. To this end certain forms of digital evidence have been accepted in India.

PARAMETERS FOR EVIDENCE TO BE ADMISSIBLE

10.11 The foremost object of the Evidence Act is to provide for uniform rules of practice. The principles of the Evidence Act are:

(a)   evidence must be restricted to the matters in issue;
(b)   best evidence must be tendered; and
(c)   hearsay evidence must not be admitted[1].

Evidence must meet certain established criteria for it to be admissible in a court of law, it. As a general rule, following requirements have to be met for the evidence to be admissible in a court of law. These are discussed below.

1   M Monir *Law of Evidence* (4th edn) p 17.

Best evidence rule

10.12 When a party seeks to put the content of a document into evidence, the best evidence rule requires that the original must be produced[1]. It is a cardinal rule in the law of evidence that the best available evidence should be brought before the court. Sections 60, 64, and 91 of the Evidence Act are based on this rule[2]. The best evidence, or original evidence, is the primary evidence and, as such, the best evidence rule excludes secondary evidence. Section 62 provides that primary documentary evidence is the evidence of the original documents. Section 91 of the Evidence Act mainly forbids proving the contents of a written document other than by the writing itself and lays down the best evidence rule. It does not, however, prohibit the parties to adduce evidence, in a case where the document is capable of being construed differently, to show how the parties understood the document[3].

In the case of *Bai Hira Devi v Official Assignee, Bombay*[4] the Supreme Court of India observed that:

> Section 91 deals with the exclusion of oral by documentary evidence. The normal rule is that the contents of a document must be proved by primary evidence which is the document itself in original. Section 91 is based on what is sometimes described as the 'best evidence rule'. The best evidence about contents of a document is the document itself and it is the production of the document that is required by s 91 in proof of its contents. In a sense, the rule enunciated by s 91 can be said to be an exclusive rule inasmuch as it excludes the admission of oral evidence for proving the contents of the document except in cases where secondary evidence is allowed to be led under the relevant provisions of the Evidence Act.

The Indian Evidence Act prescribes clear legal rules that are expected to objectively guide the judge to decide the relevancy and admissibility of evidence and rule out any unpredictability associated with subjective assessment.

1   *Clockle's Cases and Statues on Evidence* (4th edn) p 326.
2   *Sk. Siraj v State of Orissa* (1994) 100 Cr.LJ 2410 Ori.
3   *Tulsi v Chandrika Prasad* decided by the Supreme Court on 24 August 2006 in Civil Appeal No 3631 of 2006.
4   AIR 1958 SC 448.

Admissibility

10.13 Section 136 of the Evidence Act empowers a judge to decide as to the admissibility of evidence, and s 3 of the Evidence Act deals with admissibility of evidence. In order that the proof may be confined to relevant facts and may not travel beyond the proper limits of the issue at trial, the judge is empowered to ask in what manner the evidence tendered is relevant. The judge must then decide its admissibility. It is the duty of the judge to see that evidence brought on the record is relevant[1]. It is to be noted that the admissibility of evidence is to be determined with reference to the Indian Evidence Act and not with reference to any law of England[2].

In a suit or proceeding, evidence can be given only regarding those facts which are either facts in issue or are relevant, and of no others[3]. When either party proposes to give evidence of any fact, the judge may ask the party adducing the evidence to demonstrate the relevancy of the alleged fact, if proved, and the judge can admit evidence only if it is considered by the judge that the fact, if proved, would be relevant, and not otherwise. If the admissibility of the proposed fact depends upon proof of some other fact, that other fact must be proved before evidence is given of the fact first mentioned, unless the party undertakes to give proof of the other fact, and the judge is satisfied with such an undertaking. However, if the relevance of the first fact depends upon the admission of a second fact, it may be necessary for the second fact to be proved before evidence is given of the first fact. Documents are not admissible in evidence where the person who has executed the document and persons attesting them are not examined[4]. Section 3 of the Evidence Act provides for the trier of the facts to determine whether a case is proved, disproved or not proved, as follows:

'Proved'—a fact is said to be proved when, after considering the matters before it, the Court either believes it to exist, or considers its existence so probable that a prudent man ought, under the circumstances of the particular case, to act upon the supposition that it exists.

'Disproved'—a fact is said to be disproved when, after considering the matters before it, the Court either believes that it does not exist or considers its non-existence so probable that a prudent man ought, under the circumstances of the particular case, to act upon the supposition that it does not exist.

'Not proved'—a fact is said not to be proved when it is neither proved nor disproved.

Section 17 of the Evidence Act provides that any statement, whether oral or documentary or contained in electronic form, which suggests any inference as to any fact in issue or relevant fact, and which is made by any of the persons and under the circumstance mentioned under the Evidence Act, is an admission. Section 39 of the Evidence Act enables the admission of a statement that forms part of a longer statement, such as an electronic record or a connected series of letters or papers.

[1]   *Emperor v Panch Kari Dulla* AIR 1925 cal 587.
[2]   *Girdhar v Ambika* AIR 1969 Pat 218.
[3]   Evidence Act, s 5.
[4]   *Collector Raigarh v Hari Singh Thakur* AIR 1979 SC 472.

Relevance

10.14 Section 3 of the Evidence Act provides a definition of 'relevant' as follows:

One fact is said to be relevant to another when the one is connected with the other in any of the ways referred to in the provisions of this Act relating to the relevancy of facts.

The word 'relevant' in the Evidence Act means admissible[1]. The terms 'relevancy' and 'admissibility' are used synonymously, but their legal implications are distinct. The principle of 'relevance' indicates that judges are required to consider only relevant evidence and to consider whether a fact stands proved or not. In order to become relevant a fact must be admissible evidence under any one of ss 5 to 55 of the Act.

[1]   *Lala Lakhmi Chand v Haldar Shah* 3 CWN 268.

Appreciation

10.15 A fact which is relevant and admissible does not necessarily have to be construed as a proven fact. The process by which a judge concludes whether or not a fact is proved is called appreciation of evidence. It is a duty of the court to appreciate evidence minutely, carefully, and to analyse it[1]. Courts and tribunals have to judge the evidence before them by applying the test of human probabilities[2].

[1]   *Kajal Sen v State of Assam* AIR 2002 SC 617.
[2]   *Commissioner of Income Tax, West Bengal II v Durga Prasad More* AIR 1971 SC 2439.

Authentication and presumption

10.16 Section 4 and ss 79–90A of the Evidence Act deal with provision of presumptions. Authentication under the Evidence Act is not merely attestation, but requires that the person authenticating a document demonstrates the identity of the person who has signed the instrument as well as the fact of execution. It is useful to set out the presumptions in relation to electronic documents, as introduced into the Evidence Act by the provisions of Sch 2 to the IT Act. Section 85A provides 'the Court shall presume that every electronic record purporting to be an agreement containing the digital signatures of the parties was so concluded by affixing the digital signature of the parties'. Section 85B[1] provides further presumptions in relation to the use of secure electronic records:

(1)   In any proceedings involving a secure electronic record, the Court shall presume unless contrary is proved, that the secure electronic record has not been altered since the specific point in time to which the secure status relates

(2)   In any proceedings, involving secure digital signature, the Court shall presume unless the contrary is proved that—

    (a)   the secure digital signature is affixed by subscriber with the intention of signing or approving the electronic record;

    (b)   except in the case of a secure electronic record or a secure digital signature, nothing in this section shall create any presumption relating to authenticity and integrity of the electronic record or any digital signature.

In addition, s 85C provides that the 'Court shall presume, unless contrary is proved, that the information listed in a Digital Signature Certificate is correct, except for information specified as subscriber information which has not been verified, if the certificate was accepted by the subscriber,' and a presumption of the genuineness of official electronic records is governed by s 81A[2].

Provisions are made with reference to electronic messages in s 88A[3] of the Evidence Act, which enables a court to presume that where a sender sends an electronic message the content of the message is that contained in the message recorded in the sender's computer; but there is no corresponding presumption as to the person by whom such message was sent. Further, s 90A[4] provides presumption as to electronic records that are five years old.

[1]   Inserted by IT Act, Sch 2, s 13.
[2]   Inserted by IT Act, Sch 2, s 12.
[3]   Inserted by IT Act, Sch 2, s 14.
[4]   Inserted by Act 21 of 2000, s 92 and Sch II.

ADMISSION OF ELECTRONIC RECORDS

10.17 All electronic evidence falls within the generic definition of 'document' as defined in the Evidence Act and further described in the IT Act. The word 'document' in s 3 of the Evidence Act means:

> any matter expressed or described upon any substance by means of letter, figures or makes, or by more than one of those means, intended to be used, or which may be used, for the purpose of recording that matter.

The definition of evidence in s 3 of the Evidence Act 1872 has been amended by s 1 of the Sch 2 to the IT Act 2000 to include electronic records, as follows:

'Evidence' means and includes—

(1)   All statements which the Court permits or requires to be made before it by witnesses, in relation to matters of fact under inquiry; such statements are called oral evidence.

(2)   All documents including electronic records produced for the inspection of the Court; such documents are called documentary evidence.

Further, provisions relating to the accounting entries in account books in s 34 of the Evidence Act have been amended to include electronic records[1], and s 39 of the Evidence Act, providing for evidence in the form of a statement that forms part of a conversation, document, electronic record, book or series of letters or papers, has been amended to include the submission of electronic records in evidence. It is to be observed that the Supreme Court and High Court have in several cases held that tape recorded evidence is an electronic record and admissible in evidence[2].

The Evidence Act provides that the contents of documents may be proved either by primary or by secondary evidence. There are three distinct questions which are dealt with in the Evidence Act in this respect. First, there is the question of how the contents of documents are to be proved. Second, there is the question of how the document is to be proved to be genuine. Third there is the question of how far, and in what circumstances, oral evidence is excluded by documentary evidence[3]. The contents of a document must, in general, be proved by primary evidence but there are exceptional cases in which it may be proved otherwise. The evidence used to prove the content of document which is not 'primary' is called 'secondary'[4].

1   Information Technology Act 2000, Sch 2, s 12(4).
2   *Dwijadas Banerjee v State of West Bengal* 2005 Cr LJ 3115 Cal.
3   SK Sarkar *Law of Evidence* (6th edn, 2006) p 1107.
4   *Sarkar* (2006) p 1107.

10.18 Primary evidence means the document itself is produced for the inspection of the court[1]. Secondary evidence means and includes: certified copies, copies made from the original by mechanical processes which maintain the accuracy of the copy, copies made from or compared with the original, counterparts of documents as against the parties who did not execute them, and oral accounts of the contents of a document given by some person who has seen it[2].

Sections 65A and 65B provide special provision as to evidence relating to electronic record and admissibility of the electronic record[3]. The High Court of Delhi in the recent case of *M/s Societe Des Products Nestle v Essar Industries*[4], observed that:

According to Section 63(2) of the Evidence Act, secondary evidence inter alia means and includes, Copies made from the originals by mechanical processes which in themselves ensure the accuracy of the copy, and copies compared with such copies. Section 65 of the Evidence Act enables secondary evidence of the contents of a document to be adduced if the original is of such a nature.

Section 65(d) specially provides that secondary evidence of the existence, condition, or contents of a document may adduced if the original is of such a nature as not to be easily movable. By virtue of the provisions of section 65A, the contents of electronic records may be proved in evidence by the parties in accordance with the provisions of section 65B. Sub clause 1 of section 65B stipulates that any information contained in electronic record shall be deemed to be a document and shall be admissible in evidence without further proof or production of the originals, if the conditions mentioned in the said section are satisfied in relation to the information and computer in question. Sub-clause 2 of section 65B lays down the conditions required to be satisfied for admissibility of the electronic record and reads as follows:

65B(2) The conditions referred to in sub-section (1) in respect of a computer output shall be the following, namely:

    (a)   the computer output containing the information was produced by the computer during the period over which the computer was used regularly to store or process information for the purposes of any activities regularly carried on over that period by the person having lawful control over the use of the computer.

    (b)   During the said period, information of the kind contained in the electronic record or of the kind from which the information so contained is derived was regularly fed into the computer in the ordinary course of the said activities;

    (c)   throughout the material part of the said period, the computer was operating properly or, if not, then in respect of any period in which it was not operating properly or was out of operation during that part of the period, was not such as to affect the electronic record or the accuracy of its contents; and

    (d)   the information contained in the electronic record reproduces or is derived from such information fed into the computer in the ordinary course of the said activities.

In making presentation of an electronic document, the presenter may submit a readable form of the document in the form of a print-out. A question arises as to in such a case whether the print-out is primary evidence or secondary evidence. Section 65 of the Evidence Act refers to cases in which secondary evidence relating to documents may be given. However, the modifications made to this section by the IT Act have added ss 65A and 65B. Though these sections have been numbered as 65A and 65B, they are to be treated as independent sections. According to s 65A, 'Contents of electronic records may be proved in accordance with the provisions of Section 65B'. Section 65B states that 'Notwithstanding anything contained in this Act, any information contained in an electronic record which is printed on a paper, stored, recorded or copied in optical or magnetic media produced by a computer (herein after called the computer output) shall be deemed to be also a document.'

Computer-generated electronic records are considered as evidence and are admissible at a trial if proved in the manner specified by s 65B of the Evidence Act.

1   Evidence Act, s 62.
2   Evidence Act, s 63.
3   Inserted by IT Act 2000, s 92 and Sch 2.
4   Decided on 4 September 2006.

10.19 In the case of *State v Mohd Afzal*[1]the High Court of Delhi has observed that:

> The normal rule of leading documentary evidence is the production and proof of the original document itself. Secondary evidence of the contents of a document can also be led under section 65 of the Evidence Act. Under sub-clause 'd' of section 65, secondary evidence of the contents of a document can be led when the original is of such a nature as not to be easily movable. Computerised operating systems and support systems in industry cannot be moved to the court. The information is stored in these computers on magnetic tapes (hard disc). Electronic record produced therefrom has to be taken in the form of a print out. Sub-section (1) of section 65.B makes admissible without further proof, in evidence, print out of an electronic record contained on a magnetic media subject to the satisfaction of the conditions mentioned in the section. The conditions are mentioned in sub-section (2). Thus compliance with sub-section (1) and (2) of section 65B is enough to make admissible and prove electronic records. This conclusion flows out, even from the language of sub-section (4). Sub-section (4) allows the proof of the conditions set out in sub-section (2) by means of a certificate issued by the person described in sub-section 4 and certifying contents in the manner set out in the sub-section. The sub-section makes admissible an electronic record when certified that the contents of a computer print out are generated by a computer satisfying the conditions of sub-section 1, the certificate being signed by the person described therein. Thus, sub-section (4) provides for an alternative method to prove electronic record and not the only method to prove electronic record. The conditions which require to be satisfied are the ones set out in sub-section (2) of section 65B. The conditions, as noted above are—
>
> (a) The computer from which the record is generated was regularly used to store or process information in respect of activity regularly carried on by a person having lawful control over the period, and relates to the period over which the computer was regularly used;
>
> (b) Information was fed in the computer in the ordinary course of the activities of the person having lawful control over the computer;
>
> (c) The computer was operating properly, and if not, was not such as to affect the electronic record or its accuracy;
>
> (d) Information reproduced is such as is fed into the computer in the ordinary course of activity.'

In effect, s 65B of the Indian Evidence Act and s 69 (now appealed) of the Police and Criminal Evidence Act 1984 of England and Wales have substantially the same effect. Thus, in the context of s 65B(2)(c), the condition that the computer was operating properly throughout the material part of the period to which the computer operations related, has to be complied with.

Irrespective of the compliance with the requirements of s 65B, which is a provision dealing with admissibility of electronic records, there is no bar to adducing secondary evidence under the other provisions of the Evidence Act, namely, ss 63 and 65. As the Supreme Court of India observed in *State v Navjot Sandhu*[2], in relation to electronic evidence contained on servers that were not possible to physically move:

> According to s 63, secondary evidence means and includes, among other things, 'copies made from the original by mechanical processes which in themselves insure the accuracy of the copy, and copies compared with such copies'. Section 65 enables secondary evidence of the contents of a document to be

adduced if the original is of such a nature as not to be easily movable. It is not in dispute that the information contained in the call records is stored in huge servers which cannot be easily moved and produced in the court. That is what the High Court has also observed at para 276. Hence, printouts taken from the computers/servers by mechanical process and certified by a responsible official of the service-providing company can be led in evidence through a witness who can identify the signatures of the certifying officer or otherwise speak of the facts based on his personal knowledge. Irrespective of the compliance with the requirements of section 65B, which is a provision dealing with admissibility of electronic records, there is no bar to adducing secondary evidence under the other provisions of the Evidence Act, namely, sections 63 and 65. It may be that the certificate containing the details in sub-section (4) of section 65B is not filed in the instant case, but that does not mean that secondary evidence cannot be given in the circumstances mentioned in the relevant provisions, namely, sections 63 and 65.

[1]   107 (2003) DLT 385.
[2]   (2005) 11 SCC 600, and which Reva Khetrapal, J noted in *Societe des Products Nestlé SA v Essar Industries* I.A.No.3427/2005 in CS(OS) No.985/2005.

MISCELLANEOUS PROVISIONS

10.20 Section 35 of the Evidence Act provides for entries in official or public records, including those in electronic form. Under this section, three conditions must be satisfied for a document to be rendered admissible. First, the entry that is relied on must be one in any public or other official books, register, or records or electronic records; second, it must be an entry stating a fact in issue or relevant fact, and third, it must be made by a public servant in the discharge of his official duty.

The use of digital signatures is provided for by s 67A of the Evidence Act, which provides that, except in the case of a secure digital signature, if the digital signature of a subscriber is alleged to have been affixed to an electronic record, it must be proved that it is the digital signature of the subscriber. Further, s 73A provides that, in order to ascertain whether a digital signature is that of the person by whom it purports to have been affixed, the court may direct that the person or the controller or the certifying authority must produce the digital signature certificate.

Section 131 of the Evidence Act has been amended to include 'electronic records' in its remit. Section 131 contemplates cases where an electronic record belonging to another person is in the possession of the witness, and it provides that the person in possession of the document cannot be compelled to produce the documents unless the person with the right to refuse consent agrees to the production of the document by the person possessing the document.

Electronic governance and electronic filing in India

10.21 The IT Act makes it clear that the courts and the judiciary not only need to make decisions concerning new technology, but also must take advantage of that technology in undertaking their duties. For an interesting, although slightly dated, article see TK Viswanathan, 'Electronic agenda for the judiciary'[1]. At present, the website of the Supreme Court provides links to the websites of the High Courts and also provides a daily cause list online. The status of the cases filed is also available on these websites. The websites of the Supreme Court of India and the High Courts also provide judgments and orders of these respective courts. In the Supreme Court and all High Courts, fresh cases are filed before computerised Filing Counters. Judgments from 1999 onward are available via the Internet in the Judgment Information System[2].

More recently, the Supreme Court of India has, from October 2006, begun accepting the electronic filing of cases from October 2006[3]. The Delhi Police Headquarters has also launched a website[4] which can be used for lodging a first information report and the Patna High Court has decided to grant bail by way of an online bail application.

[1] (2003) *The Hindu*, 17 January, available online at http://www.hinduonnet.com/2003/01/17/stories/2003011700861000.htm.
[2] http://judisi.nic.in.
[3] http://supremecourtofindia.nic.in.
[4] http://delhipolice.nic.in.

Amendments to the Bankers' Book Evidence Act 1891

10.22 The provisions of Bankers' Book Evidence Act 1891, which provides for the copies of the entries in bankers' books being made receivable in evidence under certain conditions, have also been amended to enable banks to keep bankers' books in electronic form. The definition of 'bankers' books' has been modified to include ledgers, day-books, cash-books, account books and all other books used in the ordinary business of a bank whether kept in the written form or as printouts of data stored in a floppy, disc, tape or any other form of electro-magnetic data storage device[1]. A print-out of electronic data is acceptable, providing it is accompanied by a certificate, in accordance with s 2A.

[1] Inserted by IT Act 2000, Sch 3, s 1.

Information technology law in India

10.23 The High Court of Delhi has noted, in para 11 of the judgment in the application made in the case of *Societe des Products Nestlé SA v Essar Industries*, that

> Rapid rise in the field of information and technology in the last decade of 20th Century and the increasing reliance placed upon electronic record by the world at large necessitated the laying down of a law relating to admissibility and proof of electronic record. The legislature responded to the crying need of the day by inserting into the Evidence Act Sections 65A and 65B, relating to admissibility of computer generated evidence in the only practical way it could so as to eliminate the challenge to electronic evidence.

The IT Act is primarily based on the United Nations Commission on International Trade Law ('UNCITRAL') Model Law on Electronic Commerce and aims to provide the legal infrastructure for e-commerce and digital documentation in India. In order to meet the requirement of new digital era, the IT Act also amends the relevant provisions of existing legislations in India such as the Indian Penal Code 1860, the Indian Evidence Act 1872, the Bankers' Book Evidence Act 1891, and the Reserve Bank of India Act 1934. The IT Act also has extra-territorial effect in certain cases. The IT Act has tried to assimilate legal principles available in other laws relating to information technology enacted earlier in several other countries.

The Evidence Act as amended by the IT Act introduced the meanings assigned to the terms 'electronic form', 'electronic record', 'information', 'secure electronic record', 'secure digital signature', 'subscriber', 'digital signature', 'digital signature certificate' and 'certifying authority'. By appropriate amendments made in the Evidence Act, the concept of electronic evidence has been incorporated into law to provide the court with a framework to manage these new innovations in scientific technology.

Authentication of electronic records—digital signature

10.24 The IT Act provides for legal recognition of electronic transactions and digital signatures. Section 3 of the IT Act stipulates the method in which the electronic record should be authenticated. It provides only one method of authentication: digital signature. The digital signature as contemplated by the IT Act means the use of asymmetric crypto system and hash function which envelop and transform the initial record into another electronic record, and s 47A of the Evidence Act[1] provides that, when the court has to form an opinion as to the digital signature of any person, the opinion of the certifying authority which has issued the digital signature certificate is relevant fact.

Section 5 of the IT Act mandates that if any information or any other matter is required by law to be authenticated by affixing the signature then such requirement shall be deemed to have been satisfied if such information or matter is authenticated by means of a digital signature affixed in the prescribed manner. Section 10 of the IT Act gives power to the government to formulate rules prescribing the type of digital signature and the manner and format in which the digital signature shall be affixed.

The method of authentication of electronic records recognised by the provisions of the IT Act is technology specific and does not take into account other means of authenticating electronic records, such as electronic signatures which can be used by way of scanned handwritten signature appended to electronic message, a biometric device based on handwritten signatures (ie signing on computer screen or a digital pad using a special pen, which would analyse and store the signature as a set of numerical values), the use of personal identification number ('PIN'), and other methods, such as clicking on the 'OK' or 'I accept' button on a website.

A written notice under Indian law is capable of being satisfied by the name on a document sent by facsimile transmission, as in the case of *M/s SIL Import, USA v M/S Exim Aides Silk Exporters*[2], in which it was noted:

> A notice envisaged under section 138 can be sent by fax. Nowhere is it said that such notice must be sent by registered post or that it should be dispatched through a messenger. Chapter XVII of the Act, containing sections 138 to 142 was inserted in the Act as per Banking Public Financial Institution and Negotiable Instruments Laws (Amendment) Act, 1988. Technological advancements like Fax, Internet, Email, etc. were on swift progress even before the Bill for the Amendment Act was discussed by the Parliament. When the legislature contemplated that notice in writing should be given to the drawer of the cheque, the legislature must be presumed to have been aware of the modern devices and equipments already in vogue and also in store for the future. If the court were to interpret the words 'giving notice in writing' in the section as restricted to the customary mode of sending notice through postal service or even by personal delivery, the interpretative process will fail to cope up with the change of time.

It was held that 'if the notice envisaged in clause (b) of the proviso to section 138 was transmitted by Fax, it would be compliant with the legal requirement'[3].

The requirement of a written notice under Indian law is satisfied if the same is given in the form of a facsimile transmission or email. The notice by email can be sent instantaneously and its delivery is assured and acknowledged by a report showing the due delivery of the same to the recipient. This method is more safe, accurate, economical and quick than its traditional counterpart, popularly known as Registered Post Acknowledgement Due ('RPAD').

Although the digital signature has been legally recognised in India since 2000, its legal status has yet to be well-defined and interpreted, since the validity of digital signatures has not yet been challenged in any Indian court. The use of digital signatures is still not very common and has yet to be widely accepted. There are several reasons for this, such as the lack of infrastructure, absence of technological knowledge and cultural reticence. However, the use of digital signatures has been made mandatory in various sectors, such as banking, financial services, and filings with government departments. Since September 2006, the Indian Government has made it compulsory that all the statutory filings under the Indian Companies Act 1956 would be in electronic form only, which has to be authenticated by the use of a digital signature[4].

[1]   Inserted by IT Act 2000, Sch 2, s 7.
[2]   AIR 1999 SC 1609, (1999) 4 SCC567.
[3]   Para 19 of the judgment by KT Thomas and MB Shah, JJ.
[4]   Scheme for Filing of Statutory Documents and other Transactions by Companies in Electronic Mode, Notification No. S.O. 1844(E), dated 26 October 2006 issued by Ministry of company affairs [2006] 71 SCL 227 (St.).

Recognition of electronic records

10.25 Section 4 of the IT Act provides for the acceptance of documents in electronic format, and s 2(1)(r), in defining the term 'electronic form', provides the record can be stored in any format. The IT Act also recognises that if any law requires that any document, record or information needs to be retained for a specific period such requirement would be met by retaining the material in electronic form[1]. The attribution of an electronic record is governed by s 11, which sets out the presumption that a record will be attributed to the originator (as defined in s 2(1)(za)) if it was sent by them, under their authority, or if it was sent automatically, and the time of dispatch is determined under the provisions of s 13. Unless the mode of acknowledgement of receipt of the electronic record is agreed between the originator and the addressee, s 12 provides that the acknowledgement is deemed by any communication by the addressee either automated or otherwise or by any conduct of the address that sufficiently indicates to the originator that the addressee has received the electronic record.

[1]   IT Act 2000, s 7.

Jurisdictional issues in India

10.26 Before initiating any legal action in India it is imperative to ascertain the jurisdiction of the correct Indian court or forum to entertain and decide such action. 'Jurisdiction' means 'the legal authority to administer justice according to the means which the law has provided and subject to the limitations imposed by law'[1]. Section 61 of the IT Act provides that no court shall have jurisdiction to entertain any suit or proceeding in respect of any matter which could be decided by an adjudicating officer or the cyber appellate tribunal under the IT Act, and that no court or authority shall grant any injunction in respect of any action taken or to be taken in pursuance of any power conferred by or under the IT Act.

[1]   *Official Trustee, West Bengal v Sachindra Nath Chatterjee* AIR 1969 SC 82.

Jurisdiction for civil proceedings

10.27 As regards the jurisdiction of civil proceedings, s 9 of Code of Civil Procedure 1908 ('CPC') provides that the court shall have jurisdiction to try all suits of civil nature excepting suits of which their cognisance is either expressly or impliedly barred. Under CPC, one or more courts may have the jurisdiction to deal with subject matter such as the location of immovable property, place of residence, or work of a defendant, or the place where cause of action has arisen. When only one court has jurisdiction, it is said it has exclusive jurisdiction. Where one or more courts have jurisdiction over a subject matter, they are called courts of available or natural jurisdiction.

Pecuniary jurisdiction limits the power of the court to hear cases up to certain financial limits[1]. Subject to the pecuniary or other limitations prescribed by any law, jurisdiction also depends on where the subject matter is situated[2], where a suit is for compensation for wrong done to the person or to movable property[3], or where the defendant resides or the cause of action arises[4]. The term 'cause of action' has been judicially defined as bundle of facts and is a comprehensive term not confined to suits under the CPC, but covering other proceedings as well. Where the cause of action arises from contract, and the parties have not effectively selected the governing substantive law, the relevant criteria in identifying the appropriate jurisdiction are, the place of contracting, the place of negotiation of the contract, the place of performance, the location of the subject matter of the contract and the location of the parties.

Indian courts have followed the same policies as English courts in connection with the recognition and enforcement of foreign forum selection clauses in international commercial contracts. For commercial contracts between Indian and foreign companies, the intention of the parties would govern the question of jurisdiction[5]. Parties cannot by agreement confer jurisdiction on courts not inherently possessing such jurisdiction[6], and the choice of forum by agreement is not exercisable where only one court has jurisdiction[7].

In *National Thermal Power Corp v The Singer Co*[8], the Supreme Court of India held that the expression 'proper law of a contract' refers to the legal system by which the parties to the contract intended their contract to be governed. If their intention is expressly stated, or if it can be clearly inferred from the contract itself or its surrounding circumstances, such intention determines the proper law of the contract. Where two or more courts have jurisdiction under the CPC to try a particular suit, an agreement between the parties that any dispute between them will be tried in one of such courts is binding in India[9].

[1]   CPC, s 6.
[2]   CPC, s 16.
[3]   CPC, s 19.
[4]   CPC, s 20.
[5]   *National Thermal Power Corp v The Singer Co* AIR 1993 SC 998.
[6]   *Hakam Sing v Gammon (India) Ltd* AIR 1971 SC 740.
[7]   *G.M., ONGC, Sibsagar, Assam v Raj Engg. Corp* AIR 1987 Cal 165.
[8]   AIR 1993 SC 998.
[9]   *Globe Transport Corporation v Triveni Engineering Works* (1983) 4 SCC 707.

Jurisdiction for criminal cases

10.28 It is a principle of common law that all crimes are local unless they are intended by Parliament to be extra-territorial. Section 4 of the Indian Penal Code 1860 ('IPC') and s 188 of the Criminal Procedure Code 1973 ('CrPC') make a conspicuous departure from this common law rule. Section 4 of the IPC states that all offences under the Code, without any exception, will be extra-territorial and s 188 of the CrPC confers jurisdiction on the court within whose locality the accused is found. In other words, s 188 of the CrPC decides the venue of the trial. Where a crime is committed beyond the limits of India and the offender is found within the jurisdictional limits, the accused may be given up for trial in the country where the offence was committed, or they may be tried in India. It is significant to note that s 3 of the IPC deals with any person liable by any Indian law to be tried for an offence committed outside India. It is clear that, without leave of the government, no offence committed by Indian citizen abroad is triable in India. A person who is a citizen of India is liable to be tried by the courts of India for acts done by them, partly within and partly without the Indian territories, provided the acts amount together to an offence under the code.

Every offence shall ordinarily be inquired into and tried by a court within whose local jurisdiction it was committed[1]. Section 177 of CrPC leaves the place of trial open. Where an offence consists of several acts done in different areas, it may be enquired into or tried by a court having jurisdiction over any of the local areas[2].

[1]   CrPC, s 177.
[2]   *K Bhaskaran v Sankaran Vidhyan Balan* AIR 1999 SC 3762.

Jurisdiction for international cases

10.29 Section 75 of the IT Act extends jurisdiction to any offence or contravention committed by any person outside India. Further, the section also states that the nationality of such a person is not a relevant consideration. The only requirement in assuming jurisdiction by an Indian court is that the act or conduct constituting the offence or contravention must involve a computer, computer system, or computer network which is located in India. India has not yet adopted international co-operation or bilateral extradition treaties.

India has no specific laws regarding Internet jurisdiction. However, India's relevant laws on international commercial contracts confer jurisdiction on foreign courts to adjudicate disputes between the parties. Under Indian law, in breach of contract cases the cause of action arises where the contract is made, where the contract is to be performed, or where the performance thereof is completed; where, in performance of the contract, any money to which the suit relates is payable; where breach occurs[1].

[1]   CPC, s 20.

Civil proceedings

10.30 Under the CPC, all documents relied upon by a plaintiff are required to be produced along with the plaint, if they be with the plaintiff or, if not, the plaintiff is to specify the persons with whom they are placed. The defendant is also required to produce all the documents relied upon by them when they file the written statement.

In any case, all original documents have to be placed on record before the framing of issues by the court[1]. Adverse parties, by leave of the court, have the right to call for inspection and discovery of documents from the opposite party and, upon failure of the party to comply in situations not exempted by the court, the party refusing or failing to produce such documents shall be prevented and precluded from producing the documents later[2]. This is, of course, subject to the exception of documents produced for the purpose of cross-examination of the adverse parties.

Pre-trial

10.31 Civil proceedings are instituted by presentation of the plaint before the court of appropriate jurisdiction as provided under the CPC and rules made by the High Courts. The plaint has to be presented to the court or to its officer either in person or by a recognised agent or pleader of the interested party within the limitation specified under the Limitation Act 1963. The rules made by some of the High Courts require the plaint to be supported by an affidavit stating the genuineness of the claim of the plaintiff and of the documents upon which they rely, while no such affidavit is required under the rules made by some of the High Courts.

Summons and discovery

10.32 When the summons is issued, it should be served on the defendant within 30 days of the date of institution of the suit to enable the defendant to appear and answer the claim on a day specified in the summons[1]. Every summons must be accompanied by a copy of the plaint, and delivery of the summons can be made by means of registered post, speed post, courier services approved by the High Court, facsimile transmission or email service provided for by the rules made by the High Court[2].

Section 28 of IT Act provides powers of investigating into any contravention of the Act lie with the Controller of Certifying Authorities. Section 28 provides the powers to the Controller and any other officer authorised by him to investigate the contraventions of Ch IX. It states that the Controller shall have powers similar to those of the Income Tax Authorities as laid down in Ch XIII of the Income Tax Act of 1961. Chapter XIII of the Income Tax Act 1961 confers upon the Income Tax Authorities powers of a civil court under the Civil Procedure Code, for the following purposes:

(a) discovery and inspection of witnesses;
(b) enforcing the attendance of persons;
(c) compelling the production of documents; and
(d) issuing commissions.

Under s 30 of the CPC, all civil courts have the general powers to make any order that is necessary in respect of the delivery and answering of interrogatories, the admission of documents, facts and discovery, inspection, production, impounding and return of documents or other material objects producible as evidence; issue summonses to persons whose attendance is required either to give evidence or to produce documents or such other objects and order that any fact may be proved by affidavit. Original documents are to be produced at or before the settlement of issues.

Costs

10.33 Section 35 of the CPC provides for the ability to award costs. The award of costs is entirely at the discretion of the court subject to such conditions and limitations as may be prescribed and to the provision of any law for the time being in force[1].

[1]   *K. Madna Vati v Raghunath Singh* AIR 1976 HP 41 at 51.

CRIMINAL PROCEEDINGS

10.34 In criminal cases, the law has devised a dual system whereby the prosecution may be by an aggrieved individual or by the State. The Indian Penal Code, 1860 ('IPC') is the general penal law of the land in which various offences have been specified by statute. Legislative amendments following the passing of the IT Act have incorporated amendments to include the electronic form of documents and to include offences relevant to the electronic environment.

Section 29A of IPC provides that the words 'electronic record' mean data, record or data generated, images or sound stored, received or sent in an electronic form, or micro film or computer-generated microfiche. Whilst IPC gives meaning to the word 'electronic records' under s 29A it is necessary to resort to the meaning of the words 'computer' and 'data' as given in s 2(1)(i) and s 2(1)(o) of the IT Act. The word 'electronic form' used in the definition of electronic record is further defined in s 2(1)(r) of the IT Act which reads with reference to information, means any information generated, sent, received or stored in media, magnetic, optical, computer memory, micro film, computer generated microfiche or similar evidence.

Types of offences

10.35 Offences have been put into one of two categories: cognisable and non-cognisable. Serious offences have been categorised as cognisable cases whereby the State, through the police, may (by statutory authority), take cognisance of the offence and start an investigation and, if satisfied by the identification and arrest of the alleged offender, submit a police report (referred to as the charge sheet) to the appropriate court for prosecution and trial. In such cases, all documentary evidence sought to be relied upon by the prosecution is submitted together with the charge sheet, unless it is too voluminous or inconvenient to produce. It is incumbent upon the magistrate to ensure that copies of all documents relied upon by the prosecution are made available to the accused before the framing of the charge.

In non-cognisable cases, no police officer investigates the alleged offence without the order of a magistrate. By this means, an aggrieved party is required to file a private complaint before a magistrate seeking cognisance by the court of the complaint and for the prosecution of the alleged offender. In such cases, all documents relied upon by the complainant must be filed at the time of the filing of the complaint.

Section 2 of CrPC provides that a 'cognisable offence' is an offence for which a police officer may, in accordance with the first schedule or under any other law for the time being in force, arrest without warrant. Section 2(l) of the CrPC provides that a 'non-cognisable offence' is an offence for which a police officer has no authority to arrest without warrant. The definition of 'cognisable offence' is applicable to all offences under the IPC as well as other laws that are applicable. However, for cognisance of offences under other laws, Sch I to the CrPC provides that offences under other laws that are punishable by three years' imprisonment or more or the death penalty are cognisable and empower a police officer to arrest without warrant.

The offences under a law such as the IT Act are classified as cognisable or non-cognisable in accordance with Sch 1 to the CrPC. However, offences under ss 71–74 that are punishable by up to two years' imprisonment, and are thus non-cognisable in accordance with Sch 1, are deemed cognisable because of a special provision that enables police officers not below the rank of Deputy Superintendent of Police ('DSP') or any other authorised officer of the central government, to arrest persons for these offences without warrant.

Offences under the IT Act 2000

10.36   A wide range of offences are created under the provisions of Ch XI of the IT Act, and will be tried in accordance with the provisions of the CrPC. Offences include, but are not limited to,

(a)   tampering with computer source documents (s 65);
(b)   hacking (s 66);
(c)   the publishing in electronic form of information which is obscene (s 67);
(d)   the Controller may require a person to decrypt information (s 69);
(e)   securing or attempting to secure access to a protected system (s 70);
(f)   breach of confidentiality and privacy (s 72);
(g)   publishing false particulars in a Digital Signature Certificate (s 73); and
(h)   the creation, publication or otherwise making available a Digital Signature Certificate for any fraudulent or unlawful purpose (s 74).

Section 75 provides that the IT Act shall apply to offence or contravention committed outside India and s 76 enables the authorities to confiscate any computer, computer system, floppy disk, compact disks, tape drives or any other accessories.

Offences under the IPC

10.37 A wide variety of 'cyber crimes' under the IPC will be tried in accordance with the provisions of the CrPC. The range of offences created and relating to documents in electronic format includes, but is not limited to,

(a)   failing to produce an electronic document in court (s 172);

(b)   failing to deliver an electronic document to a public servant (s 175);

(c)   making false entries in an electronic record (s 192);

(d)   destroying a document in electronic format that is to be produced in a court, or renders illegible any such document with the intention of preventing the document from being produced or used as evidence before a court or public servant (s 204);

(e)   creating false documents (s 463);

(f)   forgery (s 466); and

(g)   the use of a forged record (s 471).

Investigation

10.38 'Investigation' means 'a minute enquiry; a scrutiny; a strict examination'. An investigation under the CrPC includes all proceedings for the collection of evidence conducted by a police officer or by any person, other than a Magistrate, who is authorised by a Magistrate. Thus 'investigation' shall include proceeding to the location of the crime, deputing a subordinate officer, ascertaining the facts of the case, discovery and arrest of the suspected offender, collection of evidence relating to the commission of an offence, examination of persons, conversion of an oral statement into writing, the search of premises, seizure of items as evidence, and concluding whether the evidence is sufficient for a charge-sheet to be drawn up.

In accordance with s 4 of the CrPC, all offences under any other law, other than the IPC, must be investigated, inquired into, tried, and otherwise dealt with according to the provisions of the CrPC, but subject to any enactment that regulates the manner or place of the investigation. Section 78 of the IT Act provides powers to investigate offences. Notwithstanding anything contained in the CrPC, a police officer not below the rank of Deputy Superintendent of Police is to investigate any offence under the IT Act.

Section 80 of the IT Act sets out the investigation procedures to be followed by police officers for investigating offences under the IT Act. Section 80(1) provides the authority to any police officer not below the rank of DSP, or any other officer of the Central Government or a State Government authorised by the Central Government in this behalf, to enter any public place and search and arrest without warrant any person who is reasonably suspected of having committed, or of committing, or of being about to commit, any offence under the Act. Section 81 of the IT Act makes it clear that the provisions of the Act shall have effect notwithstanding any inconsistency contained in any other law in force. This implies that conflicting sections of CrPC are not applicable in respect of the IT Act. Only those provisions of the CrPC that are not expressly negated by, or contradict the provisions of, the IT Act are applicable.

The Central Bureau of Investigation ('CBI') set up a special cell for investigating cyber crime in March 2000. It is called the Cyber Crime Investigation Cell ('CCIC') and is headed by a Superintendent of Police. This cell has jurisdiction to investigate cyber crime across India. Besides the offences punishable under IT Act it also has power to investigate other high-tech crimes[1].

[1]   http://cybercrime.planetindia.net/cybercrime_cell.htm.

Search and seizure of digital evidence

10.39 In India search and seizure is carried out in accordance with the provisions of the CrPC. A court has the powers to issue a search warrant to obtain any document or item under the provisions of s 93 of the CrPC for the purposes of a trial. The police also have powers to undertake a search when there are reasonable grounds to believe that it is necessary for the purposes of an investigation into an offence. The CBI has provided guidelines for search and seizure relating to cyber crime[1].

[1]   http://cbi.nic.in/AboutUs/Manuals/Chapter_18.pdf.

Cyber Forensics Laboratory

10.40 The Cyber Forensics Laboratory ('CFL'), established in November 2003, functions under the Director of the Central Forensic Science Laboratory. The responsibilities of CFL are to:

(a)   provide media analysis in support of criminal investigations by CBI and other law enforcement agencies;
(b)   provide on-site assistance for computer search and seizure upon request;
(c)   provide consultation on investigations or activities in which media analysis is probable or occurring;
(d)   provide expert testimony; and
(e)   undertake research and development in cyber forensics.

The following principles are followed by the CFL:

(a)   the purpose of the analysis shall be to use as evidence in court;
(b)   all legal formalities shall be followed;
(c)   the media should have been legally seized and chain of custody maintained;
(d)   the analysis shall be on an image of the media and not on the media itself; and
(e)   the laboratory shall have the best imaging tools and software tools for analysis.

Privacy

10.41 As far as existing privacy regulations are concerned, India has adequately dealt with some of these by the IT Act Ch XI, s 72, which provides a penalty for the breach of confidentiality and privacy where any person who secures any electronic record, book, register, correspondence, information, document or other material without prior consent and discloses the information to a third party is punishable under the Act. The punishment ranges from imprisonment or a fine, which may extend to Rs100,000, or both.

Chapter 11

IRELAND

RUTH CANNON

INTRODUCTION

11.01 The crucial statutory provision dealing with electronic evidence in Ireland is s 22 of the Electronic Commerce Act 2000 ('ECA 2000') which provides as follows:

'In any legal proceedings[1], nothing in the application of the rules of evidence shall apply so as to deny the admissibility in evidence of

    (a)   an electronic communication[2], an electronic form of a document, an electronic contract[3], or writing in electronic form[4]
        (i)   on the sole ground that it is an electronic communication, an electronic form of a document, an electronic contract, or writing in electronic form, or
        (ii)   if it is the best evidence that the person or public body adducing it could reasonably be expected to obtain, on the grounds that it is not in its original form,

    or
    (b)   an electronic signature[5]
        (i)   on the sole ground that the signature is in electronic form, or is not an advanced electronic signature, or is not based on a qualified certificate, or is not based on a qualified certificate issued by an accredited certification service provider, or is not created by a secure signature creation device, or
        (ii)   if it is the best evidence that the person or public body adducing it could reasonably be expected to obtain, on the grounds that it is not in its original form.'

---

[1]   ECA 2000, s 2(1) defines 'legal proceedings' as 'civil or criminal proceedings, and includes proceedings before a court, tribunal, appellate body of competent jurisdiction or any other body or individual charged with determining legal rights or obligations'.

[2]   ECA 2000, s 2(1) defines 'electronic communication' as 'information communicated or intended to be communicated to a person or public body, other than its originator, that is generated, communicated, processed, sent, received, recorded, stored or displayed by electronic means or in electronic form, but does not include information communicated in the form of speech unless the speech is processed at its destination by an automatic voice recognition system'. 'Information' is further defined in s 2(1) as 'data, all forms of writing and other text, images (including maps and cartographic material), sound, codes, computer programmes, software, databases and speech.'

[3]   ECA 2000, s 2(1) defines 'electronic contract' as 'a contract concluded wholly or partly by means of an electronic communication.'

[4]   ECA 2000, s 2(1) defines 'electronic' as electrical, digital, magnetic, optical, electro-magnetic, biometric, photonic and any other form of related technology.'

[5]   ECA 2000, s 2(1) defines 'electronic signature' as 'data in electronic form attached to, incorporated in or logically associated with other electronic data and which serves as a method of authenticating the purported originator, and includes an advanced electronic signature'. 'Advanced electronic signature' is defined as an electronic signature (a) uniquely

linked to the signatory, (b) capable of identifying the signatory, (c) created using means that are capable of being maintained by the signatory under his, her or its sole control, and (d) linked to the data to which it relates in such a manner that any subsequent change of the data is detectable.

11.02 Following the enactment of ECA 2000, s 22, it is no longer possible to exclude electronic evidence solely on the basis that it is in electronic form. The best evidence rule has also been modified significantly in relation to such evidence. However, there still remain a considerable number of hurdles which have to be overcome in order for such evidence to be admissible in Irish courts. In particular, the hearsay rule, although abrogated to some extent in relation to criminal proceedings[1], is still of full force and effect in relation to most civil proceedings. It will be seen that the issue of electronic evidence is something which is only starting to be considered by the courts in this jurisdiction.

[1]   Criminal Evidence Act 1992, s 5.

OBTAINING ELECTRONIC EVIDENCE IN CRIMINAL PROCEEDINGS

11.03 Members of the Irish police force (the Garda Siochana) have a common law power to seize evidence found in the course of a lawful search, irrespective of whether or not such evidence is related to the purpose of the search[1]. This power was recognised and extended by s 9 of the Criminal Law Act 1976 ('CLA 1976') which states that where, in the course of a search carried out under any power, a member of the Garda Siochana, a prison officer or a member of the Defence Forces finds or comes into possession of anything which he believes to be evidence of any offence, or suspected offence, this may be seized and retained by him for use as evidence in any criminal proceedings for such period from the date of seizure as is reasonable[2]. Section 7 of the Criminal Justice Act 2006 ('CJA 2006') extends this power of seizure to evidence found in a public place or in the course of a consensual search.

[1]   *Dillon v O'Brien and Davitt* (1887) 16 Cox CC 245; *Chic Fashions (West Wales) Ltd v Jones* [1968] 2 QB 299. This latter case appears to have been implicitly accepted by Hardiman J in *Dunne v DPP* [2002] IESC 27.
[2]   s 9(2) prohibits the seizure of documents which are represented or appears to be made for the purpose of obtaining, giving or communicating legal advice. A similar provision is included in CJA 2006, s 7.

11.04 In most cases, a search warrant is required before a search can be carried out. However a search of premises consequent on a lawful entry for the purpose of arrest does not require a warrant. A new summary search power has recently been introduced by CJA 2006, s 5(3) in respect of an area designated a crime scene. In addition there are a number of miscellaneous statutes permitting search without warrant in specified situations.

Search in the course of an arrest

11.05 Gardai lawfully entering property for the purposes of effecting an arrest have implied permission to search the part of the property where the suspect was found[1], as well as all other parts of the property under his control[2]. There is a common law right to search a person following arrest[3], although it is unclear whether or not this right extends to permit a strip-search[4].

1   *Dillon v O'Brien* 20 LR (IR) 300.
2   *Jennings v Quinn* [1968] IR 305.
3   *Bessell v Wilson* 20 LT (OS) 233.
4   The normal procedure is to rely on specific statutory provisions in order to justify a strip-search, e g the Misuse of Drugs Act 1977, s 23.

11.06 Section 6(1) of the Criminal Law Act 1997 allows a member of the Garda Siochana to enter any premises (including a dwelling) for the purpose of arresting a person on foot of a arrest warrant or pursuant to an order of committal[1]. Section 6(2) also permits entry for the purposes of effecting an arrest without warrant in respect of an arrestable offence[2]. Where the premises to be entered under s 6(2) is a dwelling other than the ordinary residence of the person to be arrested, the power of entry is subject to a number of constraints[3].

1   This provision was recently amended by the Criminal Justice Act 2006, s 8.
2   'Arrestable offence' is defined by the Criminal Law Act 1997, s 2 (as amended by s 8 of the Criminal Justice Act 2006) as an offence for which a person of full capacity and not previously convicted may, under or by virtue of any enactment or the common law, be punished by imprisonment for a term of five years or by a more severe penalty and includes an attempt to commit any such offence.
3   The Criminal Law Act 1997, s 6(2) states that in such case either the Garda must have observed the person in question within or entering the dwelling, or he or she must suspect, with reasonable cause, that that person will abscond or commit an arrestable offence before an arrest warrant can be obtained.

Search of an area designated as a crime scene

11.07 Section 5 of the CJA 2006 provides that a member of the Garda Siochana not below the rank of Superintendent may designate a place a crime scene where he has reasonable grounds for believing either that an arrestable offence has been or is being committed in that place, or that there may be in the place evidence relating to an arrestable offence committed elsewhere and it is necessary to designate the place as a crime scene to preserve, search for and collect evidence of, or relating to, the commission of this offence.

11.08 Section 5(4) states that any direction designating the place a crime scene may also permit entry and search of that place for evidence and the preservation, search or collection of any such evidence. A direction under s 5 remains in force for no longer than is reasonably necessary to preserve, search for and collect the evidence concerned[1]. Section 5(7) states that such direction, when made in relation to a place other than a public place, shall cease to be in force 24 hours after it is given. There is provision for extension of the direction by the District Court and subsequently by the High Court[2].

1   CJA 2006, s 5(6).
2   CJA 2006, s 5(9)–(11).

Evidence obtained pursuant to a search warrant

11.09 Section 10 of the Criminal Justice (Miscellaneous Provisions) Act 1997[1] provides that a judge of the District Court may grant a warrant for the search of any place[2] if hearing evidence on oath from a member of the Garda Siochana not below the rank of sergeant[3], he is satisfied that there are reasonable grounds for suspecting that evidence of or relating to the commission of an arrestable offence[4] is to be found at that place. The warrant may also extend to permit the search of any persons found on the premises the subject of the search[5].

1   As amended by CJA 2006, s 6.
2   The term 'place' is defined by the Criminal Justice (Miscellaneous Provisions) Act 1997, s 10 (as amended by CJA 2206, s 6) as a physical location including a dwelling, residence, building or abode, a vehicle, whether mechanically propelled or not, a vessel, whether sea-going or not, an aircraft, whether capable of operation or not, and a hovercraft.
3   Originally the evidence had to be given by a member not below the rank of inspector. This was amended by CJA 2006, s 6 which replaced the term 'inspector' with 'sergeant'.
4   s 10(6) states that 'arrestable offence' in this context has the same meaning as in the Criminal Law Act 1997 (as amended by CJA 2006, s 8). See 11.06 fn 1, above.
5   s 10(2)(c) specifically provides that 'anything' found at the place named in the warrant or on a person at that place may be seized if reasonably believed to be related to an arrestable offence. This provision bolsters CLA 1976, s 9. The word 'anything' is wide enough to cover electronic evidence.

11.10 There are also a number of miscellaneous statutory provisions providing for the issue of search warrants in specific situations[1]. ECA 2000, s 27 permits the grant of a search warrant by a district court judge on proof of reasonable grounds for suspecting that evidence of or relating to an offence under the ECA 2000 is to be found at a particular place[2]. Section 27(2)(c) provides for the seizure of electronic evidence obtained as a result of such a search. Where the item seized contains information or an electronic communication that cannot readily be accessed or put into intelligible form, s 27 grants the power to compel the disclosure of the information or electronic communication in intelligible form.

1   See D Walsh *Criminal Procedure* (2002) para 8.10 for a complete list.
2   An example of such an offence would be fraud and misuse of electronic signatures under ECA 2000, s 25.

11.11 A search warrant must state on its face the statutory power under which it has issued[1]. Most statutes providing for search warrants require reasonable grounds before the warrant can be issued and, if this is the case, it must be specifically stated on the search warrant that such reasonable grounds exist[2]. The warrant must also contain a description of the premises, the identity of occupier and specify the items of property within the scope of the search. However, it would appear that errors in relation to these latter matters do not necessarily render a search warrant void[3].

1   *DPP v Dunne* [1994] 2 IR 537.
2   *Simple Imports v Revenue Commissioners* [2000] 2 IR 243, specifically distinguishing the decision of the House of Lords in *R v IRC, ex p Rossminster* [1980] AC 952.
3   *DPP v Balfe* [1998] 4 IR 50, but note *The Competition Authority v The Irish Dental Association* [2005] IEHC 361.

Evidence obtained as a result of statutory provision authorising search without warrant

11.12   Certain regulatory statutes give the Gardai power to enter without a warrant and take away certain specified items[1]. These statutes apply to a variety of premises such as those used for the slaughter of animals[2], pawnbroking[3] and the sale of illicit liquor[4]. Reasonable suspicion of a criminal offence does not have to be present in order to enter pursuant to these statutes. A separate class of statutes permit entry without warrant on reasonable suspicion of a specified offence, such as the possession of explosives or chemical weapons[5], the health and welfare of a child[6], and drug trafficking[7].

1   See *Walsh* (2002) para 8.08 for a complete list.
2   Abbatoirs Act 1988, s 54(1).
3   Pawnbrokers Act 1964, s 46.
4   Illicit Distillation (Ireland) Act 1831, s 18.
5   Explosives Act 1875, s 33.
6   Child Care Act 1991, s 12.
7   Criminal Justice Act 1996, Sch 1.

Evidence obtained as a result of a production or access order

11.13   In certain limited circumstances, statute permits the making of production and access orders against third parties who, although not suspected of a crime, are believed to be in possession of information relevant to the commission of a criminal offence. Section 63 of the Criminal Justice Act 1994 permits a member of the Garda Siochana to apply for a production or access order in respect of material which he or she has reasonable grounds for suspecting is of substantial value to an investigation into drug trafficking or money laundering[1]. Such order will only be granted if there are also reasonable grounds for believing that it is in the public interest that the material be produced[2]. Production orders made under s 63 do not extend to material protected by legal professional privilege[3]. Where a production and access order is impracticable, s 64 permits the making of a search warrant in lieu.

1   That the term 'material' is clearly intended to include electronic evidence is made clear by s 63(7) which provides that where the material to which an application under this section relates consists of information contained in a computer, an order under sub-s (2)(a) of this section shall have effect as an order to produce the material in a form in which it can be taken away and in which it is visible and legible, and an order under sub-s (2)(b) of this section shall have effect as an order to give access to the material in a form in which it is visible and legible.
2   Criminal Justice Act 1994, s 63(4).
3   Criminal Justice Act 1994, s 63(8).

11.14 Section 52 of the Criminal Justice (Theft and Fraud Offences) Act 2001 also makes provision for the issue of production and access orders where there are reasonable grounds for suspecting that a person has possession or control of material which constitutes evidence of, or relating to, the commission of any offence under that Act punishable by imprisonment for a term of five or more years or a more severe penalty[1].

[1]   The Criminal Justice (Theft and Fraud) Offences Act 2001, s 52(3) is in similar terms to the Criminal Justice Act 1994, s 63(7), discussed above.

Duty to seek out and preserve evidence when obtained

11.15 In contrast to England and Wales, where the authorities have the benefit of a Code of Practice and the Attorney General's Guidelines, there are no statutory or regulatory rules in Ireland regulating the preservation of evidence obtained as a result of a search and seizure. A series of recent decisions have, however, recognised the Gardai as being subject to a common law duty to preserve all evidence relevant to the guilt or innocence of the accused[1]. This duty arises irrespective of whether the evidence assists the case that the prosecution is advancing. If it can be shown that failure to comply with this duty has led to a real risk of an unfair trial, the courts will prohibit the trial[2]. Although most of the cases have involved a duty to preserve rather than to seek out evidence, it is clear from obiter statements in these cases that a failure by the Gardai to seek out evidence may also constitute a breach of this duty. As such the rights of search and seizure set out in the first part of this section would appear to be mandatory, rather than discretionary, at least where there is a real possibility that the exercise of such rights might produce relevant and admissible evidence.

[1]   *Braddish v DPP* [2001] IESC 45, [2002] 1 ILRM 151 (18 May 2001); *Dunne v DPP* [2002] IESC 27.
[2]   It is not necessary to show that a fair trial cannot occur: a real risk that it may not occur is sufficient for this purpose.

OBTAINING ELECTRONIC EVIDENCE IN CIVIL PROCEEDINGS

Anton Piller orders

11.16 Irish courts may make Anton Piller orders requiring the defendant to consent to the plaintiff, attended by his solicitor, entering the premises to inspect and if appropriate take away any documents or articles contained in the order.

11.17 In *Microsoft Corp and Symantec Corp v Brightpoint Ireland Ltd*[1], Microsoft alleged that the defendant company had been involved in the widespread unlawful copying, use, distribution, possession and networking of the plaintiffs' software programs. An ex parte order was made by Quirke J allowing representatives of the plaintiff to enter onto to the defendant's premises for the purposes of inspection, detention and preservation of all

software appearing to be infringing copies of the plaintiff's computer programs in the possession, custody or control of the defendant its servants or
agents.

1   [2000] IEHC 194, [2001] 1 ILRM 540.

11.18 A subsequent attempt by the defendant to set aside this order was
rejected by Smyth J, who held that in the circumstances there had been strong
prima facie evidence of dishonest conduct by the defendant which, in the
circumstances, presented a high probability that the records might be
destroyed. Smyth J also rejected the defendant's argument that the in camera
hearing of ex parte Anton Piller applications and the failure to publish an
order granted on foot of such an application violated the constitutional
obligation that justice should be heard in public[1], pointing out that the
publication of the existence and contents of an Anton Piller Order in advance
of its execution could weaken the element of surprise crucial to the effectiveness of such orders.

1   The Constitution of Ireland, 1937, Art 34.5.1.

11.19 The defendant also argued that the granting of the order breached the
privilege against self-incrimination. Smyth J avoided this issue on the facts of
the case stating that, since the defendant had expressly stated that there were
no infringing copies in his premises, the issue of self-incrimination did not
apply. It may not, however, be possible to sidestep this issue as easily in future
cases. As one commentator has remarked

> While there have been few cases involving the Anton Piller orders in which
> written judgments have been delivered in this jurisdiction, such orders are being
> sought with increasing frequency and legislative intervention to at least curtail
> the ... privilege [against self-incrimination] may well be necessary if these orders
> are to be effective[1].

1   H Delany *Equity and the Law of Trusts in Ireland* (3rd edn, 2003) p 541.

Discovery

11.20 The rules in relation to discovery are set out in the Rules of the
Superior Courts 1986, Ord 31, r 12[1], which deals with discovery of 'documents'. The term 'document' is not defined in the Rules and a question arises
as to whether or not it extends to electronic evidence. In *McCarthy v Flynn*[2],
the Supreme Court held that 'document' in Ord 31 should be defined widely
so as to permit discovery of photographs and x-ray films. The ruling in this
case would appear to apply by analogy to electronic evidence[3] and, in
practice, discovery of such evidence tends to be granted on the same terms as
written evidence.

1   SI 1986/15, as amended by the Rules of the Superior Courts (No 2) of 1993 (SI 1993/265)
      and the Rules of the Superior Courts (No 2) (Discovery) 1999 (SI 1999/233).
2   [1979] IR 127.
3   In *Derby & Co v Weldon (No 9)* [1991] 1 WLR 652 it was held that a computer database
      and backup files were documents for the purposes of discovery.

11.21 Discovery will not generally be granted until after pleadings have closed[1] and should not generally be applied for more than 28 days after the matter has been set down for trial[2]. Since 1999, discovery can only be sought in respect of specified categories of documents relevant to matters before the court[3]. An applicant should first apply in writing for voluntary discovery, specifying the categories of documents in respect of which discovery is sought, and stating, in relation to each category, reasons why discovery of the documents in that category is necessary for the determination of the issues in the proceedings[4].

[1]   In very exceptional cases discovery may be granted prior to the close of pleadings: *Megaw v McDiarmid* (1882) 10 LR Ir 376; *Law Society of Ireland v Rawlinson and Hunter (a firm)* [1997] 3 IR 592; *AL v MN*, unreported, Supreme Court, 4 March 2002.
[2]   Or, in relation to a case which is not set down for trial, listed for trial: Ord 31, r 12(4)(4). However, r 12(4) specifically provides that this time limit can be extended by order of the court where it is just and reasonable to do so.
[3]   SI 1999/233 changed the law in this respect (see 11.20, fn 1). Prior to the coming into effect of this provision it was possible to seek a general order for discovery. In addition, the party against whom the discovery was sought bore the burden of showing that the discovery request was not necessary.
[4]   In exceptional cases this requirement may be waived.

11.22 If voluntary discovery is not furnished within a reasonable time, an application for an order for discovery may be made by motion on notice to the Master of the High Court. As with the request for voluntary discovery, the motion must specify the precise categories of documents in respect of which discovery is sought. It should be supported by an affidavit setting out, in relation to each category, the relevance of the discovery sought, stating that the other party is in possession of these documents and that discovery is necessary for disposing fairly of the matter or saving costs. The affidavit should also exhibit the request for voluntary discovery and confirm that this request has not been complied with. The Master has a broad discretion in relation to the granting of discovery[1].

[1]   One welcome development has been the circulation by the Master of written copies of his more complex judgments. Of these judgments, *Linsley v Cadbury Schweppes International Beverages Ltd* [2004] IEHC 18 gives, perhaps, the best overview of the approach currently being adopted in his Court.

11.23 Ord 31, r 29 of the Rules of the Superior Courts 1986 permits the making of an order for discovery against a person not a party to the proceedings where it appears that such person is likely to have, or have had, in his possession, custody or power any documents relevant to an issue arising, or likely to arise, in the cause or matter, discovery may be directed by the court. One factor to be taken into account in exercising this discretion is the oppression or prejudice which third party may suffer as a result of being required to disclose the documents.

PRIVILEGE

11.24 There are a number of grounds on which a litigant can avoid the disclosure of evidence on the basis of privilege. Legal professional privilege precludes the disclosure of communications between a client and his or her legal adviser for the purposes of giving or receiving legal advice. It also allows the client to prevent disclosure of communications between himself and the legal adviser and third parties, where such communications relate to contemplated litigation. Other examples of private privilege are sacerdotal and counselling privilege. In contrast to private privilege, public privilege involves a claim by the State to avoid disclosing information on the ground of the public interest. It is always possible for an individual to waive private privilege expressly or impliedly, however, in Ireland public privilege may also be waived[1].

[1]   *McDonald v Radio Telefís Éireann* [2001] 2 ILRM 1.

Legal professional privilege

11.25 In Ireland, legal advice privilege applies to all communications between client and solicitor made in the course of a legal relationship for the purpose of giving or receiving legal advice. It does not extend to documents prepared for the purposes of obtaining legal assistance, as opposed to legal advice[1]. Litigation privilege applies to communications between a client and a lawyer in relation to pending or contemplated litigation. Although is not necessary that the litigation be the sole purpose of the communication, it must have been the dominant purpose[2].

[1]   *Smurfit Paribas Bank v AAB Export Finance Ltd* [1990] 1 IR 469.
[2]   *Gallagher (a Minor) v Stanley and National Maternity Hospital* [1998] 2 IR 267.

11.26 Legal professional privilege can be set aside where necessary to avoid convicting innocent persons[1], or to ascertain the intention of a testator. Communications are not covered by the privilege if made for the furtherance of a criminal offence, fraud or any purpose injurious to the interests of justice[2]. The privilege may also be departed from in the case of proceedings under the Guardianship of Infants Act 1964[3].

[1]   There is no Irish authority on this matter. However, it is submitted that *R v Barton* [1972] 2 All ER 1192 is likely to be followed in this jurisdiction.
[2]   *Murphy v Kirwan* [1993] 3 IR 501.
[3]   This is a consequence of s 3 of this Act, which defines the welfare of the child as the paramount consideration: *TL v VL* [1996] IFLR 126.

11.27 Communications aimed at settling a legal dispute, and intended to be immune from disclosure if the negotiations fail, are similarly privileged from disclosure. In deciding whether or not communications fall within this category the court will examine the entire background to the making of the particular document before coming to a conclusion on the matter and will not be unduly influenced by the fact that the communication is headed 'without prejudice'[1].

[1]   *Ryan v Connolly* [2001] 2 ILRM 174 where letters were held not to be privileged under this head despite having been marked 'without prejudice'.

11.28 Priests and counsellors may also be able to claim privilege regarding statements made to them in confession and counselling sessions respectively[1]. Privilege may be claimed in respect of the identity of an informer, provided that the complaint made by the informer relates to a breach of criminal law[2]. Informer privilege is not absolute and may be set aside where the disclosure of the identity of an informant tends to show the innocence of an accused[3].

[1] *Cook v Carroll* [1945] IR 515; *Johnson v Church of Scientology, Mission of Dublin Ltd* [2001] 2 ILRM 110.
[2] *Buckley v Incorporated Law Society of Ireland* [1994] 2 IR 44.
[3] *Director of Consumer Affairs and Fair Trade v Sugar Distributors Ltd* [1991] 1 IR 225; *Ward v Special Criminal Court* [1998] 2 ILRM 493.

11.29 Public interest privilege has a narrower jurisdiction in Ireland than in England and Wales. Courts in this jurisdiction reserve the right to examine the document in respect of which public interest privilege is being claimed and come to their own decision on whether or not disclosure should be allowed[1], rather than deferring to the executive on this issue. For instance, there is no absolute privilege in this jurisdiction for communications between States[2]. It also appears that communications between police officers made in the course of duty would not necessarily be accepted as covered by public interest privilege. However, this does not mean that the courts will automatically reject a claim of public interest privilege. Rather, they will look at the particular document in respect of which privilege is sought and come to their own conclusions based on the nature of this document and the facts of the case before them.

[1] *Murphy v Dublin Corporation* [1972] IR 215; *Ambiorix v Minister for the Environment, Minister for Finance* [1992] ILRM 209.
[2] *Walker v Ireland* [1997] 1 ILRM 363.

ADMISSIBILITY OF ELECTRONIC EVIDENCE WHEN OBTAINED

11.30 Although ECA 2000, s 22 provides that an electronic communication, an electronic form of a document, an electronic contract, writing in electronic form or electronic signature cannot be held inadmissible in Irish courts solely on account of its electronic form, this does not exempt such evidence from the standard admissibility requirements applicable to evidence generally. In particular electronic evidence cannot be adduced in evidence to prove the truth of its contents unless it comes within one of the common law or statutory exceptions to the hearsay rule. The admission of such evidence may also be excluded on the basis that it was unlawfully or unconstitutionally obtained or, where it relates to past misconduct of the accused, on the basis that its prejudicial effect of adducing such misconduct outweighs its probative value. The best evidence rule, which applies to preclude secondary evidence of documents where the originals of same are still available, has however been mitigated by s 22.

Hearsay rule

11.31 Electronic evidence may be held inadmissible under the hearsay rule when adduced in evidence for the purposes of proving the truth of its contents. Irish courts accept that electronic evidence obtained as a result of a mechanical process, without the intervention of the human mind, does not come within the prohibition on hearsay and, on this basis, photographs, tape recordings and video recordings made by closed-circuit cameras have been held admissible in both criminal and civil proceedings subject to proof of authenticity[1].

[1]   *DPP v Colm Murphy* [2005] IECCA 1 (tape recordings); *Braddish v DPP* [2001] IESC 45, [2002] 1 ILRM 151 (video recordings). The principle laid down by the UK courts in *The Statue of Liberty; The Sapporo Maru M/S (owners) v Steam Tanker Statue of Liberty (Owners)* [1968] 1 WLR 739 was expressly approved by the Court of Criminal Appeal in *Colm Murphy*.

11.32 In *DPP v Brian Meehan*[1] the Court of Criminal Appeal held that a recording or other electronic data produced mechanically, without human intervention, was admissible as real evidence subject to the production of appropriate expert evidence to describe the function and operation of the electronic machinery. The impugned evidence in that case was a printout of a mobile telephone record showing calls made from a particular telephone.

[1]   [2006] IECCA 104.

11.33 However, not all electronic evidence should be regarded as having been created by a purely mechanical process. Computer files produced as result of data inputting necessarily involve an intervention of the human mind and as such require to be brought within one of the common law or statutory exceptions to the hearsay rule in order to be admissible. In *Meehan*, direct evidence was available in relation to those parts of the record (the name of the subscriber and the number allocated to him) produced by human intervention. The decision in *Meehan*, however, expressly leaves open the question of the admissibility of the printout had such direct evidence not been available.

Section 5(1) of the Criminal Evidence Act 1992

11.34 Section 5(1) of the Criminal Evidence Act 1992 ('CEA 1992') is particularly helpful in facilitating the admission of electronic hearsay in criminal proceedings. This section provides that information contained in a document compiled in the ordinary course of business and supplied by a person (whether or not he so compiled it and is identifiable) who had, or may reasonably be supposed to have had, personal knowledge of the matters dealt with therein shall be admissible in any criminal proceedings as evidence of any fact therein of which direct oral evidence would be admissible[1]. A document, for the purposes of s 5(1), is defined as including a map, plan, graph, drawing or photograph, or a reproduction in permanent legible form, by a computer or other means (including enlarging) of information in non-legible form[2]. Section 5(6) also provides that where information admissible under s 5(1) is expressed in terms that are not intelligible to the average person, an oral or documentary explanation of the evidence by a person competent to do so shall be admissible, subject to the condition that if contained in a document the document must be signed by the person providing the explanation.

¹   s 5(1)(c) imposes an additional requirement which has to be satisfied in relation to information in non-legible form produced in permanent legible form. In such case it is also necessary to show that the information was reproduced in the course of the normal operation of the reproduction system concerned. Section 5(3) excludes from the operation of s 5(1) information supplied by a person who would not be compellable to give evidence at the instance of the party wishing to give the information in evidence. Subject to two exceptions, it also excludes information compiled for the purposes of or in contemplation of any criminal investigation, investigation or inquiry carried out pursuant to or under any enactment, civil or criminal proceedings or proceedings of a disciplinary nature.

²   CEA 1992, s 2. Section 9 of the 1992 Act states that, where information is given in evidence pursuant to s 5(1), any evidence, which, if the person who originally supplied the information had been called as a witness, would have been admissible as relevant to his credibility as a witness shall be admissible for that purpose. In addition, evidence may, with the leave of the court, be given of any matter which, if that person had been called as a witness, could have been put to him in cross-examination as relevant to his credibility as a witness. Finally, evidence tending to prove that that person, whether before or after supplying the information, made (whether orally or not) a statement which is inconsistent with it shall, if not already admissible by virtue of s 5, be admissible for the purpose of showing that he has contradicted himself.

11.35 CEA 1992, s 6 requires the giving of advance notice to the other side of intention to adduce documents pursuant to s 5. A detailed certificate, outlining the documentation sought to be adduced and detailing compliance with each of the requirements in s 5, must be furnished to the other side within the time limit specified in s 7.

11.36 CEA 1992, s 8(2) gives a trial judge discretion to deny admissibility to all or part of a document qualifying under s 5 where he or she is of the view that it is in the interests of justice that the document or the appropriate part thereof ought not to be admitted. CEA 1992, s 8(2) states that in deciding whether or not the information should be admitted the court should have regard to all the circumstances, including

(a)   whether or not, having regard to the contents and source of the information and the circumstances in which it was compiled, it is a reasonable inference that the information is reliable;

(b)   whether or not, having regard to the nature and source of the document containing the information and to any other circumstances that appear to the court to be relevant, it is a reasonable inference that the document is authentic; and

(c)   any risk, having regard in particular to whether it is likely to be possible to controvert the information where the person who supplied it does not attend to give oral evidence at the proceedings, that its admission or exclusion may result in unfairness to the accused or, if there is more than one, to any of them.

Section 8(2) also states that, in estimating the weight, if any, to be attached to information given in evidence by virtue of s 5, regard should be had to all the circumstances from which any inference can reasonably be drawn as to its accuracy or otherwise.

11.37 Section 5(1), and its attendant sections in the Criminal Evidence Act 1992, are thoughtful and well-drafted provisions. However, s 5(1) does not necessarily guarantee the admission of all electronic evidence. It only applies to evidence compiled in the course of a business and, in addition, its operation is confined to criminal proceedings only[1]. There has been no general statutory abrogation of the hearsay rule in civil proceedings in this jurisdiction and such exceptions as have been created to the rule in civil proceedings are extremely narrow in scope. As such, the common law exceptions to the rule against hearsay may be of importance in securing the admission of electronic hearsay which does not comply with s 5(1).

[1] The hearsay rule is still enforced by the courts in civil proceedings: *Smithkline Beecham plc v Antigen Pharmaceuticals Ltd* [1999] 2 ILRM 190. However, the Law Reform Commission Report on the Rule against Hearsay in Civil Cases (LRC 25–1988) states at p11 that the courts freely allow hearsay evidence in civil cases when tendered by the defence. The parties are normally free in civil cases to agree between themselves for the admission of hearsay evidence. In addition the Rules of the Superior Courts, Ord 40, r 4, specifically makes provision for the inclusion of hearsay in affidavits supporting interlocutory applications.

Common law exceptions

11.38 The common law exceptions to the rule against hearsay in Ireland have traditionally been divided into four main categories: the res gestae exception; declarations of deceased persons, confessions and admissions and statements made in public documents.

11.39 Electronic hearsay will be admissible as part of the res gestae if it constitutes

(a) a spontaneous statement made by a participant/observer of a relevant event, relating to that event[1];

(b) a statement by a person performing a relevant act, accompanying or explaining it[2]; or

(c) a statement by a person relating to their contemporaneous state of mind, emotion or physical sensations it may be admitted as res gestae[3];

[1] *People (A-G) v Crosbie* [1966] IR 490.
[2] *Gresham Hotel Co v Manning* (1867) IR 1 CL 125.
[3] *Cullen v Clarke* [1963] IR 368; *Donaghy v Ulster Spinning Co.* (1912) 46 ILTR 33.

11.40 In addition, electronic hearsay statements made by a person who is now deceased are admissible if they qualify as declarations as to pedigree[1], declarations in the course of duty[2], declarations as to public rights[3], testamentary declarations[4] or declarations against interest[5]. A dying declaration by a deceased person regarding their cause of death is also admissible, albeit in murder or manslaughter cases only[6]. A confession (if valid) or, in the case of a civil case, an admission is also admissible as an exception to the hearsay rule[7].

[1] *Palmer v Palmer* (1885) 18 LR Ir 192.
[2] *Malone v L'Estrange* (1839) 2 Ir Eq R 16.
[3] *Duke of Devonshire v Neill and Fenton* (1877) 2 LR Ir 132.
[4] *Re Ball* (1876) 1 PD 154.
[5] *McKenna v Earl of Howth* (1893) 27 ILTR 48.
[6] *Smith v Cavan County Council* (1924) 58 ILTR 107. In this case the declaration was inadmissible because the trial was not one for homicide.
[7] *People (DPP) v Pringle* (1981) 1 Frewen 57 (confession in criminal proceedings); *Morrissey v Boyle* [1942] IR 514 (admission in civil proceedings).

11.41 Public documents are also available under a common law exception to the rule against hearsay if they contain matters of a public nature, have been compiled by a public official acting in the course of duty, have been intended to be available for public inspection and have remained so available[1]. A large number of public documents are also available under statutory exceptions to the hearsay rule[2].

1   *Mulhern v Clery* [1930] IR 649, where the document as held not to have been compiled in the course of a public duty.
2   Such as the County Boundaries (Ireland) Act 1872, s 4; the Pharmacy Act 1875, s 27; the Criminal Evidence Act 1992, s 11; and the Civil Registration Act 2004, s 13(4).

Miscellaneous statutory exceptions

SECTION 16 OF THE CRIMINAL EVIDENCE ACT 1992

11.42 Section 16 of the Criminal Evidence Act 1992 recognises a statutory exception to the hearsay rule in respect of criminal proceedings for offences of a sexual or violent nature[1]. Video recordings of evidence given by a person under 17 years of age through a live television link at the preliminary examination and statements made by a person under 14 years of age during an interview with the Garda Siochana or 'any other person who is competent for the purpose' are stated to be admissible in such proceedings as evidence of any fact in relation to which direct oral evidence would have been admissible. Video recordings of any statements made by mentally handicapped persons in preliminary examination or to a member of the Gardai or other competent person are also admissible under this provision[2].

1   The applicable offences are defined in the Criminal Evidence Act 1992, s 12 as follows: (a) a sexual offence (b) an offence involving violence or the threat of violence (c) an offence consisting of attempting, conspiring to commit, aiding, abetting, counselling, procuring or inciting the commission of such an offence.
2   Criminal Evidence Act 1992, s 19.

11.43 The court has discretion to exclude such recordings where necessitated by the interests of justice. In considering whether in the interests of justice the video recording ought not to have been admitted, the court shall have regard to all the circumstances, including any risk that its admission will result in unfairness to the accused

SECTION 4G OF THE CRIMINAL PROCEDURE ACT 1967

11.44 Section 4G(2) of the Criminal Procedure Act 1967 provides that a deposition taken in accordance with the provisions of the Act may be admitted in evidence if the witness is dead, is unable to attend, is prevented from attending or does not give evidence through fear of intimidation[1]. The accused must have been present at the taking of the evidence and have been given an opportunity to cross-examine the witness. The court has a jurisdiction to refuse to admit such deposition if it feels that it would not be in the interests of justice to do so.

1   The 1967 Act was amended by the Criminal Justice Act 1999, s 9.

11.45 *Ireland*

SECTION 16 OF THE CRIMINAL JUSTICE ACT 2006

11.45 This section provides for the admissibility, at a trial for an arrestable offence, of prior witness statements made by a witness who now refuses to give evidence, denies making the statement or gives evidence which is materially inconsistent with it. The statement may be admitted if direct oral evidence of the fact would be admissible in the proceedings, the statement was made voluntarily and is reliable. In addition the statement must have been given on oath or affirmation, contains a statutory declaration by the witness to the effect that the statement was true to the best of his knowledge or belief, or the court is otherwise satisfied that when the statement was made the witness understood the requirement to tell the truth. Section 18 provides for a list of competent persons, including a harbour authority, health boards and Ministers of State, to receive witness statements. Section 19 provides for the making of regulations by the Minister for Justice in relation to any witness statements which may be video recorded or audio recorded by members of the Gardai when investigating offences. At the date of writing these regulations have yet to become law.

SECTION 23 OF THE CHILDREN ACT 1997

11.46 Section 23 of the Children Act 1997 allows a statement made by a child to be admitted as evidence of any fact therein in any civil proceedings concerning the welfare of the child where the court considers that the child is unable to give evidence by reason of age or that the giving of oral evidence would not be in the welfare of the child. A statement in this regard is defined as any representation of fact or opinion however made and this definition taken together with the Electronic Evidence Act 2000, s 22 would appear to include statements made in electronic form.

11.47 As with the Criminal Evidence Act 1992, notice must be given to the other parties before this section can be exercised[1]. The notice must include such particulars of the evidence as is reasonable and practicable in the circumstances to enable the other party to deal with any matter arising from it being hearsay. The judge has a residual discretion to exclude such evidence if in his opinion it is not in the interests of justice that it should be admitted. One of the considerations that can be taken into account here is whether the admission would result in unfairness to any of the parties. Evidence may be called in relation to the credibility of the child where such evidence would have been relevant had the child been called as a witness either in examination in chief or cross-examination. Section 24 of the Act gives detailed guidelines regarding the weight to be attributed to statements admissible under s 23.

[1] The Children Act 1997, s 23(3).

BANKERS' BOOKS EVIDENCE ACTS 1879 AND 1959

11.48 The Bankers' Books Evidence Acts 1879 and 1959 provide for the admissibility of copies of entries from the books and records of a bank[1] as prima facie evidence of their contents. The term 'books and records' has been specifically amended so as to include electronic records. In order to be admissible under these provisions, the entry must have been made in the usual and ordinary course of business of the bank and the book or record must be in the custody and control of the bank.

1   The term 'bankers' books and records' is currently defined by the Bankers' Books Evidence Act 1879, s 9, as amended by the Bankers Books Evidence (Amendment) Act 1959, s 2 and the Central Bank Act 1989, s 131 to include records kept on microfilm, magnetic tape or any non-legible form, by the use of electronics or otherwise, which are capable of being reproduced in a permanent legible form together with documents which are typed, printed stencilled or created by any other mechanical or partly mechanical process in use from time to time and documents which are produced by any photographic or photostatic process.

The best evidence rule

11.49 The best evidence rule traditionally required proof of the original of a document. The rule, which has been abolished in the context of criminal proceedings by the Criminal Evidence Act 1992, s 30, still remains of full force and effect in relation to civil proceedings.

11.50 Although well-established that the rule does not require production of the originals of photographs, tapes, films or videotapes[1], its application to other forms of electronic evidence was less clear. For this reason ECA 2000, s 22 specifically provides that no objection shall be made to the fact that an electronic communication, an electronic form of a document, an electronic contract, writing in electronic form, or an electronic signature is not produced in its original form if it is the best evidence that the person or body adducing it could reasonably be expected to obtain.

1   *Kajala v Noble* (1982) 75 Cr App Rep 149.

11.51 Even in the case of electronic evidence not falling within the categories listed above, it should be possible to admit such evidence if it can be shown that the original of the document is not available, or it is not reasonably practicable to produce it in the circumstances.

Proof of authenticity

11.52 ECA 2000, s 22 does not limit in any way the rule regarding proof of authenticity, which is separate and distinct from the best evidence rule and still applies with full force and effect to electronic evidence. In the case of photographs, proof of authenticity involves the photographer proving that he took the photograph and, if he did not develop it himself, the person who did so proving that they developed it and that the negatives have been untouched since. In relation to tape and video recordings, it is necessary to prove the circumstances in which the tape or video recordings were made and to outline who had control of them from the date on which they were made to the date of the court proceedings. Where a copy of a photograph, video or tape recording is provided, the person who made the copy must also be available to swear that it is accurate.

11.53 The above principles would appear to apply by analogy to other electronic evidence, such as computer evidence. Given the susceptibility of such evidence to tampering, it is arguable that the above principles are not sufficient to ensure the integrity of electronic evidence and that further authenticity requirements guarding against possible tampering should be introduced. It is regrettable that the ECA 2000 did not deal with this issue. In *DPP v Brian Meehan*[1], the Court of Criminal Appeal stated that where electronic evidence was admitted, it would be necessary to produce appropriate expert evidence to describe the function and operation of the electronic machinery.

[1]   [2006] IECCA 104.

Unlawfully obtained evidence

11.54 In the Irish context, evidence obtained as a result of a deliberate and conscious breach of constitutional rights is inadmissible except in the context of extraordinary excusing circumstances[1]. In this context, the constitutional right most likely to be infringed is the right to inviolability of the dwelling. However, in *The Competition Authority v The Irish Dental Association*[2], business premises were searched pursuant to an invalid warrant and electronic evidence obtained. McKechnie J held that the evidence had been obtained as a result of a deliberate and conscious breach of the defendant's constitutional right to privacy, freedom of association and freedom of expression and was inadmissible.

[1]   *People (A-G) v O'Brien* [1965] IR 142.
[2]   [2005] IEHC 361.

11.55 The exclusion of electronic evidence which has been unlawfully, but not unconstitutionally, obtained is at the discretion of the trial judge[1]. In the *Irish Dental Association* case, Mc Kechnie J stated that even if the evidence had not been obtained in breach of the defendant's constitutional rights the evidence it should still be excluded as a matter of discretion balancing the interests involved.

[1]   *DPP v McMahon* [1986] IR 393.

Evidence of past misconduct

11.56 Electronic evidence relating to misconduct on the part of the accused, is inadmissible in criminal proceedings where its prejudicial value outweighs its probative effect[1].

[1]   *People (DPP) v BK* [2000] 2 IR 199.

RIGHT OF WITNESSES TO GIVE EVIDENCE BY LIVE TELEVISION LINK

11.57 The common law principle of orality remains part of Irish law[1]. Nonetheless, an increasing number of statutes now permit the giving of evidence by live television link in certain specified situations.

[1]   *Phonographic Performance (Ireland) Ltd v Cody* [1998] 4 IR 504, 521 and *Mapp v Gilholey* [1991] 2 IR 253, 262; this is a common law, rather than a constitutional principle, and as such may be abrogated by statute.

11.58 The Criminal Evidence Act 1992, s 13[1] provides for evidence, other than that of the accused, to be given via live television link ('tv link') in prosecutions for certain offences of sex and violence[2]. Where the person seeking to give evidence by live tv link is under 17 years of age or has a mental handicap[3] they will be allowed to give evidence in this form unless the court sees good reason to the contrary[4]. Other persons must obtain special leave of the court before they can give such evidence. All evidence given by live tv link must be video-recorded, and wigs and gowns are not worn by barristers in a court case involving such evidence.

[1]   As amended by the Criminal Justice Act 1999, s 18(3) and the Children Act 2001, s 257(3).
[2]   The offences to which s 13 applies are defined by s 12 of the 1992 Act (as amended by the Child Trafficking and Pornography Act 1998, s 10) as sexual offences, offences involving violence or the threat of violence to a person, offences consisting of attempting or conspiring to commit, or of aiding, abetting, procuring or inciting the commission of one of these offences, and offence under the Child Trafficking and Pornography Act 1998, s 3.
[3]   The Criminal Evidence Act 1992, s 19.
[4]   The issue of 'good reason' was discussed in *O'Sullivan v Hamill* [1999] 2 IR 9. The applicant was charged with having sexual intercourse with a person who was mentally impaired contrary to the Sexual Offences Act 1993, s 5(1). The judge made an order, without holding any enquiry as to the mental impairment of the victim, that she should be permitted to give her deposition by live tv link under the Criminal Evidence Act 1992. The applicant objected on the basis that the judge should have heard evidence to the effect that the victim had a mental handicap prior to making the order. O'Higgins J stated that an inquiry to establish mental handicap was not necessary before deciding whether or not to allow video link evidence. The trial judge had the right to grant video link evidence not only in respect of mentally impaired witnesses but in any case where he felt there was good reason to do so and in the circumstances good reason had been shown.

11.59 CEA 1992, s 18 provides that a witness giving evidence by live tv link, who testifies that the accused was known to her before the date on which offence was committed, is not required to identify the accused in court unless the trial judge, in the interests of justice, directs otherwise. In the alternative, if there is evidence by a person other than the witness to the effect that the witness identified the accused at an identification parade as being the offender, this also relieves the witness of the burden of having to identify the accused.

11.60 Where the person giving evidence by live tv link is under 17 or suffering from a mental handicap a direction may be made that questions be put to them through an intermediary in a way appropriate to their age and mental ability. Whether or not such direction should be made is a matter for the discretion of the court to be determined by the interests of justice.

11.61 Some further guidance in relation to the regulation of evidence given pursuant to CEA 1992, s 13 was provided by Kinlen J in *White v Ireland*[1]:

> The trial judge is in complete control of all the equipment. He will act in accordance with constitutional and natural justice and will ensure that there are fair procedures. If the accused is defending himself the judge can decide whether or not to make his image available to his accuser. In those circumstances his voice must personally be transmitted but not necessarily his image ...If there are any specific dangers arising out of a particular case counsel for the parties can undoubtedly deal with it and the judge in charge shall also deal with it. The usher is a very important officer. The usher should be in view of a camera in the room with the child witness. While the picture can be shut down it seems important that the sound link should not be broken. Thus the parties and the judge should be able, if necessary by earphones, to hear the conversation between the witness and the usher. Such conversations should be recorded and can be played back as required. It seems essential that there should be a constant eavesdropping of what is happening in the room. This is to prevent intentional or unintentional tutoring of the child witness[2].

[1]   [1995] 1 IR 268.
[2]   [1995] 1 IR 268 at 272–275.

11.62 Further provision for live television-link evidence in criminal proceedings is made by the CEA 1992, s 29 and the Criminal Justice Act 1999, s 39. CEA 1992, s 29 states that in the case of any criminal proceedings or proceedings under the Extradition Acts a person other than the accused or the person whose extradition is being sought may, with the leave of the court, give evidence through live TV link if based outside the State. In the case of extradition proceedings this has now been amended to permit the giving of live tv link evidence in such proceedings by persons within the State[1]. The Criminal Justice Act 1999, s 39 provides that, in any proceedings on indictment, a person other than the accused may, with the leave of the court, give evidence through a live tv link where the court is satisfied that that person is likely to be in fear or subject to intimidation in giving evidence. This statute contains provisions in relation to identification of the accused and video-recording of tv link evidence similar to those discussed in the context of the Criminal Evidence Act 1992.

[1]   The Extradition (European Conventions) Act 2001, s 24.

11.63 In the context of civil proceedings, the Children Act 1997, s 1 allows persons under 18 or with a mental disability to give evidence through live tv link with the leave of the court in any civil proceedings concerning the welfare of a child or person with mental disability. Where such leave is given, the court may also direct that questions be put through an intermediary. If evidence is given by the child or person with a mental disability that they knew the accused prior to the commencement of the proceedings, there is no need for them to identify the accused in court.

11.64 Order 63A, r 23(1) of the Rules of the Superior Courts 1986 is the most wide-ranging of the various statutory provisions permitting live tv link evidence[1]. This provision, which applies to proceedings in the Commercial

Division of the High Court, confers a general discretion on judges hearing such proceedings to allow any witnesses, whether situated within or outside the State, to give evidence by live tv link. Such evidence must be video-recorded.

[1] Rules of the Superior Courts (Commercial Proceedings) 2004, SI 2004/2.

CONCLUSION

11.65 The issue of electronic evidence has not been the subject of any detailed statutory consideration in this jurisdiction. The Electronic Commerce Act 2000, s 22 purports to provide for the admissibility of a number of significant categories of electronic evidence by making such evidence admissible on the same terms as documentary evidence generally.

11.66 However, the admissibility of documentary evidence in civil cases in Ireland is extremely limited, due to the continuing application of the hearsay rule in this context. As such, ECA 2000, s 22 in itself is not enough to secure the general admissibility of electronic evidence in civil cases where such evidence has been compiled as a result of human intervention. In many civil cases the rule is ignored or waived by the parties. However, if one party refuses to co-operate with this practice and objects to the admission of such evidence as hearsay his objection is likely to be upheld. In the circumstances legislation providing for either the abrogation of the hearsay rule in civil cases or, alternatively, the extension of criminal exceptions such as the Criminal Evidence Act 1992, s 5 to the civil context should be a priority.

11.67 Another criticism which may be made of ECA 2000 is that it fails to lay down any requirements for proof of authenticity of electronic evidence. Detailed guidelines in this area are needed as a matter of urgency. Computer evidence is peculiarly susceptible to tampering and the proof of authenticity requirements applied in relation to documents, photographs and videotapes are simply not adequate in this context. Statutory guidance would also be welcome regarding the weight to be accorded to electronic evidence, and the terms of any direction, analgous to the identification evidence warning, which might be given to a jury where such evidence is used in criminal cases.

11.68 A further difficulty, particularly acute in the context of witnesses giving evidence by live tv link, is that many Irish courts often do not have the facilities for the display and transmission of such evidence. This results in trials being delayed or moved to other parts of the country. In this regard, the proposed construction of a landmark Criminal Court Complex for Dublin, in which all courtrooms are intended to be cabled to support video conferencing and digital audio recording, is a positive development[1].

[1] Courts Services Press release, 18 November 2004; http://www.courts.ie/courts.ie/library3.nsf/16c93c36d3635d5180256e3f003a4580/81113bd5dd7b529a80256f50005e1356?OpenDocument.

11.69   *Ireland*

11.69 The willingness of Irish judges to adapt and develop the common law to deal with the challenges presented by electronic evidence, as shown in *Braddish* and subsequent case law, is also most welcome. More assistance will be needed in this regard if the statutory reforms suggested above are not forthcoming. New common law exceptions to the rule against hearsay may have to be developed in order to facilitate the admission of electronic evidence in civil cases. In the absence of statutory intervention, new safeguards, guidance and warnings will also have to be developed to properly control the use of such evidence. The benefits, and the pitfalls, of electronic evidence are only just becoming apparent in the Irish context. How we will deal with them still remains to be seen.

Chapter 12

NEW ZEALAND

LAURA O'GORMAN

SYNOPSIS OF THE EXISTING LAW OF EVIDENCE

Introduction

12.01 The law of evidence has developed significantly in New Zealand over the last decade to take account of developments in technology and, in particular, issues of electronic evidence. As referred to in this chapter, electronic material has had a major effect on disclosure and discovery of information and the ways in which electronic documents are managed and presented in court, both in civil and criminal hearings.

12.02 The New Zealand legal system is derived from the English legal system and is based on two main sources:

(a)   the common law, which is a body of law built up from cases decided in New Zealand courts and other similar jurisdictions, such as England and Wales and Australia. In the field of electronic evidence, cases from jurisdictions such as the United States are also having a significant influence on the approach to practical issues (for example, the discretion to order that parties share the costs of expensive forensic discovery to recover archived and deleted material). In New Zealand, most rules of evidence have been developed by the courts based on common law principles.

(b)   Statute law. A process has been under way for several years to codify the relevant evidential rules[1]. These reforms are contained in the Evidence Act 2006 which was enacted on 4 December 2006 but has not yet come into force[2].

---

[1]   *Evidence: Reform of the Law* (1999) New Zealand Law Commission, Report 55, vol 1 and *Evidence: Evidence Code and Commentary* (1999) New Zealand Law Commission, Report 55, vol 2.
[2]   The Act will come into force on a date to be appointed by the Governor-General by Order in Council and one or more Orders in Council may be made appointing different dates for different provisions.

Relevancy and admissibility rules

12.03 New Zealand courts in general follow the common law adversarial trial system in which the evidence produced by the parties must be both relevant and admissible.

Relevance

12.04 Evidence will be sufficiently relevant if it tends to prove or disprove a fact or matter in issue[1]. In other words, the evidence must be logically probative and persuasive[2].

1   *R v Fox* [1973] 1 NZLR 458, CA at 463.
2   *Jorgensen v News Media (Auckland) Ltd* [1969] NZLR 961 at 962.

12.05 In civil proceedings, there is an obligation prior to trial to provide discovery of all documents that 'relate to a matter in question in the proceeding'[1]. This is often described as a test of 'relevance'. However, it is of wider scope than evidence relevant to an issue at trial because it also includes information which may, rather than must, fairly lead the other party to a train of inquiry during the period leading up to the trial (see para 12.87).

1   High Court Rules, r 295(2).

Admissibility

12.06 Once the relevance of the evidence has been established, admissibility requirements must also be met. Relevant evidence will generally be admissible if there is no legal rule requiring its exclusion. These legal rules exclude evidence that is hearsay, opinion, character evidence, evidence of propensity which is not similar fact evidence, privileged information, or illegally or unfairly obtained, unless the evidence comes within an exception. Furthermore, evidence will not be admissible if it is confusing, repetitive and unnecessarily expensive or if its prejudicial effect outweighs the probative value.

12.07 Admissibility requirements are generally applied more stringently in criminal proceedings. In part, this reflects the fact that criminal proceedings have a higher standard of proof and the risk that juries may be unduly swayed by prejudicial evidence. In contrast, in civil proceedings the rules of relevance and admissibility are generally not enforced as strictly because the judge can assess these matters and take into account the weight that ought to be given to the evidence in the circumstances.

Primary and secondary evidence

12.08 New Zealand retains the distinction between primary and secondary evidence, whereby primary evidence is of a kind which 'provides best evidence of its existence and content'[1] and secondary evidence is permitted only when there is a sufficient explanation for not producing the primary version. In accordance with this distinction, the best evidence rule requires that, with regard to the content of a private document, the original should be produced or, otherwise, an explanation given as to why secondary evidence is offered.

However, this rule has been significantly relaxed in practice and in most cases no issue arises from producing copies if the genuineness of the document is not in issue[2].

1 Laws of New Zealand *Evidence* para 5.
2 See para 12.70. See also Evidence Act 2006, s 134(c).

Rules of production

12.09 Unless a specific exception applies, documentary evidence must be produced by a witness who can identify and authenticate the document and, if necessary, explain how it was created and retained, and the chain of possession leading to it being produced in court. It is necessary to lay the foundation before producing the evidence. This is usually done by the witness describing the factual circumstances and the exhibit as perceived at that time, to establish relevance and the fact that the witness has first-hand knowledge of the exhibit, having seen it at the relevant time or having been aware of its background. Then, when the evidence is shown to him or her in court, the witness authenticates it by confirming that the exhibit is what it purports to be and is in the same, or substantially the same, condition as when the witness saw it previously[1].

1 See Robertson *Introduction to Advocacy* (2000) pp 303–329.

12.10 In civil proceedings, production of evidence through witnesses in this formal way is not usually necessary because of the use of an agreed bundle of documents. The High Court Rules set out a regime whereby the parties agree to a common bundle of documents which are to be referred to by the witnesses or by counsel[1]. The documents in the agreed bundle should have been disclosed to all parties during the discovery process. Each document contained in the common bundle is, unless the court otherwise directs, considered[2]

(a) to be admissible;
(b) to be accurately described in the index to the bundle;
(c) to be what it appears to be;
(d) to have been signed by any apparent signatory;
(e) to have been sent by any apparent author and to have been received by any apparent addressee; and
(f) to have been produced by the party indicated in the index to the common bundle.

1 High Court Rules, rr 441M–441P. See Evidence Act 2006, s 130 which will introduce a procedure of notice when a party proposes to offer a document as evidence without calling a witness to produce it.
2 High Court Rules, r 441O(1). See Evidence Act 2006, s 132

12.11 If a party objects to the admissibility of a document included in the common bundle or any of the other assumptions above, that objection is to be recorded in the bundle index and the issue determined by the court. A document in the common bundle is received into evidence when a witness refers to it in evidence or when counsel refers to it in submissions, made otherwise than in a closing address. A document that is not incorporated in the common bundle may be produced at the hearing only with leave of the court[1]. Usually this will be done by agreement with the other parties by adding it to the common bundle as a supplementary document, otherwise formal production is required.

[1]   High Court Rules, r 441P.

Evidence in court

12.12   In both civil and criminal trials, witness evidence is usually given orally in court, on oath or affirmation. Traditionally, the evidence is given in the form of question and answer. The counsel who called the witness is only permitted to ask open, as opposed to leading, questions about relevant facts or issues. In civil proceedings the standard practice is now for signed written statements of each witness' evidence in chief to be filed and served in advance of the hearing. The written statements or briefs of evidence are then read in court, under oath or affirmation, as the evidence in chief of that witness. Opposing counsel is then entitled to cross-examine the witness by asking questions, including leading ones.

12.13   New Zealand courts are making progress in utilising modern technology to manage the complex system of information involved in court proceedings. New communications and information technologies allow for better management of a large volume of information and improve the ability of the parties to assemble, analyse and present information in a form that is coherent, easy to understand and more reliable. Technology can also overcome problems of distance, where evidence can be presented by video link, for instance.

12.14   Every court bench in New Zealand is equipped with a computer. However, use of information technology for the presentation of evidence still requires special arrangements with the court, as the examples set out in the following paragraphs indicate[1].

[1]   See Judge David Harvey 'Information Technologies in Court' *Electronic Issues For Lawyers: Managing Cases* (2004) Auckland District Law Society.

12.15   It is possible to make arrangements for evidence to be presented to the court by way of video link if this is appropriate because of special factual circumstances[1]. The jurisdiction of the court to allow evidence to be given by video link is derived from High Court Rules, rr 9, 369 and 496. There must be some special reason why the court should direct that evidence be given by means other than orally in open court, such as the witness being physically unable to travel for health reasons. Procedural safeguards must be put in place so that the witness is subject to a sanction for perjury and so that there is an adequate opportunity for credibility to be assessed. The requirements usually include a live two-way video link providing a clear view of the witness as well as a reasonable part of the interior of the room where the witness is located, all written materials or exhibits which the witness is referred to during the course of evidence must be clearly identified by way of a paginated agreed bundle of documents, the video link facilities should include a separate camera and monitor for documents, and the only other persons present when the witness gives evidence should be those operating the video and facsimile facilities and a notary public to take the witness' oath and assist with the implementation of any directions or requests given and made by the New Zealand judge hearing the evidence.

[1] See *B v Dentists Disciplinary Tribunal* [1994] 1 NZLR 95; *Ra Ora Stud v Colquhoun* (1997) 11 PRNZ 353; *Aeromotive Ltd v Paul Edward Page and Kyle Griebel* (2002) 16 PRNZ 329; *Ellison Trading Ltd v Liebherr Export AG (No 1)* (2002) 17 PRNZ 1; *R v MacLeod* (HC Auckland, CRI 205-404-2389, 7 June 2006, Williams J). See also r 446ZC providing for a witness giving evidence from Australia or a person appearing as a barrister or solicitor making submissions from Australia, in the case of proceedings under the Commerce Act 1986. The Evidence Act 2006 will introduce a broad discretion to make directions for a witness to give evidence in the ordinary way or in alternative ways, see ss 77, 83 and 103–105.

12.16 In addition, section 26IB of the Judicature Act 1908 now allows a judge or associate judge to preside at a hearing by video link for specific types of hearings[1]. The judicial location and every remote location must be equipped with facilities that satisfy the requirements in rule 72D of the High Court Rules and use of a video link must, in all the circumstances, be consistent with fairness and the interests of justice. The extension of the use of videoconferencing in this way was intended to increase the public's access to justice and save judicial and staff resources[2]. It will allow some civil work in provincial areas to be undertaken by video link hearings as required, rather than when a judge is able to travel. Videoconferencing has also commenced for a limited range of hearings in the Court of Appeal and Supreme Court, such as applications for leave to appeal.

[1] This provision was inserted by the Judicature Amendment Act 2006. The relevant High Court Rules, rr 72B–72E, were inserted, as from 1 September 2006, by High Court Amendment Rules (No 3) 2006 (SR 2006/211), r 5.
[2] Media release by Hon Rick Barker, Minister for Courts, 14 September 2006.

12.17 In larger trials, involving significant volumes of documentary evidence, the parties can use information technology to manage and present that evidence effectively. The Serious Fraud Office often provides electronic disclosure of documents and sets up its own network in the court so that the judge, counsel, witness and jury can see any documents referred to on their own monitor[1]. In civil cases where the parties wish to use such a system the parties must provide the technology at their own cost and make appropriate arrangements with the court.

[1] See also *Goodin v Department of Internal Affairs* [2003] NZAR 434, discussed at para 12.70.

12.18 Computers can be a valuable tool when used by experts to demonstrate or explain a situation or process, or to present a reconstruction. Such computer demonstrations are most commonly used in resource management cases, where the visual and physical effects of proposed developments can be graphically demonstrated but the prejudicial concerns do not outweigh the probative value of the evidence. The Environment Court is not bound by the traditional rules of evidence that apply to judicial proceedings[1] and is free to receive anything in evidence that it considers appropriate to receive[2]. For example, in *Infinity Group v Queenstown Lakes District Council*[3] the issue was whether a proposed extension of Wanaka town on a peninsula to the north-east should be disallowed or restricted because of adverse effects on landscape and visual amenity values. Infinity Group urged that the development provided for in that area had been very carefully assessed. This had included computer-aided inter-visibility analysis and preparation of a video-simulation based on computer-modelled dwellings built to maximum permitted heights and within the identified building platforms, taking into account controls on external colours and the requirement to retain existing vegetation[4]. In *The Inner City West Residents Association (Inc) v Christchurch City Council*[5] the issue was the height to which buildings should be allowed to be erected around the eastern and southern sides of the park-like Victoria Square within Christchurch City. The only expert evaluation offered to the court on aspects of microclimate were those effects that were derived from building shadow. Shadow effects were measurable and the court observed that video computer modelling could be a technically appropriate means to demonstrate shadow patterns realistically[6].

[1] Resource Management Act 1991, s 276(2).
[2] Resource Management Act 1991, s 276(1).
[3] Environment Court, Christchurch, C 10/05, 26 January 2005, Judge Sheppard.
[4] Environment Court, Christchurch, C 10/05, 26 January 2005, Judge Sheppard, para 143.
[5] Environment Court, Christchurch, C171/03, 19 December 2003, Judge Jackson.
[6] Environment Court, Christchurch, C171/03, 19 December 2003, Judge Jackson, para 34.

12.19 In criminal trials, the issue is broadly whether the proposed evidence is relevant, reliable and, on balance, not prejudicial. Demonstrations or reconstructions amounting to admissions or confessions are admissible[1], as are cases involving an experiment or demonstration about a relevant fact at issue[2]. However, reconstructions of an entire incident have been ruled inadmissible because of the impossibility of faithfully re-enacting the original event[3].

[1] *R v Neho* (Court of Appeal, CA 84–03, 26 March 2003, Gault P, Keith and Anderson JJ).
[2] *R v Lundy* (HC Palmerston North, T 13–01, 12 April 2002, Ellis J), involving an experiment to show the time it takes to drive from one point to another with the aim of substantiating or disproving an alibi.
[3] *Stratford v Ministry of Transport* (1971) 7 CRNZ 501.

12.20 In *R v Garrett*[1] the accused was charged with a number of offences arising out of the allegation that he gained unauthorised access to computer systems via the Internet. The Crown sought to adduce evidence of a simulated instance of computer hacking. The defence objected to the admissibility of the proposed evidence on the grounds that it constituted a reconstruction and not an experiment or demonstration. The Crown proposed that the demonstration would be undertaken on a connected computer system set up in the court using a cloned copy of the material on the accused's computer. What could be seen upon the screen of the computer would be projected onto a larger screen for easier visibility for the jury. After watching the proposed evidence, the court held that the procedure was in the nature of an experiment or demonstration and therefore evidence of it and the results were admissible. The demonstration and the experiment did not venture into the area of reconstruction and the jury would be warned as to the specific nature and purpose of the evidence.

¹   [2001] DCR 955.

12.21 In *R v Kingi*[1] the defence sought to adduce fresh evidence on appeal comprising of an experiment conducted by various boxing experts and willing participants to demonstrate that the accused could not have struck the victim with sufficient force to lift him off his feet and throw the victim backwards. After viewing the proposed evidence on a laptop, the court concluded that the proposed evidence had no probative value and could mislead the jury into believing that what it observed on the DVD was, in fact, what occurred or closely similar to it. In short, the prejudicial value, on this occasion to the prosecution, outweighed the probative value of the evidence.

¹   HC Palmerston North, CRI 2005-054-305, 17 February 2006, Wild J.

12.22 New Zealand courts are moving towards a digital audio evidence recording system which involves the recording and retention of an audio file in digital format from which a transcript may be made. On occasions, parties will arrange, at their own cost, for the provision of a real-time stenographer so that the transcript is received by counsel online in the court throughout the trial.

Role of experts

12.23 Generally, witnesses must only give evidence about facts that they personally perceived. They must not state any opinion or belief as to the meaning of those facts. It is for the tribunal of fact, the judge or jury, to draw that conclusion or inference. The ability to call expert evidence is an exception to this general rule. Before expert evidence is admissible, the court must determine that the witness is competent to provide evidence on that particular subject by virtue of the witness's training, study or experience; and that all of the evidence from that expert is within his or her special area of expertise[1].

¹   See *Mainland Products Ltd v BIL (NZ Holdings) Ltd (No 1)* HC Auckland, CIV-2002-404-001889, 28 April 2004, Cooper J, where certain paragraphs in a brief of evidence from an accounting expert were challenged on the grounds that they went beyond his expertise of financial investigation, business valuation and assessment of damages. In *Holt v Auckland City Council* [1980] 2 NZLR 124 the expert in chemical processes was not qualified to give expert evidence about the computer program used by her for analysis.

12.24 Traditionally, an expert is not permitted to provide evidence on issues within the common knowledge of the tribunal of fact, nor is he or she permitted to provide an expert opinion on the ultimate issue in the proceeding[1]. However, these restrictions have been eroded in practice[2]. The Evidence Act 2006 will abolish this 'ultimate issue' restriction and replace it with a new test of 'substantial helpfulness'. Under this new test, expert opinion evidence would be allowed if the opinion is likely to substantially help the court or jury to understand other evidence or ascertain any material fact[3].

1   *Allen v Allen* [2006] NZFLR 735.
2   *R v Eade* (2002) 19 CRNZ 470, CA at 19.
3   Evidence Act 2006, s 25.

12.25 Rule 330A of the High Court Rules requires that expert witnesses comply with a Code of Conduct for Expert Witnesses, provided in Schedule 4 to the Rules[1]. The Code states that an expert has an overriding duty to the court and is not an advocate for the party engaging his or her services. When giving evidence, the expert must state that he or she has read the Code and agrees to abide by it. The expert must state their qualifications and area of expertise, the facts and assumptions on which his or her opinion is based, and the reasons for opinion and any materials relied on. If there is insufficient data to provide a concluded opinion, or any qualifications to the opinion, this must be stated. The Code also provides that the court is able to direct an expert to confer with other expert witnesses[2].

1   These are available at www.legislation.govt.nz under High Court Rules, Sch 4. See Evidence Act 2006, s 26.
2   High Court Rules, r 330B.

12.26 Given their obligations to remain objective and impartial, experts have an increasingly important role during the process of discovery using computer forensics. Where courts exercise their discretion to make orders for a party to allow the other side to obtain access to their computer system, this is usually on the condition that such access is provided on strictly controlled terms, such as only to legal counsel and the independent technology expert. In some cases, the court appoints its own independent expert to carry out the exercise. This process better protects the party providing access in respect of issues such as privilege, irrelevance and confidentiality (see paras 12.82–12.107).

Amendments in statute for computer and Internet law

12.27 In general, the wording used in New Zealand statutes is intended to be technology-neutral so that statutory and regulatory provisions can be applied regardless of the particular type of new technology that is used at any given time. However, there are many examples of new statutory provisions being introduced to address issues arising from the use of the Internet, computers and related devices.

Electronic Transactions Act 2002

12.28 The Electronic Transactions Act 2002 ('ETA 2002') provides that legislative provisions requiring the use of signatures and signing may be met by the use of 'electronic signatures'. Under the Act, an 'electronic signature' will have the same legal effect as a handwritten signature. The concept of an electronic signature is defined very broadly in s 5:

electronic signature, in relation to information in electronic form, means and method used to identify a person and to indicate that person's approval of that information.

The provisions relating to electronic signatures are intended to be technology-neutral, in that no particular form of technology to create the electronic signature is specified. A binding electronic signature could include, for example, a name typed at the end of an email, a digitised image of a signature, or a digital signature.

12.29 The type of electronic signature that will satisfy the requirements of the Act in any given situation will depend on the nature of the transaction. The legal requirement for a signature is met by means of electronic signature if it satisfies the standards set out in ss 22(1)(a) and (b). The signature must adequately identify the signatory, adequately indicate the signatory's approval, and be as reliable as is appropriate under the circumstances.

12.30 Under s 24, the Act expressly establishes a presumption of reliability, which will result in an electronic signature being appropriate where:

(a) the means of creating the electronic signature is linked to the signatory and to no other person; and

(b) the means of creating the electronic signature was under the control of the signatory and of no other person; and

(c) any alteration to the electronic signature made after the time of signing is detectable; and

(d) where a purpose of the legal requirement for a signature is to provide assurance as to the integrity of the information to which it relates, any alteration made to that information after the time of signing is detectable(s 24(1)).

There are some exceptions as to when an electronic signature will have the same legal effect as a handwritten signature.

12.31 ETA 2002, s 24(2)(a) also allows parties to prove on other grounds or by other means that the electronic signature is as reliable as is appropriate. Some of the factors that may be relevant in this consideration include the nature of the trade activity, nature and size of the transaction, trade custom and practice, the sophistication of the technology used by the parties and the availability of alternative methods of identification.

Crimes Act

12.32 The Crimes Act 1961 has recently been amended[1] to introduce a number of crimes relating to the abuse of technology, including obtaining access to a computer for a dishonest purpose (s 249); damaging or interfering with a computer (s 250); making, selling, or distributing or possessing software for committing crime (s 251) and obtaining access to a computer without authority (s 252).

[1] Crimes Amendment Act 2003 (2003 No 39), s 15.

The Copyright Act 1994

12.33 The Copyright Act 1994 has also been amended to address new technology issues. For example, s 227 creates an offence of fraudulently receiving programmes: it is an offence to receive a television programme with intent to avoid paying any charge applicable to the reception of that programme. The maximum penalty for this offence is a fine of up to NZ$5,000 and liability to pay reparation for any loss caused.

12.34 The Copyright Act also prohibits any person from:

(a)   making, importing, selling or letting for hire any apparatus or device designed or adapted to enable or assist people to receive programmes or other transmissions when they are not entitled to do so (s 228(3)(a)); and

(b)   publishing any information that is calculated to enable or assist people to receive the programmes or other transmissions when they are not entitled to do so (s 228(3)(b)); and

(c)   making, importing, selling, letting for hire, offering or exposing for sale or hire, or advertising for sale or hire, any device or means specifically designed or adapted to circumvent copy-protection employed on an electronic form of a copyright work (s 226(2)(a)); and

(d)   publishing any information that is calculated to enable or assist people to circumvent that form of copy-protection (s 226(2)(b)).

12.35   For a breach of ss 226 or 228, the party harmed by the conduct has the same rights and remedies against the infringer as a copyright owner has in respect of an infringement of copyright. This includes the right under s 120 to bring proceedings for infringement of a property right (including damages, injunctions, accounts) subject to the provisions of the Copyright Act. The party harmed also has the right to apply to the court for an order that the infringing copy or object be delivered up, forfeited, destroyed or otherwise dealt with as the court thinks fit.

CRIMINAL LAW

Search warrants

12.36   Police may only search and detain pursuant to express common law or statutory powers, there is no general power of search. The extent to which common law powers of search and seizure remain is uncertain given the comprehensive statutory provisions that now exist[1]. The police have a common law power on arrest to search the accused and the accused's immediate physical surroundings if satisfied that this is necessary for a reason incidental to the arrest[2]. This may include safety considerations for the accused or others, protecting evidence or discovering evidence related to the offending for which the accused has been arrested.

[1]   *R v Bainbridge* (1999) 5 HRNZ 317, CA at 33.
[2]   *R v Noble* HC Auckland, CRI 2005-044-841, 3 April 2006, Winkelmann J.

12.37 In *R v Noble*[1] Mr Noble was charged with one count of possession of the class A drug methamphetamine for supply. The Crown sought an order that evidence obtained from a search of Mr Noble's car shortly after arrest was to be admissible for the purposes of the trial. The issue was whether, in the absence of any statutory power to conduct the search, the search could be justified as an exercise of the common law power to search on arrest. Mr Noble and Mr York were arrested for being unlawfully on property. When spoken to by the police, Mr Noble gave his correct details and produced his current drivers licence. Mr York did not produce identification and gave his name as Mr Yorce. Both men were arrested and taken to the police station where Mr York then gave his proper name. A police sergeant listening to communications on the police radio overheard there was a concern that the second person had given false details of his identity. He drove to a location near the place of the arrest, carried out a police check on a parked car and found that it belonged to Mr Noble. The car was locked, but the sergeant reached through a smashed window to unlock the car. His evidence was that he then searched the car looking for identity documents relating to the second individual. Nothing of relevance was located in the interior, but he found a backpack which contained cannabis in the boot. He then invoked the Misuse of Drugs Act 1975, s 18(2) to continue the search.

[1]   HC Auckland, CRI 2005-044-841, 3 April 2006, Winkelmann J.

12.38 Justice Winkelmann reviewed the relevant authorities in New Zealand, England and Wales and Canada, and concluded that the common law power to search on arrest was to search the accused and the accused's immediate physical surroundings if satisfied that it was necessary for a reason incidental to the arrest. This included safety reasons for the accused and others, protecting evidence or discovering evidence relating to the offending for which the accused was arrested. On the facts, the court was satisfied that the search was not truly incidental to the arrest, nor was it necessary to discover or preserve evidence in relation to the alleged offence. The search was both unlawful and unreasonable. It was therefore necessary to conduct a balancing exercise to consider whether to exclude the evidence. The court was satisfied that the breach of rights was serious enough to rule the evidence inadmissible.

12.39 The main statutory provision relating to search warrants is section 198 of the Summary Proceedings Act 1957 ('SPA 1957') which authorises the issue of a search warrant in relation to imprisonable offences. District Court Judges, Justices or Registrars are able to grant search warrants for crimes if they are

… satisfied that there is reasonable ground for believing that there is in any building, aircraft, ship, carriage, vehicle, box, receptacle, premises, or place:

(a)   any thing upon or in respect of which any offence punishable by imprisonment has been or is suspected of having been committed; or

(b)   any thing which there is reasonable ground to believe will be evidence as to the commission of any such offence; or

(c)   any thing which there is reasonable ground to believe is intended to be used for the purpose of committing any such offence.

12.40   Prior to 2003, there was no legal duty imposed on citizens to assist actively police carrying out a search warrant. In relation to searches of information stored on computers, this meant that there was generally no obligation to supply necessary passwords and decryption details, making the process lengthy and expensive[1]. In 2003, amendments were made to the SPA 1957 to provide that a constable, when executing a search warrant, can require a specified person to provide information or assistance to allow the constable to obtain access to data in a computer on the premises and named in the warrant (s 198B). The section is primarily for use against third parties, as persons cannot be required to give any information that might incriminate themselves.

[1]   *Electronic Technology and Police Investigations, Some Issues* (New Zealand Law Commission, Study Paper 12, 2002) paras 19–20.

12.41   In addition, there are a number of specific statutes that also provide for the issue of search warrants. For example, under section 47(1) of the Fair Trading Act 1986 the Commerce Commission may, from time to time, authorise an employee of the Commission to apply for a warrant under s 47(2) and to undertake a search under such a warrant[1]. Some statutes, such as the Arms Act 1983, Misuse of Drugs Act 1975 and Sale of Liquor Act 1989, provide for warrantless entry.

[1]   Section 98A of the Commerce Act 1986 contains a similar provision. See *R v Hewitt* (2005) 22 NZTC 19 at 309 for an example of a computer hard drive and other material seized in the context of an access warrant issued pursuant to section 16(4) of the Tax Administration Act 1994.

12.42   In *Calver v District Court at Palmerston North (No 1)*[1] the police were investigating the alleged fraudulent activities of a law firm's client. The police obtained a search warrant, issued pursuant to section 198 of the Summary Proceedings Act 1957, for the seizure of records of almost any kind relating to the client and some 39 associated companies and trusts. The warrant specifically authorised the seizure of all computer storage media and all computer hardware and software necessary to gain access to data or programs contained on the storage media. The applicants sought a declaration that the search warrant was invalid on the grounds that it was too broad in authorising the seizure of material that was privileged, irrelevant and confidential. The law firm applied to quash the search warrant and sought an order for the return of all seized material.

[1]   [2005] DCR 114, (2004) 21 CRNZ 371.

12.43   The court considered two issues: whether the warrant was lawfully issued and executed, and whether the search and seizure breached section 21 of the New Zealand Bill of Rights Act 1990. Section 21 provides that 'everyone has the right to be secure against unreasonable search or seizure, whether of the person, property, or correspondence or otherwise'. It was common ground, based on the authority of *Rosenberg v Jaine* [1983] NZLR 1, that section 198 of the Summary Proceedings Act 1957 does not authorise the issue of a search warrant which abrogates solicitor-client privilege. However, the police contended that s 198 does authorise search for, and seizure of, privileged material provided steps are taken to preserve claims to privilege for later resolution. The court held that a warrant may not be issued in respect of material that is known, or thought likely, to be privileged. Similarly, police may not seize material unless they reasonably believe at the time of removal that it is of evidential value. In breach of these principles, when the police executed the warrant, they had simply seized all of the firm's electronic records, including the firm's computer hard drives which contained the records of all the firm's 8,000 clients, without making any attempt to identify the records or files relating to the person and entities in the warrant. The court observed that conditions could be included in the warrant to allow the solicitors the opportunity of identifying the relevant material and to deal with claims to privilege by allowing police to take privileged material on terms that it is sealed and referred to a judge to resolve claims to privilege. The search and seizure authorised by the warrant was found to be unreasonable for the purposes of section 21 of the New Zealand Bill of Rights Act 1990. The court quashed the warrant and ordered the return of the material seized to the law firm.

12.44 In *R v McManamy*[1] the police obtained a warrant to search a house to which a package containing ecstasy had been addressed. During the execution of the warrant, the police obtained access to the accused's computer. The Court of Appeal held that the warrant was invalid, reasonable grounds had not been established, and therefore the search was unlawful. The court also held that the search was unreasonable. Of particular significance was the fact that it was a home that was searched and, within the home, private correspondence including correspondence on a computer specially protected by a password. This breached section 21 of the New Zealand Bill of Rights Act 1990.

[1]   CA303/02, 5 December 2002, Blanchard, Panckhurst and Salmon JJ.

12.45 The police have their own electronic crime investigation guidelines which stipulate that police officers conducting the search are not to examine the computer at the scene. Rather, it is to be removed for examination by a forensic expert. Failure to comply with these guidelines can undermine the reliability of the evidence and raises issues of admissibility[1].

[1]   *R v Good* [2005] DCR 804. This case is discussed at para 12.59.

12.46 Section 30 of the Evidence Act 2006 addresses the situation in a criminal proceeding where the prosecution proposes to offer evidence which the defendant alleges was improperly obtained. The judge must find, on the balance of probabilities, whether or not the evidence was improperly obtained. If so, the judge must determine whether or not the exclusion of the evidence is proportionate to the impropriety by means of a balancing process that gives appropriate weight to the impropriety but also takes proper account of the need for an effective and credible system of justice.

Disclosure obligations

12.47 The rationale for an obligation of disclosure on the prosecution in a criminal proceeding is the defendant's right to a fair trial[1]. There are a number of statutes that also provide express rights that can be relied on to require disclosure by the prosecution, such as the Summary Proceedings Act 1957, the New Zealand Bill of Rights Act 1990, the Crimes Act 1961, the Official Information Act 1982, and the Privacy Act 1993.

[1]   *Comr of Police v Ombudsman* [1988] 1 NZLR 385 at 392.

12.48 Section 17 of the Summary Proceedings Act 1957 provides that every information, ie the document laying the charge, shall contain such particulars as will fairly inform the defendant of the substance of the offence with which he is charged. There are greater disclosure obligations where the proceeding is on indictment, an offence punishable by imprisonment for a term of more than three months.

12.49 The right to a fair trial is entrenched in section 25(a) of the New Zealand Bill of Rights Act 1990 which provides as follows:

Section 25: Minimum standards of criminal procedure

Everyone who is charged with an offence has, in relation to the determination of the charge, the following minimum rights:
(a)   the right to a fair and public hearing by an independent and impartial court;...

Similarly, under section 24(d) of the New Zealand Bill of Rights Act 1990 everyone who is charged with an offence shall have the right to adequate time and facilities to prepare a defence. In *Herewini v Ministry of Transport*[1] the court said, in relation to that right, that, within reasonable limits, every defendant is entitled to know in advance what case he or she will have to meet. A reasonable opportunity to prepare a defence necessarily entails reasonable notice of the prosecution case. In *Simpson v Ministry of Agriculture and Fisheries*[2] the court held that when the defended prosecution hearing is in view, ss 24 and 25 of the New Zealand Bill of Rights Act 1990 implicitly require full pre-trial disclosure.

[1]   [1992] 3 NZLR 482.
[2]   (1996) 3 HRNZ 342 at 354–355.

12.50 The Crimes Act 1961 sets out the following provisions relating to disclosure:

(a)   section 329 stipulates the details that must be set out in every count of an indictment, which is to give the accused reasonable information concerning the act or omission to be proved against him;

(b)   section 344C obliges the prosecution to provide the name and address of any identification witness, along with that witness's statement and any picture or drawing made from information given by the witnesses, unless a Judge excuses such disclosure to protect that witness;

(c)   section 368 obliges the prosecution to give advance notice to the accused if any witness who has not appeared at depositions is to appear at trial.

12.51 Section 24 of the Official Information Act 1982 provides that every person has a right as against a Department or Minister of the Crown to obtain access in relation to any personal information about that person held in a readily accessible form. Personal information is defined to mean 'any official information held by an identifiable person'[1]. This provides a wide right to disclosure which would include briefs of evidence, witnesses statements and notes of interviews referring to personal information about the defendant. There are specific statutory grounds for withholding the information that may apply[2].

1   Official Information Act 1982, s 2.
2   Official Information Act 1982, ss 6, 7, 9 and 18.

12.52 The Privacy Act 1993 governs the collection, storage and dissemination of all personal information held by agencies in New Zealand. 'Personal information' is defined by the Act as 'information about an identifiable individual'[1]. The prosecution must provide access to personal information it holds about an individual whenever an information privacy request is made pursuant to Privacy Principle 6 of the Act. The only exception is when one of the grounds for refusal of access in ss 27–29 of the Act exists.

1   Privacy Act 1993, s 2.

12.53 It is generally acknowledged that the statutes governing criminal disclosure in New Zealand were not designed for the purpose and, as such, the current system has some inadequacies. These include variations in disclosure throughout New Zealand, delays in obtaining disclosure and uncertainty as to the extent of the defendant's rights[1]. However, changes are under way to improve the situation as the Criminal Procedure Bill provides for a new Criminal Disclosure Act. This proposed Act provides for a two-stage disclosure regime[2]. On the commencement of a case, or as soon as practicable, the prosecution must provide the defendant with a fair summary of the case facts, the maximum offence penalty, a list of the defendant's previous criminal convictions and inform them of their ability to request further information. On request, the prosecution must provide further information, including names of witnesses, list of exhibits, copies of interviews with defendant or witnesses and records of evidence produced by a testing device. The second stage occurs following a not-guilty plea and includes full disclosure of any other relevant information.

1   *Criminal Prosecution: Law Commission Report No 66* (New Zealand Law Commission, R66, 2000) para 197.
2   See Criminal Procedure Bill, Government Bill 2004 No 158–2, Pt 2.

12.54 A recent issue has been the developing practice of the prosecution to provide disclosure electronically by way of CD-Rom. The court has required the police to provide a copy of paper disclosure, if so requested, because some defendants may not have the means to obtain access to the contents of a CD by computer, or because printing the documents shifts the financial burden of printing onto the defendant. Review proceedings were commenced by the police in the Auckland High Court to determine whether the obligations of disclosure could be discharged by providing the documents electronically. The High Court held that the police may only meet their obligation to provide a copy when the replica provided is accessible and usable by the particular defendant. An exception is where this would impair efficient administration, but the objective of avoiding waste must be balanced against the right of a defendant to obtain reasonable and useable access[1].

[1] *Comr of Police v District Court at Manukau* (HC Auckland, CIV 2006-404-3305, 5 March 2007, AsherJ).

Consequences of non-disclosure

12.55 The response to prosecutorial non-disclosure will depend on whether it occurs pending, during, or following trial. It will also vary depending on whether disclosure was sought under a statutory regime, or pursuant to common law obligations. Requests for personal information are generally made pre-trial in accordance with the Privacy Act 1993 or the Official Information Act 1982. In a Privacy Act context, the individual concerned is able to request confirmation that an agency[1] holds personal information about them, and that the agency provide access to that information. Section 11 of the Privacy Act 1993 provides that, against a public sector agency, this legal right is enforceable in a court of law. The section has been interpreted in case law to suggest that the Privacy Act 1993 does not provide a similar right of enforcement against private agencies who refuse disclosure[2]. However, enforceability may be obtained through a complaint to persons such as the Ombudsman and Privacy Commissioner[3].

[1] Agency is defined in s 2 as 'any person or body of person, whether corporate or unincorporated, and whether in the public sector or the private sector and includes a Department ...'. However, it does not include, in relation to its judicial functions, a court.
[2] *R v R* (T 65/96) (1996) 14 CRNZ 635.
[3] *Johansen v American International Underwriters (NZ) Ltd* (1997) 11 PRNZ 22, [1997] 3 NZLR 765.

12.56 Official Information Act 1982 disclosure allows a defendant to obtain access to information about themselves from the police and disclosure can only be withheld if the reason for refusal falls within a recognised exception[1]. In certain cases, police refusal to disclose information requested will allow a court to examine the refusal and postpone or adjourn its hearing until disclosure is obtained[2].

[1] ss 24 and 27.
[2] *Commissioner of Police v Ombudsman* [1988] 1 NZLR 385.

12.57 Failure to comply with common law or statutory disclosure obligations may also result in the imposition of sanctions by the court. The High and District Courts are able to adjudicate a defence complaint that a prosecutor has not disclosed information, on the basis of their responsibility to ensure a fair trial. During trial, non-disclosure may result in an adjournment, or stay of the prosecution[1]. Issues in New Zealand have particularly arisen in relation to refusal by the prosecution to allow the examination of electronic devices, such as police Intoxilyzer machines, and disclosure of their certification records, log books and repair records. In these cases, it was held that non-disclosure could lead to exclusion of the evidence[2], dismissal of the prosecution (for breach of process or prejudice to the process of a fair trial)[3] or a warning[4]. If the trial has taken place, non-disclosure may provide a basis for setting aside a verdict if there has been a miscarriage of justice[5]. Other sanctions include a re-trial[6], or a reduced conviction[7].

[1]   *R v R* (T 65/96) (1996) 14 CRNZ 635.
[2]   *Elliot v Ministry of Transport* (HC Christchurch, M21/81, 2 December 1981, Hardie Boys J). In this case the Ministry of Transport had refused to allow the defence to examine the breath-testing device. The court held that an accused was entitled to be assured that the device was, in fact, operating properly. In certain circumstances, a refusal to allow access in order to look into that question might justify the court in disallowing evidence of the result of the testing procedure. However, on the facts, access to the device was sought for a purpose which was not relevant to an available defence, so the circumstances did not warrant any action by the court.
[3]   *John v Police* (HC Hamilton, A 155–99, 24 May 2000, Penlington J); *Allen v Police* [1999] 1 NZLR 356. In *Allen v Police* the court held that the defence were entitled to be provided with the calibration and maintenance records in advance of the trial to enable the appellant's counsel to form a view as to whether an issue of reliability of the device arose. The failure to disclose the information denied the defence this opportunity, in circumstances where there was a basis for questioning the reliability of the device, and thereby prejudiced the defence. Giles J accordingly allowed the appeal and dismissed the information on the ground of abuse of process. See also *Livingston v Institute of Environmental Science and Research Ltd* (Court of Appeal, CA148/02, 19 June 2003, Gault P, Keith, Blanchard, Anderson and Glazebrook JJ).
[4]   *Burrows v Ministry of Transport* (HC Auckland, AP 149/91, 13 August 1991, Barker J). In this case no reasonable doubt as to the accuracy of the machine had been raised in the evidence. Therefore, although the requested certification records, log books and records of repair had not been provided, Barker J decided not to take the extreme step of dismissing the prosecution but issued a warning that the court may not be so well disposed if faced with another refusal to comply with such a request.
[5]   *R v Tawhiti* [1994] 2 NZLR 696, CA. In this case counsel for the defendant accused of murder had not been told until after trial that the victim was admitted to hospital two weeks prior to his death. The court observed that, where disclosure is required, it does not follow that its absence leads to the verdict being set aside: a real possibility of a miscarriage of justice must be shown. Nothing in the evidence or in the submissions advanced by the defence counsel led the court to think there was any reasonable possibility that possession of the information would have strengthened the defence case.
[6]   *R v Chignell* [1991] 2 NZLR 257, (1990) 6 CRNZ 103; *R v Nankervill* (CA342/89, 4 May 1990, Somers, Bisson and Heron JJ); *R v Poihipi* (CA 409/89, 19 September 1990, Bisson, Hardie Boys and Williamson JJ).
[7]   *R v Wickliffe* [1986] 1 NZLR 4, [1987] 1 NZLR 55. The issue at the trial was whether the accused was guilty of murder or manslaughter when he shot a person during the course of a robbery. Job sheet notes of an interview of a key witness were not provided to the defence. The court decided that a verdict of guilty of manslaughter was to be substituted for the verdict found by the jury but that no change be made in the sentence of life imprisonment.

12.58 In *Allen v Police*, Giles J summarised the relevant principles as follows (subject always to the discretion of the trial judge as to adjournments)[1]:

(i)   if, at the date of trial, the prosecution has failed to comply with a legitimate defence request for pre-trial discovery and the prosecutor seeks an adjournment in order to comply and has an acceptable explanation for the default, it will be open to the Judge to grant that application provided there are no other implications which militate against that course (eg section 25 of the New Zealand Bill of Rights Act 1990).

(ii)   if, at the date of trial, the prosecution has failed to comply with a legitimate defence request for pre-trial discovery, and, if the prosecutor has no satisfactory explanation for the failure to comply, the Judge will be entitled to dismiss the information for abuse of process.

(iii)   if the prosecutor proceeds to a hearing and the defence establishes a failure to comply with a proper request for relevant pre-trial discovery, the defence will be entitled to a dismissal for abuse of process.

1   *Allen v Police* [1999] 1 NZLR 356 at 364.

Admissibility

12.59 Four requirements exist for admitting computer-generated records to establish real evidence, that is, facts other than the truth of human assertions[1]:

(a)   that any human involvement in the input of data or interpretation of computer reports satisfies conventional admissibility tests;

(b)   that reliability of the class of device is established;

(c)   that the reliability of the particular device used on the occasion in question is established; and

(d)   that the qualification of the particular person using the device is established.

1   The Hon Robert Fisher QC and The Hon Justice Wild *'Evidence—how it works'* (New Zealand Law Society Seminar, October 2004) at 55, citing *Holt v Auckland City Council* [1980] 2 NZLR 124.

12.60 For evidence intended to establish the truth of human assertions, for instance, the content of an email, the main admissibility issue is the hearsay rule. This applies to human statements made using electronic devices if they are put forward to establish the truth of the statements. The Evidence Amendment (No 2) Act 1980, s 2 provides some hearsay exceptions in terms of documentary evidence, which includes 'any information recorded or stored by means of any tape-recorder, computer or other device; and any material subsequently derived from information so recorded or stored'.

12.61 Documentary business records are subject to a hearsay exception in accordance with section 3 of the Evidence Amendment Act (No 2) 1980. A business record is a document made pursuant to a duty, or in the course of and as a record relating to any business, from information supplied directly or indirectly from a person having personal knowledge of the matters[1]. Relevant business records may be admitted if the person who supplied the information for the record cannot be identified with reasonable diligence, or is not available to give evidence, or cannot be expected to recollect the matters dealt with in the information supplied[2].

1   Evidence Amendment Act (No 2) 1980, s 2.
2   Evidence Amendment Act (No 2) 1980, s 3.

12.62 In *R v Good*[1] a police officer switched on a computer and searched through various files during a police search of premises. The files viewed by the police officer included the 'My Documents' folder, temporary Internet folders and the cookies folders. The unintended effect of his actions was that hundreds of files were altered and some 3.4 megabytes of data were overwritten. However, this did not affect any of the files upon which the police based the prosecution. The police officer's actions did not comply with the police's own electronic crime investigation guidelines '*E-Crime—a Guide to E-Crime Investigations*', which stipulated that in this situation a computer should not be switched on and should be removed for specialist forensic investigation. The issue for the court was whether, in the circumstances, the computer hard drive and its contents were admissible.

1   [2005] DCR 804.

12.63 The court referred to the legal authorities about the accuracy of a computer[1]. It is a matter of judicial notice that computers are not recently invented devices, are in wide use and are fundamentally reliable[2]. A court can assume that computers are accurate and do what they purport to do unless shown otherwise[3]. If there has been human intervention in computer processes that may affect its output or the information that it provides, evidence is necessary to explain that and, if necessary, expert evidence may be required to interpret such outputs or information. Such evidence may confirm the reliability of the device if the presumptions as to reliability have been put in issue[4]. Evidence that explains the circumstances of the intervention and that is able to track and interpret the consequences of the intervention may confirm pre-existing presumptions and answer any questions as to reliability.

1   [2005] DCR 804, at 5.
2   *R v Miller* (1988) 3 CRNZ 609.
3   *Marac Financial Services Ltd v Stewart* [1993] 1 NZLR 86. In this case the use of computers for recording transactions on accounts was sufficiently well-established for there to be a presumption of fact that such computers were accurate.
4   *Holt v Auckland City Council* [1980] 2 NZLR 124. In this case there was a gap in the chain of proof of the validity of the blood alcohol reading recording in a computer print out when a chemical expert gave evidence about the chemical method of analysis which used a computer as a data analyser, but no evidence was adduced about the functioning and reliability of the computer system itself.

12.64 Judge Harvey summarised the position regarding evidence of mechanical or technological devices in the following way[1]:

(a)   there is a presumption that mechanical instruments or technological devices function properly at the relevant time;

(b)   judicial notice will be taken of the output of a notorious or well-known technology. Evidence of the way in which it works to establish that it is based on sound scientific principles is not required;

(c)   new or novel technologies will not receive judicial notice. Expert evidence is required to explain the operation of the technology and the scientific principles upon which it is based. Authority seems to suggest that problems have arisen when technologically based evidence has been adduced without undertaking the inquiry whether or not the technology is 'notorious' or requires expert evidence;

(d)   there is no rule of law which says that the reliability of the device is a precondition to admissibility. In either situation set out in (a) or (b) above the evidence is admissible—it is for the fact finder to assess weight;

(e)   in some cases the presumption of accuracy of a technological device will be created by statute. The manner in which the technology is operated may have an impact upon the weight to be attributed to its output;

(f)   in some cases devices may, as a result of their own processes, create a record which is admissible[2];

(g)   however, if there is human intervention in the performance of such processes either at the input, output or any intermediate stage, hearsay issues may arise, although in some cases exceptions to the hearsay rule may apply;

(h)   whether or not there is unfairness in the process of acquiring or dealing with the evidence is a recognised common law ground to test admissibility and may be available depending upon the facts of each case. That is a matter primarily of human behaviour and is not intrinsically part of the technology.

On the facts in *R v Good*, Judge Harvey decided that the evidence of the computer hard drive should be admitted because this was neither unfair nor unduly prejudicial to the accused. The weight to be given to the evidence was to be an issue for the jury. Judge Harvey noted that his decision did not in any way deal with the admissibility of the images themselves and their probative value or prejudicial effect.

[1]   [2005] DCR 804, at 70.
[2]   *R v Spiby* (1990) 91 Cr App Rep 186, (1991) Crim LR 199.

12.65 In *R v Baptista*[1] the Crown sought orders as to the admissibility of pharmacy records of purchases, pursuant to section 3 of the Evidence Amendment Act (No 2) 1980, as 'business records'. In most cases the pharmacist was able to identify the staff member who made the record of the purchase and in some cases the employee was able to recall at least some detail of the transaction. The court ruled that the pharmacy records were admissible in some cases, but that in others further enquiries should be made to establish whether the employee in question had any independent recollection of the matter beyond making the written record of the transaction in question. The police did not want to incur the cost and delay involved in making further enquiries or obtaining the evidence identified by the judge. The Court of Appeal nevertheless upheld the High Court's decision on the grounds that the requirements of the Evidence Amendment Act must be complied with.

[1]   (2005) 21 CRNZ 479.

12.66 In *R v Chambers*[1] computer records of monthly merchandise differences were admissible to demonstrate stock discrepancies in relation to thefts of biscuits and confectionery. It was noted that 'the fact that there has been a calculation by the computer from the material entered into it cannot derogate from the fact that what the computer provides is information which at the very least has been supplied indirectly by persons with first-hand knowledge'[2].

Cooke P also indicated that, as a basis for admitting the records, there should be testimony by a witness familiar with the data entry system and information provided as to the computer's programming. The data should also be available for inspection.

1   CA 303/88, 304/88, 304A/88, 17 November 1988, Cooke P.
2   CA 303/88, 304/88, 304A/88, 17 November 1988, Cooke P, pp 4–5.

12.67 Another example is *Angell v Police*[1], where computerised business records of vehicle manufacturers were admissible in relation to charges of motor vehicle theft. The records were permitted, because the vehicle assemblers could not have recollected the details in issue given the time period and the large number of cars assembled each year.

1   HC Rotorua, AP49/90, 5 October 1990, Anderson J.

12.68 The Evidence Act 2006 will make admissibility of technology-based evidence easier. The fundamental principle is established that all relevant evidence should be admitted unless there is a policy reason not to[1]. Section 137 will also allow evidence produced wholly or party by 'a machine, device, or technical process (for example, scanning)' applying a presumption that the machine, device or technical process was performing its ordinary role on that occasion, unless evidence is provided to the contrary. In addition, if the information is stored in such a way so that a court cannot use it unless it is displayed, produced, retrieved by that machine, device or technical process, then such a document may be produced that was displayed, retrieved or collated in that way.

1   Evidence Act 2006, s 7.

12.69 In addition, the hearsay rule, notorious for its numerous exceptions, will be made more straightforward. Section 18 of the Evidence Act 2006 provides that hearsay evidence is admissible if:

(a)   the circumstances relating to the statement provide reasonable assurance that the statement is reliable; and

(b)   either—

    (i)   the maker of the statement is unavailable as a witness; or
    (ii)   in any case where the Judge considers that undue expense and delay would be caused if the maker of the statement were required to be a witness.

A maker of a statement might be not be available because he or she is dead, overseas and it is not reasonably practicable to attend a witness, unfit as a witness because of age or physical or mental condition, cannot be identified or found, or cannot be compelled[1]. Additional requirements for criminal cases include written notice of the intention to offer hearsay evidence and a copy of the document in which the hearsay statement is made or, if oral hearsay, a written statement of the contents of the hearsay statement[2]. Section 19 of the Evidence Act 2006 includes a business record exception to the hearsay rule which would allow a hearsay statement contained in a business record without having to satisfy separately the reliability test.

1   Evidence Act 2006, s 16(2).
2   Evidence Act 2006, s 22.

Best evidence

12.70 The case of *Goodin v Department of Internal Affairs*[1] discusses a number of issues relating to computer evidence, including the best evidence rule. Mr Goodin appealed against his conviction on 44 charges of possession of an objectionable publication under section 131(1) of the Films, Videos Publications Classification Act 1993. The charges related to 'electronic pictures' stored in jpg files on Mr Goodin's computer. Thirty-seven of the files were located in the directory D:\appz\donkeykong. The other seven were located in the directory E:\mirc\download. The Department of Internal Affairs had been undertaking a surveillance of Internet relay chat rooms and traced two jpg files (through Telecom records) to Mr Goodin's Telecom account. Inspectors from the Department, accompanied by police, seized Mr Goodin's computer from his home. The computer had approximately 1600 images on the computer that were sexual in nature, and of those, between 200 and 250 were objectionable by reason of the involvement of children. Mr Goodin acknowledged that the computer was his, but said that he lived with flatmates and claimed that 'hundreds of people' had access to his computer.

1   [2003] NZAR 434.

12.71 The court held that a computer hard drive could be a 'publication' for the purposes of the statutory definition ('any paper or other thing in which is recorded or stored any information that, by the use of any computer or other electronic device, is capable of being reproduced or shown as any word, statement, sign or representation'). In addition, the data stored in a computer file could be a 'picture' and therefore a 'publication', but not a 'photograph' (based on the specific wording of the statute and the purpose of the Act).

12.72 The second ground of appeal considered the point that the hard drive was not produced in evidence. The court rejected this ground given that the evidence placed before the court was taken from a clone of the hard drive which was made to prevent any alteration to the hard drive where files were opened and viewed during the course of the investigation or the trial itself. The images before the court were accurate copies of jpg files on the original hard drives. The judge expressly referred to the fact that there was no objection taken as to the admissibility of the evidence from the cloned hard drive, notwithstanding the best evidence rule. In those circumstances, there was no need to produce the hard drives in evidence given that the cloned hard drives were exact replicas.

12.73 The court accepted that proof of possession required proof of some element of knowledge. The mere presence of an objectionable publication on a computer hard drive would not amount to possession of that publication by the owner of the computer if he or she had no knowledge it was there. The defence argued that the judge found knowledge despite the fact that there was insufficient evidence to support various inferences taken. The judge had relied on direct evidence that was available about the location of the 44 jpg files and the way in which those files would be accessed by a person using the computer. The District Court hearing was conducted in a manner which enabled the judge, counsel, Mr Goodin and each witness to operate a computer to view the contents of the cloned hard drives and the procedures used to obtain access to the images in the directories in the hard drives. There was also evidence about other unobjectionable material on the computer in which Mr Goodin had a particular interest and which the judge inferred he was likely to have opened and viewed. Based on all the evidence, the judge did not accept that a regular user of the computer, which Mr Goodin was, could have remained unaware of the objectionable files. The High Court upheld this finding, noting that it largely related to the judge's assessment of the credibility of witnesses. The appeals against conviction and sentence failed.

CIVIL LAW

Pre-commencement powers

12.74 Under the High Court Rules in New Zealand, r 301 it is possible to obtain discovery prior to the commencement of the claim. The main aim of r 301 is to allow the plaintiff to formulate its claim properly. Although the Rule does not require it, applications under r 301 are usually accompanied as a matter of practice by a draft statement of claim to enable the court to assess the entitlement of the intending plaintiff[1].

[1]   *Welgas Holdings Ltd v Petrocorp* (1991) 3 PRNZ 33 at 46.

12.75 Before a pre-commencement discovery order can be made under Rule 301, the following requirements must be satisfied:

(a)   it must be established that the intending plaintiff is or may be entitled to claim relief against another person. This requires that the plaintiff must have a real, as opposed to a speculative, claim[1];

(b)   it must be impossible or impracticable for the plaintiff to formulate the claim without the documents sought. 'Impossible or impracticable" does not mean merely inconvenient[2]. It means an inability to plead the claim in accordance with the requirements of the rules[3];and

(c)   there must be grounds for belief that the documents may be or have been in the possession of the person concerned.

The courts will not permit discovery to become a fishing expedition. Therefore it is necessary to describe with some specificity the document or class of document sought. For example, a reference to 'accounting documents and other records' has been held to be insufficiently particular[4]. In addition, as a matter of discretion, the court must be satisfied that the order is necessary at the time it is made[5].

[1]   *Welgas Holdings Ltd v Petrocorp* (1991) 3 PRNZ 33 at 43.
[2]   *Gray v Trustees of the Crown Superannuation Fund* (1986) 1 PRNZ 239 at 240.

3   *Exchange Commerce Corp Ltd v NZ News Ltd* [1987] 2 NZLR 160, (1987) 1 PRNZ
    230, CA.
4   *AMP v Architectural Windows Ltd* (1986) 2 PRNZ 510.

12.76 Under this rule, an interlocutory application is made on notice to the
person from whom the pre-trial discovery is sought. Rule 303 provides that in
an application for pre-trial discovery the court may order the applicant to pay
the expenses, including solicitor and client costs, of the person from whom the
discovery is sought[1]. If the application for pre-trial discovery is unsuccessfully
opposed, the court also has the power to award costs against the party
opposing discovery[2].

1   *Jagwar Holdings Ltd v Fullers Corp Ltd (No 1)* (1989) 2 PRNZ 654.
2   *Nelson v Dittmer* (1986) 2 PRNZ 171; *British Markitex v Johnston* (1987) 2 PRNZ 535.

Urgent search and seizure (Anton Piller)

12.77 Rule 331 of the High Court Rules allows the court to make a
preservation order for the preservation of 'property' or of 'a fund' involved in
the litigation itself, or evidence relating to the litigation, so that claims are not
rendered nugatory prior to substantive hearing. In *S P Bates & Associates Ltd
v Woolworths (New Zealand) Ltd*[1] the plaintiff applied for a preservation
order relating to the defendant's electronic documents, databases and deleted
files. However, the court was not satisfied that the order was necessary.

1   HC, Auckland, CL15/02, 15 November 2002, Salmon J.

12.78 Anton Piller orders are similar to preservation orders but are more
invasive in that they permit entry into premises and removal of items. An
Anton Piller order[1] is, in effect, a mandatory interim injunction which compels
a person to permit access to premises and authorises the seizure of material so
that it can be preserved for evidence. The main purpose is the preservation of
evidence which might otherwise be removed, destroyed, or concealed, but it
may also operate as an order for discovery in advance of pleadings. Given the
grounds for such an order, it is usually granted ex parte, ie without prior
notice to the person against whom it is made.

1   *Piller (Anton) KG v Manufacturing Processes Ltd* [1976] Ch 55, [1976] 1 All ER 779, CA.

12.79 A plaintiff must satisfy the following four requirements:

(a)   a strong prima facie case: the plaintiff is required to demonstrate that it
      has a cause of action against the defendant and that the evidence is
      sufficiently strong to warrant the grant of such an order;
(b)   potential or actual serious damage to the plaintiff if the orders are not
      granted: it is necessary for the plaintiff to provide affidavit evidence
      demonstrating that if the orders sought are not granted, the damage
      suffered by the plaintiff will be serious. The essential purpose of the
      Anton Piller order is to locate and preserve evidence for use at a
      substantive trial;

(c)   evidence of possession by the defendant: the court must be able to properly infer from the evidence that the defendant has possession of the material at a particular location;

(d)   the risk of disposal or destruction: in *Busby v Thorn EMI Video Programmes Ltd*[1] Cooke J stated (at 467):

> As to the evidence that articles or records may well disappear if the defendant has notice, that will at times be difficult to provide. Generally I think that there should be enough evidence to show that the plaintiff has reasonable grounds for fearing that evidence will go. The judge must be entitled to use his common sense and to take into account the usual practices of pirates of copyright and the like. If the requirement were put too high the remedy would lose much of its value.

[1] [1984] 1 NZLR 461, CA.

12.80 The Anton Piller order was originally developed to address video piracy. It is commonly used where there is an alleged infringement of copyright or misuse of confidential information, and frequently involves the seizure of electronic evidence[1]. Given that an Anton Piller order is so invasive, any such order will be subject to a number of undertakings, conditions and procedural requirements[2].

[1] See for example *Neuronz v Tran* (HC Auckland, CP 623-SW01, 14 May 2003, Williams J).
[2] See *McGechan on Procedure,* vol 1, paras HR331.13–HR331.27.

12.81 In *Proyectos De Energia, Sociedad Anonima De Capital Variable v Loza*[1] the court made orders that the documents, including electronic documents, obtained through execution of the Anton Piller orders were to be examined by an independent barrister as well as the defendants' lawyers to identify any documents for which privilege was claimed. If the experts recovered the 'deep' memory of the computer database this was to be subject to their undertaking to the court not to disclose the contents of the documents to any party other than to the independent barrister or to the defendants' counsel.

[1] HC Auckland, CP20-SW03, 14 February 2003, Venning J.

Discovery

Introduction

12.82 During legal proceedings, the process of discovery gives the parties the opportunity, before the trial, to view any documents that are relevant to the issues raised in the proceeding. Each party is obliged to provide discovery to the other parties to the proceeding. The High Court Rules relating to discovery are intended to prevent parties from keeping cards close to their chest[1]. As a result, no party should be taken by surprise at trial. The ability of all parties to inspect all the relevant material, whether helpful or harmful to their case, is also aimed at facilitating an accurate assessment of the merits of the claim and thereby increasing the chances of settlement.

[1] *Green v CIR* [1991] 3 NZLR 8 at 11.

12.83 As referred to below, electronic information is included within the scope of discovery obligations in New Zealand. The increasing prevalence of electronic communications in society, particularly as a result of email, has had a dramatic effect on practical issues that arise with the discovery process[1]. New electronic communication and information technology allows for a larger amount of available information, presenting a challenge to the legal practitioner in fulfilling his or her professional duties by properly undertaking electronic discovery and collating, analysing, considering and presenting information that is relevant to the discovery process.

[1] G Coumbe 'Discovery of Electronic Documents' 3–37 in G Coumbe and A Forbes QC 'Obtaining Pre-trial Information' (New Zealand Law Society Seminar, September 2005).

12.84 Electronic communications such as email are often created with less concern for formality or without an appreciation of the fact that they can later be discovered. By reason of the informality of such communications, emails in particular are gaining increasing importance and are proving to be a rich source of trial evidence, often the source of a 'smoking gun'. Email communications and other electronic documents also contain data and content other than which appears on the face of the email or document. This metadata may provide valuable information such as the author of the document, when and by whom a document has been viewed, printed or edited, who an email was sent to, who received it, who opened it and when it was replied to, the mail service through which an email travelled, and file locations. Deleting emails or data files does not generally result in the eradication of the electronic data forever as computer forensics experts are often able to retrieve deleted emails and other documents.

12.85 The process of retrieving deleted data is not always appropriate for use in every case, as it can be expensive, and it takes some time for the forensics professionals to analyse the contents of a hard drive and produce a report that is suitable for use in court. However, in larger cases such forensic discovery is becoming common, particularly where there are grounds to believe that the relevant material did exist but is no longer kept in hard-copy or in an easily accessible form.

Scope

12.86 The formal process of discovery usually begins shortly after the statement of defence has been filed in response to the statement of claim. If discovery of documents is appropriate for a proceeding on the standard track the court must make a discovery order at the first case management conference, unless there are good reasons to make the order later[1]. Unless special orders are made, each side must disclose to the other side the existence of all documents that 'relate to a matter in question in the proceeding' and that 'are or have been in that party's control'[2].

[1] High Court Rules, r 294.
[2] High Court Rules, r 295.

12.87 The legal test for whether a document 'relates to a matter in question in the proceeding' remains that described by Brett LJ in *Companie Financière et Commerciale du Pacifique v Peruvian Guano Co* (1882) 11 QBD 55, CA, at 63[1]:

> ... every document relates to matters in question in the action which not only would be evidence upon any issue, but also which, it is reasonable to suppose, contains information which may—not which must—either directly or indirectly enable the party requiring the affidavit either to advance his own case or to damage the case of his adversary.

With the increase in the use of electronic business documents, this *Peruvian Guano* 'train of inquiry' test is very expansive and imposes a burden of discovery that can be extremely time-consuming and expensive[2].

[1] Cited in *AMP Society v Architectural Windows Ltd* [1986] 2 NZLR 191 at 202 and *NGC New Zealand v Todd Petroleum Mining Co Ltd* (HC Wellington, CIV-2004-485-1753, 29 March 2006, Associate Judge Gendall).

[2] Recent suggestions to narrow the scope of discovery (see *General Discovery*, New Zealand Law Commission, Report 78, February 2002) have not been taken up.

12.88 'Control' is defined in Rule 3 to mean:

(a) possession of the document;

(b) a right to possess the document; and

(c) a right, otherwise than under the High Court Rules, to inspect or copy the document.

As such, documents in the possession or custody of an agent, such as a solicitor or accountant, are discoverable on the grounds that the party is entitled to have access to them. What constitutes a 'document' is defined in wide terms in order to encompass all practical methods of information storage including those that are electronic in nature. The definition of a document in Rule 3(1) provides as follows:

> a document in any form whether signed or initialled or otherwise authenticated by its maker or not; and includes ...any information recorded or stored by means of any tape-recorder, computer, or other device; and any material subsequently derived from information so recorded or stored ...

12.89 A wide definition of document is particularly significant for the purposes of electronic discovery as it ensures that all relevant information, including electronic information, falls within the scope of the discovery process. In *S P Bates & Associates Ltd v Woolworths (New Zealand) Ltd*, Salmon J made the following observation[1]:

> it is, of course, clear that computer records, no matter how difficult they are to access are prima facie discoverable if they are relevant in any way to the issues raised in the pleadings. In that respect there is no difference between hard-copy records and computer records.

[1] HC Auckland, CL15/02, 15 November 2002, Salmon J at 3.

12.90 All discoverable documents must be listed in an affidavit which refers to the discovery order, states that the party understands the obligations under that order, gives particulars of the steps taken to fulfil those obligations, lists the documents, and identifies any documents which the party claims are confidential (in which case the deponent must set out the proposed restrictions to protect that confidentiality)[1]. As soon as a person who is required to make discovery has served an affidavit of documents, the person must make the documents listed in the affidavit available for inspection by the parties to the proceeding, with the exception of privileged documents[2].

[1]   High Court Rules, r 297.
[2]   High Court Rules, r 309.

Inspection

12.91 Traditionally the parties inspected hard copies of the other party's documents (usually paper letters, contracts, diary books, etc) and requested photocopies of the relevant pages required. With the advent of electronic discovery it is increasingly common for electronic copies of the documents to be provided, such as on a CD-ROM. This is also helpful if the parties wish to import those documents into litigation support software which improves the effectiveness of managing and analysing large volumes of material. In some cases, an issue arises as to whether the other party is able to exercise its rights of inspection properly when the underlying information needs to be opened and viewed using particular software.

12.92 In *Telecom New Zealand Ltd v AMP Property Commercial Ltd*[1] proceedings had been brought in respect of the plaintiff's computer system following an incident while the defendants were testing a high water riser at the premises. The first defendant sought particular discovery of all documents held or controlled by Telecom, including information stored in electronic format, about the plaintiff's wholesale voice refile business for the period from 1 January 1990 to 30 November 2004. This was relevant to the plaintiff's claimed loss of profits. The relevant data was held in a computer database. The plaintiff had provided some data of the nature sought in spreadsheet format, but only for a short period. The main issue was the extent to which the plaintiff could be required to create and produce another spreadsheet from its database to cover the entire period when such a report did not already exist. A spreadsheet was sought because the database was not in a readable form.

[1]   HC Wellington, CIV-2004-485-000613, 16 March 2005, Associate Judge Gendall.

12.93 The court accepted that the database was itself a 'document' for the purposes of discovery under the High Court Rules. The starting point was that the information contained in the database was discoverable, so the issue was whether the plaintiff was obliged to take the necessary steps to extract the relevant information into a readable form by creating the spreadsheet report. Based on the specific requirements to make documents 'available' for inspection[1], the court was satisfied that it had the power to order the plaintiff to put the data in question into a spreadsheet report so that efficient inspection could be achieved. The additional steps required to extract raw bitstream data from the database were not unreasonable or oppressive given the amount claimed in the proceeding (the plaintiff contended it would take two persons weeks of work to provide the spreadsheet report). Orders were made for the plaintiff to make the information held in electronic format available to the defendant for inspection and copying in 'hard-copy spreadsheet report form'.

[1]   High Court Rules, rr 309–310.

12.94 In *Fujitsu General New Zealand Ltd v Black Diamond Holdings Ltd (formerly Melco New Zealand Ltd)*[1] the defendant had been ordered to provide to the plaintiff a 'true copy of all discovered parts of the defendant's database (in a readable and useable form)'. The defendant had provided the relevant data in electronic files that were 'readable'. However, the plaintiff sought access to the defendant's computer system to determine whether the material provided was a complete set of the data that the discovered database parts contained.

[1]   HC Wellington, CIV-2000-485-000668, CIV-2000-485-000662, 31 May 2004, Associate Judge Gendall.

12.95 The court noted that the usual discovery practice in New Zealand for electronic documents is that they are described in a list of documents in the normal way, and then produced in hard-copy form or on CD-ROMs containing specific documents or files which have been downloaded[1]. However, there are occasions where it is appropriate for one party to seek to obtain access to another party's database. Three examples were provided[2]:

(a)   where the nature of the electronic information sought is such that it can only be examined in any meaningful way by access to the database[3];

(b)   where a party required to provide deleted emails or other documents claims that it is unable to retrieve the data. The party requesting discovery may wish to have its own computer expert undertake that task[4]; or

(c)   where access to metadata is required, establishing potentially important details about who obtained access to or modified a document and when.

[1]   *Fujitsu General New Zealand Ltd v Black Diamond Holdings Ltd (formerly Melco New Zealand Ltd* (HC Wellington, CIV-2000-485-000668, CIV-2000-485-000662, 31 May 2004, Associate Judge Gendall), para 14.
[2]   Referring to G Coumbe 'E-discovery' [2004] NZLJ 133.
[3]   See for example *Geddes v New Zealand Dairy Board* HC Wellington, CP52/97, 20 December 2001, Master Thomson.
[4]   See for example *North Holdings Ltd v Rodney District Council* HC Auckland, N1260/PL02, 28 May 2003, Master Lang.

12.96 In the *Fujitsu* case, the court was satisfied that the plaintiff had raised issues of genuine concern regarding its ability to inspect properly the discovered parts of the defendant's database in readable and useable form. The court therefore made an order that the plaintiff was to be given access to the defendant's database in order to obtain access to the relevant material, subject to appropriate conditions of inspection to address issues of privilege and relevance.

Privilege

12.97 The obligation is to disclose all relevant documents in a list, but the other parties have no right to inspect legally privileged communications. In this way the other parties are entitled to know the fact that the privileged documents exist, but privilege is maintained. Solicitor-client privilege protects confidential communications between a client and a legal adviser in both civil and criminal proceedings. The privilege covers communications that are made for the purpose of obtaining or giving legal advice.

12.98 Litigation privilege protects against disclosure of communications between a person or his or her legal adviser and a third party for the purpose of pending or contemplated litigation. The communication must have been made for the dominant purpose of enabling the party or legal adviser to conduct or receive or give advice in the litigation. Litigation privilege is wider than solicitor-client privilege, in that it covers communications to third parties, but narrower in that it only arises in the context of litigation.

Duties and consequences of non-disclosure

12.99 Although the discovery process will mostly be managed by lawyers, it is important for clients to be aware of the obligations. The deponent swearing the affidavit is required to state that he or she understands the obligations under the discovery orders made by the court. As soon as litigation seems likely, the routine destruction of documents that might be relevant must stop. In relation to electronic data this may require steps to ensure that any relevant back-up tapes are preserved and that emails are not deleted, whether automatically, intentionally or accidentally. In addition, it may be inappropriate to re-organise folders or files if the order or location of documents or data may be relevant. People who may hold relevant documents, for example consultants, should be informed of the possibility of the documents being required for discovery.

12.100 It is the professional obligation and duty of legal practitioners in New Zealand to ensure that evidentiary material in electronic form is provided in the discovery process, especially given that critical evidence is increasingly found in such information. Such obligations and duties of the legal practitioner are in accordance with his or her duty to the court to ensure that the integrity of the discovery process is maintained. Rule 296 of the High Court Rules creates a further obligation for a legal practitioner acting for a party to litigation to ensure, to the best of that solicitor's ability, that the party understands the obligations created by a discovery order and faithfully fulfils those obligations. The obligation of discovery continues throughout the proceeding. Therefore, if further documentation is located after the lists of documents have been exchanged, the party that has found the further material should file a supplementary list of documents listing the further material and providing an explanation for why it was not included in the initial list.

12.101 The consequences of non-disclosure during the discovery process can be serious. In *Burns v National Bank of New Zealand Ltd*[1] Mr and Mrs Burns had settled proceedings against the National Bank of New Zealand Ltd. Subsequently they alleged that the bank had failed to discover certain documents in the proceedings and that, had those documents been discovered, they would not have settled the proceedings or would have settled on more favourable terms. They sought summary judgment against the bank in respect of alleged misrepresentations and additionally alleged that the bank and its solicitor had committed the tort of 'tortious spoliation' (based on cases from the United States of America and Canada). The Court of Appeal held that an independent tort of spoliation is not recognised in New Zealand. Such a tort was not necessary given that there are numerous existing remedies for non-disclosure during discovery, which include the following:

(a) provisions in the High Court Rules, such as Rule 277, which provides for sanctions in circumstances where a party makes default in complying with any interlocutory order, including a discovery order. Possible sanctions include dismissal of a plaintiff's claim or striking out a defence;

(b) Rule 317A, which provides that a non-party who wilfully and without lawful excuse fails to comply with a discovery order is guilty of contempt of court;

(c) the possibility of disciplinary action against any legal practitioner involved;

(d) criminal sanctions, including sections 108 to 117 of the Crimes Act 1961 which define perjury and related crimes, including fabricating evidence, ss 231 and 232 proscribing fraudulent destruction and concealment of documents and ss 266, 266A and 266B relating to forgery and fraudulent use of documents;

(e) the presumption that all things are presumed against the spoliator ('omnia praesumuntur contra spoliatorem')[2]:

> If any one by a deliberate act destroys a document which, according to what its contents may have been, would have told strongly either for him or against him, the strongest possible presumption arises that if it had been produced it would have told against him; and even if the document is destroyed by his own act, but under circumstances in which the intention to destroy evidence may fairly be considered rebutted, still he has to suffer. He is in the position that he is without the corroboration which might have been expected in his case.

[1]   [2004] 3 NZLR 289, CA.
[2]   *The Ophelia* [1916] 2 AC 206 at 229–230 per Sir Arthur Channell.

Confidentiality

12.102 The commercial sensitivity of information is not a ground for excluding that documentation from discovery: the sole test in this regard is relevance. However, the confidentiality of the contents of documents may justify special orders as to the inspection and use of the documents[1]. This issue commonly arises in litigation between competitors, or in competition law cases where competitors are parties to the proceeding and would otherwise

have full rights of inspection of all discovered documents. For example, in
NGC New Zealand Ltd v Todd Petroleum Mining Company Ltd[2] Shell and
Todd were the shareholders in a company which operated a gas field. During
November 1997 Todd and Shell, as sellers of gas, entered into an agreement
with NGC as a buyer of gas. The proceeding concerned a dispute about
entitlements under that agreement. Shell sought orders for discovery of
invoices for the sale of gas to other parties. The court held that the invoices
were relevant to assess the commercial price at which Shell's alleged share of
gas was sold, therefore affecting quantum issues. However, inspection of the
commercially sensitive information was to be restricted to Shell's counsel and
expert witnesses[3]. Todd also obtained orders requiring NGC to review its
electronic back-up tapes to discover emails of current and former NGC staff
relating to knowledge of the alleged overtaking of gas[4].

[1]   *Port Nelson Ltd v Commerce Commission* (1994) 7 PRNZ 344, CA; *TD Haulage Ltd v
     NZ Railways Corp* (1986) 1 PRNZ 668, 676.
[2]   HC Wellington, CIV 2004-485-1753, 29 March 2006, Associate Judge DI Gendall.
[3]   HC Wellington, CIV 2004-485-1753, 29 March 2006, Associate Judge DI Gendall,
     para 68.
[4]   See para 12.112ff.

12.103 The discovery and examination of computer hard drives raises
important issues of confidentiality, as they will almost invariably contain a
wide range of information that is not relevant to the proceeding and which is
often commercially sensitive. In those circumstances it will be routine for
orders to be made restricting inspection to independent experts and legal
counsel[1]. In civil proceedings, any such proposed restrictions should be set out
in the affidavit containing the list of documents provided on discovery.

[1]   See, for example, *Tyco Flow Pacific Pty Ltd v Grant* HC Auckland, CIV-2003-404-
     004121, 18 March 2005, Associate Judge Sargisson.

Role of Experts

12.104 The general obligations of experts, discussed at para 12.23ff, apply to
specialists undertaking a forensic examination of computer systems or other
technology. It is critical that the evidence is preserved in its original form. This
is usually achieved by cloning the hard drive and then carrying out the
forensic work on versions of that cloned drive using recognised forensic
software[1]. The procedure must be carefully documented so that it can be fully
described in the expert's evidence in chief, taking care to record matters that
identify and authenticate the hardware or software examined, how the
forensic work was carried out, and any outputs from the analysis, such as
print-outs from searches, metadata, etc.

[1]   For example, Encase and Forensic Toolkit.

12.105 As discussed at para 12.82ff, in civil proceedings experts undertake
forensic discovery on behalf of one of the parties, or as a court-appointed
expert. They may have to review a large volume of material, including
confidential and irrelevant material, to identify the documents that are
relevant. Usually this is achieved by keyword searches[1]. In *Minter Ellison*

Rudd Watts v Gibson, the law firm Minter Ellison Rudd Watts sought to recover some NZ$70,000 in legal fees. The defendant counterclaimed that in acting for him in litigation the plaintiff breached contractual, tortious, fiduciary and ethical duties. Mr Gibson sought orders that his expert be permitted access to all electronic records held by the law firm in order to conduct a full text search to locate any records in the period prior to 1995 that may be relevant to the proceeding. The court did not make those orders because they were not regarded as necessary, particularly when issues of privilege and confidentiality clearly arose. Instead Minter Ellison was required to search its records again; it was likely that this would involve searching electronic records created by the particular staff involved at the time.

¹   See *Minter Ellison Rudd Watts v Gibson* HC Auckland, CIV 2002-404-1987, 28 June 2004, Associate Judge Lang, para 21.

12.106 In *Tyco Flow Pacific Pty Ltd v Grant*¹ the plaintiff had purchased a business called 'Water Dynamics', paying over NZ$6 million for the goodwill of the business. The sale and purchase agreement contained three-year non-competition obligations. The plaintiff alleged that the defendants, previously involved in the management of the company, had breached the non-competition obligations. The plaintiff alleged that the first defendant had assisted competing companies and that he had tried to conceal those actions by attempting to destroy email records by reformatting the laptop computer in his possession. The plaintiff sought orders requiring the first defendant to provide discovery of any emails or other communications which he received from anyone previously working for the company, if it related to the business of any of the four competing companies, and an order to enable the plaintiff's forensic expert to have unobstructed access to any computers, or computer equipment owner, operated or controlled by the first defendant that contained any such emails or communications. One of the jurisdictional requirements for an order for particular discovery is that the application must establish that at order for discovery is 'necessary at the time'². 'Necessary' does not mean 'essential', but imports a notion of being reasonably necessary³. The court must consider whether there are other ways for an application to obtain private information and, if there are not, how privacy of the discovering party can be maintained⁴. The applicant cannot use the process for 'fishing'⁵.

¹   HC Auckland, CIV-2003-404-004121, 18 March 2005, Associate Judge Sargisson.
²   High Court Rules, r 300(2).
³   HC Auckland, CIV-2003-404-004121, 18 March 2005, Associate Judge Sargisson, para 36 citing *Krone (NZ) Technique Ltd v Connector Systems Ltd* (1998) 2 PRNZ 627 at 635.
⁴   HC Auckland, CIV-2003-404-004121, 18 March 2005, Associate Judge Sargisson, para 37 citing *T D Haulage Ltd v NZ Railways Corp* (1986) 1 PRNZ 668 at 674.
⁵   HC Auckland, CIV-2003-404-004121, 18 March 2005, Associate Judge Sargisson, para 38 citing *AMP Society v Architectural Windows Ltd* [1986] 2 NZLR 191 at 196.

12.107 After considering the issues, the court decided to make orders to allow inspection of Mr Grant's email addresses and computers by an independent expert while at the same time respecting, as far as possible, the concerns about confidentiality and privilege. Rather than making the orders requested of requiring unobstructed access to any computer systems, hardware, software, storage media and any computer peripherals (including passwords or security keys), the court preferred the course of requiring Mr Grant to comply with all reasonable requests to enable the independent expert to clone the hard drives, with leave reserved to seek the intervention of the court in the event of any disagreement.

Admissibility

12.108 In civil proceedings, issues as to admissibility are similar to those discussed at para 12.59ff. However, the rules are less likely to be applied strictly because the judge is able to take into account the appropriate weight that should be given to the evidence.

12.109 The case *X v Auckland District Health Board (No 2)*[1] concerned an employment dispute. The plaintiff had been employed in a senior clinical position by the Auckland District Health Board. As a result of the discovery of a number of digital images on the plaintiff's work computer, the defendant commenced an investigation into alleged serious misconduct. In due course the plaintiff was dismissed. The plaintiff challenged his employer's treatment of him during employment and the dismissal. There were a number of challenges to the admissibility of evidence.

[1]   (2006) 7 NZELC 98 at 104.

12.110 The Employment Court has a broad discretion to admit evidence based on a standard of 'equity and good conscience'[1], including evidence that might be inadmissible elsewhere. However, rather than allowing unfettered discretion, the rules of evidence in civil proceedings in the High Court and District Courts are considered and applied, but may be modified on a case by case basis to promote the ends of employment justice.

[1]   Employment Relations Act 2000, s 160(2).

12.111 The defendant's IT expert wished to adduce evidence about archived electronic imagery that had been discovered during forensic investigations after the defendant was dismissed. The defendant could not rely on this further evidence to justify the decision, since the material was not known at the time the decision was made. However, it wished to rely on this further evidence on the issue of the appropriateness of reinstatement and the plaintiff's credibility, given that the plaintiff alleged that the material that led to his dismissal was uncharacteristic of past behaviour. The court agreed that the evidence was relevant to those issues, and rejected the argument that its prejudicial effect outweighed its probative value. Any concern that the material could be used salaciously by the media was an issue of exhibit management rather than admissibility of evidence at trial. The court could make orders restricting the extent to which the material could be copied or even described if necessary.

Costs

12.112 In *Commerce Commission v Telecom Corp of New Zealand Ltd*[1] Telecom had been ordered to make electronic discovery by retrieving and discovering electronic records. Subsequent to those orders being made, Telecom sought to recall the original decision on the grounds that further evidence was available that the probable costs of complying with the order would be in excess of NZ$823,000. Part of the problem was that, due to changes in Telecom's IT environment, the orders required the rebuilding of disused technology or directories needed to enable the data to be read. The court was referred to a number of cases from the United States where judges had ordered that the costs of comparable discovery exercises be shared, or be borne wholly by the party seeking the discovery[2].

[1]   HC Wellington, CIV-2000-485-673, 23 August 2005, Wild J.
[2]   These cases are summarised helpfully in a schedule to the decision. See also ch 16.

12.113 The court's understanding of those cases was that, under the American Federal Rules of Civil Procedure relating to discovery, the presumption is that the responding party must bear the expense of complying with discovery requests but that the court retains a jurisdiction to protect the responding party from 'undue burden or expense', which is a situation where the burden or expenses of the proposed discovery outweighs its likely benefit, taking into account factors such as the needs if the case, the parties' resources, and the importance of the proposed discovery in resolving the issues in the case. In deciding whether it is appropriate to shift some or all of the cost to the party seeking the discovery, the following factors should be considered[1]:

(a)   the extent to which the discovery is specifically tailored to discover relevant information. The less specific the request, the more appropriate to shift costs to the requesting party;
(b)   the availability of such information from other sources;
(c)   the total cost of discovery, compared with the amount at issue;
(d)   the relative ability of each party to control costs and its incentive to do so;
(e)   the importance of the issues at stake in the litigation;
(f)   the relative benefits to the parties of obtaining the information;
(g)   the importance of the requested discovery in resolving the issues of the litigation.

The court decided that a 'test' sample of the proposed electronic discovery should be completed first, with those costs shared on a 50:50 basis. Once those test results were obtained, the court proposed to give the parties the opportunity to argue why the results and the expense do, or do not, justify any further discovery.

[1]   HC Wellington, CIV-2000-485-673, 23 August 2005, Wild J, paras 37 and 39, based on the principles in *Rowe Entertainment v William Morris Agency, Inc* 205 FRD 421 (2003); *Laura Zubulake v UBS Warburg* 216 FRD 280 (2003) and *Amy Wiginton v CB Richard Ellis* 94 Fair Empl.Pract.Cas. (BNA) 627 (2004).

12.114 On appeal, the Court of Appeal accepted that Rule 236 of the High Court Rules provided jurisdiction for a cost-shifting order[1]. The *Zubulake* factors were regarded by the Court of Appeal as a commonsense encapsulation of factors which require assessment. However, the United States approach does not have legislative status in New Zealand, nor does it provide an exhaustive checklist without deviation. There was nothing in *Zubulake* to suggest that there is a fixed rule that cost-shifting can only occur after sampling. However, the *Zubulake* test was not comprehensive because it did not include as a factor a failure to preserve potentially discoverable documents[2]. After considering this factor and Telecom's decision to change computer platforms after litigation was in contemplation, the orders of the High Court were varied to delete any reference to cost sharing. The cost of the sample discovery of Telecom's stored electronic documents was to be the responsibility of Telecom in the first instance.

[1] *Commerce Commission v Telecom Corp of New Zealand Ltd* Court of Appeal, CA198/05, 13 September 2006, Glazebrook, Chambers and Robertson JJ, para 22.
[2] *Commerce Commission v Telecom Corp of New Zealand Ltd* Court of Appeal, CA198/05, 13 September 2006, Glazebrook, Chambers and Robertson JJ, para 44.

12.115 In *NGC New Zealand Ltd v Todd Petroleum Mining Co Ltd*[1] the parties were in dispute in respect of contractual rights to purchase gas from the Kapuni Gas Field. One interlocutory application was for further and better discovery by NGC of the contents of certain back-up tapes to discover emails of current and former staff containing information of NGC's knowledge of the alleged overtaking of gas by Todd and Shell. The court noted its clear jurisdiction to make the order given that 'document' was defined in Rule 3 of the High Court Rules to mean 'any information recorded or stored by means of any tape-recorder, computer or other device', referring to *SP Bates & Associates Ltd v Woolworths (NZ) Ltd*[2]. NGC contended that its back-up tapes were not readily accessible and that retrieval of the emails would impose an undue burden and cost. The costs of retrieval were estimated to be between NZ$15,000 and NZ$45,000. The court was satisfied that the back-up tapes were relevant to determine whether an account of profits may be warranted. Applying the test outlined in *Commerce Commission v Telecom Corp of New Zealand Ltd*[3], the court was satisfied that it was an appropriate case for a costs-shifting order with respect to that particular discovery exercise. The court therefore ordered that the costs of the exercise were to be shared equally between the party seeking the particular discovery and the party providing it.

[1] HC Wellington, CIV-2004-485-001753, 29 March 2006, Associate Judge Gendall.
[2] HC Auckland, CL15/02, 15 November 2002, Salmon J.
[3] HC Wellington, CIV-2000-485-673, 23 August 2005, Wild J.

Electronic document management systems

12.116 Technology has revolutionised litigation during the past five years. Today, the majority of documents that are relevant to a dispute are likely to be stored electronically. This has increased the burden of discovery. It is now relatively common for forensic computer work to be undertaken in order to identify any relevant records including, for example, deleted emails. If there have been changes to a computer system this can lead to extensive costs in the recovery of data from back-up tapes stored in an old format.

12.117 On the other hand, litigation support packages have revolutionised the way documents are managed in litigation. Electronic documents can be imported into litigation support packages, allowing full text searching. This is extremely beneficial for speeding-up the process of locating documents that are relevant to particular issues, for preparing briefs of evidence in which the witness refers to documents he or she has seen, and for generally managing large volumes of information. The challenge for New Zealand courts and the legislature is to ensure that the benefits of new technology outweigh the practical burdens.

Chapter 13

SCOTLAND

IAIN MITCHELL

THE SCOTTISH LEGAL SYSTEM

The nature of the law

13.01 Scots law is a mixed system which bridges the common law and civilian legal worlds. The preservation of Scots Law and the Scottish legal system was explicitly provided for in the Act of Union 1707[1] and, while there has been a tendency for a general convergence of at least the civil law north and south of the Tweed, Scots law has, for the most part, succeeded in maintaining its own distinct identity.

[1] In *Stuart v Marquis of Bute, Stuart v Moore* (1861) 9 HL Cas 440 at 454, Lord Campbell LC said: '... as to judicial jurisdiction, Scotland and England, although politically under the same Crown and under the supreme sway of one united Legislature, are to be considered as independent foreign countries, unconnected with each other'.

13.02 Many of the concepts of Scots Law are derived from Roman Law[1], but it is a civilian legacy that finds itself, to a greater or lesser extent, influenced by English common law. Furthermore, like any mature legal system, its formal sources include a substantial body of legislation, both primary and secondary. Those legislative sources include a handful of Acts of the pre-Union Scottish Parliament (which, along with the English Parliament, was abolished by the Act of Union 1707 to make way for the Parliament of Great Britain), Acts of the UK Parliament and of the devolved Scottish Parliament established under the Scotland Act 1998. Since 1707 the final Court of Appeal in civil matters has been the House of Lords which tended, in less enlightened times, to shape Scots Law after the English model[2].

[1] Willam M. Gordon 'Roman Law in Scotland' in R Evans-Jones, ed *The Civil Law Tradition in Scotland* (1995).
[2] See, for example, *Dumbreck v Robert Addie & Sons (Collieries) Ltd* 1929 SC (HL) 51, which supplanted the Scots Law of duty of care to persons entering premises, which had been based upon the Roman *actio legis Aquilae*, with the English category-based approach—a change which to be reversed required legislative intervention, in the form of the Occupiers' Liability (Scotland) Act 1960.

13.03 Like the common law jurisdictions, the law of Scotland is largely uncodified[1], with reliance upon judicial precedent, though Scots lawyers are more ready to argue from general principles, regarding previous cases as illustrations of those principles rather than establishing them. This can lead to a flexibility and responsiveness on the part of the courts as new problems present themselves[2].

[1]   In the sphere of criminal law, not even codified to the same extent as English criminal law.
[2]   See, for example, *Strathern v Seaforth* 1926 JC 100 (recognition of a common law offence of unlawful taking and using of motor vehicles) and *Khalik v HM Advocate* 1984 JC 23 (selling of glue-sniffing kits to children found to constitute an offence at common law).

13.04 This history has led to the development of a modern legal system which, because it is an uncodified system with civilian roots and a heavy common law overlay, bears some resemblance to the legal system of South Africa[1]. Because of this the English common lawyer, in contemplating the Scottish legal landscape, will see many things in the law of evidence, as well as in other areas of the law, which look familiar. However, such apparent familiarity may blind English lawyers to the distinct possibility that things will be done very differently in Scotland.

[1]   TB Smith 'Scotland' in *The United Kingdom, the development of its Laws and Constitutions* (1955) at p 621.

The court system

13.05 The Supreme Courts comprise the Court of Session and High Court of Justiciary[1], the former having civil and the latter criminal jurisdiction. Scotland is also divided into a number of Sheriffdoms, each of which is presided over by a Sheriff Principal. There are Sheriff Courts in the main towns and cities of each Sheriffdom, with the Sheriffs exercising both civil and criminal jurisdiction. Within each Sheriffdom there is an optional appeal in civil matters from the Sheriff to the Sheriff Principal. Additionally, throughout Scotland there are district courts presided over by lay magistrates, exercising criminal jurisdiction only.

[1]   Originally constituted by the Act of 1672 c16.

13.06 There is also a variety of specialised courts and tribunals, such as the Lands Tribunal and Land Court, the Court of the Lord Lyon, as well as many statutory Tribunals, some Scottish and some UK. A detailed discussion of these lies outwith the scope of the present work[1]. The Court of Session, which sits only in Edinburgh, is divided into the Outer House, which is a court of first instance, and the Inner House, which is primarily an appeal court[2]. The Inner House hears appeals from the Sheriff Courts (both the Sheriff and the Sheriff Principal) and from the Outer House, as well also as from statutory tribunals. There is a further appeal from the Inner House of the Court of Session to the House of Lords. The current practice of the House of Lords is to seek to ensure that Scottish judges are amongst those hearing a Scottish Appeal.

[1]   For a full treatment of the subject, see 'Courts and Competency' *Stair Memorial Encyclopaedia* (1988) vol 6, pp 329ff.
[2]   There is a very limited first-instance jurisdiction in certain matters, detailed discussion of which is beyond the scope of this chapter.

13.07 In criminal matters, cases are heard in the district court, in the Sheriff Court or in the High Court, which is nominally based in Edinburgh but which also operates as a circuit court. Apart from those crimes which, by law, require to be heard in the High Court, or in respect of which specific statutory provision is made, it is for the prosecutor to decide in which court any given offence is to be prosecuted. Although there has always been a mechanism for appealing to the High Court of Justiciary as an appeal court from the district court and a Sheriff sitting alone, there was no appeal where the accused was tried on indictment until the High Court was given the appropriate jurisdiction by the Criminal Appeal (Scotland) Act 1926.

13.08 In criminal matters there is no appeal to the House of Lords and, even in the interpretation of UK statutes, the High Court is not bound by decisions of the House of Lords, though it might find them persuasive. As Lord Hope of Craighead said in *R v Manchester Stipendiary Magistrate, ex p Granada Television Ltd*[1]:

> Thus, although there is now much common ground between England and Scotland in the field of civil law, their systems of criminal law are as distinct from each other as if they were two foreign countries.

1   [2000] 1 AC 300, [2000] 1 All ER 135, [2000] 2 WLR 1 at 5B–C.

13.09 In terms of section 29(1) of the Scotland Act 1998, an Act of the Scottish Parliament is 'not law' if it lies outside the legislative competence of the Parliament. Included in the definition of what falls outside that competence is any provision which 'is incompatible with any of the Convention rights or with Community Law'. Section 57(2) similarly limits the powers of any member of the Scottish Executive to make any subordinate legislation, or to do any other act so far as that legislation or act is incompatible with convention rights or European Community law. Both a positive act and an omission or failure to act are covered[1]. In terms of Sch 6, such questions are included amongst 'devolution issues'[2] in respect of which there is both a right of appeal[3] and a power on the part of the court to refer[4] to the Judicial Committee of the Privy Council.

1   Scotland Act 1998, s 100(4).
2   A full list of devolution issues appears in Scotland Act 1998, Sch 6, para 1.
3   Scotland Act 1998, Sch 6, paras 12–13.
4   Scotland Act 1998, paras 10–11.

13.10 Given the art 6 and art 8 Convention rights to a fair trial and respect for family life, respectively, it is not surprising that questions relating to the admissibility of evidence arise frequently in the form of devolution issues.

13.11 This new right of appeal or reference to the judicial committee is not likely to lead to a similar convergence in criminal law as has historically occurred in civil law. As Lord Hope of Craighead pointed out in *Montgomery v HM Advocate*[1]:

> It follows that members of the Judicial Committee whose background is in English law must now exercise the intellectual discipline of thinking themselves into the Scottish system of criminal law when sitting on references or appeals from the High Court of Justiciary, as members of the committee whose

background is in Scots law have always had to do of thinking themselves into the English system of criminal law when hearing appeals in criminal cases from the Commonwealth.

¹   2001 SC (PC) 1 at 13.

THE SCOTS LAW OF EVIDENCE

The common law principles

Relevancy

13.12 If evidence is relevant, which is to say 'logically connected with the matters in dispute or if it is consistent or inconsistent with, or gives rise to a logical inference regarding the facts in issue'[1], then the general rule is that it is admissible unless it is excluded by some peremptory rule of law[2]. Such peremptory rules include the prohibitions at common law against hearsay, involuntary confessions, evidence excluded by the best evidence rule, evidence which cannot be tested (such as witness statements), as well as evidence excluded on the grounds of public policy, (for example under common law principles of professional confidentiality and, under statute, evidence excluded by Public Interest Immunity Certificate[3] or by reason of having been obtained without the requisite statutory warrant[4]).

¹   *IRC v Stenhouses Trustees* 1993 SLT 248 at 251E per Lord Coulsfield.
²   *IRC v Stenhouses Trustees* 1993 SLT 248.
³   Although the Court has discretion to override such a certificate: *Glasgow Corporation v Central Land Board* 1956 SC 1 (HL); *Burmah Oil Co Ltd v Bank of England* [1980] AC 1090.
⁴   *MacNeil v HM Advocate* 1986 SCCR 288.

The best evidence rule

13.13 Peremptory rules aside, relevant evidence will be excluded if it is not the best evidence which is available. Therefore, a witness statement, or other second-hand account of what the witness said[1], will be inadmissible as evidence since the best evidence will be parole evidence from the witness himself, unless the witness is deceased or insane or (at least in civil cases) a prisoner of war[2]. Similarly, an oral description of the state of an allegedly faulty heater contained in a report on the condition of that heater was not admissible when the heater itself was available but not produced[3].

¹   For example, *Grant v HM Advocate* 1938 JC 7 (conviction quashed when a medical report containing a statement by a witness implicating the accused was read to the jury).
²   *HM Advocate v Monson* (1897) 21R (J) 5 at pp 9–10 per LJC Macdonald.
³   *McGowan v Belling & Co Ltd* 1983 SLT 77.

Hearsay evidence

13.14 The most common application of the best evidence rule is to be found in the rule excluding hearsay evidence, which is expressed thus:

13.14 *Scotland*

An assertion other than one made by a person while giving oral evidence in the proceedings is inadmissible as evidence of any fact asserted[1].

At common law, such secondary evidence (save in the situations envisaged in *Morrison v HM Advocate*[2]) was generally regarded as incompetent. However, recent statutory provisions have innovated on this. Section 259 of the Criminal Procedure (Scotland) Act 1995 defines the circumstances in which hearsay evidence might be permitted in criminal cases, in part by restating the common law exceptions and in part by widening them[3]. By contrast with this limited reform, the rule against hearsay in civil proceedings was abolished completely by section 2 of the Civil Evidence (Scotland) Act 1988.

[1] Cross on *Evidence* (6th edn) p 38, approved in *Morrison v HM Advocate* (1990) SC 299 at 312.
[2] *Morrison v HM Advocate* (1990) SC 299.
[3] For example, by allowing, in certain circumstances, hearsay evidence of statements made by a witness who cannot be found (s 259(2)(c)). At common law inability to trace a witness did not allow hearsay evidence to be adduced.

Corroboration

13.15 At common law, the facts which, in a criminal case, establish the guilt of the accused or, in a civil case, establish the defender's liability, are required to be proved by corroborated evidence, which is to say either

(a)   the direct evidence of two witnesses; or
(b)   two or more evidential facts spoken to by separate witnesses; or
(c)   a combination of the direct evidence of one witness and one or more evidential facts spoken to by other witnesses[1].

A speciality of the law relating to corroboration is the so-called *Moorov* doctrine[2], which was developed to combat one of the intrinsic problems raised by the requirement for corroboration in the case of crimes committed in private. The doctrine allows similar alleged offences to corroborate each other if one witness speaks to each.

[1] Walker & Walker *The Law of Evidence in Scotland* (2000) para 5.3.2.
[2] *Moorov (Samuel) v HM Advocate* 1930 JC 68.

13.16 In the sphere of criminal law there is a limited number of statutory exceptions to the requirement for corroboration[1]. However, in civil cases, following the recommendation of the Scottish Law Commission[2], section 1 of the Civil Evidence (Scotland) Act 1988 entirely abolished the requirement for corroboration (which had already been abolished in personal injuries actions)[3].

[1] For example, certain parking offences (Road Traffic Regulation Act 1984, s 120).
[2] Scottish Law Commission *Evidence: Report on Corroboration, Hearsay and Related Matters in Civil Proceedings* (1986) Scot Law Com No 100.
[3] Law Reform (Miscellaneous Provisions) Scotland Act 1968, s 9(2).

Legal presumptions and judicial knowledge

13.17 The Scots Law of evidence contains a number of irrefutable presumptions—for example, the common law presumption that a girl under the age of twelve cannot consent to sexual intercourse[1] and the presumption that a child under the age of eight lacks the requisite mental capacity to commit a crime[2]—and a number of refutable presumptions, such as the presumption of death after an absence of seven years[3], or that a married man is the father of his wife's children[4]. No evidence is needed to prove facts that are the subject of such presumptions.

1 ˊ Hume i 303; now governed by s 5(1) of the Criminal Law (Consolidation) (Scotland) Act 1995, as amended.
2   Criminal Procedure (Scotland) Act 1995, s 41.
3   *Secretary of State for Scotland v Sutherland* 1944 SC 79; now Presumption of Death (Scotland) Act 1977, s 1.
4   *Pater est quem nuptiae demonstrant*, discussed in *Docherty v McGlynn (No 1)* 1983 SC 202 and given statutory expression in the Law Reform (Parent and Child) (Scotland) Act 1986, s 5.

13.18 Additionally, there are also facts which fall within judicial knowledge, characterised as facts which can be discerned from sources of indisputable accuracy[1], or are notorious or a matter of common knowledge[2]. It is important to note that judicial knowledge is not necessarily the same as that which the particular judge, in fact, knows[3]. The practical result is that, in the field of information technology, it is not necessarily to be assumed that every judge, in fact, knows things which may fall within judicial knowledge[4].

1   For example, the Shorter Oxford English Dictionary: see *IRC v Russell* 1955 SC 237.
2   For example, that the prefix M in a road number denotes a motorway (*Donaldson v Valentine* 1996 SLT 643); the strength of McEwan's Export (*Doyle v Ruxton* 1999 SLT 487) but not the strength of Coors Lager (*Grieve v Hillary* 1987 SCCR 317).
3   *Brims v MacDonald* 1993 SCCR 1061.
4   See below.

Standard of proof

13.19 In Scotland there are two standards of proof: the criminal standard is proof beyond reasonable doubt[1]; the civil standard is proof on the balance of probabilities[2], even where an allegation is made that the defender in a civil action has committed a crime[3].

1   *MacDonald v HM Advocate (No 2)* 1996 SLT 723.
2   *Hendry v Clan Line Steamers Ltd* 1949 SC 320.
3   *Mullan v Anderson* 1993 SLT 835.

Burden of proof

13.20 The process of litigation in Scotland, as in England and the common law jurisdictions, is adversarial rather than inquisitorial. Thus, each party requires to take the initiative in presenting evidence that supports his case or disproves or casts doubt upon the other party's case. The initial onus generally lies upon the prosecutor in criminal matters and the pursuer in civil matters, though this onus can sometimes shift during the course of a proof[1].

[1]   *McIlhargey v Herron* 1972 JC 38.

Legislative innovation—divergence of civil and criminal rules

13.21   Although, for the most part, the law of evidence is based upon general legal principles, elaborated and developed by the courts, there has also been a history of legislative intervention and regulation. The formal sources of this legislative overlay include Acts of the UK and devolved Scottish Parliaments, together with secondary legislation in the form of Statutory Instruments and Scottish Statutory Instruments. The Supreme Courts (the Court of Session and High Court of Justiciary) have power to promulgate Rules, which have effect as Statutory Instruments, to regulate their own procedure and procedure in the Sheriff Court.

13.22   Criminal procedure is regulated by the High Court of Justiciary by means of Acts of Adjournal and civil procedure by the Court of Session by means of Acts of Sederunt. The current criminal rules are the Criminal Procedure Rules 1996[1] and the current civil rules are, respectively, the Rules of the Court of Session 1994 (RCS)[2] and, in the Sheriff Court, the Ordinary Cause Rules 1993 (OCR)[3].

[1]   SI 1996/513 the updated and amended text of which is to be found online at: www.scotcourts.gov.uk/library/rules/crimprocedure/index.asp.
[2]   For an updated and amended text see: www.scotcourts.gov.uk/session/rules/index.asp.
[3]   Act of Sederunt (Sheriff Court Ordinary Cause Rules) 1993, (SI 1993/1956) the updated and amended text of which is available online at: www.scotcourts.gov.uk/library/rules/ordinarycause/index.asp.

13.23   In recent years, the general policy of legislative intervention in civil matters has tended to be to dilute the common law principles and to simplify the rules of evidence[1] whereas, in the sphere of criminal law, the reforms tend to have been both slower to come and more cautious[2]. Thus, as noted above, the Civil Evidence (Scotland) Act 1988 abolished, in civil causes, the requirement for corroboration and the rule against hearsay evidence, whilst the changes wrought by the Criminal Procedure (Scotland) Act 1995, were more limited.

[1]   See, for example, Scottish Law Commission *Evidence: Report on Corroboration, Hearsay and Related Matters in Civil Proceedings* (1986) Scot Law Com No 100.
[2]   See, for example, Scottish Law Commission *Evidence: Report on Documentary Evidence and Proof of Undisputed Facts in Criminal Proceedings* (1992) Scot Law Com No 137 and Scottish Law Commission *Evidence: Report on Hearsay Evidence in Criminal Proceedings* (1995) Scot Law Com No 149.

13.24   As a result of this recent history, and of the different standards of proof, the rules regarding evidence in civil and criminal proceedings, though rooted in the same common law principles, are now markedly different from each other. This applies as much to electronic evidence as to other forms of evidence, and requires to be borne in mind constantly when approaching both the case law and the primary and delegated legislation.

PERCEIVED PROBLEMS SURROUNDING THE ADMISSIBILITY OF ELECTRONIC EVIDENCE

13.25 As discussed above, the Scots law of evidence remains based upon common law principles, although modified by legislation. A consequence of continuing to rely upon common law underpinnings is that the law retains a degree of flexibility. The cases of *Strathern v Seaforth* and *Khalik v HM Advocate*[1], have already been noted. However, there are limits to such innovation, especially where the problems raised by electronic evidence are perceived as conceptual, rather than merely practical, and to be solved require step-change, rather than incremental development of accepted principles.

[1]   *Strathern v Seaforth* 1926 JC 100; *Khalik v HM Advocate* 1984 JC 23.

Conceptual problems

13.26 The very nature of digital technology forces an engagement with the issue of the fundamental nature of electronic evidence. For example, the courts never had any difficulty with accepting as evidence analogue representations, such as photographs (though the strict rules of evidence require the attendance of the photographer to speak to the photograph if it is to be relied upon as evidence and not merely as a means of rendering the oral evidence of certain witnesses more explicit and more intelligible)[1]. It might, however, be thought to be different where similar evidence is originated or presented in digital form, as when a photograph is printed as a result of a series of electrical impulses encoded on magnetic or other media being processed in a microprocessor and, in turn, operating a device such as a printer. The electrical impulses are not tangible in the way that a photographic negative is. In such an instance, the nature of the evidence may be the print, the electrical impulses, or the medium on which the electrical impulses are encoded.

[1]   *Eckersley v Dempsey* 1934 SLT (Sh Ct) 46.

13.27 Similarly, letters and other documents, are clearly admissible when in physical form, but the position may differ if they are scanned and digitised. Providing the originals exist, digitised copies would clearly be inadmissible under the best evidence rule. However, if the originals no longer exist, or if the document is digitally originated and never existed in physical form, in the case of email for example, other considerations might apply. More acutely, the data created on a computer and stored as an electronic charge upon the surface of a magnetic disk, and which may never have had any real, tangible existence, has to be conceptualised within the legal framework.

13.28 In the final analysis it may questioned whether a digital document, photograph, or sound recording is itself the evidence in the eyes of the law, or a copy of something else which constitutes the primary evidence, and whether the primary evidence is the original document, where it physically existed, or, where it did not exist, is the encoded series of ones and zeros.

Practical problems

13.29 Electronic evidence potentially presents practical, as well as conceptual, problems, particularly where it engages with the best evidence rule and the rules regarding corroboration and hearsay evidence. Whenever data contained in a storage medium, be it magnetic, optical or solid-state, is opened by a computer for viewing or editing, it is copied from the storage medium into the computer's random access memory ('RAM') from where it is processed in order to make it visible to the human eye. What appears on the screen is, therefore, not the same thing as the stored binary code. The view might be taken that the best evidence is the machine-readable code on the storage medium, but such code is unintelligible to humans and requires to be processed in order to yield sounds or images which are capable of being understood. There is potential for errors to arise in the conduct of that process, or for there to be deliberate manipulation of the digital information which might change or distort the final visible image. Thus, though the final visible image may not constitute the best evidence, it may be the best that is capable of being presented to a court. When considering such evidence, it may be necessary to be alive to the prospect of manipulation having occurred just as, in an earlier analogue age, it was necessary to be mindful of the possibility that a photographic print may have been altered. This analogy, however, is not perfect: it is easier to compare a print with the original negative than it is to detect manipulation of underlying digital information.

13.30 Many digitally encoded and stored documents are themselves copies. Such a document may be a typed or scanned version of a document which originated in physical form, such as a ledger, in which case the best evidence rule would require the production of the original ledger if it still existed. In a situation where the original paper document has been lost, what is visible on a screen or printed out is, therefore, essentially a copy of a copy.

13.31 Furthermore, just as (on the whole) physical documents do not prove themselves and require to be spoken to by the author or originator, so, too, with electronic evidence. No doubt with some documents (such as digital photographs) there may be one author or originator who can speak to the print, but with computer data there might be any number of authors or other persons who were responsible for entering data into the system. This requires an engagement with both the best evidence rule and the hearsay rule—John Smith, after all, cannot speak to data entered by Jack Brown, and it may even be that no one has any idea who entered or manipulated which particular data. Thus any attempt by John Smith to speak to data entered by others is what has sometimes been characterised as 'multiple hearsay'[1].

[1]   See Scottish Law Commission *Report on Evidence, Corroboration, Hearsay and Related Matters in Civil Proceedings* (1986) Scot Law Com 100, paras 3.52 and 3.63.

13.32 It is in the engagement with these and other similar problems, both by common law and by statute, that the law of Scotland relating to electronic evidence has been developed.

SOLVING THE CONCEPTUAL PROBLEMS

13.33 The first specific reference to electronic evidence to be found in legislation affecting Scotland is sections 13 and 14 of the Law Reform (Miscellaneous Provisions) (Scotland) Act 1968 which made specific provision for the circumstances in which a statement contained in a document produced by a computer is admissible as evidence of facts stated therein. These sections are in substantially similar terms to the provision made for England and Wales by sections 5 and 6 of the Civil Evidence Act 1968. By s 15 of the Scottish Act provision was made for the procedure to be followed in the event of a party seeking to rely upon such evidence. These provisions have now been superseded by the Civil Evidence (Scotland) Act 1988 ('CE(S)A 1988'). The abolition, by CE(S)A 1988, of both the requirement for corroboration[1] and the rule against hearsay evidence[2] goes a long way to render academic the theoretical issues of the nature of electronic evidence including, in particular, whether inputted data should be regarded as 'multiple hearsay'. In the event, however, the Act went further, providing by s 5 that, unless the court otherwise directs, 'a document may in any civil proceedings be taken to form part of the records of a business or undertaking if it is certified as such by a docket purporting to be signed by an officer of the business or undertaking ...' Such a document is, in effect, self-proving, not requiring a witness to speak to it. Indeed, for the purposes of s 5, 'a facsimile of a signature shall be treated as a signature'[3].

[1] CE(S)A 1988, s 1.
[2] CE(S)A 1988, s 2.
[3] CE(S)A 1988, s 5(2).

13.34 CE(S)A 1988, s 6 provides that a copy of a document, if authenticated by the person responsible for making the copy 'shall, unless the court otherwise directs, be (a) deemed a true copy and (b) treated for evidential purposes as if it were the document itself.' It should be noted that this provision is not restricted to business documents. The interpretation section, s 9, includes in the definition of 'document':

(c) any disc, tape, sound track or other device in which sounds or other data (not being visual images) are recorded so as to be capable (with or without the aid of some equipment) of being reproduced therefrom; and
(d) any film, negative, tape or other device in which one or more visual images are recorded so as to be capable (as aforesaid) of being reproduced therefrom.

Section 9 also provides that 'records' means 'records in whatever form'.

13.35 The net result is that under s 5 appropriately certified business records in electronic form (including hard and floppy disks, memory sticks and other similar media as well as print-outs derived from such media), and under s 6 other documents (if authenticated) in electronic form, all fall to be regarded as primary evidence which is also, in effect, self-proving unless the court directs otherwise.

13.36 Change in the sphere of criminal evidence has been more limited. Sections 259–266 of the Criminal Procedure (Scotland) Act 1995 ('CP(S)A 1995') make limited provision for the acceptance of hearsay evidence in criminal proceedings. In particular, s 259(1) provides that if the evidence would have been admissible and the witness would have been a competent witness then, if there applies any of the small number of circumstances in which a witness or potential witness may be unable or unwilling to give evidence, as listed in s 259(2), hearsay evidence is permitted if either it is spoken to by a witness who has direct personal knowledge of the making of the statement or 'it is contained in a document'[1]. Section 260 allows a witness giving evidence to adopt certain prior statements which he may have made, provided that 'the statement is contained in a document'[2].

[1] CP(S)A 1995, s 259(1)(d)(i).
[2] CP(S)A 1995, s 260(2)(a).

13.37 For the purposes of ss 259–261, s 262(3) defines 'document' in the same terms as are used in s 9 of the CE(S)A 1988. This is carried through to the Criminal Procedure Rules by r 21.4, which requires a certificate which is 'endorsed on or attached to the first page of the statement or attached to the device on which the statement has been recorded.'

13.38 CP(S)A 1995, Sch 8 para 1, which allows copy documents to be treated as the principal document unless the court otherwise directs, is cast in terms analogous to s 6 of CE(S)A 1988, though there are some differences: it specifically encompasses not only the whole but also a 'material part of a document'; it expressly allows for the copy to be regarded for evidential purposes as if it were the document itself 'whether or not the document is still in existence'; it also explicitly states that 'it is immaterial how many removes there are between a copy and the original' and specifies that 'copy' includes a transcript or reproduction'. Furthermore, in place of the requirement in s 6 of CE(S)A 1988 for the certificate to be signed by 'a person responsible for making a copy', para 1 leaves the person signing the certificate to be prescribed by the Criminal Procedure Rules.

13.39 Rule 26.1, requires the certificate on the copy to be signed:

by a person who is

    (i)   the author of the original of it;
   (ii) a person in, or who has been in, possession and control of the original of it or a copy of it; or
  (iii) the authorised representative of the person in, or who has been in, possession and control of the original of it or a copy of it;

Paragraphs 2, 3 and 4 make provision for business records analogous to the civil provision in s 5 of CE(S)A 1988, but, as with the provision for copies, does so in a more detailed and explicit way. Unlike s 5(2), there is no specific provision allowing a facsimile of a signature to be treated as an original signature.

13.40 In part the greater elaboration of the criminal provisions is a consequence of the need to fit the provisions for business records and copy documents into a legal framework where otherwise the best evidence rule (particularly in relation to hearsay) and the requirement for corroboration for the most part still apply with undiminished force. It may also reflect an attempt on the part of the parliamentary draftsman to anticipate the greater readiness of criminal practitioners to take technical evidential points[1].

[1] A tendency amply vouched for by the much greater number of criminal cases cited in this chapter.

13.41 Although there are parallels between the civil and criminal provisions for copies and business records, whether in paper or electronic form, there are significant differences and a close study of the primary legislation and the rules is required by any practitioner encountering such electronic evidence in the criminal sphere.

13.42 The legislation alone does not answer all of the conceptual questions surrounding the use of electronic evidence. In both CE(S)A 1988 and CP(S)A 1995, the statutory definition of 'document' read along with s 6 of CE(S)A 1988, and CP(S)A 1995, Sch 8, para 1 will generally render academic the question of the status of computer evidence (whether on screen or in the form of a print-out) as being a copy of some original residing in binary code in the computer drive but it does not altogether eliminate such questions, especially in criminal cases where there is a chance that if the evidence is controversial, the court may direct that copies be not treated as principals.

13.43 That said, the tendency of the courts has been to deal with such questions in a realistic manner. Prior to the enactment of the provisions now found in the CP(S)A 1995, the multiple hearsay problem in relation to computer records arose in *Lord Advocate's Reference (No 1 of 1992)*[1]. That case involved allegations of fraud and corruption for the proof of which an essential element was computer-generated remittance advices giving details of payees. There was no way to identify the person who entered the data from which the forms were generated.

[1] 1992 SLT 1010.

13.44 The accused had been acquitted on the basis that, in the absence of evidence from the person entering the data, the forms amounted to hearsay evidence. In reaching that decision, the sheriff had relied upon the majority reasoning of the House of Lords in *Myers v DPP*[1]. The objectionable evidence in that case was extracts from microfilmed records of engine block numbers, where the witnesses who spoke to the records were the persons who were in charge of the records but who had not originally been responsible for making them. By a majority, the House of Lords found this evidence to be inadmissible. If the rule against hearsay were to be relaxed to make statements in business records admissible that would have to be a matter for the legislature, not the courts[2]. Such a change was effected for Scotland as well as England by section 1 of the Criminal Evidence Act 1965, and subsequently extended, for England, to bodies other than a trade or business by sections 68 and 69 of the Police and Criminal Evidence Act 1984 ('CEA 1984'). However, the 1984 Act did not extend to Scotland, where s 1 of the 1965 Act continued to apply. In the instant case, the records of the Heath Board, being a public body, did not fall within the ambit of s 1.

[1]   [1965] AC 1001.
[2]   See Lord Reid at p 1021F.

13.45   The Lord Advocate petitioned the High Court of Justiciary for a ruling. Lord Justice General Hope commented that he considered the views expressed by the minority in *Myers* to be preferable. He stated:

> This court has shown itself willing to adapt the criminal law of this country in order to meet changes in social conditions and attitudes ... And I see no reason why we should not follow the same approach when examining rules of evidence such as the rule against hearsay evidence in the light of changed circumstances[1].

[1]   [1965] AC 1001 at 1016 D–E.

13.46   In the event, however, he considered that to permit a relaxation to the extent effected by the CEA 1984 ss 68 and 69 went beyond what the court could reasonably do[1], though went on to note that it was not merely impracticable, but impossible, to identify the person who entered the data and so, in effect, the hearsay evidence became the best evidence:

> The law does not compel people to do that which is impossible. So I can see no fundamental objection in principle to recognition of the application of this exception to the case of computer records, provided always that the evidence establishes that, due to the manner of the operation of the computer or the method of organisation by which information is put into it, it is not only not reasonably practicable, but impossible to identify the authors of the entries which require to be proved[2].

[1]   [1965] AC 1001 at 1018F.
[2]   [1965] AC 1001 at 1018K.

13.47   It is notable that this result was quite different to the result achieved by the House of Lords when confronted with the similar circumstances of *Myers*. This case is now rendered largely academic by reason of the later legislative intervention, but it is illustrative of a flexible approach by the court to dealing with the questions raised by the new technology.

13.48   Of more than academic interest, however, is the case of *Rollo v HM Advocate* [1] in which the court grappled with the fundamental question of what constitutes a document. In that case, police officers were carrying out a search authorised by a warrant under section 23(3)(b) of the Misuse of Drugs Act 1971. The warrant authorised them to search for and seize any document 'directly or indirectly relating to or connected with a transaction or dealing'. In the course of the search, they recovered a Sharp Memomaster 500, an electronic notepad containing certain data protected by a password. This information was highly incriminating and formed the basis for the accused's conviction. On appeal, his counsel argued that the Memomaster was not a document in terms of the statutory provision. She referred to the statutory definitions of 'document' contained in section 1(4) of the Criminal Evidence Act, 1965[2] and Schedule 8 to the 1995 Act and argued that if Parliament had intended to give an extended meaning to 'document' in the 1971 Act it would have done so. The Advocate Depute[3] argued that, according to the Oxford English Dictionary, the word 'document' could mean 'instrument, information, evidence or proof'. Referring to the decision of Walton J, in the English case of *Grant v Southwestern and County Properties Ltd*[4], that a tape constituted a document, he further argued that 'the law of evidence must move with the times and what was important was that the Memomaster contained information'.

[1]   1997 JC 23.
[2]   It is curious that he did not refer to the cognate provision for Scotland contained in the Law Reform (Miscellaneous Provisions) (Scotland) Act 1968.
[3]   At p 25G.
[4]   [1975] Ch 185.

13.49   The Court, in rejecting the appeal, stated[1]:

> Unsurprisingly, the word 'document' in normal usage is most frequently used in relation to written, typed or printed paper documents. Where information is stored by other means on other surfaces we accept that the storing item concerned is more readily referred to by reference to the means of storage or surface for storage concerned rather than as a 'document'. Hence reference to, for example, machines or tapes. However, terminological emphasis in description in such cases on the means or surface for recording information does not deprive such alternative stores of information from qualifying as 'documents' any more so than, for example, a tombstone, which is expressly included in the dictionary definition referred to. It seems to us that the essential essence of a document is that it is something containing recorded information of some sort. It does not matter if, to be meaningful, the information requires to be processed in some way such as translation, decoding or electronic retrieval.

The court then went on to consider the potential for tampering with various media, but expressed the view that this did not invalidate the conviction: any allegation of tampering would be a question for the jury.

[1]   At p 26F.

13.50

In light of these comments it would appear that the basic philosophical approach of Scots Law is to accept the information stored, rather than the storage medium, as constituting documentary evidence. However, even if these conceptual problems are effectively sidelined, practical issues still arise, which issues will now be considered.

ACQUISITION OF EVIDENCE

Criminal procedure

Computer evidence

13.51 The gathering of evidence by the police and other investigatory bodies is governed both by common law and statute. Under section 13 of the Criminal Procedure (Scotland) Act 1995, a person whom a constable has reasonable grounds to suspect has committed, or may be committing, an offence may be required to remain with the constable while the constable verifies his name and address and notes any explanation proffered by him. Further, the police have power both to detain a suspect[1] and to arrest him[2]. The stated purpose of detention is 'facilitating the carrying out of investigations'[3].

1   CP(S)A 1995, s 14.
2   Either at common law, *Peggie v Clark* (1868) 7M 89, or under specific statutory powers, eg section 59 of the Civic Government (Scotland) Act 1982.
3   CP(S)A 1995, s 14(1).

13.52 In general, a person who has been detained[1] or arrested either with or without a warrant[2] can be searched by the police[3] and can have his fingerprints and other samples taken[4] and recorded. Since it is now the normal practice of the police to take a measurement of fingerprints electronically by using the Livescan system[5], this effectively means that what may well be a critical piece of evidence in any case will usually be in electronic form.

1   In terms of CP(S)A 1995, s 14(7)(b) a constable has the same powers of search of a detainee as are available following an arrest.
2   A warrant requires to be sought by a petition under CP(S)A 1995, s 34.
3   *Jackson v Stevenson* (1897) 24R (J) 38; *Bell v Leadbetter* (1934) JC 74 at 77 per Lord Blackburn; CP(S)A 1995, s 14(7)(b).
4   CP(S)A 1995, s 18(2).
5   Authorised by the Electronic Fingerprinting etc. Device Approval Order 1997 (SI 1997/1939).

13.53 Although, of course, real evidence will have been gathered during an investigation either by collection from the scene of the crime or by being handed over voluntarily, generally speaking, the power of the police to compel the production of evidence requires an appropriate warrant or other authorisation. Under section 134 of CP(S)A 1995, the prosecutor can apply for a search warrant, either before or after proceedings have commenced, or a warrant of apprehension. Under CP(S)A 1995, s 135, the form of the warrant is as specified by subordinate legislation[1].

1   See Criminal Procedure Rules, r 16.5(1).

13.54 A search warrant will specify the location to be searched and an arrest warrant will normally give police officers the power to search the place where the accused may be found and his dwelling house with a view to taking possession of articles relevant to the charge. However if, in the course of a search following upon the granting of a warrant, there is an item which is itself suspicious, and would be admissible evidence in relation to another offence, then the police may also take possession of that item[1]. However, the police cannot take away items, not immediately suspicious, with a view to discovering whether they might be evidence of other offences[2].

[1] *HM Advocate v Hepper* 1958 JC 39; *Tierney v Allan* 1990 SLT 178.
[2] *HM Advocate v Turnbull* 1951 JC 96.

13.55 Police powers in the case of arrest without warrant are limited to searching the person of the accused as well as his immediate surroundings when arrested: this might enable a search of the accused's premises, but only if he were arrested there[1]. The standard form of warrant is sufficiently wide to encompass both documents and other articles[2] but, as noted in *Rollo*[3], in some cases there may be a specific statutory form of warrant which is limited to documents or, again, mistakes in the drafting of the warrant may occur. However, standing the decision in *Rollo*, even a warrant referring only to 'documents' would probably suffice to enable the recovery of computers, discs, drives and other devices containing documents in the extended meaning given to that word by the court.

[1] If the accused were not arrested at home but there is an appreciable urgency, then evidence recovered without warrant might be admissible. See *HM Advocate v McGuigan* (1936) JC 16.
[2] Criminal Procedure Rules, Appendix, Form 16.5–B
[3] 1997 JC 23.

13.56 A warrant contains an implied power to break open lockfast places[1] and this should extend not only to physically breaking down a locked door, but also to overcoming electronic security devices such as passwords. Such a view finds support in the way in which the court in *Rollo* dealt with a curious subsidiary argument for the appellant who suggested that because there was password protection on the Memomaster that prevented the information from being regarded as a document. The rationale for that argument is obscure, but, in any event, the court dismissed the argument by saying that a password was 'no different to the lock on a locked diary'[2]. If the lock on a diary can be broken open so, it is submitted, may an electronic lock on an electronic document.

[1] CP(S)A 1995, ss 134(3) and 135(1).
[2] At pp 26I–27A.

13.57 Where police are carrying out a search and come upon, say, a computer, if the machine itself, as a physical object, constitutes evidence[1] then the warrant will permit its removal. However, if the evidence is in the form of documents stored on the computer the situation may be different. If the police are legitimately interrogating the computer looking, say, for documents relating to one fraud, and, in the process, come across documents relating to another, they would be in the situation envisaged in *Hepper*[2] and could properly recover those additional documents. However, if they were investigating, say, a breach of the peace or a minor assault it is difficult to see how they could justify looking at the computer.

[1]   For example, if the crime under investigation is the theft of computers
[2]   *HM Advocate v Hepper* 1958 JC 39.

13.58 The foregoing discussion presupposes that the police know how to interrogate a computer properly. This may not be an unreasonable assumption, as many forces do have specialised computer crime units. However, the police have been known to take along civilian experts. This practice has given rise to challenge.

13.59 In particular, in *Lord Advocate's Reference No 1 of 2002*[1] police recovered a computer and ten zip disks containing indecent photographs of children. The accused was acquitted on the basis that the evidence had been improperly obtained since the police had been assisted by a civilian employee of the police computer forensic unit but the warrant extended only to police officers[2]. The Lord Advocate then petitioned the High Court of Justiciary for a ruling on the issue. The court observed that a person who is not a police officer might properly assist the police in a search (for example, a locksmith who is there to open lockfast places) and, so long as that person does not actively participate in the search, there is no irregularity. In the instant case, it was a police officer who had identified the computer and disks for removal. The role of the civilian employee was merely to assist the officer in tagging and removal of the evidence. Accordingly, his presence did not have the effect of rendering the search irregular.

[1]   2002 SLT 1017.
[2]   By no means an unstateable argument: in *Hepburn v Brown* 1998 JC 63, evidence recovered in a drug raid was found to have been recovered irregularly as an officer of the Metropolitan Police had actively participated although the warrant did not extend to him. In the event, however, the Court exercised its discretion to excuse the irregularity.

13.60 This decision has come in for some criticism and McLennan, in his case commentary, suggests that the analogy with a locksmith may not be altogether helpful as the warrant envisages breaking open the premises and thereafter searching the premises[1]. McLennan poses the question of whether a civilian, not covered by the warrant, 'hacking' into a computer could be regarded as a locksmith breaking open premises. That said, it may be that the locksmith analogy would still apply, for what is being searched for is documents stored on the computer: the evidence is the documents, not the computer, so overcoming the electronic security of the computer is indeed an act which occurs prior to the search of the 'virtual premises'. However, this is a question which the court is yet to address. In the meantime, the police would be advised to try to avoid using civilians in searching for electronic evidence even if, or especially if, that search is conducted under a warrant.

[1]   See the case commentary by Angus McLennan at 2002 SLT (News) 238.

13.61 Another supposed issue may arise from the circumstance that section 14 of the Computer Misuse Act 1990 makes specific provision for search warrants in respect of offences under s 1 in England and Wales, yet omits any similar legislative provision for Scotland. However, this is unlikely to give rise to any problem as the existing common law police powers of search in

Scotland and the terms of the standard form of search warrant in use in Scotland are probably wide enough not to require the making of any special statutory provision.

Electronic communications and surveillance

13.62 Since time began, people have been intercepting letters and, since the invention of the telephone, have been eavesdropping on telephone conversations. Modern means of interception reflect the advance of technology but, in principle, are no different from steaming open an envelope or listening-in on a telephone conversation.

13.63 In the past there was a perception that such activities were largely uncontrolled, the law operating on the principle that whatever is not forbidden is permitted, and, since surveillance is not forbidden, it must be permissible[1]. This proposition does not sit well with the provisions of article 8 of the European Convention on Human Rights and was tested and found wanting in the case of *Khan v United Kingdom*[2] which led directly to the enactment of the Regulation of Investigatory Powers Act 2000, and the Regulation of Investigatory Powers (Scotland) Act 2000, both of which govern surveillance by law enforcement agencies in Scotland. A detailed consideration of the provisions of these acts lies outwith the scope of the present work but there are, perhaps, a few observations which may be made insofar as the Acts apply to electronic surveillance.

[1] In reality, the courts would intervene in flagrant cases. For example, in *HM Advocate v Graham* 1991 SLT 416, Lord Cameron of Lochbroom disallowed evidence of a conversation obtained through one of the participants wearing a 'wire' where, if the questions had been put directly by police officers without caution, the evidence would have been disallowed
[2] 8 BHRC 310 (ECHR, May 12, 2000).

13.64 RIPA Pt 1 allows interception of communications, whether postal or electronic, if a warrant has been obtained as provided for by ss 6–11[1]. Part II governs surveillance and covert human intelligence sources which, to be lawful, require authorisation and Pt III grants power to serve a notice requiring disclosure of the key to unlock encrypted data. Restrictions are imposed on the application of Pt II to Scotland by section 46, and the separate provisions for Scotland governing those cases where RIPA does not apply by virtue of section 46 are found in RIPSA. The net result is that the exercise of Pt I and III powers in Scotland will be governed by the UK Statute.

[1] Or where, in the limited circumstances set out in s 5, no warrant is required.

13.65 As the legislation is framed with electronic communications very much in mind it might be thought that few problems would arise, but this is not entirely so. In *Hoekstra v HM Advocate (No. 5)*[1], an electronic surveillance device had been placed on board a vessel which was being used for drug running. The device assisted the surveillance officers to locate the vessel and commence observation of it. The evidence at the trial related to the observations and, indeed, it was unknown to both the prosecution and the defence until a late stage in the trial that a bugging device had been used to locate the vessel. It was conceded by the Crown that the device had been placed on the vessel illegally and in contravention of art 8(1) of the ECHR[2]. The defence argued that, since the surveillance device had led to the commencement of the observations upon which the conviction had been based, the finding of guilt should be quashed.

1   2002 SLT 599.
2   It was not possible to say whether there was a breach of RIPA or RIPSA as it was not known in which port the bug had been placed on the vessel.

13.66 The court referred to its common law power, articulated in *Lawrie v Muir*[1] to excuse an irregularity in the obtaining of evidence. The court stated[2]:

> The authorities concerned with enforcement of the drugs laws had a very substantial body of information available to them to show that preparations were being made for a major transport of illegal drugs and that the *Isolda* was likely to be involved. It is difficult to see how contact with the *Isolda* could have been maintained without the use of some such device. If the illegality had consisted or resulted in the recording of conversations, for example, a very strong argument might have been presented that any such evidence was inadmissible. In the actual circumstances of this case, however, it does not seem to us that the use of the device played such a central part in the prosecution as to render the later observations tainted. What the device did was to make it possible to identify and commence observation on the *Isolda* as she approached the point at which the transfer of cargo was to be made. In these circumstances, it seems to us that the irregularity or illegality could be excused and that the judge was right to reject the objection to the admissibility of this evidence.

In relation to the broader Convention argument, the court relied on the judgement of the European Court of Human Rights in *Schenk v Switzerland*[3] to the effect that, while the Convention guarantees the right to a fair trial, it does not lay down any rules on the admissibility of evidence as such.

1   1950 JC 19 at 27.
2   At para [30] on p 609.
3   (1988) 13 EHRR 242 at pp 22–26, para 46.

13.67 A similar situation arose in *McGibbon v HM Advocate*[1], which involved a series of covert audio and video recordings, which the Crown accepted were obtained in breach of art 8 of the ECHR. However, Lord Justice-Clerk Gill[2] observed that 'while the method of obtaining evidence may infringe article 8, the leading of it may nonetheless not infringe article 6'[3]. He continued 'the underlying principle is that of fairness. In modern law that falls to be decided by means of a trial within a trial'. Since the sheriff, in allowing the evidence, had followed that procedure and it was not suggested that his decision was unreasonable, the appeal was rejected. This decision was followed in *Henderson v HM Advocate*[4].

1   2004 JC 60.
2   At para [21], p 64.
3   The right to a fair trial.
4   2005 JC 301.

13.68 The message from these cases is that the fact that electronic evidence may have been obtained irregularly does not necessarily mean that it is inadmissible or will taint subsequent evidence which follows on the back of it. It will be a question for the discretion of the court in any given case.

13.69 A more technical point was taken in *Porter v HM Advocate*[1], where HM Customs and Excise had infiltrated an operation to bring drugs from Morocco to the United Kingdom: HM Customs & Excise supplied the boat used to transport the drugs and most of the crew. In the course of the operation, HM Customs & Excise also bugged a telephone by means of placing a microphone in the handset, thereby transmitting conversations which were recorded and used in evidence. This was undertaken without any warrant under the Interception of Communications Act 1985[2]. On appeal, it was argued that this evidence should not have been allowed but the court held that what required a warrant was the 'interception' of the communication, which is to say the interception of the electrical signals within the system. The recording of the spoken word, once the signals had left the system, was lawful without a warrant. Although this case was decided under the 1985 Act, the Court observed that the language of RIPA was substantially similar. However, it is worth noting that no attempt was made to attack the surveillance as a contravention of article 8(1) of the ECHR. By similar reasoning, it was found in England that no warrant was required to intercept the signal between the handset and base station of a cordless telephone[3].

[1]   2005 JC 141.
[2]   The predecessor of RIPA.
[3]   *R v Effick* [1994] 3 All ER 458.

13.70 In *McIntyre v HM Advocate*[1] the issue was somewhat different. The police were investigating a series of threatening telephone calls, in the course of which investigation they recorded the voice of the caller. No irregularity in that process was alleged. The accused was detained by the police under s 14 of the 1995 Act and was interviewed under caution. The caution contained a warning that the interview would be recorded and might be used in evidence. Thereafter, on the direction of the Procurator Fiscal, the police obtained an expert report comparing a voice print analysis of the recording of the interview with the recording of the telephone conversation. The conclusion of the report was that the accused was the same person as the one who had made the telephone call. The accused objected to this evidence on the ground that he had not been warned, before giving the interview, that the recording would be used for this purpose.

[1]   2005 SLT 757.

13.71 The appeal failed. The Court noted that when the interview had been conducted, the police had not had it in mind to obtain a voice print analysis. The interview had therefore been properly conducted and the tape lawfully obtained. Once it had been obtained it was similar to, for example, lawfully obtained fingerprints of the accused:

[The recording] was obtained in circumstances in which, because neither the appellant nor the police officers were contemplating the possibility that the recording might yield a voice sample, there is no reason to treat it as other than an objective sample of the appellant's voice. The public interest that that sample be available for analysis and comparison is in our view clear. We do not consider that there is any clear basis for thinking that such use of the sample is unfair to the appellant[1].

[1]   at para [16].

Electronic devices

13.72 Road traffic law enforcement has become heavily dependent upon electronic devices such as Camic Breath analysers, Vascar radar devices and automatic speed cameras. Many technical points have been taken to seek to exclude such evidence. These tend, however, to be based on the precise wording of the legislation authorising their use and are of only limited interest in a treatment of the broader aspects of electronic evidence.

13.73 For example, there are several cases involving the Camic breath analysis device: *Annan v Crawford* 1984 SCCR 382 (print-out invalid as no evidence that it was served on the accused); *Gilligan v Tudhope* 1986 JC 34 and *Wilson v Webster* 1999 SCCR 747 (machine remains a 'reliable device' where unreliability is restricted to its date and time recording functions and does not affect its analytical function); *Hodgekins v Carmichael* 1989 JC 27 (similarly where the fault is in the printer); *McPherson v McNaughton* 1992 SCCR 434 (name of accused incorrectly written on print-out, but parole evidence competent to establish that the print-out related to him); *Ramage v Walkingshaw* 1992 SCCR 82 (accused taken to police station where device checked twice by police officers and each time found unreliable; on third check found to be working and accused breath tested. The machine was reliable in that the requirement to give a specimen was made at a time when the police were satisfied that it was reliable); and *Gallacher v Dick* 2000 JC 71 (blood test required because police officers relied on information from sergeant that the Camic device was not working, even though it later transpired that it was—what mattered was the belief of the officers at the time).

13.74 Examples of cases raising issues in respect of Vascar radar speed detectors include *Barbour v Normand* 1992 SCCR 331 (police observed accused travelling at what they considered an excessive speed; they measured his speed by a Vascar device and there was also produced a certificate that a device had been tested and found accurate, but there was no direct evidence from the officers that the device which they had tested was the same as the device which they had used: the court's view was that the deficiency could be supplied by circumstantial evidence); *Pervez v Clark* 2001 SCCR 138 and *Hogg v MacNeil* 2001 SLT 873 (both cases heard together—requirements in relation to measurement of marked distance used for calibration of radar speed devices).

13.75 The case of *McLean v McLeod* 2002 SCCR 127 does, however, raise an issue of wider interest. In this case the accused was charged with dangerous driving, it being alleged that he was driving at 72 mph in a 30 mph limit. He had been observed by two constables operating a radar speed trap. Although both spoke to seeing the speed displayed on the readout, only one spoke to the accuracy of the device; the other spoke to his impression that the vehicle was travelling at excessive speed. The court held that if precise speed were in issue, as it would be in a speeding charge, then the accuracy of the device would require to have been proved by corroborated evidence but, since a charge of dangerous driving did not require evidence of precise speed, the second constable's evidence of his impression gave sufficient corroboration. This does underline the need, when approaching evidence produced by automatic devices, to consider carefully in what matters corroboration may be required: it cannot be assumed that the court will accept automatic results without corroboration.

Civil procedure

13.76 The position as regards acquisition of evidence in civil causes is less complex, as the strict rules applicable in respect of evidence in criminal cases do not apply. The rule established in the case of *Rattray v Rattray*[1] is that if evidence is relevant it is admissible; the circumstances surrounding its acquisition, even if through the commission of a crime, having no bearing on its admissibility. This decision was followed with some reservation in the later cases of *McColl v MacColl*[2] and *Duke of Argyll v Duchess of Argyll*[3] where there was a suggestion that the court should have a similar discretion to admit or refuse to admit evidence irregularly obtained as exists in criminal cases. However, whatever reservations may have been expressed the rule remains.

[1] (1897) 25 R 315—a letter stolen from the post office by a jealous husband allowed as evidence of adultery.
[2] 1946 SLT (Notes) 42.
[3] 1962 SC 140.

13.77 By contrast, in *Martin v McGuiness*[1] an attempt was made by a pursuer in a personal injuries claim to exclude evidence obtained by private investigators in circumstances which, he claimed, amounted to an infringement of his art 8 Convention rights. Although he was unsuccessful, on the basis that the evidence might be permissible under art 8(2) as being in the interests of the wider community, what is significant is that the court was prepared to consider an art 8 argument to be relevant.

[1] *Martin v McGuiness* (2003) SLT 1424.

13.78 The present position is, therefore, that the rule may fall to be reconsidered at least to the extent that art 8 rights are engaged: first, it may be that in a suitable case there would require to be a balancing of infringement under art 8(1) with the wider interest under art 8(2) but then, by analogy with the situation in criminal cases, there would require to be further consideration of whether the use of evidence obtained improperly under art 8 would, in any event, result in an infringement of the art 6 right to a fair trial.

13.79 For the moment, these are issues for the future. In the meantime, a husband who uses a key logger on his wife's personal computer to spy upon her assignations, or private investigators using similar measures to detect civil fraud, would probably be able to present the results of their activities in evidence without difficulty. Not only is evidence more readily found acceptable by the court, but the abolition of the requirement for corroboration and of the rule against hearsay evidence means that most of the foregoing discussion on the use of electronic evidence in criminal procedure is of little more than academic interest to the civil lawyer.

13.80 The court also has power at common law to compel anyone possessing evidence, not restricted to another party to the action, to produce that evidence. This power extends to corporeal movables as well as documents[1]. This power is supplemented by section 1 of the Administration of Justice (Scotland) Act 1972 by which the Court of Session and the Sheriff Court are each given power subject to questions of privilege, confidentiality and public interest:

> To order the inspection, photographing, preservation, custody and detention of documents and other property (including, where appropriate, land) which appear to the court to be property as to which any question may relevantly arise in any existing civil proceedings before that court or in civil proceedings which are likely to be brought, and to order the production and recovery of any such property, the taking of samples thereof and the carrying out of any experiment thereon or therewith.

1   *Mactaggart v MacKillop* 1938 SLT 559, order to produce a typewriter.

13.81 It will be noted that this power is so wide as to be able to encompass any form of electronic evidence whether that be a 'document', in the meaning declared in *Rollo*, or any machine or device containing electronic evidence. The power is also available before or after proceedings have been commenced and may be directed at any individual in possession of evidence (who is known as a 'haver').

13.82 The detailed rules for the exercise of this power are found in RCS 35 and OCR 28[1]. An application after proceedings have commenced is made by way of a motion in the action seeking a Commission and Diligence for recovery of the evidence which is narrated in an accompanying Specification of Documents (and/or Property). The Specification is usually drafted in very wide terms. Unless there is a good tactical reason to do so, it would not be normal to specify, say, a particular letter or email but rather 'correspondence'. However, since the court will not grant a 'fishing' diligence[2] this is usually qualified, such as 'all correspondence relating to the contract referred to on Record'[3]. This motion may or may not be opposed and, if it is, there is usually a discussion between counsel or solicitors agreeing appropriate terms, failing which, the court decides.

¹ Both the Court of Session and Sheriff Court Rules are in broadly similar terms.

² ie 'one for which there is no basis in the averments or one which involves too wide a search among all the papers of the haver', *Civil Service Building Society v MacDougall* (1988) SC 58 per L.J-C. Ross at p 62; see also *St Andrews District Committee of County Council of Fife v David Wedderburn Thoms* (1898) 25 R 1097.

³ The Record is the written pleadings.

13.83 After the motion has been granted, the applicant in whose favour has been granted the Commission and Diligence may use the optional procedure under RCS 35.3¹ to enable the haver to send the documents or property direct to the applicant's solicitor, which failing the Commission is executed at the sight of a Commissioner appointed by the court. In Court of Session proceedings, the Commissioner is usually a Junior Counsel. The Commission is convened in some suitable location, usually a room in the Court building, but, in an appropriate case, there is no reason why this could not be elsewhere, say, in the case of computer evidence, the place where the computers are kept by the haver. The haver receives a citation to attend along with the evidence and is examined and cross-examined by parties' counsel. If needed, the Commission may be adjourned, for example to enable the haver to search for and produce further evidence falling under the Specification. Any evidence produced by the haver is taken into the custody of the Commissioner who may have various powers, for example to take excerpts from material falling under the Specification from a document containing other material which the applicant has no entitlement to see. If confidentiality in any document is claimed, it may be handed over in a sealed envelope for the court later to rule on a motion to allow the opening of the envelope.

¹ In the Sheriff Court OCR 28.3.

13.84 This procedure, which in its broad outline predates the 1972 Act by a considerable period, is best suited to paper documents and there are no special rules which relate the procedure to the particular exigencies of electronic evidence. However, with a Commissioner who is sensitive to these exigencies, the procedure is easily capable of adaptation. A hard drive can as easily be put in an envelope marked 'confidential' as can a piece of paper, and, as explained below, a Commissioner can easily develop appropriate protocols to preserve electronic evidence.

13.85 However, it may be that it is felt necessary to obtain evidence before proceeding to raise an action founding on that evidence or, alternatively, there may be perceived to be a risk that, if evidence is sought after the action has been raised, the evidence in question might be destroyed. In that event, a party may choose to seek recovery of evidence before any intended action is raised. The procedure for doing so is by way of a Petition to the Court of Session in terms of RCS 64¹. Electronic evidence is particularly vulnerable to being destroyed: it is much easier to wipe a hard drive than to shred a filing cabinet full of paper; the procedure is by way of Motion in a depending cause may take several weeks and there is no element of surprise. Accordingly, where such potentially fugitive electronic evidence is concerned, there is an obvious attraction in proceeding by way of pre-action Petition.

¹ There is no equivalent procedure in the Sheriff Court Ordinary Cause Rules, though it has been suggested that an application might proceed as a Summary Application under the Sheriff Court Summary Application Rules 1993 (SI 1993/3240).

13.86 Such a petition used to be a very effective tool: the petition was lodged in court, and the motion for the granting of the Commission and Diligence was enrolled. The court was empowered to grant such intimation as it thought fit, and if a good enough case were made out, the court could be persuaded to order no intimation. The motion was then usually granted at the same time as the order for service of the petition. The court customarily appointed a Senior Counsel as the Commissioner and the first that the haver knew about anything was when (it may have been literally at dawn) one day the Commissioner turned up at his door with his clerk, a computer expert engaged by him, a locksmith to break open lockfast places, a Messenger at Arms to serve the documents and the legal representatives of the petitioner.

13.87 However, this procedure, known as a 'dawn raid', and which may be seen as an equivalent to the English Anton Piller order, did not escape the effects of the Human Rights Act 1998[1]. The rules as they now exist stipulate information which is to be included in the petition[2] and require it to be accompanied by an affidavit and certain undertakings[3]. As before, it is open to the court to order such intimation as it thinks fit[4]. The Commissioner, who is still usually a Senior Counsel is required to serve the court order on the haver along with the affidavit[5] and to hand to the haver the printed Form 64.9, setting out the haver's legal rights and obligations, as well as to explain to the haver the meaning and effect of the order and his right to claim confidentiality and to seek legal advice. RCS 64.11 restricts service, except on cause shown, to Monday to Friday only between the hours of 9am and 5pm. The Commissioner is forbidden to enter the premises if they are occupied by an unaccompanied female and neither the Commissioner nor one of the persons accompanying him is female. If this provision is not to present a potential problem, it might be prudent for the one of the applicant's representatives named in the order to be female.

¹ See Ruth Charteris 'Sun sets on dawn raids' 2000 SLT (News) 271.
² RCS 64.2.
³ RCS 64.3.
⁴ RCS 64.5.
⁵ RCS 64.8.

13.88 The restrictions on service cause some blunting of the effectiveness of the dawn raid procedure, but the principal weakness, from the point of view of the applicant, lies in the effect of certain standard terms in the Order, explained in paras 5, 6 and 9 of Form 64.9. Paragraph 5 advises the haver of his right to seek 'legal or other professional advice[1]' and, though para 6 informs the haver that consultation under para 5 will not prevent the Commissioner from entering the premises, it then adds

> But if the purpose of your seeking advice is to help you to decide if you should ask the court to vary the order, he will not be able to search the premises.

Clearly this could prevent recovery of evidence for several hours while the haver attempts to contact his solicitor and to seek advice, which it might be reasonable to assume that the solicitor might not be in a position to give without consideration of the papers and time for reflection.

1 Conceivably technical advice from a computer expert.

13.89 Although para 9 tells the haver that he can ask the court to vary the order provided that he takes steps to do so 'at once', clearly this is not to be taken literally as he is entitled under para 6 first to seek legal advice as to whether to ask the Court to vary the order, and the requirement of para 9 is, in any event, to take steps. Until the Court has reached a decision on variation no search is possible though, of course, there is nothing to prevent the haver from continuing to use any computers, databases and such like specified in the order for the continued running of his business. Thus it is easy to see how, even where a haver acts entirely in good faith, a search could be stalled for days or even weeks, during which time there is a serious risk that electronic evidence may be lost or compromised. If the haver is acting in bad faith he might easily bring an application for variation, even if he thinks it has little chance of success, and, given that the Commissioner is unlikely to choose to camp, powerless, in the haver's office for a week or two, there is ample opportunity for drives to be wiped and paper records to be shredded. This is not a fanciful concern, since an order sought ex parte would have been granted in the first place only if the court had been satisfied that there was a risk of destruction or concealment of the evidence[1]. A haver who is likely to destroy evidence may not find himself deterred from doing so simply because the order forbids him to do so, even though that would place him in contempt of court.

1 *British Phonographic Industry Ltd v Cohen, Cohen, Kelly, Cohen & Cohen Ltd* 1983 SLT 137.

13.90 That said, these limitations seldom cause problems in practice[1] and the procedure can be quite effective. The order allows for the Commissioner to bring along persons to assist him and, in the case of electronic evidence recovery, it is advisable for the Commissioner to be accompanied by a computer expert. Further the order specifies named representatives of the petitioner to accompany the Commissioner 'for the purpose of identification of the said documents and other property' and, in the case of electronic evidence, there is no reason why that representative should not be a person possessing appropriate IT skills.

1 The experience of the author is that that most havers are reasonably co-operative and, at most, there may be a delay of an hour or two whilst legal advice is being sought.

13.91 RCS 64.9 empowers the Commissioner to 'take all reasonable steps to fulfil the terms of the order'. How he interprets that power is largely a matter for his discretion. In one recent Commission, the author, who attended as Commissioner along with a computer expert to assist him, carried out sufficient examination of a personal computer on site to satisfy himself that the computer contained material falling under the order (as well as other information of a confidential nature). He took the computer, as well as several floppy disks and print-outs, into his custody and then adjourned the Commission. Several days later, upon the Commission being reconvened in neutral premises and in the presence of legal and expert technical advisors for both sides, the Commissioner caused his expert to copy from the hard drive of the computer all of the files falling under the order on to a blank newly-reformatted drive and to create an audit trail by the installation of checksum software onto the new drive which was then converted to read-only, the checksum calculations performed and stored on a floppy disk which was then write-protected. The new hard drive and the checksum floppy were then received into evidence. Thereafter, in order to allow the haver the use of the material not falling under the order, the original hard drive was cloned onto a second new hard drive and there was then deleted from the clone the files which had been recovered under the order. There was then deleted from the clone a file reconstruction utility which had been present on the original hard drive and the clone was then defragmented. This second, new, hard drive was then given to the haver in place of the original hard drive (constituting, of course, the primary evidence) which was then placed in an envelope marked 'confidential'. None of this procedure was laid down in any formal rules, bur it does illustrate how the recovery procedures are sufficiently flexible to allow appropriate protocols to be developed.

13.92 Although there are the powers, noted above, to compel the production of evidence, as well as powers to require early lodging of essential productions[1] and restrictions on the late lodging of productions[2], there is, in Scotland, (unlike certain other jurisdictions) no extensive pre-trial discovery procedure. Further, even though a party might enrol a motion in terms of s 1(1A) of the Administration of Justice Act 1972 to require a person to disclose the identity of potential witnesses, as well as rules requiring the intimation of lists of witnesses for each party[3], there is no procedure for sworn depositions (a creature largely unknown in Scotland) nor is there power to compel any witness to give a precognition or statement to a solicitor if he does not wish to do so, whether because of disinclination or because his employer has ordered him not to. Accordingly, one or the other party can quite often find himself surprised by what a witness says when he comes to give evidence.

[1]   eg RCS 27; OCR 9A.2.
[2]   eg RCS 36.3; OCR 29.11.
[3]   eg RCS 36.9; OCR 9A.3.

THE PRESENTATION OF ELECTRONIC EVIDENCE IN COURT

13.93 There are no restrictions in the rules which serve to prevent or hinder the presentation of electronic evidence in court[1] and there are increasing signs that the court is prepared to welcome digitisation of evidence because of the obvious savings in time and expense that may be achieved. However, there remain a number of practical constraints and there may still be traps for the unwary in the interface with the formal rules of evidence, some of which have already been noticed in relation to the gathering of electronic evidence, especially in the criminal sphere.

1 There does exist an Act of Sederunt Computer Evidence in the Sheriff Court 1969 (SI 1969/1643) which sets out a highly elaborate procedure of notices and counter notices if computer evidence is to be relied upon. There was a similar provision in respect of the Court of Session which was revoked in 1990 (SI 1990/705) but it appears that *per incuriam* the court omitted to revoke the Sheriff Court provision, which remains extant. However, its provenance lay in section 15 of the Law Reform (Miscellaneous Provisions) (Scotland) Act 1968, which has since been repealed, and this, together with other subsequent changes in the substantive law, renders its provisions otiose and it is neither used in practice nor noted in current textbooks. It is probably safe to regard it as in desuetude.

Electronic images

13.94 It has been noted that, in criminal procedure, there still remains the requirement for corroboration. However, the court treats video evidence, such as CCTV footage, in the same way in which it treats photographs: if it is proved that the video footage was made at a particular time and place, and that the tape which is produced in court is that footage, then the requirements of corroboration are satisfied if two witnesses are able to identify the accused *from the tape* without the need for the content of the tape to be corroborated by an eyewitness who independently saw the events which are shown on the tape[1]. In effect, this means that the electronic medium becomes transparent—what is seen on it is the actual event rather than, as is theoretically possible, treating the camera as a single witness in need of corroboration.

1 *Bowie v Tudhope* 1986 SCCR 205.

13.95 However, since it is necessary to have corroborated evidence that this is the particular tape showing the event, it is fatal to have one witness who has viewed the tape and gives evidence to that effect supported by a witness who only speaks to a label which he placed upon the tape but without his then viewing the tape in the witness box to verify that this is the tape to which he originally affixed the label[1].

1 *Heywood v Ross* 1994 SLT 195.

13.96 In some cases, it may be that the role of photographs is not as primary evidence but as a visual aid to a witness in the giving of his evidence. In the civil case of *Eckersley v Dempsey*[1] a witness was shown a book of photographs of the locus of an accident and gave his evidence by reference to those photographs. However, the photographer had not been called as a witness to identify the photographs. The defender unsuccessfully objected to the evidence thus elicited and thereafter appealed. The appeal was rejected, the Sheriff[2] stating

> The photographs were produced, not as being in themselves evidence, but only for purposes of exposition—as a means of rendering the oral evidence of certain witnesses more explicit and more intelligible.

1 1934 SLT (Sh Ct) 46.
2 In 1934, the judge at first instance was called the Sheriff Substitute and the appeal judge the Sheriff. There has since been an inflation in judicial titles: the judge at first instance is now the Sheriff and on appeal is the Sheriff Principal.

13.97 Clearly the same principle applies to digital photographs and to video and other electronic visual aids. The author has variously used a video tape showing an expert witnesses recovering real evidence (a section of plaster ceiling) from a building, which real evidence was produced in court, a digital video file showing certain experiments carried out by an neurologist illustrating the effects of applying an electric current to the human body, and a screen capture file showing operations carried out by an IT expert in operating a computer program, all without objection or adverse comment[1]. There is now also available 'return to scene of crime' software which allows digitised files to be created incorporating various documents and other evidence linked to stereoscopic digital photographs permitting a virtual recreation of a location. There is no reason why such material should not also be used as a visual aid.

[1] Though arguably not necessary, *ob majorem cautelam* each of these visual aids was spoken to by the witness responsible for making it.

Remote evidence

13.98 By section 272 of the Criminal Procedure (Scotland) 1995, the court can issue a letter of request to enable the evidence of a witness who is resident outwith the United Kingdom, Channel Islands and Isle of Man to be taken and can appoint a Commissioner to take, in the United Kingdom, Channel Islands and Isle of Man, the evidence of such a witness or of a witness who is ill or infirm and unable to attend the trial. That evidence may be recorded on audio or video tape, though such a recording should be accompanied by a transcript.

13.99 In relation to civil matters, there is not made in the rules[1] similar explicit provision for video or audio recording of evidence taken on Commission or on interrogatories. However, it is to be noted that RCS 35.16, dealing with letters of request under Council Regulation (EC) number 1206/2001[2] stipulates by subpara (4) an obligation on the applicant to be liable in the first instance for certain costs including 'the use of requested communications technology at the performance of the taking of the evidence'.

[1] RCS 35.11–35.16; OCR 28.10–28.14.
[2] Letters of request in general are dealt with in RCS 35.15 and OCR 28.14. There is no equivalent to RCS 35.16 in the Ordinary Cause Rules.

13.100 In current practice evidence taken on commission is recorded only in shorthand though, given the court's inherent power to regulate its own procedure and the flexibility which it has tended to show, it would be interesting to see whether a judge, even without an explicit rule, might be persuaded to allow video recording of evidence taken on Commission or on letters of request.

13.101 Section 56 of the Law Reform (Miscellaneous Provisions) Scotland Act 1990 allowed the court to authorise the giving of evidence by child witnesses in criminal proceedings by means of a live television link. This provision has been supplanted by the Vulnerable Witnesses (Scotland)

Act 2004 which amends the Criminal Procedure (Scotland) Act 1995 to allow the evidence of children and other vulnerable witnesses to be given by means of a live television link, the specific provision being found in the new s 271J of the 1995 Act. Similar provision is made for civil cases by s 20 of the 2004 Act. If evidence is allowed to be given by way of video link it may, in certain circumstances, allow the observation to be made that an identification over such a link may be of less value than an identification made in the witness box in court[1].

---

[1] *Brotherston v HM Advocate* 1996 SLT 1154, though in that case the video link was of poor quality and had attracted adverse criticism.

13.102 Once a case comes to trial (or, in civil cases, jury trial or Proof) the evidence used to be noted by a shorthand writer but now more usually by being recorded on cassette tape and, if required, the tape is subsequently transcribed into shorthand. That is how there arose the circumstances of *HM Advocate v Nulty*[1]. In that case a trial had proceeded some way against an accused person but had collapsed. After a period a new trial was begun. In the interim an important witness who had given evidence at the first trial had become mentally unfit to give evidence at the second trial. The Crown proposed to play the tape of the evidence given at the first trial. The accused objected on the ground that this infringed his art 6 right to a fair trail. The objection was repelled on the ground that the accused was protected by the requirement for corroboration and the circumstance that the judge could give appropriate directions to the jury. What is notable for the present discussion is the circumstance that the judge commented that, while the circumstances would have justified the admittance of a transcript, it was an advantage to allow the tape[2].

---

[1] 2000 SLT 528.
[2] At p 532 L.

Computer-generated evidence and the role of experts

13.103 The status of computer evidence in general has been dealt with above, but special mention must be made here of evidence which is generated through the running of a computer program. In *Northern Metco Estates v Perth & Kinross District Council*[1], a case heard by the Scottish Lands Tribunal in which the pursuer was seeking compensation for compulsory purchase of his land, evidence was given by an expert surveyor and valuer who had carried out a project appraisal using a computer program (the identity of which was not disclosed). The tribunal observed[2]

> the program model apparently requires assumptions to be made in respect of certain variable inputs. Most of these may be open to challenge ... The mathematical formulae used to produce the output of the business plan may not be the most suitable, or may need to be recalibrated, in the light of local circumstances ... As presently advised the tribunal finds the single output from the computer model in this case ... unacceptable in the absence of the primary evidence on which it has been based. Even if the residual method of valuation had been found to be acceptable in this case, therefore, the output figure of

affordable rent for the leisure element would not have been accepted without the basis of its generation having been made explicit and subject to scrutiny by the respondents and the tribunal.

1   1993 SLT (Lands Trib) 28.
2   at p 36 F–G.

13.104   The short, sharp lesson would appear to be not to rely upon software unless you are able to examine the assumptions upon which it works. However, if that were the law it could significantly hamper the use of computer models in the giving of expert evidence, especially if the program were proprietary and the source code were not available. However, it will be noted that in *Northern Metco* the identity of the program had not been disclosed.

13.105   The only subsequent case in which this aspect of *Northern Metco* has been considered is in the unreported decision of the Lord Ordinary[1], Lord Caplan in the *Piper Alpha* litigation[2]. In that case, the defenders had sought to argue that the expert evidence based upon the running of the program should not be admitted without the lodging of the source code. An attempt was made to argue that the commercial confidentiality in a proprietary program should not prevent the court requiring the production of the source code[3].

1   The first instance judge.
2   *Elf Enterprise Caledonia Ltd v London Bridge Engineering Ltd* (2nd September, 1997, unreported) Court of Session.
3   This submission appears divorced from commercial reality.

13.106   However, commenting on the *Northern Metco* case Lord Caplan stated[1]

Nowadays there are numerous occasions when parties advance as evidence results that have been derived from a computer. Every computer is governed by the programmes [sic] fed into it. It would be extraordinary, if the extreme case is taken, that every time a party wanted to rely on a figure derived from a computer the whole computer programme had to be produced. Apart from other consideration this would be a wasteful exercise since in the average case there would be no quarrel about the adequacy of the computer programme. If not all computer programmes have to be produced to prove a case which relies on computer generated evidence then the question would arise as to where to draw the line. The defenders suggest that the line should be drawn where an expert has to rely on a computer simulation for his opinion. However I think such a rigid rule is not justified as the true test. A party really requires to decide the amount and quality of evidence required to establish the authenticity of any computer programme likely to be challenged. If for example the programme is obscure or untried or its lack of reliability is notorious then the party relying on the programme may require to produce the programme itself if the Court is to be persuaded that the programme can be relied upon. However I do not accept that the validity of a programme can only be established by the binary details of the programme itself. As Dr Bakke said the true test of the utility of a code is the extent of its validation and how it works in practice. Thus even in the situation where the binary details were produced a judge may hesitate to ascribe too much credit to a programme without knowing how it has been found to perform. Thus if parties fail to produce the programme itself (and this may in many cases reflect all that it is possible) they will have to depend for acceptance of the code on matters such as the general acceptance of the programme within the scientific community, the extent to which the programme has been validated, and how it has operated in practice.

¹   At vol 5, para 8.2.1.

The digitisation of paper evidence

13.107 It may be that the evidence lodged in the case is largely in paper form but that the volume of paper makes its use in the trial unwieldy and time-consuming. This problem recently arose in two cases, the one civil, and the other criminal. The civil case was *McTear v Imperial Tobacco Ltd*[1]. In that case, in which the judgement alone extends to 569 pages, the documentary evidence extended to 85,000 pages of which at least four sets of copies would have been needed for use in court. As the Lord Ordinary, Lord Nimmo Smith, explained[2], the material was scanned into a database and the system was operated in court by an operator 'who was able on request to cause any page to be displayed on screens for all the participants to see'. The Livenote system was used to record the evidence. The judge remarked on the considerable time and expense saved.

[1]   2005 2 SC 1.
[2]   at para 1.29.

13.108 The criminal case was *HM Advocate v Transco plc* in which the trial took place during 2005. A similar digitisation of paper records was used with, as in *McTear*, the originals being available if required. Even though Livenote had previously been used in the trial, conducted at Camp Zeist[1], of the Libyans accused of bombing Pan Am flight 103[2], an attempt by the defence in the *Transco* case to obtain the use of Livenote was rejected by the judge, Lord Carloway. Transco appealed this decision[3], but was unsuccessful on the basis that the recording of evidence in court is governed by section 93 of the Criminal Procedure (Scotland) Act 1995 which allows for the evidence to be recorded 'by means of shorthand notes or by mechanical means', and the LiveNote system did not properly fit into either category, the primary object of the legislation being to provide a record of the trial after its conclusion, rather than to facilitate its conduct by making a daily transcription available[4]. The Court added: 'It matters not that LiveNote happens to have been used, apparently by the implicit consent of parties and of the court, as the means of making the official record in the exceptional circumstances of the Lockerbie trial'[5].

[1]   Under the High Court of Justiciary (Proceedings in the Netherlands) (United Nations) Order 1998 (SI 1998/2251).
[2]   Though reported in relation to procedural maters and, subsequently, on Appeal, the verdict itself is unreported (Lords Coulsfield, MacLean and Sutherland, High Court of Justiciary, 31st January, 2001, unreported).
[3]   *Transco plc v HM Advocate* (2005) 1 JC 194.
[4]   Para [32] on p 207. It may be thought that this is a curious argument as the final record produced at the end of the trial by the LiveNote system would conform to the statutory authorisation and it is difficult to see how the fact that LiveNote could also produce daily

transcripts could prevent it from so conforming. It may be that the Court was addressing the question of what was the main object of the system against a background of resource implications.

5   *Transco plc v HM Advocate* (2005) 1 JC 194.

13.109 The impression with which one is left is that, so long as parties agree with one another, the court procedures can be adaptable but the opportunities to reach such agreements may be more limited in criminal procedure. It may also be questionable how far the existing rules which permit copies to be accepted as principals are truly fit for purpose in a world where scanning, pdf and tif are commonplace. For example, it may be dubious whether any practical purpose is served by the requirement under ss 5 and 6 of CE(S)A 1988 for a copy document to be docketed, and, indeed, what usually happens in practice is that copies are seldom so docketed, but parties are content to enter into a formal Joint Minute accepting that the copies are to be treated as principals (except, of course, in relation to those few instances when an issue as to the accuracy of a copy may arise). Further, in criminal procedure, increasing numbers of prosecutions are coming to rely upon scanned evidence, though, as with civil cases, this is by consent of the prosecution and defence, and the prosecution customarily also retains the originals 'just in case'.

Practical constraints

13.110 There are considerable resource implications if technology is to be used, especially in civil actions. Even simple applications (such as a computer on which to run software and screens on which to show it) have had to be provided by parties and, where the technology is more elaborate, the costs and the burden are greater. In the *McTear* case the IT was all provided by and at the expense of the defenders, Imperial Tobacco, and though, in the *Transco* case, the hardware was furnished by the court service, practical compatibility and reliability issues were encountered[1]. At the time, the Scottish Court service had no courts equipped to accommodate the relevant technology, so makeshift adaptations had to made to the courtroom used in order to take the technology[2]. After the trial the cabling and the equipment were removed but, anticipating changes which are more fully discussed below, the court in question has since been modified to take the necessary technology on a permanent basis.

1   The Crown and defence systems could not communicate with each other.
2   One participant described it as resembling a spaghetti factory.

13.111 The other practical constraint worth noting is that judges have differing degrees of familiarity with computers and information technology, although all are issued with a laptop by the Scottish Court Service. In the result, it cannot necessarily be assumed that all judges in fact know what falls within judicial knowledge[1]. It would be prudent, in appropriate cases, to ensure that the expert witness also gives the court a grounding in such basic principles as are necessary for a full understanding of the case, even if these may be supposed to fall within judicial knowledge.

1 The author has experience of conducting a proof regarding the terms of a software license at the end of which the judge queried why the license was referred to in submissions as a copyright license. It transpired that he was unaware that any running of a program on a computer necessarily involved copying.

ELECTRONIC SIGNATURES

13.112 We should be eternally grateful that not all human endeavour ends in litigation. Documents, both paper and electronic, are used daily in commerce and in our everyday lives. Some of these documents, especially in relation to transferring title to land, require to be self-proving. Other documents, though not requiring to be probative, require to be signed, even where the business is transacted entirely electronically.

13.113 The law of electronic signatures in the UK is dealt with in detail elsewhere in this work, but it may be worth mentioning a few Scottish peculiarities. The basic requirements for writing are contained in the Requirements of Writing (Scotland) Act 1995, but this requires to be read along with the subsequent legislation on electronic (including digital) signatures. In this regard, readers will by now be familiar with the provisions of the UNCITRAL model law on Electronic Signatures of 2001 as well as the Electronic Signature Directive[1], the Electronic Communications Act 2000 and the Electronic Signatures Regulations 2002[2]. It should, however, be noted that the Scottish Ministers possess the power the vary statutes to give effect to electronic signatures[3].

1 (1999/93), OJ 2000 L 13/12.
2 SI 2002/318.
3 Electronic Communications Act 2000, s 8.

13.114 The net effect of these measures is to accord electronic signatures the effect of written ones. However certain specific documents are excluded[1], notably documents creating or transferring rights in heritable property. This certainly covers Dispositions (conveyances) and Standard Securities but it has been suggested that the exception might also include Missives: the exchange of letters which, in Scottish Practice, creates a binding contract transferring a personal right to the property which is subsequently made real by the delivery of the Disposition.

1 Article 9 of the EC E-Commerce Directive, as given effect to by the Electronic Commerce (EC Directive) Regulations 2002, SI 2000/31.

THE FUTURE

13.115 Following on the *McTear* and *Transco* cases, the lawyers who had participated saw the need to address some of the practical resource and other problems which those cases had thrown up. In this task they had sympathetic support from the Law Society of Scotland Information Technology Committee, the Faculty of Advocates and the Scottish Society for Computers and Law. This coincided with a number of other initiatives which were bearing fruit.

13.115 *Scotland*

The Scottish Court Service had become aware of the unsatisfactory nature, both technically and in terms of equal access to justice, of ad hoc arrangements for the presentation of electronic evidence, often provided at parties' own expense, and was coming to terms with the IT implications of the Vulnerable Witnesses Act 2004. The service was preparing to start a programme of converting courts to make them suitable for IT. At the same time many 'back office' functions, such as court calendars and internal administration as well as criminal records, had been conducted electronically for some time.

13.116 Elsewhere, the Sheriff Court Rules Council, in late 2004, had published a discussion paper on the further extension of the use of information technology in the Sheriff Court. Its proposals included the electronic transmission, lodging and storage of pleadings, motions and other similar documents, and electronic transmission of interlocutors, all delivered through a website. In relation to Small Claims and Summary Causes, the proposals went further, envisaging the creation of a virtual court.

13.117 The Registers of Scotland had been working for some time on developing a project for the electronic registration of title, culminating in the making, on 4 October 2006, of The Automated Registration of Title to Land (Electronic Communications) (Scotland) Order 2006[1].

[1]   SSI 2006/491.

13.118 This happy coincidence of interests led to the formation in February 2006 of the Scottish Courts Technology forum, bringing together representatives of the Law Society of Scotland, the Faculty of Advocates, the Scottish Society for Computers and Law, the Rules Councils, the Registers of Scotland, the Scottish Court Service and other interested parties to exchange information and co-ordinate their approach to the wider introduction and use of information technology in the legal system in Scotland. An early fruit of that co-operation was agreement on the use of portable document format ('pdf') as a common standard for electronic document presentation[1].

[1]   It is understood that England and Wales may be considering the adoption of tagged image format ('tif').

13.119 In a separate development, the Scottish Parliament enacted the Criminal Proceedings etc (Reform) (Scotland) Act 2007, which received Royal Assent on 22nd February 2007. When it is brought into force it will go a long way to integrating electronic communication into Criminal procedure, allowing, by s 8, electronic citation and, significantly, by s 41 (inserting a new s 303B into the Criminal Procedure (Scotland) Act 1995) introducing a new class of 'Electronic Summary Proceedings' instituted by electronic complaint, signed by an electronic signature, with electronic citation of witnesses. It will also address one of the issues referred to above by allowing evidence to be taken on Commission by means of a video link[1]. A useful further innovation is the introduction of a procedure for recovery of documents which might be used by the defence[2]. Unfortunately, it is limited to 'documents' and not to the wider classes of evidence in respect of which a Commission and Diligence might be granted in civil procedure, though, standing the decision in *Rollo*, it ought to be wide enough to enable the recovery of electronic documents. It is also unfortunate that advantage of the opportunity has not been taken expressly to permit the Court to make use of LiveNote or other similar system as the official record of the evidence.

[1]   Section 35(3) inserting a new sub-s 271I(1A) in the 1995 Act.
[2]   Section 37, inserting a new s 301A into the 1995 Act.

13.120 In addition to these developments in the field of primary legislation, at the initiative of the Scottish Courts Technology Forum, discussions are presently underway in order to identify any areas where the various Rules of Court may be modified to facilitate the use of electronic media and assist with the presentation of electronic evidence.

CONCLUSION

13.121 Though the Scots law of evidence started life as a single reasonably coherent common law corpus, subsequent legislative and procedural developments have resulted in a substantial divergence between civil and criminal procedure. At the level of concepts and ideas there may still be common development, the principles articulated in *Rollo* as to the fundamental nature of electronic evidence are of equal application in both spheres, but for the most part they are developing along parallel, rather than common, tracks with legislative changes in the one not necessarily being mirrored exactly in the other.

13.122 The practical effect of this for the practitioner is that what is admissible, or what works in relation to electronic evidence in civil litigation, is not necessarily going to be admissible, or as practicable in relation to the same electronic evidence, in criminal trials. For example, in criminal law there have long been strict restraints on how evidence may properly be obtained, whereas in civil law traditionally all evidence is admitted, though that may be open to some increasing control by reason of Convention rights under arts 6 and 8; in civil cases, there seems to be no bar to the use of LiveNote (if the parties are prepared to pay for it, at any rate) but in criminal cases the court's view is that primary legislation prevents its use.

13.123 Some of these developments are understandable, even desirable, in light of the fundamental difference between criminal trials, which concern the liberty of the subject, as against civil litigation, which is concerned with matters of private right. Nonetheless, in both spheres, so far as is permissible within the constraints imposed by the formal rules, the courts have shown a concern with principles combined with flexibility and a desire to look beyond the rules themselves to the underlying realities, which gives considerable hope for the continuing evolution of the law in relation to electronic evidence.

13.124 *Scotland*

13.124 Also giving cause for optimism as to the continued health and vigour of the Scottish system are the many exciting developments currently in prospect[1] which, if they come to fruition, will enable information technology to attain the same central role in the courts as it has in the wider society, rather than to relegate it to being something which can be accommodated (as, indeed, it can be) by the nipping and tucking of existing procedures.

As William Shakespeare did not quite say:

O brave new world, that has such courts in it!

[1] 'Exciting' may be a cliché, but it may also be accurate.

Chapter 14

SINGAPORE

DANIEL SENG AND BRYAN TAN

ADMISSIBILITY OF EVIDENCE

Introduction to the Singapore Evidence Act

14.01 In Singapore, evidence is only admissible in judicial proceedings pursuant to the rules of evidence in the Singapore Evidence Act[1] ('Evidence Act') and in other rules of evidence contained in any written law[2]. While learned academic writings exist that suggest that the Evidence Act is little more than a codification of the English laws of evidence[3], the Privy Council has authoritatively pronounced the Evidence Act to be a codifying act[4]. The result is that, although reference can be made to the English common law to aid the interpretation of ambiguous rules in the Evidence Act[5], where any part of evidence law is expressly dealt with by the Evidence Act the courts must give effect to the relevant provisions of the Evidence Act regardless of whether they differ from the common law rule of evidence[6].

[1] Cap. 97, 1997 Rev Ed.
[2] s 2(2) of the Evidence Act states that '[a]ll rules of evidence not contained in any written law, so far as such rules are inconsistent with any of the provisions of this Act, are repealed'.
[3] James Fitzjames Stephen *The Indian Evidence Act with an Introduction on the Principles of Judicial Evidence* (1872).
[4] *Mahomed Syedol Ariffin v Yeoh Ooi Gark* [1916] 2 AC 575; *Jayasena v R* [1970] AC 618; *Public Prosecutor v Yuvaraj* [1969] 2 MLJ 89 at 90 per Lord Diplock.
[5] *Saminathan v Public Prosecutor* [1955] MLJ 121 at 124.
[6] *Public Prosecutor v Yuvaraj* [1969] 2 MLJ 89 at 90, per Lord Diplock. An English rule or principle cannot be accepted if it will thereby vary the true and actual meaning of the provision in the Evidence Act, or it will deny the provision in the Evidence Act any effect: *Mohamed Syedol Ariffin v Yeoh Ooi Gark* [1916] 2 AC 575 at 580 per Lord Shaw of Dunfermline.

Electronic evidence, computer output and the Singapore Evidence Act

14.02 The Evidence Act expressly provides for the admissibility of electronic evidence. 'Evidence' is defined to include oral statements made by witnesses as well as all documents produced for the inspection of the court[1]. A 'document' is, in turn, widely defined to mean 'any matter expressed or described upon any substance by means of letters, figures or marks or by more than one of those means intended to be used or which may be used for the purpose of recording that matter'[2]. While there is no reference to real evidence[3], Singapore courts appear to have accepted that the definition of 'evidence' includes real evidence, including computer-generated real evidence[4].

1   Evidence Act, s 3(1).
2   Evidence Act, s 3(1). In *Megastar Entertainment Pte Ltd v Odex Pte Ltd* [2005] 3 SLR 91, [2005] SGHC 84 at [35], the High Court accepted the argument that the definition of a 'document' in the Evidence Act is 'broad enough to encompass information recorded in an electronic medium or recording device, such as a hard disk drive installed in a desktop computer or server computer.
3   Referred to in evidence literature as 'Things are an independent species of evidence as their production calls upon the court to reach conclusions on the basis of its own perception, and not on that of witnesses directly or indirectly reported to it' *Cross & Tapper on Evidence* (10th ed, 2004) p 63.
4   *Public Prosecutor v Ang Soon Huat* [1991] 1 MLJ 1.

14.03 A separate definition exists in the Evidence Act for 'electronic evidence' under the definitions of a 'computer' and 'computer output'. These definitions, which are of recent origin, were inserted pursuant to the Evidence (Amendment) Act 1996 (No 8 of 1996). They state:

'computer' means an electronic, magnetic, optical, electrochemical, or other data processing device, or a group of such interconnected or related devices, performing logical, arithmetic, or storage functions, and includes any data storage facility or communications facility directly related to or operating in conjunction with such device or group of such interconnected or related devices, but does not include—

(a)   an automated typewriter or typesetter;
(b)   a portable hand held calculator;
(c)   a device similar to those referred to in paragraphs (a) and (b) which is non-programmable or which does not contain any data storage facility;
(d)   such other device as the Minister may by notification prescribe;

'computer output' or 'output' means a statement or representation (whether in audio, visual, graphical, multi-media, printed, pictorial, written or any other form)—

(a)   produced by a computer; or
(b)   accurately translated from a statement or representation so produced;

14.04 On these definitions, 'evidence' includes 'computer output'. Computer output can refer to:

(a)   an electronic version of an oral statement made by a witness, eg records of instant messaging chat statements made by two accused regarding a murder conspiracy[1] or between several defendants regarding a 'mistaken' e-commerce transaction[2], and emails and SMSs made by an accused[3] or by a defendant[4];

(b)   documents produced for the inspection of the court, eg computer print-outs of a company's business registration records[5], print-outs from the customs authorities' immigration status database[6], banking records[7] and business accounts[8]; and

(c)   real evidence, eg video cassette recordings used as identification evidence[9], drug analysis reports produced by mass spectrometers and gas chromatographs[10] medical scans and computer images[11], 'electronic' signatures and agreements for leases concluded via email correspondence[12].

1   *Ler Wee Teang Anthony v Public Prosecutor* [2002] 2 SLR 281.
2   *Chwee Kin Keong v Digilandmall.com Pte Ltd* [2005] 1 SLR 502, [2005] SGCA 2 (CA), [2004] 2 SLR 594, [2004] SGHC 71 (HC).
3   *Lim Seong Khee v Public Prosecutor* [2001] 2 SLR 342.

⁴ *Malcolmson Nicholas Hugh Bertram v Naresh Kumar Mehta* [2001] 4 SLR 454.
⁵ *Aw Kew Lim v Public Prosecutor* [1987] 2 MLJ 601.
⁶ *Roy S Selvarajah v Public Prosecutor* [1998] 3 SLR 517.
⁷ *Industrial & Commercial Bank Ltd v Banco Ambrosiano Veneto Spa* [2003] 1 SLR 221.
⁸ *Lim Mong Hong v Public Prosecutor* [2003] 3 SLR 88, [2003] SGHC 161.
⁹ *Heng Aik Ren Thomas v Public Prosecutor* [1998] 3 SLR 465.
¹⁰ *Public Prosecutor v Ang Soon Huat* [1991] 1 MLJ 1.
¹¹ *Dr Khoo James & Anor v Gunapathy D/O Muniandy* [2002] 2 SLR 414.
¹² *SM Integrated Transware Pte Ltd v Schenker Singapore (Pte) Ltd* [2005] 2 SLR 651, [2005] SGHC 58.

14.05 The breadth of the definition of 'computer output' is further reinforced by the breadth of the definition of a 'computer' to encompass all electronic devices, storage devices for such electronic devices and networks of such electronic devices[1] including the Internet[2]. Computer output may take many possible forms: audio, visual, graphical, multimedia, printed, pictorial or written. The expansive definition was legislatively intended to facilitate the use of information technology and the admissibility as evidence of information stored or produced by the use of such technology[3]. This means that almost any item of evidence that is electronically stored or processed is 'computer output' and thus calls for special treatment under the specific provisions in the Evidence Act (ss 35, 36 and 65) that deal with their admissibility. Thus, for purposes of this chapter, electronic evidence shall be referred to by the term 'computer output' where appropriate and relevant.

¹ s 3(1), Evidence Act. The definition of a 'computer' excludes (a) an automated typewriter or typesetter; (b) a portable hand held calculator, (c) a device similar to those referred to in paragraphs (a) and (b) which is non-programmable or which does not contain any data storage facility, and (d) such other device as the Minister may by notification prescribe. To date, the Minister has not prescribed any notifications that would exclude any device from the ambit of a 'computer'.
² Explanatory Statement, Evidence (Amendment) Bill (Bill No. 45/95).
³ Explanatory Statement, Evidence (Amendment) Bill (Bill No. 45/95).

Relevance and admissibility

14.06 The Evidence Act defines a fact as relevant 'when the one is connected with the other in any of the ways referred to in the provisions of this Act relating to the relevancy of facts'[1]. This definition collapses the evidential distinction between 'relevance' as referring to logical relevance—where 'according to the common course of events one [fact] either taken by itself or in connection with other facts proves or renders probable the past, present, or future existence or non-existence of the other [fact]'[1]—and legal relevance or rules of admissibility, which at the common law are rules which exclude relevant evidence for legal or policy reasons unless such evidence falls within one of the four general exceptions to these exclusionary rules: hearsay, opinion, character and conduct on other occasions[2]. James Fitzjames Stephen, the draftsman for the Indian Evidence Act 1872 (the predecessor act to the Singapore Evidence Act) thus sought to state all the 'admissibility' rules of evidence in their affirmative form, in Pt I of the Evidence Act. Although an item of evidence can be 'relevant' under different relevancy provisions in the

Evidence Act[3], the practical effect is that an item of evidence that cannot be rendered 'relevant' under any of the provisions of the Evidence Act is inadmissible.

1   Evidence Act, s 3(2).
2   James Fitzjames Stephen *A Digest of The Law of Evidence* (1886) p 4.
3   *James Fitzjames Stephen* (1886) p xii. See also Wigmore *Evidence in Trials at Common Law* (1988) p 667.
4   *James Fitzjames Stephen* (1872) p 55.

Admitting computer output

14.07 A special regime is set up in the Evidence Act for admitting computer output in evidence. Under s 35, which was amended in 1996, where computer output is tendered in evidence 'for any purpose whatsoever'[1], it is admissible only if 'it is relevant or otherwise admissible according to the other provisions of this Act or any other written law'[2] and it received in evidence under one of three alternative modes of admissibility:

(a)   by way of an express agreement between the parties to the proceedings ('express agreement')[3];
(b)   by way of output produced via an approved process ('approved process')[4]; and
(c)   by proof of the proper operation of the computer and the corres–ponding accuracy of the computer print-out ('proof of proper operation and accuracy')[5].

1   Evidence Act, s 35(1).
2   Evidence Act, s 35(1).
3   Evidence Act, s 35(1)(a).
4   Evidence Act, s 35(1)(b).
5   Evidence Act, s 35(1)(c).

14.08 This implies that there are two hurdles to admissibility for computer output under s 35 of the Evidence Act. A computer output as an item of evidence has to be independently admissible under a rule of evidence before it can be assessed for admissibility by virtue of the fact that the item of evidence takes the form of computer output. The fact that the item of evidence takes the form of computer output does not obviate the need to admit it under a rule of evidence as such[1]. Thus, in the case of *Public Prosecutor v R Sekhar s/o R G Van*, in proving various bankruptcy offences arising from the outstanding debts of the accused to a hotel where he stayed, the prosecution tendered in evidence computer print-outs of monthly summaries of invoices. Information in the summaries was extracted from the guest invoices, the originals of which were not tendered in evidence. Doubts were raised as to the accuracy of information in these summaries, the summaries were excluded in evidence and s 35 was not satisfied[2]. It ought to be noted that, while the summaries were clearly hearsay, the prosecution made no attempt to admit them under the business records exception to the hearsay rule[3], which would have militated against the need to tender in evidence the originals of the daily guest invoices.

1   cf *Industrial & Commercial Bank Ltd v Banco Ambrosiano Veneto Spa* [2003] 1 SLR 221 at [250]. Kan Tin Chu J held that once evidence is admissible under s 32(b) of the Evidence Act, it need not further satisfy the admissibility provisions in s 35.

²   *Public Prosecutor v R Sekhar s/o R G Van* [2003] 2 SLR 456, [2003] SGHC 123 at [35].
³   eg Evidence Act, s 34.

14.09   The rule in s 35 thus changes the legal position prior to 1996. Before 1996, the old s 35 was modelled after the then s 5 of the (England and Wales) Civil Evidence Act 1968[1]. A distinction was drawn in the pre-1996 jurisprudence between admitting computer output as real evidence without reference to s 35[2] and admitting computer output as hearsay under s 35[3]. This jurisprudence is prima facie[4] no longer good law as the current s 35 states that it applies 'where computer output is tendered in evidence for any purpose whatsoever'[5].

¹   1968, c. 64.
²   *Public Prosecutor v Ang Soon Huat* [1991] 1 MLJ 1
³   *Aw Kew Lim v Public Prosecutor* [1987] 2 MLJ 601.
⁴   Daniel Seng 'Computer Output as Evidence' [1997] SJLS 130 at 141.
⁵   *Lim Mong Hong v Public Prosecutor* [2003] 3 SLR 88, [2003] SGHC 161 at [38].

Modes of admissibility for computer output

14.10   The second hurdle involves satisfying one of the three modes of admissibility as prescribed in s 35. As the High Court said in *Lim Mong Hong v Public Prosecutor*, 'It is every bit as important that a computer print-out tendered should be reliable whether or not it contains hearsay'[1]. If a proponent of computer output fails to satisfy any one of the three modes of admissibility, the evidence will be ruled inadmissible, even though it is otherwise admissible by some other rule of evidence.

¹   *Lim Mong Hong v Public Prosecutor* [2003] 3 SLR 88, [2003] SGHC 161 at [38].

'Express agreement'

14.11   Under the 'express agreement' avenue, parties to the proceedings can at any stage of the proceedings expressly agree not to dispute the authenticity and the accuracy of the contents of the computer output[1]. Section 35 does not prescribe the form required for this express agreement. Thus it would appear that such an agreement need not be in writing and may even be made orally, subject of course only to questions of proof. However, for the prosecution to admit computer output as evidence in criminal proceedings, the agreement must be made with a legally represented accused[2]. In addition, an agreement that is obtained 'by means of fraud, duress, mistake or misrepresentation' is vitiated and ineffective in admitting the computer output[3].

¹   Evidence Act, s 35(1)(a).
²   Evidence Act, s 35(2)(a).
³   Evidence Act, s 35(2)(b).

14.12   The Explanatory Statement to the Evidence (Amendment) Bill also envisages agreements in multi-party proceedings[1], but s 35 is silent as to whether, in such proceedings, an agreement is required to be obtained between every party to the proceedings or only between the proponent and the opponent of the evidence concerned (or any party whose interest will be affected by its admission). It is submitted that the latter is the preferred interpretation as regards civil proceedings[2]. In contrast, in criminal proceedings, the language of s 35(2)(a) suggests that agreement must be made between every party to the proceedings and that every accused must be legally represented before this agreement is binding on all the parties.

[1]   Explanatory Statement, Evidence (Amendment) Bill 1995 (Bill No. 45/95).
[2]   See Daniel Seng 'Computer Output as Evidence' [1997] SJLS 130 at 147.

'Approved process'

14.13 As it currently stands, the 'approved process' mode of admissibility is intended to facilitate the admissibility of physical documents and records that are subsequently scanned into digital format and stored in electronic format. An approved process is a process which has been approved by a certifying authority pursuant to the Evidence (Computer Output) Regulations 1996 ('Evidence Regulations')[1]. Under the Evidence Regulations, only an 'image system' defined as 'any computer system that is capable of capturing, storing and retrieving images or generating image system output' can seek certification as an approved process[2]. In other words, physical documents that are digitally captured via a certified document imaging system may be proved by way of electronic records of the document. A certified document imaging system must provide an accurate reproduction of the contents of a document, verifiable by way of an integrity check of the physical process and the imaging system in relation to the capture, committal and output of the document images. The certification process involves a comprehensive audit of all relevant aspects of the imaging process and its surrounding procedures[3], conducted by an approved 'certifying authority' appointed under the Evidence Regulations[4] or so deemed to be appointed under the Regulations[5]. Under the Evidence (Computer Output) Regulations—Appointment of Certifying Authorities 2001 Notification, the Minister of Law had appointed three organisations as certifying authorities[6]. However, all these appointments have lapsed. The only remaining entity to serve as a certifying authority is the Auditor General[7].

[1]   Evidence (Computer Output) Regulations 1996 (1997 Rev Ed RG1 G.N. No S 93/96) which were made by the Minister pursuant to Evidence Act, s 35(5).
[2]   Evidence (Computer Output) Regulations 1996 (1997 Rev Ed RG1 G.N. No S 93/96), para 10 read with First Schedule: Compliance Criteria for Image Systems.
[3]   Evidence (Computer Output) Regulations 1996 (1997 Rev Ed RG1 G.N. No S 93/96), First Schedule: Compliance Criteria for Image Systems.
[4]   Evidence (Computer Output) Regulations 1996 (1997 Rev Ed RG1 G.N. No S 93/96), para 3.
[5]   Evidence (Computer Output) Regulations 1996 (1997 Rev Ed RG1 G.N. No S 93/96), para 4.
[6]   Evidence (Computer Output) Regulations 1996—Appointment of Certifying Authorities (S 273/2001 dated 16 May 2001): KPMG Consulting Pte Ltd (until 16 May 2002), Ernst and Young (until 24 September 2003) and PriceWaterhouse Coopers (until 20 March 2004).
[7]   The Auditor General is deemed to be the certifying authority under para 4 of the Evidence Regulations.

14.14 To tender the computer output of an imaged document, the output must be supported by proof that the output is obtained from an approved process and that it accurately reproduces the contents of the original document. This may be satisfied by way of the production of two certificates: a certificate signed by a person holding a responsible position in relation to the operation and management of the certifying authority to certify that the process has been approved[1], and a certificate by a person holding a responsible position in relation to the operation or management of the approved process, to certify that the computer output is obtained from the approved process[2]. These certifiers only need to make these certifications to the best of their knowledge and belief[3]. Where this is done, the computer output is presumed to accurately reproduce the contents of the original document unless the contrary is proved[4].

1   Evidence Act, s 35(3).
2   Evidence Act, s 35(4).
3   Evidence Act, s 35(9).
4   Evidence Act, s 35(4).

14.15 In some document imaging systems, the system or process may cause certain features of the original document, eg boxes, lines or patterns, to be removed from the reproduction. Also, some of the features of the original document such as shades, colours or graphics may be reproduced inaccurately[1]. An evidential concession has been made in this regard. Section 35(10) provides that where, notwithstanding these imperfections in the reproduction, if the accuracy of the relevant contents is not affected, the output will not be rendered inadmissible. However, if the accuracy of the contents is compromised these reproduction imperfections may vitiate the admissibility of the output.

1   Explanatory Statement, Evidence (Amendment) Bill 1995 (Bill No. 45 of 1995).

'Not unreliable output and proper operation'

14.16 The 'proof of proper operation and accuracy' avenue is the residual avenue for admission of computer output that fails to be admitted pursuant to an express agreement or is not produced pursuant to an approved process. A party tendering such output under the Evidence Act, s 35(1)(c) must satisfy two conditions. The first, a negative condition, requires the proponent to show that 'there is no reasonable ground for believing that the output is inaccurate because of the improper use of the computer, and that no reason exists to doubt or suspect the truth or reliability of the output' (the 'not unreliable output' condition)[1]. The second, a positive condition[2], is that 'there is reasonable ground to believe that at all material times the computer was operating properly' (the 'proper operation of computer' condition)[3].

1   Evidence Act, s 35(1)(c)(i).
2   cf *Lim Mong Hong v Public Prosecutor* [2003] 3 SLR 88 at [42] (describing these two as requirements phrased in the negative).
3   Evidence Act, s 35(1)(c)(ii).

14.17 Compliance with both conditions may, but need not always[1], be shown by a certificate. If a certificate is tendered, it must be signed by a person, generally the designated 'systems operator' or the 'information systems manager', holding a responsible position in relation to the operation and management of the relevant computer system. Section 35(6) further provides that such a certificate must, in addition to dealing with both conditions as set out above:

(a)   identify the output and describe the manner in which it was produced; and

(b)   give particulars of any device involved in the processing and storage of such output.

1   *Lim Mong Hong v Public Prosecutor* [2003] 3 SLR 88 at [41].

14.18 The Evidence Act recognises that for stand-alone computers and small local area networks an organisation may not have a dedicated systems operator or information systems manager. In fact, s 35 is sensitive to the fact that it may not always be appropriate to 'call an expert and it may be sufficient ... to call a witness who is familiar with the computer in the sense that that witness can attest to the fact that the computer is working properly'[1]. For instance, for wide area networks or large systems, one person alone may not have sufficient knowledge of the relevant computer output[2]. Therefore, s 35(7) provides that where a person who occupies 'a responsible position in relation to the operation or management of the computer did not have control or access over any relevant records and facts' to permit this person to make the requisite s 35(6) certification, a supplementary certificate may be signed by another person who had such control or access to the computer system. Such a person may be a part-time or contract systems operator or manager, or one of the joint managers of a system for which no one person alone has the exclusive access or knowledge. Section 35(7) therefore envisages the production of two certificates in evidence to support the admissibility of the computer output under the s 35(1)(c) mode of admissibility.

1   *Lim Mong Hong v Public Prosecutor* [2003] 3 SLR 88 at [41].
2   Evidence (Amendment) Bill, Explanatory Statement.

14.19 In the absence of a systems operator or manager[1], or where the primary certifier or supplementary certifier refuses or is unable for any reason to make the requisite certification (for instance, because he is dead or unavailable) under s 35(8), a certificate signed by a person such as an expert 'who had obtained or been given control or access to the relevant records and facts' may be tendered instead.

1   Evidence (Amendment) Bill, Explanatory Statement.

14.20 In all the above instances where a certificate is tendered, it is sufficient for the certifier to state the relevant matter to the best of his knowledge and belief[1]. However, to prevent this process from being abused and to preserve the sanctity of the certification process, especially where a certificate is used as a tool to admit false evidence, a person who knowingly makes a false or untrue statement in a certificate is guilty of an offence, which is punishable upon conviction by a fine or imprisonment of up to two years, or both[2].

1   Evidence Act, s 35(9).
2   Evidence Act, s 35(11).

Authenticating computer output

14.21 Section 35(10) of the Evidence Act describes computer output that has been admitted under the section as 'duly authenticated' evidence. The various elements that have to be satisfied under the 'approved process' and 'not unreliable output and proper operation' modes of admissibility are requirements that go towards proving that the computer output was a reliable one. In *DPP v McKeown*, in conjunction with s 69 of the Police and Criminal Evidence Act 1984, Lord Hoffman noted that s 69 was 'concerned with the way in which the computer has dealt with the information to generate the statement which is being tendered as evidence of a fact which it states'[1] and the section 'does not require the prosecution to show that the statement is likely to be true'[2]. Likewise, s 35 is concerned with supporting evidence that would substantiate the reliability of computer output. If the modes of admissibility are a condition precedent to the admissibility of computer output, the supporting evidence will be 'facts necessary to explain or introduce relevant facts' and fall within a class known as authenticating evidence, described in s 9 of the Evidence Act[3]. In this regard, it has been submitted that the modes of admissibility in s 35 may be more broadly characterised as rules calling for authenticating evidence for computer output[4].

1   [1997] 1 All ER 737, [1997] 1 WLR 295 at 302.
2   [1997] 1 All ER 737, [1997] 1 WLR 295 at 302.
3   Evidence Act, s 9: facts necessary to explain or introduce a fact in issue or relevant fact, or which support or rebut an inference suggested by a fact in issue or relevant fact, or which establish the identity of any thing or person whose identity is relevant, or fix the time or place at which any fact in issue or relevant fact happened or which show the relation of parties by whom any such fact was transacted, are relevant in so far as they are necessary for that purpose.
4   Daniel Seng and Sriram Chakravarthi 'Computer Output as Evidence' Consultation Paper, Singapore Academy of Law (2003) pp 92–105.

Authentication and electronic records

14.22 Authenticating computer output therefore entails establishing several matters. It may be necessary to establish that the output is what it is (identification), that it was produced at a certain date and time (chronology), that it came from a particular machine (attribution to machine), that the machine was working properly (calibration, operation and accuracy), that it had not been replaced with some other evidence between the time of its generation and the time of its production in court (chain of evidence), that it had not been tampered with or changed (integrity) and that, if there is human authorship or input, it can be associated with that individual either because it originated with that individual or it was written or executed by that individual (attribution to individuals)[1]. As Justice Belinda Ang observed in *Jet Holding Ltd v Cooper Cameron (Singapore) Pte Ltd*, 'there has to be an evidentiary basis for finding that a document is what it purports to be'[2]. Of course, not every item of computer output will have all these aspects of its authentication challenged. It has been submitted that the rules in s 35, regarding the modes of admissibility of computer output, deal with a subset of authentication matters, and that s 9 of the Evidence Act can be relied upon to mount and to support a challenge on the other aspects of the authentication of an item of computer output as evidence[3].

1   Daniel Seng and Sriram Chakravarthi 'Computer Output as Evidence' Consultation Paper, Singapore Academy of Law (2003) pp 106–113.
2   *Jet Holding Ltd v Cooper Cameron (Singapore) Pte Ltd* [2005] 4 SLR 417, [2005] SGHC 149, [146]. The learned judge went on to observe, rightly, that 'authentication of documents is to be distinguished from and has to be resolved before relevance and admissibility under the exception to the hearsay rule' at [150].
3   Daniel Seng and Sriram Chakravarthi 'Computer Output as Evidence' Consultation Paper, Singapore Academy of Law (2003) p 105.

14.23   Illustration (a) to s 9 of the Evidence Act states:

(a)   the question is whether a given document is the will of A;
(b)   the state of A's property and of his family at the date of the alleged will may be relevant facts.

Illustration (a) to s 9 is a useful reminder that authenticating the origin, authorship or execution of a document such as a will need not always be established by evidence of handwriting and handwritten signatures. There are provisions in the Evidence Act that expressly deal with signatures and handwriting[1], but there are no provisions in the Evidence Act that expressly refers to signatures ascribed upon electronic documents. However, the reference in the definition of a 'document' to the expression of 'any matter ... upon any substance' is sufficiently wide to encompass electronic versions of records as well as electronic versions of signatures embedded in such records. This is implicitly recognised in the Evidence Act, where s 69(1) states that 'if a document is alleged to be signed or to have been written wholly or in part by any person, the signature or the handwriting of so much of the document as is alleged to be in that person's handwriting must be proved to be in his handwriting'. Section 69(2) goes on to state that the requirement of proof of handwriting 'shall not apply to any electronic record or electronic signature to which the Electronic Transactions Act 1998 applies'[2].

1   See, e g Evidence Act, ss 69 and 75.
2   Evidence Act, s 69(2).

14.24   Section 69(2) suggests that a parallel legal regime exists for proof of 'electronic records' and 'electronic signatures' outside of the Evidence Act. However, this is not the case with 'electronic records'. An 'electronic record' is defined in s 2 of the Electronic Transactions Act[1] as 'a record generated, communicated, received or stored by electronic, magnetic, optical or other means in an information system or for transmission from one information system to another' and a 'record' as 'information that is inscribed, stored or otherwise fixed on a tangible medium or that is stored in an electronic or other medium and is retrievable in perceivable form.' So defined, all electronic records are 'computer output' as defined in the Evidence Act. Section 6 of the Electronic Transactions Act goes on to state:

> For the avoidance of doubt, it is declared that information shall not be denied legal effect, validity or enforceability solely on the ground that it is in the form of an electronic record.

[1]   Cap. 88, 1999 Rev. Ed.

14.25 As the Explanatory Statement to the Electronic Transactions Act states, s 6 'does not … establish the legal validity of any given electronic record or of any information contained in the record'[1]. Section 35 of the Evidence Act arguably does not deny an 'electronic record' admissibility solely on the ground that is in electronic form but, as explained above, it does impose requirements to authenticate the 'electronic record' as a computer output before it is admissible.

[1]   Electronic Transactions Bill 1998 (Bill No. 23 of 1998).

14.26 One aspect of the authenticity of electronic records is dealt with in the Electronic Transactions Act. Since an electronic record is inherently mutable, the integrity of the record may be in issue. The Electronic Transactions Act provides that '[i]f a prescribed security procedure or a commercially reasonable security procedure agreed to by the parties involved has been properly applied to an electronic record to verify that the electronic record has not been altered since a specific point in time, such record shall be treated as a secure electronic record from such specific point in time to the time of verification'[1]. The Electronic Transactions Act goes on to provide that in any proceedings involving a secure electronic record, there is a presumption as to its integrity— 'that the secure electronic record has not been altered since the specific point in time to which the secure status relates'[2] 'unless evidence to the contrary is adduced'[3]. However, this presumption is silent as to the other issues of authenticity of an electronic record, in particular, as to its attribution to an individual.

[1]   Electronic Transactions Act, s 16.
[2]   Electronic Transactions Act, s 18(1).
[3]   Electronic Transactions Act, s 18(1).

Electronic signatures

14.27 Like its physical counterpart, attributing an electronic record to a particular individual is often achieved by way of an 'electronic signature'. An 'electronic signature' is defined in the Electronic Transactions Act as

> any letters, characters, numbers or other symbols in digital form attached to or logically associated with an electronic record, and executed or adopted with the intention of authenticating or approving the electronic record[1].

[1]   Electronic Transactions Act, s 2.

14.28 Proof of an electronic signature is provided for in the Electronic Transactions Act. Section 8 states:

(1) Where a rule of law requires a signature, or provides for certain consequences if a document is not signed, an electronic signature satisfies that rule of law.

(2) An electronic signature may be proved in any manner, including by showing that a procedure existed by which it is necessary for a party, in order to proceed further with a transaction, to have executed a symbol or security procedure for the purpose of verifying that an electronic record is that of such party.

14.29 Thus an electronic document signed with an electronic signature may be proved in evidence, not in the manner prescribed in s 69(1) of the Evidence Act, but in the manner prescribed in s 8(2) of the Electronic Transactions Act, in that it may be 'proved in any manner'. Notwithstanding the prescriptive language of s 8(2), an electronic signature outside the scope of relevant transactions that fall within the ambit of the Electronic Transactions Act may nonetheless be proved in court. Since the issue is one of authenticating the document and the signature, as explained in s 9 of the Evidence Act, the authenticating evidence may take any form. Thus, in the case of *SM Integrated Transware Pte Ltd v Schenker Singapore (Pte) Ltd*, one of the issues before Prakash J was whether email communications constituting the terms of a lease were 'signed' by the parties, for the purpose of satisfying the formality requirements of a signed memorandum or note evidencing the terms of a lease in s 6(d) of the Civil Law Act. As the learned judge noted, s 8 of the Electronic Transactions Act did not apply since a lease was a 'contract for the sale or other disposition of immovable property, or any interest in such property', which was excluded from the scope of the Electronic Transactions Act[1]. However, the learned judge observed that the approach at common law was a pragmatic one and did not require handwritten signatures for the purpose of establishing a signature. In this case, the court found that a typewritten or printed form of the party originating the message was sufficient, even if this took the form of the email address of the originating party (as in 'From: Mr Originator originator@company.com')[2].

[1]   Electronic Transactions Act, s 4(1)(d).
[2]   [2005] 2 SLR 651, [2005] SGHC 58 at [88]–[93]. cf *Chor Pee and Partners v Wee Soon Kim Anthony* [2005] SGHC 101 at [21], [51].

14.30 The holding in *SM Integrated Transware Pte Ltd v Schenker Singapore (Pte) Ltd* suggests that every email is 'signed' for the purposes of meeting various formalities requirements. This implication is a severe one, since, unlike the use of printed, stamped or typewritten signatures which are actively applied by their signatories with the express intention of authenticating the document through the act of printing, stamping and typewriting the signatures, email client programs automatically apply the name and email address of the originating party in every email header. It is arguable that the fact that one wished to be identified as the sender of an email does not necessarily imply that one wished to sign every email[1].

[1]   cf [2005] 2 SLR 651, [2005] SGHC 58 at [92].

14.31 Of course, the fact that an email is ostensibly 'signed' by the originator for purposes of meeting the formalities requirement is no proof that the originator indeed 'signed' that email, since email client programs can be compromised and even email headers themselves can be spoofed, as the learned judge recognised in her judgment[1]. In *SM Integrated Transware Pte Ltd v Schenker Singapore (Pte) Ltd*, the defendants' representative Tan did not dispute the fact that the email originated from him, so the issue of proving that those were his emails did not arise. But as s 8(2) provides, the authenticity of an electronic signature may be proved in any manner. If a challenge is mounted on this issue, the fact that the originator of that email supplied information that only Tan was intimately familiar with could be used to prove that that was his email, as suggested in illustration (a) to s 9. Likewise, the authenticity of the email could be verified through the use of a procedure previously agreed to by the parties, such as requiring the originator to execute a symbol or use an identification code or mark in his email[2]. Where this process (described as a prescribed security procedure or a commercially reasonable security procedure agreed to by the parties)[3] carries with it the assurance that this electronic signature was unique to the originator and was capable of identifying the originator, that it was created in a manner or using a means under his sole control, and linked to the electronic record such that any changes to the record will invalidate the signature, this signature would be treated as a 'secure electronic signature'[4] and carry with it presumptions that the electronic signature is the signature of the person to whom it correlates, and that the person had affixed the signature with the intention of signing or approving the electronic record[5].

1   [2005] 2 SLR 651, [2005] SGHC 58 at [93].
2   Electronic Transactions Act, s 8.
3   Electronic Transactions Act, s 17.
4   Electronic Transactions Act, s 17.
5   Electronic Transactions Act, s 18(2).

Digital signatures

14.32 Doubts exist regarding the authenticity of electronic signatures, because of the ease with which electronic records purportedly signed with such electronic signatures, and even the electronic signatures themselves, may be manipulated. Hence the Electronic Transactions Act distinguishes between 'electronic signatures' and 'secure electronic signatures', where the latter class of signatures is rendered more trustworthy through the application of security procedures to validate the signatures. One particular technology that has been so deployed involves the use of asymmetric cryptosystems to implement a more secure form of electronic signatures. These are defined as 'digital signatures' in the Electronic Transactions Act as follows:

an electronic signature consisting of a transformation of an electronic record using an asymmetric cryptosystem and a hash function such that a person having the initial untransformed electronic record and the signer's public key can accurately determine—

(a)   whether the transformation was created using the private key that corresponds to the signer's public key; and
(b)   whether the initial electronic record has been altered since the transformation was made[1];

Because of these two special characteristics of a properly implemented digital signature, an electronic record that has been signed with such a digital signature (a secure digital signature) shall be treated as a secure electronic record[2]. A secure digital signature is, in turn, defined as one where the digital signature was created during the operational period of a valid and trustworthy certificate and is verified by reference to the public key listed in such a certificate[3].

1 Electronic Transactions Act, s 2.
2 Electronic Transactions Act, s 19.
3 Electronic Transactions Act, s 20.

14.33 Where any portion of an electronic record is signed with a digital signature in accordance with the conditions set out above, the digital signature shall be treated as a secure electronic signature with respect to such a portion of the record[1] and it shall be presumed, unless evidence to the contrary is adduced, that (a) the digital signature is the signature of the person to whom it correlates, and (b) the digital signature was affixed by that person with the intention of signing or approving the electronic record[2].

1 Electronic Transactions Act, s 20.
2 Electronic Transactions Act, s 18(2).

Other enabling legislation

14.34 Section 35(1) has made provision for its admissibility rules to be overridden by written law: 'all Acts, Ordinances and enactments ... and subsidiary legislation made thereunder'[1]. Such provisions exist in other written laws in Singapore, and various formulations are adopted. Most of these provisions pertain to the use and maintenance of electronic registries by government departments and statutory bodies and the consequent admissibility of these electronic records as evidence in court. The provisions generally state that the records as certified by the relevant registrar or officer, shall be admissible in evidence as being authentic or their contents presumed to be accurate, 'notwithstanding the provisions of any other written law' or 'notwithstanding section 35 of the Evidence Act'. Such provisions include the Companies Act[2], the Business Registration Act[3], the Customs Act[4] and the Land Titles Act[5].

1 Interpretation Act (Cap. 1, 2002 Rev Ed), s 2(1).
2 Companies Act (Cap. 50, 1994 Rev Ed), s 12A(2)–(4)
3 Business Registration Act (Cap. 32, 2004 Rev Ed), s 20(4)–(6) provides a similar provision as found in the Companies Act for copies of electronically filed documents and certificates in respect of such electronically filed documents to be admissible in evidence.
4 Customs Act (Cap. 70, 2004 Rev Ed), s 86(7) and (8).
5 Land Titles Act (Cap. 157, 2004 Rev Ed), s 164(3).

14.35 Other provisions state that certified copies of such registry entries 'shall be conclusive proof of the facts specified therein' but no express reference is made to s 35, or to override its operation. Such provisions include those in the Trade Unions Act[1] and the National Registration Act[2]. Still others merely seem to facilitate the use of electronic systems as registries and nothing is mentioned about the admissibility of information captured in these registries. Examples of such provisions include those found in the Patents Act[3] and the

Trade Marks Act[4]. In such instances, the rules of evidence in s 35 should prevail and such registry records have to be authenticated pursuant to the rules in s 35 of the Evidence Act.

[1]   Trade Unions Act (Cap. 333, 2004 Rev Ed), s 7.
[2]   National Registration Act (Cap. 201, 1992 Rev Ed), s 4.
[3]   Patents Act (Cap. 221, 2005 Rev Ed), s 42.
[4]   Trade Marks Act (Cap. 332, 2005 Rev Ed), s 66.

14.36 The last class of provisions, which are largely new ones arising from recent legislative amendments, may be found in the Goods and Services Act[1], the Income Tax Act[2], the Deposit Insurance Act 2005[3], the Road Traffic Act[4], the Property Tax Act[5] and the Regulation of Imports and Exports Act[6]. These provisions provide for alternative modes of admissibility, in that where an electronic record is filed, submitted or generated pursuant to an electronic service maintained by the relevant government department or statutory board, and it has been certified by an authorised officer as to its contents and either:

(a)   duly authenticated by the issuance of a certificate signed by the relevant officer identifying the record and giving the particulars of:

(i)   the person whose authentication code was used to submit the record; or
(ii)   the person or device involved in the production or transmission of the record; or

(b)   authenticated pursuant to the rules in s 35 of the Evidence Act,

the record shall be admissible as evidence of the facts stated therein.

[1]   Goods and Services Act (Cap. 117A, 2005 Rev Ed), ss 42 and 43.
[2]   Income Tax Act (Cap. 134, 2004 Rev Ed), s 8A.
[3]   Deposit Insurance Act 2005 (No. 31 of 2005), s 59.
[4]   Road Traffic Act (Cap. 276, 2004 Rev Ed), s 33B(8).
[5]   Property Tax Act (Cap. 254, 2005 Rev Ed), s 66(8).
[6]   Regulation of Imports and Exports Act (Cap. 272A, 1996 Rev Ed), s 8. This section is similar to the other provisions, except that there is no reference to s 35 of the Evidence Act.

14.37 These provisions are clearly an attempt at merging the admissibility provisions regarding electronic signatures in the Electronic Transactions Act with the admissibility provisions regarding electronic records in the Evidence Act. The spread of these provisions across the spectrum of legislation is as much confirmation of the parallel evidentiary regimes in the Evidence Act and the Electronic Transactions Act as testament to the urgency of consolidating these piecemeal provisions into a single provision for uniform treatment of electronically signed records in the evidence laws of Singapore.

Primary and secondary evidence

14.38 Once computer output is admitted pursuant to one of the three modes of admissibility set out in s 35(1), s 35(10)(b) provides that the same admissible computer output shall not be inadmissible merely on the ground that it is 'secondary evidence'. Secondary evidence of computer output is defined in the Evidence Act to include 'copies made from the original by electronic, electrochemical, chemical, magnetic, mechanical, optical, telematic or other technical processes, which in themselves ensure the accuracy of the copy, and copies compared with such copies'[1].

1   Evidence Act, s 65(b).

14.39 The Explanatory Statement to the Evidence (Amendment) Bill 1996 explains that the effect of this provision is to 'preclude any challenge [to the admissibility of computer output] on the basis that as the original has not been destroyed, the computer output cannot be admitted because it is secondary evidence and does not comply with the conditions in section 67 of the Act for admitting secondary evidence.' Thus the effect of s 35(10)(b) is to render inapplicable the distinction between primary and secondary evidence and the best evidence rule. Likewise the rules regarding the admissibility of primary or original evidence[1], or requiring compliance with the detailed rules regarding the admission of copies of primary or original evidence[2] and their proof[3] are not relevant to computer output admissible pursuant to s 35 of the Evidence Act.

1   Evidence Act, s 64.
2   Evidence Act, s 67.
3   Evidence Act, ss 69–75.

14.40 In a sense, the irrelevance of the best evidence rule as applied to computer output is no real loss. As the Court of Appeal observed in *Jet Holding Ltd v Cooper Cameron (Singapore) Pte Ltd*, courts have shown a persistent rescission from the best evidence principle, and the modern tendency is for the judge to be trusted to give proper weight to evidence which is not the best evidence[1]. The court referred to the judgment in *R v Governor of Pentonville Prison, ex p Osman*[2], where Lloyd LJ observed:

> [T]his court would be more than happy to say goodbye to the best evidence rule. We accept that it served an important purpose in the days of parchment and quill pens. But since the invention of carbon paper and, still more, the photocopier and the telefacsimile machine, that purpose has largely gone[3].

The court then urged legislative reform in this area of the law[4]. The same sentiments that the best evidence rule is an anachronistic one when applied to electronic records, has also been made in academic writing, where legislative reforms have also been urged[5].

1   *Jet Holding Ltd v Cooper Cameron (Singapore) Pte Ltd* [2006] SGCA 20 (CA) at [57]–[65].
2   [1989] 3 All ER 701, [1990] 1 WLR 277.
3   [1989] 3 All ER 701, [1990] 1 WLR 277, at 308.
4   *Jet Holding Ltd v Cooper Cameron (Singapore) Pte Ltd* [2006] SGCA 20 (CA).
5   *Seng and Chakravarthi* (1997) pp 151–156.

Weight of evidence in court

14.41 Even though the court may have admitted the computer output as evidence pursuant to s 35, it may retain doubts as to whether the computer output 'accurately reproduces the relevant contents of the original document'[1]. Thus the provisions under s 36 reserve for the court a discretion to call for further evidence, presumably to either prove or disprove its doubts. Section 36 allows for such further evidence to be required by way of affidavit from the certifiers whose certificates were tendered to support the admission of the computer output under s 36[2]. The court may even appoint or accept an independent expert who can contribute his evidence by way of affidavit for consideration by the court[3]. In addition, the court may require oral evidence to be given, presumably by any relevant party or witness, 'of any matters concerning the accuracy of the computer output' and, further, may require a certifier or the deponent of the affidavit to testify[4].

1   Evidence Act, s 36(1).
2   Evidence Act, s 36(2). The reference to a person (a) 'occupying a respon–sible position in relation to the operation or management of the certifying authority' is a reference to a s 35(3) certificate; (b) who occupies 'a respon–sible position in relation to the operation of the computer at the relevant time' is a reference to either a s 35(4) or a s 35(6) certificate; (c) who 'had control or access over any relevant records and facts in relation to the pro–duction of the computer output' is a reference to a s 35(6) or a s 35(7) certificate; (d) who 'had obtained or been given control or access over any relevant records and facts' is a reference to a s 35(8) certificate.
3   Evidence Act, s 36(2)(e).
4   Evidence Act, s 36(3).

14.42 The issue of the probative value of the admitted computer output is addressed in s 36(4). The section provides that the court, in estimating the weight of computer output, shall have regard for 'all the circumstances from which any inference can be reasonably drawn as to the accuracy or otherwise' of the computer output. In particular, the court must also give consideration as to whether the information reproduced in the computer output was supplied or recorded contemporaneously with the occurrence or existence of the facts dealt with in the information[1], and as to whether any information supplier or processor had any incentive or motive to conceal or misrepresent the information so supplied[2]. In *Lim Mong Hong*, the High Court summed up all these as requiring the court to direct its mind to both the accuracy of the computer output and the authenticity of the information contained therein[3]. The court then applied s 36(4) to accord little weight to the computer output in the form of a computer print-out previously admitted under s 35(1)(c) of the Evidence Act, ruling that it could at best only be corroborative evidence[4].

1   Evidence Act, s 36(4)(a).
2   Evidence Act, s 36(4)(b).
3   *Lim Mong Hong v Public Prosecutor* [2003] 3 SLR 88, [2003] SGHC 161 at [45].
4   *Lim Mong Hong v Public Prosecutor* [2003] 3 SLR 88, [2003] SGHC 161 at [46].

14.43 In this regard, it has been observed that the provisions relating to authenticity and weight in ss 35 and 36 of the Evidence Act require the court to continue to bear in mind the distinction between computer output as stored records and computer output as real evidence[1]. Issues regarding the accuracy and authenticity of computer output will be characterised differently depend-ing on whether the computer output stores information previously kept in documentary form or whether the computer output presents the results processed by some automated process. In the former, the focus is primarily on the reliability of the contents of the output, and in the latter, the focus is primarily on the reliability of the process that generated the output[2]. Thus in

Lim Mong Hong the court gave little weight to the computer output because an effective challenge was made to the reliability of the contents of the computer output (an Excel spreadsheet which contained information manually extracted from accounting records)[3]. In contrast, in *Public Prosecutor v R Sekhar* the court excluded the computer output in evidence because an effective challenge was made as to the reliability of the hotel's computer system for generating daily and monthly guest statements[4]. In both cases, the computer output played little, if any, role in the findings of fact by the court.

[1]   *Seng* (1997) pp 166–180.
[2]   *Seng* (1997) pp 166–180.
[3]   *Lim Mong Hong v Public Prosecutor* [2003] 3 SLR 88, [2003] SGHC 161 at [29], [46].
[4]   *Public Prosecutor v R Sekhar s/o R G Van* [2003] 2 SLR 456, [2003] SGHC 123, [35].

Other rules of evidence

Voluminous or complex evidence

14.44 With the growing complexity of evidence, technology has been harnessed to simplify and make cogent the presentation of such evidence. Section 68A of the Evidence Act, introduced in 1995, makes it possible for charts, summaries, computer output or other explanatory material to be adduced in evidence where such evidence would aid the court's comprehension of other relevant and admissible evidence and such evidence would otherwise be so voluminous or complex that the court considers it inconvenient to assess this other evidence directly.

14.45 However, there is an appreciation that such summaries of evidence should not be a substitute for supporting evidence, which may still take the form of direct testimony or expert evidence. Section 68A(2) thus provides that any fact or opinion asserted in such summaries of evidence, such as relationships among facts asserted in the presentations, shall be proved by relevant and admissible evidence, including any other facts or opinion whose proof is a condition precedent for the admissibility of such evidence.

Live video links

14.46 Section 62A, introduced pursuant to the Evidence (Amendment) Act 1995, inserts a new provision that would allow a witness, with leave of the court, to give evidence through a live video or live television link in civil proceedings if:

(a)   the witness is below the age of 16 years;
(b)   it is expressly so agreed between the parties to the proceedings that evidence may be so given;
(c)   the witness is outside Singapore; or
(d)   the court is satisfied that it is expedient in the interests of justice to do so.

14.47 Without detracting from the importance of having the witness testify in court, where a party applies to have a witness who is outside Singapore testify via live video or television links the court shall have regard to all the circumstances of the case, including the reasons for the witness being unable to give evidence in Singapore, the administrative and technical facilities and arrangements made at the place where the witness is to give his evidence, and whether any party to the proceedings would be unfairly prejudiced[1]. The court is also given broad powers under s 62A(3) to, amongst other things, manage the persons who may be present at or excluded from the place where the witness gives evidence, manage the persons who may be present or excluded from the courtroom where the link is received and make any other orders necessary in the interests of justice. A witness who gives evidence in accordance within s 62A shall be deemed to be giving evidence in the presence of court[2].

[1] Evidence Act, s 62A(2).
[2] Evidence Act, s 62A(8).

Courts and technology

14.48 The 1996 amendments to the Evidence Act also empowered the Rules Committee constituted under the Supreme Court Judicature Act[1] to make rules for the filing, receiving and recording of evidence and documents in court by using information technology[2]. The Rules Committee is also empowered to issue rules to provide for the authentication of evidence and documents filed or received by the use of information technology. In this regard, two sets of rules have been issued in conjunction with the infrastructure that has been developed: rules for the use of technology in the filing and receiving of court documents, and rules for the use of technological facilities in court hearings.

[1] Cap. 322, 1999 Rev Ed.
[2] Evidence Act, s 36A.

The electronic filing system

14.49 Pursuant to s 36A, the Supreme Court has implemented a case management strategy of which the Electronic Filing System ('EFS') is a part. The EFS is, in turn, made up of four services designed to meet the needs of civil litigation. These are:

(a) an electronic filing service where documents can be filed by lawyers with the court registry electronically over the Internet from their computer systems at any time at their convenience;

(b) An electronic extract service where law firms can request for the extraction of copies of cause papers from the court registry electronically or over a service bureau;

(c) An electronic service of documents facility which allows law firms to serve or 'mail' court documents electronically over the Internet to one or more law firms concurrently. This service is authenticated by a certificate of service automatically generated by the EFS and can be filed in court in lieu of the affidavit of service as evidence of service; and

(d) An electronic information service which allows law firms and members of the public to perform online search queries on the courts' databases on all classes of actions in the courts[1].

1   Electronic Filing System available online at http://app.supremecourt.gov.sg/default.aspx?pgID=56, viewed on 24 August 2006.

14.50 The relevant rules for electronic filing can be found in Ord 63A of the Rules of Court on Electronic Filing and Service[1]. In particular, Ord 63A prescribes acknowledging the validity of the electronic service of documents[2] and rules for determining the date of electronic filing of the document[3] and when time for service begins to run[4]. Presumptions as to the integrity of EFS documents and their approval through the application of electronic signatures by lawyers and their authorised agents on the documents also arise accordingly[5]. To supplement Ord 63A, practice directions exist as regards the electronic filing and service of documents for civil proceedings[6] as well as for criminal proceedings[7].

1   Rules of Court, Ord 63A.
2   Rules of Court, Ord 63A, r 12.
3   Rules of Court, Ord 63A, r 10.
4   Rules of Court, Ord 63A, r 11.
5   Rules of Court, Ord 63A, r 16.
6   Supreme Court Practice Directions (18 July 2006), Pt XII.
7   Supreme Court Practice Directions (18 July 2006), Pt XIII.

Technology facilities

14.51 The courts are technologically equipped in two respects. The first is the setting up of five Technology Courts[1] which are already equipped with various IT and audio-visual equipment and facilities for playing back and displaying various electronic media and other objects and projecting such imagery to the courts[2]. The facilities also enable computers and other audio-visual equipment to be connected to the projection facilities[3]. Videoconferencing with local and overseas parties can also be conducted[4]. The second is the availability of various audio-visual and videoconferencing equipment on trolleys (known as Mobile Info-Tech Trolleys[5]) that can be deployed in the different courts[6]. Use of such facilities is subject to prior bookings by the parties[7].

1   Technology Courts/Chambers Booking available online at http://app.supremecourt.gov.sg/default.aspx?pgID=57, viewed on 24 August 2006.
2   Supreme Court Practice Directions, (18 July 2006), Pt XIV, para 118(1).
3   Supreme Court Practice Directions, (18 July 2006), Pt XIV, para 118(2).
4   Supreme Court Practice Directions, (18 July 2006), Pt XIV, para 118(3).
5   Mobile Info-Tech Trolley Booking form available online at http://app.supremecourt.gov.sg/default.aspx?pgID=58, viewed on 24 August 2006.
6   Supreme Court Practice Directions, (18 July 2006), Pt XIV, para 120.
7   Supreme Court Practice Directions, (18 July 2006), Pt XIV, paras 119 and 121.

CIVIL PROCEEDINGS

14.52 To enable the parties in civil proceedings to effectively present their case before a court, appropriate interlocutory steps are required before leading to the trial. Under Singapore law, as in most other common law systems, the pre-trial process consists of the discovery of documents or interrogatories, the application for summons for directions, and the request for further and better particulars. In the context of electronic evidence, the discussion will be limited to the discovery of documents.

Discovery

14.53 The process of discovery is to enable a party to an action to acquire information which they do not have concerning the issues at hand so that they can prepare and present their case for adjudication at trial. This way, the parties are alerted to the causes of action they will have to meet. Each party draws up a list of documents in their possession, custody or power relating to any matter in question between them in the action and serves this list on the other party. The interests of justice require that all the relevant facts are presented before the court in order to achieve a just determination of the issues. If the parties are unable to agree on the need for or the extent of discovery then an application may be made to the court. As the First Schedule to the Supreme Court of Judicature Act states, the court may 'before or after any proceedings are commenced ... order discovery of facts or documents by any party to the proceedings or by any other person in such manner as may be prescribed by Rules of Court'[1].

[1]   Supreme Court of Judicature Act (Cap. 322, 1999 Rev. Ed.).

14.54 Discovery is only extended to documents within the possession, custody or power of a party, or information within the knowledge and belief of the party[1]. The court may order a party to discover documents on which the party relies or will rely, as well as documents which could adversely affect his own case, adversely affect another party's case or support another party's case[2]. Thus orders for discovery may be made against electronic documents such as internal email correspondence between officers of a party[3]. The duty to discover documents falling within the ambit of such order is a continuing one: a party required to give discovery under any such order shall remain under a duty to continue to give discovery of all documents falling within the ambit of such order until the proceedings in which the order was made are concluded[4].

[1]   Rules of Court, Ord 24, r 1(1) in relation to documents. In relation to information, Ord 26, r 1(1) and Ord 26A, r 1(1) provide the judicial basis for discovery of information. Although Ord 26 and Ord 26A do not stipulate any limitation on the extent of discovery of information by interrogatories, common law sets the standard at the best of the knowledge and belief of the respondent (*Douglas v Morning Post* (1923) 39 TLR 402) and where information can be obtained from documents which are in his possession, custody or power, the respondent is expected to obtain such information.

[2]   Rules of Court, Ord 24, r 1(2).

3   *Trek Technology (Singapore) Pte Ltd v FE Global Electronics Pte* [2003] 3 SLR 685, [2003] SGHC 185. In that case, the court hearing the appeal against a registrar's order for discovery reserved the right to make the discovery application before the trial judge who, with more information, was in a better position to decide on the relevance of the internal email correspondence.
4   Rules of Court, Ord 24, r 8.

14.55 The discovery process is subject to the implied undertaking that the discovering party may not use the documents or information so obtained against the other party for a collateral or improper purpose (including foreign proceedings), that is, for any purpose other than the further pursuing of the action in which the discovery is given[1]. However, the prohibition has no application to the existence of information and items seen or observed in the course of the search and the right of the raiding party. Whether the raiding party can otherwise prove such information is a matter of relevance and admissibility of the evidence. The court also has a discretion to release or modify the undertaking in special circumstances but such discretion is to be exercised only where its release or modification will not occasion injustice to the person providing discovery[2]. Such special circumstances would include whether public interest considerations were involved, whether both sets of proceedings were substantially the same, whether there would be injustice to the defendants, and where the evidence is used in foreign civil and criminal proceedings[3].

1   *Reebok International v Royal Corp* [1992] 2 SLR 136, [1991] SGHC 148 (also known as the *Riddick* principle, after *Riddick v Thames Board Mills Ltd* [1977] 3 WLR 63, [1977] 3 All ER 677).
2   *Reebok International v Royal Corp* [1992] 2 SLR 136, [1991] SGHC 148. See also *Beckkett Pte Ltd v Deutsche Bank AG* [2005] 3 SLR 39, [2005] SGHC 79 at [12] and [13]; upheld [2005] 3 SLR 555, [2005] SGCA 34.
3   *Reebok International v Royal Corp* [1992] 2 SLR 136, [1991] SGHC 148.

14.56 Discovery must also relate only to such matters in question. If the court is satisfied that discovery is not necessary, or not necessary at that stage of the cause or matter, it may dismiss or adjourn the application[1]. Neither will the court allow pre-action discovery to fish for evidence as opposed to a bona fide determination of whether there is a basis for legal action[2]. The court may also decline to permit discovery if the probative value of the documents sought is so slight so as to be outweighed by the inconvenience of discovery[3].

1   Rules of Court, Ord 24, r 7.
2   *Kuah Kok Kim v Ernst & Young* [1997] 1 SLR 169, as affirmed by *Beckett Pte Ltd v Deutsche Bank Akitengellschaft Singapore Branch* [2003] 1 SLR 321; *Ng Giok Oh v Sajjad Akhtar* [2003] 1 SLR 375; and *Bayerische Hypo-und Vereinsbank AG v Asia Pacific Breweries (Singapore) Pte Ltd* [2004] 4 SLR 39.
3   *Kahn (David) Inc v Conway Stewart & Co* [1972] FSR 169, cf *Faber Merlin Malaysia v Ban Guan* [1981] 1 MLJ 105 at 107.

The role of the solicitor and client

14.57 The duty of the solicitor is to ensure that the client is aware of their responsibilities in the discovery process and complies with them. This duty also extends to taking steps to ensure that all discoverable documents are preserved[1]. The solicitor should explain the process of discovery and the nature of the obligations to disclose documents and information when directed by the order to do so. If the client has not complied with the obligations of discovery, the solicitor must inform the court as soon as possible. In addition, if the client refuses to allow a solicitor to disclose a document requirement under an order for discovery, the solicitor is obliged to cease to act.

[1] *Koh Teck Hee v Leow Swee Lim* [1992] 1 SLR 905. See also Legal Profession (Professional Conduct) Rules (R1, 2000 Rev Ed) r 56.

Third parties

14.58 Importantly, discovery can also be ordered against other persons before the commencement of proceedings[1], or against persons who are not parties after proceedings have commenced[2]. This is especially useful in the electronic environment where the identity of the potential defendant cannot be determined and hence proceedings cannot be commenced. Therefore, pre-action discovery has become an essential part of the litigation process in order to determine the identity of the potential defendant. For instance, in suits against users who share music files on peer-to-peer networks or against publishers of defamatory remarks on the Internet, the record labels or studios or the aggrieved party would only have the Internet Protocol address of the users or publishers. Discovery against other persons allows the plaintiff to obtain information from the Internet and email service providers as third parties who may have information as to the identity of their registered users, even though formal action has not commenced. Pursuant to Ord 24, r 6, the court may make such an order 'for the purpose of or with a view to identifying possible parties to any proceedings in such circumstances where the Court thinks it just to make such an order, and on such terms as it thinks just'[3].

[1] Rules of Court, Ord 24, r 6(1) and Ord 26A, r 1(1).
[2] Rules of Court, Ord 24, r 6(2).
[3] Rules of Court, Ord 24, r 6(5). An order for the discovery of documents may
    (a)be made conditional on the applicant's giving security for the costs of the person against whom it is made or on such other terms, if any, as the Court thinks just; and
    (b)require the person against whom the order is made to make an affidavit stating whether the documents specified or described in the order are, or at any time have been, in his possession, custody or power and, if not then in his possession, custody or power, when he parted with them and what has become of them. Ord 24, r 6(6).

14.59 Of course, such discoveries may not always be successful. For instance, if the service provider has not retained the relevant information in its records or if the potential defendants have used public domain or publicly-accessible computers, the third parties would be unable to assist. Likewise, network service providers may only retain log records about their users up to a certain period of time, whereupon they are purged from the system. To assist copyright holders and performers in securing such information relating to the identity of users as potential defendants in an action for copyright infringement under the Copyright Act, provision is made in the Supreme Court

Practice Directions for such discovery applications to be expedited and heard within five days of the filing of the application[1].

1   Supreme Court Practice Directions, Pt IV, para 43(2)(b).

Non-disclosure and its consequences

14.60 The rules of disclosure do not authorise the disclosure of any documents under any rule of law which authorises or requires the withholding of any document on the ground that its disclosure would be injurious to the public interest[1]. Likewise, where a party inadvertently allows a privileged document to be inspected, the party who inspected it may only use it or its contents with prior leave of the court[2]. In addition, an aggrieved defendant may apply to the court to discharge the order relating to discovery of the documents on the grounds of privilege. Thus the privilege against self-incrimination at common law apply to pre-trial discovery by a plaintiff in actions for copyright and trade mark infringement, and entitle the defendant to refuse to disclose the incriminating documents to the plaintiff[3]. In addition, privilege may be waived by the party to which the privilege accords—in the case of legal professional privilege, by the client[4]; in the case of banking records, by the bank's customer[5].

1   Rules of Court, Ord 24, r 15.
2   Rules of Court, Ord 24, r 19.
3   *Guccio Gucci SpA v Sukhdav Singh* [1992] 1 SLR 553; *Expanded Metal Manufacturing Pte Ltd v Expanded Metal Co Ltd* [1995] 1 SLR 673, [1995] SGCA 6.
4   Evidence Act, s 128(1).
5   Banking Act (Cap. 19, 2003 Rev Ed), s 47(3).

14.61 Failure to comply with non-disclosure requirements carries four consequences. Firstly, the court may make such order as it thinks just including, in particular, an order that the action be dismissed or, as the case may be, an order that the defence be struck out and judgment be entered accordingly[1]. Secondly, any party who fails to comply with an order for discovery made against it shall be liable for contempt of court[2]. Thirdly, the solicitor of such a client who fails, without reasonable excuse, to give notice of an order for discovery to his client shall be liable to contempt of court[3]. Finally, a party who fails to produce any document required by an order for discovery made against him may not rely on those documents save with the leave of the court[4].

1   Rules of Court, Ord 24, r 16(1).
2   Rules of Court, Ord 24, r 16(2).
3   Rules of Court, Ord 24, r 16(4).
4   Rules of Court, Ord 24, r 16(5).

Costs of discovery

14.62 The general rule is that costs in discovery proceedings are borne by each party, save for discovery against third parties (where the order may be made conditional on the giving of security for the costs of the person against whom it is made)[1], or if the court otherwise makes any order to the contrary at the conclusion of any stage of the interlocutory proceedings. Where discovery against third parties is sought, the party against whom the order is sought is entitled to his costs of the application and for compliance with any order on an indemnity basis[2]. He is also entitled to ask the court for security for such costs[3].

1   Rules of Court, Ord 42, r 6(6).
2   Rules of Court, Ord 26A, r 5
3   Rules of Court, Ord 26A, r 3

Urgent search and seizure orders

14.63 A search order ('Anton Piller order') is applied when there is a grave danger of the defendant disposing of or destroying incriminating evidence. The plaintiff can apply to the court to search for, inspect and seize the relevant materials for preservation until trial. In addition, the search order may also contain directions for the retention and discovery of information eg where seized material such as hard disks are imaged and then inspected for documents evidencing infringement[1]. In the context of digital evidence, the ease with which digital evidence may be destroyed makes such an order even more critical. It has been applied in situations where computers containing evidence of breach of confidential information could have possibly been destroyed[2].

1   *Megastar Entertainment Pte Ltd v Odex Pte Ltd* [2005] 3 SLR 91, [2005] SGHC 84.
2   *Stratech Systems Ltd v Nyam Chiu Shin (alias Yan Qiuxin)* [2005] 2 SLR 579, (CA) at [14], [2004] SGHC 168 (HC) at [11].

14.64 The essential pre-conditions for the making of a search order are:

(a)   there must be an extremely strong prima facie case;
(b)   the damage, potential or actual, must be very serious for the applicant;
(c)   there must be clear evidence that the defendants have in their possession incriminating documents or things (which were the subject matter sought to be preserved in that case) and that there is a real possibility that the defendants may destroy such material before any application between the parties can be made[1]; and
(d)   the harm likely to be caused by the execution of the search order to the respondent and his business affairs must not be excessive or out of proportion to the legitimate object of the order[2].

1   *Piller (Anton) KG v Manufacturing Processes Ltd* [1976] Ch 55 at 61–62, [1976] 1 All ER 779 at 784. These three pre-conditions were approved and applied by the Court of Appeal in *Computerland Corp v Yew Seng Computers Pte Ltd* [1991] SLR 247, [1991] SGCA 28.
2   This was later added by the Staughton Committee Report and approved by the Court of Appeal in *Asian Corporate Services (SEA) Pte Ltd v Eastwest Management Ltd (Singapore Branch)* [2006] 1 SLR 901, [2006] SGCA 1.

14.65 However, the warning of the Court of Appeal in *Computerland Corp v Yew Seng Computers Pte Ltd* should be heeded. Thean J delivering the grounds of decision of the court, said:

It is also our experience that in Singapore too free a use has been made by plaintiffs of the Anton Piller orders, and all too often such orders have been applied for without sufficient grounds and on a bare allegation, without any evidence in support, that there was a fear or likelihood that material evidence would be destroyed or removed or made to disappear by the defendants. Our court has also, on some occasions, responded favourably to such applications and ... has allowed the balance to swing in favour of the plaintiffs. It is therefore imperative that on every application for an Anton Piller order the party seeking it must satisfy the stringent requirements laid down in the Anton Piller case and the court must scrutinize with care the evidence produced and must ... be very circumspect in granting such an order[1].

[1] *Computerland Corp v Yew Seng Computers Pte Ltd* [1991] SLR 247, [1991] SGCA 28 at [20].

14.66 Thus Singapore courts have discharged search orders on the basis that there was no grave danger or real risk that any evidence would be destroyed or made to disappear, or that there was no evidence of any suspicious conduct on the defendant's part[1], or that the orders were onerous and oppressive in being far too wide and extensive to be made at such an early stage of the proceedings[2].

[1] *Bengawan Solo Pte Ltd v Season Confectionery Co (Pte) Ltd* [1994] 1 SLR 617, [1994] SGCA 29; *Expanded Metal Manufacturing Pte Ltd v Expanded Metal Co Ltd* [1995] 1 SLR 673, [1995] SGCA 6.
[2] *Petromar Energy Resources Pte Ltd v Glencore International AG* [1999] 2 SLR 609, [1999] SGCA 28.

14.67 However, the very nature of electronic evidence makes it highly susceptible to destruction and erasure. In particular, if the party making an application for a search order proves the propensity of the defendant to destroy the plaintiff's company data on the plaintiff's company laptop while in the employ of the plaintiff, a strong prima facie case can be made out and the application of a search order to encompass the defendant's company's computer records would be justified[1].

[1] *Asian Corporate Services (SEA) Pte Ltd v Eastwest Management Ltd (Singapore Branch)* [2006] 1 SLR 901, [2006] SGCA 1.

14.68 It should also be noted that documents and other items disclosed pursuant to search orders are also subject to the implied undertaking that the discovering party may not use the documents or information so obtained against the other party for a collateral or improper purpose[1]. However, the prohibition in this undertaking has no application to the existence of information and items independently seen or obtained from the search, and the right of the raiding party to subsequently discover such relevant documents[2].

[1] *Reebok International v Royal Corp* [1992] 2 SLR 136, [1991] SGHC 148.
[2] *Business Software Alliance and Others v SM Summit Holdings Ltd* [2000] 2 SLR 733, [2000] SGCA 23 at [27]–[32].

14.69 Where there are concerns that the documents may be commercially confidential but which may not offer any grounds of privilege or immunity, the court may on occasion be willing to order the inspection of such documents be attended by safeguards[1]. In addition, as the court is mindful of the intrusive effect of search orders, additional safeguards have been provided in the Supreme Court Practice Directions. The Practice Directions suggest, amongst other things, that the search order be served by a supervising solicitor who is an experienced solicitor and not a member or employee of the firm acting for the applicant, and carried out in his presence and under his supervision[2], Where the items may be removed pursuant to the search order, the Practice Directions also require the applicant to insure them[3].

[1] *Format Communications MFG Ltd v ITT (United Kingdom)* [1983] FSR 473 where inspection of the source code of the other party was permitted subject to safeguards proposed by the inspecting party.
[2] Supreme Court Practice Directions, Pt IV, para 42(6).
[3] Supreme Court Practice Directions, Pt IV, para 42(6).

The use of forensic tools and the role of experts

14.70 The discovery of electronic documents and the search and seizure of computer systems and electronic records can be a highly technical process. Such processes should only be carried out with the help and presence of computer forensics experts. In particular, the process for preserving electronic evidence has to be conducted, if not supervised, by these experts. Care must also be taken to ensure that, when analysing the electronic evidence, the parties are working on exact copies or 'mirrors' of the electronic records, rather than on the electronic records themselves[1]. Using specialised forensic or data search and restoration tools, deleted information such as emails may be recovered and fragmented information reconstructed.

[1] See eg *Asian Corporate Services (SEA) Pte Ltd v Eastwest Management Ltd (Singapore Branch)* [2006] 1 SLR 901, [2006] SGCA 1 at [11]: 'computer experts ... [copied] a minor [sic] image of the hard disk and conduct a forensic analysis of the contents of the laptop computer'.

14.71 The role of the experts in such forensic processes should not be understated. To avoid issues as to the authenticity of the electronic evidence, a party seeking to execute a search order for the discovery of electronic documents would instruct a forensic expert, who would then be integrally involved from the start of the execution of the order. The expert must be able to verify that the collection of such evidence was accurate and that the electronic evidence has not been tampered with. The expert should also ensure that there is a proper physical chain of custody of the records and their copies. If necessary, the expert has to be prepared to help the court understand the process of collecting and processing the information in order to counter any allegations of tampering.

14.72 The use of experts would also be recommended in identifying any documents and information requested before drafting an application for a discovery order. It would be prudent when selecting experts to consider the expert's qualifications1. In addition, the use of experts in an urgent search order should be considered in light of the role of the supervising solicitor. For instance, the order may require the supervising solicitor to supervise the imaging by an expert of all the hard disks of computers, portable notebook computers, computer servers and any other computer media storage equipment used by the defendants found on the premises, and to ensure any equipment is retained safely. In this regard, it is prudent for the plaintiffs to ensure that the supervising solicitor notes the actions undertaken by the expert, including the manner in which the electronic evidence was produced and the devices used to process and store such evidence, as these matters may later form the basis of a s 35(6) certificate issued by the expert to support the admission of the electronic evidence.

[1]   Evidence Act, s 47.

CRIMINAL PROCEEDINGS

14.73 In Singapore, the Criminal Procedure Code applies to the investigation and trial of all criminal offences unless there are statutory provisions regulating otherwise[1]. Where there are matters of criminal procedure for which no special provision has been made in the laws of Singapore, English criminal procedure laws can be applied[2].

[1]   Criminal Procedure Code (Cap. 68, 1985 Rev Ed), s 3.
[2]   Criminal Procedure Code (Cap. 68, 1985 Rev Ed), s 3.

Criminal investigations

14.74 Generally, the powers of the police to conduct criminal investigations are found in the provisions in the Criminal Procedure Code. Under s 58, the police have the power to issue an order, known as a written order, to any person in whose possession or power a 'document or thing' is considered necessary or desirable for the purposes of any investigation, to attend and produce the document or thing or produce it at the time and place stated in the order. By analogy with the reasoning in *Megastar Entertainment Pte Ltd v Odex Pte Ltd*, a case pertaining to the seizure as 'documents' of computer records and electronic evidence under the Copyright Act[1], such a 'document or thing' could arguably encompass computer records and other items of electronic evidence. A person who, being legally bound to produce or deliver up the document to the police, intentionally omits so to produce or deliver up the same, commits a criminal offence and may be fined or sentenced to imprisonment[2].

[1]   *Megastar Entertainment Pte Ltd v Odex Pte Ltd* [2005] 3 SLR 91, [2005] SGHC 84.
[2]   Penal Code (Cap. 224, 1985 Rev Ed), s 175; Criminal Procedure Code, s 320.

14.75 Section 125 of the Criminal Procedure Code provides police officers with a range of powers to facilitate an investigation. When investigating a 'seizable case'[1] a search can be conducted if there is reason to believe a person would not respond to a written order under s 58 to produce any document or thing. The provisions of s 125A also authorise a police officer to obtain access to, inspect and check the operation of a computer that he has reasonable cause to suspect is or has been used in connection with the seizable offence; and to require the assistance of any person whom he reasonably suspects of using the computer, or otherwise concerned with the operation of the computer. In addition, s 125B of the Criminal Procedure Code enables the Public Prosecutor to issue an order to authorise a police officer or an authorised person to exercise additional powers to obtain access to any information, code or technology which has the capability of retransforming or unscrambling encrypted data into readable and comprehensible format or text. People involved with using the computer or having charge of the computer may also be required to provide reasonable technical and other assistance as may be required. This includes requiring the person to grant access to information that is encrypted by providing decryption information to enable the data to be decrypted. The Criminal Procedure Code further provides that a person acting under good faith in compliance with the requests from the police officer or authorised person 'shall not be liable in any criminal or civil proceedings for any loss or damage resulting from the act'[2].

[1] A 'seizable case' is a case in which a police officer may ordinarily arrest without a warrant in conjunction with the commission of a 'seizable offence'. These are generally serious offences such as offences against the State, piracy, offences relating to the armed forces, offences affecting the public tranquility, offences relating to currency, corruption, theft, robbery, trespass and offences affecting the body, and are set out in Sch A to the Criminal Procedure Code. See Criminal Procedure Code, s 2: definitions of 'seizable offence' and 'seizable case'.

[2] Criminal Procedure Code, ss 125A(5) and 125B(8).

14.76 Since the occurrence of international terrorism, several legislative enactments have been made. Under s 15A of the Computer Misuse Act, the Minister may authorise, if necessary for the purposes of preventing or countering any threat to the national security, essential services, defence or foreign relations of Singapore, any person or organisation specified in the certificate to 'take such measures as may be necessary to prevent or counter any threat to a computer or computer service or any class of computers or computer services'. Such measures include the exercise by the authorised person or organisation of the powers referred to in ss 125A and 125B of the Criminal Procedure Code. The powers conferred on the Minister to authorise the taking of such preventive measures are very wide. In the Second Reading of the Computer Misuse (Amendment) Bill 2003, the Minister explained that such measures may include the use of real-time intrusion detection systems and pre-emptive scanning activities[1]. The Minister also defended the breadth of the powers granted to him, saying that, in view of the nature of the cyber threats to national infrastructure, it is a better approach for the provision to be crafted to be as broad as possible without prescribing specific measures or setting out guidelines[2].

[1] Speech by the Senior Minister of State for Home Affairs, Associate Professor Ho Peng Kee, on the Second Reading of the Computer Misuse (Amendment) Bill 2003, Singapore Parliamentary Debates, Official Report vol 76 (10 November 2003) at col 3321.

[2] Speech by the Senior Minister of State for Home Affairs, Associate Professor Ho Peng Kee, on the Second Reading of the Computer Misuse (Amendment) Bill 2003.

Search warrants

14.77 Pursuant to s 61 of the Criminal Procedure Code, where a court has reason to believe that a person to whom a s 58 summons (or a related s 59 requisition order[1]) to produce a document or thing will not or would not so produce it as required, that such a document or thing is not known to the court to be in the possession of any person, or the court considers that the purposes of justice or of any inquiry, trial or other criminal proceeding will be served by a general search or inspection, it may issue a search warrant (referred to as a 'general search warrant'). The warrant may be directed to a police officer designated by name[2], or to any person or persons by name, not being police officers[3]. These persons so designated may search or inspect in accordance with the warrant and with the Criminal Procedure Code[4]. The court may, if it thinks fit, limit the warrant by specifying in the warrant the particular place or part of it to which only the search or inspection shall extend[5].

[1]   A s 59 requisition order is directed to a person in possession of a book, letter, postcard, telegram or other document that is being delivered. Although references are made in s 59, Criminal Procedure Code, to the now defunct 'Telecommunication Authority of Singapore', para 3(1)(b), Fourth Schedule of the Telecommunications Authority of Singapore Act (Cap. 323, 1993 Rev Ed) referred to this person as a 'public postal licensee'. Unfortunately, due to legislative oversight, the Telecommunications Authority of Singapore Act has since been repealed, together with the Fourth Schedule, which would have otherwise clarified the interpretation of s 59.
[2]   Criminal Procedure Code, s 61(3).
[3]   Criminal Procedure Code, s 61(3).
[4]   Criminal Procedure Code, s 61(3).
[5]   Criminal Procedure Code, s 61(5).

14.78   An alternative form of a search warrant may be issued pursuant to s 62 of the Criminal Procedure Code (referred to as an 'investigative search warrant'). Section 62 provides that where information is provided to a Magistrate's Court that stolen property, goods with false trade descriptions, forged documents or counterfeit instruments are being deposited, sold or concealed (being criminal offences), the court may, after such inquiry as it thinks necessary[1], issue an investigative search warrant. The person authorised by the warrant may also take possession of property seized as a result of the search, convey the property before a Magistrate's Court, guard the property, and take into custody and produce before a Magistrate's Court every person found in the place suspected to be privy to the offences.

[1]   *Heng Lee Handbags Co Pte Ltd v Public Prosecutor* [1994] 2 SLR 760, [1994] SGHC 123 at [28]–[30].

14.79 The differences between a s 61 search warrant (a 'general search warrant') and a s 62 search warrant (an 'investigative search warrant') are that the latter provides for additional powers in connection with the search of places and also allows for the taking into custody of suspects found in the search location[1]. As Chief Justice Yong Pung How observed in *SM Summit Holdings Ltd v PP*:

[I]t is a more difficult task to convince the court under s 61 that a search is necessary for the purposes of any inquiry, trial or other proceeding. The burden under s 61 is higher than showing that the search is necessary for investigation. The upshot of the matter is that under the legislative scheme, it is incumbent on the applicants to adduce evidence why the general search warrant is required under s 61 for the purposes of the trial or other proceeding. On this reading, the English decisions on the implied powers of search and seizure are not relevant[2].

1 *SM Summit Holdings Ltd v Public Prosecutor* [1997] 3 SLR 922 at [81].
2 *SM Summit Holdings Ltd v Public Prosecutor* [1997] 3 SLR 922 at [81].

14.80 It has also been observed, by way of comments in *SM Summit Holdings Ltd v PP*, that a s 61 search warrant only allows for the seizure of 'documents' but this has been since doubted in *Cigar Affair v Pacific Cigar Co* since s 61 refers to both 'document or other thing'[1]. The differences in the scope of powers under a general, as opposed to an investigative, search warrant are pertinent, particularly where the person designated or authorised by the warrant seeks also to seize documents such as electronic and computer data stored in computer systems and other electronic media, and to retain them in their custody[2]. Where the documents are themselves 'stolen property' or 'forged documents' no issue arises as to the scope of an investigative search warrant. Law enforcement officers are likely, in the course of executing an investigative search warrant and seizing infringing articles, to encounter documents such as invoices, delivery orders and sales orders that may prove various dealings in such articles. The question is whether these documents, some of which may be in electronic form, can be seized pursuant to the investigative search warrant as well. In *SM Summit Holdings Ltd v PP*, the Singapore High Court answered this question in the negative. The court held that, unlike the position in England[3], that there are no implied powers of search and seizure to enable seizure of items or documents which were reasonably thought to be evidence of the crimes of the same offence (or even a different offence), and that to imply such a power would be to render a s 61 general search order redundant[4]. Thus, the *SM Summit Holdings* case held that documents, including electronic documents and records, evidencing an offence may not be seized pursuant to a s 62 investigative search order[5].

1 [2005] 3 SLR 633, [2005] SGHC 108 at [25].
2 See eg *SM Summit Holdings Ltd v Public Prosecutor* [1997] 3 SLR 922 at [22], [67].
3 See eg *Chic Fashions (West Wales) v Jones* [1968] 1 All ER 229; *Truman (Frank) Export v Metropolitan Police Commr* [1977] 3 All ER 431; and *Reynolds v Metropolitan Police Comr* [1985] QB 881.
4 *SM Summit Holdings Ltd v Public Prosecutor* [1997] 3 SLR 922 at [80]–[83].
5 *SM Summit Holdings Ltd v Public Prosecutor* [1997] 3 SLR 922 at [80]–[83].

14.81 It was pursuant to this restrictive judicial reading of s 62 of the Criminal Procedure Code, as well as to give effect to the US-Singapore Free Trade Agreement[1], that the section was revised and a new provision enacted in the Trade Marks Act to legislatively provide for this implied power of seizure[2] (s 62 previously governed the search and seizure of infringing trade mark items). Likewise, the search and seizure provisions in the Copyright Act were also revised soon after the *SM Summit Holdings* decision to explicitly provide for the seizure of documents[3], to 'enable a more effective investigation and prosecution of copyright offences'[4].

1 See Trade Marks (Amendment) Bill 2004 (Bill No. 18 of 2004), Explanatory Statement to Clause 24.

2   Trade Marks (Amendment) Act 2004 (No. 20 of 2004), ss 24 and 37 (enacting the new
     s 53A, Trade Marks Act).
3   See Copyright (Amendment) Bill 1998 (Bill No. 4 of 1998), Explanatory Statement to
     Clause 24, Copyright (Amendment) Bill 2004 (Bill No. 48 of 2004), Explanatory
     Statement to Clause 36. See also *Megastar Entertainment Pte Ltd v Odex Pte Ltd* [2005]
     3 SLR 91, [2005] SGHC 84 (noting that the legislative enactments overturned the previous
     decisions to the contrary in *Lance Court Furnishings Pte Ltd v Public Prosecutor* [1993]
     3 SLR 969 and *SM Summit Holdings*).
4   Speech by the Minister for Law, Professor S Jayakumar, on the Second Reading of the
     Copyright (Amendment) Bill 1998, Singapore Parliamentary Debates, Official Report
     vol 68 (19 February 1998) at col 315.

14.82 Therefore, in relation to copyright infringements, where there is
reasonable cause upon the provision of information given under oath for
suspecting there is in any premises any article or document which is evidence
that offences involving commercial dealings in copyright works or willful
infringements of copyright[1] under the Copyright Act have been committed,
the court may issue, either unconditionally or subject to such conditions as the
court thinks fit, a warrant authorising a police officer to enter and search the
premises for the articles and documents which are specified in the warrant,
whether specifically or in any general category[2], and seize any such articles
and documents found at the premises[3]. It has been held in *Megastar Entertainment Pte Ltd v Odex Pte Ltd* that this permitted the drafting of search
warrants authorising the seizure of documents, including information existing
in computer-readable form, any computer or any hard disk integral to any
computer, which evidences any copyright offence committed in relation to
works that are set out in general categories or lists[4], and the reference to
'documents' permits the search, seizure and electronic imaging of hard disk
drives[5].

1   Copyright Act (Cap. 63, 2006 Rev Ed), section 136(1), (2), (3), (3A) and (4) ('Copyright
     Act').
2   This expression was inserted pursuant to the Copyright (Amendment) Act 2004 (Act 52 of
     2004).
3   Copyright Act, s 136(9). A similar provision in relation to performances is found in
     s 254A(9), Copyright Act. See also Copyright Act, ss 140B(7), 261A(2) and 261G(2).
4   [2005] 3 SLR 91, [2005] SGHC 84 at [20]–[24].
5   [2005] 3 SLR 91, [2005] SGHC 84 at [32]–[38].

14.83 In relation to trade mark infringements, where there is reasonable
cause upon the provision of information given under oath for suspecting there
is in any premises or conveyance any article or document which is evidence
that certain offences[1] under the Trade Marks Act have been committed, the
court may issue, either unconditionally or subject to such conditions as the
court thinks fit, a warrant authorising a police officer to enter and search the
premises for the goods, materials, articles and documents which are specified
in the warrant, whether specifically or in any general category[2]. With the
enactment of the new s 53A of the Trade Marks Act, the High Court in *Cigar
Affair v Pacific Cigar Co* explained that documents which are seized need not
be confined to those set out and cited in the complaint made that supported
the issuance of the search warrant[3]. However, as this point was not discussed
at all in *Cigar Affair*, it remains to be seen whether the expression 'whether
specifically or in any general category' allows for the seizure of documents

that may evidence another trade mark (or copyright) offence separate and distinguishable from the first offence and the information contained in the complaint made to support the issuance of a search warrant.

1   Trade Marks Act (Cap. 332, 2005 Rev Ed), ss 46, 47, 48, 49 and 52 ('Trade Marks Act'), counterfeiting a trade mark, falsely applying a registered trade mark to goods or services, making or possessing of article for committing offence, importing or selling goods with falsely applied trade mark and representation on trade marks of arms or flags prohibited.
2   Trade Marks Act, s 53A.
3   [2005] 3 SLR 633, [2005] SGHC 108 at [26]–[29].

14.84 An example of a search and seizure provision expressly empowering the production of electronic evidence can be found in the Competition Act. Under s 65 of the Act, the search warrant issued by the court authorises the Competition Commission or an inspector to, amongst other things, search the premises and any person on those premises for any document, equipment or article which has a bearing on the investigation, to take copies of, or extracts from, or possession of any relevant document, and also to require any information which is stored in any electronic form and is accessible from the premises and which the officer considers relevant to the investigation to be produced in a form in which it can be taken away and in which it is visible and legible[1]. The officer may also remove from those premises for examination any equipment or article which relates to any matter relevant to the investigation[2].

1   Competition Act (Cap. 50B, 2006 Rev Ed), s 65(1).
2   Competition Act (Cap. 50B, 2006 Rev Ed), s 65(1).

14.85 Powers of search and seizure that expressly provide for the production or seizure of electronic records or information may be found in more recent legislation such as the Human Cloning and Other Prohibited Practices Act[1], the Biological Agents and Toxins Act 2005[2] and the Private Hospitals and Medical Clinics Act[3]. Other search and seizure provisions that are potentially relevant to electronic evidence may be found in the Telecommunications Act[4], the Endangered Species (Import and Export) Act 2006[5], the Customs Act[6], the Wholesome Meat and Fish Act[7], the Exchange Control Act[8], the Internal Security Act[9], the Prevention of Corruption Act[10], the Chemical Weapons (Prohibition) Act[11], the Poisons Act[12], the Environmental Pollution Control Act[13], the Undesirable Publications Act[14], the Films Act[15], the Public Order (Preservation) Act[16], the Regulation of Imports and Exports Act[17], and the Bankruptcy Act[18]. In some of these provisions, despite the absence of an express reference to records in 'electronic form', the various references to the powers to search and seize 'documents', 'books' and 'records' arguably include the power to search and seize electronic records and other items of electronic evidence.

1   Human Cloning and Other Prohibited Practices Act (Cap. 131B, 2005 Rev Ed), ss 14(2)(c), (d) and (e).
2   Biological Agents and Toxins Act 2005 (No. 36 of 2005), s 52.
3   Private Hospitals and Medical Clinics Act (Cap. 248, 1999 Rev Ed), s 12.
4   Telecommunications Act (Cap. 323, 2000 Rev Ed), s 37.
5   Endangered Species (Import and Export) Act 2006, s 11(3)(c), seizure, removal and detention of any thing which contains evidence.
6   Customs Act (Cap. 70, 2004 Rev Ed), s 101.

7   Wholesome Meat and Fish Act (Cap. 349A, 2000 Rev Ed), s 25(1)(d), seize and detail any item which is otherwise connected with the commission of an offence.
8   Exchange Control Act (Cap. 99, 2000 Rev Ed), Sch 5, para 2(2).
9   Internal Security Act (Cap. 143, 1985 Rev Ed), s 28.
10   Prevention of Corruption Act (Cap. 241, 1993 Rev Ed), s 22.
11   Chemical Weapons (Prohibition) Act (Cap. 37B, 2001 Rev Ed), s 27
12   Poisons Act (Cap. 234, 1999 Rev Ed), s 14.
13   Environmental Pollution Control Act (Cap. 94A, 2002 Rev Ed), s 50.
14   Undesirable Publications Act (Cap. 338, 1998 Rev Ed), s 13.
15   Films Act (Cap. 107, 1998 Rev Ed), s 34.
16   Public Order (Preservation) Act (Cap. 258, 1985 Rev Ed), s 258.
17   Regulation of Imports and Exports Act (Cap. 272A, 1996 Rev Ed), s 22.
18   Bankruptcy Act (Cap. 20, 2000 Rev Ed), s 108.

Disclosure obligations

14.86 In a criminal trial, the production of evidence and the calling of witnesses are at the discretion of the prosecution and the defence, based on their assessment of their respective cases. As the law currently stands at the time of the writing of this chapter, aside from s 58, '[t]here is no provision in the Criminal Procedure Code for the discovery by an accused of documents in the possession of the prosecution. Neither is the prosecution obliged to adduce such documents as evidence'[1].

1   *Tan Khee Koon v Public Prosecutor* [1995] 3 SLR 724, [1995] SGHC 236, at [62], per Yong Pung How CJ.

14.87 Section 58 provides that defence counsel can apply to court for a summons to order any person to produce any 'document or thing' that is 'necessary or desirable for the purposes of any investigation, inquiry, trial or other proceeding under the Code by or before that court'. This section has been judicially interpreted to mean that an application can only be made before the court where the actual trial is taking place and only after the recording of the prosecution evidence has commenced[1]. Where a trial has been concluded, a summons application could be made by way of a criminal motion before a court hearing an appeal from the trial[2].

1   *Kulwant v Public Prosecutor* [1986] SLR 239; *Tan Khee Koon v Public Prosecutor* [1995] 3 SLR 724, [1995] SGHC 236 at [62].
2   cf *Chan Hiang Leng Colin v Public Prosecutor* [1994] 3 SLR 662, [1994] SGHC 207 at [34], [39]–[40].

14.88 However, the applicant for a summons to produce must be precise as to the documents or things which they wish the other party to produce. A general demand for unspecified documents or things is inadequate and will be rejected as being clearly unfair as it would enable the applicant to initiate criminal proceedings against the respondent without having first amassed sufficient evidence to make a case[1]. The court will not sanction a fishing exercise in a summons application for 'all or any documentation' relating to a particular activity:

> The document or thing must be clearly specified, that is, it must indicate the document to be produced and should be given at such time as to afford the party a reasonable opportunity for producing the document at the trial. A

general direction to produce all papers relating to the subject in dispute will not be enforced. It must be directed at a specific document[2].

Therefore it would not be appropriate, where digital evidence is concerned, to request all information relating to a specific person as such requests would be potentially onerous if the information is stored in different locations over a long period of time. Likewise, 'there is no legal provision in Singapore with respect to criminal proceedings which allows either the prosecution or the defence to obtain evidence from the opposite party by ... means [of response to interrogatories]'[3].

1   *Public Prosecutor v IC Automation (S) Pte Ltd* [1996] 3 SLR 249, [1996] SGHC 170, [65].
2   *Public Prosecutor v IC Automation (S) Pte Ltd* [1996] 3 SLR 249, [1996] SGHC 170 at [64]; *SM Summit Holdings* [1997] 3 SLR 922 at [117].
3   *Chan Hiang Leng Colin and Ors v Public Prosecutor* [1994] 3 SLR 662, [1994] SGHC 207 at [41].

14.89 The current position in Singapore has been summed up by the then Chief Justice Yong Pung How as follows:

[The prosecution] is not obliged to go out of its way to allow the defence any opportunity to test its evidence. It is not obliged to act for the defence. Only if there is an intention to hinder or hamper the defence would the possibility of a miscarriage of justice arise, requiring interference by the courts[1].

This position, however, looks set to change as it has been reported that the law is to be revised to make it compulsory for prosecutors to share their evidence with defence lawyers, before the case goes to trial[2].

1   *Chua Keem Long v Public Prosecutor* [1996] 1 SLR 510 at [77].
2   'Prosecutors to reveal all in proposed new law' (2006) Straits Times, 16 October.

Admissibility

14.90 The Evidence Act, discussed above, generally regulates the admissibility of evidence, including electronic evidence, in a criminal trial. However, the Criminal Procedure Code provides one additional avenue for admitting electronic evidence in criminal proceedings. Modelled after the UK Civil Evidence Act 1968 (which only applied to civil proceedings), s 380 of the Criminal Procedure Code, which operates 'without prejudice to s 35 of the Evidence Act', provides that if a document is, or forms part of, a record compiled by a person acting under a duty from information which was supplied by another person ('the original statement maker') who had, or may reasonably be supposed to have had, personal knowledge of the matters dealt with in that information, the statement contained in such a document shall be admissible as evidence of any fact stated therein of which direct oral evidence would be admissible, if one of three conditions relating to the original statement maker is satisfied[1].

The conditions are:

(a)   the original statement maker has been or is to be called as a witness in the proceedings;

(b)   the original statement maker, being compellable to give evidence on behalf of the party desiring to give the statement in evidence, attends or is brought before the court but refuses to be sworn or affirmed; or

(c)   it is shown that the original statement maker:

    (i)   is dead or is unfit by reason of his bodily or mental condition to attend as a witness;

    (ii)   is overseas and that it is not reasonably practicable to secure his attendance;

    (iii)   is competent but not compellable to give evidence on behalf of the party desiring to give the statement in evidence, and he refuses to give evidence on behalf of that party; or

    (iv)   cannot reasonably be expected to have any recollection of the matters dealt with in the statement, having regard to the time which has elapsed since he supplied the information and to all the circumstances[2].

[1]   Criminal Procedure Code, s 380(1).
[2]   Criminal Procedure Code, s 380(2).

14.91 Section 380 was applied in the case of *Roy S Selvarajah v PP*[1] to allow an officer with the data processing centre at the Immigration Department to testify that she had checked the immigration records which showed that one witness had entered Singapore on a social visit pass which had since expired, to prove that she overstayed. The court held that the computerised immigration records were admissible as evidence of the facts stated therein by virtue of s 380. Chief Justice Yong Pung How said:

> The records form part of the data base records compiled by an immigration officer acting under a duty from information which was supplied by a person who had or reasonably been supposed to have had personal knowledge of matters dealt with in that information. Such a person would be the immigration officer who records the names of the immigrants into Singapore, whether they were granted work permits, in-principle approvals or any extensions of social visit passes. More importantly s 380 also covers the case where the information is not supplied by that person to the compiler directly but is supplied to the compiler of the record indirectly through one or more interested persons each acting under a duty. The supplier of information need not act under a duty. In such a case, the court can take judicial notice that, having regard to the time which has elapsed since he supplied the information and to all the circumstances, he cannot reasonably be expected to have any recollection of the matters dealt with in the statement within s 380(2)(iv). The prohibition in s 380(4) does not apply because such a record is not prepared for the purpose of any pending civil or criminal proceedings, but are administrative measures[2].

[1]   *Roy S Selvarajah v Public Prosecutor* [1998] 3 SLR 517.
[2]   *Roy S Selvarajah v Public Prosecutor* [1998] 3 SLR 517 at [44].

14.92 The computerised immigration record was not actually admitted in evidence (because the records were erased by the time of the trial): the data processing officer testified as to its existence and its contents. Chief Justice Yong Pung How was prepared to admit her testimony, notwithstanding that s 380 only envisaged the admissibility of the document, on the basis that 'the investigating officer is stating facts concerning the occurrence of the record itself, not about the truth of anything contained in the record'[1]. This aspect of the reasoning must surely be doubted. The *raison d'étre* of s 380 is in the reliability of recorders of information acting under a duty to record such information. This link is surely broken when a third party who is not a recorder is allowed to testify as to an electronic record whose contents she was not under a duty to record, and which she had to recollect from memory. To admit such evidence would amount to admitting hearsay evidence on admissible hearsay evidence. Nonetheless, *Roy S Selvarajah* is a good illustration of the continued relevance of hearsay rules notwithstanding the availability of rules for admitting electronic records as evidence. It must be added that the improper admission or rejection of evidence is not grounds of itself for a new trial or the reversal or alteration of any finding, sentence or order made by the court unless the improper admission or rejection of evidence has occasioned a failure of justice[2].

[1]   *Roy S Selvarajah v Public Prosecutor* [1998] 3 SLR 517 at [45].
[2]   Criminal Procedure Code, s 396.

Illegally obtained evidence

14.93 In the digital environment, illegally obtained evidence may take the form of unauthorised interceptions of telecommunications messages[1] or secret taping of conversations and discussions. The judicial pronouncement is that evidence, though unlawfully obtained, is admissible as long as it is relevant, subject only to the judicial discretion to disallow such evidence if its reception would operate unfairly against the accused[2]. However, the court has not accepted a general rule that it will as a matter of public policy exercise judicial discretion to exclude evidence obtained by law enforcement officers by consciously unlawful means. Thus, Singapore courts have consistently refused to exclude evidence obtained via entrapment or the use of an agent provocateur[3], with the Court of Appeal making the position clear with an unequivocal pronouncement in *How Poh Sun*[4]. However, there also appears to be an acceptance of the House of Lords decision in *R v Sang*, that there is a judicial discretion to exclude evidence only where its prejudicial effect outweighs its probative value and the evidence was tantamount to a self-incriminatory confession[5]. In *SM Summit Holdings Ltd*, the High Court drew a distinction between a case where illegal investigative conduct merely induced the accused to commit the offence which he has committed and a case where the illegal investigative conduct is itself an essential ingredient of the charged offence[6]. This holding in *SM Summit Holdings* was recently reconsidered in the case of *Wong Keng Leong Rayney v Law Society of Singapore* and interpreted to mean that evidence will only be excluded in exceptional cases, such as those involving prior illegality in the procurement of the evidence[7].

[1]   See eg Telecommunications Act (Cap. 323, 2000 Rev Ed), s 42: no officer, employee or agent of a public telecommunications licensee may willfully divulge, omit to transmit, intercept or acquaint himself with or detain any message or part thereof, except in obedience to an order under the hand of the Minister or the direction of a court.
[2]   *Cheng Swee Tiang v Public Prosecutor* [1964] MLJ 291, approving of *Kuruma, Son of Kaniu v R* [1955] AC 197.
[3]   See eg *Heng Lee Handbags Co Pte Ltd v Public Prosecutor* [1994] 2 SLR 760, [1994] SGHC 123 at [32].

4 *How Poh Sun v Public Prosecutor* [1991] SLR 220, at [21], per Yong Pung How CJ.
5 *R v Sang* [1980] AC 402. See *Ajmer Singh v Public Prosecutor* [1986] SLR 454.
6 *SM Summit Holdings* [1997] 3 SLR 922 at [52], [102].
7 [2006] SGHC 179 at [87].

Chapter 15

SOUTH AFRICA

JULIEN HOFMAN[1]

BACKGROUND

15.01 Although it has been suggested that the test for admitting or excluding evidence should be whether the evidence is relevant or not, South Africa still takes an exclusionary approach to evidence[2]. This means that even relevant evidence in civil and criminal matters may be excluded if it is problematic in the sense that its value as evidence is outweighed either by the prejudice that may follow from airing it at a trial or by the time that will be lost by asking a court to consider it[3].

Electronic evidence is undeniably problematic. According to the authors of one South African work on evidence: 'In leaving paper, we have also left almost all guarantees of authenticity and reliability ...'[4]. This is true in the sense that with electronic evidence a court must not only allow, as with any other form of evidence, for deliberate or accidental human error. With electronic evidence there are the added possibilities of hardware failure[5] and defective software[6]. Tampering can also be more difficult to detect with electronic evidence than with a paper document.

---

[1] Thanks to Professor David Zeffert and Stephen Mason for valuable comments on the draft of this paper, to Louis Rood of Fairbridges for his help and to Professor Mike Larkin for his encouragement. Any shortcomings in this paper are my own.

[2] DT Zeffertt, AP Paizes and AStQ Skeen *The South African law of evidence* (5th edn, 2003) p219. This is the standard South African work on the law of evidence and will be referred to as '*Zeffertt*'.

[3] An exclusionary approach can mean a time-consuming 'trial within a trial' before a court decides whether to admit or exclude the evidence. On the other hand, an exclusionary approach can save time by not requiring a court to look at evidence on which it will not be able to rely. The rule against hearsay, in particular, can have the effect of reducing the amount of documentary evidence relied on in a case.

[4] CWH Schmidt and DT Zeffertt *Evidence*, para 133. An extract from Joubert *The Law of South Africa* vol 9, (first reissue, 1997) revised by DP van der Merwe.

[5] Dana van der Merwe *Computers and the law* (2nd edn, 2000) p 226.

[6] Andrew Marshall 'Liability for Defective Software in South Africa' (2005) LLM Minor dissertation explains how it is that all software should be treated as 'inherently and unavoidably defective':
available online at http://lawspace.law.uct.ac.za:8080/dspace/handle/2165/265.

15.02 How to treat electronic evidence has exercised the South African Law Commission ('the Law Commission')[1] since 1976 when, in a civil matter, the Appellate Division would not admit as evidence bank records generated by a computer[2]. In 1983, following a report by the Law Commission[3], Parliament passed the Computer Evidence Act making a computer print-out admissible in civil cases if it satisfied certain conditions[4]. After first, in 1987, expressing satisfaction with this legislation[5], the Law Commission, in 1995, recommended its repeal[6]. In 1998 and 2001 the Law Commission returned to this subject in two papers on computer crime[7].

Despite the recommendations of the Law Commission, there was no new legislation on electronic evidence until the Electronic Communications and Transactions Act ('the ECT Act') of 2002[8]. The ECT Act was the responsibility of the Department of Communications. The Department of Justice did take part in the consultations that preceded the ECT Act but neither the Department of Justice nor the Law Commission seems to have contributed much to what the ECT Act says about evidence[9].

In the ECT Act only s 15 deals explicitly with the law of evidence[10]. Section 15, as with many of the sections in ch 3, is based on the corresponding article (article 9) in the UNCITRAL Model Law on Electronic Commerce (the Model Law)[11]. Establishing the relationship between ch 3 of the ECT Act and the Model Law is thus essential for understanding s 15.

[1]   The Law Commission, since 2002 the Law Reform Commission, was established by the South African Law Reform Commission Act 19 of 1973 to make recommendations for improving the law. It is accountable to the Minister of Justice and is, in effect, the research arm of the Department of Justice.
[2]   *Narlis v South African Bank of Athens* 1976 (2) SA 573 (A) at 578.
[3]   South African Law Commission (Project 6: Review of the Law of Evidence) *Report on the Admissibility in Civil Proceedings of Evidence Generated by Computers* (1982).
[4]   Computer Evidence Act 57 of 1983. *Van der Merwe* (2000) pp 223–9 discusses the origins and limitations of this legislation.
[5]   South African Law Commission (Project 6: Review of the Law of Evidence) Report (1987) p 28 said: 'For the present the Commission is not convinced of an immediate need for a general investigation into the effectiveness of Act 57 of 1983'.
[6]   South African Law Commission (Project 95: Investigation into the Computer Evidence Act 57 of 1983) *Working Paper 60* (1995) p iv.
[7]   South African Law Commission (Project 108: Computer related crime: Options for reform in respect of unauthorised access to computers, unauthorised modification of computer data, and software applications, related to procedural aspects) *Issue paper 14* (1998) ch 3, paras 19–23; *Discussion Paper 99* (2001) ch 2 'The problem' paras 2.5.4.1–2.5.4.5, ch 4 'Recommendations' para 5.5.
[8]   Electronic Communications and Transactions Act 25 of 2002. Assented to on 31 July 2002 and brought into operation on 30 August 2002.
[9]   It is probably fair to say that the three-year consultation process contributed very little to the final form of the ECT Act. For details of the process see the e-commerce debate website at http://www.doc.gov.za/Ecomm-Debate/myweb/index.htm.
[10] Other sections dealing with evidence are s 92, that repealed the Computer Evidence Act 57 of 1983, and s 4(3) and (4) that authorises the exclusions in Schs 1 and 2 to the Act.
[11] United Nations Commission on International Trade Law ('UNCITRAL') *Model Law on Electronic Commerce with Guide to Enactment* (1996) with additional art 5bis adopted by resolution of General Assembly 51/162 of 6 December 1996.

CHAPTER 3 OF THE ECT ACT AND THE MODEL LAW

Status of the Model Law in South African law

15.03 Section 233 of the South African Constitution (the Constitution)[1] says that a South African court interpreting any South African legislation 'must prefer any reasonable interpretation of the legislation that is consistent with international law'.

A resolution of the United Nations General Assembly, such as that approving the Model Law and the Guide, is not an international agreement in terms of s 231 of the Constitution and does not automatically qualify as international law. The Model Law, however, has been incorporated into the domestic law of many countries. This combination of statement and usage gives the Model Law, it is submitted, the status of customary international law[2]. If this is the case, the Model Law is part of South African law and South African courts should, where the language admits, interpret domestic legislation on electronic evidence to comply with it.

In addition, the Model Law[3] requires courts to interpret domestic legislation that gives effect to the Model Law 'with reference to its international origin in order to ensure uniformity in the interpretation of the Model Law in various countries'[4].

[1] Constitution of the Republic of South Africa 1996.

[2] DJ Harris *Cases and Materials on International Law* (6th edn, 2004) p 55 cites Blame Sloan *United Nationals General Assembly Resolutions in Our Changing World* (1991) pp 71–75 in support of this view. Harris, at pp 60–61, also cites L Sohn 'The Development of the Charter of the United Nations: The Present State' in Maarten Bos, ed *The Present State of International Law and Other Essays* (1973) p 39, at pp 52–53, that States have found this form of 'instant international law making' particularly useful 'for developing new law for areas made accessible by modern science and technology'.

[3] Article 3, as explained by paras 41–42 of the Guide. The Guide is an integral part of the Model Law and, according to para 1, even addresses some issues not settled in the Model Law.

[4] The ECT Act does not refer in so many words to its dependence on the Model Law but the dependence is clear from the similarity of the wording and the UNCITRAL website lists South Africa among the countries that have enacted legislation implementing provisions of the Model Law (except for the provisions on certification and electronic signatures). Available online at http://www.uncitral.org/uncitral/en/uncitral_texts/electronic_commerce/1996Model_status.html.

Functional equivalence in the Model Law

15.04 The Model Law was drafted to promote electronic commerce by providing an electronic equivalent for written, signed and original documents. It does this by adopting what it calls a functional equivalent approach. Functional equivalence recognises the differences between written and electronic communication. Rather than using a legal fiction to create an artificial identity between the two, the functional equivalent approach regulates electronic documents so they can perform the same commercial functions as non-electronic documents[1].

The Guide does not list art 9 as one of the articles that embodies a functional equivalent approach[2]. But the functional equivalence of data messages as evidence is clearly necessary to make the functional equivalence of data messages as documents effective[3]. Treating electronic evidence as the functional equivalent of documentary evidence will ensure a 'media-neutral environment' for anyone relying on electronic evidence[4]. It will neither discriminate against those transacting electronically nor give them an unfair advantage[5]. It also does away with the incentive to engage in 'format shopping'[6].

1 Paras 15–18 of the Guide give a more detailed explanation of functional equivalence.
2 Guide para 18. This may be because the Commission felt, as the Guide says in para 136, that it was too early 'to attempt to provide legislative unification of the rules on evidence that may apply to electronic commerce messaging'.
3 Guide para 46. There is little point in making a data message legally effective in the same way as a document if the data message cannot be used as evidence in the same way.
4 Guide para 6.
5 The need for an even-handed approach is reflected in s 4(2)(a) of the ECT Act which says 'This Act must not be construed as requiring any person to generate, communicate, produce, process, send, receive, record, retain, store or display any information, document or signature by or in electronic form'.
6 Format shopping would involve converting hard-copy evidence to electronic evidence and destroying the originals or presenting a hard-copy version and destroying the electronic version in order to take advantage of differences in the law of evidence that applies to each.

Does s 15 apply to non-commercial matters?

15.05 Article 9 in the Model Law was intended only to ensure that electronic commerce should not be held back by the domestic law of evidence of any country. The Model Law limited the changes it asks for in domestic law relating to evidence because, as the Guide puts it, the law of evidence is 'an area in which particularly complex issues might arise in certain jurisdictions'.

Strictly speaking, the Model Law applies only to commercial matters. This means that the Model Law, including art 9 on evidence, does not apply to non-commercial civil or criminal cases. Footnote *** of art 1 of the Model Law[1] allows for countries expressly to 'extend the scope of the Model Law beyond the commercial sphere'.

The ECT Act has no express statement applying ch 3 to non-commercial matters. Restricting ch 3 to commercial matters, however, would not be coherent with the purpose of the Act as stated in its long title '(t)o provide for the facilitation and regulation of electronic communications and transactions'. It would also leave serious lacunae in South African law and, in particular, in the South African law of evidence.

1 As explained by para 26 of the Guide.

Implications for interpreting the ECT Act

15.06 The conclusion to be drawn from this discussion is that a South African court interpreting provisions in the ECT Act to do with electronic evidence should do so in a way that will conform with the Model Law and the Guide. In particular, a court should interpret this legislation so that the law governing electronic evidence is the functional equivalent of the law governing other forms of evidence.

DATA MESSAGES AND THEIR ADMISSIBILITY

Meaning of data message

15.07 The ECT Act follows the Model Law in referring to 'data messages' rather than electronic information or computer information[1]:

Section 1 Definitions

'data message' means data generated, sent received or stored by electronic means and includes—

(a)   voice, where the voice is used in an automated transaction; and
(b)   a stored record

[1]   Based on the definition in art 2 of the Model Law. The definition in the ECT Act differs from that in the Model Law by substituting its own examples of a data message. Example (a) in the ECT Act's definition is problematic if it is taken as a deliberate change to the wording of the Model Law meaning that the recording of a voice outside of an automated transaction is not a data message. This would make it difficult for anyone doing business by voice to comply with legislation that required a written record of a transaction. It would also override the existing interpretation of s 3 of the Interpretation Act which has included voice in the definition of writing.

Admissibility of data messages

15.08   Section 15 of the ECT Act, as already mentioned, deals with electronic evidence[1]. The heart of s 15 is s 15(1) which provides for the general admissibility of data messages and provides, in particular, for two grounds on which a data message may not be denied admissibility:

Section 15 Admissibility and evidential weight of data messages

(1) In any legal proceedings, the rules of evidence must not be applied so as to deny the admissibility of a data message, in evidence—

(a)   on the mere grounds that it is constituted by a data message; or
(b)   if it is the best evidence that the person adducing it could reasonably be expected to obtain, on the grounds that it is not in its original form.

Section 15(1) does not make every data message admissible. This follows from reading s 15(1) with s 15(1)(a) which says that a data message must not be denied admissibility 'on the mere grounds that it is constituted by a data message'. The wording assumes that a data message may be denied admissibility on other grounds[2]. Since s 15 itself contains no grounds on which a data message may be inadmissible, s 15(1) must be mean that data messages may be inadmissible on grounds contained in other laws[3]. This argument is strengthened by the way s 15(1)(b) makes a detailed change to the law on admissibility of evidence to avoid the operation of the law of evidence that would exclude data messages that are not their original form[4].

[1]   Based on art 9 of the Model Law, except that s 15(4) has no counterpart in the Model Law.
[2]   The double negative in s 15 is a rhetorical device known as 'litotes' which can be used either as a way of making an understatement or of affirming a positive. Without s 15(1)(a) it would be difficult to say which meaning was intended in the first part of s 15(1).
[3]   s 15(1)(b) will be discussed below.
[4]   The reasoning in para 46 of the Guide's commentary on art 5 'Legal recognition of data messages' seems to apply to the issue of admissibility: 'By stating that "information shall not be denied legal effectiveness, validity or enforceability solely on the grounds that it is in the form of a data message", article 5 merely indicates that the form in which certain information is presented or retained cannot be used as the only reason for which that information would be denied legal effectiveness, validity or enforceability. However, article 5 should not be misinterpreted as establishing the legal validity of any given data message or of any information contained therein'.

15.09 It is possible to argue, on various grounds, that the ECT Act makes all data messages admissible[1]. There are three reasons, given the present state of the South African law of evidence, for rejecting this position:

(a)   first, it would go against the functional equivalence between data messages and documents by treating their evidential value differently;

(b)   second, it would go beyond the purpose of the ECT Act which is to regulate electronic commerce and not reform the law of evidence; and

(c)   third, it would attribute to Parliament the intention to use detail buried in the ECT Act to bypass the wider debate about the admissibility of documentary evidence.

This chapter, therefore, takes the position that, except where the ECT Act changes it, the ordinary South African law on the admissibility of evidence applies to data messages[2].

---

[1]   There is a possible argument, for example, from the differences between the wording of s 15(3) and (4) and art 9 of the Model Law. The discussion of hearsay, at para 15.15, will look at the argument that definition of data message makes hearsay data messages admissible.

[2]   This is the approach that *Zeffertt* (2003) pp 393–395, discussing the problem of hearsay, suggests is the better interpretation of s 15(1).

Requirements for the admissibility of data messages[1]

15.10 If s 15 does not make all data messages admissible, data messages that are the functional equivalent of documents must, except where the ECT Act exempts them, satisfy the ordinary requirements in the South African law of evidence for the admissibility of documents. These are as follows.

---

[1]   For a detailed treatment of the requirements that documentary evidence must satisfy in South African law see *Zeffertt* (2003) pp 685–702.

Production

15.11 To qualify as evidence a document must be produced. When applying this to data messages it is necessary to take into account that human senses cannot directly perceive the electronic signals that make up a data message. This means a data message can only be produced as evidence by using an output device such as a computer screen, printer or data projector.

There may be questions about the reliability of a particular output device. These can be dealt with as part of the process of production. Where, however, the questions need the testimony of a witness, it will be more convenient to deal with them as part of the process of authentication.

Section 17 of the ECT Act allows a person who is required by law to produce a document to do so in the form of a data message provided the data message meets the conditions in this section about ensuring the integrity of the document[1]. Section 17 is subject to s 28, ch 4 of the ECT Act which deals with e-government services. Section 28 allows public bodies to set their own standards about when an official document can be in the form of a data message[2].

1 s 17 has no equivalent in the Model Law.
2 It is not clear, although it surely ought to be the case, that the standards public bodies set should meet the requirements in s 17(1)(a). The problem is that the wording makes s 17 subject to anything done in terms of s 18 rather than the other way round.

Original form

15.12 The rule of evidence is that '... no evidence is ordinarily admissible to prove the contents of a document except the original document itself'[1]. This means the original document must, subject to certain exceptions, be produced as evidence[2]. Section 14 of the ECT Act says that a data message satisfies the requirements of original form if it meets the conditions in the section[3]:

Section 14 Original

(1) Where a law requires information to be presented or retained in its original form, that requirement is met by a data message if—

   (a) the integrity of the information from the time when it was first generated in its final form as a data message or otherwise has passed assessment in terms of subsection (2); and
   (b) that information is capable of being displayed or produced to the person to whom it is to be presented.

(2) For the purposes of subsection 1 (a), the integrity must be assessed—

   (a) by considering whether the information has remained complete and unaltered, except for the addition of any endorsement and any change which arises in the normal course of communication, storage and display;
   (b) in the light of the purpose for which the information was generated; and
   (c) having regard to all other relevant circumstances.

Section 15(1)(b) gives data messages a further exemption from the requirement of original form 'if it (the data message) is the best evidence that the person adducing it could reasonably be expected to obtain'[4].

Section 15 Admissibility and evidential weight of data messages

(1) In any legal proceedings, the rules of evidence must not be applied so as to deny the admissibility of a data message, in evidence

   ...
   (b) if it is the best evidence that the person adducing it could reasonably be expected to obtain, on the grounds that it is not in its original form.

1 Eloff J in *Barclays Western Bank Ltd v Creser* 1982 (2) SA 104 (T) at 106.
2 For a more detailed account of this rule and the many exceptions to it see *Zeffertt* (2003) pp 686–694.
3 s 14 is based on art 8 of the Model Law.
4 s 15(1)(b) follows the wording of art 9(1)(b) of the Model Law. This is logical if the original document rule is seen as an example of the best evidence rule.

Authenticity

15.13 The rule in South African law is that anyone who wants to use a document as evidence has to satisfy the court that it is authentic: that the document is what it claims to be. Section 15(4) of the ECT Act has its own provisions for authenticating by certificate a data message that is made in the course of business but the ECT Act contains no general exemption for data messages from this rule[1].

Some documents, mostly official documents, do not need to be authenticated. Such documents usually require the signature or seal of an official. The ECT Act allows for the electronic notarisation, certification and sealing of data messages[2]. This is done using an advanced electronic signature as defined in s 1 of the ECT Act[3].

---

[1] s 15(4) will be discussed at para 15.25.
[2] ss 18 and 19(3).
[3] The definition requires that an advanced electronic signature be accredited by an Accreditation Authority provided for in s 37 of the ECT Act. The Accreditation Authority has not yet been established.

15.14 Where a data message does not fall under one of these special provisions, it will usually be necessary to call someone who was responsible for the data message to establish its authenticity.

HEARSAY

Meaning of hearsay

15.15 When a data message is used merely to establish the fact that information in it was sent, received or stored, the South African law of evidence does not exclude it. Where a data message is used to show the truth of its contents, the common law requires that the one responsible for the message should be available to be cross-examined about its contents. If this cannot be done, the data message is hearsay and will be inadmissible unless it comes under one of the exceptions to the hearsay rule.

Collier says the definition of data message in s 1 of the ECT Act is broad enough to include hearsay evidence and this means that all data messages are admissible[1]. This argument, however, confuses form with content. The ECT Act (following the Model Law) defines data as 'electronic representations of information in any form' and a data message as 'data sent, received or stored by electronic means'. The definition refers to the form in which information is kept. It does not refer to the content of the message which might, for example, be a contract, a defamatory statement or an assignment of copyright[2]. The law excludes a document as hearsay because of doubts about the reliability of its content, not because of doubts about the reliability of the technology used to record that content.

It seems, therefore, that a data message being used to show the truth of its content should be treated in the same manner as a document. Such a data message is only admitted as evidence if the author of the data message testifies about the content of the message. In the absence of this testimony a data message is hearsay and inadmissible unless it falls under an exception to the hearsay rule[3].

1   DW Collier 'Machine-generated evidence and related matters' in PJ Schwikkard and SE van der Merwe, eds *Principles of evidence* (2nd edn, 2002) p 385. Collier does not discuss the requirements of production, original form and authenticity.
2   Collier appears to have read the definition of data as electronic representations of information '*of* any form' instead of '*in* any form'. Even if the definition had read 'of any form' it is unlikely, for the reasons given in para 15.15 above, that this would have had the effect of making hearsay data messages generally admissible.
3   While there are arguments that this rule should be changed, functional equivalence requires that the same rule apply to both data messages and documents.

General exceptions to the hearsay rule

15.16 In South Africa there are two important pieces of legislation that make hearsay evidence generally admissible.

Section 34 of the Civil Proceedings Evidence Act[1]

15.17 In 1962 South Africa passed legislation which made a document admissible in civil cases as truth of its contents even in some situations where the author of the document was not available to attend as witness[2]. These provisions became part of the Civil Proceedings Evidence Act and apply to both civil and criminal cases. Section 34(1)(a)(i) is a general exception that allows 'any statement made by a person in a document and tending to establish that fact shall on production of the original document be admissible as evidence of that fact'. The exception is subject to the conditions that the person making the statement had personal knowledge of the matters and that it was impossible or difficult to call the person as a witness. Although s 3 of the Law of Evidence Amendment Act, discussed next, has lessened the importance of this exception, there seems to be no reason why this exception should not apply to a data message.

1   Civil Proceedings Evidence Act 25 of 1965.
2   Evidence Act 14 of 1962. *Zeffertt* (2003), at p 382, says that this legislation is based on the English Evidence Act of 1938.

Section 3 of the Law of Evidence Amendment Act[1]

15.18 In 1988, s 3 of the Law of Evidence Amendment Act changed the law on hearsay evidence by defining hearsay differently to the common law understanding of hearsay. Section 3(4) defines hearsay evidence as 'evidence, whether oral or in writing, the probative value of which depends upon the credibility of any person other than the person giving such evidence'. The reference to writing in the definition means that s 3 applies also to data messages which are admissible if they satisfy the conditions in s 3(1) given below.

Law of Evidence Amendment Act section 3 Hearsay evidence

(1) Subject to the provisions of any other law, hearsay evidence shall not be admitted as evidence at criminal or civil proceedings, unless-

- (a) each party against whom the evidence is to be adduced agrees to the admission thereof as evidence at such proceedings;
- (b) the person upon whose credibility the probative value of such evidence depends, himself testifies at such proceedings; or
- (c) the court, having regard to—
  - (i) the nature of the proceedings;
  - (ii) the nature of the evidence;
  - (iii) the purpose for which the evidence is tendered;
  - (iv) the probative value of the evidence;
  - (v) the reason why the evidence is not given by the person upon whose credibility the probative value of such evidence depends;
  - (vi) any prejudice to a party which the admission of such evidence might entail; and
  - (vii) any other factor which should in the opinion of the court be taken into account,

is of the opinion that such evidence should be admitted in the interests of justice.

[1]   Law of Evidence Amendment Act 45 of 1988.

Exceptions to the hearsay rule for business records

15.19   When a business record is used to establish the truth of its contents, the law expects the person who made the entry to be available for cross-examination. In a modern business, however, it may be impossible to say who made an entry or difficult to produce that person to testify. As a result, some countries have developed what is known as the 'shop-book rule' which makes business records directly admissible[1]. South Africa appears to have no formal shop-book rule[2]. There is, however, legislation that, in certain situations, makes business records admissible without the testimony of the one who made the entry. It may be that for data messages this legislation has been superseded by s 15(4) of the ECT Act. In view, however, of the doubts, discussed below, that surround the meaning and constitutionality of section 15(4), the business records exceptions that applied before the ECT Act came into force will be discussed.

[1]   *Van der Merwe* (2000) pp 204–209.
[2]   *Van der Merwe* (2000) p 204, says that in the United States, 'as in South Africa, efforts have been made to accommodate computers by means of common-law and statutory exceptions to the hearsay rule'. However, he does not cite any South African common law exception that embodies the shop-book rule.

Business records in terms of s 34 of the Civil Proceedings Evidence Act[1]

15.20   Section 34(1)(a)(ii) of the Civil Proceedings Evidence Act provides an exception for a document 'that is or forms part of a record purporting to be a continuous record, made by someone (in so far as the matters dealt with therein are not within his personal knowledge) in the performance of a duty to record information supplied to him by a person who had or might reasonably have been supposed to have personal knowledge of those matters'. Section 34, as mentioned, dates from 1962. Between 1962 and 1976 the courts interpreted the 'continuous record' requirement in a way that made it almost impossible for a computer print-out to comply with the exception and it is not surprising that in *Narlis v South African Bank of Athens*[2] Holmes JA declined to admit computer print-outs under this section.

[1]   Civil Proceedings Evidence Act 25 of 1965.
[2]   *Narlis v South African Bank of Athens* 1976 (2) SA 573 (A).

Business records in terms of s 221 of the Criminal Procedure Act[1]

15.21 Section 221 of the Criminal Procedure Act provides for the admissibility of business records:

Criminal Procedure Act section 221 Admissibility of certain trade or business records

(1) In criminal proceedings in which direct oral evidence of a fact would be admissible, any statement contained in a document and tending to establish that fact shall, upon production of the document, be admissible as evidence of that fact if—

(a)   the document is or forms part of a record relating to any trade or business and has been compiled in the course of that trade or business, from information supplied, directly or indirectly, by persons who have or may reasonably be supposed to have personal knowledge of the matters dealt with in the information they supply; and

(b)   the person who supplied the information recorded in the statement in question is dead or is outside the Republic or is unfit by reason of his physical or mental condition to attend as a witness or cannot with reasonable diligence be identified or found or cannot reasonably be expected, having regard to the time which has elapsed since he supplied the information as well as all the circumstances, to have any recollection of the matters dealt with in the information he supplied.

[1]   Criminal Procedure Act 51 of 1977.

15.22 Section 221(5) says that ' "document" includes any device by means of which information is recorded or stored'. In *S v Harper*[1] Milne J commenting on this definition, said: 'The extended definition of "document" is clearly not wide enough to cover a computer, at any rate where the operations carried out by it are more than the mere storage or recording of information.' This statement has caused confusion. If a data message is excluded from the definition of a document made by a person on the grounds that the information in the data message has been processed, few data messages would nowadays be admissible[2]. The better view is that s 221 makes data messages of any sort admissible provided, of course, they comply with the conditions in s 221(1)[3].

[1]   *S v Harper* 1981(1) SA 88 (D) at 95.
[2]   Even everyday computer operations such as composing a document or sending an email involve sophisticated processing of data messages.

3   This is the conclusion of *Van der Merwe* (2000) pp 229–230 who relies on *S v De Villiers* 1993 (1) SACR 574 (Nm). The comment of Milne J in *S v Harper* was *obiter* as Milne J did admit the computer records.

Bank records in terms of Pt 5 (ss 27–32) of the Civil Proceedings Evidence Act[1]

15.23   Section 28 of the Civil Proceedings Evidence Act says that 'entries in ledgers, day-books, cash-books and other account books of any bank, shall be admissible as prima facie evidence of the matters, transactions and accounts therein recorded, on proof being given by affidavit in writing of a director, manager or officer of such bank'. This exception will apply to bank records in the form of data messages[2]. There are some limitations to this exception. In particular it cannot be used if the bank wanting to produce the evidence is itself party to the proceedings.

1   Civil Proceedings Evidence Act 25 of 1965.
2   As Bertelsmann J accepted in *Nedbank Ltd v Mashiya* 2006 (4) SA 422 (T) at 427, para 26.

Bank records in terms of s 236 of the Criminal Procedure Act 51 of 1977[1]

15.24   Section 236 of the Criminal Procedure Act exempts bank records from the hearsay rule:

236 Proof of entries in accounting records and documentation of banks

(1) The entries in the accounting records of a bank, and any document which is in the possession of any bank and which refers to the said entries or to any business transaction of the bank, shall, upon the mere production at criminal proceedings of a document purporting to be an affidavit made by any person who in that affidavit alleges—

(a)   that he is in the service of the bank in question;
(b)   that such accounting records or document is or has been the ordinary records or document of such bank;
(c)   that the said entries have been made in the usual and ordinary course of the business of such bank or the said document has been compiled, printed or obtained in the usual and ordinary course of the business of such bank; and
(d)   that such accounting records or document is in the custody or under the control of such bank,

be prima facie proof at such proceedings of the matters, transactions and accounts recorded in such accounting records or document.

(2) Any entry in any accounting record referred to in subsection (1) or any document referred to in subsection (1) may be proved at criminal proceedings upon the mere production at such proceedings of a document purporting to be an affidavit made by any person who in that affidavit alleges—

(a)   that he is in the service of the bank in question;
(b)   that he has examined the entry, accounting record or document in question; and
(c)   that a copy of such entry or document set out in the affidavit or in an annexure thereto is a correct copy of such entry or document.

(3) Any party at the proceedings in question against whom evidence is adduced in terms of this section or against whom it is intended to adduce evidence in terms of this section, may, upon the order of the court before which the proceedings are pending, inspect the original of the document or entry in question and any accounting record in which such entry appears or of which such entry forms part, and such party may make copies of such document or entry, and the court shall, upon the application of the party concerned, adjourn the proceedings for the purpose of such inspection or the making of such copies.

(4) No bank shall be compelled to produce any accounting record referred to in subsection (1) at any criminal proceedings, unless the court concerned orders that any such record be produced.

(5) In this section—

'document' includes a recording or transcribed computer print-out produced by any mechanical or electronic device and any device by means of which information is recorded or stored; and

'entry' includes any notation in the accounting records of a bank by any means whatsoever.

It seems, in view of the definition of document in s 236(5), that this exception will apply to a banking record in the form of a data message.

[1]   For further discussion see *Zeffertt* (2003) p 693.

Business communications in terms of s 15(4) of the ECT Act

15.25 Section 15(4) of the ECT Act creates a general exception to the hearsay rule for any data message made 'in the ordinary course of business'. It is another South African excursion out of the safe harbour of the Model Law and, as with other such excursions, gives rise to difficulties.

Section 15 Admissibility and evidential weight of data messages

(4) A data message made by a person in the ordinary course of business, or a copy or print-out of or an extract from such data message certified to be correct by an officer in the service of such person, is on its mere production in any civil, criminal, administrative or disciplinary proceedings under any law, the rules of a self regulatory organisation or any other law or the common law, admissible in evidence against any person and rebuttable proof of the facts contained in such record, copy, print-out or extract.

15.26 There are six main difficulties with the way s 15(4) is worded:

(a) First, an exception for communications made 'in the ordinary course of business' is much wider than the previous business record exceptions. Taken at face value, this exception could apply to any email or even a recorded voice message made in the course of business.

(b) Second, s 15(4) is not only wider in scope than the previous business record exceptions. It differs from all of them (although not the exceptions for banking records) in making data messages not only admissible as evidence but also rebuttable proof of the facts they contain[1]. Attaching a probative value to bank records is acceptable because banks are regulated and supposedly responsible institutions whose records can be assumed to be reliable in much the way as the records of a public body[2]. However, s 15(4) applies to the records of any business. The mere fact that someone is running a business is no guarantee that the records of that business are kept either accurately or honestly.

(c)   Third, s 15(4) requires a certificate 'by an officer in the service of such person' for the data message to be admissible. This imposes less responsibility than the affidavit previously required for banking exceptions. There is also no need for the certificate to assert, as required in affidavit, that the records have been under the control of the business.

(d)   Fourth, if the person wanting to submit this form of evidence does not control the computer system which contains it, it may be difficult to get the certificate required to make the evidence admissible.

(e)   Fifth, the wide range of evidence that s 15(4) makes admissible could lead to courts being asked to consider much larger volumes of evidence than at present.

(f)   Sixth, when applied in a criminal prosecution, for which s 15(4) explicitly provides, the presumption of truth the section creates is open to a constitutional challenge as an unjustified shifting of the onus of proof onto the accused[3].

By creating such a broad exception to the rules for the admissibility of data messages, s 15(4) goes against the functional equivalence that should apply between data messages and written documents. The argument that Parliament would not have used detail in the ECT Act to make such a significant change to the law of evidence applies here[4].

[1]   This creates a presumption of truth so that, if the accuracy of a data message is not rebutted, anyone presiding at 'any civil, criminal, administrative or disciplinary proceedings' is bound to accept its accuracy.

[2]   The presumption that the records of public bodies are accurate is expressed in the common law maxim *omnia praesumuntur rite esse acta donec probetur in contrarium* discussed in *Byers v Chinn* 1927 AD 94.

[3]   For a discussion of the Constitutional Court's approach to reverse onus provisions see the judgment of Patel J in *Lodi v MEC for Nature Conservation and Tourism, Gauteng* 2005 (3) SA 381 (T).

[4]   It may be that a South African court would use the Model Law's doctrine of functional equivalence to give a restrictive interpretation to the words 'in the ordinary course of business' to bring it into line with the rest of South African law on the admissibility of business records.

DATA MESSAGES AS REAL EVIDENCE

Graphics, audio, and video

15.27 The traditional view is that graphics, audio, and video are real, as opposed to documentary, evidence. Real evidence differs from documentary evidence in that it is never excluded. Real evidence only has to be relevant and meaningful[1].

This view is conceptually simple and appeals to those who dislike excluding any evidence. However, it does not take account of the way graphics, audio and video are, to an ever-increasing extent, recorded, stored and distributed in digital form and fall under the definition of a data message. This means that graphics, audio, and video now resemble documents more than the knife and bullet that are the traditional examples of real evidence. In data message form, graphics, audio and video are susceptible to error and falsification in the same way as data messages that embody documentary content. They cannot prove themselves to be anything other than data messages and their evidential value depends on witnesses who can both interpret them and establish their relevance.

So long as South African law follows an exclusionary approach it would seem that graphics, audio, and video that are in data message form should be treated in the same way as documents. Zeffertt, relying on *S v Ramgobin*[2], submits that this is the only satisfactory way to guard against the possibility of deliberate or accidental changes in the data messages[3]. To be admissible, graphics, audio, and video that are in data message form should be produced, be original in form and be authenticated[4]. If the probative value of their content depends on someone who is not giving evidence, the statutory hearsay rule and its exceptions should apply to them.

[1]   A court will want evidence to show the relevance of a data message and will probably needs expert testimony to help understand it.
[2]   *S v Ramgobin* 1986 (4) SA 117 (N).
[3]   *Zeffertt* (2003) p 704–709.
[4]   Subject, of course, to the exceptions that the ECT Act makes for all data messages.

Computer programs

15.28   A computer program is a form of data message. It has, at some stage in its genesis, a human author and, for this reason, it could be treated as a document[1]. On the other hand, a computer program is usually only presented as evidence to show how it works. In this case a computer program is the functional equivalent of a piece of equipment and should be treated as real evidence. The logical approach is to ask what a computer program is being used to establish and treat it accordingly.

When computer program is part of equipment that produces data without human intervention, and almost every modern piece of equipment uses some sort of computer program, the data will be treated as real evidence[2].

[1]   s 2(1)(i) of the Copyright Act 98 of 1978, for example, treats a computer program as intellectual property of the same sort as literary, artistic and musical works.
[2]   In *S v Smuts* 1972 (4) SA 358 (T), for example, the court accepted that the reading calculated by a computer that was part of a speed trap machine and transmitted to a traffic officer was not hearsay.

Witnesses and experts

15.29   Real evidence, as Zeffertt points out, is little use without the testimony of witnesses to connect it to the issue[1]. When dealing with electronic real evidence expert evidence will almost certainly be needed.

[1]   *Zeffertt* (2003) p 703.

EVIDENTIAL WEIGHT OF DATA MESSAGES

15.30 Once evidence is admitted, a court needs to decide what weight to attach to it. This is a matter for the adjudicator but the law does offer some guidance in the form of presumptions and guidelines.

Presumptions

15.31 The ECT Act creates two presumptions in favour of the correctness of data messages.

Presumption in favour of the accuracy of business records

15.32 The rebuttable presumption that s 15(4) creates in favour of data messages made 'in the ordinary course of business' has already been discussed.

Presumption in favour of advanced electronic signatures

15.33 Section 13 of the ECT Act distinguishes between electronic signatures and advanced electronic signatures[1] and provides that '(w)here an advanced electronic signature has been used, such signature is regarded as being a valid electronic signature and to have been applied properly, unless the contrary is proved'[2].

[1] See fn 3 to para 15.13.
[2] s 13(4).

15.34 South Africa has not yet established the Accreditation Authority needed for advanced electronic signatures. Section 28 of the ECT Act, however, allows a public body to specify the type of electronic signature required for filing documents. This has been done by the South African Revenue Service for the filing of income tax returns using a mix of passwords and usernames[1]. What is not clear is whether this qualifies as an advanced electronic signature for the purpose, for example, of the offence created by s 104(1)(a) of the Income Tax Act[2] of signing any statement or return without reasonable grounds for believing the same to be true.

[1] For further information see http://www.sars.gov.za/eFiling/eFiling%20Default.htm.
[2] Income Tax Act 58 of 1962.

Section 15 guidelines

15.35 Section 15(3) gives guidelines for assessing the evidential weight of data messages[1].

Section 15 Admissibility and evidential weight of data messages

(3) In assessing the evidential weight of a data message, regard must be had to—

(a) the reliability of the manner in which the data message was generated, stored or communicated;

(b) the reliability of the manner in which the integrity of the data message was maintained;

(c) the manner in which its originator was identified; and

(d) any other relevant factor.

When using these guidelines a court will probably, for some time to come, need expert help to understand technical procedures such as encryption, hashing and backing-up that are used to secure data messages. In time, courts may begin to take judicial notice of how easy it is to alter an ordinary email and other less technical features of data messages[2].

When relying on expert help it is likely that South African courts will prefer the experts to refer to international standards such as the Code of Practice issued by the British Standards Institute[3].

1   These are based on art 9 of the Model Law.
2   For the nature of judicial notice see *Zeffertt* (2003) pp 715–729.
3   Issued in terms of BS7768. For more on this point see *Van der Merwe* (2000) pp 216 and 214–215.

Evidential weight of electronic signatures and data messages

15.36 Section 13(2) of the ECT Act says that data messages and electronic signatures that do not qualify as advanced electronic signatures carry evidential weight[1].

1   s 13(2), (3) and (5).

DUTY TO KEEP RECORDS AND CONFIDENTIALITY

15.37 In a modern business there are likely to be electronic records of almost everything that happens. These records will take different forms: originals, drafts and backups of documents and email messages; networked diaries and logs of telephone calls, computer, fileserver and network activity. Such information accumulates quickly, sometimes without people in the business being aware of it. It is easy to store but storing does take resources and, where there is no duty to keep it and the information serves no business purpose, it makes sense to delete it. But this evidence may be needed in civil or criminal cases, so it is important to know what records may be destroyed and what records must be kept.

Duty to keep records

15.38 There is no general duty to keep records in South African law although there is legislation, such as the Companies Act[1] and Income Tax Act[2], requiring records to be kept. Section 90 of the Promotion of Access to Information Act ('PAIA')[3] makes it an offence to damage, alter, conceal or falsify a record or make a false record 'with intent to deny a right of access in terms of this Act'. But PAIA does not say what records must be kept and, if a record has not been kept or has been destroyed before being requested, PAIA will not help anyone wanting the information.

1   The details are contained in the Regulations for the Retention and Preservation of Company Records made in terms of s 15 of the Companies Act 61 of 1973.
2   s 73A of the Income Tax Act 58 of 1972, for example, requires a person making a tax return to keep records for five years.
3   Promotion of Access to Information Act 2 of 2000.

15.39 Where there is a duty to keep records, s 16 of the ECT Act allows this to be done electronically if the conditions in the section are met[1]:

Section 16 Retention

(1)   Where a law requires information to be retained, that requirement is met by retaining such information in the form of a data message, if—

(a)   the information contained in the data message is accessible so as to be usable for subsequent reference;

(b)   the data message is in the format in which it was generated, sent or received, or in a format which can be demonstrated to represent accurately the information generated, sent or received; and

(c)   the origin and destination of that data message and the date and time it was sent or received can be determined.

(2)   The obligation to retain information as contemplated in subsection (1) does not extend to any information the sole purpose of which is to enable the message to be sent or received.

It is not clear whether the failure of s 16 of the ECT Act to incorporate art 10(3) of the Model Law[2] means that in terms of the ECT Act a person who is required to keep records may not do so in the form of a data message by using the services of another person.

1   Based on art 10 of the Model Law.
2   Art 10(3) 'A person may satisfy the requirement referred to in paragraph (1) by using the services of any other person, provided that the conditions set forth in subparagraphs (a), (b) and (c) of paragraph (1) are met'.

Confidential information

15.40 Certain information cannot be used as evidence in court.

Attorney client privilege[1]

15.41 South African law subscribes to the common law position that communications between attorney and client are privileged and cannot be used as evidence in court. The privilege, however, is the client's and a client is free to waive this privilege either expressly or impliedly.

Modern communication technology makes it more likely than previously that privileged information will become known, accidentally or deliberately, to people outside the privileged relationship[2]. When privileged information becomes known without an express or implied waiver, the common law rule is that this does not prevent evidence being given about the information. The courts have, in some situations, however, not applied this common law rule and it is possible, in view of provisions in the Bill of Rights guaranteeing a fair trial and legal representation, that the courts will modify the common law rule[3].

[1] For a full discussion see *Zeffertt* (2003) pp 556–621.
[2] Email, for example, is notoriously insecure and it might be argued that sending privileged information by unencrypted email amounts to an implied waiver of the privilege.
[3] Constitution, s 34 'Access to the courts' and s 35 'Arrested, detained and accused persons'.

Confidentiality in terms of s 29 of the ECT Act

15.42 Section 29(3) of the ECT Act provides that a cryptography provider does not have to disclose to the Director General of the Department of Communications confidential information about its cryptographic products in order to have those products registered for use in South Africa. In *Diners Club v Singh*[1] Levinsohn J relied on this provision to find that information of this sort was confidential and would not allow the employees of Diners Club to be cross-examined about the reliability of its security. The context makes it clear that s 29(3) applies only to the information required for the register. It does not give a general exemption from cross-examination and this interpretation of the section seems unwarranted.

[1] *Diners Club SA (Pty) Ltd v Singh* 2004 (3) SA 630 (D) at 673.

ELECTRONIC EVIDENCE IN CIVIL CASES

Urgent search and seizure ('Anton Piller') orders

15.43 Even where there is a duty to keep records, it is easy for someone with the necessary expertise to destroy records that are in the form of data messages[1]. To prevent potentially important information being destroyed, either maliciously or routinely, a judge may grant an order to preserve the information. The order is given *ex parte* so as not to give the person holding the information an opportunity to destroy it while disputing the order.

[1] Done properly, this can leave no evidence that the records ever existed. This is not a technical work but it should be noted that simply deleting information does not destroy it and even data that has been overwritten can sometimes be recovered. There is also the possibility that the deleted data was been backed up or copied onto other equipment.

15.44 In South Africa such an order is made in terms of r 6(12)) of the Uniform Rules of Court. It is known as an Anton Piller order after the English case. There is no standard form for the order[1]. What is clear is that an Anton Piller order must not become a 'fishing expedition' to see if there may be a claim. There must be a real likelihood of litigation and the order should ensure the information is preserved without giving the one who obtains the order access to the information[2].

1   Practice Note 18 of the Cape Provincial Division deals with Anton Piller orders and para 5 of the Note says: 'In the event that any of the listed items exists only in computer readable form, respondent or the person referred to in paragraph 3 above is ordered to forthwith provide the sheriff with effective access to the computers, with all necessary passwords, to enable them to be searched, and cause the listed items to be printed out; a print-out of these items is to be given to the sheriff or displayed on the computer screen so that it may be read and copied by him.' In *Kebble v Wellesley-Wood* 2004 (5) SA 274 (W) at 280–281 para 9. Schwartzman J referred to similar provisions in the *Practice Manual* for the Witwatersrand Local Division.
2   See *Memory Institute SA CC t/a SA Memory Institute v Hansen* 2004 (2) SA 630 (SCA). In *Kebble v Wellesley-Wood* (see fn 1) Schwartzman J also distinguished two forms of Anton Piller orders and stressed that the right to inspect the evidence only existed, notwithstanding some authority to the contrary, where the order was given to assert a proprietary right in the evidence.

Access to documents

Discovery in terms of the Uniform Rules of Court

15.45 Once litigation has begun, the Uniform Rules of Court make provision for each party to ask the other to produce ('discover') documents in their possession relating to the case[1]. This will include documents in the form of data messages. A party who refuses to produce the documents may be ordered to do so by the court. Not complying with such order will leave that party in contempt of court and may result in judgment being given against the party.

1   r 35(10) and (11) of the Uniform Rules of Court.

Access to information in terms of PAIA

15.46 PAIA was passed 'to give effect to the constitutional right of access to … any information that is held by another person and that is required for the exercise or protection of any rights'[1]. This legislation differs from similar legislation in force in some other countries in that it applies to both public and private bodies and persons. The courts have been reluctant to define what 'required for the exercise or protection of any rights' means, but a recent case made it clear that it was necessary to establish a right before requesting information in terms of the Act, and that the Act should not be used as a fishing expedition to see whether or not such a right existed[2].

1   s 9(a)(ii).
2   *Unitas Hospital v Van Wyk* [2006] JOL 17049 (SCA) p 10, para 21, per Brand JA.

Evidence improperly obtained

15.47 There used to be some doubt in South African law about whether a court had a discretion in civil cases to exclude evidence that had been improperly obtained. The law was analysed by Hurt J in *Lenco Holdings Ltd v Eckstein*[1] and he concluded:

I take the view that ..., in civil proceedings, the Court has a discretion to exclude evidence which has been obtained by a criminal act or otherwise improperly.

1   *Lenco Holdings Ltd v Eckstein* 1996 (2) SA 693 (N) at 704. This view has been approved in other High Court judgments.

Experts

15.48 It should be clear from what has gone before that experts will play an important part in helping courts evaluate evidence that is in the form of data messages. These experts, as with any other experts, will have to establish their credentials to the court and subject their conclusions to cross-examination. As with all expert evidence, the role of the expert is to help the judge come to a decision not to make the decision.

Costs

15.49 The fees of expert witnesses are recovered in full as part of an order of costs if the parties agree the expert is a necessary witness. If the parties cannot agree, the court can be asked to decide whether an expert is a necessary witness. If the court makes no ruling on the matter and the parties cannot agree it may still be possible to recover some of the expert's expenses.

Limiting the use of digital evidence

15.50 Some court records are already very long. Electronic evidence raises the spectres of excessive costs associated with discovering and reading huge volumes of evidence and of cases being deliberately submerged in unmanageable documentation.

15.51 It may be, as already suggested, that the hearsay rule will serve to control the volume of data messages being presented as evidence. South African courts have already encountered problems with excessive hard-copy evidence. They have dealt with what they consider abuse in the order of costs by depriving attorneys of the fee they would normally earn for perusing or preparing material which the court considered unnecessary[1]. In *Salviati & Santori (Pty) Ltd v Primesite Outdoor Advertising*[2] Streicher JA even ordered an attorney to pay *de bonis propriis*[3] the costs associated with unnecessary documentation. It is difficult to see how a court could reasonably use any other sanction to set limits to the amount of evidence presented in a case.

1   *Permanent Secretary, Department of Welfare, Eastern Cape v Ngxuza* 2001 (4) SA 1184 (SCA) at 1203, para 28. In *Commissioner for Inland Revenue v Estate Kirsch* 1951 (3) SA 496 (A) at 509, the court refused to allow costs for preparing a record that it found illegible.
2   Streicher JA in *Salviati & Santori (Pty) Ltd v Primesite Outdoor Advertising (Pty) Ltd* 2001 (3) SA 766 (SCA) at 775, para 18. The costs order included a provision that 'the respondent's attorney may not recover from the respondent any fees on appeal in respect of 50% of the agreed bundle'.

3   This is a common law rule that allows a court to award costs *de bonis propriis* against persons acting in a representative capacity 'if their actions are motivated by malice or amount to improper conduct' per Yacoob J in *Swartbooi v Brink* 2006 (1) SA 203 (CC) at 206, para 3.

Electronic service and filing papers

15.52 One of the purposes of the ECT Act, according to the long title, is 'to encourage the use of e-government services' and s 27, ch 4 'E-government services' says:

Section 27 Acceptance of electronic filing and issuing of documents

Any public body that, pursuant to any law—

(a)   accepts the filing of documents, or requires that documents be created or retained;

...

may, notwithstanding anything to the contrary in such law-

(i)   accept the filing of such documents, or the creation or retention of such documents in the form of data messages.

15.53 Section 19, in chapter 3, is also relevant:

Section 19 Other requirements

(1) A requirement in a law for multiple copies of a document to be submitted to a single addressee at the same time, is satisfied by the submission of a single data message that is capable of being reproduced by that addressee.

(2) An expression in a law, whether used as a noun or verb, including the terms 'document', 'record', 'file', 'submit', 'lodge', 'deliver', 'issue', 'publish', 'write in', 'print' or words or expressions of similar effect, must be interpreted so as to include or permit such form, format or action in relation to a data message unless otherwise provided for in this Act.

Electronic service

15.54 When it comes to instituting proceedings against a person outside South Africa, r 5 'Edictal citation' of the Uniform Rules of Court allows a person to apply to court for 'such order as to the manner of service as to it seems meet'[1]. For persons within South Africa, r 4(1) expects the sheriff to serve founding papers. Rule 4(2) provides that, where the sheriff cannot effect service in terms of r 4(1), a person may follow the procedure in r 5(2) and apply to court for directions as to how to effect service[2].

1   r 5(2). From private communications it seems that, in some cases, the court has authorised that this be done by email.
2   From private communications it appears that service by email has been used for this purpose. The dangers of email service emerge from *Bernuth Lines Ltd v High Seas Shipping Ltd* BLD 2212055836, [2005] EWHC 3020 (Comm), [2006] 1 All ER (Comm) 359. Available online at
http://alliott.butterworths.co.uk/construction/dataitem.asp?ID=225939&tid=3.

Electronic filing

15.55 Rule 1(3) of the Constitutional Court Rules requires an electronic version of documents that are lodged with the Registrar. Rule 1(4), however, says that 'if a notice or other communication is given by electronic copy, the party giving such notice or communication shall forthwith lodge with the Registrar a hard-copy of the notice or communication, with a certificate signed by such a party verifying the date of such communication or notice.' Practice Direction 2 of 1999 of the Constitutional Court allows for lodging records and documents 'on a computer disk' or by email in WordPerfect format. As an incentive for lodging electronically, point 3 provides: 'Where a disk or an electronic copy of a document other than a record is provided, the party need lodge only 13 copies of the document concerned with the Registrar'.

15.56 There is no provision in the Uniform Rules of Court for the electronic filing of papers. Parties do sometimes serve court process on each other electronically, by facsimile transmission or email, but the papers so served must be filed in hard-copy with the court after electronic service and they must contain the service address of an attorney practising within eight kilometres of the court. The practice is to follow electronic service with physical service on the other party so as to have the papers stamped and signed as evidence that the papers were filed.

ELECTRONIC EVIDENCE IN CRIMINAL CASES

Interception centres and the Office for Interception Centres

15.57 The Regulation of Interception of Communications and Provision of Communication-related Information Act[1] ('RICA') governs the interception of electronic communications. Chapter 6 of RICA allows the Minister responsible for intelligence services[2] to set up interception centres that will be permanently connected to telecommunications systems and will implement any interception direction. These centres are accountable to an Office for Interception Centres that is run by a Director assisted by representatives of the departments responsible for the following areas of government: communications, defence, intelligence, police and justice.

Chapter 5 of RICA makes service providers responsible for storing communication-related information and for making it possible to intercept communications[3].

---

[1] Regulation of Interception of Communications and Provision of Communication-related Information Act 70 of 2002. Although assented to on 30 December 2002 it only came into operation in September 2005. Section 40, dealing with providing cell phone and SIM card information, has since been suspended.

[2] Constitution section 209, Intelligence Services Oversight Act 40 of 1994.

[3] The Independent Communications Authority of South Africa, established by s 3 of the Independent Communications Authority of South Africa Act 13 of 2000, determines what equipment service providers must install to allow communications to be intercepted.

Interception directions

15.58 RICA envisages various orders or 'directions' which allow data messages to be intercepted. These directions have their own complex conditions but the applicant must be from the police or state security services, the application must usually be in writing[1] and the direction obtained from a judge[2]. There are four directions:

(a)   an interception direction[3];
(b)   a real-time communication-related direction[4];
(c)   a combined interception direction, real-time communication-related direction and archived communication-related direction or interception direction supplemented by real-time communication-related direction[5]; and
(d)   an archived communication-related direction[6].

Section 51 makes it an offence not to comply with an interception direction and conviction does not relieve anyone of the obligation to comply with an interception direction.

[1]   s 23 allows for an oral real-time communication-related direction to be issued, subject to detailed conditions, in urgent cases.
[2]   s 24 allows the judge to ask for progress reports and to cancel the direction if this seems warranted.
[3]   s 16. Section 22 allows anyone applying for an interception direction to apply for an entry warrant to install an interception device. It is clear from s 22(4)(b) that this is intended to be a last resort.
[4]   s 17. A real-time communication-related direction is to obtain 'real-time communication-related information' which s 1 of RICA defines as 'communication-related information which is immediately available to a telecommunication service provider: (a) before, during, or for a period of 90 days after, the transmission of an indirect communication; and (b) in a manner that allows the communication-related information to be associated with the indirect communication to which it relates'.
[5]   s 18.
[6]   s 19.

Decryption directions

15.59 Where a data message is encrypted its contents are unintelligible without the encryption key. Section 21 of RICA allows a judge to issue a decryption direction, which s 1 defines as 'a direction ... in terms of which a decryption key holder is directed to disclose a decryption key; or provide decryption assistance in respect of encrypted information'. Section 29 explains what is meant by disclosure and assistance.

Section 51(4)(a) imposes the same penalties for failing to comply with a decryption direction as for failing to comply with an interception direction.

Foreign evidence

15.60 Section 47 in ch 9 of RICA 'Criminal proceedings, offences and penalties' allows for the admissibility of evidence obtained in another country through an interception direction. Presumably evidence obtained in a foreign country is subject to the ordinary South African law on admissibility[1]. Where the information is in the form of a data message, the guidelines in s 15(3) of the ECT Act will apply when evaluating it.

[1] An additional requirement is that s 47(2) requires written authority from the National Director of Public Prosecutions.

Proof of issuing of a direction of entry warrant

15.61 Section 48 provides that a certificate asserting that a direction was authorised is prima facie proof that the direction was issued.

Search warrants

15.62 Data messages that are stored on a computer but not transmitted will not be accessible in terms of the interception directions provided for in RICA. Anyone who needs such information as part of a criminal investigation will have to apply for a search warrant either in terms of ch 2 of the Criminal Procedure Act or the other legislation that provides for search warrants[1].

Section 20(b) allows the State to seize 'anything (in this Chapter referred to as an article) that may afford evidence of the commission or suspected commission of an offence, whether within the Republic or elsewhere'. 'Anything' has been held to extend to documents and money and will certainly extend to a computer or hard drive in which data messages are stored[2].

The warrant must be issued by a magistrate, justice of the peace, judge or judicial officer and must, as the name implies, be in writing. The terms in which warrant is issued may refer to merely copying the data messages or to removing a computer or hard drive. It is important to get the terms of the warrant correct. There might be grounds to object to a warrant, for example, if it allows for the arrest of a computer when the evidence required is data messages stored on the computer.

[1] Criminal Procedure Act 51 of 1977. Among this other legislation is s 83 of the ECT Act that allows a cyber inspector to apply for a warrant.
[2] There have been high-profile cases where search warrants have been used to seize computers and the data on the computers but none seem to have found their way into the law reports. See, for example, the *Mail and Guardian* report of 4 July 2006 that a challenge to the search warrant seizing computers and data belonging to French arms dealer Thint had been dismissed, available online at http://www.mg.co.za/articlePage.aspx?articleid=276177&area=/breaking_news/breaking_news_national/.

Evidence obtained without the required authority

15.63 Where evidence is collected without a warrant or direction, or with an improperly obtained warrant or direction, or without following the conditions set out in the warrant or direction, a court must decide whether to admit it or not. Kriegler J summed up the position in *Key v Attorney-General, Cape Provincial Division*[1]:

What the Constitution demands is that the accused be given a fair trial. Ultimately, ... fairness is an issue which has to be decided upon the facts of each case, and the trial Judge is the person best placed to take that decision. At times fairness might require that evidence unconstitutionally obtained be excluded. But there will also be times when fairness will require that evidence, albeit obtained unconstitutionally, nevertheless be admitted.

[1] *Key v Attorney-General, Cape Provincial Division* 1996 (4) SA 187 (CC) at 196, para 13. Admitting such evidence will not exempt the one who collected it from the possibility of civil or criminal action.

Using electronic equipment in court

15.64 Project 113 of the Law Commission concerns using electronic equipment in court proceedings. In July 2003 the Commission published a Report on using an audio-visual link to postpone criminal cases without having to transport the accused persons to court[1]. The Report found that there were no constitutional objections to doing this but the proposal has yet to be implemented.

[1] Available online at http://www.doj.gov.za/salrc/reports/r_prj113_2003jul.pdf.

ELECTRONIC FORENSICS

15.65 Given the ease with which data messages can be altered, it is essential in both civil and criminal cases that there should be reliable procedures for ensuring that evidence in the form of data messages is not tampered with. These procedures are part of what is sometimes known as electronic forensics. Of particular importance is preserving a 'chain of evidence' or 'chain of custody' for data messages[1].

Chapter 12 of the ECT Act envisages the Director General of the Department of Communications appointing cyber inspectors with powers ensure compliance with the provisions of the ECT Act. It might have been the intention that the cyber inspectors would be responsible for electronic forensics. In practice, the Director General has appointed no cyber inspectors. The South African Police Service and the Directorate of Special Operations ('Scorpions') have electronic forensics capability and they can also, if necessary, enlist the support of the business sector[2]. Government departments are said to be working to put in place the structures for dealing with electronic crime which will include, presumably, procedures for collecting and presenting electronic evidence[3].

Similar procedures would be helpful in civil cases. One way to produce and distribute these procedures would be in terms of the Rules of Court or practice directions.

[1] For example, the US Department of Justice has at least two websites on electronic evidence: http://www.usdoj.gov/criminal/cybercrime/tecpa.html and http://www.cybercrime.gov/s&smanual2002.htm.
[2] Mariette du Plessis 'SA's e-crime strategy takes shape' (2005) *iWeek*, 14 July. Available online at http://www.iweek.co.za/ViewStory.asp?StoryID=155069.

[3] Any such code will have to be tested in court for compliance with existing legislation and the Constitution rights to privacy and a fair trial. For a general discussion see Thami Magele 'E-Security in South Africa' 2005 White Paper prepared as a delegate brief for the ForgeAhead e-Security event held 16/17 February 2006 and available online at http://209.85.129.104/search?q=cache:6gXQRd8cDZcJ:www.forgeahead.co.za/E-Security%2520in%2520South%2520Africa%2520-%2520final.doc+sa-cert&hl=en&gl=za&ct=clnk&cd=6.

CONCLUSION

15.66 Apart from the matters of detail mentioned in this chapter and the more serious problems associated with s 15(4) of the ECT Act, the South African law of electronic evidence has followed what, in 1995, the Law Commission saw as the tendency in other countries not to prescribe special rules for the admissibility of computer evidence but to deal with electronic evidence on the same basis as other documentary hearsay evidence. Section 15 of the ECT Act is based on the Model Law and as such conforms to international practice and presents no major domestic obstacles to electronic commerce. Any further reform of the law governing electronic evidence should be seen as part of the general reform of the South African law of evidence.

15.67 What is missing in the South African law of electronic evidence are detailed procedures that the courts have approved as complying with the general law and with the Constitution for collecting electronic evidence, storing it and presenting it in court. Only when these procedures are in place will the South African law of electronic evidence be fully effective.

Chapter 16

UNITED STATES OF AMERICA

BRIAN W ESLER[1]

16.01 'More than 99% of new human information now being created and stored is stored electronically'[2]. Over three billion emails are sent by businesses each day in the United States alone[3]. In 2002, computers were estimated to be storing at least five exabytes of data, and the amount of computerised data continues to grow[4]. Since the lifeblood of a lawsuit is information, it is understandable that an increasing percentage of discovery requests, discovery disputes and evidentiary issues involve the access to, and admission of, such electronic information. It is now estimated that email alone makes up as much as 80 percent of discoverable communications in civil litigation[5]. In many respects, electronic information can be treated much like its cellulose-based cousins. However, electronic evidence presents unique problems, especially in the realm of discovery and document production.

Many of those problems are addressed by the new amendments to the Federal Rules of Civil Procedure, which took effect on December 1, 2006[6]. The new rules address issues likely to arise regarding discovery of electronic evidence in civil cases, although there remain unanswered questions. The rules were drafted against a background of increasing uncertainty among practitioners as to how far their and their clients' obligations to preserve and produce electronic information in discovery would extend. Those new rules, and their effect, will be a central focus of this chapter.

Because most states' procedural and evidence rules are derived from or to some extent reflect federal procedural and evidence rules, this chapter deals primarily with the Federal Rules of Civil Procedure, the Federal Rules of Evidence, and case law interpreting those rules. The chapter is organised to address chronologically issues that are likely to arise in dealing with potential electronic evidence in a typical civil case, with a brief section at the end noting some of the issues that may arise in the criminal arena.

---

[1] Special thanks go to C. Dean Little, of Blank Law and Technology, P.S. in Seattle, Washington, for providing helpful comments on drafts of this chapter. However, any mistakes herein are solely the author's responsibility.

[2] David K Isom, 'Electronic Discovery Primer for Judges,' 2005 FED. CTS. L. REV. 1

[3] *Isom* (2005) at 18.

[4] Comment, 'The New Electronic Discovery Rules: A Place for Employee Privacy?' 115 YALE L. J. 1481 (2006).

[5] Paul R Rice *Electronic Evidence: Law and Practice* 3 (2005).

[6] The rule changes are recited, with background on their drafting, in the September 2005 'Report of the Judicial Conference Committee on Rules of Practice and Procedure' located online at http://www.uscourts.gov/rules/Reports/ST09–2005.pdf#page=110 (last visited on 9 October 2006). Appendix C to that Report contains the 'Report of the Civil Rules

Advisory Committee' ('Committee Report'), which discusses the changes to the Federal Rules of Civil Procedure. See also Comment 'Paper or Plastic?: Electronic Discovery and Spoliation in the Digital Age' 42 HOUSTON L. REV. 1163, 1168–69 (2005–2006).

PRE-FILING INVESTIGATION AND RETENTION

16.02 Most civil disputes involve a certain amount of investigation and negotiation before any lawsuit is filed. Yet, even at this very early stage, counsel must pay close attention to issues regarding the preservation and production of electronic evidence. Obviously, the Federal Rules of Civil Procedure, which only apply after a lawsuit is filed, do not directly command counsel's and client's pre-filing duties. Nonetheless, case law (as well as the new amendments to Fed. R. Civ. P. 37) make clear that both counsel and client must be diligent in their efforts to investigate and preserve probative electronic information.

'If documents are lost or destroyed when they should have been preserved because litigation was threatened or pending, a party may be prejudiced'[1]. Thus, it is commonly understood that a party's duty to preserve relevant, discoverable information arises as soon as that party reasonably anticipates that litigation might ensue—even though that may be well before any complaint is ever filed in court[2].

The more difficult question to answer is what information or evidence must be preserved. The preservation obligation is a highly fact-dependent inquiry, in which few clear lines may be drawn. Certainly, emails and other electronically stored information that involve any of the key people during the time period relevant to the dispute should be preserved[3]. What is most important, however, is that counsel and client establish as early as possible the nature and extent of relevant electronic evidence, and act swiftly and comprehensively to preserve that information for future use.

Thus, in *Zubulake v. UBS Warburg* ('*Zubulake IV*'), Judge Scheindlin summarised a party's pre-litigation responsibilities:

> The scope of a party's preservation obligation can be described as follows: Once a party reasonably anticipates litigation, it must suspend its routine document retention/destruction policy and put in place a 'litigation hold' to ensure the preservation of relevant documents. As a general rule, that litigation hold does not apply to inaccessible back-up tapes (eg, those typically maintained solely for the purpose of disaster recovery), which may continue to be recycled on the schedule set forth in the company's policy. On the other hand, if back-up tapes are accessible (ie, actively used for information retrieval), then such tapes *would* likely be subject to the litigation hold [italics in the original][4].

[1] *Zubulake v. UBS Warburg*, 220 F.R.D. 212, 214 (S.D.N.Y. 2003) ('*Zubulake IV*'). As will be discussed, there were at least seven separate decisions in this case, most of which dealt with electronic discovery, and which are now recognised as 'setting the benchmark standards for modern discovery and evidence preservation issues', *Consolidated Aluminum Corp v. Alcoa*, 2006 U.S.Dist. LEXIS 66642 (M.D.La July 19, 2006). In addition to the above-cited *Zubulake IV*, the other opinions are: *Zubulake v. UBS Warburg LLC*, 217 F.R.D. 309 (S.D.N.Y. 2003) ('*Zubulake I*') (allowing discovery of deleted emails that resided only on back-up media and addressing the legal standard for determining the cost

allocation for producing such emails); *Zubulake v. UBS Warburg, LLC,* 230 F.R.D. 290 (S.D.N.Y. 2003) (*'Zubulake II'*) (addressing Zubulake's reporting obligations, and refusing to order release of confidential transcript); *Zubulake v. UBS Warburg LLC,* 216 F.R.D. 280 (S.D.N.Y. 2003) (*'Zubulake III'*) (allocating back-up tape restoration costs between Zubulake and UBS); *Zubulake v. UBS Warburg LLC,* 229 F.R.D. 422 (S.D.N.Y. 2004) (*'Zubulake V'*) (finding that defendants willfully destroyed relevant emails, granting plaintiff an adverse inference instruction regarding those emails; and ordering monetary sanctions as well); *Zubulake v. UBS Warburg LLC,* 231 F.R.D. 159 (S.D.N.Y. 2005) (*'Zubulake VI'*) (refusing to allow defendant to assert new affirmative defense due to unexplained delay in asserting defense and undue prejudice in forcing plaintiff to reopen discovery); *Zubulake v. UBS Warburg LLC,* 382 F.Supp.2d 536 (S.D.N.Y. 2005)(*'Zubulake VII'*) (refusing to allow plaintiff to offer as evidence pre-trial sanctions decisions or correspondence regarding discovery, and refusing to allow plaintiff to call opposing counsel to testify regarding preservation of evidence).

2   Eg, *Zubulake IV,* 220 F.R.D. at 216; *Fujitsu, Ltd v. American Express Corp,* 247 F.3d 423, 436 (2nd Cir. 2001); *Silvestri v. General Motors Corp,* 271 F.3d 583, 591 (4th Cir. 2001); *Capricorn Power Co v. Siemens Westinghouse Power Corp,* 220 F.R.D. 429, 434 (W.D. Pa. 2004).

3   *Zubulake IV,* 220 F.R.D. at 216.

4   *Zubulake IV,* 220 F.R.D. at 218. But see *Arthur Andersen LLP v. United States,* 544 U.S. 696 (2005) (reversing Arthur Andersen's conviction for 'knowingly ... and corruptly persuading' employees to shred documents relevant to a federal investigation when such shredding was within the parameters of a document retention policy).

16.03   Any back-up tapes containing the documents or electronic information of the main personnel (ie, so-called 'key players') should also be preserved in any instance where the party can easily identify such tapes, and the information on those tapes is, or may become, inaccessible from other sources[1]. As will be seen, the new Rule 26(b)(2)(B) codifies this distinction between reasonably accessible and inaccessible electronic records.

The duty to enact a 'litigation hold' is reciprocal; thus, plaintiff's counsel also must ensure that relevant electronic evidence is retained as soon as litigation is contemplated[2]. A 'litigation hold' must involve more than merely a letter from counsel instructing the client to preserve relevant information. Rather, as observed in *Zubulake V,* counsel must take affirmative steps to familiarise himself or herself with the client's document retention policies, data retention architecture, and how the key players stored relevant information[3]. This will involve talking not only with potential client witnesses, but also the client's information technology ('IT') personnel who are actually in charge of electronic information retention. Finally, counsel must instruct 'all employees to produce electronic copies of their relevant active files' and make sure that all 'back-up media which the party is required to retain is identified and stored in a safe place'[4].

As will be discussed further below, the revisions to Rules 26 and 37 potentially provide limited relief for failure to produce electronically stored information that is 'not reasonably accessible because of undue burden or cost'[5] and 'electronically stored information lost as a result of the routine, good-faith operation of an electronic information system'[6]. Nonetheless, it is questionable whether courts will relieve a party from its broad discovery obligations if the party cannot show a good-faith, well-documented and organised attempt to preserve relevant electronically stored information.

1   *Zubulake IV,* 220 F.R.D. at 218.

² *Consolidated Aluminum Corp v. Alcoa,* 2006 U.S.Dist. LEXIS 66642 (M.D.La. July 19, 2006).
³ *Zubulake V,* 229 F.R.D. at 432.
⁴ *Zubulake V,* 229 F.R.D. at 434.
⁵ Fed. R. Civ. P. 26(b)(2)(B).
⁶ Fed. R. Civ. P. 37(f).

DISCOVERY OF ELECTRONIC EVIDENCE DURING LITIGATION

Rule 26 conferences and initial disclosures

16.04 Once the complaint is served, the Federal Rules of Civil Procedure facilitate the discovery and disclosure of relevant evidence. As the Supreme Court stated 60 years ago, the discovery rules[1] are meant to be a means 'to narrow and clarify the basic issues between the parties, and [serve] as a device for ascertaining facts, or information as to the existence or whereabouts of facts, relative to those issues'[2]. Even before the new rules amendments, it was considered 'black letter law that computerised data is discoverable if relevant'[3]. As made clear by the new amendments, disclosure of relevant electronic evidence is now explicitly required.

Indeed, in drafting the new amendments, the Rules Committee concluded that the existing definition of 'document' in Rules 26 and 34 was too restrictive to ensure inclusion of electronic evidence. Thus, the new amendments add a new category of discoverable material—'electronically stored information'—that is considered to be both broader than, and separate and apart from, the term 'documents.' As explained by the drafting committee:

> [I]t has become increasingly difficult to say that all forms of electronically stored information, many dynamic in nature, fit within the traditional concept of a 'document'. Electronically stored information may exist in dynamic databases and other forms far different from fixed expression on paper ... The change clarifies that [the discovery rules apply] to information that is fixed in a tangible form and to information that is stored in a medium from which it can be retrieved and examined[4].

Thus, to the extent that there was any previous doubt, it is now clear that electronic evidence—of whatever type, format or location—is discoverable.

In most cases, federal courts will require a scheduling conference or the submission of a scheduling order under Rule 16(b) in order to compel initial evidence disclosure requirements. Thus, at least three weeks before the scheduling order is due, or the scheduling conference is held, the parties must meet and confer to discuss the case, possible early resolution, and how initial evidence will be disclosed[5]. Under the new amendments to Rule 26(f), discussion of electronic evidence issues is mandated. In addition to existing obligations, the new amendments require the parties to discuss:

(a)   any issues relating to preserving discoverable information;
(b)   any issues relating to disclosure or discovery of electronically stored information, including the form or forms in which it should be produced;

(c)   any issues relating to claims of privilege or work-product protection of trial-preparation material, including—if the parties agree on a procedure to assert such claims after production—whether to ask the court to include their agreement in an order[6].

The scope of discussion and disclosure of electronically stored information depends on the nature of the case, and the likelihood that relevant or discoverable evidence is to be found in electronically stored information. Assuming that electronic evidence may play a role, the new rules require counsel to pay attention to three broad areas of concern: preservation, the form of production, and privilege issues.

1   Fed. R. Civ. P. 26–37, 45.
2   *Hickman v. Taylor*, 329 U.S. 495, 501 (1947).
3   *Anti-Monopoly, Inc v. Hasbro, Inc*, 1995 WL 649934, at *2 (S.D.N.Y.).
4   Committee Report, at C-73, 74. It should also be noted that the former reference to 'data compilations' has been eliminated, on the assumption that the broader 'electronically stored information' will encompass data compilations.
5   Fed. R. Civ. P. 26(f).
6   Fed. R. Civ. P. 26(f)(3), (4).

Preservation

16.05 As discussed above, the duty to preserve relevant or discoverable electronic evidence attaches as soon as litigation becomes likely. Parties may want to discuss, or independently move for, preservation orders in order to ensure that discoverable data is preserved, to define what must be preserved, and to lay the foundation for future sanctions should the evidence fail to be preserved.

Although there has been some controversy regarding whether parties must meet the more demanding standards for a preliminary injunction in order to have a preservation order entered[1], most courts now accept that the provisions of Rule 65 regarding preliminary injunctions are not applicable to mere preservation orders. Instead, the court should examine principally whether the order is 'necessary' and whether the order is 'unduly burdensome'[2]. To show that a preservation order is 'necessary,' the proponent must show that there is a significant risk that relevant evidence will be lost absent a court order[3]. The court must seek to minimise the burden on the party subject to the preservation order:

> The volume and dynamic nature of electronically stored information may complicate preservation obligations. The ordinary operation of computers involves both the automatic creation and the automatic deletion or overwriting of certain information. Complete cessation of that activity could paralyze a party's operations ... A preservation order entered over objections should be narrowly tailored. *Ex parte* preservation orders should issue only in exceptional circumstances[4].

The presumed authority of the Federal courts to enter such preservation orders has now been buttressed by Fed. R. Civ. P. 16(b)(5), which explicitly authorises courts to include in the initial scheduling order 'provisions for disclosure or discovery of electronically stored information.'

1   *Re African-American Slave Descendants' Litig,* 2003 U.S.Dist. LEXIS 12016 (N.D.Ill.).
2   *Pueblo of Laguna v. United States,* 2004 U.S. Claims LEXIS 49, 60 Fed. Cl. 133 (2004);
    Capricorn Power Co v. Siemens Westinghouse Power Corp, 220 F.R.D. 429, 435–46 (W.D.
    Pa. 2004).
3   *Pueblo of Laguna,* 2004 U.S. Claims LEXIS 49, 60 Fed. Cl. at 1387.
4   Committee Report, at C-34, 35.

The form of production

16.06 Amended Rule 26(f) will now explicitly mandate that the parties discuss 'the form or forms in which [electronically stored information] should be produced'[1]. Such a discussion is mandatory in order to 'avoid the expense and delay of searches or productions using inappropriate forms'[2].

Although discussion is required, agreement is not. Thus, the new rules sensibly permit that the party requesting documents or electronically stored information under Rule 34 'may specify the form or forms in which electronically stored information is to be produced'[3]. The responding party may then include in its written response 'an objection to the requested form or forms for producing electronically stored information, stating the reasons for the objection'[4]. Nonetheless, an objection does not relieve the responding party from its obligation to produce the requested information: 'If objection is made to the requested form or forms for producing electronically stored information—or if no form was specified in the request—the responding party must state the forms or forms it intends to use'[5].

If the Rule 34 request for production fails to specify any particular form for producing electronically stored information, the responding party 'must produce the information in a form or forms in which it is ordinarily maintained or in a form or forms that are reasonably usable'[6]. However, a party that fails to request a particular form for production may find itself at a serious disadvantage, as in the absence of a court order or agreement of the opposing party, 'a party need not produce the same electronically stored information in more than one form'[7]. New Rule 45 (governing non-party subpoenas) follows the same basic format.

1   Committee Report, at C-32.
2   Committee Report, at C-34.
3   Fed. R. Civ. P. 34(b) (found at Committee Report, C-71).
4   Fed. R. Civ. P. 34(b) (found at Committee Report, C-72).
5   Fed. R. Civ. P. 34 (found at Committee Report C-72).
6   Fed. R. Civ. P. 34(b)(ii) (found at Committee Report C-73).
7   Fed. R. Civ. P. 34(b)(iii) (found at Committee Report, C-73). Note, however, that the 'one
    form of production' rule is only applicable to responses to requests for production under
    Rule 34, not to initial disclosures under Rule 26(a). Rule 26(a) gives parties the choice of
    producing 'a copy of, or a description by category and location' of documents, and now
    electronically stored information, and it is common practice to produce copies as well as a
    description. Ironically, the 'one form of production' rule may cause parties to refrain from
    actually producing electronically stored information at the beginning of the case for fear
    that they may be required to produce that information again in a different form in response
    to a Rule 34 request for production. Hopefully, the requirement to discuss the form of
    production of electronically stored information as part of the Rule 26 conference will
    alleviate that hesitancy.

Privilege issues

16.07 Some of the most innovative reforms contained in the new rules involve the difficult issue of privilege and, in particular, the effect of inadvertent disclosure during discovery on claims of privilege. First, the new rules require the parties to discuss during the Rule 26 conference 'any issues relating to claims of privilege or protection as trial-preparation material, including—if the parties agree on a procedure to assert such claims after production—whether to ask the court to include their agreement in an order'[1]. The rather bland description of this topic in the rule may obscure its importance, but the multiple paragraphs of explanation in the Committee Notes show that issues of privilege, and how to lower the cost of privilege review, were of central concern in the formulation of the new rules. As stated by the Committee:

> The Committee has repeatedly been advised about the discovery difficulties that can result from efforts to guard against waiver of privilege and work-product protection. Frequently parties find it necessary to spend large amounts of time reviewing materials requested through discovery to avoid waiving privilege. These efforts are necessary because materials subject to a claim of privilege or protection are often difficult to identify. A failure to withhold even one such item may result in an argument that there has been a waiver of privilege as to all other privileged materials on that subject matter. Efforts to avoid the risk of waiver can impose substantial costs on the party producing the material and the time required for the privilege review can substantially delay access for the party seeking discovery[2].

As noted by the Committee Report, privilege issues become more acute when electronically stored information is sought because of the volume of information to be reviewed, because of the informality and ubiquity of electronic communications, and because embedded data or metadata that is not apparent to the ordinary reader may also contain privileged information[3]. In an effort to lower the costs attendant in reviewing voluminous electronically stored information for attorney-client and work-product privilege, several procedures are outlined in the Committee Notes that can be used to facilitate discovery and privilege review. Two of the most commonly used procedures are:

(a)   the 'Quick Peek': Here, the responding party provides documents or electronically stored information within the scope of a broad request for an initial, superficial examination without waiving privilege. Once the requesting party designates the documents or information out of that initial production that it wishes to have produced, the responding party then reviews only those documents for privilege.

(b)   'Clawback Agreements': Here, the parties agree to expedite production without completing a privilege review but also agree that the producing party may later identify documents or information as privileged, and such documents or information will then be returned without any waiver of the privilege[4].

---

[1]   Fed. R. Civ. P. 26(f)(4). Further, Rule 16(b)(6) now explicitly provides that such agreements regarding privilege may be memorialised in the court's scheduling order. Nonetheless, counsel must remain aware that any agreed protective order to preserve the confidentiality of documents and information among the parties will not bind non-parties and may not ultimately determine whether the evidence can later be submitted, or remain, under seal.

Foltz v. State Farm Mut. Auto. Ins. Co, 331 F.3d 1122 (9ᵗʰ Cir. 2002) (finding blanket protective order overbroad, and ordering unsealing of certain evidence, including disc containing computerised records).
² Committee Report, at C-35.
³ Committee Report, at C-35, 36.
⁴ Committee Report, at C-36.

New Rule 26(b)(5)(B)

16.08 The new Rule 26(b)(5)(B) now mandates that parties must respect claims of inadvertent disclosure and may not use such privileged information, absent a court order, once the disclosing party has alerted the opposing party of the inadvertent production:

> If information is produced in discovery that is subject to a claim of privilege or of protection as trial-preparation material, the party making the claim may notify any party that received the information of the claims and the basis for it. After being notified, a party must promptly return, sequester, or destroy the specified information and any copies it has and may not use or disclose the information until the claim is resolved. A receiving party may promptly present the information to the court under seal for a determination of the claim. If the receiving party discloses the information before being notified, it must take reasonable steps to retrieve it. The producing party must preserve the information until the claim is resolved[1].

Thus, the new rules, and more especially the Committee Notes, suggest that inadvertent production of privileged material should not constitute an automatic waiver of attorney-client or work-product privileges[2]. In that respect, the new rules follow the guidance of many courts, the American Bar Association and many commentators in suggesting that, in most instances, inadvertent production of privileged material does not constitute a waiver and such material should be returned upon request[3]. Nonetheless, counsel is reminded that the failure to produce in a timely manner a privilege log of documents or electronically stored information withheld may result in a waiver of the privilege[4].

[1] Fed. R. Civ. P. 26(b)(5)(B) (Committee Report at C-57–58).
[2] However, the new rule does not directly decide that issue: 'Rule 26(b)(5)(B) does not address whether the privilege or protection that is asserted after production was waived by the production' Committee Report at C-58.
[3] *Mendenhall v. Barber-Green Co,* 531 F. Supp. 951 (N.D. Ill. 1982); *Georgetown Manor, Inc v. Ethan Allen, Inc,* 753 F. Supp. 936 (S.D. Fla. 1991); *Kansas-Nebraska Natural Gas Co v. Marathon Oil Co,* 109 F.R.D. 12, 22 (1983); *Helman v. Murray's Steaks, Inc,* 728 F. Supp. 1099, 1104 (D. Del. 1990); *City of Worcester v. HCA Management Company, Inc,* 839 F. Supp. 86, 89 (D. Mass. 1993). See also American Bar Association Section of Litigation *The Attorney-Client Privilege And The Work-Product Doctrine* (2nd edn, 1989) at p 66, noting that only client, not attorney, can waive privilege, so inadvertent production by lawyer should not waive privilege; ABA Formal Ethics Opinion No. 92–368 'A lawyer who receives materials that on their face appear to be subject to the attorney-client privilege or otherwise confidential, under circumstances where it is a clear they were not intended for the receiving lawyer, should refrain from examining the materials, notify the sending lawyer and abide the instructions of the lawyer who sent them'.
[4] *Burlington Northern v. Dist. Ct,* 408 F.3d 1102, 1149 (9ᵗʰ Cir. 2005) (holding that boilerplate privilege objections, coupled with a failure to produce any privilege log for months after discovery responses were due, resulted in a waiver of all claims of privilege).

Proposed Fed. R. Evidence 502

16.09 In the summer of 2006, the Federal Standing Committee on Rules of Practice and Procedure approved for public comment a proposed new evidence rule, Federal Rule of Evidence 502, that also specifically addresses attorney-client and work-product privilege waiver, especially in the context of electronic discovery[1]. As currently promulgated, the new rule states:

Rule 502. Attorney-Client Privilege and Work Product; Limitations on Waiver

(a) **Scope of Waiver.** In federal proceedings, the waiver by disclosure of an attorney-client privilege or work product protection extends to an undisclosed communication or information concerning the same subject matter only if that undisclosed communication or information ought in fairness to be considered with the disclosed communication or information.

(b) **Inadvertent disclosure.** A disclosure of a communication or information covered by the attorney-client privilege or work product protection does not operate as a waiver in any state or federal proceeding if the disclosure is inadvertent and is made in connection with federal litigation or federal administrative proceedings—and if the holder of the privilege or work product protection took reasonable precautions to prevent disclosure and took reasonably prompt measures, once the holder knew or should have known of the disclosure, to rectify the error, including (if applicable) following the procedures in Fed. R. Civ. P. 26(b)(5)(B).

(c) **Selective waiver.** In a federal or state proceeding, a disclosure of a communication or information covered by the attorney-client privilege or work product protection—when made to a federal public office or agency in the exercise of its regulatory, investigative, or enforcement authority—does not operate as a waiver of the privilege or protection in favor of non-governmental persons or entitities. The effect of disclosure to a state or local government agency, with respect to non-governmental persons or entities, is governed by applicable state law. Nothing in this rule limits or expands the authority of a government agency to disclose communications or information to other government agencies or as otherwise authorised or required by law.

(d) **Controlling effect of court orders.** A federal court order that the attorney-client privilege or work product protection is not waived as a result of disclosure in connection with the litigation pending before the court governs all persons or entities in all state or federal proceedings, whether or not they were parties to the matter before the court, if the order incorporates the agreement of the parties before the court.

(e) **Controlling effect of party agreements.** An agreement on the effect of disclosure of a communication or information covered by the attorney-client privilege or work product protection is binding on the parties to the agreement, but not on other parties unless the agreement is incorporated into a court order.

(f) **Included privilege and protection.** As used in this rule:

(1) 'attorney-client privilege' means the protection provided for confidential attorney-client communications under applicable law; and
(2) 'work product protection' means the protection for materials prepared in anticipation of litigation or for trial, under applicable law[2].

The two main purposes for proposing this new evidence rule are to resolve long-standing disputes among the various federal courts regarding the effect of inadvertent disclosure and selective waiver and to address the widespread concern that the costs of privilege reviews, especially 'in cases involving electronic discovery', have become prohibitive due to the concern that any inadvertent disclosure of privileged material will operate as a general subject matter waiver[3]. It remains to be seen whether the proposed rule will be adopted.

1   The Committee's report can be found online at http://www.uscourts.gov/rules/
     Excerpt_EV_Report_Pub.pdf#page=4 ('FRE 502 Committee Report').
2   FRE 502 Committee Report at 4–7.
3   FRE 502 Committee Report at 8.

Discovery of electronically stored information that is not 'reasonably accessible'

16.10 A recurring problem in conducting discovery of electronically stored information is that relevant or discoverable information may be contained in back-up tapes or similar emergency archival storage systems that are not designed to be searched in any traditional sense. As explained by the Committee Report:

> Although computer storage often facilitates discovery, some forms of computer storage can be searched only with considerable effort. The responding party may be able to identify difficult-to-access sources that may contain responsive information, but is not able to retrieve the information—or even to determine whether any responsive information in fact is on the sources—without incurring substantial burden or cost ... Examples from current technology include back-up tapes intended for disaster recovery purposes that are often not indexed, organised, or susceptible to electronic searching; legacy data that remains from obsolete systems and is unintelligible on the successor systems; data that was 'deleted' but remains in fragmented form, requiring a modern version of forensics to restore and retrieve; and databases that were designed to create certain information in certain ways and that cannot readily create very different kinds or forms of information[1].

While such sources of information may contain useful evidence they may also, at a high cost, fail to offer any evidence of note or produce evidence that can be more easily obtained from other, more accessible, sources. The rules amendments deal with the problem by creating a two-tier system of discovery.

Thus, the new discovery rules specifically exempt parties from searching data sources that they self-certify as 'not reasonably accessible':

> A party need not provide discovery of electronically stored information from sources that the party identifies as not reasonably accessible because of undue burden or cost. On motion to compel discovery or for a protective order, the party from whom discovery is sought must show that the information is not reasonably accessible because of undue burden or cost. If that showing is made, the court may nonetheless order discovery from such sources if the requesting party shows good cause, considering the limitations of Rule 26(b)(2)(C). The court may specify conditions for discovery[2].

Importantly, the responding party's duty is only discharged if that party actually identifies the sources that have not been searched. The responding party must thus 'provide enough detail to enable the requesting party to evaluate the burdens and costs of providing the discovery and the likelihood of finding responsive information on the identified sources'[3]. Further, a party is not freed of its obligation to preserve such evidence merely because a party

495

has identified the source as 'not reasonably accessible'[4]. In producing a party's initial disclosures or responding to document requests, parties will have to identify all potentially responsive repositories of information and also have a well-documented argument as to why some sources have not been searched.

1   Committee Report, at C-42.
2   Rule 26(b)(2)(B). Rule 26(b)(2)(C), which is referred to in the proposed rule, provides that courts may limit discovery it is unreasonably cumulative, duplicative or expensive, the requesting party has had ample opportunity to obtain the information sought, or the burden and expense of the proposed discovery outweighs its likely benefit.
3   Committee Report, at C-48.
4   Committee Report, at C-44, 48.

Cost-shifting

16.11 Normally, the party responding to a request for production bears the cost of locating and making available the requested documents or information and the requesting party only incurs the costs of its own review and copying[1]. However, when dealing with the discovery of electronic evidence the responding party's costs to collect, much less review, all available repositories of responsive evidence can be enormous[2]. Thus, courts are increasingly willing to entertain motions for a protective order to shift some of the costs of production to the requesting party.

However, such cost-shifting 'is potentially appropriate only when *inaccessible* data is sought'[3]. Absent a showing of inaccessibility, the responding party should typically bear the costs. Indeed, '[e]lectronic evidence is frequently cheaper and easier to produce than paper evidence because it can be searched automatically, key words can be run for privilege checks, and the production can be made in electronic form obviating the need for mass photocopying'[4].

One of the leading decisions on cost-shifting is *Rowe Entertainment v. William Morris Agency, Inc*[5]. There, the court promulgated an eight-factor balancing test to determine who should pay for the production of requested documents:

(a)   The specificity of the discovery request: the more general and far-reaching the request, the more appropriate it is to shift the expense to the requesting party.
(b)   The likelihood of a successful search: if the requested documents or electronically stored information are likely to contain relevant evidence, the more likely it is that the producing party should pay for production.
(c)   The availability of the information from other sources: if equivalent information has already been provided, or if the information is likely available through a less expensive source or process, the more likely it is that the requestion party should pay for production.
(d)   The purposes for which the documents or electronically stored information was retained: If the requested information is used, or likely to be used, for current business purposes, then the producing party should expect to pay for production. However, if the evidence is solely

maintained on archival storage devices, such as back-up tapes, that are only retained for emergency purposes, the requesting party should probably pay for production.

(e) The benefit to the parties: if the responding party might benefit from the search in question (eg, by finding information useful to its claims or defenses in the current litigation) then cost-shifting is less appropriate.

(f) The total costs to produce the information: the higher the costs to produce the requested information, the more likely it is that the court will consider cost-shifting[6].

(g) The ability and incentive to control costs: generally, the costs of production should be allocated to the party who has the most control over the costs to be incurred.

(h) The parties' respective resources: in a true 'David and Goliath' battle, it may be more appropriate to make Goliath Corporation pay the costs.

[1] *Oppenheimer Fund, Inc v. Sanders*, 437 U.S. 340, 358 (1978).
[2] *Friedman v. Superior Ct*, 2006 Cal. App. Unpub. LEXIS 7588 (Cal. App. Aug. 29, 2006) (third-party subpoenas seeking electronic evidence held overbroad when responding party would have to spend US$1.4 million to gather and review potentially responsive emails).
[3] *Zubulake III*, 216 F.R.D. at 284.
[4] *Zubulake I*, 217 F.R.D. at 309.
[5] 205 F.R.D. 421, 430–32 (S.D.N.Y. 2002).
[6] Although the estimated costs of production at issue in *Rowe* were in the hundreds of thousands of dollars, the court cited Supreme Court dicta opining that US$16,000 could not be viewed as 'an insubstantial burden' 205 F.R.D. at 431 (citing *Oppenheimer Fund, Inc v. Sanders*, 437 U.S. 340, 358 (1978)).

16.12 Although *Rowe* is much cited, it is not the last word. Judge Scheindlin took issue with a number of the *Rowe* factors in *Zubalake I*, eliminating some factors, adding others and reordering the rest in the order she felt were most important. Thus, in her eyes, the specificity of the discovery request and the purposes for which the responding party maintained the data were irrelevant, but the amount in controversy and the importance of the issues raised in the litigation were very important. Her weighted seven-factor test consists of the following:

(a) the extent to which the request is specifically tailored to discovery relevant information;

(b) the availability of such information from other sources;

(c) the total costs of production, compared to the amount in controversy;

(d) the total costs of production, compared to the resources available to each party;

(e) the relative ability of each party to control costs and its incentive to do so;

(f) the importance of the issues at stake in the litigation; and

(g) the relative benefits to the parties of obtaining the information[1].

The factors a court will follow in determining cost-shifting will depend upon many variables, including other precedent in that circuit[2]. Nonetheless, all federal courts will be guided by Fed. R. Civ. P. 26(c), which explicitly provides that a court has the authority to 'protect a party or person from ... undue burden or expense.' This provision gives courts considerable discretion in determining when or how cost-shifting should occur[3].

Neither the *Rowe* formulation nor the *Zubulake* formulation is likely to be the last or definitive word on the factors a court will consider in deciding when it is appropriate to shift some of the costs of discovery onto the requesting party, although the Committee Notes to proposed Rule 26(b)(2) suggest a seven-factor test similar to that of *Zubulake* for determining when discovery into sources 'not reasonably accessible' should be ordered[4]. Moreover, because claims of undue costs are often exaggerated, courts are frequently resorting to (and the proposed new rules encourage) ordering sample productions first, with detailed costs affidavits, in order to test the veracity of the responding party's claims of undue burden or cost[5]. In the realm of electronic discovery, courts are also increasingly willing to engage special discovery masters to facilitate the orderly discovery and disclosure of electronic evidence[6].

1 *Zubulake I*, 217 F.R.D. at 322. Of the seven factors, Judge Sheindlin pronounced the first two to be the most important, *Zubulake I*, 217 F.R.D. at 323.
2 *Hagemeyer North America v. Gateway Data Sciences Corp*, Case No. 97-C- 635, (E.D. Wis. 2004) (identifying four different approaches used by district courts to decide cost-shifting, and concluding that *Zubulake* approach is the most appropriate); *Wiginton v. C.B. Richard Ellis, Inc*, Case No. 02-C-6832 (N.D. Ill. 2004) (identifying three different approaches used for determining cost-shifting, and determining that a modified hybrid of the *Rowe* & *Zubulake* approaches was most appropriate).
3 *Spears v. City of Indianapolis*, 74 F.3d 153, 158 (7th Cir. 1996). See also Fed. R. Civ. P. 34, Advisory Committee Notes, 1970 Amendments 'the courts have ample power under Rule 26(c) to protect respondent from undue burden or expense, either by restricting discovery or requiring that the discovering party pay costs'.
4 Committee Report, at C-49 suggesting that appropriate considerations may include: (1) the specificity of the discovery request; (2) the quantity of information available from other more easily accessible sources; (3) the failure to produce relevant information that likely existed but is no longer easily available; (4) the likelihood that relevant responsive information cannot be obtained from more easily accessed sources; (5) the likely importance and usefulness of the additional information; (6) the importance of the issues at stake in the litigation; and (7) the parties' resources.
5 *Zubulake I*, 217 F.R.D. at 324; *McPeek v. Ashcroft*, 202 F.R.D. 31, 34–35 (D. D.C. 2001). See also Committee Report, at 48–49 noting that a requesting party may need discovery to test the responding party's assertion that data is not reasonably accessible, and suggesting that the responding party be required 'to conduct a sampling of information contained on the sources identified as not reasonably accessible'.
6 Fed. R. Civ. P. 53. See generally *Electronic Evidence* at 43–44; David K. Isom 'Electronic Discovery Primer for Judges' 2005 FED. CT. L. REV. 1, 11–13 noting especially that the 2003 amendments to the Federal Rules of Civil Procedure substantially amended Rule 53 to encourage judges to appoint special masters with much broader functions.

Sanctions for spoliation

16.13 Spoliation consists of both the failure to preserve relevant evidence and the failure to prevent significant alteration of such evidence[1]. With good reason, most lawyers' biggest worry regarding electronic discovery is that relevant evidence will be destroyed, and that the party or lawyer with putative control of that evidence will be sanctioned for such spoliation. Given the dynamic nature of much electronic evidence it is difficult, if not impossible, to preserve all potential sources of evidence. Nonetheless, the various *Zubulake* decisions, as well as other decisions in this area, have pointed to an increased willingness of courts to sanction parties and counsel for failure to preserve electronic evidence[2].

The authority for such spoliation sanctions arises from both Fed. R. Civ. P. 37 and the court's inherent power[3]. Rule 37(b) provides that 'if a party fails to obey [a discovery order], the court ... may make such orders in regard to the failure as are just'. Rule 37(c) allows a court to 'impose other appropriate sanctions' if a party 'without substantial justification fails to disclose information required [by these Rules], or to amend a prior response to discovery'. Nonetheless, the civil rules do not require counsel to warrant the completeness of any production of documents, or electronically stored information[4].

The presence of potential spoliation can have a significant effect on the outcome of a case, as the court may impose more than just monetary sanctions for the destruction of evidence. Remedies for spoliation generally fall into four categories[5]:

(a)   default judgments against the spoliator[6];
(b)   adverse evidentiary inferences against the spoliator, such as evidence preclusion or adverse inference instructions[7];
(c)   contempt orders[8]; and
(d)   monetary fines, including awards of damages and attorneys fees[9].

Federal courts have not been consistent in explaining the level of culpability that is necessary before imposing sanctions for spoliation, nor have they been entirely consistent in explaining the degree of prejudice that must be shown for sanctions to be imposed. It is clear that bad faith is not absolutely necessary to impose sanctions[10]. Nonetheless, at least some circuits hold that a finding of wilful or bad faith destruction of evidence is necessary to support the most severe sanction of default or dismissal[11]. Often, the issue of prejudice to the opposing party dominates the decision regarding sanctions[12]. Although sanctions are usually imposed when a party violates a court order regarding preservation and production or destroys electronic evidence, courts may decline to impose sanctions if there was a lack of wilfulness or bad faith[13], or a lack of prejudice, or both[14]. Thus, in her survey of 66 recent cases in which sanctions for alleged electronic evidence spoliation were discussed, Judge Scheindlin concluded that 'the more prejudice there is, the less wilfulness courts require before sanctioning a party for e-discovery violations, and vice versa[15]'.

The new rules take notice of the dynamic nature of electronic evidence, and provide parties a so-called 'safe harbor' from sanctions for electronically stored information lost because of the routine operation of the storage system. New Rule 37(f) provides that:

> Absent exceptional circumstances, a court may not impose sanctions under these rules on a party for failing to provide electronically stored information lost as a result of the routine, good-faith operation of an electronic information system[16].

Much debate surrounded this provision[17], especially regarding the culpability standard necessary to shelter in the 'safe harbor'. As originally published, the rule contained two alternate variations: one calling for a mere negligence standard, and the other setting a higher culpability standard[18]. Ultimately, the Committee settled on an intermediate standard: the 'good faith' routine operation of the system[19]. Although 'good faith' is not explicitly defined, '[t]he steps taken to implement an effective litigation hold bear on good faith, as does compliance with any agreements the parties have reached regarding preservation and with any court orders directing preservation'[20]. Thus, a party may be required to suspend the routine destruction of electronically stored information, even information contained in sources that the party believes are not 'reasonably accessible' under Rule 26(b)(2), depending on the circumstances of the case[21]. Even under the new rules, sanctions for spoliation of electronic evidence are likely to be a continuing part of electronic discovery.

1   Eg, *Thompson v. United States Dept of Hous. & Urban Dev.*, 219 F.R.D. 93, 100 (D.Md. 2003); *Zubulake IV*, 220 F.R.D. at 216; *Trigon v. Ins. Co*, 204 F.R.D. 277, 284 (E.D. Va. 2001). See generally Comment 'Spoliation of Discoverable Electronic Evidence' 38 LOY. L. A. L. REV. 1803 (2004–2005).

2   Eg, *Metropolitan Opera v. Local 100*, 212 F.R.D. 178 (S.D.N.Y. 2003). See generally *Isom* (2005) at 25, noting that there are more reported spoliation cases in the 10 years from 1994 to 2004 than the 200 years before.

3   Shira A. Scheindlin and Kanchana Wangkeo 'Electronic Discovery Sanctions in the Twenty-First Century' 11 MICH. TELECOMM. TECH. L. REV. 71, 72 (2004).

4   'Rule 26(g) does not require the signing attorney to certify the truthfulness of the client's factual responses to a discovery request. Rather, the [lawyer's] signature [on a discovery response] certifies that the lawyer has made a reasonable effort to assure that the client has provided all the information and documents available to [the client] that are responsive to the discovery demand.' Fed. R. Civ. P. 26(g), Advisory Committee Notes to the 1983 Amendments.

5   *Isom* (2005) at 26.

6   Eg, *Computer Task Group Inc v. Brotby*, 364 F.3d 1112 (9th Cir. 2004); *Metropolitan Opera v. Local 100*, 212 F.R.D. 178 (S.D.N.Y. 2003); *AdvantaCare Health Partners, LP v. Access IV*, No. C 03–04496 JF, 2004 U.S. Dist. LEXIS 16, 835, at *15 (N.D. Cal. Aug. 17, 2004). As noted in the *AdvantCare* decision, because entry of default is the most severe sanction available, it should be reserved for only those cases where the spoliation 'eclipse[s] entirely the possibility of a just result'.

7   Eg, *Zubulake IV*, 220 F.R.D. at 219; *Thompson v. United States Dept of Hous & Urban Dev.*, 219 F.R.D. 93, 100 (D. Md. 2003); *Re Heritage Bond Litig.*, 223 F.R.D. 527 (C.D. Cal. 2004); *Network Computing Services v. Cisco, Inc*, 223 F.R.D. 93 (D.S.C. 2004); *Stevenson v. Union Pac. R.R.*, 354 F.3d 739 (8th Cir. 2004); *Minn. Mining Co. v. Pribyl*, 259 F.3d 587 (7th Cir. 2001).

8   Eg, *Bradley v. Am. Household, Inc*, 378 F.3d 373, 378 (4th Cir. 2004).

9   Eg, *Computer Task Group, Inc v. Brotby*, 364 F.3d 1112 (9th Cir. 2004); *Stevenson v. Union Pac. R.R. Co*, 354 F.3d 739 (8th Cir. 2004). In a survey of recent sanctions decisions, attorney's fees and costs were the most frequently granted sanction. Shira A. Scheindlin and Kanchana Wangkeo, 'Electronic Discovery Sanctions in the Twenty-First Century,' 11 MICH. TELECOMM. TECH. L. REV. 71, 77 (2004).

10   Eg, *Stevenson v. Union Pac. R.R. Co*, 354 F.3d 739, 750 (8th Cir. 2004); *Young v. Gordon*, 330 F.3d 76, 82 (1st Cir. 2003); *Melendez v. Illinois Bell Telephone Co*, 79 F.3d 661, 671 (7th Cir. 1996).

11   *Yeti by Molly, Ltd v. Deckers Outdoor Corp*, 259 F.3d 1101, 1106 (9th Cir. 2001); *Bank Atlantic v. Blythe Eastman Paine Webber, Inc*, 12 F.3d 1045, 1049 (11th Cir. 1994). But see *Young v. Gordon*, 330 F.3d 76, 82 (1st Cir. 2003) ('a finding of bad faith is not a condition precedent to imposing a sanction of dismissal').

12   Eg, *Re Heritage Bond Litig.*, 223 F.R.D. 527 (C.D. Cal. 2004); *Trigon Ins. Co v. United States*, 204 F.R.D. 277 (E.D.Va. 2001); *Sheppard v. River Valley Fitness One, L.P.*, 203 F.R.D. 56, 60 (D.N.H. 2001).

13   *Morris v. Union Pac. R.R.*, 373 F.3d 896 (8th Cir. 2004); *Convolve, Inc v. Compaq Computer Corp*, 223 F.R.D. 162 (S.D.N.Y. 2004); *United States v. Murphy Oil*, 155 F.Supp.2d 1117 (W.D. Wis. 2001).

14   *Convolve, Inc v. Compaq Computer Corp*, 223 F.R.D. 162 (S.D.N.Y. 2004).

15   Shira A. Scheindlin and Kanchana Wangkeo, 'Electronic Discovery Sanctions in the Twenty-First Century, 11 MICH. TELECOMM. TECH. L. REV. 71, 89 (2004). Thus, Judge Scheindlin concluded 'that the profile of a typical sanctioned party is a defendant that destroys electronic information in violation of a court order, in a manner that is willful or in bad faith, or causes prejudice to the opposing party' at 80.

[16]   Committee Report, at C-86.
[17]   Committee Report, at C-84. See also 'Comments of Federal Magistrate Judges Association Rules Committee on Proposed Changes to the Federal Rules of Civil Procedure, Criminal Procedure and Evidence' 2005 FED. CT. L. REV. 2, 8–9 (opposing any 'safe harbor' from sanctions); Richard L Marcus 'E-Discovery & Beyond: Toward a *Brave New World* or *1984*?' 25 THE REVIEW OF LITIGATION 635, 656–57 (discussing some of the arguments for and against the 'safe harbor' provision).
[18]   Committee Report, at C-84.
[19]   Committee Report, at C-85.
[20]   Committee Report, at C-85. As noted there, an earlier version of the rule explicitly made the 'safe harbor' unavailable for parties that violated a court order requiring preservation. That provision was removed in the final rule, as the Committee was concerned that such provision would lead to all parties moving for preservation orders immediately in order to vitiate the safe harbor. Committee Report, at C-84, 85.
[21]   Committee Report, at C-87.

ADMISSION OF ELECTRONIC EVIDENCE AT TRIAL

16.14   Most civil cases, and many criminal cases, settle before ever going to trial[1]. However, for those cases that actually do proceed to trial, admissibility of electronic evidence will play an increasingly important role. There are still surprisingly few decisions dealing directly with the admissibility of electronic evidence. Nonetheless, there are some common issues that often reappear, which are discussed below.

[1]   Judith Resnick 'Trial as Error, Jurisdiction as Injury: Transforming the Meaning of Article III' 113 HARV. L. REV. 924, 928 n. 10–11 (2000). According to Ms Resnick, 70% of all civil cases filed in federal court settle, 24% are disposed of by dispositive motions or pre-trial dismissal and only 6% proceed to trial.

Authentication

16.15   Authentication of evidence is governed by FRE 901, which requires the proponent to produce 'evidence sufficient to support a finding that the matter in question is what its proponent claims'. Certain documents, such as certified copies, commercial paper, and newspapers and periodicals, do not need to be independently authenticated to be admitted[1]. However, for most other evidence, authentication is the first step to admission[2].

US courts now recognise that there is nothing intrinsically unreliable about electronic evidence[3]. FRE 901 lists a number of non-exclusive means of proving authenticity[4]. Often, authenticity issues will be handled before trial via procedures such as requests to admit authenticity and pre-trial conferences and orders[5]. However, merely putting on a witness that will testify that printed emails look like printed emails, without more, will not suffice to meet the minimal burden of authentication[6]. Generally, courts will require only a minimal showing to satisfy the requirement of authenticity and, absent sufficient evidence to raise a substantial issue regarding authenticity, deem that questions regarding alteration or chain of custody go to the weight, not the admissibility[7].

How electronic evidence is authenticated depends on the type of evidence, the availability of witnesses and, most importantly, the purposes for introducing the evidence. 'Few jurisdictions have attempted to enunciate a formula or fixed set of guidelines to govern the establishment of a foundation for computer-generated evidence'[8]. Often, electronic evidence will be authenticated using a combination of means listed in FRE 901[9].

Indeed, FRE 901(9) was specifically crafted to assist in the authentication of computer-generated or computer-stored documents or information, by allowing authentication to occur through 'evidence describing a process or system used to produce a result and showing that the process or system produces an accurate result'[10]. FRE 901(b)(9) is usually satisfied if there is sufficient demonstration that the records are trustworthy and the opposing party has had adequate opportunity, before the evidence is proferred, to inquire into the accuracy of the records[11]. A print-out of computer records that are automatically generated and kept in the ordinary course of business can be authenticated by a witness who has no expert knowledge of the functioning of the program[12].

[1] FRE 902.
[2] It is important to remember that the rules of evidence apply to evidence used to support written motions as well as evidence at trial. Thus, especially with respect to dispositive motions, authenticating the evidence may become important. *Orr v. Bank of America*, 285 F.3d 764 (9th Cir. 2002) (finding trial court properly refused to consider many of plaintiff's proposed exhibits in opposition to summary judgment because plaintiff failed to properly authenticate the evidence).
[3] *United States v. Vela*, 673 F.2d 86, 90 (5th Cir. 1982).
[4] The examples listed in the rule include testimony of a witness with knowledge, non-expert opinion, expert opinion, distinctive characteristics, witness identification, circumstantial evidence, evidence that a document is a public record or more than 20 years old, and evidence showing that a process or system was used to produce a result and that the process or system produces an accurate result.
[5] FRE 901, Advisory Committee Notes to 1972 Proposed Rules.
[6] *Richard Howard, Inc v. Hogg*, Case No. 12-96-5, 1996 Ohio App. LEXIS 5533, at *7–*8 (Ohio Ct. App.) (employee of company could not authenticate emails where employee was neither sender nor recipient and had no personal knowledge regarding whether the messages were actually sent or received); *Monarch Fed. Sav. & L. Assoc v. Genser*, 383 A.2d 475, 489 (N.J. Super. Ct. Ch. Div. 1977) (refusing to admit computer print-outs because of insufficient authentication). See also *Orr v. Bank of America*, 285 F.3d 764 (9th Cir. 2002) (discussing means of authenticating documents used with summary judgment motions).
[7] *United States v. Bonallo*, 858 F.2d 1427, 1436 (9th Cir. 1988) 'The fact that it is possible to alter data contained in a computer is plainly insufficient to establish untrustworthiness'.
[8] *Bray v. Bi-State Dev. Corp*, 949 S.W.2d 93, 99 (Mo. Ct. App. 1997).
[9] *United States v. Siddiqi*, 215 F.3d 1318, 1322–23 (11th Cir. 2000) (holding email was properly authenticated because email address was a variant of defendant's name combined with the uniform resource locator for defendant's employer, the email address was consistent with another email introduced by defendant, the contents indicated the author knew of defendant's conduct, the email referred to the defendant by his nickname, and the emails were consistent with other unchallenged telephone conversations); *United States v. Simpson*, 152 F.3d 1241 (10th Cir. 1998) (print out of chat room session authenticated because defendant used his first initial and last name during session, provided his email address during session, and pages near computer in defendant's home contained address and telephone number that detective provided defendant during chat room session). See generally Mark D Robins 'Evidence at the Electronic Frontier: Introducing email at Trial in Commercial Litigation' 29 RUTGERS COMP. & TECH. L. J. 219, 228–232 (2003).
[10] The 1972 Advisory Committee Notes specifically note that this portion of the rule is designed for computers, which were relatively novel at the time. See, eg, *Bray v. Bi-State Dev. Corp*, 949 S.W.2d 93 (Mo.App. 1997); *Pierce v. State*, 718 So.2d 806 (Fl. App. 1997) (discussing authentication of computer-generated evidence under state analogues to FRE 901).

11   *United States v. Briscoe*, 896 F.2d 1476, 1494–95 (7ᵗʰ Cir. 1990) (computerised telephone records); *United States v. Moore*, 923 F.2d 910, 915 (1ˢᵗ Cir. 1991) (computerised tax records).
12   *United States v. Linn*, 880 F.2d 209, 216 (9ᵗʰ Cir. 1989).

16.16 For emails, the most common means of authentication is usually through a witness with knowledge, who can authenticate the email chain in a manner similar to the means of authenticating reply letters[1]. Additionally, emails or websites whose address utilises a company's tradename (eg, worker@company.com) may be held to be self-authenticating under FRE 902(7), which states that extrinsic evidence of authenticity is not required with respect to 'inscriptions, signs, tags, or labels purporting to have been affixed in the course of business and indicating ownership, control, or origin'[2].

Web pages pose a particular challenge, as there can be a certain amount of reasonable scepticism regarding materials posted on the Internet. Indeed, one court referred to materials taken from the internet as 'voodoo information'[3]. Nonetheless, so long as there is some evidence to suggest that a print-out or electronic copy of a website is the same as what appeared on that website at the particular time in question, there is little reason not to deem the evidence authentic and leave questions about tampering or alteration to the finder of fact[4]. However, if the website evidence is being offered to show that the owner of the website made the statements at issue and it is clear that the website operates as a bulletin board, such that any user may be able to post messages or content, the court may require heightened evidence of authenticity before allowing admission of the website postings[5]. As websites rapidly replace newspapers and periodicals as a source of information it may be that courts will begin to deem them self-authenticating under FRE 902(6), which allows 'printed materials purporting to be newspapers or periodicals' to be accepted as prima facie evidence of what they appear to be. Moreover, information from government websites should be self-authenticating under FRE 902(5) as 'books, pamphlets, or other publications purporting to be issued by a public authority', although counsel would be wise to have available testimony from a government official supporting authenticity if challenged[6].

1   Eg, *People v. Downin*, 357 Ill. App. 3d 193, 203, 828 N.E.2d 341 (2005) (defendant's emails properly authenticated by testimony of witness receiving the emails).
2   *International Casings Group, Inc v. Premium Standard Farms*, 358 F.Supp.2d 863, 874 (W.D. Mo. 2005) 'by hitting the send button, [each party] intended to presently authenticate and adopt the content of the emails as their own writing'; *Elliot Assocs v. Banco de la Nacion*, 194 F.R.D. 116, 121 (S.D.N.Y. 2000); *Superhighway Consulting, Inc v. Techwave, Inc*, No. 98CV5502, 1999 U.S. Dist. LEXIS 17910, at *6 (N.D.Ill. Nov. 16, 1999).
3   *St Clair v. Johnny's Oyster & Shrimp, Inc*, 76 F.Supp.2d 773, 774–75 (S.D.Tex. 1999).
4   Eg, *Perfect 10, Inc v. Cybernet Ventures, Inc*, 213 F.Supp.2d 1146 (C.D. Cal. 2002) (web page print-outs authenticated by testimony that the print-outs were true and correct copies of pages printed from the Internet, along with internet domain name showing on copy); *Johnson-Woolridge v. Woolridge*, 2001 WL 838986, at *4–5 (Ohio Ct. App. 2001) (Board of Education records taken from Board's web page admissible because person who copied them could testify what he did to retrieve them); *Daimler-Benz Akteingesellschaft v. Olson*, 21 S.W.3d 707, 717 (Tex. App. 2000) (website print-out authenticated through affidavit stating 'within [affiant's] personal knowledge, the attachments are accurate copies of the original documents'). Cf *United States v. Whitaker*, 127 F.3d 595 (7ᵗʰ Cir. 1997) (holding that computer print-outs were properly authenticated and that any issues of tampering by a co-defendant went to the weight, not the admissibility).

[5]   *United States v. Jackson,* 208 F.3d 633, 638 (7th Cir. 2000) (holding that trial court properly excluded website postings where the defendant failed to show that website postings were actually posted by website's owner, as opposed to being slipped onto website by defendant herself).

[6]   *Sannes v. Jeff Wyler Chevrolet, Inc,* 1999 U.S.Dist. LEXIS 21748, at *10 n.3 (S.D.Ohio Mar. 31, 1999) (admitting Federal Trade Commission press releases printed from FTC's website). But see *State v. Davis,* 141 Wn.2d 798, 854, 10 P.2d 977, 1010 (2000) (holding population statistics printed from state website did not qualify as a self-authenticating document).

Hearsay issues

16.17 Except as otherwise provided by the Federal Rules of Evidence, hearsay is not admissible as evidence[1]. The Federal Rules of Evidence define hearsay as 'a statement, other than one made by the declarant while testifying at the trial or hearing, offered in evidence to prove the truth of the matter asserted'[2]. Hearsay does not include prior statements by the witness testifying[3] or admissions by a party-opponent[4]. Since hearsay is limited to statements made by 'persons', a 'statement' generated by a computer is also not hearsay[5]. In addition, statements that are hearsay may still be admissible pursuant to the at least 29 separate exceptions to the hearsay rule[6].

[1]   FRE 802.
[2]   FRE 801(c).
[3]   FRE 801(d)(1). This includes prior inconsistent statements made by the witness under oath, prior consistent statements made by the witness and offered to rebut a charge of recent fabrication, or statements identifying a person made after perceiving the person.
[4]   FRE 801(d)(2). This includes any statement offered against a party that is the party's own statement, a statement that the party has adopted or affirmed as true, a statement by the party's authorised representative, a statement by the party's agent while acting as agent, or a statement by a co-conspirator made in furtherance of the conspiracy.
[5]   Paul R Rice *Electronic Evidence: Law and Practice* (2005) at 275–276.
[6]   See FRE 803, 804 and 807. Additionally, the Federal Rules of Evidence contain a general residual hearsay exception for statements not covered by any other specific exception, but 'having equivalent circumstantial guarantees of trustworthiness' FRE 807. The residual exception has not been adopted in all states, so state evidence codes may be more strict on this issue.

Admissibility of emails

16.18 The admissibility of email will depend upon the purpose for which the email is offered. Obviously, an email sent by a party-opponent will be admitted[1]. Similarly, an email offered for reasons other than the truth of its contents (eg, notice, state of mind, motive) will also be admissible[2]. An exchange of emails that forms the parties' contract constitutes legally operative facts, and thus is not hearsay[3].

Emails often beget emails, forming long and varying chains among various participants. The admissibility of such email chains creates special problems, as part of an email may be clearly admissible (for instance as an admission of a party-opponent) but other portions may appear to be inadmissible hearsay[4]. FRE 106 may solve this problem, although it is not without controversy. That rule states that '[w]hen a writing or recorded statement or part thereof is introduced by a party, an adverse party may require the introduction at that time of any other part or any other writing or recorded statement which ought in fairness to be considered contemporaneously with it'. While the rule clearly prescribes the time at which the opposing party may offer (or more correctly, force the proponent to offer) a related statement (ie, 'at that time'), there has been some controversy regarding whether the rule also contains a 'trumping function' whereby the proponent essentially waives objection to related statements by offering the statement at issue[5]. Although federal (and state) courts are by no means unanimous on the subject, the better reading seems to be that, either under FRE 106 itself or pursuant to the common law 'doctrine of completeness', otherwise inadmissible (but relevant) evidence should be admitted if that evidence is necessary in order to render the offered statement complete[6]. Thus, otherwise inadmissible emails that are part of a chain of emails relating to the proffered email may be admitted 'in fairness' to place the proffered email in its proper context[7].

Often, emails will be offered under the 'business records' hearsay exception. This exception provides generally that records 'kept in the course of a regularly conducted business activity' that were made 'at or near the time' of the event or transaction by 'a person with knowledge' are admissible if it 'was the regular practice of that business activity' to make the record in question[8]. Many emails regularly generated in the course of business activity will not meet this criteria[9]. Most often this is because '[a]lthough systematic use of email to communicate about business matters is the norm for numerous businesses, far less often have those businesses established procedures requiring that email be used to collect specific types of information in a particular format in regular fashion'[10].

However, emails can be used and often admitted via various other hearsay exceptions. Some successful examples include:

(a)   present sense impression under FRE 803(1)[11];
(b)   then-existing state of mind under FRE 803(3)[12];
(c)   prior consistent statement under FRE 801(d)(1)[13]; and
(d)   statement against interest under FRE 804(b)(3)[14];

---

[1]   *United States v. Siddiqui*, 235 F.3d 1318, 1323 (11th Cir. 2000), *cert denied* 533 U.S. 940 (2001); *Everett*, 2002 Tex. App. LEXIS 2579, at *4; *Bloom v. Commonwealth*, 542 S.E.2d 18, 20–21 (Va.Ct.App. 2001) *aff'd*, 554 S.E.2d 84, 87–88 (Va. 2001).

[2]   Eg, *Perfect 10, Inc v. Cybernet Ventures, Inc*, 213 F.Supp.2d 1146 (C.D. Cal. 2002) (emails admissible to show notice); *Brill v. Lante Corp*, 119 F.3d 1266 (7th Cir. 1997) (email admissible to show belief); *United States v. Siddiqui*, 235 F.3d 1318, 1323 (11th Cir. 2000), *cert denied*, 533 U.S. 940 (2001) (email admissible to show two persons knew each other); *Mota v. Texas Houston Health Center*, 261 F.3d 512 (5th Cir. 2001) (email admitted as a verbal act, and not offered for the truth of the matter).

[3]   *International Casings Group, Inc v. Premium Standard Farms*, 358 F.Supp.2d 863, 870–72 (W.D. Mo. 2005) (finding exchange of emails sufficient to form a contract). This case also contains a good discussion of the meaning of 'signature' under the statute of frauds provision of the Uniform Commercial Code (U.C.C. § 2–201), and the intersection of the UCC's signature requirement with the Uniform Electronic Transactions Act ('UETA'). Although not all the emails exchanged contained the sender's typed name or other signature block at the bottom, each email contained a header with the name or email address of the sender, and it was clear that each party 'by hitting the send button, intended to presently authenticate and adopt the content of the emails as their own writing' *International Casings*, 358 F.Supp.2d at 874. Thus, the Missouri District Court joins many

other courts in holding that 'an electronic signature in an email satisfies the statute of frauds'. *International Casings,* 358 F.Supp.2d at 874. See also *Cloud Corp v. Hasbro, Inc,* 314 F.3d 289 (7ᵗʰ Cir. 2002); *Roger Edwards, LLC v. Fiddes & Son, Ltd,* 245 F.Supp.2d 251 (D.Me. 2003); *Central Illinois Light Co v. Consolidation Coal Co,* 235 F.Supp.2d 916, 919 (C.D. Ill. 2002; *Commonwealth Aluminum Corp v. Stanley Metal Associates,* 186 F.Supp.2d 770, 774 (W.D. Ky. 2001); *Shattuck v. Klotzbach,* No. 01–1109A, 2001 Mass. Super. LEXIS 642, at *6–*7 (Dec. 11, 2001); *Amedisys, Inc v. JP Morgan Chase Manhattan Bank (Re National Century Financial Enterprises Inc),* 310 B.R. 580, 595 (Bankr. S.D. Ohio 2004).

4   FRE 805 requires that hearsay within hearsay be excluded unless all portions fall under an exception.

5   See, eg, Mark D Robins 'Evidence at the Electronic Frontier: Introducing email at Trial in Commercial Litigation' 29 RUTGERS COMPUTER & TECH. L.J. 219, 259 (2003); Wright and Graham, FEDERAL PRACTICE AND PROCEDURE: EVIDENCE 2d § 5072.1 (2005).

6   Wright and Graham, supra § 5072.1, at 401. See also *Beech Aircraft Corp v. Rainey,* 488 U.S. 153, 171 (1988) (district court abused discretion in excluding completing material even if Rule 106 did not apply); *United States v. Awon,* 135 F.3d 96, (1ˢᵗ Cir. 1998) (the 'doctrine of completeness' is 'codified in Fed. R. Evid. 106, [and] holds that an otherwise inadmissible recorded statement may be introduced into evidence where one side has made a partial disclosure of the information, and full disclosure would avoid unfairness to the other party', citing cases). But see *United States v. Woolbright,* 831 F.2d 1390 (8ᵗʰ Cir. 1987) (FRE 106 does not empower court to admit otherwise inadmissible hearsay).

7   Since such other emails are only being offered to provide context and completeness, they are not being strictly offered for the truth of the matter, and thus are not hearsay. See *United States v. Dupre,* 462 F.3d 131 (2ⁿᵈ Cir. 2006) (affirming admission of otherwise inadmissible emails because they were only offered to provide context to defendant's email, and thus were not offered for the truth of the matter). See also *Robins* (2003) at 259, (suggesting same result); *Rathje v. Scotia Prince Cruises, Ltd,* No. 01–123-P-DMC, 2002 U.S. Dist LEXIS 4078 (D.Me. Mar. 13, 2002) (admitting email for completeness over objection that it constituted an inadmissible settlement offer under FRE 408).

8   FRE 803(6).

9   *Monotype Corp v. International Typeface Corp,* 43 F.3d 443, 450 (9ᵗʰ Cir. 1994); *United States v. Ferber,* 966 F.Supp. 90, 98 (D.Mass. 1997); *Re Hechinger Liquidation Trust,* 298 B.R. 240 (D.Del. 2003).

10 *Robins* (2003) at 266.

11 *United States v. Ferber,* 966 F.Supp. 90, 99 (D.Mass. 1997).

12 *Mota v. University of Texas,* 261 F.3d 512 (5ᵗʰ Cir. 2001); *People v. Jovanovic,* 269 A.D.2d 182 (N.Y. App. Div. 1999). See also *Arachnid Inc v. Medalist Mktg Corp,* Case No. C89–204C, 1991 U.S. Dist. LEXIS 9055, at *8–*9 (W.D. Wash. Feb. 15, 1991), *aff'd* 972 F.2d 1300 (Fed. Cir. 1992) (holding that evidence of customers attempting to order defendant's products from plaintiff would be admissible as statements of then existing state of mind).

13 *People v. Lee,* No. A078429, 1999 WL 595455, at *5 (Cal. Ct. App. July 27, 1999).

14 *Everett v. State,* No. 14-01-00588-CR, 2002 Tex. App. LEXIS 2579 at *4–*5 (Tex. Ct. App. Apr. 11, 2002).

Computer-generated and computer-stored records

16.19 As mentioned above, a hearsay objection can only serve to exclude a statement by a 'person,' and thus 'statements' by computers are not hearsay[1]. The Louisiana Supreme Court articulated the distinction well:

> The print-out of the results of the computer's internal operations is not hearsay evidence. It does not represent the output of statements placed into the computer by out of court declarants. Nor can we say that this print-out is a 'statement' constituting hearsay evidence. The underlying rationale of the hearsay rule is that such statements are made without an oath and their truth cannot be tested by cross-examination. Of concern is the possibility that a witness may consciously or unconsciously misrepresent what the declarant told

him or that the declarant may consciously or unconsciously misrepresent a fact or occurrence. With a machine, however, there is no possibility of a conscious misrepresentation, and the possibility of inaccurate or misleading data only materializes if the machine is not functioning properly[2].

Thus, a properly-authenticated computer-generated record should be admissible.

Conversely, a human statement that is merely stored on a computer may be hearsay, depending upon who made the statement and the reason for it being proffered. Often, but not always, such computer-stored evidence can be admitted as a business record under FRE 803(6) [3]. Proper authentication of the records is crucial, which should include evidence regarding the reliability of the computer records[4]. However, courts generally will not require extensive testimony disproving any possibility of error before admitting business records stored on a computer[5].

[1]   See FRE 801(a) ('statement' is assertion or conduct 'of a person, if it is intended by the person as an assertion'); FRE 801(b) ('A declarant is a person who makes a statement').

[2]   *State v. Armstead*, 432 So.2d 837, 840 (La. 1983). See also *United States v. Fernandez-Roque*, 703 F.2d 808, 812 n.2 (5th Cir. 1983) (automated telephone records not hearsay because 'the fact that these calls occurred is not a hearsay statement').

[3]   Eg, *Sea-Land Service v. Lozen International*, 285 F.3d 808, 819–20 (9th Cir. 2002); *United States v. Cestnik*, 36 F.2d 904, 909–10 (10th Cir. 1994); *United States v. Moore*, 923 F.2d 910, 914 (1st Cir. 1991); *United States v. Catabran*, 836 F.2d 453, 457 (9th Cir. 1988); *State v. Ben-Neth*, 34 Wn. App. 600, 663 P.2d 156 (1983).

[4]   *Re Vinhnee*, 336 B.R. 437 (9th Cir. BAP 2005). This case is a good lesson on the importance of foundation, as here the appellate court affirmed the trial court's exclusion of proffered computerised business records as inadequately authenticated, even though the opposing party never appeared for trial and the plaintiff was essentially seeking entry of a default judgment. The appellate court emphasised that the proponent of computer-stored business records must still demonstrate 'the accuracy of the computer in the retention and retrieval of the information at issue' 336 B.R. at 449. See also *Harveston v. State*, 798 So.2d 638 (Miss. Ct. App. 2001) (refusing to admit computer database print-outs because proponent offered no testimony as to reliability).

[5]   *United States v. Moore*, 923 F.2d 910, 915 (1st Cir. 1991); *United States v. Glasser*, 773 F.2d 1553, 1559 (11th Cir. 1985); *United States v. Vela*, 673 F.2d 86, 89–91 (5th Cir. 1982).

Websites

16.20 Again, the admissibility of information found on websites will depend upon who is the author of the site and the purposes for which the evidence is offered. Web pages certainly do not qualify as the business records of the Internet service provider ('ISP') who merely hosts the website on its server[1]. On the other hand, the internal records of an ISP regarding a customer's activity online are the ISP's business records and can be admitted if properly authenticated[2]. Statements made on an opposing party's website will constitute the admissions of a party opponent, which are not hearsay and are admissible[3]. However, anonymous statements posted on a website may be inadmissible, even if the party offers a witness who can testify that he used software to trace the internet protocol ('IP') address of the anonymous poster, and that the address belonged to the defendant[4].

[1]   *United States v. Jackson*, 208 F.3d 633, 637 (7th Cir. 2000). Cf 17 U.S.C. § 512 exempting ISPs from copyright infringement liability for merely hosting infringing content in most circumstances.

2 *Bowers v. Bowers,* 758 So.2d 405, 414–15 (Miss. 2000).
3 *Florida Conf. of Seventh Day Adventists v. Kyriakides,* 151 F.Supp.2d 1223, 1226 (C.D.Cal. 2001).
4 *Ezra v. American International Group Data Center, Inc,* Case No. 04-CV-641 WDS (S.D. Ill. March 15, 2006). On the face of it, this case appears to have involved 'computer-generated' data, rather than 'computer-stored' data, such that the court's discussion of the business records exception seems misguided. However, given the proffering party's failure to even identify the software used to generate the result, the outcome is understandable. See also *United States v. Jackson,* 208 F.3d 633, 637 (7th Cir. 2000) (postings on web bulletin board inadmissible).

CRIMINAL ISSUES

16.21 Electronic evidence in criminal proceedings presents many of the same issues that arise in civil proceedings. However, one issue unique to criminal proceedings is the defendant's constitutional right to confront any witness that will testify against him or her[1]. Thus, hearsay issues become even more difficult in criminal prosecutions. The most recent pronouncement on the confrontation clause by the Supreme Court in *Crawford v. Washington*[2] held that 'testimonial' hearsay could not be used against a criminal defendant. While the Court was not clear on what effect this would have on established hearsay exceptions, it did seem to exempt some exceptions from the rule, such as the business records exception and statements in furtherance of a conspiracy[3]. How this new and stricter requirement regarding the use of hearsay in criminal proceedings will affect the admissibility of electronic evidence remains to be seen, though it would appear to affect some of the decisions cited above.

Computer-related searches can also raise difficult Fourth Amendment issues[4]. There are 'heightened [search warrant] specificity concerns in the computer context, given the vast amounts of data they can store'[5]. Courts are becoming increasingly aware and vigilant regarding the government's ability to use technological means to obtain evidence without necessarily obtaining a warrant[6]. As noted by one court,

> The contours of [the Fourth Amendment's] protections in the context of computer searches pose difficult questions. Computers are simultaneously file cabinets (with millions of files) and locked desk drawers; they can be repositories of innocent and deeply personal information, but also evidence of crimes. The former must be protected, the latter discovered. As society grows ever more reliant on computers as a means of storing data and communicating, courts will be called upon to analyze novel legal issues and develop new rules without our well established Fourth Amendment jurisprudence. The fact of an increasingly technological world is not lost upon us as we consider the proper balance to strike between protecting an individual's right to privacy and ensuring that the government is able to prosecute suspected criminals effectively[7].

Nonetheless, the government is not inherently forbidden from using technological means to search other technology, so long as the search complies with the Fourth Amendment[8].

1 U.S. CONST., Amend VI ('the accused ... shall enjoy the right ... to be confronted with the witnesses against him').
2 541 U.S. 36 (2004).

3   448 U.S. at 56.
4   'The right of the people to be secure in their persons, houses, papers, and effects, against unreasonable searches and seizures shall not be violated, and no warrants shall issue but upon probable cause, supported by oath or affirmation and particularly describing the place to be searched and the persons or things to be seised' U.S. CONST., Amend. IV.
5   *United States v. Adjani*, 452 F.3d 1140, 1149 (9th Cir. 2006).
6   *Kyllo v. United States*, 533 U.S. 27 (2001) holding that government's use of technology—here, an infrared detector—to explore details of a private home that would previously have been impossible without physical inspection constituted a 'search' such that a warrant was required. Nonetheless, the USA Patriot Act seems to permit such warrantless electronic searches in some instances. See generally *American Civil Liberties Union v. Dept. of Justice*, 265 F.Supp.2d 20 (D.C. 2003) describing some of the salient searches now allowed under that Act. It remains to be seen how courts will respond to this development.
7   *Adjani*, 452 F.3d at 1152.
8   *United States v. Hill*, 459 F.3d 966 (9th Cir. 2006).

16.22   One other issue that often arises is what constitutes 'possession' when the object possessed is purely electronic. That issue is well illustrated by a recent pair of Ninth Circuit decisions *United States v. Romm*[1] and *United States v. Kuchinski*[2]. In *Romm*, the defendant connected to the Internet and visited and viewed websites containing images of child pornography and the images were automatically saved in his computer's internet cache, although the defendant himself admitted only to having viewed the images for a few minutes and consciously sought to delete any images of which he was aware. Nonetheless, the court held that the defendant 'knowingly possessed' illegal pornography, as he could view the images in his computer's internet cache on the screen, and print them, enlarge them, copy them to more accessible areas of his hard drive or send them by email to others[3]. Thus, the computer's automatic, normal operation led to his conviction despite his conscious attempts to avoid possession.

A few months later, the Ninth Circuit released its decision in *Kuchinski*. There, the defendant admitted to knowingly receiving and possessing 110 images of child pornography. However, he was charged and sentenced on the basis of an additional 13,904 to 17,984 images, all of which were solely found in his internet cache files and about which he disclaimed all knowledge. The Ninth Circuit explained the presence of such 'unknown' files as follows:

> [W]hen a person accesses a web page, his web browser will automatically download that page into his Active Temporary Internet Files, so that when the site is revisited the information will come up much more quickly than it would have if it had not been stored on the computer's own hard drive. When the Active Temporary Internet Files get too full, they spill excess saved information into the Deleted Temporary Internet Files. All this goes on without any action (or even knowledge) of the computer user[4].

Acknowledging that *Romm* dealt with many of the same issues, the court nonetheless distinguished *Romm* on the basis that the defendant in *Romm* admitted to obtaining access to the cache files in order to delete them (and thus could also view them, print them and the like). The defendant Kuchinski claimed to have no knowledge of the files still stored in his computer's internet cache. Hence, the court held that:

> Where a defendant lacks knowledge about the cache files, and concomitantly lacks access to and control over those files, it is not proper to charge him with

possession and control of the child pornography images located in those files, without some other indication of dominion and control over the images. To do so turns abysmal ignorance into knowledge and a less than valetudinarian grasp into dominion and control[5].

Ironically, in the digital crimes arena, it may be that ignorance is the best defence.

It cannot be denied that '[a]n increasing number of criminals use pagers, cellular phones, laptop computers and network servers in the course of committing their crimes'[6]. But, as pointed out in the dissent from another case involving the search of a suspect's computer, '[i]n this age of increasing government surveillance, lawful and unlawful, and of the retention of all our deeds and thoughts on computers long after we may believe they have been removed, it is important that courts not grow lax in their duty to protect our right to privacy and that they remain vigilant against efforts to weaken our Fourth Amendment protections'[7]. It remains to be seen how courts will deal with the evolving ability of the government to trace the activities of its citizens through digital footprints and how the balance will be struck between security and civil rights[8].

[1]   455 F.3d 990 (9th Cir. 2006).
[2]   469 F.3d 853 (9th Cir. 2006).
[3]   *Romm*, 455 F.3d at 1000.
[4]   *Kuchinski*, 469 F.3d at 862.
[5]   *Kuchinski*, 469 F.3d at 863.
[6]   United States Department of Justice 'Searching and Seizing Computers and Obtaining Electronic Evidence in Criminal Investigations' (July 2002) found online at http://www.cybercrime.gov/s&smanual2002.htm#preface (last visited on December 4, 2006).
[7]   *United States v. Gourde*, 440 F.3d 1065, 1074 (9th Cir. 2004) (en banc) (Reinhardt, J. dissenting).
[8]   For more about that balance, see Eric Klumb 'Hard Drives and Hard Ethical Issues: Some Legal, Ethical and Practical Concerns for Prosecutors Conducting Their Own Searches of Digital Storage Media' (October 2003), found online at http://www.usdoj.gov/usao/eousa/ole/video_info/eta_computer_forensics_ethics.pdf (last visited December 4, 2006).

Appendix 1
SELECTED LIST OF SOURCES

JOURNALS

Subscription only

Digital Investigation: The International Journal of Digital Forensics & Incident Response (Elsevier)
> http://www.compseconline.com/digitalinvestigation/

Journal of Digital Forensic Practice (Taylor & Francis)
> http://www.tandf.co.uk/journals/titles/15567281.asp

Transaction on Information Forensics and Security (IEEE)
> http://www.ieee.org/organizations/society/sp/tifs.html

Digital Evidence Journal (Pario Communications)
> http://www.digitalevidencejournal.org

Free

International Journal of Digital Evidence
> http://www.ijde.org

Forensic Science Communications (considers all aspects of forensics)
> http://www.fbi.gov/hq/lab/fsc/current/index.htm

PRACTICE GUIDES

Australia

HB 171–2003: Guidelines for the management of IT evidence (note: the editor has not had sight of this document and cannot comment on the contents)
Seizing Computers and other Electronic Evidence Best Practice Guide, February 2003, Australian Centre for Policing Research
> http://www.acpr.gov.au/pdf/Seizing%20Computers.pdf

CTOSE

Cyber Tools On-Line Search for Evidence, CTOSE 'Project Results'
> http://www.ctose.org/

511

Appendix 1 *Selected list of sources*

European

European Network of Forensic Science Institutes, Forensic Information Technology Working Group, Guidelines for Best Practice in the Forensic Examination of Digital Technology, (v5, 28 July 2006)
http://www.enfsi.org/ewg/fitwg/

International

International Organization on Computer Evidence G8 Proposed Principles For The Procedures Relating to Digital Evidence
http://www.ioce.org/G8_proposed_principles_for_forensic_ evidence.html
IETF RFC 3227 Guidelines for Evidence Collection and Archiving
http://www.rfc-archive.org/getrfc.php?rfc=3227

Interpol

Interpol, IT security and crime prevention methods, (an introduction to what an investigator needs to know about Information Technology (IT) security measures in order to be able to carry out investigations in an IT environment and to give advice in crime prevention methods)
http://www.interpol.int/Public/TechnologyCrime/CrimePrev/ITSecurity.asp

Scientific Working Group for Digital Evidence (SWGDE)

SWGDE/SWGIT Guidelines & Recommendations for Training in Digital & Multimedia Evidence, Version: 1.0 (November 15, 2004)
http://ncfs.org/swgde/documents.html
SWGDE Best Practice for Computer Forensics (v 2.1, July 2006)
http://ncfs.org/swgde/documents/swgde2006/Best_Practices_for_Computer_
Forensics%20July06.pdf
Scientific Working Group for Digital Evidence Best practices for digital evidence laboratory programs
http://ncfs.org/swgde/documents.html

United Kingdom

Association of Chief Police Officers and National High-Tech Crime Unit, *Good Practice Guide for Computer based Electronic Evidence* (v3.0, 2003)
http://www.nhtcu.org/ACPO%20Guide%20v3.0.pdf
The Litigation Support Technology Group (LiST)
Data Exchange Protocol: Part 1: the exchange of Electronic Disclosure Documents, (v. 1.1, 4 May 2006)
Part 2 Exchange of electronic Disclosure Data
http://www.listgroup.org/
(Note: the editor has not had sight of the BSI documents listed below and cannot comment on the contents)
BIP 0008–1: Code of practice for legal admissibility and evidential weight of information stored electronically
BIP 0008–2: Code of Practice for Legal Admissibility and Evidential Weight of Information Communicated Electronically
BSI BIP 0008–3: Code of Practice for Legal Admissibility and Evidential Weight: Linking Electronic Identity to Documents

BSI BIP 0009: Legal admissibility and evidential weight of information stored electronically
BSI PD 0010: The principles of good practice for information management

United States of America

The National Centre for Forensic Science, *Digital Evidence in the Courtroom: A Guide for Preparing Digital Evidence for Courtroom* Presentation Master Draft Document Revised March 12, 2003
> http://www.ncfs.org/DE_courtroomdraft.pdf

Searching and Seizing Computers and Obtaining Electronic Evidence in Criminal Investigations, Computer Crime and Intellectual Property Section, Criminal Division, United States Department of Justice (July 2002)
> http://www.cybercrime.gov/s&smanual2002.htm

US Department of Justice Office of Justice Programs National Institute of Justice *Electronic Crime Scene Investigation A Guide for First Responders* (July 2001)
Forensic Examination of Digital Evidence: A Guide for Law Enforcement Special Report (April 2004)
http://www.ncfs.org/digital_evd.html
Police Scientific Development Branch, *Digital Imaging Procedure* 02–02, (Version 1.0, March 2002)
http://scienceandresearch.homeoffice.gov.uk/hosdb/publications-2/cctv-publications/02–02_DIP?view=Standard&pubID=356166
Colleen Wade, editor and Yvette E Trozzi, associate editor, U.S. Department of Justice Federal Bureau of Investigation Laboratory Division *Handbook of Forensic Services* 2003, Electronic Devices Examinations pp 45–46; Image Analysis Examinations pp 63–68; Crime Scene Search pp 155–168.
http:// www.fbi.gov/hq/lab/handbook/forensics.pdf
Forensic Examination of Digital Evidence A Guide for Law Enforcement, U.S. Department of Justice, Office of Justice Programs, April 2004
http:// www.ncjrs.gov/pdffiles1/nij/199408.pdf
Richard Van Duizend, Reporter *Guidelines For State Trial Courts Regarding Discovery Of Electronically-Stored Information*, (Conference of Chief Justices, August 2006)
http:// www.ncsconline.org/WC/Publications/CS_ElDiscCCJGuidelines.pdf
Open Source Digital Forensics
> http://www.opensourceforensics.org/

United States of America: books for lawyers

Michael R Arkfeld *Electronic Discovery and Evidence* (Law Partner Publishing, 2003)
Adam Cohen and David Lender *Electronic Discovery: Law and Practice* (Aspen Publishers, 2003)
Brent E Kidwell, Matthew M Neumeier and Brian D Hansen *Electronic Discovery* (Law Journal Press) Looseleaf
Joan E. Feldman *Essentials of Electronic Discovery: Finding and Using Cyber Evidence* (Glasser Legalworks, 2003)
Gregory P Joseph *Modern Visual Evidence* (Law Journal Press) Looseleaf
Jay Grenig and William Gleisner *eDiscovery & Digital Evidence* (Thomson-West Publishing, 2005)
Michele CS Lange and Kristen M Nimsger *Electronic Evidence and Discovery: What Every Lawyer Should Know* (American Bar Association, 2004)
Paul R Rice *Electronic Evidence—Law and Practice* (American Bar Association, 2005)
Sharon Nelson, Bruce A Olson and John W Simek *The Electronic Evidence and Discovery Handbook* (American Bar Association, 2006)

513

Appendix 1   *Selected list of sources*

MISCELLANEOUS INTERNET RESOURCES OF INTEREST

A wide range of websites offer a variety of information on the Internet. Below is a list of a few of the websites available. In many instances, websites will have mutual links and links to other websites that may be of interest.

Sources with a wide remit

The Electronic Evidence Information Center
http://www.e-evidence.info/
Computer Forensics, Cybercrime and Steganography Resources
http://www.forensics.nl/

United Kingdom

First Forensic Forum F3
http://www.f3.org.uk/

Unites States Resources

Ken Withers
http://www.kenwithers.com/
Michael Arkfeld
http://arkfeld.blogs.com/
Electronic Discovery Law, published by Preston Gates Ellis LLP
http://www.ediscoverylaw.com/
International Association of Computer Investigative Specialists, volunteer non-profit corporation based in the USA
http://www.iacis.info/iacisv2/pages/home.php
LexisNexis Applied Discovery
http://www.lexisnexis.com/applieddiscovery/default.asp
Kroll On-track
http://www.krollontrack.com/
New York Law School Visual Persuasion Project
http://www.nyls.edu/pages/2734.asp
Eric Klumb Trial Attorney, *Hard Drives and Hard Ethical Issues Some Legal, Ethical and Practical Concerns for Prosecutors Conducting Their Own Searches of Digital Storage*, Media Computer Crime and Intellectual Property Section October 2003
http://www.usdoj.gov/usao/eousa/ole/video_info/eta_computer_forensics_ethics.pdf
The Sedona Conference
> *Best Practices Recommendations & Principles for Addressing Electronic Document Production* A Project of The Sedona Conference® Working Group on Best Practices for Electronic Document Retention & Production (WG1) July 2005 Version
> *Best Practice Guidelines & Commentary for Managing Information & Records in the Electronic Age* A Project of The Sedona Conference® Working Group on Best Practices for Electronic Document Retention & Production September 2005
> http://www.thesedonaconference.org/

MAJOR PORTALS

Australasian Legal Information Institute
http://www.austlii.edu.au/

514

British and Irish Legal Information Institute
        http://www.bailii.org/
Canadian Legal Information Institute
        http://www.canlii.org/
Hong Kong Legal Information Institute
        http://www.hklii.org/
Pacific Islands Legal Information Institute
        http://www.paclii.org/
World Legal Information Institute
        http://www.worldlii.org/

GENERAL COUNTRY-SPECIFIC WEBSITES OF INTEREST

Canada

Uniform Law Conference of Canada, Uniform Electronic Evidence Act, with commentary
        http://www.ulcc.ca/en/us/index.cfm?sec=1&sub=1u2
Uniform Law Conference of Canada *Uniform Electronic Evidence Act: Consultation Paper* March 1997
        http://www.ulcc.ca/en/poam2/index.cfm?sec=1997&sub=1997hka
PracticePRO, links to resources on Electronic Discovery
        http://www.practicepro.ca/practice/eDiscovery_Rlist.asp
Ontario Bar Association, Discovery Task Force E-Discovery Guidelines and Resources Page
        http://www.oba.org/en/main/ediscovery_en/default.aspx
Library of Parliament, Telecommunications and Lawful Access: I. The Legislative Situation in Canada
        http://www.parl.gc.ca/information/library/PRBpubs/prb0565-e.html
Telecommunications and Lawful Access: II. The Legislative Situation in the United States, the United Kingdom and Australia
        http://www.parl.gc.ca/information/library/PRBpubs/prb0566-e.html

England & Wales

England

JUDGMENTS

House of Lords Judgments
        http://www.publications.parliament.uk/pa/ld/ldjudgmt.htm
        http://www.worldlii.org/uk/cases/UKHL/
House of Lords Judicial Work
        http://www.parliament.the-stationery-office.co.uk/pa/ld/ldjudinf.htm
Court of Appeal
        http://www.bailii.org/databases.html
Court Service website
        http://www.hmcourts-service.gov.uk/

Parliament

United Kingdom Parliament
        http://www.parliament.uk

Appendix 1 *Selected list of sources*

Office of Public Sector Information
http://www.opsi.gov.uk/
Official Documents
http://www.official-documents.gov.uk/
UKOP Online—Official Publications
http://www.ukop.co.uk/
The UK Statute Law Database (the official revised edition of the primary legislation of the United Kingdom)
http://www.statutelaw.gov.uk/

Wales

Statutory Instruments for the National Assembly for Wales
http://www.opsi.gov.uk/legislation/wales/w-stat.htm   National   Assembly   for Wales
National Assembly for Wales
http://www.wales.gov.uk

Portals

Access to Law
Run by Active Lawyer and Inner Temple Library, this site covers general resources, legal subject areas in the UK, Commonwealth and other jurisdictions
http://www.accesstolaw.com/site/
British and Irish Legal Information Institute, covering England & Wales, Ireland, Northern Ireland, Scotland, and links to other collections around the world
http://www.bailii.org
eagle-i service, Institute of London, University of London: good gateway to the Institute of Advanced Legal Studies library catalogue and hyperlinks to numerous sources
http://ials.sas.ac.uk/links/eagle-i.htm
Intute: Law, Social Science Information Gateway
http://www.intute.ac.uk/socialsciences/law/
University of Kent at Canterbury: Excellent portal of the same quality as eagle-i service
http://library.kent.ac.uk/library/lawlinks/

Hong Kong

Primary sources
Free online access to legislation and regulations
http://www.legislation.gov.hk
http://www.hklii.org
Link to cases
http://www.judiciary.gov.hk
Secondary sources
Legislative Council website for access to bills and Legco briefs
http://www.legco.gov.hk

India

Online legal research from Manupatra
http://www.manupatra.com/asp/home.asp

516

Supreme Court and High Court cases on-line
  http://judisi.nic.in.
Supreme Court of India
  http://supremecourtofindia.nic.in.
Delhi Police department
  http://delhipolice.nic.in.
Cyber crime planet India
  http://cybercrime.planetindia.net/cybercrime_cell.htm.
Central Bureau of Investigation
  http://cbi.nic.in/AboutUs/Manuals/Chapter_18.pdf

New Zealand

Auckland District Law Society has a list of useful public legal links at
  http://www.adls.org.nz/links/
Free online access to legislation and regulations
  http://www.legislation.govt.nz/
New Zealand Parliamentary Debates (Hansard)
  http://www.parliament.nz/en-NZ/PB/Debates/Debates/ and http://www.vdig.net/
  hansard/index.jsp
New Zealand Gazette—the official newspaper of the Government of New Zealand
  &&&http://www.dia.govt.nz/diawebsite.nsf/wpg_URL/Services-New-Zealand-
  Gazette-New-Zealand-Gazette-On-
  Line?OpenDocument&Start=1&Count=1000&ExpandView
Full text access to all unreported Supreme Court decisions, Court of Appeal from
1 January 2003 and High Court decisions from 1 September 2005
  http://203.97.11.181/jdo/Introduction.jsp
Recent decisions from the Supreme Court, Court of Appeal and High Court, which are
published shortly after being delivered and then removed from the site after 28 days
  http://www.courtsofnz.govt.nz/from/decisions/judgments.html
Commerce Commission—full text access to decisions from 1997 located under the
Public Registers tab
  http://www.comcom.govt.nz/index.aspx
Links to cases including the Supreme Court, Court of Appeal, Commerce Commission
and Privacy Commission, and some university law journals, Law Commission papers
and legislation
http://www.nzlii.org/

Northern Ireland

Northern Ireland Legislation
  http://www.opsi.gov.uk/legislation/northernireland/ni_legislation.htm

Scotland

Primary Sources

UK Legislation applying to Scotland
  http://www.opsi.gov.uk/legislation/scotland/s-act-si.htm
Acts of the Scottish Parliament
  http://www.opsi.gov.uk/legislation/scotland/s-acts.htm
Scottish Statutory Instruments and Executive Notes
  http://www.opsi.gov.uk/legislation/scotland/s-stat.htm

Appendix 1 *Selected list of sources*

Scottish Parliament
>   http://www.scottish.parliament.uk

Scottish Executive Links
>   http://www.direct.gov.uk/Dl1/Directories/DevolvedAdministrations/fs/
>   en?CONTENT_ID=4007267&chk=I7beYy

The Scottish Courts website has a fully searchable database of every judgement (whether or not reported) issued by the Court of Session and High Court of Justiciary since September 1998 (January 1998 in respect of commercial cases) and a selection of significant Sheriff Court judgements. It also has an html text of the Rules of the Court of Session and an html and pdf text of the Sheriff Court Rules. Both texts are kept updated. There is access also to practice Notes, Memoranda, Directions, announcements etc. for each of the Court of Session, High Court of Justiciary and Sheriff Courts, as well also as the Rolls of Court (the published daily business of these courts) and Fee information for the Court of Session and Sheriff Courts.

>   http://www.scotcourts.gov.uk

There are also many other resources available. Of special relevance to the present publication is a fully searchable and constantly updated list of every court (The High Court of Justiciary, Court of Session and every Sheriff Court in Scotland) with an inventory of the electronic resources available in each court. There is also a link to a pdf version of a power point presentation discussing the work of the Scottish Courts Electronic Delivery Unit. All of this is to be found at

>   http://www.scotcourts.gov.uk/resources/courtroomtech/courtroomtech.asp

The Scottish Courts Technology Forum is hosted on the Scottish Courts Website
>   http://www.scotcourts.gov.uk/courttechnologyforum/index.asp

Secondary Sources

In addition to providing information on their own activities, the undernoted websites also contain useful web links to other websites dealing with Scots Law:

Scottish Law Online
>   http://www.scottishlaw.org.uk/scotlaw/index.html

Scottish Lawyers European Group
>   http://www.sleg.co.uk/home.html

Scottish Society for Computers & Law. Hosted on the Website of the Society for Computers and Law (www.scl.org)
>   http://www.scl.org/groups.asp?i=91&r=4£0

Singapore

Lawnet, a comprehensive resource for Singapore case law and legislation (by subscription only)
>   http://www.lawnet.com.sg

Supreme Court of Singapore, for the latest Singapore cases
>   http://www.supremecourt.gov.sg

Singapore Academy of Law
>   http://www.sal.org.sg/

Attorney-General's Chambers—Law Reform and Revision Division, Law Reform Reports
>   http://www.agc.gov.sg/publications/law_reports.htm

Appendix 2

THE SEDONA GUIDELINES FOR MANAGING INFORMATION & RECORDS IN THE ELECTRONIC AGE (SEPTEMBER 2005)

These guidelines are included in this text with the permission of the Sedona Conference, and are available in electronic format at http://www.thesedonaconference.org/

1. An organization should have reasonable policies and procedures for managing its information and records.

a. Information and records management is important in the electronic age.
b. The hallmark of an organization's information and records management policies should be reasonableness.
c. Defensible policies need not mandate the retention of all information and documents.

2. An organization's information and records management policies and procedures should be realistic, practical and tailored to the circumstances of the organization.

a. No single standard or model can fully meet an organization's unique needs.
b. Information and records management requires practical, flexible and scalable solutions that address the differences in an organization's business needs, operations, IT infrastructure and regulatory and legal responsibilities.
c. An organization must assess its legal requirements for retention and destruction in developing an information and records management policy.
d. An organization should assess the operational and strategic value of its information and records in developing an information and records management program.
e. A business continuation or disaster recovery plan has different purposes from those of an information and records management program.

3. An organization need not retain all electronic information ever generated or received.

a. Destruction is an acceptable stage in the information life cycle; an organization may destroy or delete electronic information when there is no continuing value or need to retain it.
b. Systematic deletion of electronic information is not synonymous with evidence spoliation.
c. Absent a legal requirement to the contrary, organizations may adopt programs that routinely delete certain recorded communications, such as electronic mail, instant messaging, text messaging and voice-mail.
d. Absent a legal requirement to the contrary, organizations may recycle or destroy hardware or media that contain data retained for business continuation or disaster recovery purposes.
e. Absent a legal requirement to the contrary, organizations may systematically delete or destroy residual, shadowed or deleted data.
f. Absent a legal requirement to the contrary, organizations are not required to preserve metadata.

519

4. An organization adopting an information and records management policy should also develop procedures that address the creation, identification, retention, retrieval and ultimate disposition or destruction of information and records.

a. Information and records management policies must be put into practice.

b. Information and records management policies and practices should be documented.

c. An organization should define roles and responsibilities for program direction and administration within its information and records management policies.

d. An organization should guide employees regarding how to identify and maintain information that has a business purpose or is required to be maintained by law or regulation.

e. An organization may choose to define separately the roles and responsibilities of content and technology custodians for electronic records management.

f. An organization should consider the impact of technology (including potential benefits) on the creation, retention and destruction of information and records.

g. An organization should recognize the importance of employee education concerning its information and records management program, policies and procedures.

h. An organization should consider conducting periodic compliance reviews of its information and records management policies and procedures, and responding to the findings of those reviews as appropriate.

i. Policies and procedures regarding electronic management and retention should be coordinated and/or integrated with the organization's policies regarding the use of property and information, including applicable privacy rights or obligations.

j. Policies and procedures should be revised as necessary in response to changes in workforce or organizational structure, business practices, legal or regulatory requirements and technology.

5. An organization's policies and procedures must mandate the suspension of ordinary destruction practices and procedures as necessary to comply with preservation obligations related to actual or reasonably anticipated litigation, government investigation or audit.

a. An organization must recognize that suspending the normal disposition of electronic information and records may be necessary in certain circumstances.

b. An organization's information and records management program should anticipate circumstances that will trigger the suspension of normal destruction procedures.

c. An organization should identify persons with authority to suspend normal destruction procedures and impose a legal hold.

d. An organization's information and records management procedures should recognize and may describe the process for suspending normal records and information destruction and identify the individuals responsible for implementing a legal hold.

e. Legal holds and procedures should be appropriately tailored to the circumstances.

f. Effectively communicating notice of a legal hold should be an essential component of an organization's information and records management program.

g. Documenting the steps taken to implement a legal hold may be beneficial.

h. If an organization takes reasonable steps to implement a legal hold, it should not be held responsible for the acts of an individual acting outside the scope of authority and/or in a manner inconsistent with the legal hold notice.

i. Legal holds are exceptions to ordinary retention practices and when the exigency underlying the hold no longer exists (i.e., there is no continuing duty to preserve the information), organizations are free to lift the legal hold.

Appendix 3

THE SEDONA PRINCIPLES FOR ELECTRONIC DOCUMENT PRODUCTION (JULY 2005 VERSION)

These guidelines are included in this text with the permission of the Sedona Conference, and are available in electronic format at http://www.thesedonaconference.org/

1. Electronic data and documents are potentially discoverable under Fed. R. Civ. P. 34 or its state law equivalents. Organizations must properly preserve electronic data and documents that can reasonably be anticipated to be relevant to litigation.

2. When balancing the cost, burden, and need for electronic data and documents, courts and parties should apply the balancing standard embodied in Fed. R. Civ. P. 26(b)(2) and its state law equivalents, which require considering the technological feasibility and realistic costs of preserving, retrieving, producing, and reviewing electronic data, as well as the nature of the litigation and the amount in controversy.

3. Parties should confer early in discovery regarding the preservation and production of electronic data and documents when these matters are at issue in the litigation, and seek to agree on the scope of each party's rights and responsibilities.

4. Discovery requests should make as clear as possible what electronic documents and data are being asked for, while responses and objections to discovery should disclose the scope and limits of what is being produced.

5. The obligation to preserve electronic data and documents requires reasonable and good faith efforts to retain information that may be relevant to pending or threatened litigation. However, it is unreasonable to expect parties to take every conceivable step to preserve all potentially relevant data.

6. Responding parties are best situated to evaluate the procedures, methodologies, and technologies appropriate for preserving and producing their own electronic data and documents.

7. The requesting party has the burden on a motion to compel to show that the responding party's steps to preserve and produce relevant electronic data and documents were inadequate.

8. The primary source of electronic data and documents for production should be active data and information purposely stored in a manner that anticipates future business use and permits efficient searching and retrieval. Resort to disaster recovery backup tapes and other sources of data and documents requires the requesting party to demonstrate need and relevance that outweigh the cost, burden, and disruption of retrieving and processing the data from such sources.

9. Absent a showing of special need and relevance a responding party should not be required to preserve, review, or produce deleted, shadowed, fragmented, or residual data or documents.

10. A responding party should follow reasonable procedures to protect privileges and objections to production of electronic data and documents.

11. A responding party may satisfy its good faith obligation to preserve and produce potentially responsive electronic data and documents by using electronic tools and processes, such as data sampling, searching, or the use of selection criteria, to identify data most likely to contain responsive information.

12. Unless it is material to resolving the dispute, there is no obligation to preserve and produce metadata absent agreement of the parties or order of the court.

13. Absent a specific objection, agreement of the parties or order of the court, the reasonable costs of retrieving and reviewing electronic information for production should be borne by the responding party, unless the information sought is not reasonably available to the responding party in the ordinary course of business. If the data or formatting of the information sought is not reasonably available to the responding party in the ordinary course of business, then, absent special circumstances, the costs of retrieving and reviewing such electronic information should be shifted to the requesting party.

14. Sanctions, including spoliation findings, should only be considered by the court if, upon a showing of a clear duty to preserve, the court finds that there was an intentional or reckless failure to preserve and produce relevant electronic data and that there is a reasonable probability that the loss of the evidence has materially prejudiced the adverse party.

COMMONWEALTH DRAFT MODEL LAW ON ELECTRONIC EVIDENCE

The model law was drafted by an Expert Group convened to develop a model law on electronic evidence for the needs of small Commonwealth jurisdictions. This model law, together with a Model Law on Computer and Computer related Crime, is available on-line at http://www.thecommonwealth.org/Internal/38061/documents/ and is included in this text with permission of the Commonwealth Secretariat.

1. Law Ministers and Attorney-Generals of Small Commonwealth Jurisdictions, at their 2000 meeting, recognized that common law rules of evidence were not adequate to deal with technological advances and needed to be modernised. They welcomed the convening of an Expert Group to develop model legislation on electronic evidence to address the needs of small Commonwealth jurisdictions.

2. The Expert Group examined the admissibility of electronic evidence and the question whether the rules that apply to other forms of documentary evidence can be applied in a like manner to electronic documents. Computer records are sophisticated systems that may be more prone or vulnerable to alteration and degradation than are records on paper. Therefore it was thought that the admissibility rule should take account of this risk. The Group noted that most jurisdictions seeking to impose a minimum level of reliability for admissibility of documents do so by focusing not on the document itself but rather on the method (system) by which the document was produced. This is because it is very difficult to show anything about the electronic document per se. By showing the reliability of the system one can lay the basis for admissibility of the document which is the product of that system. The Group agreed that system reliability is the most sensible measurement.

3. The model law contains provisions on general admissibility, the scope of the model law, authentication, application of best evidence rule, presumption of integrity, standards, proof by affidavit, cross examination, agreement on admissibility of electronic records, and admissibility of electronic signature.

4. On the basis of these deliberations, the Commonwealth Secretariat decided that because of the complexity of the issues, a separate model law on electronic evidence should be drawn up in order to ensure admissibility of such evidence. The model law draws on the Singapore Evidence Act Section 35 (1), the Canada Uniform Electronic Evidence Act and UNCITRAL Model Law on E-Commerce. Member countries wishing to make use of the model E-Evidence Law may choose to do so as—

- a separate piece of legislation; or
- part of a law on electronic transactions; or
- as amendments to existing laws on evidence; or
- as an addition to the proposals contained in paper **LMM(02)4** which deals with modernisation of evidence laws but concentrates primarily on criminal law matters and business records in their more traditional sense.

5. The model provisions on electronic evidence are annexed to this paper.

Action by law ministers

6. Law Ministers may wish to endorse the annexed Electronic Evidence Model Law and commend it to member countries for adoption (or adaptation to national circumstances) as a Commonwealth model of good practice.

Commonwealth Secretariat

Marlborough House

London SW1Y 5HX

September 2002

ANNEX

ELECTRONIC EVIDENCE MODEL LAW

AN ACT to make provision for the legal recognition of electronic records and to facilitate the admission of such records into evidence in legal proceedings.

BE IT ENACTED by the Parliament *[name of legislature]* of .... *[name of country]* as follows:

Short Title

1.   This Act may be cited as the Electronic Evidence Act, 2002

Interpretation

2.   In this Act,

"data" means representations, in any form, of information or concepts;

"electronic record" means data that is recorded or stored on any medium in or by a computer system or other similar device and that can be read or perceived by a person or a computer system or other similar device. It includes a display, print out or other output of that data.

"electronic records system" includes the computer system or other similar device by or in which data is recorded or stored, and any procedures related to the recording and preservation of electronic records.

"legal proceeding" means a civil, criminal or administrative proceeding in a court or before a tribunal, board or commission.

General Admissibility

3.   Nothing in the rules of evidence shall apply to deny the admissibility of an electronic record in evidence on the sole ground that it is an electronic record.

Scope of Act

4.(1)   This Act does not modify any common law or statutory rule relating to the admissibility or records, except the rules relating to authentication and best evidence.

(2)   A court may have regard to evidence adduced under this Act in applying any common law or statutory rule relating to the admissibility of records.

Authentication

5.   The person seeking to introduce an electronic record in any legal proceeding has the burden of proving its authenticity by evidence capable of supporting a finding that the electronic record is what the person claims it to be.

Application of Best Evidence Rule

6. (1)   In any legal proceeding, subject to subsection (b), where the best evidence rule is applicable in respect of electronic record, the rule is satisfied on proof of the integrity of the electronic records system in or by which the data was recorded or stored.

(2)   In any legal proceeding, where an electronic record in the form of printout has been manifestly or consistently acted on, relied upon, or used as the record of the information recorded or stored on the printout, the printout is the record for the purposes of the best evidence rule.

Presumption of Integrity

7.   In the absence of evidence to the contrary, the integrity of the electronic records system in which an electronic record is recorded or stored is presumed in any legal proceeding:

   (a)   where evidence is adduced that supports a finding that at all material times the computer system or other similar device was operating properly, or if not, that in any respect in which it was not operating properly or out of operation, the integrity of the record was not affected by such circumstances, and there are no other reasonable grounds to doubt the integrity of the record.
   (b)   where it is established that the electronic record was recorded or stored by a party to the proceedings who is adverse in interest to the party seeking to introduce it; or
   (c)   where it is established that the electronic record was recorded or stored in the usual and ordinary course of business by a person who is not a party to the proceedings and who did not record or store it under the control of the party seeking to introduce the record.

Standards

8.   For the purpose of determining under any rule of law whether an electronic record is admissible, evidence may be presented in respect of any standard, procedure, usage or practice on how electronic records are to be recorded or preserved, having regard to the type of business or endeavour that used, recorded or preserved the electronic record and the nature and purpose of the electronic record.

Proof by Affidavit

9.   The matters referred to in sections 6, 7, and 8 may be established by an affidavit given to the best of the deponent's knowledge or belief.

Cross Examination

10. (1)   A deponent of an affidavit referred to in section 9 that has been introduced in evidence may be cross-examined as of right by a party to the proceedings who is adverse in interest to the party who has introduced the affidavit or has caused the affidavit to be introduced.

(2)   Any party to the proceedings may, with leave of the court, cross-examine a person referred to in subsection 7(c).

Agreement on Admissibility of Electronic Records

11. (1)   Unless otherwise provided in any other statute, an electronic record is admissible, subject to the discretion of the court, if the parties to the proceedings have expressly agreed at any time that its admissibility may not be disputed.

(2)   Notwithstanding subsection (1), an agreement between the parties on admissibility of an electronic record does not render the record admissible in a criminal proceeding on behalf of the prosecution if at the time the agreement was made, the accused person or any of the persons accused in the proceeding was not represented by a solicitor.

Admissibility of Electronic Signature

12. (1) Where a rule of evidence requires a signature, or provides for certain consequences if a document is not signed, an electronic signature satisfies that rule of law or avoids those consequences.

(2) An electronic signature may be proved in any manner, including by showing that a procedure existed by which it is necessary for a person, in order to proceed further with a transaction, to have executed a symbol or security procedure for the purpose of verifying that an electronic record is that of the person.

Index

Index

Index

Index

Index